VENEZUELA

GUYANA

COLOMBIA

SURINAM

FR. GUIANA

Manaus

Amazon River

Belem

PERU

Fortaleza

Natal

Olinda

San Francisco River

Recife

B A H I A

BRAZIL

BOLIVIA

M I N A S   G E R A I S

Salvador

Belo Horizonte

PARANÁ

Ribeirão Prêto

Vitória

Desengano

Vassouras

Campos

Petropolis

São Paulo

Lizzieland

Juquia R.

Rio de Janeiro

Iguaçu R.

Iguape

PARAGUAY

Curitiba

Florianópolis

Pôrto Alegre

A R G E N T I N A

C H I L E

URUGUAY

A T L A N T I C   O C E A N

John morris

RIVER OF DREAMS

RIVER OF DREAMS

Gay Courter

WOODCUTS BY DAVID FRAMPTON

Houghton Mifflin Company / Boston

1984

Library of Congress Cataloging in Publication Data

Courter, Gay.
River of dreams.

1. Brazil — History — Fiction.   I. Title.
PS3553.086185R5   1984   813'.54   83-22747
ISBN 0-395-35301-7

Printed in the United States of America

V 10 9 8 7 6 5 4 3 2 1

Endpaper map by John Morris

For Philip, Blake, Joshua, and Robin

From the Iguaçu to the Amazon:
intrepid travelers!

Acknowledgments

For the ideas, inspiration, research assistance, technical and professional guidance, and experiences they generously shared with me I am immensely grateful to Mary Ann Boline; Bonnie Bonsall; Jane Buchanan; Miriam and Monroe Cohen; Jacqueline Fontaine; Julie Houston; Alfred Hower; Walter and Nininha Lundgren-Illi; Martha Braden Jones; Ralph Keyes; Larry Ladrido; Christina and Gilmar Lins; Maria and Ramiro Muniz; Anna Madalena Moutinho Nery; Laura Oliveria Rodrigo Octavio; Leah B. Pedena; Bob Reynolds; Margaret Schmidt; Roberta Teixeira; Cecilia and Charles Wagley; Signe Warner; Elsie, Leonard, and Robin Weisman; and the staffs of the Crystal River Library and the University of Florida Libraries and Latin American Collection.

And how can I thank my family — Philip, Blake, and Joshua — for all the hours they put up with (and managed without) me while I was mentally in Brazil?

I'm also indebted to Donald Cutler for his creative input and nurturing advice and to Anita McClellan, Sarah Flynn, and Nan Talese for their incisive editorial contributions.

Author's Note

This is a work of fiction. But readers should know that Confederate Americans did immigrate to South America after the Civil War; and yes, there was a Lizzieland, a Vassouras, a Desengano, and, of course, a Rio de Janeiro — which is, for me, the most sublimely beautiful city in the world.

But here is a Brazil rearranged and adapted to the needs of the novelist. The characters are imaginary, or were when the story was begun. Though never flesh and bones, they now have pasts on paper and futures in the mind of any reader who may choose to wonder what might have happened next.

Contents

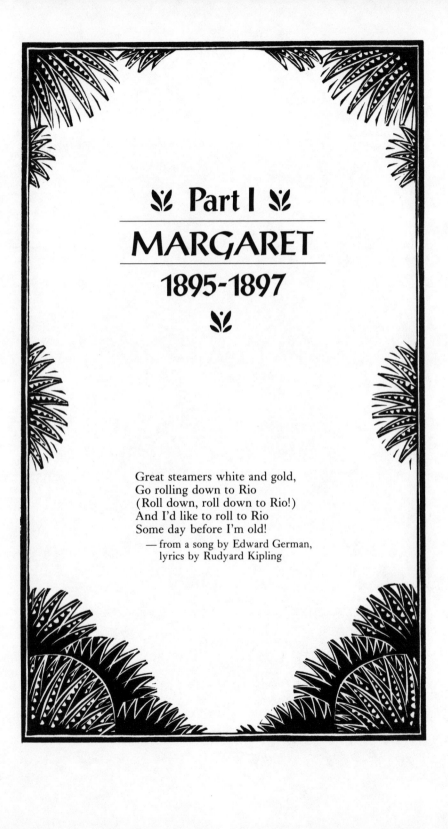

❧ Part I ❧
MARGARET
1895-1897
❧

Great steamers white and gold,
Go rolling down to Rio
(Roll down, roll down to Rio!)
And I'd like to roll to Rio
Some day before I'm old!
— from a song by Edward German,
lyrics by Rudyard Kipling

The Serpent

1 "All my voyages should be this unremarkable," the captain of the *Oceania* announced at the dinner table to the six unescorted women who were traveling from New Orleans to Rio de Janeiro under his protection. "You've not even had to suffer the dreadful pitching motion that a following sea can create in a vessel this size. It'll make you a far sight sicker than rolling on high waves any day, I promise you that."

During the past two weeks at sea, he'd regaled these, the least confident of his passengers, with tales of more torturous trips, believing that if they understood how many hardships he'd weathered already, they'd be more apt to trust their safety to him now. But his cheerfulness produced just the opposite effect on the one he most wanted to please: the beguiling yet disappointingly aloof Margaret Claiborne.

Every day, every hour, she grew more apprehensive. No matter that the ocean had often been mirror-smooth, no matter that the winds had remained continuously in their favor. Neither clement weather nor kind words could make this forced journey away from everything familiar, away from the life for which she'd painstakingly practiced and studied, acceptable to her.

Noting that Margaret was especially glum that evening, Captain McCormick turned to face her. "Miss Claiborne, you'll feel

better in the morning, for that's when we'll all be seeing terra
firma again," he said in his usual jovial tone.

"But didn't Melville say that 'a ship is a bit of terra firma cut
off from the main' ?" Margaret replied with a wry smile.

The captain was enormously pleased. "So, you've found the
copy of *Moby-Dick* I left in your cabin, have you?" He could not
help openly admiring the favorite of his charges. What a waste to
send a bright, pretty thing out to one of those mosquito-plagued
plantations only to bear babies and wither in the brutal sun! "Do
you remember these words from Chapter Fifty-eight? 'For as this
appalling ocean surrounds the verdant land, so in the soul of man
there lies one insular Tahiti, full of peace and joy, but encompassed by all the horrors of the half-known life.' "

Margaret looked puzzled as she tried to comprehend the captain's meaning. Realizing he'd gone against his intention to lift
her from her barely concealed misery, he changed the subject
abruptly. "If these winds hold their course, we'll be around Cabo
Frio twelve hours early. Mark my words, the first sight of land
will be the perfect tonic for what ails you."

Not likely, Margaret thought to herself, but for the sake of the
kindly man she tilted her chin bravely. "I'm sure you're right."

After the coffee and pastries were finished, Captain McCormick personally escorted Margaret, her Brazilian companion,
Francisca Larson, and the four others in his care to their cabins.
Margaret was far from being ready to retire. She would have preferred an hour or two in the salon where the men and married
women conversed. It was so unfair that Raleigh, her older
brother, was free to roam the ship while she was all but locked
below decks "for her own protection." How she resented being
treated like a child who couldn't be trusted! This was but one
more reminder that her own concerns took second rank to those
of her brother simply because he was a man.

Nine years earlier, their parents, desperate after their many financial failures, had made the heart-rending decision to settle in
Brazil, leaving their two eldest children behind to be educated in
New Orleans. In 1867 Margaret's paternal uncle, Lester Claiborne, had been one of the first to heed the advice of the charis-
matic Reverend Ballard S. Dunn, who from his New Orleans

pulpit lectured that "in the light of history no Southerner would be blamed if he sought a land where the night of vengeance had not yet come." In the aftermath of the War Between the States, Reverend Dunn set out on a journey to find a new homeland for Southerners, finally discovering in Brazil a place that held the "promise of accumulation," a country where slavery was still practiced, vast lands were available for nominal sums, and immigration was encouraged by government policy. Dunn and his followers purchased from the government, at extremely favorable terms, a sixty-four-by-forty-kilometer tract of land. He named it Lizzieland, to honor his daughter, a yellow fever victim, and set about to re-create the cherished Confederate way of life five thousand miles south of Louisiana.

Among the men in his family, Charles Claiborne, Margaret's father, was the only one to return safely from the war. He promptly married Lucretia Davis, a girl from a neighboring county who'd originally been promised to the elder brother he lost at Shiloh. The young couple, their combined ages totaling less than forty, undertook the challenge of resurrecting what remained of the Claiborne plantation, Moss Oaks, with no experience, no capital, no field hands, no guidance, and no luck. Within five years, they had produced three babies and as many mortgages. Eventually they lost the plantation to the bank, only a few months after two of the children died in a measles epidemic. Distraught and disheartened, they and their surviving infant son, Raleigh, moved to New Orleans, where Lucretia's prosperous brothers grudgingly gave Charles a clerk's job in their dry-goods store.

Margaret was the first Claiborne born in the city. Her childhood world was bounded by the geranium- and fern-fringed courtyard where she was safe from the market wagons bustling down Felicity Street. Perhaps to justify the space the gilded and carved instrument demanded in the tiny parlor crammed with the most valuable furnishings preserved from Moss Oaks, Margaret was given lessons on the family's grand piano as soon as she could sit on its bench and reach the keys. By the time she was six, she had demonstrated a musical talent worth nurturing.

Independent and idealistic, Charles Claiborne never forgave

himself for losing his legacy nor for taking orders from his tyran-
nical brothers-in-law. But now that he was responsible for three
new babies — a total of five living children — his options were
few until suddenly his uncle Lester died in Lizzieland, having
made Charles his heir. For the first time since the war, there was a
promise of opportunity.

Lucretia balked. It had been one matter to move from Moss
Oaks to the city, but it was quite another to suggest leaving her
homeland entirely. To persuade her, Charles read aloud from
Uncle Lester's early poetic descriptions of his "fazenda" and Reverend Dunn's proselytizing book on Lizzieland. At last Lucretia
was convinced that in Brazil there might be a chance to live well
and create something substantial for all their children.

The *Oceania* barely rocked on the docile sea, but Margaret was
still unable to fall asleep. She lay in her berth, trying to grasp
what Melville had meant by "the horrors of a half-known life."
She'd been especially enchanted with the book because she had
read it at sea. All the images were so alive and meaningful, she
wondered if anyone on dry land had ever appreciated them as
much as she had, though she knew she probably wouldn't have
turned to page one if Melville's writings hadn't been forbidden
reading at the Ursuline convent school she attended in New Orleans. Reaching for the volume, she flipped to Chapter 58,
searching for the quoted passage. "Consider . . . the universal can-
nibalism of the sea . . . and then turn to this green, gentle, and
most docile earth; consider them both, the sea and the land; and
do you not find a strange analogy to something in yourself?"
Margaret closed her eyes, trying to sense the author's meaning.
All she could identify in the words was a yearning for dry land
and an aversion to the uncertainty of the sea. The next few sentences contained that peculiarly upsetting reference to "the horrors of the half-known life." She read the end of the paragraph.
"God keep thee! Push not off from that isle, thou canst never return!"

She shut the book firmly. Never return! I didn't need Captain
McCormick to tell me that! Margaret pounded the hard pillow
with her fist. That she had no say in where she was to live or
what future she was to have was never more evident than the day
she'd boarded this ship. Was "the half-known life" the one she

was leaving behind? A life in which she might have freely chosen her own destiny instead of dutifully followed the orders of others? Was the horror the knowledge that somewhere else choice could be a reality instead of a myth?

Infuriated, Margaret curled her body around the pillow and willed herself to think of something else, anything else, until she finally slipped into a dark, blank sleep.

☙ ☙ ☙

In the middle of the night there was a distinct change in the air. Since the ship had neared the equator and crossed beyond, the atmosphere had been so sweltering that even with the porthole opened, Margaret had been unable to sleep in comfort. Now the sudden chill startled her awake. She drew the sheet high, but it was hardly enough protection. As she huddled to warm herself, Captain McCormick's irritating quotation surfaced. "Push not off from that isle . . ." she silently repeated over and over until she settled into an uneasy sleep.

"Cabo Frio! Margaret! Cabo Frio!"

The unexpected voice at the door caused Margaret's heart to thump wildly.

"Who is it?" she moaned.

"It's me. Francisca!"

Shivering in the draft, Margaret let her convent classmate in.

"Cabo Frio! I promised I'd call you." Francisca Larson was completely dressed in a heavy traveling skirt, vest, fitted jacket, and waterproof cape. "I've been watching for hours. Now you must hurry on deck. From here on there will be so much to see!" Margaret allowed Francisca to tie her robe snugly about her and wrap her own long silk scarf around Margaret's neck. "That will do for now. You don't want to miss the first sighting of Brazil!"

At the starboard rail, Francisca pointed to a high green headland barely visible in the dawning mists. This was Cabo Frio, or Cape Cold, the first landmark on the approach to Rio. For almost a week they had been sailing on a southerly bearing parallel with the coast that, for thousands of kilometers, runs approximately north to south. But now the ship had turned to follow an indentation that begins at Cabo Frio and stretches east to west. Rio de Janeiro, Margaret's immediate destination, lay in the middle of this dimple, facing not east toward Africa, as many imagine, but south toward Antarctica.

Delicate shapes first appeared as low-lying clouds, but then, as the sun rose higher, they revealed themselves as voluptuous coastal hills. Rolling waves licked the rocky clefts at the shoreline like rasping tongues. Since she was more suitably dressed to break the wind, Francisca stood in front of her friend. At school, the Ursuline sisters had been quick to pair Margaret and the daughter of a wealthy Brazilian merchant when she arrived three years earlier. Surely Margaret, lonely without parents of her own nearby, would be sympathetic to the timid foreign student; and, wasn't it a heavenly sign, the sisters agreed, that the new one could teach Margaret Portuguese, the language she most needed to learn?

From the first Francisca was different, not only because she didn't speak English (though it would come easily to her) or because of her shyness (which was to be expected in a new student); there just was something about the liquid quality of her soft brown eyes, the paleness of her skin that hovered between the unhealthy and the fashionable, and the fragility of her slender frame that worried the sisters. They took special care to be certain she ate properly, received prompt medical attention for the slightest ailment, and slept at least ten hours a night.

At times, Francisca seemed almost too perfect. "A porcelain doll" was the way Margaret came to think of her friend. She sat with a studied stillness, moved with a metered grace, rarely laughed aloud. Margaret believed Francisca's total control over her words and motions was imperative, for if she ever faltered, she'd somehow break into a thousand fragments.

"Golfinho!" Francisca shouted.

Margaret didn't understand until she followed Francisca's wild gesturing toward the ship's bow.

"There! There!" Margaret's heart leapt as she caught sight of the great herd of porpoises, which relished the cold currents off the cape.

"Over here!" Francisca called as one silvery hump appeared at almost the height of the railing. They could see just under the surface the flash of the torpedo-shaped bodies swimming effortlessly, yet keeping pace with the steamer. Every few seconds one would nose down slightly, disappear, suddenly shoot forward, and blow a spray of water in their direction.

When three porpoises arched out of the water simultaneously, Margaret hugged Francisca in delight. "Oh, they're so wonderful!" As they finally veered off in another direction, she turned and saw tears streaking Francisca's cheeks.

Francisca struggled to find her handkerchief. "The wind . . ." she mumbled as her lace square fluttered wildly.

Now the jagged outline of the Organ Mountains wreathed by black-blue cumulus clouds came into focus in the background. In front of them was the dense weave of tropical forests, rocky inlets, and jutting peninsulas bathed in an exotic violet light. Rolling shadows from the clouds laid patchwork patterns over the distant hills. The sun climbed atop the amorphous haze to send out celestial beams radiating across the continent like spokes of a wheel.

Margaret's hands on the polished wooden rail became raw in the wind. Still she did not move. Francisca's head was lifted resolutely, waiting . . . waiting . . . for that first view of the city of her birth.

"My father used to say that the man he most envied was Magellan."

"Why?" Margaret asked.

"To have been one of the very first to have seen Rio from the sea . . ." Francisca paused. "You'll understand what I mean in less than an hour." Her usually wistful voice rose in pitch, alarming Margaret.

Raleigh, who had just come up from behind, stared at his sister's dressing gown and disheveled hair. "Margaret Claiborne!" His voice was thick with disgust.

There was no family resemblance between the two eldest Claiborne siblings, and Raleigh's jealousy over his sister's beauty was but one of the reasons they had never become friends. Not that Margaret's features were perfectly balanced. She thought her nose was too long and narrow, her chin too bony and pointed, but few noticed these imperfections once they saw the intense glow that radiated from her deep azure eyes. Unfortunately, Raleigh's face was an unattractive amalgam of asymmetrical parts. A childhood fall had caused a twist in his nose, and his ears were so oversized that playmates had cruelly likened them to the wings of bats. While Margaret's head floated above a swanlike neck, Raleigh's neck was stubby and short, a description that aptly suited the rest of his body as well.

Margaret deliberately turned from his disapproving gaze and faced the sea. "I didn't have time . . . The porpoises . . ."

"Have you no shame? I promised our parents that I would watch out for you. Now what ever will I tell them?"

"Are you forgetting that I'm not your responsibility? My papers, like Francisca's, say that I travel in the care of the captain, not of my brother."

Raleigh's face contracted in anger. The borrowed scarf had come unknotted and Margaret's creamy throat was bare. He could not stop himself from staring at the V in her robe, which revealed the low neckline of the nightgown underneath. Only the barest fillip of lace at her cleavage prevented a direct view of a soft curve of breast. When Margaret realized how she must have appeared to her brother, she momentarily regretted her harsh tone; still, she resented his authority to criticize her. Why, the entire voyage he had acted as more scrupulous a chaperone than any maiden aunt or teaching nun!

"Oh, Raleigh," she said sweetly, mistaking his gaze as sympathetic. "You're the first person we've even seen this morning . . . though perhaps we were a bit indiscreet with the fish!"

Raleigh blanched. Ever since he'd taken a fervent interest in religion, he'd lost the witty sense of humor he'd had as a child. His clever puns and practical jokes had warmed their stern father's heart more times than she could remember, saving many a dour mealtime. He grabbed his sister's shoulder with one hand and with the other slapped her loudly across the left cheek. "You are a disgrace! Perhaps our mother will be able to put some sense into your empty head and deliver you from the teachings of idolatry."

Francisca recoiled, both from the blow and from the slur to her own religion, but Margaret stood firm. "I shall never forgive you for that!" she hissed, waiting until Raleigh retreated before releasing the hot tears that stung her wind-chapped cheeks.

❀   ❀   ❀

"Hurry, Margaret ... We can't miss the entrance to Rio!" Francisca handed Margaret her linen shirtwaist, then helped her button the tiny closures at the back while Margaret hooked her skirt. "Shall I button the top of the collar?"

Margaret took a deep breath. "Raleigh will think me a sinner if he sees even an inch of my bare neck!" She let out a furious gasp. "Even my father never laid a hand to me! What do you think got into him?"

Francisca blinked rapidly but didn't respond. "I'll lace one shoe, you do the other."

In a few moments the girls were back on deck. Now almost all the passengers swarmed at the starboard rail. A waiter dressed in white with a red sash at the hip and highly polished black shoes served small cups of strong, sweet coffee and fried bread dusted with cinnamon sugar, a seaboard cousin of the New Orleans beignet.

The ship passed humpbacked rocks that, in the wandering mists, looked like resting whales. "There it is!" Francisca pointed to a harbor lighthouse facing the middle of a shipping lane. "That's Raza Island and this is the entrance to Guanabara Bay." The steamer approached the balloon-shaped natural harbor on whose western shore the center of Rio lies.

"It's like another sea!" Margaret gasped.

"That's how it must have seemed to the Portuguese navigator Gaspar de Lemos. When he first entered the bay on January 1, 1502, he thought he'd discovered the mouth of a great river. In fact, that's how the city got its name: Rio de Janeiro actually means 'River of January.' "

"Then it really isn't a river?"

"No, only a huge bay."

"I can understand someone making that mistake at first, but why did they keep the city named after something that doesn't exist?"

"Perhaps to remind us that nothing in Brazil is as it first seems!" Francisca laughed.

A few minutes later she pointed to the silhouette of the mountain range on their left. "Can you see the 'sleeping giant'? " She drew an outline in the air to show how the mountain peaks spread around from the north to resemble a human form stretched on its

back. "Look, the giant's head is in the Tijuca Mountains behind
the city, and the peak of Tijuca is his hooked nose."

"Oh! Now I can see it!"

"Look at the granite mountain at the left of the harbor entrance. We call it Pão de Açúcar."

Margaret stared at the prodigious stone monolith that seemed
to have a decided tilt. "Sugar Loaf?" she asked quizzically.

"The Portuguese from the Madeiras used to produce refined
sugar in that conelike shape."

Soon the sights became too numerous to explain, so Francisca
only translated the evocative names bequeathed to the mountains:
"the Widow, the Hunchback, the Two Brothers, the Finger of
God." Next came the zigzagging beaches, each a brilliant ellipse
of white sand. "Copacabana, Ipanema . . . and there's . . . Flamengo — that's where we live!" Francisca squeezed Margaret's
hand too tightly.

When Margaret turned to stare at her friend's expectant face,
she did not see the total excitement she'd anticipated. Her own
stomach churned wildly as the steamer made its final, hectic run
through the currents outside the harbor and then took the great
plunge over the bar. Francisca gripped Margaret's hand once
again as the ship glided regally into the placid harbor. Margaret
took a calming breath and filled her lungs with the sultry, moist
air that felt soft as a feather across her cheek. A pungent scent
floated out to greet them — the scent of the tropics, at once intoxicating and seductive. Before them the city of Rio lay open like
scenes on a fan. Margaret whispered to Francisca, "It's not what I
expected. It's more like a dream."

As the ship moved closer to shore, the mountains, forested
from chin to toe, loomed larger. Every summit, each incline, had a
different texture. Some were soft and green, others grey and
rough. Soon Margaret could see not only the many churches that
crowned each hill but a patchwork of red-tiled roofs, friezes of
swaying banana fronds behind ivory walls, individual plumes of
windswept palms. The last detail to come into focus was the people: dark-skinned women carrying baskets of snowy laundry,
children running down black stripes of paths, a gang of laborers,
their skin luminous with sweat, hauling sacks to the docks.

Margaret was amazed to see how crowded the harbor was with

warships, sailing vessels, and other steamships flying flags of a dozen nations. Before the anchors were down, they were surrounded by a welcoming fleet of ferries filled with people waving up at them. With an unexpected surge of loneliness, Margaret turned away from the flotilla. Although they were to be met by Francisca's family, Rio was but the first stop on her journey to be reunited with her parents. Tomorrow, whether she liked it or not, she'd be boarding a smaller ship that would take her several hundred kilometers south to Santos, where she would transfer to a third vessel for the voyage to Iguape. Then there would be one last boat ride to complete her journey upriver to the colony of Lizzieland. If it had been left to her to make the decision, Margaret knew she would have chosen to remain in New Orleans with her music teacher, whose dreams had been far more dazzling than the prosaic marriage arrangements her parents had in mind.

☙   ☙   ☙

Six bronzed Negroes rowed the Larsons' private launch in silent precision. The strong odor from their bodies blew across Margaret's seat. She turned to avoid the peculiar smell that reminded her of burning nuts. While Francisca and her father chatted happily in Portuguese, Margaret realized that even after three years of studying she understood hardly a single word of the spoken language. Raleigh held his back stiffly and stared straight ahead.

Once on the wharf, another gentleman stepped forward and hugged Francisca. "Chiquinha!" He swung her around, kissed her on both cheeks, and set her down directly in front of Margaret.

Margaret had heard much of her companion's older brother and had imagined he would be more like Raleigh, not this startlingly handsome man with eyes an even purer blue than her own. His gaze was so intense, she had to turn slightly aside while they were introduced formally.

Francisca saw her friend's discomfort and chided, "Gigo! You're the first Brazilian man Margaret's ever met! Don't you think you're setting a very bad example?" Her effort at lightness failed to put anyone at ease.

Hesitantly, Margaret asked, "Why do they call you Chiquinha?"

"Most all Brazilians have nicknames. Chiquinha is the diminutive of my name. Erik is called Gigo in the family only. It's Erico to most everyone else in Rio."

Erik lifted Margaret's hand and kissed it softly. "May we call you Margarida?"

"If you like . . ." Margaret stammered.

Erik placed his arms around Raleigh, giving him a typical abraço, a masculine hug. "Welcome to Brazil. I hope you will permit me the honor of showing you what others, more traveled than I, call the most beautiful city in the world," he said in measured but meticulous English.

"Gigo! You've been studying!"

"My dearest sister, you're not the only one in this family to be educated!" he teased.

"So, it seems you are doing more trading with the British," Francisca replied in a knowing voice. She turned to Margaret. "Gigo was born an entrepreneur, not a scholar. He can convert any currency in a second, but cannot add a simple column of figures on a university exam!"

Erik grinned. "Just the opposite of Chiquinha. She's forgotten nothing she's ever been taught since the day she was born," he said affectionately.

"Come, children," his father called. "The carriages are waiting."

❦ 2   In Sweden, Sven Larson had been a particularly impetuous young man. After he was arrested at an antimonarchist demonstration, his parents had sent him to sea as a sailor until he matured sufficiently to join the family textile business in Norrköping, a provincial industrial center on a narrow inlet of the Baltic Sea. But a series of circumstances — a missed ship, an introduction to a cotton broker, a thwarted love affair — all led to his remaining in Rio. Eventually, he imported Swedish factory parts to Brazil and developed a highly profitable textile mill and retail business of his own.

Larson's astuteness at trade was but one of his assets in a colonial society where three hundred years of interbreeding among the Portuguese, Indians, and African slaves had resulted in the darkening of pigment among even the highest social classes. To

marry lighter, to have children whiter than oneself, was the goal
of most every Brazilian family. Sven's blondness alone made him
one of the most sought-after bachelors of his day.

Yet the first girl he chose had been promised in infancy to the
son of a family who owned contiguous lands. So disappointed
was Sven, it took ten years before the Swede proposed to eigh-
teen-year-old Guilhermina de Lourenço, the daughter of a
wealthy Portuguese-descended landowner who held title to a
piece of wharfside property he coveted. Though at twenty he had
decried marrying a woman for her property, at thirty the idea
was infinitely more acceptable. Besides, Maria Guilhermina possessed the same soulful eyes and blue-black tresses of his earlier
love, Christina, and fortunately Gilberto de Lourenço was easily
convinced, as part of the nuptial bargain, to give his son-in-law
the land where Larson would eventually build his largest mill and
warehouse.

Guilhermina was expected to fulfill her duty by producing a
crop of, if not blond, then light-skinned children. Unfortunately,
it took a distressing four years for her to conceive Erik. Another
decade passed before her second and last child, Francisca, was
born.

For ten years Erik had been his mother's sole occupation.
Though nurses and servants were plentiful, no one besides Guilhermina was permitted to change, bathe, or feed her son. She had
rigid ideas about what he might be permitted to eat: only the rip-
est mangos — washed, peeled, and mashed with honey; the whit-
est farinha — boiled, dried, and strained; the freshest fish, picked
over for bones and impurities; no meat until he was four, at which
time he was weaned completely from her own generous breast.

Sven Larson almost competed with his wife in proving his devotion. He taught Erik Swedish, German, and French; supervised
his tutors; read every paper and corrected each mathematics sum
the boy completed. He personally ministered to insect bites and
scrapes, and though he agreed the child would be raised in the
Roman Catholic Church, taught him Lutheran traditions as
though they were historical, rather than religious, in nature.

Instead of resenting Francisca's appearance, ten-year-old Erik
welcomed the respite from the constant parental attention. When
his mother did not recover from her second confinement for al-

most a year, he taught the baby to clap her hands to call the servants and to say her first words. After his precocious sister began
to speak at the age of nine months, Erik taught her a clever gib-
berish that combined Swedish, Portuguese, and French all in one
sentence. At parties she was paraded about and asked questions
by the guests, who delighted in her adorable, high-pitched multi-
lingual responses.

Erik knew that Francisca was probably brighter than he, but
their age difference prevented them from becoming rivals. Erik
protected his sister with a fierceness that his parents rewarded,
and Francisca believed that her brother was the most wonderful
person in the world. When Sven suggested that Erik travel to
Sweden for a few years of advanced training, Francisca's protests,
combined with Erik's lack of interest, prevented them from being
separated. It wasn't until the hasty decision was made to send
Francisca to North America that brother and sister had ever been
apart.

                        ❧   ❧   ❧

After winding up and down a maze of narrow rutted streets that
led from the port to a more elegant residential section, the Larsons' carriages arrived at a wider avenue lined with row after row
of royal palms, each more than thirty meters high. Every house
was hidden behind a high wall topped with shards of jagged glass.
At their approach, armed sentries opened the bronze gates
wrought in the form of two matching pineapples, the symbol of
hospitality. The Larsons' impressive seaside mansion was situated on a small rise to take advantage of the views of both the
Corcovado (the humpback) Mountain to the west and the open
bay to the east.

As soon as they were greeted by Francisca's tearful mother, an
elaborate meal was served. They sat around a long polished oval
table, served by six liveried waiters. After the blandness of the
steamship's cuisine, Margaret relished the tiny quail eggs, creamy
corn soup, fresh hard rolls, and cold sliced chicken with a tangy
orange sauce. When, at the end of the meal, a tray of custard-
filled pastries crowned with chocolate swirls was passed around,
Margaret noted, to her delight, that everyone was expected to select more than one. The tiny gold-rimmed coffee cups were re-

filled as soon as they were emptied, but the viscous drink was too bitter for her taste.

"So, you leave for Santos tomorrow, is that correct?" Senhor Larson asked Raleigh warmly.

"We sail at eight in the morning."

"Nonsense, the tides aren't till twelve," Erik interrupted. "But still, if we begin our tour this afternoon, you can still see most of our city's finest attractions."

"I don't want you to take all this trouble . . ." Raleigh protested weakly.

"For almost three years Margaret's been hearing my tales and descriptions of Rio; now she must see how beautiful it is for herself." Francisca looked across the table at her friend. Margaret was studying her empty plate, for the slightest eye contact with Erik, seated directly opposite, seemed somehow to be dangerous. "What do you most want to do?" Francisca asked her softly.

Margaret turned to Francisca, skillfully avoiding Erik. "To go to the top of Corcovado! You said the city was the best from above!"

"I think it would be a mistake to go there first," Erik interjected firmly. "The mountain should be the finale, not the overture."

Margaret was charmed. "Is Erik a musician?" she asked Francisca.

"Not my brother! But Erik, you should hear Margaret play the piano. The sisters said that she had a divine gift. She was always asked to entertain when dignitaries visited the school."

"Won't you play for us this evening?" Erik inquired politely.

"I'm so terribly out of practice. More than two weeks without an instrument can have a disastrous effect."

"But Margaret . . ." Francisca pleaded.

"Next time I visit I will prepare especially."

"Will your parents have a piano?" Erik asked.

"They wrote that there is one in the settlement, but not in their home. I'll be content if I can practice two or three times a week . . ." Margaret sighed.

"It isn't as though you're a professional," Raleigh said with an envious edge Erik could not help noticing.

❧ ❧ ❧

"As you probably know, Brazil was officially discovered by the Portuguese in 1500. The new land was first called Vera Cruz, then Santa Cruz, and finally Brazil, because of the abundance of red dyewood — pau-brasil," Erik began.

From his Swedish father Erik Larson had inherited a love of thoroughness. His idea of a tour of Rio was a fastidious year-by-year history and street-by-street guide. He directed the carriage driver to take them to the waterfront area of Botafogo at a very slow pace.

"And we might be speaking Spanish if it weren't for the Treaty of Tordesillas, which Pope Alexander VI signed in 1494, giving the Portuguese the right to exercise their sovereignty over all territories discovered up to a line three hundred seventy leagues west of Cape Verde."

Francisca groaned. "Gigo! I'm sure our guests are far more interested in the sights than four hundred years of history."

Erik smiled engagingly at his sister and pointed across the bay, the shores of which formed a reverse letter *S*. "This harbor, second only in size to your San Francisco's, is nearly one hundred and sixty kilometers in length, yet the entrance is only three hundred meters wide. It is easily defended by two small forts. Any unfriendly vessel passing through these fortifications could be sunk by our cannons."

Erik raised his arm to the distant shore and pointed. "Look over there and you will see that portion of the bay where the warships of the nation lie at anchor. In the west is Rio proper, to the east we see Jurujuba, where the asylum for epidemic diseases is located."

Francisca groaned. "Must we even be told about the hospitals? I'm certain Margaret would be more interested in the cultural districts or at least in the elegant shops on the Rua do Ouvidor."

Erik's arm dropped to his side. "My apologies," he said contritely. "I am quite proud of my city, its history, the great renovations it is undergoing." He turned to Raleigh. "My sister will be surprised how much has been done in her absence under the forward-thinking guidance of Presidente Prudente de Moraes. He's giving real meaning to Brazil's motto, 'Ordem e Progresso.'

Even in this period of financial depression, swamps have become parkland, the marshes have been drained, whole new sections electrified."

"It's more modern than New Orleans," Raleigh volunteered brightly. "I am quite enjoying every minute of this."

Before replying, Erik looked to Margaret for a sign she also wanted to continue. Though exhausted by the mounting heat and the lack of sleep, she did not want to be the one to offend her host. Also, she was flattered that he, for some unfathomable reason, valued her opinion. She looked out across the amethyst bay, then back at the green velvet-swathed hills. "I must know everything," she answered. "Start from the beginning, for surely this is the most beautiful place I have ever been."

"You are not the first to feel that way. In the year 1552, one of our first explorers, Thomé, wrote, 'Everything here is of a beauty which can hardly be described,'" Erik said victoriously before helping Margaret into the carriage beside his sister.

"Now, as Rome was built on seven hills . . ." He droned on as the carriage horses plodded wearily up and down each street, with the two gentlemen in front blissfully unaware that the two ladies in the back had fallen asleep.

❧ 3 Anxious not to miss the ship to Santos, Raleigh was dressed at dawn the next morning and woke Margaret shortly thereafter. Before joining her brother in the dining room, Margaret walked around the silent mansion. No relation or friend in New Orleans lived in a style to match the Larsons'. The evening before, when Francisca had given her a complete tour, she'd counted more than two dozen servants to handle every task. A mere clap of the hand brought someone running, who then summoned the most appropriate person for a given task. Three or four dark-skinned boys were available just to transmit messages from one part of the vast house to the other.

"Our home was originally built for my mother's grandmother as a wedding present," Francisca had explained. "It was passed on to the brides in the family as part of their dowries. Three times it has been renovated in accordance with the styles of the day, almost everything being imported from Europe." Room by room, she'd pointed out the Portuguese tiles, English oak mantles and balustrades, French ironwork balconies, Italian marble floors, and local woods set in elaborate chevron parquets by foreign-trained craftsmen.

"Will you inherit it when you marry?" Margaret knew Francisca was promised to Augusto Cavalcanti in an arranged marriage between prominent families.

"No, I've always wanted a house of a simpler design. I've even made drawings of what I'd like someday."

"Have you really?" Margaret was surprised that she concerned herself with such practical matters.

That night Margaret had slept in a canopied bed covered with two layers of thickly woven mosquito netting. The sheets were hand-trimmed with Valenciennes lace and her coverlet was cro- cheted in a pattern of birds and stars. Even more elaborate was Francisca's room, with furniture of tooled burgundy leather cush- ions inset in dark Brazilian jacarandá frames. Lucretia Claiborne's florid descriptions of the luxuries of her childhood plantation house, even allowing for the embellishments of her nostalgia, did not begin to compare with the opulence and comfort the Larsons enjoyed.

"Margaret, where have you been?" Raleigh called through the door of the dining room.

When she was seated, a waiter offered platters of colorful fruits. Margaret passed over the ordinary pineapples, bananas, oranges, and watermelons, pointing to the papayas topped with glistening black seeds. As the fruit was passed to her, she lifted the mesh- domed tent that protected the food from flying insects and helped herself to a small portion. Next the waiter served slices of a pressed white curd cheese and hot rolls that had been glazed with honey; he also poured her a large cup of dark coffee, thinned for breakfast with an equal amount of steaming milk.

"Raleigh, this fruit is the sweetest I've ever had!"

"It looks inedible to me! If I were you, I'd be cautious today to avoid suffering on the voyage."

Margaret ignored this advice and resumed her meal with gusto. Between bites she studied the charming room where the Larson family took their daily meals. The wall above the sideboard was decorated with panels of blue-and-white Portuguese tiles called azulejos. The night before, Senhora Larson had explained that the girl and boy feeding the geese and ducks in the bucolic scene were taken from portraits of Francisca and Erik as children. Though the face of the handsome boy, from his high brow and piercing eyes to the dimple on the left side of his cheek, was obviously that of Erik, any trace of the carefree little girl with the impish smile could hardly be found in the grown Francisca's unusually solemn expressions.

Raleigh rudely interrupted her reverie. "If you are quite finished, perhaps you'll see to your luggage."

Margaret nodded permission for the servant to pour a second cup of coffee. "It would be impolite not to wait for Francisca and her family," Margaret answered resolutely.

Traveling with Raleigh had turned out to be far more irksome than she had imagined. Though they had both been students in New Orleans, Raleigh had boarded with relatives while attending a preparatory school and later Tulane University, while Margaret had lived in the more protected environment of a convent school. On the infrequent holidays when Margaret was permitted outside visits, she usually opted to spend them with her beloved piano teacher, Mlle Evangaline Doradou. With Mademoiselle she was offered more love and warmth than in the home of her mother's brothers, who looked upon her as merely another Claiborne mouth to feed. Whenever brother and sister were reunited, however, Raleigh would boss her mercilessly, lording the privileges of both his seniority and his sex over his little sister. Though Margaret realized Raleigh was as sad, sensitive, and lonely without his parents as she had been, she had developed a vehement intolerance for his criticisms and bullying ways.

Mademoiselle had advised her to be patient with him, saying, "I suspect Brazil will make a man out of him." Margaret had then asked, "What will Brazil make of me?" But Mlle Doradou had turned back to the music at hand without further comment. Now, as Margaret looked across to where Raleigh sat stiff and anxious, she wished she could think of something to break down the barrier between them, for whether they liked it or not, they'd be traveling and living together for a long time to come.

"Good morning, Miss Claiborne." Margaret recognized Erik's

distinctively accented English that rang closer to Swedish than Portuguese. Quickly she swallowed the bite of bread in her mouth before turning to greet him.

Francisca's older brother was resplendent in a dark grey Prince Albert suit, stiff wing collar, and striped tie — a costume that must have been uncomfortable for the heat of the midsummer January day. A tingling sensation so disarmed her, Margaret could barely respond. At last she mumbled, "Bom dia," attempting to say the *d* with the harmonious "gee" sound that Francisca had taught her was the correct pronunciation in Rio.

"Muito bom! You sound like a Carioca already!"

Raleigh rose from the table. "If you would be so kind as to arrange transportation to the wharf . . ."

"There is no need for haste. As I said, you have many hours yet."

"If we miss this boat there won't be another for a week. While I have very much appreciated your hospitality, we would not wish to inconvenience you further."

"It would be our great pleasure to have you stay the week or as long as we could persuade you to be our guests," he said, facing Margaret. "Besides, I regret that darkness fell before we could take you up Corcovado yesterday."

Raleigh walked into the foyer as he replied, "I very much hope we shall have the opportunity to return one day and see everything that we have missed, but after all this time away from our family, we cannot disappoint our parents." He turned to his sister. "Margaret, are your trunks in order?"

"All but one," she replied tensely.

"Then get finished at once!"

Recoiling from acute embarrassment, Margaret spoke her mind. "I believe Senhor Larson knows what time we must depart better than you do," she said angrily. "Besides, I, for one, don't really care if I do miss the boat. So, if you must leave now, you'll do so without me!"

Erik turned so that Raleigh couldn't see his eyes crinkling in amusement and said in a most tactful voice, "Mr. Claiborne, I have no desire to see you distressed and assure you that you will reach your ship in good time. The servants will see that your sister's luggage is packed, but first she must go to Francisca, who is too upset to come down to breakfast. Will that be satisfactory with you?"

With his mouth tightened into a grim line, Raleigh nodded.

※ ※ ※

Francisca sat in bed surrounded by pearly satin pillows. She was pale and shaking as she whispered her farewells to Margaret.

"You promise you'll come for my wedding?"

"When do you think it will be?"

"Not for many months."

"I will do everything in my power. But I cannot promise . . ."

"But you must!" Francisca began to cry.

Margaret propped the pillows and held Francisca's hand. "Tell me about him."

"Who?"

"Augusto Cavalcanti, of course. You once said he was a very good match. Aren't you excited that you'll be reunited with him soon?"

"I haven't seen him in three years. He could've changed."

"Wasn't he your choice?"

"No, he wasn't."

"Surely your parents wouldn't force you in this matter!"

"I must follow their wishes."

"It's your life!"

Francisca shrugged. "Will it be so different when the time comes for you? Aren't your parents expecting you to pick one of the sons of their North American friends?"

Margaret paled. "I expect to marry for affection, not convenience."

"I thought you wanted to be a musician, to play on every great concert stage in the world."

"A schoolgirl's dream. Besides, whatever happens, I'll still have the pleasure of my music. No one could ever take that from me."

"You make it all sound so simple."

"It will be for you, too; just wait and see."

"You don't understand," Francisca wailed. "I don't want to marry anyone at all!"

Margaret guessed her friend's building hysteria had more to do with her own departure than with any future marital plans. She hugged Francisca close. In the distance she could hear Raleigh's impatient voice calling her.

Francisca lifted a small crystal jar from her bedside table and poured the contents onto the satin coverlet. Topazes, ranging in size from a child's fingernail to a small apricot and cut into a dozen different shapes, tumbled out. Their colors, from the palest yellow to a smoky amber, mingled and twinkled. "I started to receive these gifts when I began to lose my teeth!" Francisca giggled. "They come from Belo Horizonte, northwest of Rio in the state of Minas Gerais, where Father owns a share of one of the mines."

Margaret let the gems roll in her fingers and held a multi-faceted stone up to the light. "They're beautiful! What will you do with them?"

"Someday I'll have them set into rings or necklaces, but for now I enjoy just looking at them like this." She stretched Margaret's skirt and placed a few of the precious rocks in her lap. "For you."

"Oh, no! I couldn't!"

"For remembrance, for the future . . ."

There was a knock at the door. Erik called, "Miss Claiborne, I am afraid the time has come. Your brother is most anxious."

Francisca took a small velvet sack with a golden drawstring and filled it with the stones before Margaret could protest further. "I can't watch you leave. Forgive me for not coming downstairs." She pressed the sack into Margaret's hand and once more began to cry.

Margaret crossed the room, turned, and mimicked the voice of their sternest Ursuline nun. "Maria Francisca Larson, that is absolutely enough!"

Francisca almost smiled as Margaret closed the door.

Across the corridor Erik waited. As soon as Margaret appeared, he took her arm gently. "My sister will be inconsolable."

Margaret had refused to cry in front of Francisca, but was now finding it more difficult to control herself. She nodded at Erik briefly, then turned and started for the stairs. Erik didn't move to follow, and when she realized this, she stopped and looked back over her shoulder. Finally he spoke. "If you meant what you said, it can be arranged."

Margaret looked perplexed.

"About not caring if the ship left without you."

Though Margaret wanted to protest that her remark had been said in haste, a pounding pulse in her forehead warned that it was imperative to say exactly what was in her mind. "It's true that I'm not looking forward to living on the remote lands my parents have chosen. Perhaps . . ."

"If you could choose for yourself, what would you most like to do instead?" Erik was whispering so softly that she had to move closer to catch his last words.

"To study my music, to be with my friends" — she stumbled — "with Francisca. I have always lived in the city and know nothing of rural life. Besides, I hardly remember my family. I've lived almost longer without them than with them."

"Nothing says you must . . ."

She tightened her lips into a thin line. "I should not be speaking to you like this."

This time Erik narrowed the distance between them. Now Margaret could not descend the staircase unless he permitted her to pass. He leaned back on the railing and half-closed his eyelids. "Nor should I speak to you like this, but Rio is where you belong. I want you to miss the boat, not for your sake, but for mine."

Margaret heard his voice but could not absorb his meaning. All she could think was that she must get away from him before he forced her to reveal even more of her feelings, and these were too jumbled to begin to comprehend. As she tried to pass him on the stairs, the shoulder of her white linen suit momentarily caught against the grain of his grey jacket. Her skin burned at the touch.

"Please . . . ah, por favor . . ." Margaret murmured. Reluctantly he moved aside and she somehow found her way downstairs through a mist of tears.

"My dear sister, this is hardly a funeral!"

"Please, Raleigh, let us just go, please . . ." As she took his arm, the pattern of the black-and-white marble foyer danced in front of her eyes. She would not have found her way to the door on her own.

❧ 4 After twenty-four stifling hours of traveling on the rusty steamer *Neptuno*, which made numerous calls along the coastline, they arrived in Santos and transferred to a third vessel,

the *Juparana,* whose stained hull and oil-slicked water line made
it look both unsafe and uninviting. The port of Santos was littered with the skeletal ribs of abandoned hulls that rotted in the
sluggish ooze of low tide. On deck, the Claibornes made the acquaintance of Dr. Boline, an English-speaking passenger traveling
south to the River Plate. He explained that crew after crew had
died in the harbor from yellow fever, their corpses along with
their plague ships burnt in a deliberate attempt to wipe out the
hideous scourge.

"Who'd want to live in a place like this?" Raleigh asked.

"As few people as possible," the doctor replied. "While Santos
is the seaside port, the major metropolis of São Paulo is sixty kilometers inland."

"Why so far away?" Margaret wondered aloud.

"Legend says it was the first place a traveler could shake himself dry after coming through the cloud belt on the coast."

As soon as they were out of the stinking port, Margaret was
overcome by the obnoxious smell of oil from the machinery mixing with the odor of burnt beans and onions. She excused herself
from Raleigh and the doctor and went to her cabin. There she lay
on her bunk, trying to keep from vomiting, until she fell into a
fitful sleep. In the middle of the turbulent night, Margaret followed Raleigh's lead and stumbled into the small launch that
would ferry them to the port of Iguape. Still disoriented from
seasickness, Margaret let Raleigh sort the luggage handed down
by the deck hands.

The boat plunged over the rough waves that glimmered at the
channel entrance like beckoning fingers in the moonlight. The
final passage over the treacherous sandbar sprayed everyone and
left several inches of water sloshing in the bottom of the boat as it
pulled up to a crumbling stone wall. Inside the cove, the roar of
the ocean diminished to a faraway hiss. Since the tide was so low,
Margaret had to climb a steep staircase from the water line to the
top of the sea wall. At least the land felt safer, warmer, the heat
absorbed by the stones during the day, radiating back in a most
welcome way.

Margaret seated herself among the first of their bundles and
counted as each article was lifted from the launch and placed on
the ground. The largest of her trunks, containing the items she'd

collected for her trousseau — linens embroidered during her convent days, silk undergarments, her finest dresses, and the antique family laces her aunts had given her to someday stitch into a wedding dress — seemed to be missing. She became agitated. "Raleigh, they've forgotten my trunk, the one that wouldn't fit in the cabin."

"I'm sure it's here; I counted everything."

"No, it's not. Ask them to go back for it. In fact, you'd better go with them or they might not return, since we're the only ones who disembarked in Iguape."

"I've already been soaked enough by one pass over that sandbar!"

"Then make them understand!"

"You're the one who supposedly studied their language."

Margaret went over to the deck hand and frantically tried to explain. Although she spoke the words for *lost* and *trunk* and *return to get it*, he shook his head with incomprehension.

"Milton! Vem embora!" called the sailor at the oars.

Shrugging an apology, the deck hand untied the line, pushed off the bow of the launch, and jumped aboard.

"Espera! Wait. Um outro baú ... mais bagagem!" she called hoarsely after the departing boat. "Raleigh!" she pleaded hopelessly.

"I think he finally understood. He'll come back with it."

"He won't," she said furiously.

"I hope you don't blame me! I did all I could and without any help from you!"

"Perhaps they'll return it on their next trip here ..." Disbelieving her own words, she lay down amongst the baggage and wept.

ꕥ ꕥ ꕥ

Never before had Margaret watched the birth of a new day from the first shimmer of light christening the sea with a rosy halo to the glittery second when the sun's edge sparkled out like the most glorious of diamond rings being lifted onto a black velvet tray. Concentration on the breathtaking palette of colors that dappled both the sky and scudding foam had calmed her. She no longer felt an intense ache when she stared at the spot where the

wretched steamer had lifted anchor and departed without returning with her trunk.

In the pale daylight, Margaret could see the narrow passage in
the sandbar that the launch had plunged through and realized
why the sailors were not about to row over it twice. The unpretentious town of Iguape was, by navigational standards, unsuitable as a port, but because it was the first settlement of any
significance one hundred kilometers south of Santos, a few steamers found it profitable to anchor outside the bar and send rowers
to the quay for passengers and cargo.

Asleep among the bundles, Raleigh looked more pathetic than
pious. Poor Raleigh, Margaret thought with unexpected sympathy, he faces as dismal a future as I do. While she might be able
to extend her horizons with a fortuitous marriage, he would have
to manage with whatever meager holdings his father could provide, and do so under his dictatorial thumb.

Margaret decided she'd let Raleigh sleep another hour so
he'd be in a better humor. She stood, stretched, and wondered
where she could ask directions to the home of Ralph Gunter, the
gentleman who was to arrange their passage upriver to Lizzieland.

Looking toward the village, Margaret could see only a quiet
group of stuccoed commercial buildings, each painted a different
pastel shade. On a slight rise above the port, within the twin
towers of the Bom Jesus church, bells began to peal. Perhaps the
Gunters would even have a bathtub, she thought wistfully. Her
hair was matted with salt spray and her dress had been soaked,
then dried so stiff it chafed as she walked into town.

Because the name *Iguape* had been printed with letters almost
as large as *Santos* on the map, she had expected a grander spot
with a large bay rather than only a sandy inlet. Where were the
freighters, the docks piled high with sacks of coffee and sugar, any
sign of prosperous industry? The tide had gone out even farther,
and the stinking mud flats stretched almost to an offshore island.
The smell of the putrid seaweed and shellfish seemed unhealthy,
and Margaret, remembering Santos's plague ships, worried that
Iguape's marshlands might be similarly infested.

All around were droning noises of what probably were virulent
insects. As the last notes faded from Bom Jesus, a clear-throated

ringing melody greeted her. Margaret searched the treetops for the bird that trilled such a divine song. Rustlings in the underbrush revealed a small group of barefoot children who stood silently beyond a fringe of palmetto leaves, their wide, solemn eyes curiously watching the fair newcomer. One bright-eyed little boy scurried forward and began to babble in a dialect Margaret couldn't begin to fathom.

She gestured to the trees and whistled an imitation of the birdsong.

One child giggled. "Sabiá."

"Sabiá," she repeated. Then she asked slowly, "Conhece a casa do Senhor Gunter?"

"Ah, sim!" The boy smiled so Margaret could see that he was missing his front teeth. Then he gestured to her to follow him.

5 "What a tragedy!" remarked Mrs. Gunter with great sympathy when she heard the story of Margaret's missing luggage. "You look quite green, my dear. You must sit outside and let me get you a proper breakfast of eggs and fruit while Mr. Gunter sees to your brother and the safety of the remainder of your possessions."

Margaret sipped a cup of hot tea and basked in the attention of a maternal woman who spoke English with a gentle drawl not very dissimilar to her own.

The Gunters had been early emigrants from Sumter County, Georgia. Ralph Gunter had established himself as the shipping agent for the settlers in the region, later becoming the customs inspector, empowered to sign and stamp any number of government documents. One by one, their seven children had settled into their own plantations, sending coffee, cacao, corn, rice, sugar, and timber to their father to export at the highest prices. The Gunter house was modestly built from local materials, but the interior contained priceless pieces of European furniture, porcelains, sterling utensils, and a surprising collection of Sèvres clocks.

A barefoot servant girl brought Margaret a plate of perfectly poached eggs on slices of a hard roll, a pot of citrus marmalade, and a pitcher of a juice she didn't recognize.

"It's amora, a mulberrylike fruit. Do you care for it?" Mrs. Gunter asked.

Margaret took another taste. "I think so," she answered truthfully. "Do you make the marmalade yourself?"

"No, but it's my recipe. I'll write it out for you. You'll be able to show your mother's cook how to make it."

After breakfast Mr. Gunter offered to take Raleigh to his wharfside office. "You'll stay here with me and get a proper rest," Mrs. Gunter said to Margaret solicitously. She pointed to a hammock. "I think you'll find this much cooler than the divan."

When Margaret awoke several hours later, she heard a loud pounding on the palmetto roof and Mrs. Gunter saying "Muita chuva" while she bustled about closing shutters.

Mrs. Gunter noticed Margaret was awake. "I can't send you upriver in this weather. You'll have to spend the night with us."

"I wouldn't want to trouble you ..."

"Not at all. Besides, I'll certainly make you pay your way." She caught Margaret's worried expression. "By telling me about New Orleans, your journey, even Rio. You can't imagine how I yearn to hear news of the world ... in English!"

"How long has it been since you've been outside of Iguape?"

"Fifteen years since I've been farther than Santos."

"Do you miss it?"

"I could travel if I chose, so if I don't I can't very well complain, can I?"

"I've always lived in a city ..."

Mrs. Gunter observed Margaret thoughtfully. "There is a pleasure in the slow ways, a secret pulse you must heed. Otherwise you will suffer by feeling out of step, as so many of the original North American colonists did. Eventually, though, more adapted than returned. You look like a sensible girl and I am certain you will do very well."

"Thank you for your confidence, but I don't think ..."

"When you have a family of your own you will be quite busy with them, and here, more than in the city, you can have an influence over them."

"Look!" Margaret pointed to the doorway. A stream of brown rainwater was beginning to soak the edge of the frayed carpet.

Mrs. Gunter took notice but did not rush to roll it up. "The

rainy season." She sighed. In a steady, methodical way she began
to get out buckets and position them in the places of the most frequent leaks. To her, it was all very ordinary; to Margaret, it
seemed a thankless, disheartening task.

❦ ❦ ❦

The next morning, the Iguape River was a chocolate brown, its
usual tannic-acid blackness churned lighter by the storm. Since
no passenger barges were headed upriver that day, an oversized
canoe with two oarsmen was made ready, trunks and bundles
were stowed, and two chairs were placed for the benefit of the
foreigners. Mrs. Gunter insisted Margaret carry her own white
parasol to protect her from the sun. With a flurry of waves and
good wishes, the Gunters sent the young travelers up the winding
turns of the unknown river.

The loudest noises during the long journey were the oars'
rhythmic splashing and the whining of insects that sounded more
industrial than natural. Margaret soon was dappled with bites
that swelled and itched. It took all her attention to watch where
the black devils landed and to kill them before they could puncture her skin.

Traffic on the river was sparse. Occasionally a barge carrying
timber or sacks of produce moved downriver. Passing small settlements with stilt houses built close to the river's edge, they saw
spindly-legged children and skinny dogs running along the
beaches, men fishing from hand-hewn canoes, women washing
their clothes in the tea-colored water and stretching the linens to
bleach in the sun. There were no large houses or prosperous com-
munities to be seen.

"Any hope I've held that Lizzieland's going to be a pleasant
surprise is fast fading." Margaret sighed.

"You've never had a positive outlook," Raleigh responded.

"Does it seem to you as if anyone's prospering around here?"
Margaret pointed toward some riverfront shacks. "This doesn't
begin to resemble Father's early descriptions of Lizzieland."

From a small bag between her knees Margaret pulled a frayed
letter and read, " 'Our colony is beautifully situated on a pranc-
ing, playful little river. I have never enjoyed any scenery more
than this. The mountains tower above on either side of the

stream, presenting a most inviting soil of a deep, dark vermilion hue covered with gigantic trees of useful and ornamental woods, while the ever-varying luxuriant undergrowth make me almost believe that the hands of sylphs have been about, festooning and rendering still more pleasing nature's exceedingly perfect works. I do not see how you, dear Gettie, could have an ear so dull or a heart so heavy as not to also respond to Brazil's rich and varied song as I have.' " Margaret made a sour face.

Catching her expression, Raleigh spoke sternly. "You'd do well to adopt our father's view of the place. It's not as though you have any choices."

No choices . . . His words hung in the moist air as the boat moved inexorably upstream. "The horrors of the half-known life . . ." reverberated in her head. No! she thought. It won't be that way for me! "At least I'll always have my music," she said aloud to convince herself she hadn't given up everything.

Seven hours after they had left Iguape, a simple floating dock appeared around a bend. A small faded sign on a pole unmistakably read, WELCOME TO LIZZIELAND.

"There it is!" Margaret shouted, her face glowing with excitement.

Raleigh leapt out before the oarsmen had completely brought the boat up alongside the dock. Margaret scrambled beside him and ran down a rickety boardwalk to a clearing in front of a semicircle of stilt houses.

At the door of a hut two men were grinding cane and catching the juice in a primitive machine. Two posts with rollers attached were driven into the ground; one of the rollers was turned by a lever that passed through the end. Cane stalks were crushed between these rollers while the resulting sweet juice was caught in a round calabash gourd below. The men looked up and, realizing these were the new Norte Americanos, pointed up the hill.

"It must be this way," Raleigh said, repeating their gesture. The path turned sharply to pass alongside a waterfall where native women were washing clothes and chattering like birds. At least our clothes aren't going to be done in the muddy river, Margaret consoled herself. At the top of the ridge a circle of houses appeared. Several of the larger dwellings had wide verandahs with plaid hammocks hung between the porch poles, flowering shrubbery, and neatly swept paths. None was particularly grand, but all were decidedly more substantial than the stilt houses along the river.

A familiar sound from one of the first buildings caused Margaret to pause and draw closer. Inside were rows of children, the girls wearing blue jumpers, the boys in white shirts and blue shorts.

". . . With the cross of Jesus going on before! Christ, the royal Master, Leads against the foe: Forward into battle — See His banners go . . ." they sang sweetly.

One of the children pointed to the doorway, and their music teacher stopped the group and scrutinized the two strangers for a long, silent moment before stepping out into the intense sunlight. She blinked and rubbed her eyes.

"It's . . . it's . . ." Her voice broke. ". . . Gettie!"

"Mama!" Margaret cried. "Yes, Mama, it's me!" As she hugged her mother she was surprised to find a woman who was not only much shorter than she expected but so frail she worried that she might have injured her with the intensity of her embrace.

Raleigh waited on the edge of the circle of children who gathered around curiously until his mother caught sight of him. "Raleigh! My boy!" She pulled away from Margaret and ran to her son, throwing her arms around his neck.

For a moment Margaret felt abandoned. A stocky girl of about sixteen she recognized as the leader of the children's chorus came forward with tears in her eyes. "Nell?" Margaret asked tentatively.

The girl nodded happily. "And this is Kate." A child with brown braids came forward and shyly touched Margaret's hand. "Marshall? Where's Marshall?" Nell called. A towheaded boy jumped out from behind Kate.

Margaret bent down and studied her younger brother. He'd been but a babe in arms when he'd left for Brazil. As she touched his freckled cheek, she suddenly felt acutely the loss of watching him grow to the age of ten, and began to weep.

❦ 6   "But you wrote that you had a piano!" Margaret's initial disappointment quickly turned to fury.

"No, what we wrote was that there had been a piano in the colony. By the time we arrived, it virtually had rotted away. We hoped it could be repaired . . ." Lucretia Claiborne explained defensively.

Margaret's father answered with the strained politeness he felt was due this stranger who was his daughter. "When you are settled in a home of your own, we will make every effort to produce a suitable instrument for you. There's no point in trying to get a piano all the way upriver and then have to move it a second time."

Instead of comforting, his words hurt Margaret more deeply, for he'd made her feel, only hours after being reunited with him, that she was merely an encumbrance to be disposed of as soon as someone could be found who would take her away.

Without an instrument to play, books to study, or any assigned tasks, Margaret's first weeks in Lizzieland were achingly long. Initially, she offered to help her father with the accounts. "I've had good training in figures and I helped Sister Antoinette with the paperwork in the convent library. Surely I could do some of the bookkeeping."

"That's to be Raleigh's job. I've had enough of you two squabbling over unimportant matters and am not about to create another issue for you both to dispute."

"Then how shall I occupy my days fruitfully?"

"You can always help your mother with the little ones," he replied. Nell, Kate, and Marshall hardly needed tending, and there were enough servants to handle mundane chores.

In desperation Margaret thumbed through sheets of music, drumming out favorite phrases on a tabletop in an attempt to keep the muscular memory of the music alive. Eventually she made a rough wooden keyboard with a Kalkbrenner hand-guide and practiced silently, almost in accusation of her parents' failure to provide an instrument.

"Why do you practice with that thing?" Margaret's mother asked one afternoon as she watched her daughter's tortured exercises.

"I spent so many years developing a special firmness of touch and suppleness of wrist that I don't dare permit my arms to relax into lazy habits."

Margaret's teacher had been a student and acolyte of the Louisianan composer and America's first internationally known pianist, Louis Moreau Gottschalk. When he was thirteen, Gottschalk had been sent to Paris to study with Camille Stamaty, Kalkbrenner's prize pupil. Although he'd found the technique of the hand-guide tedious, he'd returned to New Orleans praising its value. Mlle Doradou was the first to adopt it for her pupils.

"It's a shame that nobody hears your music," her mother replied. "Though sometimes I feel as though I almost can."

"Then that's two of us who do."

"Why don't you stop and have a nice cool drink with me on the verandah before the children come in from school?"

"All right." Margaret shrugged, not unwilling to leave her futile, mute exercises.

"Who's Leonard Fontaine?" she asked as she took the second most comfortable seat on the shaded side of the porch. The name had been mentioned so often recently that Margaret had begun wondering if he wasn't one of her father's marriage prospects for her.

Lucretia poured mint tea into two of her least-chipped glasses. "No one for you to concern yourself about. He has only daughters."

Margaret beamed with relief. "So he's someone for Raleigh to worry about!"

"Possibly." Lucretia tried to rearrange her pillows on the only chair she felt she could sit in. "This heat seems to cook the flesh from my bones."

"Mother!" Margaret frequently groaned at her mother's outlandish complaints. "New Orleans was hardly much cooler."

Lucretia gulped the lukewarm liquid. "We never had this choking red dust, the miasmic mists, the incessant damp, when we lived there."

"You forget."

"A privilege of age, my dear. Pour me a second glass and I'll tell you about Fontaine's daughter if you promise not to talk to Raleigh . . . yet."

Delighted to have her mother's confidence, Margaret put her finger to her lips. "I wouldn't breathe a word."

Lucretia took a long drink, settled back, and closed her eyes. "Like his father before him, Leonard Fontaine was trained to be a

Mississippi riverboat pilot on the Natchez–to–New Orleans run. As soon as he arrived in Brazil, he set up a barge fleet to transport the products of the other colonists to the coast. He charges either a flat fee or a percentage of a crop's value in Santos. While most of us struggled at a subsistence level, he reinvested his considerable profits in boats, not land. Today he's probably one of the wealthiest men in the state of Paraná."

"Now I see why Father keeps bringing up his name. Tell me, Mother, if Raleigh's worth a barge or two, what would someone pay to get me?"

"Gettie! We aren't planning to offer our children to the highest bidder. We just want them to be comfortable and secure."

"So Raleigh will be married off first."

"Only if he agrees. I think you both need more time for . . . adjustment, but your father . . ."

"This year's watermelon crop has barely covered expenses, so he's especially anxious, isn't he?"

"How do you know about the crop?"

"I can read the numbers in the ledgers as well as anyone, better than some! Raleigh's made a mess of them. His totals don't anywhere near balance."

Her mother's narrowed eyes filled with angry tears. "Now I understand what the sisters' reports meant when they called you spirited. Or do I also remember their concern about a certain degree of impertinence?"

Margaret squirmed under her mother's critical gaze. "Tell me about Fontaine's daughters," she said to placate her.

"I've never met any of them, but Charles has visited them at their large homestead at the river junction near Juquiá. He says the two youngest are real beauties, but still too little to marry." Lucretia sipped her drink thoughtfully. "Marianne is their eldest."

"What's wrong with her?"

Lucretia looked away from her perceptive daughter. "I hear she has a very passable demeanor, is reasonably intelligent, though she's never been educated outside of Brazil."

"And . . ." Margaret waited.

"Well, she does have one small defect. She was born with a

badly twisted foot, a clubfoot. She walks with a limp and requires
a cane, but Charles says she is a very practical girl. Better someone who will be grateful for a boy like Raleigh, better a father-in-
law who owes a favor."

"So, you've found Raleigh a rich cripple . . ." A sob caught in
Margaret's throat. "I can't imagine what you've planned for me."

"That's unfair! I'm told Marianne's a delightful girl!" Lucretia
answered firmly. "Besides, your father and I have seen too much
unhappiness from forced alliances to command either of you
to follow our will in this matter. We are here to suggest, to
guide . . ."

"But choose we must . . . and soon!"

"Oh, Gettie! Your father isn't an impossible man. All he wants
for you is someone who comes from our background, someone
who can provide for you properly. You should've heard him the
night after he saw you again. He called you 'God's flower' and
wondered how two people as plain as us could have produced
someone as sweet as you."

❧ ❧ ❧

No matter her mother's conciliatory words, Margaret knew that
everything was leading to the big planters' reunion held at Carnaval time each February. While the Brazilians had their traditional celebration, making it impossible for anyone to get any real
work done for several weeks, the colonists arranged their own
version of a New Orleans–style Mardi gras and watermelon harvest festival. The event was so important that their voyage had
been timed to guarantee that Margaret and Raleigh wouldn't miss
this year's opportunity to meet the other eligible men and women
from the district. Despite what anyone said, Margaret knew that
she was expected to select a husband or have one chosen for her.

That night she heard her parents arguing again. From their
heated words she understood that their financial difficulties were
serious and that the arrival of two unmarried grown children had
added considerable strain.

"If you blame anyone, blame your poor, departed uncle Lester,
not me!" Lucretia hissed. Though she attempted to lower her
voice, every nuance of their argument wafted through the shut-

ters of Margaret's bedroom. It was rare to hear her mother, who gave every appearance of obedience, snap back at her husband.

Margaret heard her father mumble incoherently, which fueled her mother's anger even more.

"Or better still, blame Princess Isabel, or Lincoln, or Beauregard, but certainly not me! God knows I followed you to Moss Oaks, to Felicity Street, to the wild ends of the earth to see that you've had every opportunity. I buried two babies before I was twenty, abandoned my eldest, and still you weren't satisfied." Lucretia began to sob. Margaret listened to her father's futile efforts to calm her, feeling desperately sorry for them both.

Finally, Lucretia sighed. "We'd better get some rest, Charles."

He turned on his side and settled back onto his pillow. "Tomorrow I'll be supervising the construction of the storage pavilion. What are your plans?"

"Working on Margaret's clothing. She really has nothing suitable for Carnaval."

"You needn't worry about Gettie. She won't need finery to catch a man." Charles's voice softened with paternal pride. Hearing those words, Margaret turned over in bed, finally able to sleep.

❧   ❧   ❧

Within five years of their immigration, Uncle Lester and the other Lizzieland pioneers had begun, with the help of slave labor, to prosper. Their crops of melons, mangos, and rice brought profits so quickly to their remote settlement that they felt no need to follow the political changes taking place elsewhere in Brazil. In 1871, after six months of parliamentary struggle, the Rio Branco law, which abolished slavery in principle, was passed. The provisions of the "law of the free womb" declared that all children should henceforth be born free and remain only until their majority in the service of their mothers' masters in order to pay for the expenses of rearing and education. The law also made it obligatory for all masters to register their slaves or have them considered free. Since a bill passed forty years earlier forbade the importation of slaves, the Rio Branco law was to serve as the death knell of slavery within a generation, but it was intended to allow for the gradual changeover to a paid labor force.

In Lizzieland the passage of the law was not considered an important event because leaders of the community had pointed out the potential loopholes it offered slave proprietors. In fact, the end of their old way of life came far sooner than predicted. A strong abolitionist movement remained bitterly unsatisfied with the Rio Branco law. While the emperor, Dom Pedro II, was out of the country for a year, his appointed regent, the Crown Princess Isabel, granted immediate liberty to all slaves, without restriction, on the thirteenth of May, 1888. The consequence of this unexpected action was a violent economic blow to the unprepared colonists. When Charles and Lucretia arrived in Brazil in 1886, they had no idea that the whole economy of the expatriates was about to be shattered.

Even though the beauty surrounding the riverside colony could not be denied, the taming of the land, especially without a ready supply of free labor, became a brutal task. If Charles had ever regretted the move, he never spoke of his disappointment to anyone except his wife; but his authoritarian stubbornness deepened. Once the slaves had been freed by the sudden imperial decree, the peasants who were left to work the land adopted their own easygoing manner of serving Senhor Claiborne, whose name they found impossible to pronounce; instead they called him Seu Claro, "Mr. Light," enjoying the pun on his fair complexion.

Charles's once coppery blond hair had turned a shade of tarnished silver in the tropical sunlight. Only a few golden highlights remained in his long bristling mustache and triangular beard. With great difficulty he had learned to speak Portuguese, but he never mastered the intonation, dialect, or abbreviated phrases favored by the local inhabitants. When a farm worker took an order, he would repeat it back to Seu Claro in precisely the stilted words the landowner had used, though the North American never sensed the faint mockery in the response. While deference was expected, even Charles Claiborne was quick to realize that a respectful nod and a "Sim, senhor" did not necessarily mean the job would be finished or even begun. Perhaps this impossible chasm of expectation and response, made even deeper because few of the colonists ever understood the essence of the problem, was what really doomed the residents of Lizzieland.

All Lucretia's private longings had been transformed into hopes for Margaret. She had to admit her elder son was a recalcitrant and unattractive child, and even Charles tolerated his impulsive, often naughty son only barely. When the Claibornes decided to emigrate, it seemed best, from several viewpoints, for the fractious fourteen-year-old boy to remain in New Orleans, if only to spare Raleigh his father's belt.

But Margaret was another matter. She was the daughter every parent dreamed of having. This charming little girl had fortuitously inherited the best of the Claibornes and the Davises. Her hair sparkled with her father's blondness, yet she'd also received the same soft curls and fiery highlights that set off her mother's plain face. Even though her father's angular chin and mother's long, thin nose had at times seemed out of place when she was younger, in adulthood they served to give her a strength of expression that was more appealing than the fragility of a helpless beauty. Lucretia was especially pleased that their grey and blue eyes had merged to produce Margaret's outstanding shade of deep blue ringed with a dark grey border.

Gettie spoke early and distinctly. From a very young age she had been permitted to accompany her parents to Dr. Clapp's Congregational church in New Orleans, where she delighted everyone with her precise singing of the hymns. Lucretia, who had taken a brief course of music lessons as a child, began to introduce Margaret to the piano when, at age three, her thin fingers prematurely lost the pudginess of infancy, showing signs they would be elegantly tapered. When her daughter's precocity and attentiveness combined to make her an exceptional piano student, Lucretia began searching for the perfect teacher to mold Margaret into more than a just passable drawing room musician. Early tutors who shied from demanding too much of the tiny child were replaced until Mlle Doradou, an immensely talented woman who shared Lucretia's vision of Margaret's abilities, came into the Claibornes' life when the child was eight.

By the time Margaret was ten, her talent had blossomed. She was asked to perform at small public recitals as well as for anyone who ventured into the house. The sweet sounds of her practicing rose from the windows, enchanting passers-by on Felicity Street. Because of all the attention and compliments, the child also began to dream of what her mother and devoted teacher promised would be a bright future. But when her father had spoken of moving to Lizzieland, Margaret saw it all coming to an end.

"How can Margaret have a musical career in the jungle?" Lucretia had actually shouted. "It will destroy everything Mlle Doradou and I have worked for!" This was the first time Margaret had ever heard her mother question her father's authority.

"While I agree that Raleigh can go to your brothers, work in the store to pay his board, and finish his schooling, there is no one I can ask to shoulder the responsibility of so young a daughter," Charles had responded firmly.

Lucretia then pleaded, "How can you waste everything, ruin all our plans? What will there be for her in Brazil?"

"Her home, her parents, eventually a suitable marriage."

"Gettie is only twelve. To ask her to give up her lessons with Mlle Doradou now . . ."

"I'll think about it" was all Charles said. But that was enough for Lucretia to believe she'd won.

Charles Claiborne was proud that his daughter possessed all the best of him, even what should have rightly gone to a boy — courage, resilience, intelligence. With the sparkle in her sapphire blue eyes, an insouciant skip down the street, her golden curls flying . . . Ah, she was irresistible!

Finally it was Mlle Doradou who proposed the solution. Since Charles would not permit his daughter to stay with her because her reputation had been compromised by her long associations with musicians and artists, she suggested that Margaret could continue to study with her but live at the Ursuline convent school, clearly a safe haven for any young lady. Charles relented, settling on one condition. "She must continue to attend our church and not be permitted to bow before those saints and candles!"

Lucretia had agreed immediately. "Of course! My brothers will see to her religious training in our church."

For Margaret, not accompanying her family to Brazil had been the most unsettling event in her life. What had she done to change her parents' feelings for her? Hadn't she always tried to do as they wanted? Hadn't she worked to smother any rebellion at the endless lessons that pushed her further than she herself had ever wanted to go? After all the effort, she was being thrust from the family's center, and the very talent that had made her special now worked against her and made her life miserable.

It had taken some time for her to adjust to life without her family. But the Ursulines expected decorum and studiousness, and the well-disciplined Margaret did not find it difficult to capitulate to their rules. In time she had friends, girls with whom she spent her every free hour, girls who, like her, were denied the warmth of a close family and who banded together for security.

There was also Mlle Doradou, who educated her in areas far beyond the blacks and whites of notes and keys. In her unconventional home, cluttered with musical memorabilia and frequented by visiting celebrities, Margaret was introduced to the delicacies of Creole cuisine and European wines, taught how to appreciate everything fine, from paintings to lace, and shown how to dress simply yet fashionably. Mademoiselle's worldly salon, a shrine to the memory of Gottschalk, became Margaret's refuge from the starkness of the school, while the cloistered simplicity of the convent was often a welcome relief from the complications created by the artistic types who made her teacher's French Quarter home their local headquarters.

From the time, more than thirty years earlier, when Gottschalk, "mon petit Moreau," as Mademoiselle still affectionately referred to him, had accepted her as somewhere between protégée and sycophant (and, it was rumored, mistress for a time), Evangeline Doradou had won herself the enviable position as the musical doyenne of New Orleans. Her home was a magnet that attracted the most interesting artists of the day. They came to play Gottschalk's own Pleyel piano, drink from his engraved wine glass, and copy from the original scores of "The Union" and "The Banjo" that he left her for safekeeping before leaving on his last, and fatal, concert tour to South America. Though she was but a young woman when Louis Moreau Gottschalk died, Mademoiselle's whole life had been dedicated to his memory and music until Margaret's talent had changed her focus from preserving the past to promoting the child's future.

During her years away from her family, Margaret maintained a dutiful correspondence with her parents. In a few years, the memory of close family life all but forgotten, she found herself one of the main attractions of the Doradou salon. Mademoiselle had begun to promote her as "America's prettiest prodigy" and had visions of becoming Margaret's manager and chaperone as soon as she'd finished her last year at the convent school. "Together we'll see every concert stage in the world, ma chère," she'd promised. But her hopes were dashed, because as soon as Raleigh had completed his first few semesters at Tulane, the indifferent student, who wearied of serving the whims of his autocratic uncles, wrote his father that he now felt adequately prepared to meet the challenges of Brazil and requested passage south. Claiborne immediately responded, sending two tickets. Margaret could never have been permitted to remain in New Orleans alone.

When the news came, Margaret had loudly proclaimed she had no intention of leaving school, especially not in the middle of the term. Though sympathetic to the distress of one of their favorites, the sisters explained that her duty was to obey her parents. Mlle Doradou, however, was firmly on Margaret's side. In a barrage of letters, she had insisted that her pupil at least be permitted to finish out the school year, hoping by then to have thought of another excuse to keep Margaret with her. Not only didn't she want to lose her most talented student, she also retained a morbid fear of Brazil because her beloved Gottschalk had died there. But the result of her efforts was only to delay the journey a few months until the end of the semester, a small but important victory, since she had scheduled Margaret to play at a gala concert that autumn. Margaret had also been delighted at the postponement because it enabled her to travel with one of her classmates, Maria Francisca.

❧7 Eligible men. They were all Lucretia ever thought about. Even though the discussions frequently repulsed Margaret because she felt by joining them she was agreeing to the barter of her life, it was, if nothing else, the least boring topic of the day.

"Have you ever met Captain Shippey?" Margaret asked as she sat with her mother, who was deliberating on whether to alter one of her plainer dresses for Carnaval.

"No, but your father met him once in Iguape. He served in General Lee's Army of Northern Virginia and has recently purchased a plantation on the Rio Capivari, though I don't know who'd want to live in a place with such a terrible name."

"Why?"

"Well, I think it's named after a capivara, the world's largest rodent. Can you imagine a hundred-pound rat?"

"Isn't it considered a delicacy?"

"I'd rather starve!" Lucretia shivered. "Anyway, your father says that Shippey is phasing out his other crops and will grow coffee exclusively." Her mother fingered the simple eyelet trim. "What if we remove this and add the lace from my tea gown?"

Margaret, bored with the clothes, pressed on. "How many sons does he have?"

"Two. Or is it three? Still, the Shippeys live so far away, we'd rather find someone closer."

"Father seems keen on this Royce Burrows, the one whose parents lease part of the Gomes estate, but he's just thirty and has already buried his second wife."

"No fault of his. The man has been grief-stricken over each loss. Besides, they say his soil may be the best in this region for sugar cane."

"The best for breeding mosquitos! I won't be lured into that pest hole, no matter how sweet the bait!"

"Gettie! There's no need for more of your thoughtless remarks. Your father and I are only trying our best, and insolence is all we get for our efforts!" Lucretia's anger turned quickly to tears. Before Margaret knew what was happening, she was comforting her mother. "You have no idea how I've suffered without you and Raleigh. When you've babies of your own . . ."

Gradually, Margaret learned more about her prospects. The youngest possibility was the twenty-year-old son of Dr. Gaston from South Carolina who was studying medicine abroad and was not expected to return for several years (as far as Margaret was concerned, this delay was a point in his favor); the oldest was a fifty-year-old widower with grown children and a magnificently situated estate north of Iguape on the Rio Pariquera. In between were a motley selection of planters' sons, one not appreciably better-sounding than the next.

Recently, few marriages between the children of the colonists had taken place, so this year the colonists were even more anxious to make the effort to come together at Carnaval to prevent their "pure" population from dwindling further. Word had it that several young men living on remote parcels of land scattered over hundreds of miles of South American wilderness had been so imprudent as to wed Brazilian women. Already these local girls, themselves daughters of well-established landowners, were developing a reputation for being extremely suitable, undemanding, hardworking companions.

"But they're Roman Catholics!" Charles had roared when he had heard the news of one of these liaisons. "And who knows what kind of mixed blood they carry in their veins?"

Lucretia hadn't dared mention that the young men had been pressured to convert. "Even more reason our Gettie will be a welcome sight. Why, she'll be this year's sensation," she promised her husband.

Still, Charles worried. Margaret's musical training had been a fine diversion for an active youngster's mind, but it held no practical value. Worse, her talents had made her expectations unrealistic. If only she could learn to dedicate herself to a husband's needs, she'd find security and happiness. Yet every time he thought of her in another man's home, he felt pained. He had sorely missed watching her youthfulness ripen to succulence. She had turned out so well, with golden hair and a face so artlessly individual that any man would be blessed to have her. Still, without his hand in her training over the past nine years, there were some rough edges. His daughter didn't express the proper deference to him or her mother, and there were those endless struggles with Raleigh. Why, those two were worse than the three little ones put together! Just last night they'd gone after each other again. It had started when Margaret criticized Raleigh's rudeness with one of the workers and ended with another of his son's lectures on religion. Odd that a child of his would become so devout, but Charles supposed it was better for his son to have gone in the direction of the Lord than of the devil. Whatever religion had done for Raleigh, it had given him greater satisfaction with his lot, something that Margaret definitely lacked. Already Raleigh had made a far better adjustment to Lizzieland than Margaret, who, with all her charms, was simply not content to be what she was — an enchanting young woman — instead of striving for

what she seemed to want and could never obtain — the freedom
and choices of a man.

8 Life in Lizzieland was worse, far worse, than Margaret
had ever imagined. Most nights she dreamed of escape. In
futile attempts she had paddled small boats into cataracts, fallen
into sucking pits of sienna mud, been clawed by saw-toothed
palms blocking her path. For once, instead of running through an
endless, impassable forest filled with vicious insects, Margaret
dreamed she possessed a mysterious ability that enabled her to
fly. With a few deep sighs she was able to raise her body, and
then, by regulating her breathing into a rhythmic intake and out-
flow, she magically hovered above her damp and tangled bed like
a hummingbird. The bolted bedroom shutters flew open with
hardly a touch and she was away.

Higher and higher she rose, following the four shrill notes of
the mãe-da-lua. The odd mother-of-the-moon bird, its mouth as
big as its body, nested by the Iguape River, which wound its way
east to the sea. Once the aggravating disturber of her sleep, the
bird's call was now a sentinel for her journey. As soon as she
could see the black ribbon of waterway glistening in the moonlight, Margaret followed its circuitous curves, dipping low and
swooping high, reveling in the precise flying maneuvers that
came with practice. The mother-of-the-moon bird quieted.
Ahead dawn's coppery gleam reflected in the rolling Atlantic sea-
swells. Sand fingers along the shoreline reached out to touch the
foaming waves. At last she could see north, north to Rio.

Margaret's eyes fluttered open. She wished she could've retained the sensation of flight, but it dissolved in the glare, the unusually strong glare of morning sun. She turned her head toward
the window. Outside, an iridescent green hummingbird, its wings
shot with gold, was sucking from a freshly opened pink hibiscus
with its long down-curving bill. Each night the hibiscus flowers
died; each morning enormous new blossoms offered themselves,
their dazzling cores inviting insects and birds to partake. The
wooden shutters had truly come open during the night. Had she
forgotten to bolt them fast before retiring? In any case, Margaret
realized she was too distracted to fall back to sleep, though sleep
was the best way to fill the formless, shapeless hours that lay be-

fore her. Now her day, always agonizingly long, punctuated only
by meals or petty family squabbles, had prematurely begun.

Just as Margaret made a move to sit up, slowly turning on her
side and pushing with her slender hand, she caught sight of something so shocking that all went black. Her eyes refocused on a
spade-shaped head held alert by the largest snake Margaret had
ever encountered.

How long could the snake have been there? Had she shared her
bed most of the night with this creature, or had it slithered in
only moments before she'd awakened? How had the shutters
come undone? she mused nonsensically, that mystery crowding
out the rising hysteria.

She commanded her trembling limbs to remain still as she tried
to detect any nuance of expression in the reptile's mask of a face,
any blink of its diamond eyes. She concentrated on breathing so
shallowly that the bedcovers barely rose or fell. Thank God her
mother's fear of this place included snakes! Lucretia lectured her
about the skins tacked to colonists' walls so earnestly that the lessons had stuck. Immediately, Margaret recognized the golden
skin decorated with brown rhomboid markings rimmed in black,
the lance-shaped viper head with the characteristic pit between
the eyes. This very similar snake must certainly be a jararaca,
which meant "arrow," the most common poisonous snake of the
region. Margaret hastily calculated that each of the snake's four
thick coils had to be more than a foot long; unwound, it would
probably be taller than her own body.

Thankfully, she heard stirrings in the house. She recognized
Raleigh's footsteps and dared a whisper. "Ral . . . eigh!"

No answer. Panic overcame Margaret's caution. She called
loudly. "Raleigh, help me! There's a snake in here!"

The snake's javelin head, aimed at her chest, wavered notice-
ably. Margaret's action became instinctive. Her body rose in one
deft motion, and throwing the bedclothes onto the creature, she
leapt from the bed, through the opening door, and into her
mother's astonished arms.

She sobbed and hugged her mother around the waist. "There's
a snake in my bed!"

"Have you been having another of your bad dreams?"

"No, I really saw a snake! I called to Raleigh" — she pointed

toward her brother, who had come in through the side door —
"but he wouldn't help me."

Margaret could see doubt clouding her mother's watery
grey eyes. "Poor darling, you're letting your imagination run
away . . ."

"There was a snake!" Margaret protested. "I threw my bedding
over it . . . It must still be somewhere in the room."

Lucretia Claiborne clapped her hands. "Berto! Berto!"

A servant who had been quietly sweeping leaves from the path
came into the house through the kitchen. "Senhora?"

"Uma cobra!" Margaret trembled and pointed to her room.

Berto looked toward the door with disbelief, his nut-brown face
a map of wrinkles from working under the incessant sun all his
life. With one hand he pulled a peixeira, his ever-present knife, from
his hip pocket and knocked the door open with the broom handle.
There, on the floor to the left, was indeed a large coiled snake,
frozen in the striking position. Raleigh chuckled in the background as Berto nudged the stiff creature with his broom handle.

"It's dead! I saw it on the road last night and shot it!" Raleigh
tugged at his sister's single golden braid. "I meant it as a harmless
joke and you fell for it."

"Raleigh!" Lucretia's voice was exasperated. "I'd have expected
something like this from a boy like Marshall. A man your age
should have been done with pranks years ago!"

Under his breath Raleigh muttered, "I just thought my sister
might benefit from a Biblical reminder that temptation is ever-
present."

His mother's disapproving expression brought him up short
and he turned away, obviously upset that she hadn't fallen for his
excuse.

Margaret crossed her quivering arms to cover her thin batiste
gown. "You're wrong! It's alive! I know I saw it move!"

Just as Berto lifted the dead snake with the broom, a glittery
flash whipped across the floor and wound itself around his naked
calf. This second snake drew back its head and struck, burying its
fangs into a spot just above a knob of ankle bone. The reptile's
mouth was hinged so wide that its long fangs were visible as they
dug into the flesh a second time. It seemed to happen so slowly
that the snake's final strike became clearly etched in Margaret's

mind: the fangs curving back in its jaw, the sickly yellow venom oozing from the puncture wound.

With indifference to his injury, Berto thrust the bristle end of the broom onto the five feet of writhing, winding muscle. Momentarily immobilizing the snake, he grabbed it behind the head, unwound its tail from his ankle, and stood on it. With a quick movement of his peixeira, he sliced through the three-inch-thick body, cutting it in half before tossing the offending head section toward the wall. Blood arced across the bedroom, spraying the linens, the plaster, the bleached mosquito netting. Margaret fled the room before the severed creature crashed to the floor.

Within minutes after the attack, all the servants had crowded around the verandah to see Berto's injury and to comment, admiringly, on the snake's corpse.

"Such a grand one! What beautiful markings!" Both dead snakes were unwound and laid side by side. The one that had been alive in Margaret's bed was almost two feet longer than the one Raleigh had placed in her room.

"Uma cobra casada," a villager murmured as Colonel Willis Demaret, given an honorary title because he was the oldest living Lizzieland resident, made his way into the center of the excited crowd. He kneeled beside the victim. Though initial attempts to stop the bleeding and suck the poison had already been made by one of Berto's friends, Colonel Demaret, who functioned as community pastor, historian, and medic simply because he had seen, read, or heard more than any of the other colonists, began to take charge.

"A pity the man's honest and sober," he said after he examined the jagged double V fang wound. "I've only seen them survive these snakebites when their system has been pickled with pinga. The rum dilutes the poison. Even now he should drink as much of the stuff as is humanly possible; if nothing else, it'll help with the pain."

While Berto's friends tried to force him to drink cup after cup of caustic cane spirits, Colonel Demaret sent for his small cache of medical supplies. He did the best he could to stop the flow of blood from the steadily oozing wound.

"What's 'uma cobra casada'?" Margaret asked the colonel.

"A married snake. When one of these reptiles is captured or

killed, it will often be followed by its mate." He turned toward where Raleigh was cowering in the corner of the porch. "What made you try such a stupid, dangerous trick?"

"How was I to know about the other snake?"

Openly disgusted by the young man's puerile response, the colonel turned back to where Margaret was leaning over Berto. "From now on you must remember to keep your shutters tightly closed at night," he spoke kindly. "There are so many unwanted nocturnal creatures: bats, scorpions, wildcats, and, of course, snakes . . ."

"I always bolt them! Raleigh must've opened my shutters to provide a convincing way for his serpent to have entered my room." Margaret made no attempt to disguise the bitterness in her voice.

In less than an hour Berto's leg had swollen past the knee. By the time Demaret's servant returned with his supplies, Berto was complaining of a terrible thirst. "Aiii!" he moaned pathetically. "I see only yellow, everything is yellow . . . Why?"

"Poor fellow!" Colonel Demaret sympathized as he prepared a potassium permanganate compress. "I've heard there was some kind of a cast that forms in the eyes when the poison nears the brain."

"Let me help," Margaret insisted. As she bound the purple-stained gauze to the servant's ankle, she asked in a shaky voice, "Is there nothing more we can do?"

Colonel Demaret, his silvery white hair contrasting handsomely with his high sun-stained forehead, touched her shoulder gently. "My dear, the venom of this snake is almost always lethal. Once I heard of a woman in Iguape who grated coconuts for candy and consequently had numerous small scratches on her fingertips. When her husband, a plantation laborer, was bitten by a jararaca almost six feet in length, she tended him by bathing the bleeding punctures. Despite her efforts, and those of the local 'snake doctor,' the man died. Even more dreadful, a few days later, the wife, who must have absorbed some of the venom through her lacerated fingertips, succumbed with the same symptoms as her husband."

Margaret shuddered uncontrollably. Soon more men from the village arrived, wrapped Berto in a striped cotton hammock, and carried him down the hill to his home. All day long neighbors appeared with more cachaça rum, herbs, and amulets. A small statue of Nossa Senhora do Rosario was brought from the chapel and placed outside his hut so that prayers could be offered by everyone who came to visit and comfort his family.

❧ ❧ ❧

The next morning Margaret walked down from the colonists' hillside enclave to the dusty peasant village on the riverbank to learn firsthand if there had been an improvement in Berto's condition. Littering the crossroads were candle stubs, dead chickens, neatly arranged bones of newborn animals — all signs of the healing rituals performed by the devotees of macumba, the uniquely Brazilian form of black magic.

Berto's wife huddled inside their hut. A baby sleeping on a pile of rags began to cry. Margaret caressed the infant until it quieted.

"What's your name?" Margaret asked the woman gently.

"Florinda, senhorita."

"How many children do you have?"

"Five . . . living, senhorita."

Florinda herself looked so young that Margaret thought it impossible for her to have produced so many babies. "How old are you?"

"Twenty, senhorita."

Margaret was stunned to realize that Berto's wife was a year younger than she. Even after so many pregnancies, the bronze-skinned girl retained a youthful, if slightly voluptuous, figure. With her large, alert black eyes and sensuous mouth, it was hard to imagine her aging into one of the withered, prematurely old women most of the village girls became.

The baby tossed back his head and began to cry more forcefully. Florinda rose, shuffled over, lifted him up, and prepared to put him to her breast. She nodded toward a doorway covered by a handwoven curtain. Margaret could postpone her duty call no longer.

The smell in the back room was an overpowering mixture of smoke, sweat, and burnt feathers. Optimistically, Margaret had imagined that the puffiness of his skin would have subsided somewhat or that his pain-clouded stare would have cleared, but

Berto's condition had obviously deteriorated. Wherever there had been old injuries on his body, huge bluish-red marks had blossomed and then begun to blacken. He gave a low, guttural moan. Even though a sheet had been loosely draped over his genitals, Margaret could see they too had become grossly swollen. Every few seconds the barely conscious man was ravaged by long, excruciating spasms.

Colonel Demaret caught Margaret running blindly up the path. "My dear, you shouldn't have gone."

"I had to . . . All my fault . . . and Raleigh's," she stammered. "But he doesn't seem to care."

"I agree that your brother showed little judgment, but you must believe that it was God's will."

"How can you say such a thing!" Margaret choked. "Poor Berto's body is slowly turning . . . black!"

"As your dear old uncle Lester used to say, 'What man is he that liveth, and shall not see death?' "

She bowed her head. "But to die in such agony, all because he came to help me. It's so unfair!"

"Remember the words of Isaiah, 'The Lord will have mercy upon his afflicted.' " The colonel lifted Margaret's chin. The pretty child's eyes were luminous with tears.

"You speak as though he cannot possibly live."

The old man took her hand and patted it compassionately. "He must have absorbed a vast quantity of the poison. Snakes do not have venom strictly to defend themselves. This they do more effectively with skin coloration and rapid movements. The function of their poison is to break down the blood and tissues of their victims so as to aid digestion."

Though Margaret's eyes began to glaze, Colonel Demaret continued with the technicalities of his explanation. "You've seen for yourself how the blood at the site of the wound continued to trickle; that's called the hemotoxic reaction . . ."

Margaret's legs began to shake violently. She slipped against the colonel and fainted. The next she knew, Margaret was in her own bed being sponged by her mother. Faces and voices seemed very distant.

"She's always been too sentimental, a sweet child, but not as strong as she appears. I worry about her adjusting."

"You worry about the wrong things!" Charles said too forcefully.

"Hush! Let her rest."

He lowered his voice to a hoarse whisper. "We've tolerated both Gettie's and Raleigh's nonsense far too long. If Raleigh had been called home to us years ago maybe he wouldn't have been so misguided by those . . . fanatics. And, so far as I'm concerned, our daughter would have been better off married before she was eighteen. The only thing those nuns at that convent school seem to have done is to indoctrinate her with all that Roman Catholic rigamarole."

Lucretia left her husband's side and stared out across the valley where clouds were gathering for an afternoon storm. "Charles, our daughter's a God-fearing Christian, with a good heart. Look how concerned she's been over this accident."

"That's exactly what I'm talking about! All this sentimentality over a half-breed servant! Gettie's tender sensibilities have been misplaced. We've let both of them behave as children far too long. Now they must become the man and woman you and I were at their age."

"Maybe Raleigh is ready, but Gettie? There's really no one suitable for her to marry."

Charles was adamant. "They'll both be wed within the year. Raleigh first, then Gettie."

A hard, fast rain began to hammer against the tiles on the roof, dripping through the ceiling cracks that no one ever remembered to repair between storms.

Margaret stirred. "Mother, I . . ."

Lucretia patted her daughter's hand. "You're fine, you just became overly excited." She tried to silence her husband with her eyes.

Charles bent over his daughter and spoke close to her face. "I forbid you to go to the village again!"

❧ ❧ ❧

Margaret awoke in the middle of the night to the reverberating voices of the villagers chanting prayers to Omulú, the ancient African macumba goddess with the power to confront the spirit of the dead. She stepped out onto the verandah to listen.

Omulú, hear your child!
You have the strength,
The strength your child needs!
Come to his aid!
You are old,
But you are wise and powerful!

The primitive sounds, churning amid outbursts of wind and rain, quieted as the birds began to sing. Margaret shivered in the morning chill and wondered if Berto's condition possibly could have improved. If she dressed quickly she could check on him and be back before her father realized she'd been down to the village. Perhaps Colonel Demaret had been wrong; perhaps the potassium permanganate had worked or a miracle had been accomplished.

From the back door Margaret could see the palm-thatched rooftops of the huts floating above the rising river mists like rafts in a delicate sea. So she wouldn't be noticed by an early riser, she slipped through the forest trails that goats had worn through the undergrowth. Candles burned close to the ground and the macumba signs still littered the periphery of Berto's hut. A chicken in the doorway startled her. Margaret shooed it before she entered.

Nobody was in the front room, so Margaret bravely moved toward the back of the house. The bedroom smelled of paraffin and sulfur. In the dim shadows, Florinda stood watch over Berto's very still body.

"Senhor?" Margaret asked politely.

"He does not see nor hear, Dona Margarida." Florinda dipped a rag into a bucket and wiped her husband's face, rinsed it, then slowly repeated the movement, again and again and again.

Blood oozed in a thin continuous line from Berto's mouth, from his nose, from his ears, from open sores all over his body. The colonel had explained that hemorrhaging was the precursor of death. "May God grant him peace," Margaret gasped, and rose quickly to return home before her family awoke.

Within a few hours Margaret watched the red dust rising from the small funeral procession. Berto's body had been placed in a black casket, the traditional color for a husband and father, and rolled on a small cart pulled by his eldest children. Behind them his young widow shuffled barefooted, holding her youngest in her arms. Only a few other relations and close friends joined the march to the cemetery. Death was too commonplace to interrupt work. Though the sun was at its highest, Margaret shivered as the last mourner passed out of sight. She could not stop worrying about Florinda's plight. Strangled, stifled, locked in a life she never would have chosen for herself, Margaret recognized another trapped spirit when she saw one.

"I won't let them suffer," she promised silently. Any help she'd provide would have to be without her family's knowledge. All the colonists warned against any favoritism toward one of the villagers, calling it divisive. But to Margaret, Christian charity dictated no less than what she intended.

9 "Carnaval, Mardi gras, whatever you call it! I still don't see why everything stops for it!" Charles grumbled as he came to the breakfast table. Lucretia quickly poured his coffee. "I wouldn't mind two or three days of celebration, but the preparations alone slow productivity for over a month!"

"One egg or two, dear?" Lucretia cracked a soft-boiled egg on a piece of dry toast, breaking the yolk precisely in the center so it would coat the jellied white the way her husband demanded it.

"And those damned drums have been beating all night. How're we supposed to get any sleep?"

"Charles!"

"It's part of their religion, isn't it?" Margaret asked naively.

"If this is a religion, then Satan's in his glory!"

Lucretia shot a warning glance at Margaret to indicate she wasn't to disagree with her father until after he'd eaten. "There's no harm done by a bit of celebration now and then." Lucretia's tone was placating. "I'm even looking forward to this week. It's been more than a year since I've seen many of my dearest friends."

"As far as I'm concerned, it's a wasteful interruption!" Charles muttered.

A whistle blast from a river barge startled them.

"Could that be the Fontaines already?" Lucretia beamed. "They must have traveled all night! Gettie, your father, Raleigh, and I will go down to the wharf. In case they're exhausted, you

stay here and ready the rooms for them. Raleigh will move in
with Marshall; you'll bed with your sisters; move the divan into
the parlor ..." she fluttered on unnecessarily, since the details
had been organized weeks in advance.

✻   ✻   ✻

"What do you think?" Nell whispered to Margaret as they helped
to decorate a long table with wildflowers and fruits for the
luncheon buffet.

"Of what?" Margaret asked innocently.

"Her!" hissed Nell. "I mean, how can Father think that Raleigh would ever agree! I've never seen such a toad!"

"Nell." Margaret giggled. "I think she's absolutely perfect!" In
a second she regretted her meanness.

Marianne appeared painfully shy. The girl knew all too well
that she was being paraded before the Claibornes as a marriage
prospect. After the meal, Margaret sought out Marianne and
asked if she would like to take a walk. Marianne nodded and
reached for the engraved silver handle of her cane. They strolled
without speaking for a few moments, until Margaret purposely
broke the awkward silence. "Have you ever been to Lizzieland
before?"

"Once, about five years ago. I don't remember it very well. It
rained every day and the roof leaked in the house where we were
staying. I caught such a severe chill I had to be carried back to the
boat in a hammock."

"We do have frequent showers, something to do with the elevation." Margaret pointed across a ridge. "I love to watch the
storms as they creep across the valley."

"Excellent coffee country."

Her confident appraisal of the land surprised Margaret. "It's
not grown here. The colonists have always stayed with more familiar crops."

"A pity, there's so much more profit in coffee."

Margaret studied Marianne's small, pinched face and, seeing a
quickness in her green eyes, realized that Marianne's withdrawn
nature cloaked a ready intelligence. Just what Raleigh needs,
Margaret thought, this time without malice.

"Do you know the history of Lizzieland?" she asked.

"It was the first North American settlement in this area, wasn't it?"

"That's right." Margaret pointed to a house a hundred yards across from where they were standing. "That's number twelve, the home of Colonel Demaret. He's the last person remaining from the first wave of colonists. In 1867 he sailed from New Orleans with my uncle Lester and a party of three hundred sixty-five men, women, and children — about eighty families — in two ships heading for Mexico."

"Mexico! Then how did they end up in Brazil?"

"Their timing was terrible. The Mexican insurrection was at its most turbulent. In fact, Emperor Maximilian was executed just before they landed. So, to avoid political troubles, the ship refueled and started for South America. The first Confederate settlement was in a town known as Xirica, but they quickly found it too low and damp there. So, the group dispersed to various localities. My uncle and the Demarets were among the first to join Reverend Dunn, who was just forming Lizzieland farther south."

"Be glad they didn't remain along the river. Where we live it's so humid that green fungus grows in the folds of our clothes overnight."

"No!"

Marianne laughed out loud. "Maybe not overnight, but I would much prefer to live at this elevation."

For the first time, Margaret realized there might be an even worse location than Lizzieland.

"How is it that all your houses were built so close together? I thought you owned individual plantations." Marianne gestured toward the almost identical rectangular houses. The only differences were the styles of landscaping.

"Since there were twelve original families in the settlement, they divided the holding in a unique circular fashion, based on the face of a clock. I told you that the Demaret house is called twelve. Now ours, directly opposite, is called six. Can you now see how it works?"

Marianne pointed to the Confederate flag that was still raised each morning. "The flagpole is where the hands of the clock might be."

"Right, and everything immediately surrounding it is considered 'the common.' Each family is taxed a percentage for the building and upkeep of the meeting hall, the church, a schoolhouse, and the warehouses for the crops."

"What is privately owned?"

"Only the wedge-shaped initial parcels. Each family built their house as close to the narrowest point as possible. The land just behind was used for kitchen gardens, widening into fields for the melons and other major crops. The rim still contains the unharvested forests."

"It seems almost too practical," Marianne mused.

"You're correct. While it must have seemed ideal on paper, it really didn't work out fairly, since not every piece of land was equal in value. Some portions contained more rocks and untillable land; other sections had cliffs instead of forestable trees. My father's piece is quite large in the backlands because he bought out a section when number five's husband, Oliver Pyle, died. My father has an option on the house, too. He'll probably settle it on Raleigh when he marries."

"Which is the Pyles'?" Marianne asked with renewed interest.

"Over there." Margaret pointed to the house with the sagging verandah. "When you face our house, it's the one to the left, a bit hidden under the guava tree."

If Marianne was disappointed by its shabby exterior, she didn't convey it. On the way back to the house, she seemed to walk with more assurance, and for some unexplainable reason, Margaret thought her limp was much less noticeable.

❧ 10 "If we can't get our products on the wharf at Santos at a competitive price, we might as well all sell out and save the aggravation!" Cunningham Lee shouted, his porcine cheeks reddening. The other gentlemen on the Lees' verandah murmured their approval. A distant cousin of the great general, Lee commanded respect for his name alone.

Mrs. Lee directed the servants to refill their guests' glasses with cool fruit juice and pass platters of smoked ham sandwiches.

"We all know who's responsible for our runaway costs, don't we?" Walter Phillips said snidely.

Since traveling to Lizzieland posed a multitude of inconveniences and considerable expense, the planters expected their time together to be worthwhile from more than one point of view. Eschewing most of the frivolities, the men gathered daily to discuss the commodities prices in Santos, Rio, and London; new varieties of seed and fertilizer; labor management; and the rising threat of banditry in the backlands. But the most serious matter under consideration was the escalating cost of river transport. The Brazilian-owned ships, while less expensive, were also less reliable than those that Leonard Fontaine owned, but the expatriates were chafing at being gouged by one of their own.

As Charles Claiborne watched the shipping fees press higher each year, he also had kept his eye on the old man's eldest daughter. Now that his plan to stabilize prices for his personal cargo through a marriage alliance was almost realized, he had little interest in antagonizing Fontaine. Still, he could not publicly defend the policies that had squeezed profits from the majority. His diplomatic solution was to remain uncharacteristically quiet throughout the heated debate.

Oscar Shippey chewed off the tip of his cigar and spat it into the jasmine vines that wrapped themselves around the roof supports. "No more mélancia! We no longer have a monopoly on watermelon and they're just too difficult to transport, wagon to wharf, barge to ship! I'm converting to coffee one hundred percent!"

Breaking his own vow to keep silent, Claiborne jumped into the fray. "You'll wait three years before you even know if you've got the right soil, five years for a real crop, and if there's ever a freeze . . ."

"Then the price will go up," Shippey said smugly. "You see, my dear Claiborne, coffee, unlike your precious melons, has a world market. They can't get enough of it in Europe, in the States. Those nice little brown berries can be stored for months to take advantage of peak prices. Pile up your melancia and you have nothing but slime!"

"Our first attempts at cotton were a disaster, rice turned only a passable profit, sugar thrives in but a few of our lowlands. It's about time we made a more organized study of a crop before haphazardly planting something else that looks good on paper," Cunningham Lee added forcefully.

"What do you know about coffee?" Claiborne countered. "All

you ever think about are those damned chocolate beans of yours!"

"Who suggested anything about planting cacao in the high-lands?" Lee burst out. "It's only because the seaside piece my son's working has a climate rivaling the famous groves in Bahia that I'm even considering the crop."

"That brings us to the point at hand, doesn't it?" Shippey interjected. "If we are going to succeed, we must unemotionally look at the raw land, the climate, the world marketplace, before making a decision as to what to plant where or when."

Charles listened, but not exactly with the same motives as the others. Both Shippey and Lee had eligible sons. This was a perfect opportunity to ascertain both the character and financial worth of the families. He was so impressed by Shippey's remarks that he made a point to seek out his one unmarried son for some private conversations later that day.

Soon the heads of the families, their meeting adjourned, maneuvered into smaller groups. They smoked and chatted about less volatile topics in the shadow of the Lee house, which, with its additions and outbuildings, was the largest and most substantial in the colony. The women congregated across the common on the Demaret porch so they could tend their babies sleeping under mosquito netting, have a vantage point to observe their toddling youngsters, and prudently observe, but not interfere with, the young people who congregated near the bakery.

Lizzieland boasted one of the few ovens in the region. Servants from the different families took turns tending the brick fires all night so fresh breads were available at dawn. Young women, without babies to watch or business discussions to attend, hovered around the bakery to guard the crusty sourdough breads as they were set out to cool. Since Lizzieland did not have a well-established dairy, butter was a luxury. Knowing this, the Shippey family had brought earthenware tubs of sweet butter wrapped in moistened banana leaves to keep them cool and fresh. The table laden with the sliced warm loaves, the sunny bowls of butter, and the rainbow of exotic fruit jams was the bait to lure the young men who roamed the perimeters of the common.

As planned, two dozen or more young men and women were enmeshed in a ritual of avoidance and attraction. For the first time, Nell, now sixteen, was permitted to join the group of young adults. Knowing that no match would be considered for her that year, she was confused as to how to behave.

Too self-conscious to engage anyone in conversation, she walked around the table, testing the jams and jellies. She came back to where Margaret and Marianne were standing. "I've tried every sweet on the table!" she said a bit too loudly, "and the blue-ribbon prize should go to Mrs. Shippey's caju fruit preserves! Heavenly! Have you tasted them?"

"No, I haven't. Which one is it?" Marianne asked.

"In the blue willow bowl. It has chunks of lemon or orange! If everything Mrs. Shippey cooks is as good as that, I'd marry her son myself — that is, if Margaret decides she doesn't want him for herself."

Margaret blanched. "Shhhh . . ."

"Do you know which one he is?" Marianne asked.

Nell twisted around, flashing her petticoats. "I think he's the one with the thin mustache. Shall I find out for sure?"

"*No!*" Marianne and Margaret said in unison and then began to laugh.

"Here come your 'bookends.'" Nell referred to the two men who'd been staying as close as possible to Margaret.

The taller of the two, Farley Williams, had pocked skin but a kindly manner. He claimed he played the banjo and tried to keep Margaret's interest with discussions along musical lines. The other, Andrew Hudgins, was extremely fidgety. He never seemed to know where to put his nervous hands, so he usually had them jammed into his pockets. Unfortunately, he had a grating, squeaky voice that made him terribly shy about speaking his mind, but he was an apt listener. Margaret did her best to put them both at ease and was rewarded with an attentiveness that she had to admit was rather appealing. They laughed at her every joke and followed her every gesture. She'd tease them just enough to keep them amused, but was careful not to hurt either's feelings. In every way possible, she attempted to dissuade them, because neither, in her mind, was a serious candidate. However, the realization that they thought her so special was irresistibly pleasing.

In less than an hour, a wind kicked up from the ridge and began to blow across the common, swirling a fine-grained red

dust over the tables spread with delicacies. The girls jumped to
cover everything, but in a few seconds the crusts, plates, and
bleached tablecloths were powdered with grit. This mishap mus-
tered the more reluctant young men into action. They sprang
forward to salvage what they could. By the time the breeze had
changed direction, a familiarity had developed and everyone had
regrouped. Margaret and her retinue moved to one side. While
she half-listened to Farley's tale of a bandit's capture near his settlement, she observed Marianne talking solemnly to Raleigh and
Nell.

"For a while I thought I'd become a preacher," Raleigh was
saying.

When Nell groaned out loud at this clumsy preamble, Margaret stepped forward and steered her back to her group. "You
must hear Mr. Williams's story. It's quite incredible." From the
corner of her eye, Margaret could see Marianne resting her
weight on the side of the table to balance her stance. Raleigh
leaned as close to her as could be thought proper, his attention
riveted to her soft and guileless face.

"What made you change your mind?" Marianne's low voice
carried well.

"I don't know that I have," Raleigh continued a bit shakily. "I
returned to Brazil out of a sense of duty to my parents. Yet surely
we all have been sent to live in this wilderness for a greater purpose than we may understand at this moment."

Marianne smiled tentatively. " 'I am the voice of one crying in
the wilderness. Make straight the way of the Lord.' "

With great emotion, Raleigh stared at the girl, his dark pupils
dilating. Droplets of sweat formed along his brow and he felt his
hands moisten. His voice quaked as he asked, "Have you accepted
Christ as your personal savior?"

Marianne's chin wavered. "I have been taught to believe in the
word of God."

"Have you truly opened up your heart to Him? Have you
dedicated your life to Him?" Raleigh spoke with even more intensity.

Confused by the serious questions being thrust at her in the
first hours of an acquaintance, Marianne had no immediate answer. What did she believe and how could she sum it all up in a

few crucial moments when her whole future was obviously at stake? She had been raised as a Protestant, the Bible was read daily in their home, and her mother was especially devout. Still, she knew there was no way she could pretend her belief was as profound as Raleigh's.

Another gust of wind stirred the red dust at her feet. A flock of black-capped canaries flew across the common to take shelter in the high trees by the river. Mothers were calling their young children inside, and a flurry of bright skirts swirled around the tables as the women quickly carried the food to safety. Raleigh steered Marianne under one of the pendulous banana trees. Sheltered by the great fanning leaves, they stood side by side, saying not a word. Marianne did not look at Raleigh critically. Instead of seeing his large ears or crooked nose, she was riveted to a few individual elements — his deep brown eyes, the pinkness of his lips, his brow that stretched appealingly taut during his most fervent speeches.

To Raleigh, Marianne was beguiling. Her bones were fine and her face was a delicate oval, with quick, green eyes a beacon of intelligence and benevolence. Though unusually thin, her arms were well developed from assisting her crippled leg, giving her a powerful maternal quality that he found deeply affecting. When he reached across and touched Marianne very lightly on her arm, she quivered. Her face registered alarm at the unexpected intensity of her response to him. "You feel what I do?" he asked.

Aware of the powerful charge in the air, Marianne nodded. "This isn't what I expected . . ." Her voice was so thick she could barely make herself heard.

"I feel I must tell you everything I am thinking, for after knowing you, even this briefly, I believe that something far greater than our parents has brought us together."

Marianne somehow found the courage to respond. "I can't explain why, yet I know you speak the truth."

"When were you baptized?" Raleigh asked suddenly.

"As an infant."

"That was before you accepted Jesus as your own personal savior! Would you consider being baptized again, before we are wed?"

No fantasy of what a proposal of marriage would sound like had prepared Marianne for his blunt words, though it seemed perfectly natural to respond, "I would do so with all my heart!"

Dark clouds washed across the hillside. The rumbling, beating sounds of the encroaching storm went unnoticed and unheeded by the couple whose eyes were locked in mutual fascination. With a graceful gesture, Raleigh took Marianne's delicate face between his hands. Both ignored the fat raindrops. "We have been blessed to have been brought together, for surely He has a purpose for us, a task for us to perform together. I have often read about grace, the kindness and love of God that our Savior has toward man; but never, never before this moment, have I felt its presence so wholly."

A voice called from the nearest house. "Marianne! Raleigh! Everyone is looking for you!"

Raleigh finally noticed Margaret beckoning him. He stepped away from Marianne.

"What shall we tell them?" Marianne asked.

"That you and I . . . that we have decided . . ." Raleigh stopped himself. "We have agreed . . . to be married . . . Have we not?"

Marianne laughed, not her usual nervous high-pitched trill, but deeply and fully. "We have!"

Raleigh disregarded the rain that now beat so fiercely the tree offered insufficient shelter. "Then when shall it be?"

The words came rushing out before she could rearrange them. "It would be most convenient if . . ."

"With everyone already gathered . . ."

Marianne was beginning to shiver as the rain pelted her thin dress. "It need not be very elaborate . . ."

"And the baptism . . . Could it be tomorrow?"

Marianne cupped her palm under a dripping bough. "If this doesn't count, then it shall be tomorrow," she replied, victory bubbling in her voice.

Her last words were blurred as Raleigh modestly kissed her shining face.

❧ 11   The Fontaine and Claiborne families were equally unprepared for so swift a wedding. Yet neither dared complain about two such dutiful children who had, before their very eyes, fallen into a love so compelling that the young couple was oblivious to everything else. Marianne's clubfoot had never been mentioned; some believed Raleigh hadn't even noticed. Old sayings about marriages being made in heaven and the Lord moving in mysterious ways were bandied about as the hasty preparations for the ceremony were made.

As often as possible, the newly engaged couple abandoned the hectic festival on the hillside, preferring to spend their courtship talking quietly along the riverside docking area, which was now crowded with the assorted craft of the visitors. Sometimes they would sit on the deck of the Fontaine barge (whose interior was too elegant for the term to be truly apt) always in full view of anyone along the waterfront. While they craved privacy, both were so concerned about maintaining a flawlessly respectable appearance that another family member was always present as chaperone.

Just before dusk on the fourth evening of Carnaval, Marianne and Raleigh sat sipping coffee. Leonard Fontaine's personal servant, who seemed especially anxious to join the peasants' celebrations, hovered about, waiting for the cups to be drained. Marianne's little sisters fished off the back of the boat, their squeals and shouts punctuating Raleigh's ongoing saga of his life. He believed it vital that his fiancée know his past completely before the wedding. "My Davis uncles were not cruel men; it's just that they never cared for me especially."

"Surely you were very helpful to them."

"I tried my best, though I always seemed to end up the butt of their crude jokes. I'd overhear them calling me their 'clay that had to be borne.' "

"How terrible for you!" Marianne was filled with sympathy. "I can't imagine being left with relatives when I was just fourteen, having to work for my keep, and study too! You are a remarkable person to have survived so well."

Raleigh was so relieved by his fiancée's compassion that he dared reveal the details of the religious conversion that changed his life. "My parents had been led away from their Baptist upbringing when, after moving to the city, they joined the church founded by Reverend T. S. Clapp, who started the First Congregational Unitarian Church in New Orleans. I think they were attracted more to his choir and flowery sermons than his ministry."

They were interrupted by Marianne's exuberant sisters. "There it is! Get the net!" The barge rocked as the two little girls ran back and forth, chasing something in the water.

Raleigh steadied his coffee cup before continuing. "My uncle Mortimer Davis, with whom I boarded, was not a faithful churchgoer, so when one of their other clerks, Henderson Potter, invited me to accompany him to the Jackson Avenue Evangelical Church, I was most pleased to have been asked. How would I have known that this simple offer of comradeship would illuminate my entire life?"

"Everything changed after only one service?"

"Oh, Marianne!" Raleigh grasped her hand. "If I could turn back time, I would ask to have you beside me that evening! The guest preacher was Billy Sunday, surely the most eloquent man I have ever heard! When he spoke about the fires of hell, I really believed I was a sinner who needed — no, wanted — to be saved. The choir sang the invitation, 'Out of my bondage, sorrow and night; Jesus, I come, Jesus, I come; Into Thy freedom, gladness and light, Jesus, I come to Thee.' " Raleigh paused and wiped his tearing eyes.

Marianne encouraged him to take a few more sips of the syrupy coffee. With a nervous gesture, Raleigh brushed back the lock of hair that slipped in front of his eyes every few seconds. To Marianne, every one of his movements was so much more endearing than the last that she had to force herself to follow what Raleigh was saying about his early attempts at proselytizing.

"Even though my heart desires to bring the Lord to my fellow men, I've failed time and time again. Though I want more than anything to spread the word of the Lord, sometimes I do not feel fit to preach the Gospel."

"Do you remember the parable of the sower?" Marianne spoke thoughtfully. "Jesus said that some seeds will fall by the wayside. You mustn't see everything as a failure, for 'blessed are your eyes, for they shall see: and your ears, for they shall hear.' "

"How well you know the Scriptures!"

Marianne laughed. "When the Bible is your only book written in English, you become a very attentive student indeed!"

"I know everyone will not be converted, but when even my

own sister won't open her heart to the Lord ..." He stood and nervously paced the bow of the barge. The younger Fontaines had begun splashing each other, and he eyed them severely.

"Margaret? I can hardly believe she isn't a Christian."

"Oh, she claims to be! But she has never made a personal commitment to Christ. All those years with the Ursuline nuns ... I think their papist teachings took root. To be fair, I don't believe Margaret knows the full extent of her indoctrination. No matter how often I've tried to show her the true path to salvation ..." He broke off, guiltily remembering how miguided he'd been with the snake. He had meant no harm, though harm had certainly resulted. Raleigh decided to explain that incident to Marianne, for she would surely hear of it from someone with malicious intent, perhaps even from Margaret herself. "So you see ..." He stumbled over his clumsy explanation. "I believed the dead snake would remind her of Satan's power and help her repent her sins. Do you understand?" he asked hesitantly.

Though Marianne was confused by his tale, at least she formed a clearer concept of why there was a rift between brother and sister. "It must be very difficult to have a sister who's so ..."

Before she could finish, Elizabeth raced her younger sister to the front of the boat. "Look! Look what we caught!"

Abigail, with glowing pink cheeks and ringlets of auburn hair framing an angelic face, shoved a fishy basket at Marianne. "Isn't he the most enormous crab you've ever seen?"

"Indeed!" Marianne laughed and pushed it away.

"Shall we take it up to Mama?" the eight-year-old asked. "Or ..." she said knowingly, "are we supposed to wait for you?"

"We'll follow you up the hill, Abigail." Marianne stood to prove that the couple had almost completed their conversation.

The servant rushed to clear the crockery, taking the cup from Raleigh's hand. The little girls jumped from boat to boat and then to the floating dock with great agility. Marianne, her clubfoot a useless encumbrance, needed Raleigh's aid, as well as her cane, to negotiate the swaying floorboards, barrels of fuel, nets, and treacherous planks. As Raleigh helped Marianne ashore, she noticed a momentary change in his expression. He turned away, filled with shame, when he realized that she had read his unworthy thoughts.

"I'll never run like Elizabeth and Abigail; I'll never be a normal woman," Marianne said, her voice strong and clear. "I don't want you to marry me out of pity, out of filial duty, or Christian charity either!"

Raleigh had not concerned himself before with her affliction. Now, when he privately had yielded to one weak impulse, she had known instantly what he had been thinking. "I only want you to be happy . . ." he stammered awkwardly.

Marianne took a few steps up the path and turned so that Raleigh would have to look up at her when she answered. "If I were to become a burden, I could not live with myself."

Raleigh's eyes stung with tears of embarrassment. He turned to face the river, trying to compose himself. In the distance, a lone nerve-wracking cigarra droned louder and louder, like a fiddler endlessly tuning a hopeless violin. Raleigh wondered how one tiny insect could cause such disruption. Then, a solitary fish leapt into the air, sending circles eddying toward the bank that gently disturbed every weed and craft. Smoke from supper fires in the riverside village settled in the low places, and a soft wind carried the hazy veil downstream. The musty odor would linger for miles.

Marianne stumbled down toward him and touched his hunched shoulder blade. "Raleigh, I'll tell them I am the one who isn't yet certain . . ."

"No!" He spun around to face her. His voice was tender, but assured. "I beg you to understand!" He stared at Marianne with bright, fervent eyes. "I have been blessed, especially blessed by this moment. In my confusion, the true purpose of our union has been made clear."

Marianne trembled at his intensity.

"Listen! Do you hear the cigarra? He's one tiny insect, yet he's heard for miles around. And look! You can still see the undulations created by the only fish to jump from the still waters."

Marianne took Raleigh's hand in hers.

He took a deep breath and sighed audibly. "The smoke from one hearth will change the air along the length of the riverbank. Do you see my meaning?"

"I think so . . ."

"In this way the Lord has revealed His plan to me . . ." Raleigh said and, with his next words, began to explain how the course of both their lives was to be changed irrevocably.

❧ 12 All week, while the peasants had their night-long Carnaval revels, the colonists gave more subdued galas with ballroom dancing and an abundance of homemade spirits. The night of the final Mardi gras–style celebration, Raleigh and Marianne sat watching the dancers, fascinated with each other and nothing else.

The Claiborne parents were triumphant over the match. "She's done wonders for him already," Charles crowed. "Wasn't I right? Like any healthy young man, all he needed was a woman to settle him down."

"Yes, dear, you've been right all along," Lucretia agreed easily. "If she's managed all this before the wedding, he'll be putty in her hands afterward."

"Are you suggesting that a son of mine will be at the beck and call of a woman?"

Lucretia had to turn away so her husband wouldn't catch her amused expression. "Of course not, Charles, I'm agreeing, not arguing, with you."

After witnessing her brother's passionate discovery of his life's partner, Margaret guessed that her turn was coming all too quickly, for her father was glorying in the belief that he was a brilliant matchmaker. Interviews with each of the eligible young men present were soon arranged, tea parties were held by their mothers and sisters, and solemn analyses of their financial prospects were made. Each boy who'd made her father's final list of prospects was lined up to dance with her on Friday evening.

During a break for refreshments, Margaret complained to her mother. "I feel as though I'm being auctioned to the highest bidder."

"Don't talk like that! Just have a good time. When everyone leaves, it will be dull enough around here!"

Reluctantly, Margaret did as she was told, finding herself just as bored whirling around with one of the hopefuls as with the next.

Early the next morning, Margaret found her mother sewing in the small parlor. "Why are you up so early?" she asked sleepily.

"I'm not the one who danced all night. Besides, I have three daughters to dress for this wedding and I haven't yet started on something for myself," she continued distractedly.

Preparations for Raleigh's marriage to Marianne had proceeded with festive dispatch. Four native seamstresses, who had been promised extra pay if they'd stop their dancing a day or two early and begin sewing, sat on the Claibornes' porch and stitched Marianne's gown, chattering melodically in the local dialect.

"If only my trousseau trunk hadn't been lost," Margaret groaned. Everything she had brought from New Orleans was much finer than could be created in this remote village from mildewed scraps.

"Come sit by me for a while," Lucretia suggested, "and stop fretting about something that can't be changed."

"Do you remember a Mardi gras a long time ago when you took me to see the Zulu king arrive at the wharf in New Orleans?" Margaret asked wistfully.

Her mother put down her sewing and smiled. "Certainly, but I'm surprised you do. You couldn't have been more than six or seven."

"They came down the river on a barge with a canopy made of sacking and decorated with a sorry array of paper flowers. The Negro playing the king wore a suit of knitted black to keep him warm, and wasn't there a silly grass skirt on his hips?"

Lucretia peered up from her handiwork. "You have an amazing memory for details!"

"On the bank were all kinds of Negro men wearing evening clothes with long red and purple scarves about their necks."

"They called out, 'Ain't yo' brought us no queen?' " Lucretia mimicked.

Margaret bent over, laughing.

"Have you ever seen the Zulu king since?"

"No, every year the nuns would lock us into the convent for the whole week of Mardi gras."

"As they should!"

Margaret walked over to a pile of petticoats. "I'll work on Nellie's hem."

Lucretia looked up quickly, started to say something, but changed her mind. Instead she handed Margaret the needle she had just threaded. "I suppose Nell won't mind a few stray stitches on her underthings."

"It isn't my fault that I was taught to play the piano instead of sew." She gave a nervous little laugh. "Though needles, threads, and fabrics are far more accessible in a place like this."

Lucretia tried to avoid a conflict. "It's hard for me to believe that anyone living in New Orleans could've missed Mardi gras completely."

"Well ... though they wouldn't let us out," Margaret continued warily, "we'd sneak up to the attics and look down at the flickering torches that would pass along the avenue. Great wreaths of black smoke wafted up past us, and then, in the clearing air, we could catch glimpses of the floats, which were only blurs of color and light, and hear the cheering, the rippling applause; but the music was only a faraway beat."

"They say that Carnaval in Rio is the grandest in the world. Cunningham Lee's been there; ask him to tell you about it sometime."

Margaret pulled her thread through the cloth so quickly it ripped from the eye of the needle. "I'd rather see it for myself!"

Once rethreaded, Margaret's needle stubbornly refused to slide in and out of the stiff muslin as she tried unsuccessfully to stitch neat little tracks like her mother's. "Ouch!" she cried and held up a pricked finger with a droplet of red forming on the tip.

"How could such a little needle do so much damage?" Her mother dropped her own work to rescue the petticoat from becoming stained.

Lucretia decided to change the subject entirely. "Don't you agree the Pyle house would be ideal for them? . . . So much easier for Marianne . . . Children might come soon; she'd never be able to chase a two-year-old . . ."

Margaret's long-festering rage welled up and burst. She grabbed her mother's frail wrist with a hand strengthened by hours of mute keyboard exercises. "Why? Why did you do this to me? How could you take my life and purposely twist and smash it?"

Lucretia could not look at her daughter but tried to shake herself free of Margaret's iron grip.

"Why, Mother?"

"I've given you every advantage, taken from the others so that you might have lessons, so you might remain in New Orleans and have the education that neither of your sisters will be fortunate enough to have."

Margaret let go and backed against the white stucco wall. It felt cold against her burning skin. "Lessons! For what? So I can hem petticoats in the jungle? So I can bear babies for one of those . . . those 'bookends' you want me to bed with! First you raise me with dreams and promises, then you snatch them away. First you tell me my life is music, then you drag me to a place where there isn't even a piano to play!" Margaret stared at her hands, flexed her fingers, and stretched them out in supplication.

Falling back into her cushioned chair, Lucretia looked very small and very tired. "I thought music would make you happy." Her voice gathered strength. "That's the only reason I allowed you to remain in New Orleans. Do you think the long separation was easy for me?"

"I never wanted to stay. I wanted to be with you, Mama!"

Margaret choked, her anger melting into tears. She wanted to slip into her mother's arms and be comforted, but she remained standing, gasping and sobbing. "For once, tell me the truth . . . Tell me why you made me into a pianist when there was never, never any chance . . ."

Sounds of children running up the wooden stairway and across the verandah startled them both for a moment, but Lucretia didn't move from her seat. "I liked to hear you play. I liked it that you were better . . . better than I ever could have been. It made me feel important to be your mother . . . so . . ." She paused for several long seconds and took a deep breath. "I did it to please myself."

Margaret's mouth formed an astonished *O*, but no words came out.

"Perhaps your father was right. I shouldn't have let it go on so long. You'll see; after you're married, you'll make a new life for yourself and music won't seem so all-important. A man like Donald Lee with his cacao plantation has such fine prospects, I know he'd be pleased to have you . . ."

"Never!"

"If he doesn't appeal to you, you still have such a wide choice. Imagine if you were poor little Marianne . . ."

"Marianne has done quite well for herself!" Margaret's tremulous voice caught, then deepened. "There is only one man I would even consider."

A tiny smile creased Lucretia's thin lips.

"Nelson Cable."

The name hung in the air between the two women. The prosperous fifty-year-old widower from Georgia had told Charles of his interest in Margaret but had been politely dissuaded. Yet all week he had been discreetly attentive to Margaret, behaving in a gentlemanly, circumspect manner that she had found a welcome relief from the panting, fawning younger men.

Finally, Lucretia choked. "You would pick Mr. Cable over all the others? Why in the world?"

I did it to please myself, echoed in Margaret's head. To do something, to be someone, to make another person do what you want purely for your own pleasure was a revelation. "I'll marry Nelson Cable because he's the only man who owns a piano," Margaret replied decisively. Before her mother could respond, she ran out to join Nell and Kate on the verandah.

❧ ❧ ❧

After Raleigh's wedding, after all the guests had gone back to their own districts, life at Lizzieland returned to the same stultifying routine. Margaret was always the first in her family to awaken. After packing a small basket with clean scraps from the evening meal, she'd often walk down to Florinda's hut in the village. Margaret admired the native dwellings constructed from the simplest of materials: poles lashed together with vines, then plastered with mortar made from local clay and water, and thatched with palmetto branches. It was primitive yet practical, and Margaret was amazed at how much more suited to the climate these simple quarters were than the more elaborate structures the colonists had constructed.

"Bom dia," Margaret greeted the widow.

Florinda, who was sweeping the dead hibiscus blossoms from the path in front of her house, kept her head lowered. "Bom dia, Dona Margarida."

As was her custom, Margaret went inside and unwrapped what she had brought. She gave the baby a kiss on the cheek, handed a sweet, a *doce*, to one of the older girls, then went quickly off to follow the winding route beside the river. She filled her basket with fresh flowers and greens as she walked, enjoying the music of the early morning forest.

In the distance she thought she could hear parrots and decided to see if she could find them. The birds seemed to have a great instinct for camouflage when in their covert, hiding their bright markings beneath their leaf-green wings and tails. Once before, Margaret had come across a large flock roosting in the guariroba trees, their foreheads and crowns having the exact coloration of the yellow and pink fruit. Nearing the same grove, she watched for the smallest flutter of a leaf that might indicate a bird was readying for a burst of vivid flight.

Today, her eyes fastened to the canopy of trees, Margaret thought about Mr. Cable. Neither parent was especially pleased by her choice. Her mother was trying to convince her that he was too old for her; her father would only refer to him as "that damned goober-grabber," a slur on his Georgia farming background, and wouldn't discuss the subject of a formal engagement further. Although Nelson Cable was an unlikely mate, Margaret found him a man of quiet charm. His forehead was high and his hair had thinned, but it had greyed only around the ears and the nape of his neck. His beard, speckled with silver, appeared to be more silky than bristly. Though she had always preferred clean-shaven men, Margaret wondered how his face might feel against her cheek. His body was stocky, still more muscled than flabby, and Mr. Cable had a firm and decisive bearing that was not unattractive in a man his age.

Mr. Cable. That's how she still thought of him. Though when she'd told him she would seriously consider accepting his proposal, he'd asked her to call him Nel, as all his friends did.

"I can't use my sister's name." She giggled.

"My mother called me Sonny, but I suppose that would sound amusing to you as well."

"Yes, Mr. Cable."

"There you go again. I suppose you'll have to invent a name

you like, then, and why not? I'll be a new man with a wife as young and lovely as you."

Though Margaret had been pleased by his suggestion, she hadn't thought of what to call him by the time he'd left.

The last morning of Carnaval, he had stood at the base of the steps leading up to her verandah. After a few brief farewell words and a promise that they'd meet again soon to discuss their future plans, he'd kissed her hand gravely. Instead of turning when she'd expected him to, he'd waited, back straight, arms folded, staring up at Margaret. With one bushy eyebrow cocked upward like an accent mark, he had smiled out of the corner of his mouth, not exactly from happiness, or amusement, but from some grand comprehension of who she was and what she was doing. Margaret had found his expression so unexpectedly appealing that this image of him, frozen like a memorial statue, was all she could re- member distinctly. Would he always stare at her that way, or would the day come when he'd be as crass as her father and she'd have succumbed to the same bland meekness as her mother? Marriage and its realities were almost impossible to imagine.

A quickening sound, then a raucous call, diverted her. Several parrots burst out of the tree with a voice that could be heard up and down the river for miles. The flight of the birds was a vibrant display of reds and blues as their breasts and underwings were revealed. They flew higher and faster, their long tail feathers trailing like ribbons in the sky.

"Good morning," Margaret called up the path to her mother, who was resting on a creaky settee on the verandah. "I've brought back some ripe papayas. Would you like to share one with me?"

Lucretia's thin arms and spindly feet were propped up among her many cushions. "Sounds lovely . . ." She closed her eyes.

Margaret placed her basket on the table outside the kitchen door, sorting out the fruit, flowers, and a twig decorated with bunches of bright berries.

"Aren't there enough flowers around the house without bring- ing more inside?" Lucretia's voice was tense and quarrelsome.

"It's only something to do, Mother," Margaret answered tersely. She stopped arranging her treasures in an assortment of bowls and vases. "Are you feeling poorly?"

"Just tired after all the excitement." Lucretia loosened the lace fichu at her neck. "I only hope Raleigh will be taking the Pyle house after all."

"What are you worrying about? He promised he'd be back after his trip to the Fontaines'."

"How would I know what he's planning? Before he left, he said he was going to speak to Leonard Fontaine about some idea of his, though I hardly think he's suited to the barge business, do you?"

Margaret didn't think Raleigh was qualified to handle any business, but she willed herself not to respond truthfully. A lingering tension between mother and daughter could only make the day even more impossible to endure. She turned to a subject that her mother might find more agreeable. "Before he left, Mr. Cable asked if I would consider a wedding trip on the River Plate to Buenos Aires. If we married after Easter, we would be there for the best season."

Lucretia eyed her daughter warily. "Would you like that?"

"Any change would be welcome." Margaret spoke blandly.

As Lucretia stretched her arms and felt her aching joints, she thought about the petty pains that came with age. Surely a man like Nelson Cable would have his share of weakness and miseries, disabilities that Margaret didn't need to cope with at so young an age. If only she could help her daughter see how many difficulties there would be in such a marriage! But Margaret was not in a frame of mind to listen to a mother's opinion.

"Mr. Cable's plantation is even more remote than ours, is it not?" was all Lucretia mentioned.

"He says he is on a major tributary with frequent mail-boat traffic, and he does get to São Paulo once a year."

"Once a year . . ." Lucretia repeated grimly. She closed her eyes and lay back on her cushions. "Once a year."

❧ 13 "Nellie, you're to be General Johnston, and Katie, you're to be General McDowell. I'll be Beauregard," Marshall shouted.

"You're always Beauregard," Kate complained to the youngest Claiborne. "Besides, I'm tired of that stupid game. C'mon, Nellie, let's see if Gettie wants to go fishing."

Marshall stomped his foot. "I wish Ned Brady didn't have to

help his father today. He's the only one who knows how to do the battle properly. Besides, Mama said you were to stay with me this morning."

Kate looked up at her older sister. "All right, Marsh, but we absolutely refuse to play Bull Run one more time. Don't we, Nell?"

"If you'll stop quarreling, I'll take you both fishing."

Kate jumped gleefully. "Out in the boat? To the shallows?"

Nell nodded, though she wished she wasn't the one who perpetually had to mind the little ones. Kate was active and exuberant, but nothing compared to Marshall, who had lived in Brazil since the age of two without apparent discipline. In recent years, Marshall had gravitated toward Colonel Demaret, who'd won the boy's affection with his tales recounting his service with General Beauregard. In retrospect, all the colonel's battles had been victorious, so Marshall couldn't understand how it had been possible that Beauregard's side had lost the war.

As they hurried toward the river, Marshall kicked stones and complained. "Fishing! I'd rather be hunting or doing target practice. Fishing's boring."

Nell shook her head. Only things violent interested her brother. Marshall knew the name and gauge of every shotgun in Lizzieland and had pestered his father mercilessly until he received his own Winchester for his birthday.

"Ah, look, low tide," he moaned. "Gee, the mud stinks! I should've gone to the barn and waited to shoot whatever's been into the grain. Might've been a paca or even . . ."

"Marsh!" Kate cried. "Pacas are so adorable with their funny stripes."

"They're only pests, and besides, I hear they're delicious to eat . . . All white meat!"

Nell winced. "You'd shoot beetles if they were big enough!" Though everyone in the family knew of his interest in weaponry and warfare, they smiled at the irony of these masculine attributes in a boy with the face of a freckled cherub.

As soon as they passed the wharf, they heard a familiar whistle sounding downriver.

"The mail boat!" Nell shouted.

"I'll run up to the common and sound the bell," Kate volunteered.

Marshall elbowed her out of the way. "I'll go. I'm faster." He began a succession of whoops that he'd been taught were the official rebel yell and dashed up the hill.

Though it was scheduled to arrive weekly, the mail boat's appearance was erratic. By the time it docked, a crowd had gathered at the quay.

"Maybe there will be something from Raleigh," Nell suggested. It had been over a month since they'd had word of the newlyweds and their activities.

"Demaret, Brady, Lee . . ." Letters and parcels were passed hand over hand until they were retained by the recipient or someone who would deliver the item.

"Here's one from Louisiana." Nell waved a small package at Kate. "It's from Mama's brothers."

A stout, especially anxious woman shoved her way forward. "Anything for Worthington?"

"Claiborne!" The mail-boat skipper shouted to be heard.

Nell saw a thick white envelope being waved over his head. "Here! Claiborne! Here!" By the time it reached her, the important-looking letter was smudged by a dozen damp fingerprints. She turned it over and read the flowery calligraphy. "It's from Rio, for Gettie," she said as she passed it to Kate.

The skipper held his sack upside-down to prove it was empty to the disappointed members of the throng. As he began to take the outgoing post aboard, Marshall came barreling down the hill so quickly it seemed he might not stop before he hit the water. Deliberately he bumped into Kate. "Here's what we're sending out. What'd we get?"

Kate kept the letters behind her back, but Marshall dashed around and grabbed at her. In the struggle, Margaret's envelope flipped in the air and landed in the sucking mud. "See what you've done!" Kate moaned. She tried to wipe the worst of it off. "Gettie will be furious."

"All your own fault." Marshall spat, then disappeared.

"He's . . . he's impossible!" Kate shrieked.

Nell shuffled through the remaining stack of correspondence. "Here's one from Raleigh and Marianne — no, two from them."

"Who sent the one to Gettie?"

"M. F. Larson, her friend from the convent." Nell held up the grimy envelope. "It's awfully thick for just a letter . . . Wonder what it could be?"

"Don't know, but it certainly got soaked. Better get it to her before the whole thing falls apart."

"You tell her how it happened . . . Let her take care of Marsh."

Nell stopped and stared at her little sister. "You were holding it . . . You tell her!"

"Tell whom what?" Margaret asked brightly. She stood in the shade at the edge of the path, the lace on her hem blowing gracefully in the breeze. "I hurried out as soon as Marshall said there was something for me. Who's it from? Mlle Doradou?"

"Kate, give it to her," Nell ordered.

Kate slowly withdrew the envelope from behind her back and quickly explained what had happened. Margaret frowned but didn't berate them. "Mother's waiting for the rest. Go on without me."

She sat on the edge of a large flat rock alongside the path and gently unfolded several sheets of fine paper, laying them out to dry in the sun. The first part of the letter was a wedding invitation written in the most delicate hand. Some of the letters had been blurred by water stains, but it was clear that Francisca was finally to be married to Augusto Cavalcanti.

"My dear Margaret," her letter began formally. "Though I hope to hold you to your promise to attend my wedding, I realize that this entails considerable travel expenses for you and your chaperone, which neither I nor my family feel free to burden you with at this time. You would do me the greatest of honors if you would agree to stand by my side when I am given in marriage to Senhor Cavalcanti, for you are as dear as a sister to me. My father insists that you accept the enclosed passages so that we will not feel we are making too presumptuous a request."

Margaret checked to be certain that the ship vouchers weren't disintegrating and then anxiously read on.

"The prenuptial celebrations will commence in early May, and we would hope you could be with us from that time through the wedding day later in the month. Rooms for you and your chaperone will be readied at our house, and so you suffer no additional hardships, we are having the piano tuned properly for you to play while you are here."

Margaret skipped quickly over several pages describing the wardrobe ordered and the possible designs for Margaret's own dress, the decorating of the house her father was having built for the couple, and the dates of the various festivities. Finally, Margaret spied the name she had been looking for and began to read more slowly.

"Erik sends his congratulations to your brother on his marriage. He also says to tell you that he looks forward very much to your arrival."

Francisca closed with a list of possible boats and their timetables for Margaret's journey. The two fully paid round-trip tickets were stiffening in the sun. As Margaret turned them over to dry, she wondered how she should broach the subject to her parents.

❧   ❧   ❧

That night all the letters were read aloud to the assembled family. The Davis brothers bragged about their prosperity in New Orleans and repeated their promise that a job awaited Charles should he ever decide to return. As usual, Charles gritted his teeth at their assumption of his failure. They also mentioned that a wedding gift had been shipped for Raleigh.

"We'd best ask the Gunters in Iguape to watch out for it," Lucretia suggested.

"What did Raleigh write?" Nell asked.

Lucretia read his first letter, describing how nicely he had been treated at the Fontaines' and closing with warm wishes from Marianne.

"When was that dated?" Charles asked.

"The tenth of March."

Charles brought out the second envelope. "This one was written four days later. He skimmed the first few paragraphs and announced, "They're coming back for a visit this week."

"A visit?" Lucretia looked puzzled. "What about the Pyle house?"

Charles took a sip of tamarind juice, his favorite. "He refused to make a decision until he had talked it over with Marianne and her family. That boy won't move an inch without her approval." He stroked his neatly trimmed beard. "Still don't know if I like that."

Kate made a face that her father couldn't see. "Gettie, aren't you going to read your letter, too?"

Margaret unfolded the invitation and passed it around the table as she read Francisca's plea for her presence at the wedding.

"Oh, Gettie!" Kate clapped her hands. "You're so lucky! I'd give *anything* to go to Rio."

"Me, too . . ." Nell sighed. "You'll be in the wedding party and everything."

Lucretia twisted her napkin and waited for Charles to swallow his mouthful of coconut pudding. Everyone watched as he put down his spoon, methodically wiped his bearded chin, and pushed back his chair. "Impossible." Her father rose and stepped outside without another word.

Margaret's voice was thin. "They've even sent us the tickets."

"I don't believe he wants to accept their . . . charity. Also, there would be other expenses: a proper gift, clothing for all those events, both of us would be gone many weeks . . ."

"You've always wanted to see Rio; now's your chance. As for the dresses, I'll need just as many when I wed Mr. Cable, won't I?"

"Then there is Mr. Cable to consider now, isn't there? Do you think he'd be content to have you off in Rio when you've practically promised yourself to him?"

"You'd be with me the whole time. How could he possibly object?"

"He might. And for politeness' sake you should ask his permission first. Also, your own wedding trip would have to be postponed if you go to Rio in May, and you can't expect a man his age to wait forever."

"I won't ask his permission!" Margaret replied fiercely. "If he cannot wait a few extra months, then he certainly is too demanding for me. Above all, I want a kind and patient husband." She continued dangerously, "I well know what a disaster the other can be."

Nell gasped and Kate buried her face behind her hands. Fortunately, Marshall had been excused earlier.

Lucretia gestured for the younger girls to leave the room. When the women were alone, she whispered. "I'll talk to Charles later, in private, but don't get your hopes up."

"Why?" Margaret asked contritely. "Why can I never have anything I want?"

"Perhaps you'll have better luck with your husband than your father," Lucretia responded flatly. "Though if you marry Mr. Cable, I doubt that your life will change a whit."

❧ 14 Lucretia suggested that the subject of Margaret's journey not be discussed again until Raleigh and Marianne's visit, believing that once Charles saw his son settled into a happy marriage he'd be more inclined to be generous with his daughter. However, within the first hours of his arrival, Raleigh had already upset his father.

"I know this'll disappoint you, Father," Raleigh began at the start of their first meal together, "but all around us people are hungry, dying of disease, living in ignorance. Most of all, they are starving for the knowledge of Jesus Christ. They are lost without knowing how Jesus can save them from their sins. Some people may be content to worship one day a week or feel virtuous putting a little money in the collection plate, but I know that Jesus wants more of me."

Lucretia spoke up. "You've always studied the Bible faithfully; you've shared your convictions with all your friends, with the family, with your bride. What more can you ask of yourself?"

"Mother, don't you see? It's not what I ask of myself, it's what He asks of me."

Lucretia choked on her words. "No, I don't see."

"God has led me to Marianne and now He wants us to spread His word together."

"Missionaries? Both of you?" Margaret asked.

Quickly Marianne jumped in. "My father has already agreed to my husband's plan."

Noticing the smooth way she said *husband,* Margaret felt an odd twinge of envy.

"Mr. Fontaine has generously offered to give us a barge outfitted with everything we need." Raleigh beamed with victory. "We'll travel the rivers and speak to the settlers, to the natives, to whomever will listen and be saved from eternal damnation."

"But, son," Charles pleaded, "Lizzieland needs young men if it's going to survive. These last years have been difficult, but . . ."

"Father, I'm sorry, but I have a more powerful calling."

"The Pyle house . . . I thought it was all settled . . ." Charles sputtered. He could not think of an argument that would win against his son's intense commitment.

"Most missionaries are trained and brought to Brazil at great expense. Can't you see how wonderfully He has arranged it by having me already here, by giving me Marianne, and by showing Mr. Fontaine the importance of supporting our endeavors?"

Any objections were silenced. Raleigh turned toward Marianne to meet her triumphant gaze.

❧ ❧ ❧

The morning after Raleigh's announcement, Margaret asked Marianne's help in preparing some sweets for the evening meal. When Marianne was with Raleigh she seemed a totally different person. Margaret wondered how someone so strong of heart could become so mesmerized by her brother. Still, as long as Raleigh was otherwise occupied, she sought Marianne's intelligent companionship.

As the two young women were peeling guavas for the cream dessert, Margaret confided how much she wanted to go to Rio.

"Why shouldn't you have the chance?" Marianne's voice was adamant. "I think you should talk to your mother again. If she's excited about taking the trip with you, your father might let you go just to please her."

"I can see you don't understand how my father's mind works, but still, I'll try anything. And what about Mr. Cable? Would you ask his permission if you were me?"

"It's only fair. If he objects, perhaps you should know that now. It might make a difference in your choice." Marianne paused. "Margaret?" It was clear she wanted to say something else but didn't know if she dared.

"Yes?"

"Do you really feel that you and Mr. Cable were . . . meant for each other?"

"I . . ."

"It's only because I am so content with Raleigh . . . Everything has been so perfect so far . . ." She blushed. "I would just want you to have the same blessed happiness . . ."

"Do you find something wrong with Mr. Cable?"

"No, he's a very fine man. My father respects him immensely, but . . ."

Margaret turned her back to her sister-in-law and began layering the slippery slices of fruit in an enamel kitchen bowl. "I've got to choose someone soon, and he's so much more sensible than the others."

"I understand. Raleigh's also quite serious about life."

Margaret held her tongue, mashing the soft fruit with a fork a bit harder than necessary. She would never understand how a girl as practical and sweet as Marianne could have fallen in love with her brother. "Then, you know how I feel about Mr. Cable."

Marianne looked at Margaret warily as she reached for the pan of orange-colored pulp. "Shall I add the lime juice now?"

"Yes, it keeps it from discoloring." Margaret took a wire beater and began to vigorously pound the soft guavas into an even finer purée while Marianne squeezed in the citrus.

"Stop, I've lost some seeds in there." Marianne fished around until she found them and began to lick her fingers. "Mmmm . . ." She smiled demurely. "Delicious."

As soon as Margaret started beating again, Marianne asked, "Who's Erik?"

"Erik?" Margaret stopped and stared into the slimy-sided bowl. "Who told you about him?"

"Raleigh," Marianne said guilelessly. "He was talking to your father about our plans when your father mentioned that you might be going to Rio to a wedding . . ."

"Father said that I *might* be going? That's a change!" Margaret's eyes glowed with excitement.

"Raleigh said the reason you were so anxious to go was not because of the girl who is getting married but because you couldn't wait to see Erik Larson again."

The wire beater dropped from Margaret's hand and clattered to the floor. Orange spots of guava splattered her dress and the white floor tiles. "How could he tell such a lie? Mr. Larson is Francisca's older brother. Why would that matter to me?" Margaret's cheeks flamed.

Marianne's bad leg buckled for a moment. She held on to the table, her knuckles whitening. "Raleigh told me that this man had behaved rather shamelessly toward you, though I'm certain your parents will listen to your side of it if . . ."

Angrily, Margaret thrust the guava bowl at Marianne. "Here, add one hundred grams of castor sugar and a pinch of salt. I'm going to have a talk with my brother! He had no right to say that about Mr. Larson, no right at all!"

Marianne spoke in a pathetic little croak. "I'm sure he meant no harm."

"I'm not certain he didn't. My brother . . ." She caught herself. No need to involve Marianne in the old feuds; poor thing, she'll suffer enough just being his wife.

❧ ❧ ❧

"It's no use," Lucretia said with resignation. "Your father is absolutely adamant."

"All Raleigh's fault." Margaret sobbed on her bed.

"Don't be too harsh. Charles was never in favor of such a long journey for such a frivolous purpose. He only wants to see you safe and settled."

Margaret buried her head in her pillow. "You both can't wait to be rid of me!"

Her mother sighed and started to pace the room. Idly her fingers felt the rough stucco walls where the faint stain of snake blood could still be noticed by someone who knew what it was. She shuddered involuntarily. "You must start thinking less about what might have been and more about your future with Mr. Cable. He is quite a figure of a man! I believe he will be kind, very kind to you." Lucretia waited three long beats. "And very gentle."

She noticed that Margaret's back stiffened. Ah, I was right! she thought. Sometimes my little girl puts on such a brave and knowing front that I forget her innocence. An experienced man like Nelson Cable might be far more tolerant of a young woman's fears than one of these impetuous boys who won't know anything except how to satisfy himself. She sat on the bed and patted Margaret's loosened braid. It was hard to imagine her daughter with a man almost thirty years older than she. Margaret would spend more years as nursemaid than wife. Still, if that's whom she chooses . . .

Margaret's crying subsided. She'll get over this, Lucretia thought. She reached for the handkerchief tucked in the sleeve of her dress, turned Margaret around, and dabbed her tear-stained face. Unexpectedly, Lucretia had an intuitive grasp of her daughter's dilemma. "Tell me about Erik Larson."

Margaret swallowed hard. "He's Francisca's brother." Margaret spoke warily. "He was very polite to both Raleigh and me."

"Then why does Raleigh dislike him so?"

Margaret sat up in bed. Though her pulse beat rapidly, she was able to steady her voice. "Because Raleigh has always been exceedingly jealous of me. But really, Mr. Larson was only being a generous host." Margaret guessed she was speaking too fast, but she blurted out her thoughts anyway. "In fact, he arranged to show Raleigh the sights of the city that especially interested him and expedited our departure to save Raleigh the trouble."

The brightness in Margaret's eyes did not go unnoticed by her mother. "Mr. Larson must be an exceptional man . . . ."

Margaret tried to meet her mother's gaze, but turned from its intensity.

". . . to have won you over in so short a time. I'm not surprised. It happens more frequently than anyone guesses. It happened to Raleigh and Marianne; it happened to me and your father."

"You? But I thought your marriage had been arranged."

"True, I was supposed to marry Henry. He was the first Claiborne to visit our home, and my parents actively supported the alliance. But the very first time I visited Moss Oaks I met your father and, after that moment, hardly ever thought about Henry again. In those days, all his younger brother Charlie did was tease me, chase me, take me riding in the bayou. No one thought anything of it; after all, I was only fourteen at the time. Yet from the very first I preferred Charles, dreamed about him, wished that my parents had chosen him instead of his more serious older brother. Then, when the war started, they all enlisted in the Delta Rifles. When Henry was reported missing at Shiloh, I didn't mourn, I only prayed for Charles's safety and hated myself for feeling as selfish as I did."

"And he was the only one who returned?"

"That's right. At first I was so thankful, but later . . . ." Lucretia knotted the handkerchief's lace border. "To have what you want at the great expense of another . . ."

"Surely you know that you weren't responsible for Henry's death."

"One always wonders what would have happened if life had been different."

"Wouldn't it also have been terrible to have married Henry when you loved Father?"

"Yes." Lucretia stood and methodically straightened her skirt. "It would be tragic to marry one man when you think you might love another." She stared at Margaret meaningfully. "Better to love no one than always to be wishing for someone you couldn't have."

Margaret's chin trembled. "You don't believe I should marry Mr. Cable, do you?"

"I think you should go to your friend's wedding and then make your decision."

"But how?"

Lucretia grasped her daughter's hand so tightly that Margaret winced. "I've made many mistakes with you. I hope this isn't another." She took a deep breath. "I'll get you to Rio. It will be our secret."

❧ 15 The daring, covert nature of the adventure brought mother and daughter closer than they'd ever been. Neither thought the trip would have any disastrous consequences. At worst, Margaret would return to Lizzieland contrite and apologetic after the festivities in Rio. Her father would have to forgive her, and if Mr. Cable did not, then someone else would be found. At the other end of the spectrum of possible outcomes were the private dreams that each of the women held but were too restrained to share.

The night of the journey the rains began shortly after supper. From the ferocity of the wind and the intensity of the pelting drops, Margaret realized the storm would continue well into the morning. Lucretia hoped nobody noticed her extreme anxiety at this turn in the weather. Both found excuses to go to bed early, but Margaret became so agitated she started to dress hours too soon.

"Gettie," Lucretia whispered as she slipped into the room once the others were asleep. "You haven't been to bed?"

"No, I couldn't rest, too much to think about. What if the boat is late, what if . . ."

"It's early yet." Lucretia tried to sound calm, but even in the shadows Margaret could see her mother's hands twisting her handkerchief.

"You're shivering, Mother." Margaret wrapped her own quilt around her and the two women huddled together on the bed.

"This reminds me . . ." Lucretia said dreamily.

"Of what?"

"When I once left my home in the middle of the night."

"You did?"

"My mother, sisters, and I were all running from General Butler, that beast who occupied New Orleans. I was furious! Rather than submit, I thought that we should have burned our houses and taken our own lives. How I ached to don breeches in those days!"

"You ran away?"

"We all did. It was May of sixty-two. We were staying with my aunt Muriel Gordon in Baton Rouge. Not a man among us. When the shells started landing on our street no one wanted to leave the house, but Dr. Castleton rode up and told us we must walk to Greenwell. It became dark and began to rain. It was a heart-rending scene. Women searching for babies along the road where they had been lost and no one knew whether Baton Rouge was in ashes or being plundered. Still we sang 'Better Days Are Coming' and 'I Hope to Die Shouting, The Lord Will Provide.' "

Margaret let her mother ramble on to pass the long night of waiting. Even though Lucretia had taken the defeat of the South as a personal loss, she still spoke of those terrible times as the most glorious moments of her life. While she listened to how the Confederates had set their own cotton bales afire and sent them downriver in defiance of the encroaching enemy, Margaret tucked a few final items into her straw bag.

"Why, a single barrel of whiskey that was thrown on the cotton cost Freddie Pickney one hundred and twenty-five dollars! Doesn't that prove what a nation in earnest is capable of doing?"

Margaret was trying to rearrange everything to accommodate a hairbrush and small pillow when Lucretia slipped something cold into her hand. Even in the darkness, Margaret could recognize the outlines of a small pistol.

"I don't need that."

"Yes, you do. I carried it with me everywhere."

Margaret had never seen the weapon before. "Have you ever used it?"

"In the old days I had so many fewer fears. Once I sewed a tiny Confederate flag above my bosom and walked right out in front of the Federal sentinels. I told my sisters that the man who says to take it off would have to pull it off himself; the man who dared attempt it — well, a pistol in my pocket filled the gap!"

"You shot someone?"

"No, but don't think I wasn't capable of it!"

"I can't see why I would need it. Florinda will be with me at all times . . ."

Lucretia shook her head at her daughter's trusting innocence. "Florinda won't have the strength to save you if any man presses to have his way with you."

"Who would . . ."

"Hush now. I'll just feel better knowing you have it."

A sudden thunderclap shook the room and the gun clattered to the floor. Lucretia picked it up and briefly tried to demonstrate its use. "It's called a pepperbox pistol. It has a separate little barrel for each shot, and these revolve when the hammer is cocked." She demonstrated with the empty gun. "I'll show you how to load it. My father always said there was no point in having a gun if it wasn't loaded."

Margaret heard the clicks in the dark and wanted to protest, but nonetheless she slipped it into her traveling cape pocket. A trunk containing her better dresses had been secretly taken to the wharf the night before.

The women listened to the rain. "It seems to be quieter now. I think you should go at least as far as Florinda's house. From there you'll be better able to hear the boat's whistle."

"I wish you or Nell could have come with me!"

"Your father will be impossible enough as it is!" She took Margaret's black cape trimmed with grosgrain from the hook by the door, buttoned it tightly around her daughter's shoulders, and steered her toward the kitchen. Lucretia unlatched the door and peered out. The water poured off the verandah roof in wide sheets. "It's time."

Margaret hesitated. "Mama . . . I . . ."

Lucretia pulled Margaret's hood over her head and resolutely pushed her out into the night. "God be with you."

A jagged streak of lightning briefly illuminated her daughter's rushing silhouette as she turned the corner and disappeared into the raging night.

Night-Blooming Cereus

❦ 1 Thunder rolled across the skies. Turbulence churned the river into a froth of dark mud. From the moment the Fontaines' barge pulled away from the wharf at Lizzieland, the rain had been relentless. Most of the passengers, huddled under sheets of deck canvas, appeared to be strange lumps of cargo. Seeing a small deckhouse aft, Florinda motioned Margaret to take shelter, but the dank room was so crowded with sticky barrels of oil and molasses that Margaret could neither stand nor sit.

Florinda yelled to a deck hand who seemed impervious to the elements. "Vem cá! Move these for the senhorita!" Ignoring her, the man continued to chew his cigar. "Don't you realize that this is the sister of Seu Leonardo's new son-in-law?"

"Bem, bem . . . Why didn't you say so?" he answered before he clamped his charuto between his teeth and cleared a small place for Florinda to hang a hammock.

Inwardly Margaret smiled at the authority that had come into the servant's voice.

"You rest," Florinda said firmly. Arms folded, she waited until Margaret not only lay down but closed her eyes.

She'll sleep, Florinda thought. Just as she knew when a child was exhausted, she could see the same signs in Dona Margarida. Her sweet children . . . How would they fare with her sister and mother? The eldest, Carlota, would help mind the little ones, but the baby hardly knew anyone else. Would he accept the taste of her sister's milk? Would he notice the difference? Her lips could almost feel the warm spot on her baby's neck where she'd kissed him less than an hour ago, whispering, "Justininho, querido, my darling boy, don't forget your mamãe."

But she hadn't cried. When the senhorita had asked her to be her companion, she had not hesitated for a second. "Não tem problema." She'd nodded willingly. Anything for the good lady who'd taken care of her family since Berto's death; anything for one chance to leave the village where she'd lived all her life.

As Florinda stared out into the bleak night with only the whooshing water telling her they were traveling to an unknown place, she surprised herself by her lack of fear. She could only remember being afraid once before, eight years ago, when she was only thirteen and Berto had asked her mother for her.

"It's just a bend in the river" was the way her mother had explained what marriage was like. "You think something terrible must be on the other side because you've never been there, but when you turn the corner you'll see that the banks are as green, the waters as blue, as the place you knew before."

Now she was going around the bend of a real river; now she was finally leaving the tiny settlement where she'd been born and had expected to die. Even if it was only for a few weeks, she'd have something to tell her children stories about for years to come, just like the stories her mother had told her about her own village upstream and her father's tales of cutting cane in the north.

The barge moved from wharf to wharf to take on cargo, mostly sacks of rice and ground manioc. At one stop, Margaret stirred. She heard voices mumbling in Portuguese. Opening one eye, she saw, in the lee of the shelter, the profiles of two men. Their voices were so hushed and tense that Margaret instinctively held her breath so as not to move. Through the loose weave of the hammock, their gesticulating hands could be seen against the hazy predawn sky. The man in a hard leather hat, the style worn by the vaqueiros, or cowboys of the backlands, pulled out a package wrapped in rags. His hawk-nosed companion opened it, quickly counted the bills, then gave a few clipped instructions. Rough slang in an unfamiliar dialect made it difficult for Margaret to make out more than a few phrases. "Capitão Virgulino . . . os cangaceiros . . . Pontaria fina, tática e espera." The hawk-nosed one laughed and pounded the vaqueiro's back before disappearing into the mist.

"Fine point, tactics and hope . . ." The words didn't mean anything to Margaret. Perhaps she'd gotten them wrong.

The rain had relented to a fine drizzle, but it was still too wet to go out on deck. Margaret tried to fall asleep, but the ominous nature of the men's voices kept her awake. She wound her fingers through the coarse threads of the hammock, listening to the familiar grating sound of the engine, a signal that the boat would dock at yet another wharf. She braced herself for the bump of contact and the slap of ropes against the hull, but heard only voices calling. In a moment the barge was under way again at full speed.

Florinda carried in a cup of tepid coffee. "What was that?" Margaret asked.

"Someone got off onto another boat going upriver. Must've forgotten something." Florinda gestured for her mistress to come out on deck. "The rains have stopped."

A deck hand standing at the bow shouted directions to the pilot. "À direita ! To the right!" Margaret prayed there would be no delays, for if the boat became stuck on a sandbar, her father might overtake her.

"Você está com frio?" Florinda asked, mistaking Margaret's shiver. "Come over here." She indicated the brighter side of the deck.

Margaret followed without protest. As she turned the corner, Margaret caught sight of the hawk-nosed man leaning over the rail. Just as she passed him, he turned and grinned malevolently. Had he seen her come out of the shelter, or was she making too much of the stare? After all, Brazilian men were often obvious in their admiration for a woman, especially one with golden hair. Still, his expression had been devoid of any such approval. Margaret slipped her hand over the little pepperbox pistol tucked deep into her cape pocket. Mother was right, she realized, it does give me courage. The sickening feeling of fright that had gripped her stomach slowly receded. She lifted her eyes to the treetops. Gulls sliced through the whitening sky, and she could almost hear the howl of the breakers on the bar. Iguape, almost Iguape, and whatever lay beyond.

❧ 2 As soon as the riverboat docked at Iguape, most of the passengers scrambled up to the pier without waiting for the gangplank to be set in place. Margaret took the time to straighten her hair and tidy her dress before entering the town. Her first time there, the waterfront marketplace had seemed hopelessly provincial compared to Rio or New Orleans. Now she thought it wonderful to see such substantial architecture again. Margaret thought she remembered her way to the Gunters and headed down the cobbled street, carrying the basket and her cape over her arm. Florinda followed with the rest of the bundles.

"Don't offer elaborate explanations about why you're traveling with Florinda," Lucretia had instructed. "If you take everything as a matter of course, no one, least of all Mrs. Gunter, will suspect a thing. She's one of the kindest creatures on the face of the earth."

The moment she knocked on the garden gate, Mrs. Gunter came running and hugged Margaret as if she were a lost relation. "What in the world are you doing here?"

"I'm on my way to a friend's wedding in Rio."

"You're a very lucky girl."

"Yes, I can't wait to see Francisca again."

"No, you misunderstand me, I have a wonderful surprise for you."

Mrs. Gunter called to a servant. "I've been waiting for someone trustworthy to be heading up to Lizzieland. It's been safely stored at the foot of my bed for so long I'll miss it when it's gone."

Margaret heard a scraping sound and then saw her trousseau trunk being dragged onto the patio.

"The crew from the *Juparana* brought this out the next time the steamer had to stop here. Must've been two, maybe three, months ago."

Margaret beamed. "And to think how hard my mother worked to fix up a few poor dresses so I wouldn't embarrass myself in Rio!" ·

"Now you'll have all your pretty things for the wedding parties, won't you?"

"How soon can I get a boat?" Margaret tried to conceal her anxiety.

"In the morning there's a small coastal steamer in from Florianopolis. Not very grand, but it's fast. Or you can wait till next week when a larger ship comes by."

Thinking that her father, if he really tried, could reach her by the next day and force her to return to Lizzieland, Margaret answered smoothly, "I'm expected in Rio this week."

"Pity you won't stay with me longer. I could use a fresh face around here. Besides, I want all the news from upriver."

"On the way back there'll be no need for me to rush home. Also . . ." Margaret was wondering how to phrase her request. "I do have one immediate problem . . ."

"Yes?"

"As you might imagine, there're not many wedding presents to be found upriver." She managed a contrived laugh.

Mrs. Gunter smiled easily. "What do you think she'd want or need?"

Margaret described more about the Larsons. "So you see I can't come without anything, and they will hardly permit me to shop once I am there, so I was wondering . . ." Margaret unwrapped her small velvet sack filled with Francisca's topazes.

Mrs. Gunter eyed a pear-shaped topaz expertly. "Must be over five carats. Where did you get them?"

"A gift from Francisca."

"Do you think it right to barter something she wanted you to have?"

"The truth is I have very little else of any value. Won't you even consider my offer?"

Mrs. Gunter led Margaret into her dining room. A specially constructed railing along two walls held her clock collection. "Here's one I might be convinced to part with." Gingerly, she lifted down a porcelain clock. "It's only about thirty years old, mind you, and not really one of my finest pieces." She turned it over and pointed to crossed swords marked in the blue underglaze. "That's the Meissen factory mark. It's got a very fine Brocot suspension."

Margaret looked at the florid romantic design. The bell-shaped top was latticework decked with china flowers, while two embracing cherubs encircled the base. "It's perfect." Margaret handed Mrs. Gunter the two largest topazes.

Mrs. Gunter rolled them in her fingers and then passed the darker one back. "One would easily cover the clock's value. I couldn't take them both."

Though Margaret couldn't determine the worth of either the clock or the stones, she had been hoping for just such an opening. "Could you . . . might you consider purchasing the other stone?"

Mrs. Gunter caught on immediately. She knew how tight money had been for the failing colonists. Fortunately, the Gunters' profitable import-export business had insulated them from these problems. "I'd only need one large stone for a necklace. But if you could see your way to selling me three matching smaller ones for earrings and a ring . . ."

"How can I ever thank you?" Margaret kissed her on both cheeks.

"You've become quite a Brasileira," Mrs. Gunter replied, returning the double kisses in kind.

❧ 3 "Be certain you are not seated in the dining room with any gentlemen, unless they are traveling with their wives. I'd expect the steward to seat you with suitable companions, but do not hesitate to request a change if you feel the situation might be even the slightest bit dishonorable." Mrs. Gunter fussed at Margaret as they watched the ship lower anchor on the far side of the reef. "Remember that Brazilians are very observant of all the rules of etiquette, and their standards are every bit as high as ours. In Rio, they will dress formally every evening unless they say otherwise." She looked over at Florinda hovering near the baggage. "Your maid should stay with you in your cabin tonight, but she isn't to sit with you at table."

"I'll try to remember everything."

Florinda was staring uneasily at the high rolling waves. "O mar está muito bravo," she said in an awestruck voice.

Margaret spoke in English to Mrs. Gunter. "She's never before seen the sea."

Mrs. Gunter sighed deeply but didn't mention the anxiety she felt for these two unworldly travelers. At least the voyage would be very short.

Florinda pointed to the sky. "O que é que são aqueles pássaros?"

"How do you say 'seagulls'?" Margaret asked Mrs. Gunter.

"Gaivotas."

"Ah, sim, gaivotas!" Florinda's face was glowing with childlike expectation.

"There's the launch!" Mrs. Gunter pointed out beyond the bar. "In this surf the sailors will only want to hold it off but a few minutes. I'll direct the baggage while you take care not to slip down those slick stairs." She reached across and hugged Margaret.

During the embrace, Margaret looked back toward the town. At the edge of the quay, she saw the hawk-nosed man from the barge. Margaret clutched Mrs. Gunter and whispered in her ear. "That man, behind you, do you know him?"

Pretending to adjust Margaret's cape, Mrs. Gunter looked over her shoulder. She froze when she caught sight of the disreputable man.

"Who is he?" Margaret asked shakily.

"I never thought I'd . . ." Mrs. Gunter started, then stopped. She seemed to force her voice to be less concerned. "I'm happy to see that your instincts are so sound. Take care to stay away from characters like that and you'll do just fine."

"Why is that?"

"Tubarão stirred up some trouble here several years back. I expect he's just passing through."

"Tubarão?"

"One of those typical bandido . . . ah . . . backland names. It means 'shark.' I'll have to tell Mr. Gunter about this so he can inform the authorities. Tubarão's not welcome in Iguape for too long, I'll tell you that."

"Is he some kind of criminal?"

Seeing Margaret's distress, Mrs. Gunter softened her tone even further. "Just a nuisance. If he's looking for trouble, it's more than flirting with you. You've got to learn to be more like the Brazilian girls."

"In what way?"

"They know how to look through a man as though he's made of glass."

As the launch approached the crumbling sea wall, the few departing passengers gathered nearer to the edge. Mrs. Gunter brushed back a few loose strands of Margaret's silky hair and tucked them under the hood of her cape. "We'll wire ahead so you'll be met."

Margaret took Florinda's hand to guide her down the slippery stairs. Frightened by the lapping fingers of surf, Florinda jumped up to the top and wouldn't budge. An impatient sailor reached for her and, with one firm gesture, placed her in the bow seat facing the sea wall. Margaret swiftly took her place next to her.

Just as the launch was pushed off, Tubarão leapt aboard and slunk onto the last seat in the stern. The rowers quickly plunged in the oars to keep the boat from crashing into the wall. The land receded surprisingly quickly behind a curtain of lizard-green water. In a brave attempt to appear serene, Margaret sat up straight and tightened her mouth into a fixed smile while an agitated Mrs. Gunter wildly waved her bright scarf on shore, whether to bid Godspeed or call her back, Margaret couldn't tell.

❧ ❧ ❧

"Let's go directly to our cabin," Margaret said as soon as the ship was under way.

"Are you sick, Dona Margarida?" Florinda asked. Her own stomach was feeling extraordinarily queer.

"Não," Margaret demurred. "Just tired. I think we both need to rest."

Since most of the cabins had been taken by the passengers who'd come from the south, Margaret was thankful to be given a tidy inside room with two hard bunks. She locked the door securely behind her.

Almost immediately, someone knocked. Margaret stepped back to let Florinda answer the door. The steward poked his head in to ask, "Cafezinho para a senhorita?"

Wishing only to lie down, Margaret declined the offer of coffee and secured the door once more so she could nap.

Florinda took Margaret's cape and hung it on a peg behind the door. Next she unwrapped Margaret's food bundle and laid out some bread and fruit. "Mais tarde, later . . ." Margaret yawned, sat on the bed, and began to unlace her shoes.

Florinda kneeled and helped with the second boot. "Ai!" she cried when she saw the red welts caused by the hooks and laces. She took a pillow from the top berth and placed it under Margaret's swollen calves.

"Muito bem, Florinda, obrigada."

As she tried to surrender to sleep, Margaret couldn't help but remember "the shark's" guttural voice and the penetrating way he had stared at her on the launch. "Hand me my cape, Florinda," she asked. Even though she wasn't chilled, she pulled it over her and reached into the pocket. She stroked the pistol, feeling the intricate engravings on the barrel and the raised section of bone set into the handle with a single screw. The metal warmed in her hand. "My little pepperbox," her mother had said. What a comforting name! It brought images of their kitchen on Felicity Street and of old Tildy. Margaret remembered their cook's calloused black-and-pink hands refilling her small boxes of fragrant Creole spices: filé, herbsaint, saffron, crushed bright peppers, and chicory. Still gripping the pistol, Margaret slept.

❧ 4 The grinding sound of an anchor being lowered vibrated the metal walls of the cabin. Margaret stirred.

"Is it Rio, Dona Margarida?"

The air in the tiny room was palpably moist. Margaret's traveling clothes felt glued to her skin. "No, just Santos. Would you like to see the port?"

"Oh, sim, senhorita!"

When Margaret stood, she noticed that a basin of fresh water waited next to her combs and hairpins. "Muito bom, Florinda," she complimented as she changed into a fresh linen shirtwaist.

Florinda unbound Margaret's hair and openly admired the golden cascade. "Tenho permissão?" she asked before taking a comb to the fine strands that were so different from her own dark, coarse ones. Reluctantly Margaret agreed, but she was surprised how swiftly Florinda managed to rearrange her tangled curls into a neat coiffure.

They could smell the stench of the mud flats of Santos even before they reached the deck. The odor of dried salt and putrid shellfish was so nauseating Margaret thought she could almost taste the pestilence in the air. As soon as the bales of coffee were loaded, the ship quickly was under way again. A simple luncheon was served on deck. Florinda filled for Margaret a platter with ordinary Brazilian fare: dried beef, called carne sêca, prepared both broiled and stewed, rice, as well as black feijão beans and the tasteless, sawdust-textured farinha mixed with pieces of hard-boiled egg. Margaret ate a bit of the rice and tried to swallow a few pieces of the rubbery egg but immediately spit it into her napkin.

The boat pitched wildly from stern to bow. Perhaps this was the "following sea" about which Captain McCormick had warned her. In any case, it was decidedly unpleasant. Margaret felt heavy and full, her stomach was a knot of pain, and her head pounded in rhythm with the noises of the ship. Florinda tucked her into a deck chair with a wool steamer rug and gave her a few slices of oranges on which to suck. At least these refreshed the bitter taste in her mouth.

"If you don't need me, senhorita, I'll go sit with the others." She pointed to the area around the stern where all the servants were congregating. One old "preto," black and wizened, was playing a melody from the interior on a guitar. Margaret nodded.

Buffeted by a strong, warm wind, Margaret felt like closing her eyes, but she knew she should remain watchful in case the bandit might also be about. But only the most reputable types were strolling this deck, she noticed with relief. Either he stayed below or, more likely, he had disembarked at Santos. At least that's what Margaret hoped. Slowly, she adjusted to the ship's rhythms and began to enjoy the long regular rollers that stretched to the sky.

When she felt steadier, Margaret walked to the rail and watched the fork-tailed petrels fly above the ship's wake. The setting sun turned their dark brown bodies almost chestnut, though when they faced away from the brilliant rays they appeared quite black except for their conspicuous white rumps. Their flight was so arrowy it was only just possible to see the tips of their toes stretched beyond the edge of their tails, but as they swooped to pick up some tempting morsel floating below, they would let their legs dangle and their toes skim the surface of the water that was churned by the engine's screws into a milky froth. The wide swath of whiteness seemed to stretch endlessly back toward the laziness of Iguape, the tedium of Lizzieland, the boredom of the backlands.

Backlands. Margaret recalled Mrs. Gunter saying, "One of those typical bandido . . . ah . . . backland names."

In Lizzieland she'd heard some of the bandido legends told in heroic songs and apocryphal tales. Their crimes, most of which could be traced to century-old familial rivalries, had never affected the colonists, she comforted herself as she watched an elderly couple, arm in arm, approach the port rail to watch the sunset. The sun slipped from beneath a screen of clouds, like the yolk of an egg breaking over the ocean, and bathed the water in an acid light. Orange and pink tentacles, like an incandescent octopus, reached out across the sky. The water, losing all contours, seemed cast in steel. The bow of the boat slapped its way forward with an insistent rhythm.

Blessed with an excellent musical memory, she thought she could hear the second movement of Mozart's Piano Concerto in B-flat. Mlle Doradou had taught her the piece as an elegiac farewell, with a serenity both tender and noble. As the mood of the soft tropical wind and the motion of the cresting moonlit waves blended with the music only she could hear, Margaret yearned to touch a keyboard, actually to pick up the graceful melodic arch of the second theme, sweeping over a two-octave span. A sudden spray from a wave brought her back from her imaginary concert hall to the ship's deck.

Florinda was nowhere to be found to help her dress for dinner. Most of the second-class passengers had left the wave-spattered deck to bed down along the closed inner passageways. Where was the servant? Crossing to the starboard side of the ship. Margaret wove her way among the hammocks and sprawled peasants. As she rounded the corner near the dining saloon door, she heard a strange moan and stopped abruptly. All she noticed at first was a confusing tangle of arms and flailing legs that made spidery shadows on the underside of a lifeboat. She permitted her eyes to drift downward.

In the waning light, the silhouette of the grappling couple revealed more than enough for Margaret to realize what she was witnessing. She hesitated. If she opened the door to the saloon, light from the interior would illuminate the couple, or worse, might reveal the identity of the onlooker. If she moved in any direction, they would know she had been watching them. In the shadows, frozen by indecision as well as curiosity, Margaret waited.

As the deck pitched on the churning waves, the half-naked bodies rose and fell, darkened and glistened in the reflection of a deck light. Their bodies exuded a scent that Margaret found not exactly unpleasant. The man lifted himself on his elbows, momentarily displayed the girl's nipples, black, protruding, then raised his clenched buttocks before falling on the yielding body beneath him.

Margaret shut her eyes tight and tried not to gasp out loud. Slowly she reopened them, praying the couple had disappeared. Instead, the girl had become slightly distracted and stared up at Margaret. In the darkness, the shape of her face, her coloration, looked remarkably like Florinda's. Margaret blinked. It wasn't Florinda, thank heavens!

"Aiii! Chico!" The woman gasped, bit into the man's shoulder, and spread her legs even wider.

Margaret ran back to her cabin alone.

❧   ❧   ❧

Dutiful Florinda had Margaret's lime-green dinner suit neatly arranged on the bed. A fresh basin of water and snowy towel were waiting. What if that had been Florinda? Margaret considered as she scrubbed herself with great thoroughness. This was one of the few times she'd ever considered another person's sexuality. She admitted musing about the intimate side of Raleigh's marriage, and she had sometimes wondered which of Mademoiselle's visitors received more than a private concert and bowl of her famous gumbo. Now, after witnessing something so graphic, she was intrigued about Florinda. Here was a girl who was almost the same age as she was, but while she had no idea of the feelings that transpired between a man and a woman, Florinda had children as proof of her years of conjugal experience. In her own simple way, Florinda was still very attractive. Margaret could easily see her charming another man.

When she'd finished washing, Margaret said to Florinda, "I don't want you to be on deck with any of the others this evening!"

"Sim, senhorita," Florinda agreed without the slightest question in her voice.

"You'll have your dinner in the cabin and wait for me here."

Florinda handed Margaret her cloak. "Sim, senhorita."

Margaret started down the corridor in the direction of the main dining saloon. She felt the hard little pepperbox pistol inside her pocket pressing to her with every rolling motion of the ship. But the passageway led to another maze of closed cabin doors. She tried to make her way back by following the room numbers, but they changed unexpectedly. The ship lurched. Margaret grabbed the handrail and closed her eyes. She tried to force herself to remain calm. Just find an outside door, she told herself, then follow the promenade deck around to the dining saloon door. No! She didn't want to have to pass those lifeboats again. Images of twisting bodies and the eyes of the excited girl who'd looked so much like Florinda caused her heart to pound uncontrollably.

"Now don't be so silly," she said aloud, knowing that if she could just get to the other passengers she'd be fine.

With a deep breath she opened the first outside door she came to. Believing that the dining saloon was to her right, she rounded the corner. A firm hand grabbed her shoulder and pushed her into a dark passage under the stairway leading to an upper deck.

"Tubarão!" she gasped just as his hand clapped over her mouth. Reflexively, she reached into her pocket for the pepperbox and slipped her finger through the trigger guard. The little five-shot .24-caliber weapon was instantly ready.

"O que você sabe?" he demanded gruffly. "What do you know?"

Margaret pretended not to understand. He menacingly lunged his left leg toward her stomach. The sudden jolt sent Margaret reeling backward, and without really intending to, she pulled the trigger and fired blindly.

"Meu Deus!" Tubarão clutched his thigh and howled. "Você está louca?"

Margaret leaned against the rail and stared at the pistol blankly.

"What happened?" asked a well-dressed passenger who'd come running at the sound of the gunshot.

"I shot him." Margaret pointed to the injured man who was bent double. What seemed like a tremendous quantity of blood seeped through his trousers, quickly coating the deck crimson.

The passenger briefly inspected the wound. "Not so serious," he pronounced to the crowd gathering under an eerily quavering deck lamp. "He seems to have lost more than he really has because the blood mixes with the moisture on the deck."

Florinda pushed her way forward, screaming. Even after Margaret showed her that the only damage was a powder-ringed hole in her cape, Florinda was still unconvinced that so much blood had come from only one victim and loudly berated herself for leaving her lady alone.

Rigid with shock, Margaret was led into the captain's lounge behind the bridge while the assailant was laid out on the deck and ministered to by two deck hands.

"Do you know the man?" Captain Jorge Lopes asked Margaret gently.

"He's called 'Tubarão.' In Iguape I was warned to avoid him. He has a bad reputation there."

"Do you know anything else?"

Margaret shook her head and began to cry. "It was accidental; when he grabbed for me, I reached for my pistol. Somehow it just fired!"

"Great fortune for you, my dear. Who knows what the man might have done?"

"Is the injury serious?"

"Not serious enough." The captain smiled charmingly. "Don't trouble yourself about it. We'll turn him over to the authorities in Rio in the morning. I ask only that you be my guest on the bridge this evening so I can properly watch over you. I'll have your meal served here."

While Margaret tried to swallow some broth, the captain continued to question her discreetly about where she was going, who would be meeting her, and what she knew about her assailant. Margaret kept repeating the same information until he was convinced that she could add nothing more. For some unexplainable reason she resisted mentioning what she'd seen and overheard on the barge. Too confusing, not enough information; besides, she just wanted to be done with the whole incident.

"You're certain he won't die?" Margaret kept asking.

"The wound's very minor, really," the captain assured her. "The bullet will be removed by the police doctor." He poured her a cup of cafezinho.

"Police?"

"There must be a brief inquiry, but nothing for you to worry about. They'll ask much the same questions as I did."

"Did he tell you anything?"

"Only that his real name's Valdemar Barreto, that he's a resident of Sete Barras, a very small place in the interior. He's carrying plenty of money, too much for a man of his type, but there's no real crime in that. He claims he's on his way to Rio to purchase supplies." The captain shrugged in disbelief. "Have some more to drink," he encouraged. Brazilians thought everything could be cured by coffee. He refilled Margaret's apparently bottomless demitasse cup and watched the grace with which she drew its chipped rim to her lips and took a tentative sip.

Captain Lopes settled back into his worn leather chair and sighed aloud. Such a mouth! He stared with satisfaction at the twin peaks of her upper lip. A perfect pink line. What a lovely young thing . . . So dangerous for her to be alone in this country with unscrupulous men like Barreto around. A girl like that . . . Such a temptation. If I were her father, I'd keep her behind high walls. If I were her husband I'd . . . He watched Margaret's head lean back against the cushion her maid had provided. She closed her swollen eyelids. The captain wiped the sweat that beaded on his forehead, stood, and stared boldly at the way her soft breasts spread as she reclined. The outline of nipples was just visible through the stretched creamy linen of her bodice. Damp tendrils of an exquisite sunny color framed her pale face. An angel . . . a golden angel . . .

"Capitão . . ." One of his aides entered the room. Lopes pretended he'd been checking the water pressure gauge. Though he appeared intent on his work, he saw nothing . . . The numbers had blurred.

❦ 5 The police launch was the first to approach the ship. Sven Larson came on board with three officers. Their spokesman wore a badge with the name Feitosa. After only a few brief questions, Margaret was told she could disembark.

"Is that all?"

The Larsons' private launch pulled aside. "The matter is quite settled," Sven Larson replied briskly. "You are hardly the guilty party, my dear." He pointed to the swaying ladder. "Do you think you can manage the climb?"

"Yes, I can, but I think Florinda is afraid."

Sven looked at Margaret's timid servant sternly. He pointed to the launch. "Agora!" he ordered.

Florinda jumped to obey, and Margaret followed her into the smaller boat.

"Now let's get you home to Francisca, who has been making herself ill she is so excited to be with you." Sven Larson spoke haltingly in English so Florinda would not understand. "Only one thing . . ."

"Yes?"

"Please don't mention this incident to my daughter; she would be so upset for you. He paused meaningfully. "I can understand that you might not have wished to give those . . . men . . . the entire story. However, is there anything else you would like to tell me? Confidentially, of course."

What was there really to say? Margaret wondered. The only part she hadn't told about was a few senseless words, the roll of money, nothing that made any sense. To explain further would be to complicate the matter endlessly. Barreto's wound was slight, he'd recover, and as long as she'd never have to see him again, it was simplest to say "No, nothing."

"Then put it out of your mind. For your sake, I'm glad the fellow has a minor injury. For mine . . ." His voice turned surprisingly bitter. "Gostaria que tivesse matado o miserável! I wish you had killed the bastard!"

❧6 When Margaret arrived at the Larsons', she was greeted, given a light luncheon in her room, and put to bed. All day Florinda tiptoed in and out of Margaret's room, replacing uneaten foods with fresh ones. Francisca's maid, the buxom Zefinha, stopped her in the corridor.

"Your senhorita still sleeps?"

"The trip was very . . . difficult." Senhor Larson had warned the servant never to mention the shooting to anyone in his house.

"I'll bring Dona Margarida green coconut water. It will settle her stomach."

Florinda bristled. "There's nothing wrong with her stomach," she replied shrilly. "She just hasn't slept for two nights."

Zefinha smiled knowingly. "She'll be even more excited tomorrow."

Florinda stared blankly.

"When she sees Seu Erico, Dona Francisca's brother."

"Quem?"

Zefinha gave a throaty laugh and pulled Florinda into the linen pantry. "Have you not wondered why a young girl would come so far only for the wedding of a school friend?" she whispered.

"Ai! I didn't think!" Florinda giggled.

Margaret slept twenty hours. As soon as she was awake, Francisca came to her room and stood beside her bed. The elegant four-poster was carved in the eighteenth-century manner of Dona Maria I, with flowers and ribbons intertwined around pineapples, and painted in pastel combinations of yellow, sky blue, and pink. A matching armoire was directly across the room.

Francisca pulled back the mosquito netting and smoothed the pink brocade covers across Margaret's lap. "You look so much better today!"

"Was I so awful yesterday?"

"Anyone would've needed to recover from so miserable a journey." She propped the bolster behind Margaret's back. "Papai told me you had very severe weather on the Atlantic and that you had taken ill. You did so well from New Orleans, I was surprised."

Margaret demurred purposefully. "The *Oceania* was a much larger ship . . ."

Francisca fluttered about the room, opening draperies, rearranging flower vases. "If you are well enough, my dressmaker will fit you this afternoon for several gowns. I hope you'll like the fabrics. I've picked sapphire blue for the wedding . . . to match your eyes. Then something in a greenish gold for the first dinner party."

"I've brought all my dresses from New Orleans. If someone could only clean and mend them, I won't need much else."

"We've already purchased the silks!"

"You're the bride. I'll do whatever you wish."

"Then, afterward, Mamãe has some ladies coming to tea to help arrange the wedding gifts." Francisca rushed on, describing her plans with great animation. Margaret only half-listened until, at the end of her ramblings, Francisca blurted, "Last week Gigo personally saw that our piano was tuned properly."

"How kind of him to go to so much . . ."

"Not at all. *He* was the one who insisted it be ready for you. I've told him about your playing so many times that he doesn't want to miss this chance to hear you."

Margaret flexed her fingers, hoping she hadn't lost too much of the strength in her hands. "I guess I'll have to trim my fingernails," she said with a high laugh. "I let them grow long in Lizzieland since I had nothing but a mute keyboard there."

"What a pity!" Francisca cocked her head to one side like a little bird. "Once, when I asked how you could play without sheet music, you told me, 'The muscles remember, the eye forgets.' "

"And you forget nothing," Margaret replied lightly.

Francisca was very still.

Margaret wondered what she had said to effect the change of mood. "Tell your mother that I will be delighted to join her at tea . . ." Her voice trailed. "My mother wanted so much to come to Rio, but she couldn't leave the little ones and . . ."

Francisca patted Margaret's shoulder. "You mustn't worry about anyone thinking it improper. Didn't I travel all the way from Louisiana in the care of the captain?"

"I was worried that I might have offended someone."

"If anything had deterred you, I would've been heartbroken!" Francisca lifted a glass of a viscous fluid and passed it to Margaret. "Drink this; it's Zefinha's cure."

Margaret wrinkled her nose. "What is it?"

"Green coconut water. It's very refreshing."

Margaret tasted, then nodded. "Not as awful as I expected." She sipped again. "Muito bom."

"We'll be having a light supper with just my parents tonight, since Gigo and most of the guests are dining in Boa Vista." She watched Margaret's face for a sign, and she was rewarded with a momentary flicker of interest. "They sent him there to entertain some of the guests who could not be accommodated here, mostly managers from our textile plants and our cousins from the northeast. You'll see him Saturday evening. All the Cavalcantis are coming for dinner, and afterward we're having a party for all the cousins. We were . . . I was hoping you might play for them."

Margaret massaged the back of her weaker left hand with her right. "I haven't played for ages!"

"I was hoping you might play that Chopin etude that always made me cry."

"Opus ten, number three, in E?"

"I can never remember the numbers or letters, but it had a romantic beginning, then a whirlwind of chords in the middle. Your fingers flew over the whole keyboard when you played it. The main part was something like this." Francisca hummed the lilting theme in her thin soprano voice.

Margaret leaned back on the bolster and heard the music swell in her head. "That's it, that's opus ten." She closed her eyes, allowing her mind and her fingers to review the piece that she had played hundreds of times. In a moment she had slipped back to when her teacher had insisted she play all twenty-four etudes each day for a month. She'd complained, "But Mademoiselle, after playing them all each day, I am too tired to practice my regular music."

"You exaggerate, ma chérie. Done at the proper tempo, they take less than an hour. You'd still have time for your Czerny exercises, a few preludes, and finally one of the neglected mazurkas . . . for energy."

Energy! No one realized the sheer physical strength it took to perfect her playing. Sometimes Mlle Doradou had forced Margaret to practice till exhaustion. Though she loved the woman, even worshiped her skills and knowledge, at moments her mentor and musical guardian had also been her tormentor and cruelest jailer. As she thought about Mlle Doradou, with her auburn curls streaming unbound down her back, Margaret could almost smell the fading roses in the dusty parlor, hear the woman's gravelly voice counting out the beats of a difficult passage. Margaret stretched the long fingers that had easily made an octave before she was ten. The tendons seemed to have shortened. I'll have to relearn my Czerny studies from the school of velocity, all the scales, arpeggios, and trills, even Brahms's exercises for the thumb . . . The simplest, most basic techniques to strengthen the fingers, retrain the hands. Czerny! That's where I'll begin. Margaret sighed contentedly. Tomorrow.

❧ 7 Tea that afternoon was held in the most elegant room in the mansion, the gilded sala de visitas. Not knowing Guilhermina Larson's relations or intimate friends, nor understanding their clipped Carioca accents very well, Margaret concentrated her thoughts on the grand piano set in front of the massive bay windows, wondering what kind of sound and action it had and what palette of tone color would be available. Would it be especially suited to Chopin or would Schumann, her favorite, sound better?

Impatient to play, Margaret awoke early the next morning and made her way directly to the drawing room. Slowly she opened the unlocked doors and saw the piano's silhouette haloed by the morning sun. Someone had already raised the lid, and the twinkling bronze harp beckoned her closer. She peered inside and saw the felt-covered hammers waiting patiently. As a youngster she'd thought of the hammers as her "mice." She'd worked to make them dance faster and faster as her fingers flew up and down the boring scales. She smiled at the childhood memory. "Dance, little mice, dance!" she said aloud.

Reverently, Margaret stroked the smooth ivories. On the fall board in front of her were the words *André Charles Roule, Paris.* She repositioned the little bronze candleholders at either side before seating herself on the tooled-leather double piano bench.

Mademoiselle's hoarse voice echoed from the past. "Remember your Czerny rules even before you begin!" How Margaret had come to hate the grinding sound of that authoritative name! Czerny! Still, before sounding a note of the Larsons' piano, she mentally reviewed his rules: "The seat of the player must be placed exactly opposite the middle of the keyboard, and at such a distance from it that the elbows, when hanging down freely, shall be about four inches nearer the keys than the shoulder. The position of the hand and of the chest should be upright, dignified, and natural." Margaret inhaled slowly and then, with trembling excitement, began her preliminary exercises. The piano's responsive action compared amazingly well with Mademoiselle's treasured Pleyel.

Even a few mandatory scales, after so long an absence, brought immense pleasure in their playing. Margaret was delighted to find her fingers more fleet and her touch more precise than she had expected. She was relieved that her facility to play had not been lost entirely. When she was fully warmed up, she hoped the missing accuracy would return completely. She tried a few simple melodies, such as passages from Schumann's "Papillons," consciously bringing each finger up equally high. Next she attempted techniques with mezzo staccato or dropped note touches, always working for a pearly sound with roundness and finish. The notes rang out clear and distinct.

Her breath came quickly as she turned to a more difficult passage from a Bach bourrée. She watched the little mice flutter as her hands worked their way, albeit often inaccurately, up and down the keyboard. It was frustrating to be so stiff! It seemed as if she'd grown a few extra fingers that refused to glide over the intervals or land on the right black key.

As she stopped to rub her aching lower arms and shoulders, Margaret had the feeling that someone was near. Wordlessly, she walked toward the door, flung it open, and caught Florinda listening by the wall. "Come in, por favor." Margaret gestured to a gilded chair. "I'll play something special for you."

Margaret returned to the bench and stared out into the garden, willing the tension in her neck and back to dissolve. Spiky palms were twisting in an uneven breeze. A bougainvillea was bursting with bright orange blooms. "Always keep your audience firmly in mind" was another of Mlle Doradou's dictums. What should I play for Florinda? Margaret wondered.

The wind outside reminded her of the beginning ripples of Mozart's Fantasy in D Minor. Without further thought, she began to play the introductory andante, which began so slowly it was easy for her fingers to recall. The faster phrases came tumbling, slicing the air with delicate tones. To herself Margaret hummed the unassuming slow arpeggios, trying to squeeze life into every note. It was really not a difficult piece, but romantic, and with enough short passages to permit her to exhibit some florid technique to her audience of one.

❧ 8 In their bedroom directly above the drawing room, the Larsons could hear Margaret practicing.

"Oh, she plays so wonderfully. It sounds like butterflies," Guilhermina remarked as she dressed.

"Such a gift!" her husband replied. "Has anyone asked her to play on Saturday evening?"

"Chiquinha hinted. But she isn't certain Margarida is willing."

"Mininha," Sven said affectionately, "she's our guest, not a performer." Sven Larson sat down on a slipper-shaped divan to tie his shoes. "Besides, she needs to rest for a few days longer. Remember how green she looked when she arrived? She's done remarkably . . . considering everything."

Guilhermina stopped tugging at her corset. "Vivo." She used her intimate name for him. "Is there something I don't know?"

Larson hadn't actually meant to tell his wife about Barreto, but he'd had some disquieting news the day before. The police, with no evidence of any crime committed, had released the hoodlum without penalty. If the man really was a bandit, instead of a peasant who'd been unfairly treated, as he claimed, Larson worried he might be tempted to avenge his honor in some way, to satisfy the crazy codes that ruled in the uncivilized backlands. Now his guest would have to be guarded more thoroughly. Since it would be impossible to make the complicated arrangements without his wife's knowledge, he explained the situation in the lightest tone possible. "I'm certain the man only stumbled, the way he said, and she reacted like a frightened child. However, we can't take any chances, can we?"

"Extraordinary that the girl would even have a firearm, let alone know what to do."

"That's my point. She pulled the trigger without meaning to when he jarred her. The injury was very slight. Still, he might harbor a grudge. You can never tell with these matutos . . . these peasants."

"Even against a woman?"

"Who knows how they think? He might let it pass for just that reason, or . . ."

"He might think it a mark against his manhood," Guilhermina finished for him.

Sven took his wife's hand. "Then, you'll agree to my precautions?"

"Do as you must, but say only that there have been some suspicious people about or that you are just protecting our guests, their jewels, anything but . . ."

"I agree that Chiquinha mustn't ever hear about Margaret and this man . . ."

Guilhermina lowered her voice and spat, "Nunca! Never!" with such vehemence that her husband dropped her hand as though he had been burnt.

❧ ❧ ❧

After Margaret finished her practice, Florinda pointed to the family dining room. "Café?" she asked.

"Is anyone else awake?"

"I think the parents take breakfast in their rooms. About the others I know nothing."

A man's voice surprised Margaret as she entered the dining room. "Good morning, Miss Claiborne." Margaret started as she quickly recognized Erik's distinctive English accent, but his easy smile was even more compelling than she'd remembered.

"They've tried their best to keep us apart, but they'll soon learn it's a hopeless endeavor."

"Apart? But why?"

Erik cocked his head to one side and opened his palms to the ceiling. "I suppose I'm considered a great danger to beautiful young ladies."

Margaret couldn't imagine what she had done to encourage the man to speak like that, but in an odd way she hoped he wouldn't stop.

"At least you will do us the honor of staying more than one day on this visit, will you not?" Erik led her to a seat and clapped his hands. A servant poured coffee into a gold-rimmed cup and placed a flour-dusted roll on her silver plate.

"Last time darkness fell before you could see the view from Corcovado. You should have stayed longer then."

"I would have liked to," she blurted. "But my brother . . ." She trailed off weakly.

Luckily, Francisca came into the room before she'd shamed herself further.

"Are you ready to go to the Rua do Ouvidor?" she asked before she saw Erik. "Gigo! You're supposed to be at Boa Vista!"

Erik hung his head theatrically.

"Just came for some clothes and" — he winked at Margaret — "to be certain I wasn't needed." He gulped his coffee. If you'll take me in the carriage, I can get to the wharf from the shops. It will be our secret."

Francisca laughed easily. "Oh, Gigo! You're crazy. But, yes, you can come with us."

9 En route to the Rua do Ouvidor, Rio's most fashionable shopping district, murky, inactive clouds hung over the city like a broken tiara. Erik sat up front with the driver, while Francisca, Margaret, and Zefinha rode under the canopy in the rear.

"Today is going to be very hot. I'm glad we got such an early start." Francisca's voice seemed strained. "I guess I should be pleased we'll be going to the mountains after the wedding. The Cavalcantis' place in Petropolis isn't far from where the emperor had his palace."

"Petropolis? Is that near Boa Vista?"

"No, it's much farther. Boa Vista is only half an hour from the city by tram, longer by carriage."

"Do you go to Boa Vista often?"

"For holidays and every summer. Up in the hills the air changes completely. There are constant breezes, freshwater streams, heavy forests with cool shaded patches. I love the gardens there. To me they're much more beautiful than the ones in town."

"How's that possible?"

"I prefer gardens less tidy, less formal. It's the difference between a well-mannered house cat and a trained but slightly dangerous circus leopard."

"Francisca!" Margaret laughed gaily. "What an unusual comparison!"

The carriage turned and twisted through the winding streets of
Rio, past its mist-stained buildings and an ancient drinking fountain rich with the mossy marks of time. Francisca pointed to a
plaza ringed with small varicolored houses. "That was the old
slave market."

They skirted poorer districts, making their way past the more
affluent houses shaded by the thick leaves of the banana and tamarind trees.

"Look at that!" Margaret pointed to street vendors making their
rounds from door to door. She was fascinated by everything: the
bread man, dressed in a salmon-colored shirt and wide-striped
trousers, who carried a day's supply of baked goods for each family in a little green-roofed reed house on his head; the sweetmeat
seller, who balanced a small tray of fruit cakes and coconut candies; the poultry man, who juggled a huge wicker basket with the
heads and necks of his domestic menagerie protruding at the
sides.

As they rounded the corner into a large cobbled area called the
Largo de São Francisco de Paula, Francisca pointed to the statue
of José Bonifácio de Andrada e Silva, the father of Brazilian independence. "Sergio, please leave us here and we'll meet you at the
other end of the street near the quay."

The carriage halted. Erik leapt down, waved farewell, and ran
off to catch a passing streetcar.

"My brother!" Francisca shrugged. "Louco!"

"Wonderful . . ." Margaret murmured under her breath.

"The Rua do Ouvidor is known worldwide, but visitors are
always surprised when they see it. It's less than eight meters
wide; that's why street carriages and horses are not permitted
through." Francisca pointed up at the bronze arches that supported ornate street lamps. "It was one of the first streets in all
Rio to be electrified." Francisca pulled a list from a small silk
purse that hung from her wrist. "Mamãe and I always walk from

one end to the other, stopping in all our favorite shops. Today we begin at number one oh one, the Casa Moreira, Joalharia."

The ladies entered the narrow brass-trimmed door at the apex of the triangular building on the corner. Zefinha, carrying a large straw bag to hold their purchases, waited outside. The junior partner in the jewelry firm stepped forward and bowed. "Dona Francisca, muito prazer. The ring is ready for your approval." Senhor Machado ushered the young women into a private area in the back of the showroom, inserted a key in a glass case, and removed a filigreed silver box.

The wedding ring's center was set with a stone the size of a small nut. Margaret gasped.

"Papai brought the diamond from Minas Gerais and had me choose the setting. I think it came out beautifully, don't you?"

Margaret nodded mutely while Francisca tried on the ring. For a moment she wondered why Francisca's fiancé hadn't purchased the stone himself. Perhaps that's the custom in Brazil, she decided.

"You approve, Dona Francisca?"

"Oh, sim!" Francisca handed the ring back to the jeweler.

"Won't you take it with you?" Margaret asked.

"No, too great a risk. Senhor Machado will have it delivered very discreetly."

While Francisca gave further instructions, Margaret peered into some of the cases that featured elaborate settings of sapphires, rubies, topazes, and amethysts. Through a parted curtain, she could see into a workroom where the stones were being polished and set by small children. Once on the street again, she mentioned it. "Such young workers! I saw boys who looked barely ten."

"It is an honor to be taken in by a company such as Moreira's. They must apprentice very young to develop the precise skills needed for that type of work," Francisca said matter-of-factly. "Next we're going to buy something for you."

Margaret protested while Francisca steered her past an elegant leather-goods shop. Some of the buildings were splendid, with brass-trimmed windows or gaily painted exteriors; others were shabby examples of unrehabilitated colonial architecture. They went into Casa Arthur Napoleão. There, in the center of the showroom, was a massive piano made entirely of bronze. It was supported by thick legs that tapered into ferocious clawlike feet. "That was the piano of Senhor Napoleão himself. He was a well-known pianist in Rio, and he founded this business with his partner, the composer Miguez." In the rear, Margaret noticed some less pretentious pianos and a sign indicating the store specialized in the Bechstein and Blüthner brands. But she was more impressed by the floor-to-ceiling cases of sheet music.

"If there is something you would like to have . . ."

Margaret had intended to save the little money she had for an emergency. "No, not at this time. I have a small box of scores in my trunk and much more at home."

"You misunderstand," Francisca said, taking her hand. "My parents ordered me to buy you some music, as a gift, in gratitude."

"But I haven't even played for you yet."

"Even your practicing delights us all. You should've seen everyone hovering outside the sala de visitas yesterday while you were playing the Mozart."

"Then you heard me stumbling through the closing rondo!"

Francisca shook her head in mock disapproval. "You do need more music; that proves it!"

Margaret understood that it would be impolite to refuse. "Perhaps something by one of your Brazilian composers. I am completely unfamiliar with them."

Francisca was touched by Margaret's choice. In a few moments Zefinha's straw bag was filled with heavy musical scores by Carlos Gomes, Leopoldo Miguez, Joaquim Freire, Alexandre Levy, Alberto Nepomuceno, and Henrique Oswald.

Stepping out on the white-hot street, Francisca consulted her shopping list, then wiped her brow. "If I don't have a coffee, I can't possibly continue. Fortunately, the Confeitaria Colombo is just around the corner."

Momentarily blinded by the sun, Margaret walked to the left while Francisca turned right. As soon as she realized she was going the wrong way, she tried to push through the shoulder-to-shoulder throng and catch up to her friend. Edging her way to the curb, she caught sight of a man leaning against a sidewalk stand. A curtain of bright-colored lottery tickets hanging in rows partially blocked the all-too-familiar hawk-nosed face. Was it really Barreto? Margaret caught up to Zefinha before looking back over her shoulder. The man had disappeared. Couldn't have been him, she thought. Her heart pounded mercilessly.

"You look worse than I feel." Francisca waited under the café's awning. "Let me just give Zefinha a few coins to buy herself something from a street vendor," she said before steering Margaret inside.

The two young women were shown to a cool table directly under a high ceiling fan in the immense double-tiered restaurant. The waiter, dressed inappropriately for the weather in a grey frock coat, took Francisca's order for cafezinho and turned to Margaret. "Refrêsco de laranja, por favor," she said weakly. Turning to Francisca, she chided, "How can you drink something hot?"

"The quickest way to fight the heat is to treat like with like." Francisca fanned herself with her menu. "Maybe it doesn't sound sensible, but it's effective."

The burning flush in Margaret's cheeks slowly subsided. She admired the walls of the café, which were lined with sixteen-foot-high beveled mirrors in carved rosewood frames that simulated wrought iron. "Look at that!" Margaret leaned back, the better to see the enormous stained-glass skylight above.

"I prefer what's behind glass over there!" Francisca pointed out the elaborate pastries encrusted with layers of icing, which were displayed like jewels in the cases in the front of the café.

Now Margaret began looking around the room at the elegantly dressed patrons. She was surprised at how many of the ladies who were taking their refreshments had dark, mulatto skins. She'd somehow assumed all upper-class Brazilian women were as fair as the Larsons. Before Margaret had a chance to phrase a question on the subject, a lady in a rose silk dress waved to Francisca from across the room. "Alô!"

Francisca nodded back happily. "Some of my wedding guests are here. Probably shopping for me on 'poor husbands' row'!" she said brightly. Then more somberly, "Only six more days."

"At least on Saturday I finally get to meet your groom," Margaret said. "If I don't approve, will you cancel the ceremony?"

"Not without the attorneys." Francisca made a helpless gesture. "There were many legal documents to be signed. If it all weren't so complicated . . ."

The waiter set a tall glass of iced orange juice and a demitasse of coffee on the round marble table. Francisca took a sip from her cup before continuing in a different vein.

"And Saturday you'll see Gigo again, or rather that's when you were supposed to see him. We'd better not say anything about this morning. All right?" Francisca raised her thick brown eyebrows meaningfully.

"I still don't understand why he must stay at Boa Vista."

"Don't think that Gigo didn't beg to remain at Flamengo! Papai had to remind him that it would be extremely impolite to leave the Souto and Araujo cousins without a member of the family to entertain them." She paused dramatically. "This might surprise you, but he's never forgotten you. Since you were here, every other woman has bored him. I could tell."

"I knew him only for a few hours . . ."

The pastry cart was rolled up to their table. They each selected a few slim sandwiches and one voluptuous pastry. Francisca squirmed in her cane seat. "Before he sees you again, Gigo wanted me to tell you . . ." She took a deep breath. "He has been married."

Margaret's hands momentarily wavered in front of her face before she pressed them into her lap. "Why didn't anyone tell me before now?" She was conscious of the shrill edge that crept into her voice. "Now I really know why he stays at Boa Vista!"

"No, no . . . I said it badly. He *was* married . . . while I was in Louisiana . . . to a Swedish girl, a distant relation. I never met her."

"I don't understand . . ."

Francisca stared at the dark pool of coffee that shimmered in her cup. "Gunilla Bergson was her name. They tell me she was a very sweet, shy girl who was brought to Brazil especially to become Gigo's wife. He was almost thirty, and up to that point, he'd refused to make a choice on his own. They say that Gunilla wasn't happy in Brazil." She wiped her forehead with her napkin. "It's so close in here."

Margaret pressed her juice glass to her friend's cheek. "Cool is better, isn't it?"

"Yes ... yes ..." Francisca nodded distractedly. "Erik and Gunilla had a child. Her name is Astrid."

"What happened to Gunilla?"

"She died as a result of the birth. She bled to death the second night."

"Oh, that's terrible!" Margaret was quiet for a few seconds. "And Astrid?" As she said the name, Margaret felt a sudden sharpness in her chest.

"She still lives with the woman who cared for her as an infant."

"At your holiday home in Boa Vista?"

"No, not with Gigo at all. It's very ... complex. Eventually, when my brother has a home of his own again, Astrid will live with him."

Margaret lifted her fork, then put it down again immediately. The trouxinha, a sweet of whipped eggs and sugar, had melted into a sticky soup. All this seemed too much of a confession. After all, she'd only flirted with Erik briefly. "Why are you telling me all this?"

"My dearest friend, certainly I could not be happier than to have you for my real sister someday. But if it is not to be ..."

"How can you presume ... when I've met him but once?" Margaret raged unexpectedly.

Delicately Francisca reached out to touch Margaret's stooped shoulder. "It's just a feeling I've always had, even at school. I was so dreadfully disappointed when I received the news Gigo had married that I didn't tell you about it. Now, wasn't that odd? Why should you have cared that my brother thousands of kilometers away had married? Then, when you met each other in January, he was so taken with you my hopes soared! He's asked me hundreds of questions about you ever since. He even devised a business scheme, something to do with rice exports, that would've taken him to Iguape of all places. Unfortunately, my father saw it for what it was and put an end to it."

"Rice!" Margaret's tension dissolved into laughter. "Rice!"

"If you hadn't come for my wedding, he surely would have been negotiating in melancia by now! I'll tell you something else about my brother," Francisca continued in a conspiratorial voice. "When we were younger, he'd point out the eligible girls everyone paraded before him. 'See that one,' he'd say. 'The other boys follow her like moths to a flame. At fifteen she's at her best, but in two years . . . finished!' Then he'd snap his fingers like this, and tell me, 'I want a woman of promise.' "

"What did he mean?"

"He was always looking for someone whose beauty was not only in the youthfulness of her skin, the slenderness of her body, but someone with interests, talents of her own. Most of the girls here are educated only a few years at home or at a church school. Many make marriages before they are sixteen."

"How old was Gunilla?"

"Nineteen. That's ancient by Brazilian standards."

"I guess both of us qualify for a place in the cemetery."

"My father has more European thinking on such matters."

"Your brother, too, it seems."

Francisca tossed her head back to loosen a stiffness in her neck. "If you're ready, I must collect the corsets and lingerie I'm having made and the ribbons and candles for the church."

Zefinha, who noticed the ladies standing, rushed to join them. Francisca and Margaret opened their parasols and walked down the Rua do Ouvidor. Anxiously, Margaret looked about for the man who resembled Barreto. Misreading the tenseness in her face, Francisca touched Margaret's gloved hand lightly. "My brother has a very discerning eye," Francisca said almost under her breath.

Margaret spun around.

"The first words he said after he'd met you were that he thought you were, without a doubt, 'a woman of promise.' "

❧ 10 "Bonito!" Zefinha lifted a few strands of Margaret's hair and wound it around her fingers. "Dourado."

Florinda shook her head. "Não, prateado."

The two maids continued to argue whether her hair was more a shade of gold or of silver while each worked to fashion the fine metallic strands into ringlets to frame her face. As soon as they were satisfied, Margaret sent them from the room so as to finish dressing herself. She'd selected a costume of lavender moiré silk that had been in her trousseau trunk, a farewell gift from Mlle Doradou. The crocheted neckline had a modest scoop, but the skirt had a sensual drape. Twirling in front of the mirror, Margaret was aware of the effect she would have on all the men in the room, but most especially Erik.

The tortured curls suddenly looked blatantly artificial. Margaret pulled at the pins and attempted to structure the complicated arrangement into something more natural. Restrained by the tightness of her corset, she couldn't reach around to unwind the twisted chignon, and the front pompadour refused to lie back against her head at the proper angle. Weeping with frustration, she anxiously fussed at every crease in her skirt.

Downstairs Margaret was first introduced to the elder Cavalcantis and Francisca's fiancé, Augusto.

"You remember my son, Erik," Senhora Larson said at last. Margaret smiled tensely and allowed him to kiss her hand. With the faintest gesture, he put her finger to his lips as though to warn her to remember to keep their little secret. She was so unnerved by his glistening blue eyes and his penetrating gaze that she quickly moved on to meet Augusto's brother and sister.

For the few minutes it took to serve bebidas of lime juice and rum, Margaret appraised Francisca's future husband and his family. Augusto was not the man Margaret had envisioned. He was younger than Erik, but his body was shorter and more compact, with square shoulders and a thick neck. His skin seemed tough and leathery, with the added coarseness of a difficult beard. His mustache, even more wiry than his hair, was thick and upswept, but the size of it, unbalanced for his face, appeared unintentionally amusing. Though he wore a well-tailored jacket and silk cravat, Augusto seemed misplaced among the elegant visitors in the drawing room. Was it his eyes with their deep aboriginal set or the prominent ridge of his cheekbones? Margaret wondered. Augusto laughed aloud. At once Margaret realized that, next to him, Francisca, in her iridescent gown of ivory silk studded with a triple row of pink pearls and coral sequins, appeared aristocratically pale. His skin tone was by far the darkest in the room. Lucretia would have mistaken him for a black man, and Margaret's father would never have sat at the same table with him. While she understood that Brazilians were far more tolerant of mixed blood than North American Southerners, Margaret also knew that they admired Nordic blood. Francisca, with her Swedish father, ob-

viously was bringing more than her substantial wealth to the
match.

"You have the eye of an expert, Dona Antonieta." Erik's deep
voice carried easily from the other side of the room. "It was
painted by Henrique Nicolau Vinet." Erik pointed to a view of
sailing ships in Rio's harbor. Margaret couldn't help noticing
Senhora Cavalcanti's acquisitive gaze. For a brief second Erik met
Margaret's critical eye. She luxuriated in the warmth of his wry
smile.

Guilhermina Larson led the way into the festively decorated
formal dining room. The huge oval room boasted a ceiling mural
of the goddess Diana surrounded by paintings of hanging game
birds, fish tied on strings, baskets of fruits, vegetables, pastries,
and cakes. Around the polished table were tall chairs, their backs
carved with a fruit-and-nut pattern.

"Senhor Carlos, will you do me the honor of sitting beside
me?" Guilhermina Larson said, pointing to the chair at her right.
"And my son-to-be, Augusto, on my left."

Sven Larson pulled out the chair on his right for the enormously fat Senhora Cavalcanti, who had dressed in black to show
off her diamond-studded pearl choker. Francisca took her place,
beside her future father-in-law and directly across from her fiancé. Augusto's younger sister, the petite and flirtatious Maria
Edna, was given the seat between her brother and Erik, while
Margaret was positioned next to Raimundo, Augusto's corpulent
younger brother. With Erik too far away to talk to, Margaret felt
her skin prickle in dismay.

Not knowing what to say to either Raimundo on her left or
Senhor Larson on her right, Margaret stared at the luminescent
cattleya orchids floating in Waterford goblets at each place. In the
candlelit room, the facets of the glass reflected the brilliant color
of the purple petals across the lacy white cloth. Margaret realized
that her choice of gown had proved fortuitous, for its color was in
perfect harmony with the setting.

"Ah, parece delicioso!" Margaret said to Raimundo as the first
course of empadas de camarão was served. She noticed he helped
himself to six of the dainty pastries stuffed with shrimp while everyone else took no more than two. Momentarily annoyed by his
greed, she turned away and caught Erik's eye winking diagonally

opposite her. As soon as he had her attention, he twisted his mouth into a broad clown grimace. To keep from reacting, she concentrated on neatly splitting the crumbly pastry into bite-sized pieces.

Above the centerpiece of cascading cymbidium orchids, Margaret could see Maria Edna, gulping her food and then chattering to Erik like a frantic little bird. He was nodding unenthusiastically, much to Margaret's relief. Sven Larson politely turned the conversation in her direction. "Chiquinha tells me you have become interested in our Brazilian musicians."

"I'm particularly enjoying the piano part of a trio by Henrique Oswald. Now all I need are a violinist and cellist to hear how he meant it to sound."

"That can be arranged," Larson said, his heavy white mustache bobbing merrily. "In fact, several fine musicians, old friends of the family, are invited to the wedding reception. I'll make certain you are introduced, and — who knows? — we might all profit from the association!"

"You are very kind. Rio is spoiling me for life in the backlands."

"I would agree that our great metropolis would suit a woman with your talents better."

"My parents have only permitted me to come for the wedding."

"I understand." He lowered his voice and bent quite close. "But I will not allow you to return until safer arrangements can be made for your passage."

The wine waiter paused behind Francisca and waited to catch Sven Larson's eye. He nodded his approval and the waiter refilled her glass. Larson smiled at Margaret. "I suppose I must relinquish my right as a father. Soon my daughter's husband shall judge whether or not she should have a third glass of wine."

Margaret wondered why anyone needed to watch over Francisca quite that closely, but held her tongue. She picked up her own glass of wine, but put it back without a taste because she didn't want to drink before the performance. Margaret glanced past Raimundo to Francisca, who was smiling across at Augusto in a most beguiling manner. Despite Francisca's fears, Margaret thought they were attracted to each other.

"We are searching for someone suitable who is traveling in that direction to accompany you, at least as far as Iguape," Sven Larson added.

Margaret turned her attention back to Francisca's father. "Will that delay my return?"

"Possibly. My wife will write to your mother and explain everything, without alarming her unnecessarily."

Margaret looked properly compliant. "I admit I'm still somewhat anxious about what happened. Even yesterday on the Rua do Ouvidor, I thought . . ." She caught herself. This was not the proper time for such a discussion.

"Sim?"

"Probably my imagination or the heat, but a man in the shadows looked very much like . . . But it couldn't have been, could it?"

Larson tried to hide his concern. "No, not likely!"

Senhor Cavalcanti interrupted with a loud compliment on the roast lamb. "I am glad it pleases you," Sven Larson said.

"It's marinated in garlic and vinegar before being stuffed with bacon and vegetables and basted with a brown gravy," Guilhermina added. "Our cook prefers a vinegar from her native Bahia. We'd be happy to send some over to your kitchen."

"You are very kind," Senhora Cavalcanti responded.

Larson turned back to Margaret. "Now don't you worry about anything. You're perfectly safe here with us," he said, closing the matter with her. Before the sweets were served, however, Larson excused himself, called for the head vigia, and gave him very direct, very specific orders in a voice distinctly less calm than the one he had used with Margaret.

ꖴ   ꖴ   ꖴ

Maria Edna was quick to take Erik's arm after the meal and to follow him into the drawing room, where the prenuptial party was due to commence. Augusto's sister was quite short, and her little chin bobbed up at her almost-brother-in-law as she chattered on and on. Erik barely disguised his impatience as he slowly walked over to Senhora Cavalcanti, who was educating Margaret about the groom's ancestors, emphasizing that her side of the family, the Prados, were by far the more illustrious. Finally, the couple found themselves alone as the Cavalcanti and Larson parents were called to stand beside Francisca and Augusto to receive their guests.

Erik shifted his weight as he searched for an opening remark. "Now, aren't you impressed by the groom's distinguished background?"

Margaret was sufficiently agitated by Erik's proximity that she could only manage a silly smile.

"Our family will never have the credentials of a Cavalcanti."

Looking around the sumptuous drawing room, Margaret realized that his remark was in jest. The incomparable salon, designed to have flowing, rounded lines, was capped with a domed ceiling painted in the classical manner with scenes of nymphs in a sylvan glade. The curving theme was continued in the massive bay windows and the huge circular crystal and bronze chandelier. It contained more than a hundred lights, which reflected a thousand times over in the floor-to-ceiling beveled mirrors. All the furnishings were carved in a delicate black jacarandá wood, bordered by a golden groove, and upholstered in a vibrant French yellow brocade.

"This is my favorite room in your house." Margaret's voice was steadying. "It's so sunny during the day, but at night" — she pointed to the infinity of images created by the lights — "it's magical."

Erik took a step closer and daringly touched the sleeve of Margaret's shimmering gown. "Only with you in it."

Margaret's breath caught in her throat.

The room was beginning to fill. Margaret looked at the dozens of people milling around the receiving line and was surprised to see many more than the few young adults she had expected. "I thought this evening was only for the cousins."

"The invitations were sent to the cousins, but in Rio the entire family escorts young people when they go out in the evening. Whenever I had a birthday, Mamãe would invite twelve children but would prepare to serve at least fifty."

"Even grandparents?" Margaret was staring at a white-haired woman tastefully dressed in black silks.

"That's Dona Serafina, Augusto's great-great-grandmother."

"How's that possible?"

"She married at fourteen or fifteen and so did her daughters."

"So young!"

"It's still the custom in many families. Most of Francisca's childhood friends have had many babies already."

"Gigo! What's new?" A group of young men and women swarmed toward them.

Erik began the introductions. "Senhorita Margarida Claiborne, I would like you to meet my cousins. This is Maria Marietta Pederneiras Rodrigo, called Sinha; Frederico Rodrigo Octavio, called Didi; Laura Pederneiras Octavio, called Laurita; and her cousin, Laura Rodrigo Octavio, called Laurinha . . ."

Each person seemed to have three or four names at least, and since they were all interrelated, the names were distressingly similar. Seeing Margaret's confusion, Erik laughed. "You'll learn soon enough."

When the group moved on, Margaret asked, "I can understand a nickname such as 'Laurinha' from Laura, but how did they get 'Gigo' from Erik?"

"My father, when he came from Sweden, was called the galego, which means 'the blond one.' When I was a baby, they called me the galeguinho, for 'the little blond one.' But that was much too clumsy. Eventually it was shortened to Gigo."

Margaret's eyes wandered to where Francisca stood, framed like a portrait by the open doorway. Augusto was unenthusiastically shaking each hand on the receiving line. "What do they call Augusto, then?"

Erik thought for a moment. "It's something like Gustinho; we'll ask him later. Augusto suits him better. He always was a serious fellow."

Margaret stared at Augusto's stern face. In contrast, Francisca's head was tossed back and she was laughing. The unnatural timbre of her friend's voice so grated on Margaret that she excused herself to walk closer to her. Instead of the demure appearance that Margaret had always associated with Francisca, the spirited, almost giddy young woman who laughed so loudly at every teasing remark was acting like a stranger. One of Augusto's friends was so encouraged by her responses, his words were becoming more and more outrageous. Francisca's laugh seemed to verge on hysteria.

As Margaret tried to move forward, she was blocked by a family group waiting impatiently to be greeted before entering the room. Suddenly aware of the slowdown in the receiving line, the elder Larsons and Cavalcantis turned to their children.

"Did you hear what Bernardo just said . . . about his recipe for love . . . darling?" Francisca poked Augusto with her elbow. "Meu querido . . ." she said and reached up and kissed his cheek to get his attention.

Augusto blanched and roughly pushed her aside. "What do you think you're doing?" he asked too loudly.

Everyone turned toward the couple. Margaret finally realized that Francisca had had far too much wine. "Poor thing!" she said as she took Francisca's hand. "You've been on your feet all evening. Come sit by the windows; you need the fresh air." She signaled for one of the waiters. "Agua, por favor."

"Those two-faced Cavalcantis!" Erik muttered bitterly. He spoke close to Margaret's ear. "If you knew what everyone else chooses to ignore . . ."

"Gigo . . . don't . . ." Francisca said weakly.

"All their noble ancestors and fancy airs won't buy them the paper to wipe their . . ."

"Gigo!" Francisca begged.

A waiter brought the water. Margaret held the glass, insisting Francisca drink. In a few minutes the flush on her cheeks lessened. "I'm so sorry . . ."

"Shhh . . . It's been a very difficult day. It'll . . ."

"Would you . . . perhaps . . ." she gestured toward the piano weakly.

Erik brightened. Under his breath, he said, "This is what I've been waiting for." He clapped his hands. The raucous voices in the room hushed only slightly. With elaborate graciousness, he said loudly, "Won't you consider playing for us tonight, Dona Margarida?"

Bowing her head shyly, Margaret stepped over to the piano. Erik pulled out the bench for her. When he tried to help her adjust it, she signaled that it was perfect. The tone in the rest of the room was so sour, her nervousness increased. This would be the first time she played in front of an audience in more than a year.

She quailed at the possibility of appearing foolish before all of Francisca's relations, but most especially Erik. She lifted the lid that protected the keyboard and stared at the flickering shadows that played across the blacks and the whites. In sunlight the keyboard appeared entirely different than it did now under the chandeliers. Because so much of her concentration involved the visual perception of her fingers on the keys, she was tempted to replace the lid and flee from the room. Margaret looked over at Francisca's forlorn figure. Moments earlier her friend had appeared so sublimely happy; now she looked meek and exhausted. I must play . . . for Francisca, she told herself. But what? Something to gladden everyone, something rousing to bring Francisca back to the way she was at dinner . . . bright, triumphant.

Margaret stretched her long arms toward the keyboard with the grace of a bird landing. The room was silenced. Then, without further thought, her fingers began the sixteen-bar introduction to Chopin's Polonaise no. 6 in A-flat Major, projecting the main theme with so grand a flourish she could feel her audience sit up straighter.

Erik and Francisca sat directly to the side of the piano. It was for them she performed. The anger she felt toward Augusto's pompous behavior gave Margaret the intense burst of energy she required for the powerful right-hand crescendos that Mlle Doradou had often accused her of minimizing. Next she concentrated on the stately melody, advancing it like a phantom apparition of an immense conquering army. During the long, murmuring monologue in the right hand, so free that it almost sounded like an improvisation, she felt inspired by the image of Francisca, her selflessness and generosity winning over the mean-spirited Cavalcantis. Bringing in the main theme once again in all its splendor, she ended the piece on its surprisingly quiet note.

Unsure the music had truly died away, everyone was in a trance. It was only when Margaret placed her hands in her lap and bowed that the audience clapped their approval, rhythmically in the Brazilian fashion. Margaret glanced only at Erik and Francisca.

The power of music, Margaret thought to herself. The power to heal, to cleanse, to make people feel what someone else had felt a century before. She'd always loved to imagine the composer himself listening, then appraising her performance, and she hoped that Chopin would not have been greatly displeased with her impulsive interpretation.

"Always play *for* someone," Mlle Doradou had insisted. "If not me, think of the composer." Her teacher's voice, so soft, yet raspy, with its distinctive Creole intonation, had cut deeply into Margaret's unconscious. "It matters not if you play with love or hate in your heart, as long as you feel something so powerful that words could never have expressed it as well as the music."

Francisca's head was held higher, and one look at Erik, his face transformed from his usual bemused grin into something alarmingly complex yet tender, told Margaret her music had touched both its marks.

Sven Larson stood. "You've honored us greatly, Dona Margarida. Would you be so kind as to play just one more short piece?"

The piano warmed under her fingers. The huge, inert instrument held vast secrets that she could unlock at will. Everyone waited for her response. The room breathed the request.

"O prazer é todo meu," she agreed sincerely, then stared at the keys, wondering again what to choose.

First she'd selected Chopin . . . Now perhaps she'd turn to Schumann or Mozart to vary the program? She procrastinated out of fear. Nothing came. She still retained an image of Chopin listening to her. Chopin with Erik's eyes. Chopin at Erik's age with George Sand. She remembered how shocked she'd been when Mlle Doradou explained that Sand was really a she — a Mlle Dudevant. After that Margaret always imagined Chopin writing the etudes for her. An etude . . . the loveliest one . . . opus 10, no. 3, in E, Francisca's favorite.

Margaret's hands quavered above the keyboard. She'd played the polonaise to give Francisca courage; but she would play the etude for someone else as well. She took a deep breath, tried not to be disquieted by the uneven light that dappled the keys, and prayed not to fumble the difficult passage of diminished sevenths that sometimes tripped her. Then, as though she were departing on a fearsome journey, she began the lyrical, lilting theme of a vast aching love, touching the keys with great softness, gradually increasing the tempo and tone, so the music wouldn't reach full climax until the forte con bravura. Now as she played the theme once more in reprise, so hauntingly perfect, she understood why it was said to have been Chopin's favorite. The sounds spilled from her fingers. Her eyes followed her right hand for a moment until she could glimpse Erik through the piano's open lid. His eyes were half-closed; he seemed transported by the music. She played as in a dream, finishing the piece as naturally as a river flows out to sea.

❧ 11 Margaret leaned against the banister of the staircase in the grand vestibule and tried to catch her breath. As soon as possible, she'd fled from the room. A vigia silently watched to see if she was planning to return to the drawing room or if she was heading upstairs to retire. Margaret turned from the servant's unrelenting gaze and tried to cool her burning forehead by placing it against the brass railing.

The drawing room door opened. The rhythmic clapping that not only signaled approval but demanded her return echoed across the marble corridor.

Erik rushed to her side. "Margaret, are you ill?"

She straightened and looked into Erik's eyes, which reflected the hundreds of tiny lights from the chandelier overhead. Mesmerized by the effect, she stared and stared.

"Margaret?"

She blinked several times. "Yes?"

"Won't you join the family again?"

"Not yet, please . . ."

"It must be very exhausting. You play with such . . . vigor. Would you prefer to rest quietly for a few moments?"

"I'd like that." Margaret indicated the guard. "But . . ."

Erik took her hand and led her away from the clatter of guests being offered champagne to toast Francisca and Augusto. "Follow me," he said, opening a narrow doorway.

"What's this?"

"A servant's passage. It was built to keep the slaves from using the main halls."

"Where does it lead?"

"Everywhere. I spent my childhood learning the mazelike routes just so I could pop out and surprise everybody."

Margaret pretended to be shocked. "You spied on your own family?"

"Their activities were boring compared to those of the servants!" He opened the door to a study, lit a desk lamp, and whispered, "All their intrigues, fights . . . romances."

Very gently, Erik took her hand in his and led her out to a private atrium. A narrow path led around its sheltered perimeter. "This is my father's orchid garden. He breeds rare varieties." He picked up a tag on a specimen and read clumsily, " 'Cattleya Juno (forbesii × velutina).' I think that's one of his newest crossbreeds, though you'll have to ask my father to explain it properly, since I can't tell the difference between a cypripedium and a cymbidium."

Margaret admired the unusually colored flower with a spotted lemon lip and delicate ecru petals. "It's absolutely lovely."

The air seemed to drip with scent. Margaret breathed deeply. The specially transplanted mosses and jungle mulches that nourished the flowers smelled palpably fertile. As she followed Erik through the garden, avoiding the barely tamed lianas and waxlike flowers that nested in tangled webs of hanging sphagnum, the hem of her dress caught on an itinerant aerial root. Margaret worried that she might have injured a valuable specimen. "Should we be here at all?"

"This is where I did my lessons when I was a boy."

An image of a towheaded Erik hunched over his desk, struggling to make straight letters, touched Margaret. She squeezed his hand. He took this as a signal and drew her to him, buried his face in her hair, and took a long deep sniff that was shockingly erotic to the young woman barely emerged from convent school.

"That's called a cheiro." He nuzzled her neck and once again inhaled. "Ahhh." He exhaled and placed his arm around her waist. "Now that I have your scent within me, I can begin to know you."

"Erik . . . what?" Margaret quivered.

"That's how a Brazilian greets someone he likes. It's quite proper."

"I've never seen anyone . . ."

"But of course not." He was determined not to frighten her. The muscles in the small of her back were soft and yielding. When he stroked her, she didn't stiffen. He brushed his lips across her cheek and then lightly passed his mouth across hers. "That's a beijo."

"Beijo," Margaret repeated in a husky voice.

Erik lifted her dimpled chin and ran his finger across the narrowing point that gave her face its sometimes unbalanced, yet distinctive, appearance. "Last year . . ." He lowered his lips to kiss her again, this time lingering a bit longer. Then, holding her cheeks between his wide hands, he murmured, "I should have begged you to stay in Rio. We've wasted so much time!"

Margaret felt his heart pounding wildly. Unnerved by the closeness, she stepped back just enough to alter the mood.

"Francisca's told you everything about me, hasn't she?"

Margaret could feel herself nodding numbly.

"Then you'll accept Astrid and the church?"

Wasn't he making too many presumptions? she wondered. And yet it all seemed to be happening naturally, as though it had always been planned. "I'd very much like to meet your daughter" was all she replied.

"Of course you shall! She'll be in the wedding party. And I'm so happy you won't be reluctant to join the church."

The closeness of Erik's breath, the overpowering smell of the garden, the heaviness in the night air, made it impossible to think clearly or respond with just the right words. What had he said? The church? Had Francisca been expected to ask Margaret a question about religion even before Erik had spoken his feelings to her?

"I don't understand . . ."

Erik took one step back and placed his hands at his side. "I've done it all in the wrong order, haven't I? I shouldn't have left this to anyone else. You must think me quite cowardly, when the truth is I only wanted to spare you the difficulty of refusing my requests." He hesitated and then, lifting a large elephant-eared frond so she could pass under without scraping her head, he beckoned her toward a narrow marble bench beside a small pond. Silently, they focused on the reflection of the moon rippling in the water as though the crescent image held answers to their private questions.

"For me . . . From the moment I first saw you . . ." Erik cleared his throat. "I believe, with all my heart, that we were meant to be together."

Margaret was captivated by the warmth and sincerity in his voice.

"If you will consent, I will promise to make your life very . . . happy and . . ."

"You know so little about me."

"What must I know?

"There's a North American gentleman in the south, also a widower . . . He's . . ."

Erik's voice lowered in pitch. "You've given him your word?"

"Not exactly. But my father would never approve of this . . ."

"Your mother?"

"Perhaps. She's always wanted someone who might understand the importance of my music, who might permit me to . . ."

Seeing this chance, Erik jumped in. Unable to select the correct English words, he spoke rapidly in Portuguese. "At first when Francisca told me about your talents I assumed they were very minor, but now that I've heard . . . I realize that it may be the essence of your life, perhaps the reason you are what you are." He stopped and began again in English. "You understand? There's no reason, for my sake, that you should ever interrupt your musical studies. It would give me the greatest pleasure to listen to you play for the rest of my life." Impulsively, Erik reached over and kissed her again, this time with force.

Margaret collapsed against him, leaning her head on the hollow of his shoulder. "It must be contagious." She smiled up at him. Indeed, she felt peculiarly feverish. "My mother warned me about this climate!"

Erik laughed and kissed her forehead. "I assure you that the treatments for this condition are very, very pleasurable." He kissed her again, caressing her arms with his strong hands. "And very frequent."

Margaret felt as if she were melting. Between embraces, she tried to think over her choices sensibly. Erik or Lizzieland, Erik or the "half-known life." Erik or Nelson Cable, Erik or some other planter's son. Was this how Raleigh had felt when he met Marianne, how her mother had felt when she'd first seen her father at Moss Oaks? Or was she just drawn to Erik because he offered her a life of luxury and sophistication? Still, he was a kind man, an utterly exciting man, a person who had tempted her like no other.

"Is it your wish that I become Roman Catholic?"

"Not for me, but in Brazil it is best. My father converted to please my mother. But if you cannot . . . we need only promise that our children . . ."

Briefly, Margaret thought about Raleigh, with his antipapist preachings, and easily guessed her family's reaction to conversion. "I would have to study your faith further before I could make a decision."

In the moonlight Erik's glistening eyes looked like a turbulent night ocean. "That's all I could ever ask, minha querida, minha namorada, minha Margarida."

"You never call me Margaret."

"Margarida's so much more . . . musical, don't you agree?"

"Yes, I admit I like it. Better than 'Gigo.' "

Erik pretended to be insulted. "You don't like 'Gigo'?"

"No." Margaret repressed a laugh.

"Then I forbid anyone to use that name again!"

"I didn't mean that . . ."

"Don't you see how much your opinion means to me?"

They sat quietly for a few moments, daring only to touch each other's fingers tentatively. Amazed at the heat she exuded, Erik flattered himself by thinking that her reaction to him had elevated her temperature.

"Don't you think we're missed?" Margaret asked.

"Everyone will understand."

"Everyone?"

"Brazilians are very perceptive."

"How would anyone guess?"

"Minha querida, you're the one who gave away our secret."

"I did?"

"You cannot play a piece like the last one without everyone, at least every Carioca, knowing what you were feeling."

"That etude's Francisca's favorite."

"I see." Erik shrugged his shoulders. "Then you made her very happy."

"I hope I did, but the truth is that . . . I . . . I played only for you."

Lifting her hands, he kissed each finger. "Don't be ashamed; there is no dishonor in love. Not in this house."

Margaret thought of Augusto's anger at Francisca for her kiss and wondered if he spoke the complete truth. "There might be dishonor if we do not return to say good night to the guests and your family." Margaret stood and reached up to straighten the chignon that had slipped too low on her head. Pins had shifted to unfamiliar places, and as she struggled to discern the pattern, several slipped out onto the ground. She bent over, trying to feel them in the dark, when suddenly an exotic, almost primal, odor wafted toward her. "What do I smell?"

"The perfume? I thought it was yours."

"No, it's not."

Erik walked to the far side of the garden, sniffing his way like a puppy. "Over here! No wait, you'll never see it properly." His voice was excited and anxious. "Stay here while I bring a light from inside."

The lamp chimney jangled on its brass handle as Erik rushed toward the center of the garden. When he positioned the lamp at knee height, Margaret could see, hanging from a narrow stalk, the outline of a most enormous white bloom.

"Flor-da-noite, the night-blooming cereus. It opens but once a year and only at night. Usually, Papai knows just when one will bloom. Perhaps he was so busy with the wedding plans, this one, so hidden in the center of the garden, escaped his notice."

"Is it an orchid?"

"No, it's actually in the cactus family. Father made an exception when he planted them, but in fact they've become his favorites. On blooming nights he invites special friends to drink champagne while waiting for the moths to come."

"The moths?"

"The flowers are fertilized by beautiful night moths attracted by the perfume that gets stronger by the hour. Some people call the plant 'flor-cheirosa,' the fragrant flower."

"How can you predict which night it will open?"

"At sundown the flower is swollen but still tightly closed, waiting. Then it expands very slowly. If you watch intently, you can actually see movement as the sepals pull back and the petals unfold."

"I've never seen any flower so huge!"

"Look inside," Erik said reverently. He held the lamp so she could stare deep into the center. The corolla, a gossamer ring of transparent featherlike white petals, guarded a rich treasure sunk deep into a cavernous vault. At the center, golden-tipped stamens clustered around an immense star-shaped pistil.

Margaret bent over to study the misshapen stalks. "Without the flower, it's really quite ordinary, if not actually ugly."

Erik barely heard what Margaret was saying, for the sight of the silk folds of her gown sculpting her rounded bottom had distracted him completely. That he could not yet touch her . . . hold her completely, that he had to restrain himself . . . was almost unbearable!

"And it has no spines?"

He twisted his hands behind his back, trying to banish the passionate yearnings from his mind. "What?" he asked, inwardly reproaching himself for his lewd thoughts.

"Just these thick leaves that stick out all over?"

He bent down to examine the plant more closely. "Some of the most ordinary objects hold the most extraordinary secrets."

Margaret smiled at his double meaning. "Do you ever pick the flower and bring it inside?"

Erik gasped. "Nunca!" His own frustrations made his voice sound more vehement than he intended. With great effort he modulated his next words. "It would be a waste, since the flower is always dead by sunrise."

"There's no way to preserve it?"

"No, dear one, it is like your music, fleetingly beautiful, but while it blooms it is magnificent beyond anything more permanent."

"You're a poet!"

Erik helped her to her feet. He brushed dried leaves and earth from the folds of her skirt. "I am a tradesman, a man of commerce, nothing more. If you like my words, it's because you inspire me to speak the truth." He turned her around and helped adjust her hairpins, smoothing the golden ringlets around her forehead. "One truth is that I will promise to never harm you, to keep you safe, to nourish and protect you, to let you bloom always."

"Once a year?"

"As often as you like, minha querida."

"May Florinda stay with me?" Margaret asked suddenly.

Erik looked chagrined. "Do you have to ask such a question? Do I not want what you want? Will not what is mine be yours?"

How could she have doubted him? How could she ever have worried that she might be making the wrong decision? Margaret looked at the magnificent flower that lived its whole life in one night — its roseate sepals beckoning, the elliptical petals waving in a wild and tempting dance. Now she dared admit her secret hopes to herself. Had she not really journeyed to Rio to be with him?

The sound of carriages lining up in the courtyard, servants being called, and happy laughter was heard in the distance. Erik lifted the lamp and signaled Margaret to follow. "Come, minha querida."

At the edge of the study door she lingered, staring back at the cereus, a beacon in the night garden. Just above the bloom, fluttering and hovering, the bright wings of a moth glinted momentarily in the moonlight before it descended to savor the fragrant delights embraced in the flower's secret center.

❧ 12 Nossa Senhora da Candelária was not the Larsons' or the Cavalcantis' usual place of worship. However, the groom's family had insisted the couple be married in Rio's most impressive cathedral. It had the largest choir and seated the most guests, but everyone knew that Dona Antonieta favored it because of the loudness of Our Lady of Candlemas's famous bells.

The tremulous bride had not objected. Except for two rehearsals at the church and the mandatory dinner parties, Francisca took little part in the complex arrangements, leaving everything to be decided by her mother, rearranged by Senhora Cavalcanti, and finally negotiated by the fathers, who had a complicated financial arrangement to protect.

"Nervous exhaustion" was Dr. Bandeira's pronouncement.

The family physician prescribed a fasting diet and strict bed rest between social engagements.

In the afternoons, Margaret helped Francisca open wedding gifts and arrange them in the sala de visitas. The day before, a huge grandfather clock had been sent by one of the Cavalcanti uncles. Margaret admired it openly. "My little timepiece looks quite silly compared to it!"

"It's a monstrosity," Francisca had whispered. "I doubt that the ceilings in our new house will be high enough for it." She walked over to the table where the tiny clock Margaret had presented to her privately was surrounded by a glittering silver service. "Your gift is the real treasure. I will keep it beside my bed always. It will be a great comfort," she added forlornly.

Margaret could do nothing but pat Francisca's hand gently, while the broth prepared from Dr. Bandeira's own recipe was served in mugs. Margaret guessed that Francisca's problem could not be cured with beef teas. Though Margaret realized she was hardly an authority on matrimony, she believed she knew more than her sheltered Brazilian friend. In supplement to the limited convent education regarding marriage and family life both girls had received as part of their preparation for womanhood, Margaret had been instructed on more than musical matters by Mlle Doradou, who was filled with aphorisms about men and romance.

"You know, the Creoles have an expression," she'd begun. " 'Beware of a man with le coeur comme un artichaut' — a heart like an artichoke — 'because he has a leaf for everyone.' That is not to say you should avoid men entirely, for one cannot express oneself in music unless one knows every feeling: passion and despair, happiness and sorrow, adoration and hate."

"My mother always said that a lady wasn't to know about such matters until . . ."

"Ignorance." Mademoiselle drew out the word by emphasizing its French pronunciation. "Een . . . yor . . . ahnce! That's the black shadow that plagues every institution of learning, clothes with bigotry and intolerance those who claim to be the apostles of religion. Most mothers raise their children like moles, with only the rudiments of eyes. But you, ma chérie, have powers which those other quadrupeds have not, and you must place yourself in the light which is ready to shine upon you."

Once, after Margaret had finally memorized a complex sonata, Mademoiselle ordered chicory-flavored coffee and sugar-dusted beignets brought into the garden. Weeks earlier, the teacher had slipped in the startling details of procreation in just such a setting, so Margaret felt a curious excitement mounting as Mademoiselle lectured on.

"Did you know that you are a lucky child, a child born from a proper union, unlike me?" Mlle Doradou had sighed deeply. "Have you ever wondered how you escaped all of my afflictions?"

Margaret was well acquainted with Mademoiselle's major and minor physical conditions. Polite "How are you feeling today?" greetings were always answered with a long description of her teacher's latest migraine or rheumatoid attack.

"Most people are ignorant of the fact that their own physical condition at the moment they yield the germ that starts a human being has an everlasting influence upon that being. Many a child like myself has been conceived when its father was under the influence of compounds, spirits, or other sickness and today suffers physically from the effects. I've often wondered what state of health the parents of Robert Schumann, who suffered from melancholia, or the parents of the poor diseased Chopin were in when they brought forth these great men."

"Perhaps the same destructive element which affected their health also caused their genius," Margaret added thoughtfully.

"Hmm . . ." Momentarily diverted by the incisive remark, Mlle Doradou continued. "There are thousands more children with disordered nervous systems and no hint of prodigy who are so because they were conceived by quarrelsome parents."

Margaret remembered wondering if this theory explained Raleigh's odd temperament. Had her father done something to her unwilling mother? Had either parent been ill? Or were the tragic aftereffects of the War Between the States somehow transmitted through the parents to the child? And what of Mademoiselle? Had her father been a drunkard? Margaret never recalled a time when there had not been a wine bottle open beside her piano. "My cure," Mademoiselle would say by way of explanation.

Now, sitting beside Francisca, Margaret worried that her friend's nervous condition might be an inherited one. If Mademoiselle's theories were true — and why should she believe they were not? — then Astrid, Erik's little daughter, could also be the unhealthy product of a loveless union. Margaret was filled with concern for the child who, for some still mysterious reason, was not living with the Larsons. There was so much she didn't understand that she vowed to make a bolder attempt to find answers to her endless list of questions before she took her own marriage vows.

❦   ❦   ❦

"Tell me about the Cavalcantis," she asked Erik after he'd listened to the last half-hour of her morning practice.

"There's nothing to tell." Erik was unusually abrupt. "What was the last piece you played?"

" 'Variations on the Name Abegg.' I always try to play something by Schumann every day."

"Why's that?"

Margaret realized that Erik was drawing her away from her own concerns. "The piano system that my teacher favored was developed by Clara Schumann's father, Friedrich Wieck. Clara's still my idol, as a woman and a musician. Her husband's music always had a special meaning for me."

"I don't understand. If it is the wife you admire . . ."

"A pianist is but a vehicle for someone else's music. When I lift my fingers from the keyboard, my music dissolves into the air as if it had never been played. But a composer lives on forever in his work. I like to think that Schumann captured much of his wife's personality in his music. I feel as though I know her when I play the notes that she must have interpreted first."

Impressed with the intensity of Margaret's expression, Erik slipped beside her on the piano bench and took her hand in his. "I am very unschooled in music, but every word you speak fascinates me. 'Abegg' is a very curious name. What does it mean?"

Immensely pleased at his interest, Margaret expounded further. "It's a musical anagram. Schumann dedicated the piece to a Countess Pauline von Abegg, probably because he was trying to win her patronage." Margaret placed her hands on the keys. "This is the note 'A,' now 'B,' now 'E,' 'G,' and 'G.' You see how

the music spells the name? The rest is a variation, though I must
say the piece is a bit contrived."

Erik was clearly delighted by Margaret's explanation. "Can
you do a variation on my name?"

"There isn't an 'R,' 'I,' or 'K' in music!"

"What a pity! Tell me more about the Schumann family."

"That's a very long tale ... and quite romantic." Margaret
squeezed his hand. "First you must answer my question about
the Cavalcantis."

"They're no worse, no better, than the rest. Augusto and I
went to school together. The alliance will be good for Francisca;
you'll see."

"She's so upset at the thought of the marriage. I believe that it's
because she doesn't have deep feelings for Augusto ... not the
way you and I ..."

Erik wrapped his free arm around her waist and drew her
beside him. "This is a very rare thing. I know. I've never felt
like this before. Francisca's marriage will be more like my first
one."

"Do you wish the same unhappiness on her?"

"I was not discontent with Gunilla because at that time I didn't
know what was lacking, and neither will Francisca."

"Are you certain?"

Erik nodded. "The worst time for Francisca is now. She's always been very shy away from the family. All this public fuss
about the wedding, meeting so many people, frightens her. As
soon as she and Augusto are alone ..." Impulsively, Erik turned
his head and kissed Margaret's lips. Flooded with emotions she
could not begin to describe, Margaret returned his affection without a thought for propriety. She stroked the Saxon-white hair
that curled at the nape of his neck while he tenderly caressed the
delicate curve of her back. Both were oblivious to the fact that the
Larson parents were standing in the doorway.

Margaret saw them first and instantly drew back. Erik grinned
boyishly as his parents approached.

Sven Larson moved a parlor chair beside the piano and offered
it to his wife. "My son ..." he said as Guilhermina rearranged her
skirts. "We have a responsibility to Margaret's parents."

"Sim, Papai," Erik replied. "We did not come to you yet because we wanted Chiquinha to be the one to shine this week."

"That's very thoughtful of you, Gigo," Sven said. "But you should have given equal consideration to our guest."

"In these few short days of our renewed friendship, I've come to believe that Senhorita Claiborne is the woman I wish to marry." He swiveled to face Margaret. "She's agreed about Astrid and the church ... All we need is the approval of her parents — and yours, of course."

Larson kept his eyes, the same vibrant blue as his son's, focused on Margaret. The girl's expression was one of honest devotion. Clearly, here was a young woman of great intelligence and talent, but there was a vague uneasiness that troubled him still. "Margarida," he said with measured politeness, "Gigo's mother and I would welcome you into our family. Your dearness to our daughter goes without saying, and you have captivated not only the heart of our son but that of everyone who has had the pleasure of hearing your music. But we cannot begin to consider such an arrangement without the permission of your parents."

"She is of age ..." Erik blurted.

Sven Larson drew his mouth into a tight line. He stared meaningfully at Margaret. "You expect opposition?"

"I believe my mother will approve. My father ..."

"Vivo, my parents were against us at first," Guilhermina reminded. "Margarida, what will he object to, our church?"

"Yes. Also the distance from them. They'd hoped I'd choose a North American living in their district."

"Would you be breaking a promise to a particular Norte Americano?" Larson asked sternly.

Margaret thought about Nelson Cable. He'd be disappointed, but not surprised, at her change of heart. "No," she said honestly. "No promises have been made."

Guilhermina's sigh was audible. She pulled herself up from the chair and walked around to Margaret's side of the bench. Margaret stood dutifully. Erik's mother kissed her on both cheeks. "Tudo bem, minha filha. Very well, my daughter, everything will be arranged." She kissed her son in the same manner. "It may be complicated, but your father and I have handled difficul-

ties far worse than this one. All we want is our son's happiness."
She took her husband's arm, led him from the room, and very deliberately closed the great carved doors behind them.

❧ 13 As soon as the morning mists burned off, the glaring sun proved again the wisdom of planning the wedding ceremony for early in the day. Though Francisca had capitulated to most of her mother's plans for the ceremony and reception, she had refused to select an older, married woman to be her "madrinha de casamento," insisting that Margaret have the honored role of escorting her to the ceremony. "That's how they do it in North America," she'd explained, easily winning her way in the matter.

Francisca was openly perspiring in her high-necked satin gown. "Just think how cool and fresh you'll be by evening!" Margaret said with a touch of envy in her voice as she proudly rode beside Francisca in the gaily decorated carriage.

The bride's soft brown eyes were somber under the floor-length veil. "It's a long trip to Petropolis ... and I won't know anyone."

"After all the confusion these past few days, I think you'll find it a pleasant change."

"I suppose so. There's not even a breeze off the ocean today," Francisca complained. The carriage wound north along the wharfside road. Francisca's veil began to stick to her face and hands.

Margaret pulled it away from her face and patted the bride's damp forehead with her own handkerchief, taking care not to muss her elaborately swirled coiffure. "I think the men will be more uncomfortable than us in those heavy morning coats. Why did they ever have them made from woolens?"

"It's always been the fashion." Francisca became more animated. "Margaret, do you really like him?"

"Of course! You always knew I would."

"Do you think him handsome?"

"By far the most wonderfully attractive man I've ever met."

"Now I know you are being insincere. Augusto is very presentable, but there are others who surpass him in looks."

"I thought you were talking about Erik!" Margaret laughed at her mistake. "But Augusto is very . . . masculine . . . strong. I'd feel very protected by him. I think he's also a bit shy, more like yourself than you think."

"Why do you say that?"

"Mlle Doradou always said that men were less confident than women but took more trouble to hide it."

Francisca laughed. Margaret purposely kept up her chatter with tales of Mademoiselle's early associations and the rumored romance with Gottschalk.

"Do you think she really ever . . . ?" Francisca asked.

"That's a secret she'll take to her grave."

"Do you still hear from her?"

"She writes me regularly on the first day of every month. I find I miss her very much, although when I was her student I thought her terribly overbearing at times. I never really appreciated her until I had to leave her."

"It's the same with so much in life . . ." Francisca's voice faded off as they drew closer to the large square. A crowd had gathered around the wide steps that led up to the cathedral. On the fringes, flower sellers hawked bouquets and little peasant girls waited to touch the bridal train for good luck.

Francisca hugged Margaret unexpectedly. "Tell me that what I suspect is true?"

"What do you . . . ?"

"That you and Gigo might . . ."

Margaret kissed Francisca's cheeks. "It's still a secret, until my parents give their consent . . ."

"A secret from me?"

"No, never. We would've told you before you left for Petropolis."

"I'm so happy! It's what I always dreamed would happen!" Francisca started to weep just as the carriage slowed in front of Nossa Senhora da Candelária.

Senhora Larson stepped up to greet them. "Chiquinha, what's the matter?"

Francisca quickly dried her eyes. Her mother and Margaret gathered the yards of material in the bride's train as she stepped outside. A thin flaxen-haired child dressed in a long pink gown with a crown of matching roses ran to greet them.

"Tia Chiquinha! Tia Chiquinha!" The child threw her arms around the bride's waist without realizing she was stepping on the veil's beaded hem.

Margaret heard a small ripping sound and rushed to pull the little girl away before any serious damage was done.

"Ow! Ow!" Even though Margaret had used a firm grip, she didn't think she could have hurt the girl enough to justify her kicking and screaming.

A few of the guests entering the cathedral turned to see what was the difficulty while Francisca tried, unsuccessfully, to muffle the childish cries. "Astrid, my little darling, don't be upset. Astrid . . ."

Hearing the commotion, Erik ran over. Astrid flew into his arms and sobbed more loudly. "Papai, Papai, she hurt me!"

"Who would hurt my little kitten?"

When Astrid pointed to Margaret, Francisca blurted, "Oh, Erik, you know how she likes to make a fuss. It's because Isabel doesn't . . ."

Francisca was silenced by her brother's warning glance. "Now, kitten, you must behave and walk down the aisle like a princess, remember? Princesses don't cry, do they?"

The cathedral's famous bells tolled ten o'clock. Guilhermina Larson gave the bridal party hurried instructions and saw that Astrid was in her proper place between Francisca and Margaret. The three front doors of carved bronze were opened by pages dressed in blue-and-white livery. Margaret turned to give Francisca one last smile for courage, but the only thing that caught her eye was little Astrid's tiny face twisted in the most contentious of scowls.

❧   ❧   ❧

The music swelled as Margaret marched down the long aisle festooned with white ribbons and pink flowers toward the high altar. The cathedral, unpretentious except for size from the exterior, shimmered inside with gilt, stained glass, and elegant murals commemorating the seamen who, when caught in a storm, had vowed to erect a church in honor of the Virgin if she saved them. Their subsequent guidance into the harbor by an apparition of a candle was the miracle the edifice celebrated. A huge pipe organ set to the side of the great choir played the theme from a concerto that echoed a joyful yet solemn mood. Margaret immediately recognized it as having been written by Antonio Soler. She marveled at this original choice.

Sven Larson led his only daughter down the flower-strewn aisle to take her place by the altar under a glass dome, the light from which beamed down celestially on only the priest and the wedding party. On either side, stained-glass angels hovered in perpetual prayer. The immediate family stood in a circle. Margaret was directly opposite Erik. As the priest took his place, the Benedictine choir began to sing the opening of the nuptial mass. "Kyrie eleison, Christe eleison, Kyrie eleison . . ."

Though she had been worrying that she'd too hastily agreed to join the Larsons' church, Margaret now realized that she might be spiritually drawn to the conversion. She wouldn't be relinquishing her love of Christ; she wouldn't have to forfeit her Christian ideals; she would just embrace a different form of worship — one filled with song, saints, candles, and new rules of piety. The music swelled. Her heart seemed to welcome the peace and joy it signified.

"Deo gratias," the congregation responded. The Latin words reverberating from the carved wooden ceilings to the mosaics in the nave filled her with mystical yearnings. How different this was from the austere approach that Raleigh preached, warning of the evil perpetrated by Satan rather than exalting in God's glory and power.

In a few minutes the priest was asking Francisca if she consented to marry Augusto.

"Quero, I will," she responded.

A mantle of peace descended. Margaret felt bathed in happiness. "Quero," she repeated silently.

A member of the chorus began an elegant solo, his voice clear and touched with grace. The priest added, "O que Deus uniu, o homem não separa."

The congregation responded in unison, "Amen."

Calm and self-assured, Margaret raised her eyes for the priest's blessing over a solemn Augusto and a glowing Francisca. She rotated slightly to where Erik was standing between his daughter and his mother.

"In nomine Patri et Filii et Spiritus Sancti."

Erik caught Margaret's gaze and held it securely.

"Amen," she said aloud. Her decision was sealed.

ꙮ   ꙮ   ꙮ

The bells pealed and pealed. Astrid skipped out the door and Erik swung her around. Francisca's face was finally beaming. Margaret backed away from the door to make room for others leaving the church. Family and friends gathered in the plaza, creating an impasse for the normal traffic as well as the carriages of the many guests. Street urchins pressed forward, hoping to be bribed with "nuisance coins" that would keep them from annoying the newlyweds with rude remarks.

Senhora Cavalcanti touched Margaret's arm politely. "Would you care to ride back to the house with Raimundo and Maria Edna?" she asked kindly.

Realizing that her place in the carriage she had arrived in would be taken by Augusto, Margaret accepted with thanks.

Dona Antonieta pointed to the far corner of the square. "It's over by the fountain, the one with the purple-and-white trim. I'll have my children join you as soon as I find them."

Almost deafened by the still-tolling bells, Margaret headed toward the gaudy carriage with its brightly painted exterior and tooled red leather seats. As she crossed the square, someone bumped her rudely. Margaret turned and saw the sun-wizened face of Valdemar Barreto close to hers. His thick eyebrows met in a sharp point above his angled nose and his mouth had a lopsided, evil turn. "Filha da puta!" he swore and spat a foul mixture of green tobacco juice and saliva. It hit her flat on the cheek before dribbling down the bodice of her powder-blue lace gown. She was so stunned she didn't move.

"Something for my trouble . . ." he mumbled, then ripped the tiny gold crucifix and chain from around her neck and bolted across the crowded square.

Breakbone Fever

1 The turmoil that surrounded Margaret had the surprising effect of making her calm. The more Florinda fussed, the more steady she felt. A peach brocade gown from her trousseau trunk was substituted for the dress the bandit had soiled. Margaret was secretly pleased, for its lower neckline was more flattering than the one the Larsons' dressmaker had made for her to wear during the ceremony.

As soon as she was presentable, the Larsons and the police inspector were led into the sitting room off her bedroom. Guilhermina kissed her warmly. "Minha filha, tudo bem?" She rubbed Margaret's icy hands. "Are you all right? Did he hurt you?"

Margaret loosened the wide velvet ribbon that Florinda had tied around her neck. "Only here."

Shaking her head, Guilhermina stepped back to allow her husband to see the welt that encircled Margaret's throat.

"You are certain it was Barreto?" Larson asked. "Not just some street urchin?"

Margaret nodded. "Every time it has been the same man."

"Muito ruim," Inspector Alvaro said when he examined the

swelling on Margaret's tender skin. "Very bad . . ." He was really thinking something quite different about the lovely North American's creamy neck.

Larson guided his wife and the inspector into the corridor. "I was afraid of a reprisal," he muttered. "Revenge is to be expected with these types. In fact, I'm quite relieved it happened like this. It could have been worse."

"Vivo!" Guilhermina admonished. "Where was her vigia?"

"No one knows."

"He's finished here!"

"Of course, minha querida. See to Margarida while the inspector and I finish our business. And remind her that the fewer who know of these events, the better."

Guilhermina walked back into the sitting room. "Have you been introduced to Joaquim Freire and the musicians yet?"

"Não, Dona Guilhermina," Margaret answered.

"Maestro Freire's one of Rio's most esteemed composers. He was sent to Paris when he was a boy and received all his training there. One of the other musicians, Delgado de Mello, is a very charming fellow who plays violin. He's married to a cousin of mine."

"I'm looking forward to meeting them."

"They're going to perform a piece to honor Francisca and Augusto and, when they heard of your talents, wondered if you would play the piano part."

"It takes practice to play with a group, and I wouldn't even know the piece."

"They assure me that the music is very short and simple."

"Yes, but . . ."

"Erik thought it would be a wonderful opportunity for you to meet some musicians. The cellist, a woman named Nicia Netto, is delightful. But if you are not able, especially after what's already happened today, we'll understand."

Margaret's mind swirled. How well Erik understood her isolation from those who shared her interests!

"I'd be delighted to try."

"Ótimo!" Guilhermina replied. "Splendid news." She patted Margaret's coronet of braids. "Such lovely hair. The color alone

will be the envy of every woman in Rio. Brazilians are wild for
blonds. I should know! When I saw my 'galego' I looked no further." Guilhermina clapped her hands.

Florinda rushed into the room. "Florinda, get more pins for the
back of Margarida's hair so it won't come loose."

Margaret stood respectfully as Senhora Larson started to leave.

"Take your time in getting ready, and don't you worry, they'll
catch that jagunço . . . that hoodlum!"

Margaret smiled bravely. But as soon as the door closed,
she fell back into her chair and pressed her forehead with her
hands.

Florinda was alarmed at the strange cast in Margaret's eyes.
"What's the matter?"

"It hurts . . . here . . . Oh, it's terrible!"

"Agua quente!" Florinda shouted to a passing laundress.

As soon as the steaming bowl arrived, Francisca's maid dipped
a wide strip of cloth in the water, wrung it out, and wrapped it
around Margaret's forehead. "It takes away the pain?"

Margaret nodded. The stabbing feeling behind her eye sockets
receded almost as suddenly as it had come. Must've been the
fright, she told herself. "Much better now."

She stood shakily at first, then checked herself in the mirror.
The graceful curve of the neckline in the back would look perfect
when she sat at the piano. Spinning around, she threw back her
shoulders and smiled at herself. Her glowing image banished any
memory of Tubarão.

※ ※ ※

"I've missed you!" Erik said as Margaret met him outside the
drawing room.

"We haven't been apart."

"We haven't been together."

Margaret laughed. "Well, I suppose we must be parted once
again. I promised your mother to try the piece your friends wish
me to play, but I'm not certain I'll be able to learn it in so short a
time . . ."

"It's they who'll have to work to keep up with you. Then,
later . . ."

"Yes?" Margaret tilted her head prettily.

"After Francisca and Augusto leave, we'll have supper together. Won't you like that?"

"It can't be soon enough for me." Margaret started for the door and turned. "Erik, I told Francisca about us on the way to the church."

"I told her too!"

"When?"

"First thing this morning."

"She pretended I'd surprised her!"

"Maybe she didn't believe me."

"Why ever not? She trusts you above everyone."

"My sister trusts no one completely."

"But . . ." Margaret stopped herself, feeling, in some indefinable way, that Erik was right. She looked around for Dona Guilhermina. "Your mother was to introduce me to the musicians."

"She's so much to do, won't you allow me the honor?" Erik stroked Margaret's cheek tenderly with the back of his hand. "Minha querida."

"Shhh, someone will hear you."

"I want the whole world to know!" Erik said as he opened the large double doors to the salon.

The three musicians who were gathered by the piano looked up as one.

"What is it that you wanted us to know?" a man holding a violin asked.

"How brilliantly our guest plays the piano," Erik responded smoothly.

Erik took Margaret's arm and led her toward the sullen group. He bowed to a middle-aged woman balancing a cello at her side. "Dona Nicia, may I introduce our North American guest, Margaret Claiborne. Margaret, this is our esteemed cellist, Senhora Netto."

Next Erik greeted the violinist. His dimpled cheeks promised a more cheery personality. The two men hugged each other warmly. "Delgado de Mello is not only one of Rio's finest musicians but one of the best cousins-in-law a man could have. His wife is my father's cousin."

"Mother's cousin," de Mello corrected.

"A hundred apologies." Erik bowed deeply. "And this is Henrique Braga."

The man who stood to shake Margaret's hand was so thin and retiring that it seemed as though he might almost disappear behind his huge polished bass. Though the musician grinned shyly, he said not a word.

"Where is Maestro Freire?" Erik asked.

Henrique Braga started to clear his throat, but the cellist responded for him. "Since he wasn't needed for the run-through, he decided to find something to eat."

"Weren't refreshments brought in to you?" Erik asked.

"We sent them away," Nicia Netto replied frostily. "I, for one, can't hold a bow and a fork simultaneously. Could you?"

"Well, I'm certain you're anxious to get on with your music. In any case, I must get back to the ballroom ..." Erik glanced over to see if Margaret was going to be all right.

She smiled slightly. "Yes, there's not much time to practice ..."

After Erik had departed reluctantly, Margaret asked, "Is Senhor Freire your regular accompanist?"

The cellist suppressed a smirk. "Not exactly."

Margaret regretted her faux pas immediately. Guilhermina Larson had explained he was a composer, not a performer.

Delgado de Mello's conciliatory voice was syrup-smooth. "Quincas — that's our nickname for him — is a very fine composer, but an aggravating ensemble member. He puts frills and flourishes in unexpected places and is impossible to follow." The musician was speaking English with a decidedly British accent. "And he never performs a piece the same way twice. Though as a conductor, he can be quite superb."

"You've also studied in Europe?" Margaret asked, hoping to make up for her previous gaffe.

"We all have. Nicia in Italy, Henrique and Joaquim in Paris. I spent two years in London. Eventually, Joaquim will probably go back to the Conservatoire. There's not much more he can achieve here."

Margaret gestured toward the score opened on the piano. "Is that the piece we are to play?"

"Yes. Would you like to run through it alone first?"

Margaret took her seat on the bench. The violinist turned the music back to the first page. It was titled "Nuptial Souvenir."

"It was written especially for them?" Margaret turned the handwritten pages.

"By Joaquim Freire."

"Really? This first section is a variation on Brahms, isn't it? I like the way he's woven in this second theme."

The cellist raised her eyebrows in surprise. Delgado de Mello glanced at her for a meaningful moment. Margaret's hands sounded the first chords with an unexpected firmness. She played flawlessly through the opening allegro. "This break is for the violin?" she stopped and asked.

De Mello answered, "Yes, then the cello comes in at the top of the next page."

Margaret quickly sight-read the next adagio section and played a few tricky measures before saying, "I think I have the idea. Won't you join me now?"

De Mello picked up his bow. "Muito bem, Senhorita Claiborne."

By the second run-through, the musicians had warmed considerably.

"How do you like it?" de Mello asked as they rested.

"It's quite charming. And clever. He's taken a theme that Brahms wrote as a variation on one of Handel's and made his own variation into a sonata. I especially like the fugue theme near the end of the scherzo."

"I'm so happy that my little souvenir pleases one with so great and unexpected a talent." The composer, a tall man with skin the color of warm molasses, stepped out from the shadow of one of the marble pillars.

As soon as Margaret saw him, she thought that this couldn't possibly be the man who wrote the elegant music she'd just played.

"I apologize for not being here when you arrived. I'll admit to not wanting to hear my music played — how shall I say it? — by an amateur." Joaquim Freire spoke in Portuguese, but the intonation and gestures were more Gallic than Latin. "The piece was not written for any parlor pianist, but as a tribute to the daughter of this esteemed household, and I was afraid . . ."

". . . that a mere guest of the Larson family couldn't play it at all." Nicia Netto finished for him. De Mello chided her sarcasm with his eyes and she quieted.

Waiters carrying trays of pastries, fruits, and drinks served the musicians. Freire pulled a chair up to the bench where Margaret sat and watched intently as she took a few sips of water. She hoped she was hiding the immense discomfort she felt. How could the Larsons permit someone of his obviously mixed racial background to be received as a guest in their home? she wondered. And how could *he* be the composer everyone had told her so much about?

Freire didn't shift his eyes away from her for a moment. Please don't let him know what I'm thinking, she prayed silently. Thankfully, he was diverted when a platter of a dozen varieties of sliced fruits arranged like a rainbow was passed. Margaret declined when it was offered to her. "Não, obrigada."

Suddenly, Margaret was jarred by a memory of her mother's prejudices of anything the least bit unusual. "Hybrids!" She'd spit the word with obvious disgust. Lucretia had made it a point not to eat anything she hadn't tasted first in Louisiana, believing she could be poisoned by the unfamiliar milky goiabas, pungent jambos, prickly graviolas, or acidy pitombas. "Hybrids! Even the fruits in this country are hybrids! Like the people!"

Though Margaret had always felt her mother's fears of miscegenation were a bit excessive, she still was shocked to find a man with Freire's physical characteristics accepted by the upper echelons of Rio society. Was this really the man who studied in Paris and wrote the glorious music she'd just played? In New Orleans, no matter his achievements, Freire would never have been received in any decent home, though she couldn't help realize that he was still an attractive man despite the slight brown cast to his skin.

"Where did you study piano?" Freire was asking Margaret.

Startled to be addressed directly, she spilled some water on the keyboard. A waiter wiped it up immediately.

"New Orleans."

"Nowhere else?"

Margaret shook her head. His voice was strangely soft and so mellifluous she wished he'd keep on speaking until she could gather her scattered thoughts.

Freire looked at her hands thoughtfully. "Very strong attack! I have another piece I'd like you to play sometime." His voice was smoother than syrup. "It's called 'Encantamento.' In English I believe that means 'enchantment.' I'm certain you could interpret my meaning very easily." As he leaned nearer to her, Margaret could smell the fine cologne he wore. A rush of confusing feelings disarmed her. His skin was really not as dark as it first had seemed. In fact, if he stood side by side with Augusto, he might be only a shade darker. But while Augusto's features were obviously a reflection of his Portuguese and Moorish ancestors combined with some native Brazilian stock, Freire's were a curious amalgam of his European and African heritage. His cheekbones were high, his nose was thin and aquiline, but his hair was wiry and formed a tight cap on his beautifully proportioned head. Unexpectedly, Margaret decided that he was a very attractive man. Shaken by the thought, she looked away from Freire and quickly realized that the other musicians had strolled across the room. She and Joaquim were completely alone.

"Who are your favorite composers?" he was asking.

"Chopin, Mozart, Bach, Brahms. At the top of a very long list would be Schumann."

"Did you know that Brahms used to show all his pieces to Schumann's wife, Clara, first?"

"Oh, yes!" Margaret thought it extraordinary that Freire had just mentioned her childhood idol. "I used to dream of studying with her at the Frankfurt Conservatory. But now it's too late . . . She's gone."

"Yes," Joaquim replied sadly. "Only this month. Who knows, you might be the one to take her place."

"My talent couldn't compare to . . ."

"A performer can never judge her own work."

The compliment unnerved her for a moment; then she neatly turned the tables. "And you, what do you wish to accomplish?"

"If you desire to be Clara, I'd want nothing more than to be Robert."

Margaret blushed, but recovered quickly. "But Robert Schumann went insane and died tragically."

"I don't intend to be precisely like him. It's the complexity and perfection of his music that I admire."

"Which pieces especially?"

"His Fantasie, opus seventeen, is a masterpiece." Freire paused. "Did you know that Schumann once wrote a piece with a Brazilian theme?"

"No! Did he really?"

" 'Carnaval'!" Joaquim teased.

"That's based on the characters of the commedia dell'arte!" Margaret protested.

The composer laughed heartily. "I thought I could get you to believe me, but you're far too quick. So, if I can't be Schumann, I'll be happy to settle for the lot of Johannes Brahms."

Margaret laughed a bit uncomfortably. "At least you're half-way!"

"If you think my music half as good as his, I'm flattered indeed."

"That's not exactly what I meant." Margaret was becoming flustered. "It's just that . . . your names . . . They're so similar."

"Joaquim . . . Johannes . . . I've never thought of that before. I'm sorry to disappoint you, but my father named me after the great Brazilian statesman Joaquim Nabuco."

Transfixed by Freire's silvery voice and attentiveness, Margaret could think of nothing more to say. Suddenly, her head pain returned. She cried out involuntarily and pressed her hands to her temples.

Freire placed his warm brown hands over hers. "What's the matter?"

Margaret gasped for breath. The pain felt as though a shaft had penetrated her head and was slowly being withdrawn. She grasped the sides of the piano bench to keep from falling forward. The pain receded enough for her to speak. "My head . . . There's a pain."

"You've strained yourself playing in this heat."

She stared up at his face. His eyes were not the flat dark brown she had expected; they were flecked with tones of gold and bronze. His lashes, too, had metallic tips. His mouth turned upward, giving him the most benevolent of expressions. Altogether, his warm, honey-colored face seemed to have sprung from the pages of a child's storybook. He looked like a foreign prince or, better still, a conjurer. As his riveting gaze drew her deeper, Margaret wondered what she might say to break the spell.

"Many great musicians feel ill before every performance. Vertigo, nausea, true suffering, have been endured by the likes of Thalberg, Kalkbrenner, even Liszt."

"No, no, this has never before happened to me," Margaret insisted. Already some of the wedding guests were being ushered into the sala de visitas, followed by footmen carrying trays of champagne glasses.

Freire bent close. "I'll play the piece if you cannot."

"I promised." Margaret stood shakily by the piano while the bride and groom were led to their seats of honor. The other musicians had taken their places behind her. Freire tossed one last worried glance at Margaret before raising his hand to silence the audience.

"For Senhor and Senhora Augusto Cavalcanti, I dedicate my 'Nuptial Souvenir,' with apologies to Johannes Brahms." His hand dropped as a signal, and Margaret began to play, the music swelling just enough to block the insistent pain that throbbed inside her head.

❧2 "May I present my wife, Constança." Delgado de Mello was standing in front of the buffet table.

"Muito prazer," Margaret replied brightly. Much to her relief, the musical tribute had gone splendidly. "Would you like some of the shrimp pastries? They are one of the cook's specialties."

At Margaret's suggestion, the plump musician's wife held her plate out to be filled. Constança gestured to a small table where Nicia and her husband, Tobias Netto, were already seated with Henrique Braga. "Won't you join us?"

Margaret's eyes searched the room for Erik. Even though the newlyweds were well on their way to Petropolis, Erik was still busy entertaining business associates. Though he kept nodding to her from across the room, she could see he wouldn't be able to sit with her yet. "I'd be delighted," she agreed halfheartedly.

Senhora de Mello misunderstood the slight resistance in Margaret's voice. "Oh, her . . ." She used her chin to indicate Nicia Netto. "She makes it a point to be difficult. Inside, though, she's as tender as a lamb. Pay her no mind and she'll be licking your fingers by tomorrow."

Skillfully balancing an overflowing plate of food and a glass of champagne, Constança wove her way to a table that had been set up near the garden windows. Margaret followed along, guarding her plate from a tangle of elbows that poked from all sides.

When she had settled her plate on her lap and her glass on the small round table, Freire took the chair by her side. "Senhorita Claiborne, you must eat more than just a few pieces of bread and cheese."

"I've never had an appetite after a performance."

"Just the opposite with me," Delgado de Mello said as he speared three codfish balls with his fork, dipped them in a red sauce, and swallowed them all at once.

Freire stared solicitously until Margaret made an attempt to eat. "At least let me get you a fresh glass of champagne. It's a Veuve Clicquot '55. With a cellar like his, it's a pity Larson doesn't have more daughters to marry off!" He snapped his fingers sharply and a waiter scurried to his side. He handed Margaret's champagne glass to her, smiling paternally. "Your pain?"

"Much better, thank you." Margaret concentrated on cutting the thin cheese slices into even smaller portions. The composer's consideration made her uneasy, especially in front of the others. She wished Erik would rescue her soon. To herself she admitted that despite the darkness of his skin, she was drawn to Freire's brilliance and charm. It was not as unnatural for her to be conversing with him as she would have expected, though she could easily imagine her mother's horrified reaction if she were to see her daughter at that moment.

Freire leaned forward and spoke like a conspirator. "Do you know the work of Debussy?"

"No, I don't. Is he French?"

"Yes, he is. No one since Chopin has written so freshly for the piano. I believe his music would suit your style."

"I don't think my interpretation of one piece gives any hint of my style. All it proved was I could follow the notes."

Freire stroked his cheek thoughtfully with the edge of his thumb. "Perhaps."

Margaret waited. Not so much for what he would say, but for him to just speak again. The mellow intensity of his voice was enchanting. Just then, Erik hurried to her side. She beamed at his approach.

"So, have you met every one of Rio's greatest talents?" he asked sincerely. "I was so hoping you'd all get along, because Margaret will probably be wanting to study at the Academy of Music."

"You'll be remaining in Rio?" de Mello asked.

Without giving away their secret, Erik replied, "I have every intention of convincing her."

Surprisingly, Nicia Netto spoke with an affectionate tone. "Erico, if you truly want to keep her here, you'll have to have the middle register of that piano worked on."

"Thank you for telling him," Margaret agreed. "I hadn't the courage myself."

Everyone except Freire laughed easily.

When Erik led Margaret away, Delgado de Mello, always the astute observer, said to Freire, "I thought your family was very close to the Larsons."

"What of it?"

"I noticed you didn't say three words to Erico. Are you feuding with him?"

"Certainly not!" he bristled.

Nicia Netto touched Freire's arm. "You're quite taken with the newcomer, aren't you?"

"Every new musician interests me."

"Every new woman interests you!" Nicia snapped.

Delgado de Mello tried to play referee. "Nicia, darling . . . She plays piano, not cello!" he said consolingly. "She might really be an asset to our little musical community."

"You've mistaken my feelings," Nicia defended. "I think she has great possibilities. With her on my side, I might have a chance to get my way in the choice of program sometimes." Nicia sipped her champagne, then smiled naughtily. "I wonder if she plays that Mozart sonata you've never been willing to learn."

"What?" Freire hadn't heard her last words. He was completely distracted as he watched Margaret walking beside Erik.

The cut of her gown was particularly erotic from the back. "Did you say Mozart? I'm sure she'd be eager to work with you on it."

"Unless, of course, she marries Larson," Nicia added tartly.

"Don't be so melodramatic, Nicia," Joaquim insisted. "You've been married for twenty years and you can still lift your bow to the strings."

"It was different for me."

"Why was that? Was your music always more important than your husband?"

"Depends whom you ask," Tobias Netto said in good humor.

"I doubt that she's the kind of woman who could ever make a practical separation between marriage and music. She's far too romantic for that." Nicia placed her glass down with a clatter. "Why, she's bewitched Quincas already!"

"What do you mean?" Freire looked back in Nicia's direction. "Just because you won't be the only hen in the barnyard anymore . . ."

The cellist sniffed in mock contempt. "That's not it at all. You gentlemen don't understand what it must have taken for a girl as young as she is to have progressed so far in music." She shot a glance toward Erik and Margaret. "She's lovely, enchanting, and, yes, I'll admit that I wish I were twenty years younger myself. But inside she's more. Only another woman, another musician, would recognize the fortitude, the single-mindedness, that it took to play as incredibly well as she did today. Just her prodigious sight-reading skills required years of concentration, years of giving up the usual pastimes of a pretty girl. I'm afraid she'll plunge into a marriage with exactly the same intensity. A woman with a personality like hers gives her all to the task at hand. Eventually she'll have to make a choice: music or a man. Not both."

Freire's voice became distant. "You have your opinions, I have mine. At least we probably agree that if Larson gets his way, he'll ruin her."

"Olhe ali!" Henrique Braga pointed to where Margaret had been standing. "Look!"

They all turned in time to see Margaret very slowly leaning against Erik. She clutched the sides of her head with her hands before tipping backward. Freire was the first to bound to her side and lower her to the floor.

3 Fever! The word shattered the Larson household. That year the cases in Rio had been fewer because sanitary measures to fill the swamps and pour kerosene on stagnant water had greatly diminished the numbers who fell victim to deadly seasonal epidemics. In wealthy quarters like Flamengo, epidemic outbreaks were even rarer.

It was too early to tell exactly which disease Margaret had contracted, but her symptoms did not rule out the worst possibility: yellow fever. The night of the wedding Margaret's body was racked with chills so violent that her bedstead vibrated. Dr. Bandeira stayed by her side all night, spelled by his assistant, Sister Piedade. By morning her temperature was so high that her skin seemed aflame. Florinda and Zefinha took turns with the herbal compresses and tried, in vain, to get Margaret to take sips of a tea made from the bark of the root of the quina-cruzeiro tree. At noon, when the fever had risen still higher, the beleaguered doctor poured water on her head while the maids fanned vigorously with wet towels.

"Very bad ... Terrível!" Dr. Bandeira reported dejectedly to the Larsons, who were keeping vigil in their upstairs parlor.

"How could this have happened?" Dona Guilhermina's voice was almost hysterical. "We haven't had a case of fever in our family in seven years."

"I don't think the girl contracted it here. By all signs, she's brought it with her. Might have been bitten by a mosquito on her river journey or, in that worst sewer of them all, the port of Santos. To be truthful, these cases are always more dangerous for foreigners. That's why there's such a high mortality with sailors."

Erik, who had numbed his fear with brandy, lunged forward. "She won't die!"

The doctor steadied him. "It's a very bad sign when the fever rises so sharply the first night."

"What if it wasn't the first night?"

"What makes you think she's been sick for a longer period of time?"

"The night the Cavalcantis came to dinner, I noticed she was not well."

"Anything else?"

"Her skin was flushed and felt hot to my . . ."

The doctor shook his head. "There are a dozen different diseases. All take different courses but may appear quite similar at first. Even the febre amarela can be so mild as to never cause concern. On the other hand" — he turned toward Sven Larson — "the last Norte Americano I saw with the yellow jack was a very sad tale indeed. I treated him for three days for an only intermittent fever and thought him cured. The next evening I saw him walking in the rain and sent him home to bed. When I was summoned, mortification had already set in; his body was all discolored from the throat downward. Eighteen hours later, he died."

Guilhermina Larson gasped, but the doctor, caught up in his grisly story, didn't notice. "The funeral was to be the afternoon of the same day. I remember it well because even though the coffin lid was screwed down, the gases generated so quickly that when the box was lifted to be placed on the hearse, the screws gave way. Why, the effect was so awful that mourners fainted from the odor!"

❧   ❧   ❧

"I know a cure," Zefinha whispered to Florinda. "Better than that medicine from the farmácia. It was taught to me when I was a little girl by an old black woman, the preta velha, Maria-José. It works for many things: bleeding, fever, even snakebite."

Florinda shuddered, but Zefinha, knowing nothing about Berto, thought only of Margaret. "Your lady is a strong one, not like my Francisca." She crossed herself. "I hope my little girl is all right. They should have let me go to Petropolis, but Dona Guilhermina wouldn't hear of it, thought she needed to be on her own. Stupid woman!" she spat. "What does she know?"

"The cure . . ." Florinda reminded.

Sister Piedade was ministering to Margaret, so they backed into the small linen room across the hall. Zefinha withdrew three small candles from her apron pocket, placed them on a shelf, and lit them. "Say the words after me. 'Cursed fever . . .' " She bade Florinda to get down on her knees.

"Cursed fever . . ." Florinda echoed.

"I bury you three times in the bowels of the earth. The first in the name of the Father, the second in the name of the Son, and the third in the name of the Holy Ghost, with the grace of the Virgin Mary and all the saints."

Sister Piedade burst in. "What are you doing?" She blew out the candles. "Devil worshipers!"

Before Zefinha could respond, a surprising sound came from the bedroom. "Nell, it *is* a ginger cake!" Margaret's voice rang out clear and natural.

"Graças a Deus!" Florinda ran into the room expecting to see her mistress fully recovered. Instead, Margaret was sitting in bed, staring at something only she could see and talking to someone who wasn't there.

Sister Piedade stared at the delirious girl and crossed herself. "What is it? What's the matter, Dona Margarida?"

"Don't tell me it isn't a ginger cake," she continued in English. "It is a ginger cake! Now let me have some, you silly girl, or I'll find Mother and I'll . . ." She stopped, fell back against her pillows, and was quiet once again.

The sister shook her head. "Fevers. They do the strangest things to the brain, bring terrible visions. Do you know what is 'ginger cake'?"

Florinda shook her head.

"Ask Dr. Bandeira to come at once."

Dr. Bandeira ordered Sister Piedade to write down everything Margaret said. "Part of the patient's record" was the only explanation he'd give. In the back of his mind, though, he thought that the girl's parents would like some last word from their daughter and that the English words, even written phonetically by the nun, might have a special meaning to them in their grief.

❧ ❧ ❧

The next morning Margaret had shown no improvement, but neither had she gotten any worse. Sister Piedade had scrupulously transcribed her every utterance before falling asleep in her chair just after dawn.

Dona Guilhermina stopped in before breakfast and read the list on the bedside table. Ridiculous to tire a nurse with such trivia, she thought. How can anyone expect her to tend to Margaret and also keep writing notes like: "ginger cake . . ." "put it on the

Chickering," "D-flat, not C-sharp," "tell Mr. Cable . . ." "pontaria fina . . ." Nonsense! The only Portuguese phrase was "pontaria fina," meaning, in cowboy terms, "sure shot."

She touched Margaret's burning face. The girl's bow-shaped lips were caked and dry; sweat had coated her beautiful golden hair with an oily film. Tenderly, Guilhermina felt around the crown of her chignon for pins that might be uncomfortable and unbound her hair. She'd have Zefinha braid it loosely later. Margaret's head flopped back on the pillow without resistance. She moaned slightly.

Taking her hand, Guilhermina stroked the palms briskly to stimulate her circulation. Such gifted hands, such talent! What a waste if she couldn't be cured! And Erik — what would he do if anything happened to her? A mother knew the boy beneath the man who had cried behind closed doors when Francisca had left for New Orleans, was inconsolable after his young wife's death, and now was sleepless over this lovely North American.

She looked at Margaret's brow shining with perspiration, like a laborer in the hot sun. Good, she thought, work to live. Struggle against the fever and come back to us. Guilhermina had grown up in a city where these seasonal plagues carried away thousands in a week, yet she had no inner sense that this girl would die. Margaret possessed a strength that far surpassed her fragile bones, a power vividly expressed in her forceful approach to her music. Perhaps that fierceness of purpose in one so young and feminine was exactly what had captivated her son so quickly.

Guilhermina took the cloth steeping in cool rose water, squeezed it almost dry, and began to wipe Margaret's cheeks and neck. My son, she thought, he's also an enigma. No one would ever have guessed his softness, his generosity, his love for children and women. Any other man would have treated his mistress quite differently. How hard they'd worked to convince him to marry someone more suitable, like Gunilla. And when she'd died, he'd gone right back to Isabel's bed, like a devoted puppy. Some men were like that. They just couldn't do without the comfort of a woman, even for a night. If it weren't for Margaret, they might have had another fight over his marrying Isabel on their hands. Good thing the North American's a strong one with a mind of her own. She'll know how to handle Astrid and Erik when, and if, the time comes.

Margaret moaned again. The guttural sound seemed unnatural. Guilhermina crossed herself. With all that had happened to the girl — the bandido, now this fever — perhaps she needed a medicine Dr. Bandeira couldn't provide. Three times a day Guilhermina had been saying her prayers in front of her private collection of favorite saints: Nossa Senhora do Livramento, who absolved from sin, Nossa Senhora da Bom Parto, who gave healthy children, and Nossa Senhora da Fatima, whose plaster face was filled with the benevolence and generosity to which Guilhermina aspired daily. Candles burned day and night beside her bedroom altar. Still . . . What would it hurt to try one more way to change Margaret's luck? Though she'd never admit it to anyone, Guilhermina couldn't completely disbelieve the rites the servants practiced. What harm could be done by sending Severino to the macumbeiro for some potions . . . just in case?

❧   ❧   ❧

"At least let me see her!" Erik pleaded.

Breakfast had been served in his parents' parlor, but no one had done more than take a few sips of coffee.

"Nunca!" His mother's voice was unnaturally shrill. "She would never forgive me if I let you in her room."

"Even for a few minutes?"

"No! A woman shouldn't be seen at such times."

"Perhaps you are too harsh," Sven interjected. "It must be difficult for Erik not to see for himself . . ."

"Not without her permission."

"And if" — Erik's voice wavered — "she's unable to ever give it again . . ."

"Don't say such things!" Guilhermina shouted. "Dr. Bandeira has great hopes. There's no sign of vomiting and her tongue is pale, not red, as it would be by now if she had yellow fever."

"Then what is it?"

"Could be many things, but possibly it's the dengue."

"I've never heard of it!"

"The doctor says it's more common down in Paraná."

"Is it fatal?"

"Sometimes."

Erik leapt from his seat.

"Where are you going?"

"To find the doctor."

"He's examining Margaret now. If you promise to act sensibly when he returns, I'll permit you to remain for his report."

Nervously, Erik chewed on a crusty piece of bread.

"You've wired her parents, Vivo?"

"Yes," Sven replied, "but the lines only go as far as Iguape, so it will take several days to reach the colony."

"We had no choice except to send for them."

Her husband nodded. "With them here it will be easier for you both to make your plans."

"What if they disapprove?" Erik asked.

"A disobedient daughter will be a disobedient wife," Sven chided.

Dr. Bandeira entered the room. "The fever is down slightly and she's perspiring heavily."

"Is that a good sign?" Guilhermina asked.

"It's not the typical course for yellow fever. Have you sprayed the gardens with kerosene?"

"All the standing tubs, pools, basins, everywhere you suggested," Larson answered. "Even in the orchid garden. The fumes are overpowering the flowers."

"Bom, bom. It's just a precaution, of course. I want her kept under mosquito netting, for reinfection in her weakened condition would be disastrous. She'd recover faster in a less miasmic climate."

"We could take her to Boa Vista, com o seu consentimento, Doctor . . ." Sven suggested.

Erik added hurriedly, "We could move her at night when it's cooler and the streets are less crowded." He was also thinking how much more difficult it would be to keep him apart from Margaret in the smaller, less formally run house.

"Impossível!" Guilhermina was adamant. "She's much too weak."

Larson waited for the doctor to mediate.

Dr. Bandeira stroked his beard thoughtfully. "Tomorrow will

bring the answer. If the fever is still down, we'll talk of a journey to Boa Vista."

❧ ❧ ❧

The next morning, on the fourth day of her illness, Margaret woke up screaming. Florinda, who refused to sleep anywhere but beside her lady's bed, raced to her side and, seeing what caused such distress, joined in the wailing.

Fully expecting to find her patient had suddenly expired, Sister Piedade rushed into the room, her white robes flying. When she saw Margaret sitting up in bed, howling at the condition of her skin, she laughed with relief.

"The dengue! The dengue!" she cried, adding to the confusing cacophony.

In his bedroom down the hallway, Erik heard the women's wails and panicked. Since the talk of moving Margaret to Boa Vista and the signs that the fever was diminishing, he'd cheered in the belief that she would surely recover. But now . . . it could only be the worst! He prayed it was not too late to at least kiss her farewell.

The doors of her room were already flung open. Thick layers of mosquito netting hung about the bed, and his view was further blocked by Florinda, his mother, and the nurse. Without waiting for permission, he pushed his way forward, flung back a flap of the gauzy fabric, and stared at Margaret in disbelief.

"Oh, no!" she moaned. "Please . . . please go! You can't see me like this!" Her eyes blazed intensely and her voice had its normal spirit back, but her body! Her face, hands, chest, almost every visible skin surface, had erupted in a brutal red scaling rash that gave her the appearance of a boiled reptilian creature.

As quickly as possible, Florinda tried to hide Margaret under the linens, but even so, her face, masked in red tracery, was still visible.

"Gigo! I ordered you to stay away from this room!"

But Erik seemed oblivious to his mother's fretting or to Margaret's mortified expression. "This means she'll recover?" he asked Sister Piedade.

"You'll have to ask the doctor."

"But what is it?"

"The dengue, the breakbone fever. When the rash comes, you know for certain."

Through the sheets, Erik clasped the hand Margaret had snaked under the covers. "I'm sure that's the sign he's been waiting for, the sign to tell him it wasn't something more serious."

For the first time Margaret was speaking without a fevered slur. "What could be more serious than this?"

When he realized that she was well enough to jest, Erik stammered, "Oh . . . Margarida . . ." while his mother pushed him out the door.

"Mais tarde . . . Gigo . . . por favor . . ."

Once again he faced the bed. Behind the shrouded netting Margaret appeared a small rosy speck, shrinking under the covers. "You look wonderful in pink!" he shouted before his mother slammed the door.

4 The diagnosis was dengue fever. From the onset of the postorbital pains and the fever that rose rapidly after the first few nights to the rashes, Margaret had developed a classic case. Weakness and nausea prevented her from eating, and the itching hindered her rest. Her bones throbbed, her joints swelled, and at times, it was all she could do to keep from crying out from the pain. Paradoxically, it was when these aches worsened that Dr. Bandeira knew she was out of mortal danger.

"Now we must guard against the remote possibility of her being reinfected by a mosquito carrying the vector."

"Do you think she'll survive?"

"Sim, she'll survive indeed, but she'll need a long convalescence. Periods of extreme discomfort are to be expected."

"Then you'd advise our taking her to Boa Vista?" Sven Larson asked.

"As soon as it can be arranged."

To Margaret, almost worse than the pain was the violent, patchy, measlelike rash that erupted all over her body. The palms of her hands and the soles of her feet swelled and became bright red. Night fevers were still common and the severe sweating only compounded the itching. Margaret was grateful that Erik's mother had forbidden him to see her.

Not that Erik had agreed. When he was not permitted to ride

in the carriage that carried Margaret to Boa Vista, he had traveled to the downtown district, taken the bonde, or streetcar, up into the hills, and established himself wordlessly in his usual room in the summer house. Finally his mother agreed to let him stay on as long as he understood he could talk to Margaret only from outside the door.

The summer house, or chácara, had been placed in a cozy niche in the mountains at a site where three rushing streams met in a series of natural pools, several of which had been expanded and dammed for swimming and irrigation. It was the perfect place to convalesce. Margaret remembered her first days there as a series of aromatic smells: the greenness of the air; the ripeness of the oiled wood plank floors and sturdy carved furniture in her room; the bowls of bananas, oranges, and mangos placed at her bedside to tempt her.

From the window to the right of her bed she had a view of the bald granite escarpments and the fringes of tropical greenery on the less steep slopes. If she looked out the window to the left, she could see the terraced gardens that had been etched from the convoluted hillsides and planted with an incredible array of vivid flowers. These plants seemed a natural, rather than designed, part of the landscape, rooted by an irreverent gardener who, despite his ill-conceived intentions, had created colors and patterns that surpassed anything that an orderly mind could have planned. Three shades of bougainvillea — a riotous pink, violent orange, and livid purple — entwined to produce a flowering cluster of breathtaking blooms. Moss-draped stone walls, randomly sprouting trails of ivy and asparagus ferns, provided a backdrop to sensational specimens of seemingly wild laelia orchids. Trees that weren't in flower were improved upon by hanging baskets of poinsettia, called asa-de-papagaio, meaning "parrot's wing," in Portuguese. The tree trunks were surrounded by pots of waxy red anthuriums, their yellow spadices jutting out brightly. Occasionally, howling monkeys held a noisy caucus overhead or a flock of bright parrots glided swiftly across the tall, bending bamboos.

"You are looking so much better," Florinda said brightly one morning at the end of their first week at Boa Vista. "A good night?"

Margaret nodded.

Florinda touched the linens. "No sweats?"

"Não. Nothing."

"Muito bom!"

"Something to eat?"

"Sim." Margaret surprised herself. "I'd like . . . canja, bread, and . . . perhaps cheese."

"Canja!" Florinda's wide smile revealed the gaps in her teeth. She hurried to order the nutritious chicken soup, the first actual food Margaret had requested since she'd become ill.

"May I come in?" Guilhermina Larson asked softly.

"Um momento." Margaret quickly arranged her covers.

"So, Florinda was correct! You do look so much better. Now, if you'll only begin to eat, your strength will return rapidly."

"I'm sorry to have been so much trouble."

Guilhermina came closer to the bed. "May I?" she asked before sitting. "Your skin is clearing beautifully. There won't be a mark."

"One place heals, but another worsens."

"Dr. Bandeira's sent some special powders for the itching. He also recommends fresh air and sunshine to speed your healing."

Margaret turned her head aside. "I couldn't go outside . . ."

"You're worried about Erik?" Guilhermina patted Margaret's hand. "I'll make certain he won't be around when you are outdoors. He needs to start going to the city with his father every day, and this weekend he'll go to visit his daughter. Astrid stays very close by."

"Who does she live with?"

"Her nursemaid. She still takes her milk from her. That's why she cannot be separated yet."

"At *four?*"

"It's not so unusual, not in Brazil."

"She'll come to live with us after we're married, won't she?"

"I know that's what my son wishes."

"There's so much I don't understand."

"Yes?"

A certain wariness in Guilhermina's inflection warned Margaret off.

"I just thought that the nursemaid would've cared for Erik's child in your home."

"It was more complicated than the usual situation." Guilhermina chose her words thoughtfully. "Isabel has other children, so it would not have been fair to bring them into our house and to treat one as our own and the others as . . . less desirable. Astrid's been well cared for and Isabel's been well rewarded," she concluded crisply.

Florinda came to the door followed by a kitchen girl carrying an overflowing tray. A steaming bowl of chicken soup was placed on Margaret's bedside table. Guilhermina stirred it with a spoon while Florinda placed a crocheted napkin across Margaret's chest and propped her back up with more pillows. Guilhermina herself filled the spoon with broth and a glistening piece of yam.

Pleased that Margaret was accepting the soup, Guilhermina sighed. "It's good?"

"Just what I wanted." Margaret tried to take the spoon.

"You must allow me to do this, minha filha." Guilhermina kept feeding the invalid. She offered Margaret a piece of buttered toast. "Is your throat too sore for this?"

The yeasty aroma was wonderful. "I'll try it."

Guilhermina passed a platter of peeled fruits. When Margaret reached for her second slice of guava, she grinned. "You'll be back to that piano in a very short time if you keep this up. But we can make plans now."

"Plans?"

"For the marriage. I'm certain that you'll agree we should have the ceremony as soon as the doctor permits."

"Why?"

"A matter of practicality. You came to visit us for a wedding and you stay on with us now that you are ill; there's no harm in that. But, if we go on for too long without announcing the marriage, there will be much talk. Rio can be a surprisingly small town in matters of gossip."

"I see. But my parents . . ."

Guilhermina paused. "We've . . . My husband has . . ." She stopped herself. "When your fever was its most severe, we thought it best to contact your parents. We've been expecting them to arrive any day."

"My father is coming here!"

"There was nothing else to do. If something had happened —

graças a Deus, it did not, but if — we would never have been for-given for not bringing them to your bedside, would we?"

"You did what you thought best." Margaret's voice quavered. "Did they respond?"

"No, not yet, but I have a sense, a mother's sense, that your family will be here soon."

"My father . . ."

"Am I not a mother? Do I not know how a parent feels? Be-lieve me, Margarida, when they see you recovered from such a dangerous illness, they will only want your happiness."

"I hope you're right, Dona Guilhermina."

"In this I am." She patted Margaret's mouth with her napkin. "Now we have a few practical matters to attend to."

"Yes?"

"When you are willing, I will have the priest at Boa Vista come to see you for instruction. What better time to study?"

"I suppose you're right."

"If you learn quickly, the wedding can be held soon . . . with your mother and father by your side. Won't that be lovely?"

As hard as Margaret tried to imagine herself saying her wed-ding vows at the altar of Candelária with her parents beside her, the illusion blurred. Her father kneeling in a Roman Catholic church? Never! Margaret pushed the fruit platter away and fell back on her pillows.

"You must rest now."

With her eyes closing almost against her will, Margaret didn't object. "Erik . . ." she said. There was something else she wanted to ask about Erik, but what was the question? She felt dizzy and disoriented. Her stomach churned mercilessly and her face broke out into a sweat. Florinda, seeing the familiar paleness, ran across the room with a wet towel and a basin just in time. Margaret retched painfully.

"Too bad . . . Coitada!" Guilhermina commiserated at the piti-ful sight.

5 Later that afternoon, Erik knocked on the door to Mar-garet's room. He opened it slightly and turned his chair with the back toward the six-inch opening, as was his daily cus-tom during the time when the rest of his family took their naps in the verandah hammocks. "Margaret? Do you hear me?" he whispered loudly.

When she didn't answer, he called again. "Margarida, querida?" He listened and heard only a deep sonorous breathing from under the covers. Unusual. She always had looked forward to this quiet time of day when they could talk privately while everyone else rested. He'd been telling tales of his childhood holidays at Boa Vista, and Margaret had been so enchanted with his descriptions of the waterfalls in the nearby forest of Tijuca that he'd promised to take her for a picnic with Francisca and Augusto as soon as she was well enough.

Just yesterday she'd been in such good spirits, asking him questions about his business, something she had known little about but seemed to grasp immediately. He thought her the most exceptional woman he'd ever met. He crossed himself as he gave thanks for her recovery. Last Sunday he'd noticed that the chapel at Boa Vista was falling into disrepair. Must send a donation, he reminded himself.

He opened the door wider. "Margaret?"

The draperies were closed. He moved nearer to the bed. Erik was quick to notice the brown bottle of sleeping medicine, the still-sticky spoon, and the tangled knots of blond hair that peeked from under the blankets. Very gently, he pulled back the sheet and saw her beautiful head cradled by her thin arms. Margaret's hands were much more delicate than they'd appeared before she'd become ill, with bony protuberances around the flushed wrists. Erik touched one to see if it was really as hot as it appeared. It was so unexpectedly moist and infant-soft, he could not bring himself to release it.

Margaret stirred. The only sound in the house was the ticking of the upstairs and downstairs hall clocks. All the servants, even Florinda, had been sent back to their quarters. Guilhermina treasured silent afternoons with nary a servant's foot permitted to creak a board. He stroked Margaret's long neck, running his forefinger across the fragile hollow that pulsated with life. Only the faintest rash remained on her face, but even the brighter spots that crusted on her forearms did not disgust him.

Erik pulled the covers down even further and saw she was wearing only the thinnest batiste shift. Just that morning he'd seen Florinda hang half a dozen of them on the laundry line and had been captivated by the idea of the nightclothes against her body. Good girl, that Florinda. Margaret was lucky to have someone so devoted. As he ran his finger across the rosebuds embroidered on her bodice, his palm touched a protruding nipple. The feeling that shot through him was so sharp his breath caught, and he almost stumbled.

I should leave, I shouldn't be here . . . he thought for the briefest of seconds. Unable to control himself, he kissed the sweet cleft at her throat and allowed his hands to flutter over both nipples again, feeling them erect slightly. Afraid the stimulation would waken her, he moved downward to feel the sharp bones of her pelvis and the very soft, flat belly between. So thin! She must eat more! Her hips were also too prominent, but her thighs were still soft and pliable. His heart pounded so hard he thought the sound might rouse her.

The floor-length gown had tangled around her knees, so it was not difficult for him to lift it and see that the woman who lay in the bed wore nothing but the sheer shift. An odor both pungent and sweet assaulted him. He took a long, slow whiff of her secret feminine perfume. His hand hovered above her naked belly before he dared lower it just enough to brush the curly, tempting triangle between her legs. Summoning a modicum of control, he withdrew his arm and straightened her gown. Staring hungrily, he tried to memorize her form. His mind whirled with wild fantasies; the blood surged through his loins with unbearable swiftness. Margaret's lips moved silently and her eyeballs could be seen shifting eerily behind her lids. Erik tried awkwardly to replace the covers exactly as they had been, before fleeing from the room in a guilty panic.

※　※　※

No sooner had he reached the kitchen than Erik heard an unexpected sound. His father's carriage was arriving hours earlier than expected. From the back door Erik could see that two unfamiliar women were his guests. He ran to wake his mother.

On the front verandah, Lucretia and Nell Claiborne were welcomed first by Guilhermina. Erik stood silently in the background, feeling most contrite.

"And this is my son, Erik."

Erik stepped forward and bowed. Margaret's mother was a much plainer woman than he'd expected, considering the exceptional loveliness of her daughter. He turned and made a slightly briefer bow to Nell, thinking that the family resemblance was closer in the sister, although she lacked Margaret's fine bone structure and compelling eyes.

Sven Larson spoke stiffly. "I've already told Senhora Claiborne how well her daughter is doing and how pleased we were to discover Margaret's illness was not the fever we feared." He looked to his wife for help.

"Your journey was not too difficult?"

"We were so worried about Margaret that our discomfort didn't concern us." Lucretia spoke haltingly in Portuguese. "How relieved we were to learn that she will recover completely."

"You arrived this morning?"

"Yes, very early. We went to your home, as instructed. The servants sent for your husband at his place of business. He insisted we drive out immediately to see my daughter, though he told us she was out of danger, praise the Lord!"

"We're sorry to have troubled you, but at the time it seemed . . ."

"Charles and I were very grateful to hear from you." Lucretia knew that the Larsons were wondering where her husband was. "You can't imagine how he wanted to travel with me, but there were so many difficulties on our fazenda, I insisted that he remain home to settle them. My Nell will help me nurse my little girl back to health."

"Is this your first trip to Rio?" Guilhermina asked.

"Yes, for us both."

"Now that Margaret's doing so well, we shall endeavor to make your stay as enjoyable as possible." She turned to where Erik was nervously pacing in the background. "Gigo, send the boy for Florinda. I'm sure Margaret will want to be presentable."

"Won't you come inside and have some coffee?" She showed them into a dim parlor decorated with family portraits and large stuffed furniture built more for comfort than beauty. A few claps roused the kitchen girl, who came running with tiny china cups and a platter of fruit. "Would you prefer a refrêsco de maracujá?" she asked Nell.

"Sim, senhora," Nell responded, her accent flawless.

When they were seated, Guilhermina spoke in a warm but serious tone. "Your daughter has progressed better than expected, although I must warn you, she has been a very sick young lady. Some days are better than others. I'm afraid today has not been her best." Guilhermina placed her hands in her lap and leveled her voice. "She ate very well this morning, a good sign, but perhaps she shouldn't have taken quite so much. Her stomach was quite distressed. After her medication, she fell asleep. We haven't had the heart to wake her all afternoon."

Lucretia listened for any sign that she wasn't hearing the whole truth.

"Do you know about this fever they call the dengue?"

"In New Orleans we dreaded yellow fever, but this other one . . . It's not so serious, is it?"

"Not usually. There is the same high temperature, but the dengue's followed by rashes."

Lucretia seemed startled.

"I wanted to explain . . ." Guilhermina went on. "So you won't be surprised when you see your daughter. Every day I notice the difference, but for you . . . it might be a shock."

"Does she have much pain?"

"At first the headaches were so terrible she cried. Afterward it was her joints and bones. That's what gives the dengue its common name: breakbone fever. Even now she must be carried, for it hurts too much for her to walk."

Lucretia sighed pitifully. "My poor child!"

"Senhora Claiborne, the doctor assures us that your daughter will recover completely."

Florinda tiptoed into the room and made a slight bow to Mrs. Claiborne.

"Hello, Florinda. How are you?" Lucretia asked.

Florinda nodded, then lowered her eyes. "My children?" she whispered.

"They're all very well."

Florinda smiled shyly.

"Have you seen to Dona Margarida?" Guilhermina asked.

"Sim, senhora. She is ready."

"Did you tell her who was here?"

"Não, senhora."

"Muito bom, Florinda." She dismissed the servant. "A very good girl. She's devoted to your daughter."

"Now may we see her?"

"Certainly." Guilhermina pointed the way up the narrow wooden staircase. Nell went ahead, barely able to control the urge to race up the stairs two at a time.

※   ※   ※

During Margaret's groggy but happy reunion with her family she jabbered in English, telling all about Francisca's wedding. Lucretia pretended to listen but was more concerned with the vast changes in her daughter's appearance. The grey hollows under her eyes and the awful scabs on her exposed skin showed clearly the ravages of this serious illness.

"What's this?" Nell pointed to a glass of murky liquid.

"Coconut water. It's about all that stays down."

"Can't you eat anything?"

"It wasn't until today that I even wanted food. Tomorrow I'll try some canja again."

"But that's a peasant food!" Lucretia cried, before purposefully lowering her voice. "You'd think a family with their means would serve something more . . . substantial."

"Their house in Rio!" Nell exclaimed. "I've never seen such a palace!"

"It's beautiful," Margaret agreed. "Did you see the piano?"

"No, we were there less than an hour before Senhor Larson came and brought us here."

Lucretia handed Margaret the glass of green coconut water. "You must drink it."

Margaret sipped slowly.

Nell was bursting to speak. "You can't imagine what happened when Father discovered you were gone! He wanted to send someone out after you, but then Mother . . ."

"Nell!" Lucretia admonished.

Margaret blanched. "Oh, Mother, will he ever forgive me?"

"His anger was directed solely at me. After he'd raged on for a while, I simply explained that if he did not settle down and understand that your life was to be your own, then I would take all my children back home."

"You said that?"

"You would've been so proud of her!" Nell said. "There's more news! Marianne's expecting a baby."

"Already? Where are they living?"

"On a barge somewhere upriver. Your brother's taking missionary life very seriously." Lucretia waited a few beats. "As for other news, Mr. Cable has contacted us. He's very anxious for your return."

"Does he know of my illness?"

"I wrote him before I left."

Margaret gasped. "Do you think he'll try to find me here?"

"No, we didn't tell him exactly where you were. Only that we were bringing you home."

"Home?"

"You don't want to come home?" Nell asked suspiciously.

"Mother . . ."

Lucretia looked from Margaret to Nell and began to glow. "So . . . there is more to tell, isn't there?"

"I knew it!" Nell jumped around the room. "I knew it right away! You're going to marry Erik! You are!"

"Before I became sick, we were going to write for your permission."

"He's a dream, isn't he, Mother?" Nell cooed. "A dream come true!"

"You'd be well cared for, wouldn't you?"

"It's more than that, Mother. I have a feeling for him, something different from . . ."

"Mr. Cable?"

"From anything I've ever felt. He's . . . he's . . ." Margaret stopped and remembered her mother's description of falling in love with her father. "It's unexplainable, isn't it?"

Lucretia closed her tired eyes. Margaret could see her mother had changed somewhat even in a few brief weeks. Was it the worry over her, the journey north, or was she hiding something else? "Tell me everything, Margaret. Then I'll decide."

6 When it came to religion, Lucretia was as pragmatic as her daughter. In New Orleans the Creole Catholics far outnumbered the Protestants, so she well understood the wisdom of her daughter converting and raising her children in Brazil's most popular faith. True, Charles and Raleigh would object, perhaps vehemently, but even Charles would realize the significance this marriage could have for the whole family. Their holdings in Lizzieland held no rich legacy for their children, but with Margaret well secured, there would always be somewhere to turn.

Yet there was something else, something less tangible, that worried Lucretia about her daughter's alliance. Behind Erik's gentle manners, his sparkling eyes and ready wit, was a man far older, far more experienced, than her daughter. He had been married and he had a child. Even though the same could have been said for Mr. Cable, Lucretia was still troubled. Why had his daughter been hidden away in some servant's house, instead of being cared for by the Larsons? She knew Brazilians did things differently, but in family matters they were usually kindhearted to a fault. Even the peasant, Florinda, thought first of her children. When Lucretia had brought the news that all her children were well, Florinda had cried with gratitude. Florinda . . . Maybe she could be of help now.

That evening, after Florinda had finished with Margaret's sponge bath, Lucretia pulled her aside.

"Senhora?" said Florinda, folding the towels into a bundle for the wash house.

"Do you know where the daughter of Senhor Erico lives?"

"Not exactly."

"Could you find out?"

"Sim, senhora."

"Muito bem. But this is our secret. I do it to help my daughter, compreendes?"

"Sim, senhora."

By lunchtime the next day, Lucretia knew that Astrid was only a few miles from Boa Vista with a woman called Isabel da

Silva. When she heard they lived in a resort hotel called the
Parque Panorama, her suspicions diminished somewhat. It sounded
like a well-run, healthy country place for a child. Perhaps Erik
had chosen wisely after all. Even so, Lucretia was determined to
see Astrid, if only to be certain that the Larsons weren't conceal-
ing an idiot or deformed child.

She had to wait two more days until Dona Guilhermina, relieved of having to chaperone and nurse Margaret around the
clock, was in Rio preparing Francisca's new home for her arrival.

Lucretia sat on Margaret's bed and dipped pineapple slices into
honey. "Try one," she encouraged.

Margaret held one in her mouth and sucked.

"It won't do any good unless you swallow."

Margaret fanned her mouth. "It burns. My throat is still so
raw."

"Maybe a banana?" Nell offered. "They were picked ripe, just
down by that rock wall near the front gate."

"I'll try."

"Dona Guilhermina says that we are the best medicine of all
. . . that you ate nothing until we arrived," Nell boasted.

"It's true. Every day I feel slightly better. If only these rashes
would disappear; but as soon as they clear up in one spot, they
move to another."

"Your face is almost perfect again, and your hands are looking
better," Nell said cheerfully.

"The Larsons are bringing the doctor back with them this afternoon. Perhaps he'll have more good news," Lucretia added.

Florinda asked if she could clear the plates. Small portions of a
dozen fruits, two kinds of soup, bread and butter, corn pudding,
and a prune dessert littered the dresser and bedside table. Lucretia kept the sweets and told Florinda she could take the rest.

"Nell," Margaret asked, "do you like Rio and Boa Vista?"

"I haven't seen *anything!*" Nell complained, then caught herself. "Not yet, but we will, won't we, Mother?"

"As soon as Margaret's well."

"Mother, you don't have to sit with me day and night. I always
sleep in the afternoons anyway. Why don't you and Nell do
something together? Erik's told me there's a beautiful view

nearby, the Alto da Boa Vista, and there's a waterfall in the Tijuca Forest. He's promised me a picnic there when Francisca comes home."

Lucretia was delighted with how well this fitted in with her own plans. "Are you certain?"

"Absolutely. The Larsons took the carriage to town, but there's always a smaller one-horse charrette here that the servants take to the market. Florinda . . ."

Florinda's hands were filled with china. "Sim, Dona Margarida?"

"Who drives the charrette?"

"Aldemar."

"Ask him to take my mother and sister to the Alto."

"Sim, senhora."

"Good. Now I'll be able to rest without wondering if I'm being force-fed in my sleep!"

❧ ❧ ❧

"Isn't it beautiful?" Nell stared dreamily across the splendid view of the narrow valley. Thin cascades of falling water wetted the ragged spurs of grey rock.

Anxious to get on with her real mission, Lucretia barely noticed the lush surroundings. "Very nice." She walked toward the carriage as a signal to Nell.

Petulantly, Nell followed her mother and got into the carriage.

"Hotel Parque Panorama," Lucretia said to the driver.

"Aren't we going to the waterfall in Tijuca?"

"I'm desperate for a cool drink, aren't you? There's supposed to be a very nice hotel nearby."

As the horses rounded the next bend, the mountains closed in on each side. The palms and tropical vegetation sprouting from the rock buttresses drew so close to the vehicle that it would have been an easy matter to pluck a pink blossom or pull a gossamer fern by merely stretching out an arm. Then, suddenly, as though a door had been flung wide open, a valley unfolded before them, complete with a view of Rio's bay far in the distance.

"Oh, Mother . . . look! It's a sight that only birds ever see. Doesn't it almost hurt to take in so much at once?"

For a moment Nell's enthusiasm distracted Lucretia. She took the time to admire the wonderment in her daughter's eyes. Had she ever perceived the world with such unbridled joy?

A few more miles down the mountain the carriage turned into a rutted lane. Many years earlier, the Parque Panorama, cantilevered on a rocky ledge to take advantage of a breathtaking view, was a wonder of design and construction. Wealthy travelers between Rio, Petrópolis, and other mountain resorts must have found it an elegant stopping point. Clearly those days were over.

From the end of the drive the slanted building appeared less formidable than a child's tower of blocks. The only attempt to maintain what had once been extensive gardens was to keep the narrow roadway from becoming reabsorbed by the forest itself. Several of the posts that supported the verandah roof had been destroyed by voracious insects. A few thin boards had been propped as a brace by a somewhat wishful handyman.

"Is this the right place?" Nell asked hesitantly. "They probably don't even have a restaurant. Don't you think we should take our coffee back at Boa Vista?"

"No, Nell, I don't. You wait here while I go inside."

"But Mother . . ."

"Nell!"

Lucretia ducked under a broken sign, crossed the rotted porch, and entered the dark central hallway where a few tables were littered with old whiskey and beer bottles. "Alô!" she called into the back room.

"Estou chegando," a rough voice answered. "I'm coming." After a few loud bumps and groans, a man stumbled into the room. Lucretia couldn't help but notice that he had just fastened on his wooden leg without bothering to roll down his pants to cover the apparatus. The man was equally surprised to see the unescorted North American lady. "The senhora wants a room?"

"Não, obrigada. I've come to see the child of Senhor Larson."

He coughed and sputtered. "The child?"

"The child's not here?"

"Sim, but of course. It's only a matter of which child."

Lucretia wondered if her awkward Portuguese was the trouble. "The child of Senhor Erico Larson," she said as crisply as possible.

The man scratched his stained muslin shirt. "I'll get my daughter, Isabel."

"Isabel da Silva?"

"Sim, the mother."

"There must be some mistake."

The man went up the uncarpeted stairs, his wooden leg banging against each hollow step.

Lucretia took a seat in the nearest chair and tried to compose herself. How could Erik's daughter live in a place like this? Certainly a hotel in such disrepair could only attract the poorest of itinerants. Looking around, she saw the remnants of better times in the tulip wall sconces and broken chandeliers. What once must have been a ballroom or dining area was partitioned into smaller rooms, but even the dividers were made of cloth and paper, not wood. What worried her even more was the possibility that Isabel was the mother of Astrid. If that was so, then the story about Erik marrying a Swedish girl was a deliberate fabrication.

"I am Isabel da Silva, senhora. How may I help you?" The girl's voice was sweet and deferential, but her large brown eyes stared with an unexpected self-assurance.

For a moment Lucretia was speechless. Isabel was not the middle-aged maternal nursemaid she'd expected but a tall, cocoa-colored young mulatto woman dressed immaculately in a long white cotton dress with a crocheted border and waist. Her father, following close behind, was waiting to hear what the foreign lady wanted.

"I'm a friend of the Larson family," Lucretia said as she stood. "I would like to see Senhor Erico's child."

"Little Astrid?" Isabel's voice was stronger than Lucretia's and her bearing more formidable.

"Astrid, sim."

"This time of day she sleeps for several hours. She cries much if awakened."

"No mother likes to awaken a child." Lucretia waited a few beats. "You are the mother, then?"

"Oh, no!"

Why did she have so much trouble with the language? This should all be so simple. "The man ... Your father ... said ..."

Turning swiftly to where her father stood in the doorway chewing a cigar butt, Isabel asked, "What stupidity did you say now?"

He spit on the floor. "É verdade! I only tell the truth. You are the mother of Erico's children, are you not? And the milk mother of the blond one, too, I might add."

"You wish to see my children?"

"I suppose so," Lucretia replied in a dry, raspy voice.

"The older children are in the back. Would you care to follow me?" Isabel led the way through the hotel's kitchen, now abandoned to a rooster and his flock, across a smelly passageway and a hard-packed dirt courtyard where wash lay on bricks, drying in the sun. They passed through a wing where sparse but tidy guest rooms — each containing a bed, sturdy side table with candleholder, and washstand — opened onto an atrium. Finally, they reached the family's quarters. An obese black woman was stirring a pot of onions and beans over an open fire.

"Crianças!" Isabel called out the back door and clapped her hands.

"Mamãe?" called a curly-headed ragamuffin who ran into the house and buried his nose in her skirt. The boy of five or six was naked except for a long shirt that came to his knees.

Self-consciously, Isabel kissed the top of the child's head. "Senhora, this is Xavier, my son."

An older girl of about seven or eight stood shyly in the doorway. She was dressed in a pale rose shift of good-quality cloth and design; her black hair was braided neatly and trimmed with matching pink ribbons. The child's skin color was not as dark as her mother's or younger brother's. It was merely the faintest cinnamon tan. Lucretia was stunned by the girl's regular, European features. The set of her eyes was the same as Erik's; their color was unmistakably the warm chocolate color of her mother's.

"Come here and meet the senhora."

The girl hid behind her mother during the introduction. "Minha filha, Eulalia."

Lucretia willed herself calm. If what she guessed was true, it could irrevocably alter her daughter's future. "These . . . are your children?"

Isabel bowed her head. "Sim, senhora."

"And Senhor Erico's children?"

"Sim."

"And Astrid? Is she older or younger than little Xavier?"

"Younger by more than a year, although Astrid already is taller."

Now Lucretia began to understand. The stridency left her voice. "How fortunate that Astrid had you when her own mother died."

Though wary, Isabel had no real reason to distrust the foreign lady.

"You still had milk for the little girl?"

"For a while I fed the two. Now I just have Astrid."

"You still feed her?"

Isabel shrugged. "When she needs it, mostly to sleep."

"Mother . . ." Nell said, coming into the room. "Mother . . . I was worried . . ."

In English, Lucretia spoke rapidly, "Nell, go back and wait for me as you've been told."

Nell knew enough to obey instantly but wondered what was so secretive about the grimy servants' quarters of the hotel.

When Nell had gone, Isabel asked, "Shall I get Astrid, then?"

"Não é necessário. When does she come to Boa Vista again?"

"When Senhor Erico asks. Usually on Sundays, but not lately. There is sickness in the house. The father doesn't permit the child around sickness. I keep her perfect." Isabel's soft brown eyes hardened momentarily, and Lucretia could see the protective feeling the woman had for Erik's daughter.

❧ ❧ ❧

The carriage zigzagged down the narrow road carved from a ledge of rock, the horse gaining speed after every turn. Nell seemed excited by the closeness of the wheels to the precipitous edge, but Lucretia's terror sprung from an internal cleft far more treacherous. When they arrived at Boa Vista, she was in such turmoil that she sent Nell to sit with Margaret and went directly to her room.

"Senhora Claiborne?" Guilhermina asked softly at the door. "May I talk with you?"

Lucretia let her in.

"You've been to the Parque Panorama?" she began. Lucretia felt a rush of relief when Erik's mother opened the subject of Isabel first.

"As a mother of a daughter myself, I understand completely. As someone who's come to care very much for Margaret, I have worried about this matter."

"Then you see how impossible it would be for her," Lucretia said. Tears spilled down her bony cheeks. "I don't know how to tell her; she's been so ill."

"Why tell her at all?"

"Secrets like this cannot be kept forever."

"Perhaps not forever, but later, when she and Erik are married, she'll understand so much more about men."

Lucretia's voice became high and shrill. "Do you think my daughter would ever understand that her husband has had children with a brown-skinned native woman?"

"In Brazil these things are thought of quite differently than in your country perhaps. My husband and I felt it was better for a young man to have one woman, not many. It's safer for the man — not so many difficulties, diseases, you know? Both of Isabel's children are his; that alone speaks well of the woman. And that there have been no children since Astrid speaks well of my son. If he marries again, I'm certain he will be the model husband he was with poor Gunilla."

Lucretia calmed slightly. "I don't understand why you don't have your granddaughter living with you."

"The child is so attached to Isabel that we wanted to wait until she'd have a new mother who could take her place."

"But a child that age not even being weaned!"

Guilhermina smiled wryly. "You must make allowances for a motherless child."

"I think you're more interested in Astrid's future than my daughter's."

Guilhermina's eyes narrowed. Aware of exactly how much was at stake in this conversation, she needed to form her words precisely. "Only you know what is best for your daughter. I can truthfully tell you that my son has never given his heart to any woman the way he has to Margarida. From what I've seen, she feels much the same for him. Once she is well and strong, their future looks as bright as that for any two young people I've ever known. We have a saying in our country: 'Marry equal; marry well.' Don't you think that applies to your daughter and my son?" Guilhermina added cagily. She guessed that Lucretia could not help being flattered at being considered equal to someone with her obvious status and wealth.

"Yes, I see what you mean."

"I only wish my Francisca could have been so fortunate as to make a love match." Guilhermina sighed loudly. "Perhaps there is a better life for Margaret where you live?" She paused and watched the other mother.

Lucretia was thinking about Margaret's prospects in Lizzie-land. If the truth were told, Nelson Cable's own reputation was not that impeccable either. Every man was a compromise of one sort or the other. Even Senhora Larson admitted as much about her daughter's alliance. Not even her own beloved Charles was without his considerable faults. At least this Larson boy was not about to lead her daughter into the same economic ruin for which the rest of the Claibornes seemed destined. Whether she chose to admit it or not, this was Margaret's best chance.

She looked over at Dona Guilhermina's benevolent face. Just a crease of a smile was forming on her wide lips. She was a good, kindly woman who'd nursed Margaret back to health. This was a family that took good care of its own. Erik, too, seemed to have inherited a generous streak that could prove valuable someday. "Do you think your son — and the others — could be trusted not to tell her anything?"

"I will personally guarantee that everyone will be discreet in this matter." Guilhermina's smile broadened.

"And Erik?"

"I know just what to say to him."

"He must end his alliance with that woman completely, of course."

"That is understood."

"But the two children . . ."

"He's always met his responsibilities. They'll be looked after properly." Guilhermina reached out to Lucretia and kissed her on both cheeks. "You worry about helping our Margarida recover completely. I'll manage the rest."

❧ 7 On the day of Francisca's homecoming Margaret was still too weak to consider making the journey to town for the welcoming luncheon at Flamengo. Her legs were so rubbery that they could not support her weight, even though she had lost so many pounds that she feared her expensive Louisiana gowns would hang limply from her shoulders. Dr. Bandeira was more concerned about the ghostly hollows under her eyes, the signs of dehydration on her skin, and her visual problems that, thankfully, were receding. Blindness or permanent lameness, not unknown side effects of these fevers, would have been an especially tragic burden for the talented young woman. On his most recent visit, he had ordered that each day Margaret should be carried down to a hammock hung between the verandah posts beside the rock garden. Sunshine and fresh air circulating through the crocheted mesh was the prescription to aid the healing of her skin eruptions, while herbal drinks and rice puddings were ordered to help her regain her strength.

After being settled in her hammock, Margaret was usually devoid of any ambition. She spent the hours listening to trilling birds, smelling the ripening fruits, watching flower petals drift in the wind, pleased just to be able to do so. At first her world was a blur of vivid colors, a life-size palette of an indiscriminate artist, but each day a few new details sharpened until even the vibrations of the hummingbirds were thrillingly distinct. In an hour or so, the lulling breezes would rock the hammock just enough to coax Margaret into a short nap before being awakened to sample Florinda's familiar tray of tempting foods. The great waves of nausea and pounding head pains came less frequently. She ate better and seemed to be recovering slowly but uneventfully.

After everyone had gone to town to greet Francisca, she expected to be especially lonely. Even her mother and Nell had joined the celebrations.

"You must go," Margaret had insisted. "I want you both to meet Francisca. I'm only going to doze and eat, doze and eat."

"If you really won't mind . . ." Lucretia was eager to meet more of the Larsons' family and friends.

"Sometimes all this attention tires me more than it helps. And Nellie needs the change. Being my nursemaid hasn't been any fun for her."

"Don't worry about that!" Lucretia stroked the braid that cascaded down Margaret's neck. A small sheaf of hair fell out into her hand. She tried to hide it, but Margaret noticed. Without warning, Margaret began to cry. The hair loss that had come with the high fevers had worried her more than she'd admitted. Fortunately, longer strands from the crown covered the bald areas on the back of her head.

"Maybe we ought to stay?" Nell asked worriedly.

"She's just overtired . . . Rest is the best cure." Lucretia kissed Margaret's tear-stained cheek. "We'll be back after dark. Florinda will help you to bed this evening."

Partially because of her throbbing joints, partially because of her seclusion, Margaret had sobbed herself to sleep. The breeze rocked her slight form in the hammock like a cocoon on a twig. When she woke, she believed she was in the middle of the most wondrous of dreams. Erik was bending close to her, his wide hands firmly holding her shoulders. "Margarida, minha querida . . ."

She blinked several times before she believed he was really there.

"Francisca's day . . . Why aren't you at Flamengo?"

"No one will ever miss me as long as I'm back for dinner."

A great swelling of happiness shot through her, giving her body more strength than she'd had in weeks. Margaret flung her arms around Erik's waist and pulled him down to her. He sniffed deeply at her neck and kissed her cheek where the faintest blush of the rash still remained. Margaret held him tightly against her, and instead of pulling out of the contorted position, Erik lowered himself to his knees and remained bent over the hammock that cradled his beloved.

Margaret loosened her grasp and looked down at where he was kneeling on a mosaic of red and white tiles. "You can't be comfortable. Bring that chair over to this side and sit with me."

When his back was turned, Margaret rearranged the thin cotton quilt that protected her modesty.

"Do you realize how long it's been since we've been alone together?" He remembered the stolen moment when he'd touched
her as she slept and felt not only a guilt pang but sexually
stirred.

Margaret's face was wreathed in an enigmatic smile. "We're
not completely alone. Florinda comes by here every half-hour to
check me or feed me."

"Not today," he winked suggestively.

Margaret's eyes widened.

"I took the opportunity to speak with your mother this morning before Francisca arrived," he began nervously. "I took her to
my father's orchid garden so we could be alone. It seemed the
perfect place to ask her permission."

"And?"

"I like your mother very much, she's a very good ... a
very" — he searched for the word — "sensible woman." Now it
became more difficult for Erik to continue with what he'd
planned to say. That morning he'd promised Lucretia that he'd
never tell Margaret about Isabel. At first he'd argued, but believing that she knew her own daughter best, he'd agreed to her demands.

"She won't object?"

"No, but she won't officially speak for your father."

"Will she send for him?"

"Our mothers agree it's best not to wait much longer. In Rio all
the families know each other. Without a wedding in the near future, the gossip will begin, words that could harm you and my
family for many years to come."

"Who'd want to harm us with idle words?"

Erik shrugged. "I can't be responsible for the small minds of
others, but I know from experience the hurt that sharp tongues
can inflict. If you are willing, and if you are strong enough, the
priest from the local chapel will begin your instruction tomorrow.
Then . . ." He bent over and kissed her on her cracked lips. "We'll
marry sometime next week."

"Next week?" Margaret tried not to let him see her fear.
"We've planned nothing . . ."

"We'll have a very simple ceremony and postpone the reception until you are completely well. Once we are united in the

church, we can be together freely. That's what I desire with all my heart!"

Margaret's throat felt painfully dry. "My mother consented to a wedding next week?"

"Only if you agree. She said all she wants is your happiness."

A bitter taste rose in Margaret's mouth. Mother'd only wanted her happiness when she'd forced her to stay behind in New Orleans, leaving her orphaned for nine years; she'd only wanted her happiness when she'd aborted her musical career and summoned her to Lizzieland, tried to marry her off to the first ignorant colonist who'd have her; she'd only wanted her happiness when she'd sent her to Rio to be stalked by a bandit and felled by a virulent fever. If it weren't for Erik ... She looked up into his brilliant blue eyes and saw the clearest reflection of concern for her. She wished she knew what he was thinking.

Thankfully, she would never know. Torn by his promise to her mother and his desire to open himself completely to Margaret, he was in a final struggle of conscience. Lucretia had told him about her visit to Isabel. He'd denied nothing. She'd asked him to remove Astrid before the marriage and to have no further contact with Isabel. He'd understood all Lucretia's points. It was enough to ask Margaret to raise Astrid, who couldn't be helped, but to flaunt two mulatto children, the constant evidence of an illicit alliance, in front of his bride might destroy any faith Margaret had ever had in him. It was the difference, she'd explained, the difference between the way Brazilians and North Americans saw these things.

"I know my own daughter best," she'd said over and over. A mother did ... didn't she? Erik ached to do the right thing.

Finally Margaret spoke in a raspy whisper. "I can barely walk; you might have to carry me to the altar."

"Gladly." He brushed his lips on the rosy palms. "So beautiful, like a flower ..."

The lilies swaying near the pond caught her eye and she laughed. "Perhaps more like one of those ... How do you say in Portuguese?"

Erik saw the spotted tiger lilies she meant and chuckled. "Lírio-tigrino. Which are you, the tiger or the lily?"

"After we're married, then you shall see!"

Erik cradled her head in the crook of his arm. He stroked her forehead, her cheeks, her neck, the cleft above her breasts, and murmured endearments. Margaret leaned toward him. She moaned involuntarily.

"What is it? Have I hurt you?"

"No. It's just that everything aches whenever I move in the slightest direction."

With extreme gentleness, Erik cupped his arm around Margaret's shoulder, then, with fingertips only, caressed her arm. "Does that bother you?"

The tightness around her mouth had softened. "Not at all. It feels wonderful, as though you are lifting the soreness with your fingers."

Kissing her cheek, Erik spoke close to her ear. "Let me heal you." He stroked her other arm in the same delicate manner, his forearm brushing her breasts. Though Margaret could have complained, she remained perfectly still, trying to absorb the pleasant sensations that whirled within. When she'd first become ill, so many once-ignored places in her body had swelled and ached, she'd been forced into the exquisite self-awareness that pain induced. Now, as Erik touched her, she began to perceive another world of feelings that replaced torment with something equally mysterious, equally intense.

Opening her eyes, she saw that Erik had removed the coverlet and was staring at the curves of her body that were easily visible through the sheer gown. Even though a brief wave of shame washed over her, she didn't protest. Erik's face had been completely transformed. Instead of the capricious charmer, she saw a man so earnest that if she hadn't just felt his gentleness, she might have been frightened. His hooded half-closed eyes had darkened to the color of a stormy sea; his brow furrowed, his nostrils flared with every breath, and his lips had thinned to a tense line. Unnerved by his expression, Margaret looked out at the garden. A bright butterfly folded back its wings and dipped bravely into a lily trumpet that seemed to swallow it whole. She concentrated on watching its escape instead of thinking about what Erik was doing. He methodically massaged her right leg, from ruddy-soled foot to yielding thigh. Finally he slid his hand between her legs.

Not a word was spoken. Erik kneeled beside the hammock and

placed his head on Margaret's chest. Reaching down, she felt the soft curls of his hair tangle under her fingers. She idly made semicircles at the nape of his neck while he, proving his experience in the matter, mirrored her movements as he parted her secret lips with trembling fingers.

All at once Margaret lost the terrifying feeling of helplessness she'd had during the illness. Blood surged through her body, reminding her what it had been like to feel strong and well. Without flinching in pain, she pulled her knees up and allowed — no, insisted — Erik do whatever would sustain the mounting craving that welled up unexpectedly. Sensing her urgency, his fingers concentrated on moving while he kissed the soft mounds of her rash-dappled breasts, then licked their raspberry tips with abandon. If Margaret dared speak aloud, she would have asked him to go faster, to suck harder, but he stayed at his own relentless pace. In the last shattering moment, she opened her eyes long enough to see Erik's mask of concentration before clinging to him to keep from being swept away by the terrifyingly new force that had lain dormant within her until this sorcerer had broken the spell and freed it forever.

❧ Part II ❧
ERIK
1901-1905
❧

Beyond the equator, everything is permitted.
— fifteenth-century Portuguese sailors' motto

Black Powder

1 "It was a mistake. Buying this house was a terrible mistake," Erik railed. He stormed into the upstairs sitting room and stared out the rain-streaked windows. "The streets are the worst they've ever been."

Sitting at the table, dressed immaculately in a tight lace bodice and tailored skirt, Margaret knew that as soon as her husband had something to eat, he'd be more reasonable. "You love this house as much as I do," she said in a conciliatory voice. "How were we to know that Oswaldo Cruz would begin his sanitary reforms on our doorstep?" She looked dolefully at the fomenting skies and the flooded plaza across from their home.

Since dawn that morning, gangs of chanting workers had begun repairing the damage that the overnight storm had brought to the waterfront improvement project. Their once tranquil view of the exclusive Largo da Gloria's promenade of royal palms and bougainvillea had turned to ugly mounds of sludge. Swamps were being drained and filled, roadways, parks, and promenades built, causing great inconvenience over an extended period of time.

"The mud on our doorstep is already a foot thick!" Erik's cup clattered as it touched the saucer. "How do they expect anyone to live here?"

She passed a platter to Erik. "Have a sweet roll, darling."

He bit into the yeasty pastry. "You're not eating anything this morning?"

"No, I might take communion."

"Will you need the carriage today?"

"No, I don't think so," Margaret replied sweetly. "So don't risk the Protos in the mud." She referred to their elegant German automobile, a fourth anniversary gift from Erik's parents.

"Then how will you get to mass or to Francisca's?"

"Tomorrow will do as well."

"Don't disappoint her," Erik replied firmly. "With the new baby it's more difficult for her to come to you."

"Please send my regrets home with Augusto."

"Augusto won't be at the fábrica today. He's already left for Pernambuco."

"You've sent him to buy cotton himself?"

"He's gone with Father twice, the price has been set, so there's not much damage he can do. I, for one, think the responsibility will be good for him."

"Your father doesn't?"

"I'm trying to make him see that Augusto won't become useful until he feels he has some authority."

Margaret sighed. "Yes, but Augusto has never shown the slightest . . ."

"Minha querida . . ." he cut her off. "Francisca will be alone for many days now. Why don't you ride downtown with me? Then Severino can take you to her house in Catete."

"But . . ."

"You wouldn't even have to miss your morning practice. You've said yourself how much you admire the tone of Francisca's piano."

"Very well." Margaret went to gather her music.

❧   ❧   ❧

As they rode to the factory in the closed carriage, Erik stared at his wife. He openly admired the straightness of her back and the optimistic, slightly defiant thrust of her dimpled chin. That the first years of their marriage had not been as perfect as he might have designed was unfortunate, but neither of them could be blamed. Only God could give them the child they both craved; he certainly had done his part in the matter. Feeling contrite for being so difficult earlier, he made a suggestion he knew would please her. "I have time to escort you to communion."

The rains had finally stopped and the wet streets were shimmering in sunlight. On the hill directly in front of them, the whitewashed exterior dome of Nossa Senhora da Gloria do Outeiro, Our Lady of Gloria on the Hill, sparkled brightly. Margaret squeezed her husband's hand. "I'd like that."

Erik directed the driver to take them to the picturesque chapel where they had been married. Since the road to the top was steep and narrow, the carriage stopped at the base of the incline. Erik helped Margaret into the cog railway's tiny compartment, offering her a seat along the side. As usual, he chose to stand by the front window and stare out at the two iron rails that angled sharply to the crest. The car jerked forward. Erik appreciated the engineering that had gone into such a simple yet practical machine. When they neared the halfway point, the descending weight box went under them between the tracks. "It always amazes me," he said, "that all this is operated with one cable."

Grimacing at the grating noise, Margaret squeezed her eyes shut.

"How many times do I have to tell you there's nothing to fear? Those ratchets will prevent the car from rolling back, even if the cable were to break."

"I believe you, I always do." Margaret forced a tight smile.

The car stopped with a jerk. Erik took Margaret's arm and steered her around the wheel house. Almost reverently, he looked back over his shoulder at the cable spool and modern electric motor. "Beautiful machine," he said under his breath.

The wind on the high stone piazza whipped Margaret's skirt between her legs. Memories of a blowing veil and a shaky bride touched Erik. His own sentimentality surprised him sometimes. "Do you remember how it was the day we were married?"

"Only that it was so difficult just to stand upright beside you . . . Also, the pain in my legs when we kneeled for the prayers. Without my mother and sister supporting me, I could never have survived that day."

"We should've waited until you were stronger."

"No, I'm glad we didn't." Margaret looked up at the small octagonal church. "It's still my favorite, like a crowning jewel to the hill. No wonder the imperial family worshiped here."

A loud explosion shook the treetops. Erik rushed over to the eastern view and looked toward the sea. "Veja! It's not far from our house." He pointed toward some rising smoke. "They're blasting for the canal."

"If we'd known, I could've had the windows sealed!" Margaret moaned.

"Progress. In another year every swamp will have been drained, all the sewage will be removed with underground pipes."

Margaret pointed to the saffron dust cloud blowing rapidly inland. "It will be over our house in minutes."

Ignoring the ravaged streets and massive construction that made their miniature palace appear to be floundering in a churning brown sea, Erik sighed. "If it weren't for this mess, our house would be the most exquisite one in Rio."

The church bell tolled eight. Erik took Margaret's hand and led her into the cool vestibule, its eight walls lined with Portuguese blue-and-white azulejo tiles representing Old Testament scenes. Together they entered the sanctuary, genuflected, crossed themselves. After the mass, they approached the high altar. Margaret knelt before the image of the Virgin robed like a fashionable lady in silks and laces and festooned with precious stones, gifts from generous devotees. An immense diamond brooch, vowed to the Virgin by the consort of the Prince of Joinville after the restoration of her highness's health, sparkled on her breast. The flowing curls that clustered around Our Lady's brow were also offerings — clipped by anxious mothers from the locks of ailing children.

Margaret stood shakily. Erik followed her to the vestry in the rear of the church where the ex votos, wax representations of diseased limbs, hands, and eyes that needed curing, were placed around a more modest altar. Erik grimaced at what he considered a pagan custom, but one that all the women in his family seemed to embrace. Under several large wax legs, he spied the infant model his mother had given Margaret. When she touched it, the heavy dust from it smearing her fingers, Erik winced. "Come, it's time to . . ."

"One last prayer." Margaret knelt again.

As Margaret whispered her pleas to the Virgin, Erik wished, with all his heart, that her prayers would be answered. Dr. Bandeira had warned him that the dengue fever had left Margaret very weak. He'd listened to the doctor's counsel and had made certain not to overtax Margaret physically the first few months of their marriage. Hadn't he taken her home to Flamengo after the wedding, put her to bed with only gentle kisses and tender words? What other husband would have shown such restraint? When he'd finally thought her well enough, he'd worshiped her body. The sweetness of their first year together could almost be tasted. Suddenly Erik remembered where he was. He placed his arm around his wife guiltily and led her from the church.

❧ ❧ ❧

Erik rushed into his father's wharfside office in the textile plant later than usual. "I went to church with Margaret," he explained hastily.

Sven Larson lifted one of his bushy grey eyebrows. "Again?"

"At least she let me take her to Gloria this time. Last week she insisted we drive all the way to Nossa Senhora da Pena in the Barra da Tijuca because Mother'd told her that Our Lady of the Pen had had much success with barrenness."

"Who'd have guessed that your Protestant bride would've become so devout?"

"These days she needs a strong belief."

"Better leave that to the women. With Augusto in the nordeste, and Diniz going to Santos tomorrow, you're required here."

Erik cloaked his irritation. "If we left babies to the women entirely, the problem would never right itself, would it?"

Abruptly, Sven changed the subject. "These are last year's figures for export revenues. Compare them to the first three months of this year and bring me a report on the reason for the unexpected decline."

"I thought we were going to go over the designs for the new looms."

"Perhaps we'd better reconsider the expansion."

"You know I'm better with equipment than accounts."

Sven Larson started to speak severely, but his obvious love for his boyish, often impetuous son undermined his harshness. "I want you to know everything that's happening and why." He pointed to the minuscule numbers on the page in front of him. "Most of the answers are right here. Find them!"

Erik rolled the long ledger sheets into a tube, telescoped the papers, then peered through one end. "I'll look into it," he teased.

❧ ❧ ❧

In his own office above the vibrating looms, Erik enjoyed his panoramic view of the harbor, as good as one from a captain's bridge. It made up for the incessant clamor of the machines below. A skinny black boy dressed in clean white shorts and a bright yellow shirt brought him a cup of coffee. Erik rubbed Americo's small head affectionately. "How goes it, Rico?"

"Tudo bom, Seu Erico." Rico placed the cup on the senhor's desk and glanced curiously at the scratchy numbers on the papers.

"Can you read that?" Erik asked.

"Leio um pouco, senhor."

"Do you still study in the evenings?"

"I try, senhor, but sometimes I fall asleep."

"Bom, Rico. Someday, if you learn to read, you can have a job at a desk like Seu Vicente, my secretary, or Seu Adherbal who knows all about money, which is so important, right?"

"Sim, Seu Erico. Anything else?" Rico asked, knowing full well his weekly errand came next.

"The flower market is open today?"

"Sim, senhor, it's Wednesday."

Erik took some change from his pockets. "Buy the largest bouquet for my wife."

Grinning from ear to ear, Rico ran down the stairs two at a time. Every week the senhor bought flowers from Rico's widowed mother. If he hurried, he could be back just as Seu Erico would be ready for his second cup of cafezinho. Seu Erico liked one about every hour, and Rico attempted always to be on time.

Erik smiled after Rico. He's such a good lad. I must remember to do something about getting him in school for at least a few hours a day. He turned to the distasteful paperwork, making notes on each column total, then comparing the figures month by month. Though Erik didn't care for desk work, he attacked it with the same systematic approach he used on any task — from organizing his collection of starched linen collars and cuffs in his bureau drawer to ordering wines for his cellar. In this, at least, he took after his father.

One of Sven Larson's first jobs in Brazil had been supervising commodity exports with the British investment firm of Sullivan and McClellan. He shone at the job because of the meticulous research he brought to his investment decisions. In the 1860s, when the War Between the States effectively eliminated the North Americans as a source of raw cotton for European markets, Larson had personally invested in cotton to the extent of providing improved seed and credit to local planters. At the height of the Brazilian cotton boom, Larson was riding the peak with private holdings that yielded fifty thousand tons a year.

Unlike his British counterparts, Larson propitiously predicted that the end of the North American war would curtail the wild profits. Instead of reinvesting in other crops, he began importing textile machinery and built factories to produce finished goods, figuring that with Brazil's cheap labor he could still undercut prices for fabric on the world market. When the cotton bust came as predicted, Larson, by his crucial maneuverings, had avoided losing any money. This coup not only was the foundation of his vast personal fortune but won Larson the deep respect of Rio's financial community. The Swede had done everything correctly — dealt honorably in business, even married into the right family, thus launching himself into society as well.

Now, as Erik scanned the thick ledgers, he realized that although they were shipping more finished goods each month, the cost for the raw cotton was higher but the price on the world market was lower, making the profit margin slim indeed. The biggest earnings were being shown in the few retail outlets that they had opened the previous year. Named Casas Margaridas because Margaret had been the first to suggest that the goods from the Larson mills should be available locally, the textile stores had proven unexpectedly successful.

Is this what his father had been wanting him to see? Surely a few more outlets in other cities would do as well. He could almost imagine a Casa Margarida, with its bright yellow daisy symbol, in every Brazilian town. Bolts of hammock plaids, fine mosquito netting, and ordinary dress cottons lined up in sturdy stalls on every market street. Why, they could expand indefinitely all over Brazil!

After a few additional calculations, Erik realized that they'd never be able to fill the stores without a dramatic increase in production, straining the limits of the current factory. Conservatively, they'd have to double the size of the plant, order new machinery from Europe, and expand to the second wharf that was currently leased to Lloyd Brasileiro Shipping. By the time Rico had served the fourth cup of coffee, Erik's mind had raced years ahead into his own prosperous industrial future.

2 "Campinas, Ribeirão Prêto, Araraquara, Rio Claro, Limeira . . ." Sven Larson circled cities on the map of Brazil that he'd laid out on the long mahogany table in his office. "All centers of the coffee market, all good prospects."

"What about Taubaté, São José dos Campos, Mauá?"

"They're secondary towns, but also possibilities. You'll have to check them out for yourself and give me a full analysis." Sven clipped the end of a fresh cigar and fumbled for matches.

Erik handed his father a box from his pocket, then formulated his words with care. "You expect me to travel to all those cities?"

"Who else? Your classmate Diniz is well trained, but it's always preferable to have a family member handle the transactions. And when you return, you'll go north to Salvador, Recife, possibly all the way to Natal and Fortaleza."

"That will take months, maybe a full year."

"Gigo, this is your idea and I believe you have developed a viable, if not brilliant, scheme." Sven paused to check the effect of his praise, a device he used infrequently but shrewdly. For some reason his son was not responding as he'd expected.

"Who would take over my responsibilities in the plant?"

"You've organized everything so well that the machines run themselves. We've two Swedish mechanics already and I can easily hire a third, but who else can I trust to make the proper judgments on store locations, to negotiate fair terms? . . . Surely not . . ." Diplomatically, he didn't mention the name of his son-in-law.

Though he knew he was right, Erik wondered how his father could expect him to leave his wife. The doctor had just recommended a long summer vacation at Boa Vista, suggesting that time away from the confusion of the waterfront construction might help Margaret to conceive.

Sven strolled to the windows that overlooked the port. Dockhands were loading bales of cotton onto a German freighter. Smiling mischievously, he remembered receiving the valuable wharfside property as part of his wife's dowry. *Pity we didn't have more sons, though; the business has grown too large for only one.* He spoke perfunctorily so that Erik wouldn't realize that he'd just had a fresh thought. "I thought Margarida might enjoy a change. Astrid could stay with us and you two could have a long trip, the kind you should've had after your wedding. We've many fine friends in that region, the Schmidts, the Ludwigs, the Krausses. You'd be very comfortable in their homes and on their fazendas."

As soon as he'd included Margaret in the plan, his son brightened perceptibly.

Erik kept his excitement under control. "Very well, I'll discuss it with Margaret. If nothing else, I need to get her out of that house until the blasting is finished."

"Good." Sven crushed his cigar and put his arm around his son. He walked him to the door. "One more thing. Does Margarida still see Chiquinha often?"

"Almost every day."

Sven stopped to run his fingers across his balding head. "What does she say?"

"I think I've heard more than enough about little Emilia's every gurgle."

Nodding knowingly, Sven smiled. "When it's your own, it's different. Still, I'm worried. Chiquinha hasn't been home to lunch with your mother since the baby was born and your mother says that even when she goes over to Catete to visit, your sister never bothers to dress."

"Maybe with Augusto away so frequently . . ."

A shadow crossed Sven's face. "It's better that way."

"I don't understand."

"Too many babies, too soon."

"I would have thought the babies would have brought her more happiness."

Sven pounded his fist in his hand, but remained silent.

Both men stood quietly, thinking their own angry thoughts about a past that could never be changed.

"Do you think Augusto knows about Francisca?"

Sven raised his palms to the ceiling. "His father brought it up several times when we were negotiating the marriage settlement."

"Meu Deus!" Erik roared. "It's all so unfair."

Sven gave his son a tight abraço. "Basta de tolices! Enough of this nonsense, eh? If your new stores are a success, I'll give you full control of them."

"Father! You give your word?"

"It will all be yours in the end." He threw up his hands. "Margarida will agree, won't she?"

"Certainly she will," Erik answered, hoping that for once he'd figured her right.

❧   ❧   ❧

Severino opened the front door for his employer. "Boa tarde, Seu Erico."

Erik preferred all his servants to use the provincial abbreviation "seu" instead of the more formal "senhor" that his parents' retainers used. He'd tried to run his own household with grace and style, though he'd eliminated much of the pretension he'd been brought up with. After all, these people were employees, not slaves; they lived in a republic, not a monarchy. He'd always been proud that his father had never owned a slave. Such an idea had been anathema to the young Swede, who on his marriage day had granted manumission to those his wife still retained. Erik's own servants, ten in their house (eleven, if you counted Florinda's eldest daughter, Carlota, who now earned a few coins for work in the laundry), were younger, perhaps lazier, than his parents', but he and Margaret were content.

Eager, as usual, to see his wife, Erik bounded up the spiraling marble staircase, the showpiece of the house, two steps at a time. Just thinking of her welcoming smile and what would soon follow always spurred him back to the Gloria district as soon as he could respectably leave the textile mill.

Erik loved what Margaret had done to restore and decorate their home. It had been designed by the German architect Gustav Waehneldt in 1858 for an eccentric mistress of an Amazonian rubber baron before he'd lost his fortune when Malay rubber won the world market. Although the house had been in disrepair when they'd purchased it, the original details were restored by painstaking workmen. Flea-ridden Oriental rugs had hidden mosaic floors in the hallways and unusual parquetry in the public rooms. Moldings were regilded, brass polished, chandeliers electrified, murals cleaned and retouched.

With surprising zeal, Margaret had seen that even such minor features as the scallop-shaped lintel decoration were recast, carrying the shell motif throughout the house. She made certain that the new paint for the plaster exterior was the precise shade of coral that she'd admired inside a conch shell. Erik had installed an imported Otis elevator that held five people, because Dr. Bandeira had warned against Margaret walking up and down too many stairs. Now only Astrid used the contraption, endlessly taking her dolls for rides.

As Erik turned toward their private rooms, he checked the ormolu clock on the hall table. There was still enough time. Astrid would be eating in the kitchen with Florinda and her two oldest children. Set out on the table in the middle of the drawing room was a cut-glass decanter filled with Erik's favorite Portuguese sherry. He poured himself half a glass, then followed it with an equal amount of filtered water. Erik smiled up at the oval ceiling mural that the rubber baron, whose sordid reputation had made the house a bargain, had commissioned. Though his parents had expected him to have the ceiling repainted, he couldn't bring himself to obscure the dancing ladies whose rounded pink buttocks and breasts had been so artfully shaped. Often he wondered what erotic events had transpired in this fanciful room with heart-patterned parquetry floors and beveled mirrors on every wall.

The drawing room, obviously meant for evening entertaining, was just too hot that time of day. It was a relief to step into the marble-lined coolness of Margaret's dressing room. She'd stripped away the heavy wine velvet draperies hemmed with golden tassels, leaving only sheer lace curtains that didn't block the breeze.

"Boa tarde," Margaret said, looking up expectantly from the open book on her lap.

At the sight of her so ready for him, Erik's heart pounded fiercely. "You look so much better this afternoon," he said sincerely, for her cheeks were brighter and the tense lines around her mouth had softened. "You had a good day with Chiquinha?"

"She slept most of the morning. I played with the children. Do you know that Marcelino has a musical ear?"

"He's still a baby!"

"Mozart performed in public before he was seven."

"Augusto fathered a Mozart?"

"Not exactly. But Marcelino sat beside me on the piano bench and hummed along in perfect pitch. Then I played a simple song and he repeated it almost exactly. Maybe I'll start giving him lessons."

"What about Astrid? I thought you were teaching her."

Margaret drew her lip in sharply. "She doesn't want to concentrate. Perhaps next year . . ."

"That's probably best." Erik did not want, at this of all times, to explore a controversial subject. He removed his jacket.

Margaret placed her book on the table beside the grey velvet slipper-shaped chaise longue, then unbuttoned the loose dress she wore in the afternoons. "I like this so much," she said. Erik began helping her. "After supper I'm too tired; in the mornings you're too rushed."

He kissed the hollow at her throat. "Isn't this what the doctor ordered?" Unexpectedly, Margaret blushed. Erik kissed her quickly, murmuring, "So it wasn't your idea?"

"Not entirely." She wriggled free of her last remaining undergarments.

The curtains danced in the open window. The shouts of laborers could be heard from over the walls.

Erik stared without touching. Her body, warm, inviting, with legs parting, was far more perfect than those of the goddesses on the ceiling. For a moment he hesitated to press himself alongside his wife, whose skin was so white, so cool, so dry. With delicious impatience she reached around his muscular back, pulled him down to her breasts, and wordlessly offered a nipple to his eager mouth.

❧3 That evening Erik decided not to tell Margaret of his father's plan until after their meal, which was served in their upstairs sitting room. He talked of more general business matters, the details of which always seemed to interest her. When the dessert was served, Astrid was permitted to join them.

"Papai!" Eight-year-old Astrid flung herself at her father's chest, spilling the wine in his glass.

"Querida, you must watch where you're going," he admonished lightly.

Though Astrid sat down, she barely kept still. She twisted in her seat and kicked the table leg. It took great strength of will for Margaret to hold her tongue. She knew from experience that any correction from her could lead to one of Astrid's deep sulks or, worse, childish fits. Whenever Astrid was crossed, she'd whine for Isabel, uncannily knowing that this was the quickest route to getting her way.

Isabel. It had been six weeks since Erik had seen her or his other children. Margaret always accepted his infrequent visits with Astrid to the Parque Panorama, never guessing the truth.

"The attachment's quite natural. She's the only mother the baby ever knew," Margaret had said naively. "I'd have no objections to the woman coming to live with us."

"But Isabel has children of her own, a crippled father . . ." Erik had insisted nervously.

"Florinda's whole family is under our care. Five children, her mother. What are three or four more? There's plenty of housing on the hillside."

"No," he'd answered quickly. "If Isabel's here, Astrid'll never really need us. If we're ever to have an influence over her . . ."

Fortunately for Erik, Margaret had seen the wisdom in his logic. She'd also recognized that the child's ties to Isabel couldn't be severed entirely. So Erik discreetly weaned Astrid from Isabel, lengthening the intervals between visits, waiting until either Astrid complained or he felt a strange ache signaling the time had come to see his other children again.

The silver dessert trolley was wheeled across the room. Astrid jumped to examine the selection of sweets. "Oooo! Quindims! My favorite!" She poked her finger into one of the bright yellow sweet cakes and tasted the coconut custard filling.

"Please serve that one to Astrid," Margaret said sternly.

"I don't want that one!" Astrid wailed. "I want the other one. It's bigger."

"You'll take the one you touched."

"No I won't! Papai, tell her . . ."

Erik cringed whenever Astrid demanded that he contradict her stepmother. Margaret made every attempt to treat her fairly, even lovingly, he knew that, but she just didn't see what he did. Astrid had Gunilla's pale eyes and fragile, almost translucent, skin, but none of the solid, stoic upbringing that had made Gunilla bland and tolerant to a fault. The child's wildness and dramatic flair reminded his parents of his own youthful rambunctiousness, which had been smilingly accepted in a male but was the antithesis of the way a little girl should behave. He could insist, he could demand, but he hesitated to stifle that part of himself he saw in this child, perhaps the only legitimate offspring he'd ever have.

That night, with far more important matters to negotiate later in the evening, he especially didn't want to cross Margaret. "Have the quindim, Astrid, then you can have something else as well." He pointed to the trolley. "Look, cook's made pudim ambrosia, papos de anjo, and creme de abacate."

Astrid indicated two desserts.

"Your father said one other . . ."

A large dollop of the sugar and fruit pudding was placed beside the little cakes and then the tiny babas in syrup, called angel's cheeks by the nuns who'd invented the dessert, were mounted in the remaining space on the overloaded plate.

"Just a bit of the avocado mousse," Margaret said to the waiter.

Noticing one of his favorites on the second tier, Erik pointed to three prunes shaped like boats and stuffed with a cinnamon-flavored coconut filling. A whole clove in the center of each concoction made it look like the pupil of an eye.

"Why do they call it 'ôlho-de-sogra'?" Astrid asked.

"Because it looks like an eye, doesn't it?"

"But why the eyes of a mother-in-law?"

"Don't know."

"Tell me!"

Erik controlled his voice. "I'd tell you if I knew."

"Why do *you* think, Astrid?" Margaret asked.

"Because they're so ugly and taste so . . . ." She made a sour face, then brightened. "Do you have a mother-in-law, Ridi?" Ridi was the strange nickname that Astrid had chosen for Margaret, refusing any form of "Mother." Everyone knew Margaret disliked it, so no one else ever used it.

"Yes, my mother-in-law is your grandmother Guilhermina."

"And you?" she asked her father.

"Well, I suppose I have two."

"I know!" Astrid said brightly. "Grandmother Bergson who lives in Sweden and sends me a doll every Christmas and Grandmother Claiborne who lives in Brazil and never sends me anything."

Margaret frowned. Her mother sewed adorable dresses and bonnets for the child, but those practical items hardly competed with the exquisite porcelain dolls that arrived yearly from Europe.

Aware that she'd begun to upset Margaret, Astrid hurriedly chatted on. "I know something else. You have *three* fathers-in-law, Papai! Grandpa Bergson, Grandpa Claiborne, and Grandpa da Silva."

"He's not your grandfather," Margaret mechanically corrected her stepdaughter.

"Oh yes he is! More than the other two. They've never bothered to come to see me, but Isabel's father took care of me for years and years."

"That still doesn't make him your grandfather or your father's father-in-law," Margaret insisted gently.

"He should've been! If Papai'd married Isabel . . ."

From the corner of his eye, Erik saw Margaret replace her fork and hold very, very still.

Astrid suddenly became suspiciously quiet.

Margaret stared at the wasted food on Astrid's plate. "Don't you want to finish?"

Fighting back tears, she said, "No, I don't."

Margaret tried to rescue the evening. 'Would you like me to play something for you before you go to sleep?"

"No!"

"Not even some of those little butterfly pieces by Schumann? You can try to find the diminished chord."

"I hate that game!" Astrid started to shriek. "I hate it!"

Margaret pulled the child back from the table to avoid her breaking anything or hurting herself. Astrid rolled off the chair onto the floor and thrashed about. Having been kicked often enough during one of these episodes, Margaret knew to stand back. Erik waited helplessly until the rage subsided.

As soon as Astrid's screams had faded into choking sobs, Florinda arrived. Perhaps because she'd had five of her own, she seemed to know just what to do. Firmly, wordlessly, she lifted Astrid in her strong brown arms and carried her to her room.

❦ ❦ ❦

Erik poured his second glass of port. Fortunately, Margaret seemed in better spirits than he'd expected. She was becoming accustomed to Astrid's scenes; she was learning they were unavoidable and not really caused by anything she had done.

"They're Gunilla's fault," Margaret had said one morning after a fit that had ended with Astrid's nose bleeding. "The child's furious that her mother left her."

"That's ridiculous! She never knew her mother."

"She did for nine months."

"Children don't remember that."

"How can you be so sure? I've heard that what a woman eats, thinks, even sees during her pregnancy can affect the unborn child. Astrid expected her mother to be there when she was born, but she wasn't. She was given to a stranger, with a different colored skin, a different smell, a different tasting milk."

The whole idea was far too complex for Erik to contemplate for long, but he saw the kernel of wisdom in her words and took them to heart. It helped him to forget that many of his daughter's problems might be his fault too. He'd been so distraught at Gunilla's death that he'd no idea of what being a father meant. Once he'd given the baby over to Isabel, he'd concentrated, perhaps for the first time, on his work and surprised himself when he'd discovered great satisfaction in seeing his ideas not only adopted but turning a tidy profit.

Margaret was playing a Bach prelude on the harpischord.

"If you want to keep Margaret happy, keep her busy with her music," the composer, Joaquim Freire, had suggested to Erik shortly after their marriage. "That great monstrosity of a piano is fine downstairs in the public rooms of a house, but every musician needs a more intimate instrument close at hand."

That great monstrosity! That's how the maestro had insultingly referred to the most expensive piano in all of Brazil: the bronze showpiece at the Casa Arthur Napoleão! Erik had been so enraged he'd almost made a few comments of his own about "a musician's intimate instrument," but had refrained for Margaret's sake. He knew how much her association with Freire and the other Academy of Music members meant to her. Still, he always felt uncomfortable with Margaret's musical friends. He found them uninterested in his work and thought their artistic pretensions a bit hard to take most of the time. If Margaret wished to occupy her afternoons with practice sessions and lofty conversations of clefs and keys, he indulged her, but he went to great lengths to avoid entertaining them in his home too frequently or accepting their invitations to an interminable number of evening soirées.

Though he'd taken Freire's suggestions and ordered for Margaret a harpsichord from France (for which she'd been genuinely grateful), he'd never warmed to the composer who preferred to speak in French and affected more European than Brazilian manners. Didn't he realize there was no other country in the world where a man of his color could have achieved as much as he had?

"What's that you just played? I don't recognize it." Erik had struggled to learn the names of most of Margaret's pieces so he could speak intelligently about them.

"Bach's Prelude number two in A."

Everything with numbers, letters, opuses, and movements. It made it all so difficult. But he did have a good memory for melodies.

"I didn't recognize that last part."

"I always improvise the chords differently."

"Are you supposed to do that?"

"The baroque custom was for the performer to embellish the endings."

Shaking his head, Erik went to stand by her side. Her loose satin dressing gown parted at the knee. He wished he could remove it completely and begin with her again. He often wondered if she felt as he did, but then a woman wasn't expected to put those feelings into words. Though she rarely refused him, he sometimes thought that was only because she didn't want to miss an opportunity for a baby; other times he sensed her desire was equal to his own.

He sat beside her on the needlework cushion that Francisca had made for the bench and placed his arms around her waist. Maybe he shouldn't approach the subject of the Casas Margaridas expansion plan that night. Traveling would be a major interruption in her musical engagements. Sometimes he worried that if she ever had to choose between him and her music, he would be the loser. A few weeks earlier, when he'd asked her to give up a charity concert to entertain a visiting British buyer, he'd been foolish enough to let her see his jealousy.

"I can't let the whole ensemble down. Why don't you bring him to the Lyric Theater? Afterward he can join us at Maestro Freire's table," she'd suggested.

"You'd use any excuse to be with Quincas, wouldn't you?" he'd yelled unfairly, since her plan was a sensible compromise.

As it turned out, Alistair Gregory was a devotee of music and had been enthralled with the performance. He'd complimented Erik lavishly. "I've heard Fanny Bloomfield-Zeisler and Olga Samaroff, two of Europe's leading ladies of the keyboard, and your wife is an equal to either of them!"

Even after Erik had told Margaret she'd been right, she had sulked for weeks after his outburst. Tonight he couldn't afford to react so stupidly. He decided to stall while he thought everything through more clearly. "Please, won't you play one more?"

"What would you like? A prelude and fugue?"

"Yes." He picked a random number. "Number ten."

"In 'E'?"

"I think so."

"That's the easiest one of all. No challenge, just two voices."

"I'm a simple man; I like simple music."

"That's not true."

"It is."

"Is not." As Margaret pressed closer to Erik, he pretended she'd pushed him off the bench, sprawling like a rag doll on the carpet.

Sometimes she loved his clowning; other times she had little patience for it. Tonight she laughed. "All right, I'll play it if you promise to behave!"

"I'd never promise such a thing. No man would!"

Margaret sighed and placed her hands on the keyboard. Erik stood behind her, enjoying the confidence with which she pressed the keys, the complicated rhythm flowing effortlessly from her fingers.

The piece had increased in pace and Margaret seemed to be playing it with more intensity than usual. He was disappointed when her fingers came to rest.

"Are you very tired?"

"You want another piece?" she said with mock impatience.

"No, I want to ask you something." He walked over to the couch and patted the buttery leather cushion beside him. "Come sit with me." Now that he'd figured out how to tell her, he was anxious to hear her response. After four years, he still had no idea what she'd say. That was the best part — her unpredictable nature. Not in the sad way that Chiquinha was unpredictable — you never knew if she'd be weeping or laughing, sickly, or over-zealously redecorating the house. Margaret's mind was difficult to fathom, yet sometimes her reasoning was better than his own. He loved her questioning the whys of everything.

Margaret retied her dressing gown to prove she was ready to listen seriously, catching Erik's silly pout as she buttoned it above her bosom. "Well, you wanted to *talk* didn't you?" She sat primly beside him.

Erik placed his hands in his lap and looked at her intently. "I

need your advice." He used precisely the words that he knew
would intrigue her. Then he told her the plan.

4 To sweeten the prospect of a long journey in the south,
Erik had offered Margaret a trip to Lizzieland as part of
the itinerary. But even after two months of traveling, she'd shown
a surprising reluctance to see her family again. Once they'd arrived at the riverfront outpost, Erik better understood Margaret's
averseness to returning there.

On their first afternoon in the colony, they sat on the verandah
of the Claibornes' house, sipping the milky cajuada drink that
Lucretia had served. Erik discreetly spit out a cashew seed.

"The cook should've strained it," Lucretia apologized. She noticed Margaret's glass was still full. "Shall I have her strain yours
now?"

"No, thank you, Mother. I don't care for any."

"I didn't like the taste either," Charles Claiborne added, "until
I realized that caju meant 'cashew.' Wonderful fruit, eh? With
that nut on the outside and the white flesh on the inside,
nothing's ever wasted. Too bad we can't raise enough of them
here. The elevation's either too high or too wet, can't remember which. They grow better in the north, don't they, Senhor
Larson?"

Erik bristled. It was the man's way of stating politely that he
considered him a stranger, a stranger who happened to have married his daughter without his approval. For his wife's sake he remained outwardly polite. "My father has a small caju orchard on
some land he inherited in the state of Minas Gerais. When I was a
child I always wondered which were the ripe ones, the yellow or
the red. It took me a long while before I understood that both are
ripe versions of the same fruit. Funny that there's no difference in
taste." Erik realized he was going on a bit, but he always talked
too much when he was tense.

Erik knew his mother-in-law wondered if he'd kept his promises about Isabel. He'd never slept with her again, but her con-
nection to Astrid, and the fact that he still cared for his and
Isabel's children, had made it impossible to banish his former
mistress from his life. At least he'd made certain that Margaret
knew nothing of his past. Deus! His mother-in-law made him feel

guilty, though he'd done nothing for which he needed to be ashamed.

"What do you know about bananas?" Charles asked unexpectedly.

"Bananas?"

"They require less labor than watermelons and are a year-round crop in this climate. I've tried a few experiments with the Caturra strain. The tree is by no means tall but produces enormous bunches, with an average of a hundred and fifty bananas per bunch. The exports to Argentina alone amount to more than thirty-five hundred contos de mil-reis, and I've read reports that banana flour will assume significant importance in the near future. That's not even mentioning the value of the trunk fibers. I hear they're much in demand for, of all things, men's neckties."

"Is that so?" Erik politely tried to stay with the conversation, but his eyes wandered to where Margaret was standing in the doorway talking heatedly with her mother. Probably his mother-in-law was inquiring, as all of their family and relations eventually and discreetly did, about her barrenness, a subject that upset Margaret deeply. At least his mother had been especially sympathetic, since she'd experienced a similar delay in conceiving her children.

Blocking out Claiborne's agricultural ramblings, he strained to hear what the women were talking about. He caught a few sensitive words: "half-breed mother," "effect of past conduct," "a doctor could tell . . ." Erik felt Margaret's pain, but didn't interfere. His own mother had been told that the reason she'd had trouble conceiving was her marriage to the "galego." Nonsense! If miscegenation caused fewer babies, Brazil would be an unpopulated country. He'd often heard his mother rail on the subject of racial stupidity and prejudice among society.

"Who are they to criticize?" she'd asked. "Where in this country can you find consanguinity? Tell me the name of one pure Brazilian, even one with a fancy Portuguese pedigree like mine!"

"What I don't understand," Margaret had asked during one of these outbursts, "is why everything happened so differently in Brazil. After all, in the United States we had Indian natives, then Negroid slaves, but at home it was absolutely forbidden to marry someone of a different color. Here it's possible."

Because Sven Larson had thought about the differences between the two countries, he'd given a ready answer. "It all goes back to the reasons the Europeans went to the two areas. Your country was colonized initially by whole families rushing to escape religious persecution. They founded towns, intermarried among themselves, never mingling with nativos or pretos. With the Portuguese, it was different. First, because they were seafaring people and sailors who saw so much of the world, they tended to get their prejudices rubbed off. Second, they already retained habits and customs acquired during three centuries of mingling with the Moors, who were dark-skinned themselves. And finally, the Portuguese explorer who arrived in Brazil without a European woman naturally sought and took his pleasure with a native woman. Later, when the Africans came, their women were not considered altogether unattractive to the Portuguese."

"Did they marry them?"

"Not in great numbers. That didn't stop them from procreating. And since later generations were mostly mixed, with the children of landowners sometimes the same shade of color as the children of slaves, the distinctions blurred. A person's class became more important than his race."

"You chose to marry lighter than yourself," Margaret whispered to her mother-in-law.

"Erik's father had many charms besides his blue eyes and fair skin. But, yes, to marry whiter, to lighten one's children, has always been considered desirable — perhaps *fashionable* would be the better word."

"Although to be dark is no disgrace in Brazil," Sven had added. "Look at your friend Freire. He has so much Indian, African, and Portuguese blood in his veins he'd be considered inferior in North America, wouldn't he?"

Margaret had agreed with her in-laws, but Erik knew that the rest of the Claibornes had a far less enlightened outlook on the matter. Now, as he saw Margaret storming away from her mother, he ached to discover what had so disturbed his wife. If only he could get away from Claiborne and his infernal interest in bananas!

"Actually, the Pacova is the largest of the species, but its fruits are fewer in number, the bunches smaller. I've heard of some new varieties from India that are easier to digest . . . but too insignificant to market, don't you agree?"

"I'm afraid you know more about it than I do, sir."

As Erik listened to the old man's chatter, he looked around at the dilapidated buildings, the unweeded fields, the disheartened expressions of the remaining settlers, and doubted that anything would be left of the place in five years. A pity. The high land was the equal of the best coffee fields he'd seen around São Paulo.

"Have you considered coffee, sir?"

Claiborne coughed excessively. "Coffee? Ruination! Everyone I know who's planted the damn stuff is still waiting for berries. Six years before the first conto is brought in."

"But after that . . ."

"One year for bananas . . . One year! They almost grow wild. No need for all that cultivation, worry over too much or too little rain. Every year we've been here they say it's the worst flood in half a century or the worst drought in ten years. There's no such thing as *normal* weather, for God's sake! And, you tell me, who doesn't like bananas?" Claiborne pointed menacingly. "You like bananas, don't you?"

The old fellow was not rational. Erik nodded vigorously so as not to invite further conflict. But as soon as he could, Erik excused himelf and followed the downhill path his wife had taken. He found her standing in front of a mud-walled hut.

"That's where Florinda lived." A sob caught in her throat. The once-tidy yard was filled with rubble. A few workmen bunked there now. One dozed in the hammock inside the open doorway. Margaret turned away and wiped her eyes.

"What's wrong?" Erik asked.

"We shouldn't have come."

"It's not what I expected, either," Erik admitted.

"Mother tells me that Nell won't be able to visit us while we're here. I had so hoped to see her!"

Erik remembered how upset Margaret had been last year when her sister married Royce Burrows, one of the men who had once been interested in Margaret. "Isn't she well?"

"She's going to have a baby in five months."

"Aren't you pleased for her and Royce?"

Margaret began to cry. "I miss her, more than I thought I would. Now Katie . . ."

Erik liked the dark-haired youngest sister better than the paler, less fiery version of Margaret that he'd remembered in Nell. Kate, who'd turned eighteen the week before, was bursting with bright remarks and flirtatious smiles. "She's a wonderful girl. Why are you worried about her?"

"What kind of life will she have here? She can't teach school for the rest of her life."

"I thought there was a man . . ."

"Her heart was set on some young doctor, but he married a Brazilian girl; isn't that awful?"

"You make it sound like a terrible fate! After all, I'm Brazilian."

Margaret pulled away from his embrace. "I don't think of you as Brazilian."

"But I am," he said coldly.

"Not like Augusto . . ."

"No, I should hope not. What else did your mother say?"

"She asked ridiculous questions, she warned me . . ."

Erik held his breath. Her mother wouldn't bring up Isabel now, would she? "What do you mean?"

"Don't know . . . I'm all confused."

"Your father is very ill, worse than he lets on. That kind of worry can make a person say or do things they wouldn't otherwise." He clasped Margaret's hand in his. "Now, about Kate. What can I do to help?"

"Mother would . . . I mean, I'd like to bring her back to Rio with us. Introduce her to some of our friends . . ."

"They're all Brazilians."

"I know, but . . ."

"And we're not going directly back. We've six weeks more of traveling at least."

"Could she join us later?"

"Perhaps," Erik said affably, realizing he'd as much as promised.

❦   ❦   ❦

A few nights later, when they were in bed, Margaret complained again about Lucretia to Erik. "If my father is the one who is ill, you'd never know it listening to my mother. All she does is moan about how her rheumatoid pains are worse than ever."

"Do you know what I think?"

"What?" Margaret snuggled closer, but Erik lay on his back stiffly.

He stared at the ceiling, trying to moderate his fury at having everyone expect so much of him. "She wants us to move the whole family to Rio."

"You're wrong. Father would never leave Lizzieland, and she's never hinted anything about Marshall, has she?"

"Goodness, no! He's an odd sort of child. They'd better watch him. Your father said he prefers the companionship of the fishermen's sons, sometimes sleeping in their huts, eating their food. What he didn't say is that he's also lying with their women."

"He's only seventeen!"

"That's not too young . . . Even I . . ."

"At that age?"

"For a man it's not unusual."

"Then why are you worried about Marsh?"

"Your parents give him too little guidance."

"I wish we could go home to Rio."

"Raleigh comes in two more days. Don't you want to see him again?"

"Actually, I'm more interested in seeing Marianne and the babies."

"They made quicker work of it than Francisca. Did that surprise you?"

"No, not really." Margaret had never forgotten the passion that had so quickly flamed between the couple. "I saw for myself the way it can be for two people, even after only a few hours."

"When I see your brother, I'll have to thank him."

"For what?"

"For teaching you a lesson that was later quite valuable to me."

"You wouldn't!"

"Why wouldn't I?" Erik's hand strayed between her legs.

"No, not here."

"We'll be very quiet." He kissed her even though she tried to wriggle away. Ever since they'd arrived, she'd turned her back to him at night.

"Only if you promise . . ."

"I'd promise you anything . . ." He smothered her with kisses. This time she stilled and kissed him back. In a few seconds her reluctance vanished and she welcomed his lovemaking with as violent a surge as Erik had ever before aroused.

❧5 "The cangaceiros, they've overrun the backlands." Raleigh spoke heatedly after supervising the docking of his barge, *O Salvador*, at Lizzieland's wharf.

Erik hardly recognized this emaciated, intense man as the stodgy, overprotecting brother he'd met five years earlier. "Are you certain? I've never heard of bandits in this part of Brazil. What do these outlaws look like?"

"Most have taken to wearing the leather hat of the cowboy with the brim turned up at the front. They're well armed. The band that delayed us for three days wore cartridge belts across their chests."

Marianne and her children had been hurried into the Claibornes' house by Lucretia and Margaret. Filthy with dust, bitten by numerous bugs, and exhausted from lack of sleep, they needed tender ministering. Raleigh lingered to share his tale with his father and Erik.

"Were you harmed or robbed?" the old man asked.

"No, you don't understand. When we heard their camp wasn't far from the river, I made my way up there myself. I knew that if I could bring the word of God to these lowest of men who sowed murder and destruction, if I could convert but one to preach the Gospel instead of vengeance . . ." Raleigh stopped to stare across the dry hills. "Too little rain this year. It's always more violent when its dry, they tell me. Got to go back, there's so much more to be done." Raleigh paused long enough to sip some coffee, then greedily bit into a slice of hard cheese.

"There was one of them, one of their strongest men, called Mergulhão, The Diver. When he was a child his father was killed by a bloodthirsty lot, and he vowed to live and die a bandit forever. When I talked with him, I endeavored to show him the errors in his thinking. It wasn't until I read the Scriptures that he began to listen. In Deuteronomy, Chapter Thirty-two . . ."

Raleigh rubbed his exhausted dark-ringed eyes and quoted, " 'To me belongeth vengeance, and recompence; their foot shall slide in due time: for the day of their calamity is at hand, and the things that shall come upon them make haste.' "

"That's all very well . . ." his father replied, bored with Raleigh's incessant preaching.

"Don't you want to know what happened to The Diver?" Raleigh waited a few beats. "Last week we rebaptized him José; now he's traveling with us. What a witness he'll make to the power of the Lord's message!"

"Where's he now?" Charles asked in alarm.

"On the barge, guarding it."

"You're a fool!" his father exploded. "How can you trust a man like that with your family?"

"Perhaps he's good protection." Erik rushed to support Raleigh. "A man who's lived by his wits for so long can sense danger miles off."

"The only protection I need is my prayers," Raleigh responded righteously.

Margaret called from the doorway. "Raleigh, there's hot water in the tub for a bath. Marianne thinks you should use it now; then we'll put out something for you to eat. We've already fed the children."

Raleigh followed her inside.

Charles Claiborne tilted back on his chair and stared at Erik. All at once he saw his son-in-law in a different light. In comparison with Raleigh, Erik was wonderfully secure, urbane, settled. He smiled at Erik for the first time. The lined, tired face behind the triangular beard reminded Erik of an old ram with its head lowered. He wondered what request might be coming next.

❧ ❧ ❧

Early the next morning, Erik and Charles met in the kitchen. "Can't sleep the way I used to," Charles complained. "My pains are worse at night."

"Is there nothing to be done for it?"

"It's bad, very bad. I don't like to alarm the ladies, but between you and me . . . there's blood in my urine. More each week. Could go on for years they say, but I don't think so. A man knows, especially when it's that part of him."

"I'm sorry, sir."

"Sorry won't help. But Erik . . ." He stared with icy blue eyes, trying to convey something that he couldn't quite say.

Erik returned his gaze steadily. "I'll do whatever I can, sir."

"Obrigado," Claiborne's voice choked. "I thank you."

Erik placed his half-filled coffee cup in the tin sink. The tasteless, anemic coffee these North Americans made was hardly worth drinking. "I'd like to see this barge of Raleigh's."

"I'll walk with you down to the docks and show you around. Fontaine made certain his daughter would have every possible comfort."

The only sound along the path was the droning of the cigarras, whining like huge machines even though their insect bodies were barely the size of a man's thumb. A light mist feathered up from the riverfront. The men had to get very close to the shoreline before they could see anything. The barge was nowhere in sight.

Claiborne pointed upstream. "I thought he'd anchored over on those pilings. It's the safest place to leave a craft for several days. Gives the ferries room to turn around."

A light wind swirled the fog into eerie patches. "Where else could he have left it?" Erik asked.

"Don't know, unless they moored it on the other bank to keep it completely out of the way of night traffic."

"Who's on board?"

"They usually have a crew of four or five. Now they've added this reformed bandido . . ." Claiborne stopped. Something floating in the murky water caught his eye. "What's that?"

Erik crouched down on the dock and tried to focus on the partially submerged shape. "Get me a pole or a stick."

Charles handed him a grappling hook. For a second Erik hesitated, then pulled the mass toward him. "Bom Deus! It's a woman." The hook was tangled in her hair. He turned the dangling neck so that Charles could see the bloodless face.

"She's the children's nurse," he sputtered.

"Her throat's been cut. Maldito!"

"We've got to fish her out," Charles answered weakly. He let Erik inch the body into shore.

"He was very foolish to trust so blindly." Charles held his head in his hands and moaned. "I wish I could believe something like this would bring him to his senses."

"Meu Deus!" Erik shouted. "Look, there are more of them." Three bodies were being carried downstream on the fast current. Steadying the grappling hook so that it wouldn't do further damage to the corpse, he struggled to lift the nursemaid's sodden body onto the dock. "We almost have her. Take the legs and swing them around."

Charles bent down and grabbed a limb, but then fell back screaming. He flailed about, trying to pull something off his arm. "Eels, she's covered with eels!" Wildly, he threw a slippery creature in the air. As the old man's terror increased, Erik felt his own ease. He steadied his father-in-law and half-carried him back to the house.

☙ ☙ ☙

"Do you think they were dead before he threw them overboard?"

"Margaret, must you?" Raleigh asked. "None of that's important now. We've lost our home, our good kind servants . . ."

"There's every chance the boat will be found," Erik suggested.

"Do you know how many small rivers, streams, and inlets there are? José knew every one." Raleigh pressed his palms to his temples and rocked his head back and forth. "All my books, my sermons . . . everything we've worked for . . ."

Marianne was not quite so agitated. "No, we have each other and the children. That's all that really matters." She held her youngest baby, Ethan Lawrence. "Perhaps it's for the best. Our Lord Jesus must have another road for us to take."

"Jesus!" Erik cried out. "How can you think that Jesus had something to do with the murder of four innocent people. It was stupid to get involved with those outlaws, to take one into your home. He could just as easily have killed you and the children if you'd been aboard. Can't you see that he tricked you to get the boat, that this was his plan from the beginning?"

"It wasn't like that," Raleigh protested.

"You've never seen a man more serious, more penitent," Marianne added, though her wavering voice belied her words.

"If your José wasn't responsible for this, who else could it have been?"

"Don't know," Raleigh groaned. "The others were remorseless, couldn't be touched by the word of the Lord."

Margaret, who had been listening in the background, spoke up nervously. "Have you ever heard of one of them . . . a bandido . . . with a name like Tubarão?"

Raleigh stared at Margaret suspiciously. "Where have you heard that name?"

Erik didn't give her long enough to answer. "My father had some run-ins with a man by that name several years ago. Margaret's heard us speak of him. I'm sure he's still wanted by the Rio police."

"The name's familiar. He might be with a band that's in opposition to the one Mergulhão was with. Crazy fools, they're always after someone's blood."

"Isn't that the band who call themselves the 'pontaria finas'?" Marianne added.

"Pontaria fina!" Margaret's voice rose with anxiety. "What does it mean?"

"Good shooting — it should only take one bullet to kill an enemy."

"How could you be so stupid? . . ." Charles grumbled.

"There's no point in arguing now." Marianne spoke sorrowfully. "We couldn't have stayed on the river forever."

"But you never complained . . ."

"I know, Raleigh, but the time was coming quickly when we would have had to move ashore. Already Mary Lee's fallen into the river twice."

Lucretia gasped.

"Luckily she's always been tethered, so we just fished her out. But with three of them . . ."

Raleigh, distracted by the tragedy, placed his head back in his hands. "I'll have to bury them, all of them. They trusted me, they trusted the Lord. How will I ever live with myself?"

Marianne smiled encouragement. "Jesus will give you strength. He always has."

"I don't know, I don't know where to turn."

"You've kept at this long enough without any assistance," his father said sensibly. "Don't you think you might enlist the help of some of the organized missionaries?"

"The only one I know is Tucker Fitzhugh of the American Bible Society in Rio, on the Rua Sete de Setembro. Do you know where that is?"

Margaret nodded.

"Then you should go and see him," Charles suggested. "If you put the same energy into business as you have into religion, you'd be a great success. But you've never listened to me before, so . . ."

"I'm listening now, Father. What would you do if you were me?"

Suddenly Erik became more attentive.

"I'd go to Rio, offer to work for the Bible Society. I'd meet with other missionaries, learn from them, and decide if this was what I really wanted."

"I know what I want!"

"You think you do now. At your age I thought I wanted Moss Oaks . . ." He began to cough.

Lucretia spoke up. "I think Rio's a fine idea. You've never lived in a city, have you, Marianne?"

"No, Mother."

"The children would have more advantages and you'd be close to Margaret. Wouldn't you like that?"

Marianne nodded agreeably.

Everyone waited for Margaret to respond. Though she was horrified at the idea of having Raleigh close enough to interfere with her life, this was not a moment she could be selfish. "Erik and I won't be home for several weeks, so you'd be welcome to stay in our house. When we return . . ." She shot a glance at Erik. His impassive face didn't reveal his emotions. "We'd be happy to help you find a place to live," she finished.

"I'm sure Erik would know what would be a suitable location for your family," Lucretia added.

Now they turned to Erik. He wondered how to appease them. "Whatever arrangements Margaret makes will be agreeable with me," he answered smoothly. "I'd better get back to the river." He left to attend to the grisly work of recovering the bodies, which at that moment actually seemed the preferable of the tasks at hand.

6 After two weeks surrounded by the drabness and despondency of Lizzieland, Erik and Margaret both welcomed traveling north to the towns surrounding São Paulo in the hub of the coffee economy. On paper it had appeared that these prosperous areas would be excellent locations for stores.

Margaret was enchanted with the landscape in the vicinity of Ribeirão Prêto and was especially impressed with the Krauss fazenda, the largest in that region. "How do they keep the plants and grounds so beautifully organized?" she asked, looking out from the open-air dining area. "In all of Brazil I've never seen anything to match it!"

The fazendeiro's residence was artfully placed on a little eminence, like a ship on the crest of a wave. At a glance she could survey an ocean of dark green shrubs planted in perfectly even lines, stretching in unbroken symmetry as far as the eye could see.

"Colonos," Erik explained. "The Italian immigrants who were imported to solve the labor problem after abolition are the primary reason for the success of these coffee fazendas. Without them, all would be chaos."

Their host, Colonel Krauss, nodded. "Your husband is correct."

"How much do you grow?"

"Over ten thousand tons of coffee a year," he said in a modest tone.

"Ten thousand tons!" Margaret echoed.

"That's why they call our host the 'Coffee King,' " Erik explained.

"Hardly a king," the colonel replied with more than a trace of a German accent. "When I arrived here thirty years ago, I was an impoverished lad."

Margaret was genuinely enthralled. "You've accomplished a miracle in so few years . . ."

"Hardly. What did I do? Plant a seed, wait six years, pick it, and . . . deposit the gold in my account!" He refilled everyone's glass with the imported beer he'd insisted they try. Erik noticed Margaret had hardly touched her first glass.

"Isn't it hard to cultivate all those plants on hillsides?"

"The best coffee grows on sunny slopes," the colonel explained.

"Doesn't it also have something to do with the earth's rich red color?" Margaret couldn't help remarking on the carmine tint of the soil. It was a stunning contrast to the glossy emerald coffee leaves.

"Your wife is very observant, Erico. Our famous soil contains the perfect mixture of nutrients: silicic acid, oxide of iron, alumina, phosphoric ..."

"I don't know which is more beautiful," the colonel's wife interjected, "when the bushes are in flower or now, with the berries ripening."

The colonel exhaled slowly and sighed as he replaced his beer stein. "Do you want to know when I like them best?"

"When is that?" Erik asked politely.

"When the beans are converted to currency."

Erik laughed heartily. "Don't you ever worry that the boom will end?"

"Impossible. Every year the price gets higher; every year the demand increases."

"That's what they said about rubber."

"How could a Wickham affect me?" Krauss asked testily.

"What's 'a Wickham'?" Margaret asked.

The colonel settled back in his chair, ready to amuse his pretty guest with one of his favorite tales. "Black gold was in such demand that the Amazonian rubber barons who controlled the entire world supply could set any price they wanted. At least that was true in 1876 when a daring Englishman named Henry Wickham made his way up the Amazon and filled his cases with seventy thousand seeds of *Hevea brasilienis*, the rubber tree. He carried them safely back to Kew Gardens in London. There, in carefully controlled hothouses, the seeds were germinated. Later that year, he took his baby seedlings to Ceylon because he believed that island offered the most similar climate under the British flag to that of the Amazon. Nine years later, the young rubbers flowered successfully.

"Why did they permit the seeds to be exported?" Margaret asked.

"After Wickham's coup was discovered, a law was passed forbidding the export of rubber seeds, but this was a classic case of locking the stable door after the loss of the steed."

"My father remembers that period well," Erik added. "No one in Rio thought Ceylon rubber could ever be a threat. Everyone believed the plants would die, or if they did not die they would not yield latex; and if they yielded latex, it would be of a lesser grade."

"But they succeeded?"

"Plantation rubber has almost surpassed the output of Amazonian rubber. And it's far cheaper to harvest in neat little rows, rather than in the wilds of the jungle. But coffee is already cultivated. If any nation wished to compete, why aren't they doing so already?"

"Your point is well taken, Colonel," Erik interjected. "But how do you explain the cotton bust? My father barely escaped losing everything in '74."

"You can blame your North American friends for that. But nobody challenges Brazil's authority in the coffee market."

Margaret tried to divert Erik from starting an argument. "Your father used to grow coffee at Vassouras, didn't he?"

"Still does. We've always had a small area under cultivation, but never expanded it."

"If the price keeps getting higher, don't you think it might be worth the effort? After all, your land is so much closer to Rio."

"My father's land. I'm not a fazendeiro, remember?"

The colonel seemed bemused at Erik's disinterest in agriculture. "And what's wrong with that?"

"It takes an expert like you, Colonel Krauss, to be truly successful. I'll stick to something I understand."

"Your charming wife might like the country life."

Erik's eyes crinkled. "No, my wife prefers the city. She's a musician."

"Ah, I remember. I'd hoped you would consent to play for my family this evening."

"With pleasure, Colonel," Margaret said graciously, though her mind was filled, quite unexpectedly, with questions about coffee. "Are any of these lands for sale?"

"There are many estates around Ribeirão Prêto ripe for investment. I could show you Fazenda Aurora, which is only two kilometers from the Palmeiras station on the Mogyana railway. If you
would like to have me speak with the owner, Carlos Caetano
Dantas . . ."

Offended by his wife's direct talk on business matters, Erik interrupted. "I am not interested in anything but small buildings to
lease for my Casas Margaridas. In fact, if you'll excuse me, I'm already late for a meeting in town."

"Will you permit me to give your lovely wife a tour of our coffee drying and husking areas?"

Erik shrugged. "Whatever pleases her, pleases me."

Margaret nodded diffidently and took the colonel's arm. "So
you prefer growing the Bourbon variety to the Murta or
Creoulo," she was saying as they left the room.

As he rode into town, Erik began to wonder if it had been a
mistake to bring a woman along. Maybe his error had been to
discuss business matters with her and take her opinions into serious consideration. Perhaps Augusto and the others had been
right! He should have left Margaret in Rio, traveled by himself,
and experienced the delights of being temporarily single. By the
time he reached Serrana, Erik's anger had dissipated. But still,
she'd have to learn that some kinds of questions could not be
asked by a woman in Brazil, at least not in public!

Later that evening, when Margaret played impressively for
some of the colonel's neighbors, Erik sat back, smoked his cigar,
and basked in the fact that Margaret was his and his alone. Afterward, she was content to remain quietly with the other women
while the men discussed the recent meetings in Paris of the Pure
Food Association, which was seeking to obtain worldwide pro-
hibition of the name "coffee" being applied to any product that
had been adulterated.

"If the French agree, it will set a precedent," the colonel was
explaining to Erik. "For years we've been hurt by something they
call 'coffee,' containing chicory, sprouts, and other cheaper addi-
tives. Few people outside Brazil have ever tasted the true flavor of
one hundred percent coffee."

"I understand that it's unlikely that we'll receive a ruling in our
favor," interjected the Italian landowner Vincenzo Puccianti.

"Because these mixtures are not prejudicial to health, they say there's no need to condemn them."

"In that case, we'll have to implement the other scheme we discussed," the colonel continued. "We've got to support the opening of more 'pure' coffeehouses in the larger cities. The name alone connotes that the other is less desirable."

"I'll bring it up at the commission next month," the Italian agreed as the women drifted back into the room.

Margaret looked especially radiant. Her gown, cut low in the back to look appealing when she played the piano, was shaped so snugly around the buttocks she couldn't walk without causing the men in the room to stir. Krauss in particular had been openly admiring, though he hadn't stepped over the bounds of politeness. Nevertheless, at moments Erik resented how eagerly he moved to position himself near Margaret. With the arrangements for the stores all around Ribeirão Prêto almost complete, Erik was more than ready to move on. Only two more cities and it would be time to return home. He was weary of these endless discussions of adulterated coffee, the diseases of beans, husking inventions, and the numbers of kilos exported this month versus last month.

For some reason Margaret was not. "Is *café* a Portuguese word?" she was asking Krauss.

"Not at all. Coffee itself is supposed to be native to Abyssinia, and its name is derived from the Arabic word spelled 'q, a, h, w, e,' pronounced *kahveh* by the Turks."

"Erik, did you know that?"

"No, I didn't."

"Tell me, Colonel, when did people discover the beverage?"

Krauss began an extended historical explanation. "It's been known since the third century, but up until relatively modern times, perhaps the fifteenth century, coffee was taken in the form of a paste."

"Really! Erik, isn't that fascinating? How did it come to be grown in Brazil?"

"There are two stories. One says a deserter brought some seeds from Cayenne to Pará in 1761, the other that a Belgian monk introduced some plants to Rio de Janeiro in 1774. Perhaps both are true, but up to the end of the eighteenth century coffee was considered a medicine to stimulate the nerves and was to be found only in pharmacies." He went on with coffee lore, until Erik, yawning broadly, convinced his wife it was time to retire.

"I'll be happy to be home again," he whispered to Margaret that night in bed. "Won't you?"

"Yes, in a way, and then again . . ." She turned and reached out to him. "I find I like this life because I am with you so many hours of the day. At home it is just a few in the evening."

Her words were softening. Erik turned over and stroked her cheek.

"I don't miss all the daily details in Rio. So many servants to watch out for, all the staples to procure, the endless ordering of butter from Denmark, wines from Portugal, and I don't know what else."

"I thought you hated the backlands. You ran away from Lizzieland as soon as you could."

"I wasn't running away."

"You were."

"Anyway, that was Lizzieland." She hugged Erik close. "There'd be no life for me anywhere if it weren't for you."

"I live in Rio."

"Then I live in Rio."

"Are you certain?"

"How could you doubt me?"

"I thought you might have preferred to stay with Krauss," Erik said sulkily.

"That windbag! Never! But if you should want to invest in some good coffee land . . ."

"Margarida! You are serious?"

"Not really," she giggled, then kissed his downy chest.

He pulled back for a moment. "I never know with you, I never know."

❧7 "Your problem is wood," Colonel Krauss announced after he'd heard Erik's concerns about expanding his factory to meet the demands of all the new stores. "It all comes down to wood in the end."

"I don't understand . . . " Erik said, bringing his horse alongside his host's. They had taken the afternoon to inspect a timbering operation on the western portion of the Krauss fazenda.

"You've the property to extend your fábrica, all the labor you need. Raw cotton is produced in quantities far greater than you can use in the mills. All that stops you is the energy to fuel the equipment, right?"

Erik shrugged. "Perhaps . . ."

"Your lands around Rio cannot possibly produce enough trees, nor can they be transported to your wharfside site economically. What you've got to do, my boy, is buy wood from coastal areas, load the trunks on barges, and ship them by sea directly to the plant."

"All the good forests are to the north."

"Right, so you travel north and purchase up whole blocks of trees. If you locate forests that not only have good hardwoods to generate steam for the mills, but also areas rich in imbaúba wood, you'll make a fortune."

"How is that?"

"Because it's so soft and light it's the most perfect wood for the making of charcoal. I've a small amount of it on my own land, but I'd give anything to have an endless supply."

"Not much money in charcoal, Colonel."

Krauss raised his left eyebrow meaningfully. "But charcoal is the prime ingredient for something much more valuable — black powder."

"You make your own gunpowder?"

"A tidy profit for very little work, plus I have a continuous supply for my personal use." He reined his horse around and headed back toward the casa grande.

Erik kicked his horse smartly in order to catch up. "Why are you telling me this?"

"I'd like to see the son of an old friend succeed. When your father and I were but poor little immigrant boys in Rio, we shared much!" He winked. "Has your father ever told you about it?"

Erik's curiosity was aroused. "Not exactly."

"There was a woman from Bahia who lived in a tiny house in Laranjeiras and was very beautiful, but too expensive for one young man to keep. So we each paid half, until your father married. After that, I couldn't afford her alone. Taking your father's cue, I found myself a Portuguese beauty whose father just happened to have a few extra thousand hectares of prime coffee land and married her!"

Unexplainably, Erik felt annoyed. He allowed his horse to canter ahead of the colonel's. He'd known that his father could hardly have been a saint during the ten years between his arrival in Rio and his marriage. Yet for him to have shared a woman with this pompous German seemed so unlike his staid Lutheran father.

Krauss quickly came up behind. "Erico, you didn't know about any of that? Forgive me. I thought a father would have told his son." As the two horses trotted side by side, Krauss continued smoothly. "I understand she died a few years back. Your father looked after her in her later years. If he'd asked, I would've contributed something for old times' sake."

"The imbaúba wood . . ." Erik reminded.

"Yes, yes, back to business. Follow me; I'll show you something quite interesting."

In the packed earth courtyard between the farm buildings, the men turned their horses over to the stable boys. Krauss led the way to the barn. "Black powder is a mixture of saltpeter, sulfur, and charcoal. In Europe the supply of saltpeter was always the critical item. They scraped cellar walls for the saltlike crust, but in Brazil it is quite easy to create the material in our dung barns." Krauss opened the door to the dank stone building.

"How does one do it?"

"Ah, Erico, it is so simple. The mineral forms naturally in humid soil containing decaying vegetable or animal matter. Look!" Krauss pointed to wooden barrels lined up on benches against the walls. Underneath the benches, smaller pans were placed to catch a liquid dripping out slowly. "We place manure and humus in the upper tiers and dissolve out the raw saltpeter, which then falls into the bottom ones. Later, we'll further purify this by evaporation and recrystallization."

"That's all there is to it?" Erik tried to conceal his mounting excitement. With the massive reconstruction around Rio, particularly the dredging and sanitation projects along the waterfront, blasting powder was in high demand.

They walked across the courtyard, where two workers were minding large boiling kettles and stirring them with long paddles.

"Finally, we boil down the saltpeter solution until the cooling precipitates crystals that can be skimmed off with a strainer. In Germany regulations required refining it through three such recrystallizations to provide the high grade of powder the army required, but here that is unnecessary. Come this way."

Krauss led Erik to a long shed separated from all the other buildings. No one was then at work inside. "Here are the mortars." He pointed out some simple hard wooden containers. "I've seen whole batteries of power-driven mortars at Essonnes, but we do things more simply here. The process begins with nine parts of saltpeter, two of pulverized sulfur, and three of powdered charcoal moistened with two liters of water and then placed in each mortar. We have the men pound the mixture for an hour, after which the contents from the second are scraped into the first, the third into the second, and so on. The process is repeated at three-hour intervals with occasional moistening until all the powder has been beaten in each of the four graduated mortars."

"Isn't it extremely hazardous work?"

"Certainly. That is why the mortar men are the highest paid on the fazenda. In twenty-four hours one man in this shed can earn what would take a month picking coffee."

"They're willing to take the risk?"

"The minute we lose one, another runs to take his place."

"Are accidents frequent?"

"Not really. We're well prepared for them. In order to channel the damage upward, the roof planks are not nailed down; they are simply laid across the rafters."

"That protects the men in the shed?"

"Not the mortar men, but those in the surrounding area are usually spared." Krauss noticed Erik's grim expression. "So, you think me heartless? There is risk with every work, is there not? Does your father not lose men at his mill? Are there not snakes and scorpions in the fields? Yes, this is hazardous work, so the men are compensated for the danger. We hold no slaves anymore, but even when we did, they did not shirk this work. A slave who agreed to be a mortar man was freed after five years."

"How many men have you lost?"

"Six," Krauss said flatly.

To himself Erik admitted that was not many, though he didn't realize that Krauss had meant six so far that year and not the sum total since he'd begun the operation. "I apologize if I sounded critical, Colonel. It's quite an amazing business."

"You understand, the key to the high grade we are able to achieve with such simple methods is the wood. Nowhere in Europe can such a fine charcoal be found as we can make from the imbaúba. It's black gold, easy to find, easy to mine."

He put his arm around Erik and steered him across the courtyard. "Now I'll take you to the pulverizing mill, also the drying and graining rooms."

A slight wind churned the pale red earth into a fine dust that billowed around their feet. Erik began to choke. Krauss handed him a dipper of water. "You must learn when to hold your breath, my boy!" He patted him on the back, then launched into his explanation of the next process. "After the roller mill pulverizes the gunpowder, it is dried, then sifted. The explosive characteristics depend, in very large part, on the size of the granules." He let some powder fall through his fingers. "This grade is excellent for blasting caps. Kilo for kilo, you can find little to match it for cost against profit."

As they rounded the corner, Leandra Krauss called to them. "Erico, your wife . . ."

"Is Margaret still feeling poorly?" She'd declined Krauss's offer to accompany him and Erik on their tour of the property and had gone back to bed after breakfast.

"Not at all. My herb tea worked wonderfully. But I think you should go to her now."

"Will she be able to travel tomorrow, or must I beg a few more days of your hospitality?"

"It would be our pleasure to have you stay even longer, but why don't you ask her yourself."

"Leandra, I was just going to take Erico to see how I've converted the old sugar engenho."

"Later, Franco, mais tarde."

Erik caught the gleam in her eye. His heart soared. A woman with eleven living children should know about these things. He started to run toward the house. Smudged from charcoal and black powder, he burst into their large, airy bedroom. Margaret sat in a chair, looking out across the flanks of coffee bushes in the distance.

"Well?" he asked.

Her hands were folded in her lap and she remained unusually quiet. "I think so."

"When can we know for certain?"

"It could be weeks . . . to be absolutely sure. But Dona Leandra has much experience . . ." Her words were oddly punctuated. "She says that it's without a doubt, so . . ."

In the soft light Margaret looked serenely beautiful. "Are you happy?" he asked, knowing the question foolish the moment he'd spoken.

Margaret turned slowly toward him. Now the light created a shimmering aura behind her. "If I am, then I've never been happy before. This feeling is so different from anything I've ever known."

Erik wanted to be as thrilled as she was, but often pregnancy captured all of a woman's attention. It had happened with Gunilla, even with Isabel, but somehow he hadn't expected the same with Margaret. Right now she looked so fragile and rare, like one of his father's blossoming orchids. This time it would be different, he pledged, as he bowed like a courtier and kissed her hand.

❦8 "Diversity!" Though Erik had resolved not to raise his voice, his father's stubbornness had forced him to shout. "All I'm asking is that you consider the plan on its own merits without condemning it because it wasn't your idea first."

"Nor was it yours, my son," Sven Larson snapped. He opened the doors from his study that led out into the orchid garden, took a deep breath of the balmy air, then continued. "Krauss may be a very successful agriculturalist, but he knows nothing of textiles. I'll allow him to tend his coffee beans in peace if he'll permit me the same courtesy with my mills. And may I add once and for all, munitions are entirely out of the question!"

"Let's take it from the beginning, Father. The most profitable part of our business is the retail stores, right? You and I agree that we should expand the stores. We now have fifteen locations and thirty-five more ready to open. By my calculations, we can barely keep the ones we've opened stocked and still meet our export orders, so we must expand. You've already contracted for the new machinery; you've begun the addition to the plant. But how are we going to run the machinery without power? Power from wood. Even you cannot deny that we must find new sources for inexpensive trees. We've often talked about the need for someone to go on a buying expedition. The colonel's idea of working along the coast instead of going inland is brilliant; at least you must concede that."

"I'd thought of it myself, but until now our reserves were satisfactory."

"Let's not argue over whose idea it was — Krauss's, yours, mine, or Nossa Senhora herself! The point is that it will work, but it will take barges, men, a logging operation. All I'm saying is that while we're hauling wood to burn for running the factory generators, let's also select some of the desirable specimens of fine furniture woods like jacarandá and mahogany for resale in Europe and also imbaúba wood for charcoal. All three needs can be met from the same forests. If only you'd seen Krauss's operation, the simplicity of it, the profitability from so little effort!"

Sven Larson lifted a small brass pruning tool from a crockery container on his desk. "How do you propose you do everything?" He stepped into his atrium. "It would take a year or more of traveling the coastline to purchase the trees, supervise the lumbering and transport. And what about your Margarida? Do you think she'd tolerate your absence, especially in her condition? You forget she's not the typical woman. If she was, it might be simpler." He began to clip some withered orchid blossoms.

The uneasiness that Erik had felt at the beginning of the discussion welled into an unexpected rage at his father's attitude toward his wife. Typical! Did he mean not passive like Francisca or his mother, not content to remain behind high walls and grow fat on sweets and successive pregnancies? Silently he watched his father ministering to his prize cattleya crossbreeds. Sven corresponded with orchid growers all over the world and dreamed of visiting others' collections one day to swap stories and collect seeds. The man was a complex adversary. A pity we don't have a larger family, Erik thought. With a brother or two he'd have been able to gain wider support for his new plan. As it was,

Augusto had been siding with his father-in-law on this issue, perhaps seeing it as a way to ingratiate himself.

Erik followed the old Swede to the small pond where the night-blooming cereus grew. Its odd thick leaves, each spawning identical branches, had grown several feet larger in the last few years. To support its tentaclelike growth, his father had staked it in numerous places. Erik watched as he tied some straggling branches back.

"When did it bloom last?"

"About six months ago, the night of your mother's birthday. Sixteen blossoms in one evening! The odor was overpowering! It's amazing how many times it has bloomed for special occasions. Sometimes I think this is one plant with a soul."

"I wouldn't be surprised!" Erik remembered his first night in the garden with Margaret. Though he hadn't told his father it had bloomed, so as not to compromise Margaret, he'd always wondered if his father, on seeing the dead blossom, had regretted missing it. "My wife is very fond of the plant. Perhaps you might give her a cutting some day."

"I'd be most pleased to start one for her. Perhaps in six or seven months I can force it to bloom."

"How?"

"The plant can be fooled by how many hours it's exposed to sunlight, how much water it receives. It chooses to flower in summer, so I'll take a cutting indoors, and rearrange the seasons for it. It'll be an interesting experiment."

The horticultural discussion had lightened his father's mood to the point where Erik decided to broach the second part of his plan.

"I understand your worries about sending me on a wood-buying mission; that's why I'd like to propose someone else for the task."

"Whom did you have in mind?"

"Margarida's brother, Raleigh."

"What makes you think he could act as our representative in very complex business arrangements?"

"First, I believe he can be trusted. Also, the man's traveled widely throughout Paraná on his religious missions, preaching to all sorts of people: matutos, fazendeiros — just the sorts he'd encounter working for us. I could instruct him in the financial side. He's had several years of education at a university, so he's not stupid."

"But this devotion to religion . . ."

"Frankly, I think he took it up because he saw no future in his father's landholdings. After seeing Lizzieland myself, I'd have to agree that he made a wise decision on that matter."

"Gigo, you are blind to everything that concerns your wife and her family!" Sven's eyes soared to the blue, cloudless canopy above the atrium. His tone turned sardonic. "What kind of judgment put a bandido in charge of his boat?"

Erik willed the irritable edge out of his voice. "I agree he made a tragic error, but he learned his lesson. Lately, I've been impressed with his modest conduct in Rio. He's made no demands on our family, though he very well might have. I don't know how Marianne manages with Raleigh's small subsistence payments for his work at the Bible Society. They've only one servant in the house."

"I admit I like his wife. Lots of courage in that one . . . and sense."

"All the more reason to have confidence in them."

Holding a broad smooth cereus leaf in his hand, Sven brooded over his son's arguments. "This one's quite mature." He poised the clippers at the point where the leaf emerged from the plant's woody stem. "Notice all the root hairs and budding edges? I think this will make a fine specimen for your Margarida, don't you?"

Though he knew nothing about plants, Erik grinned agreeably. "And Raleigh? Shall we give him a try?"

"You'll take full responsibility for training him?"

"I will."

"All right, then," Sven answered gruffly. Using the clippers with great precision, he separated the cereus cutting from the mother plant.

29 From the moment Margaret entered his wharfside offices one blustery July morning, Erik was on his guard. His wife rarely came downtown, though when she did it was for a specific reason, for she understood that no man should be dis-

turbed at his office too frequently. This time she'd needed to
oversee the shipment of gifts to some North American friends
and relatives. For more than six months she'd had seamstresses
and lacemakers from Bahia working on elaborately embroidered
table linens, and now that they were finished, she'd insisted on
supervising their packaging and addressing herself.

Rico served Margaret cafezinho at a small table beside Erik's
desk. "The largest package goes to Mother's aunt and uncle. The
smaller one is for Mlle Doradou and includes a rose-embroidered
scarf for the piano." Margaret chattered on.

"I'm sure they'll be delighted with the gifts, but you'd better
repeat this all to my secretary. Rico, call Seu Vicente, por
favor."

"Sim, Seu Erico."

"What's this?" Margaret idly lifted an envelope addressed in
swirling calligraphy that had been set on top of some accounting
sheets on her husband's desk.

"I think it's some sort of announcement," he replied noncha-
lantly.

Margaret pulled out an invitation engraved on heavy buff stock
and read aloud. "It's for a party given by Celso Tavares. Do I
know him?"

"No, I don't think so." Already Erik was on guard. Tavares,
while a business acquaintance for many years, did not enjoy one
of the best reputations in Rio. "He's actually more a friend of
Augusto's than of mine. We've done some work with his father's
law firm, so I suppose that's why he's invited me. I think he's in
construction himself."

"I'd like to meet him."

"Some other time. In your condition, I'm certain you wouldn't
want to have a late evening out."

"I barely show at all. Besides, the dressmaker made me some
'transitional' dresses that should do very nicely."

"You'll hardly know anyone there."

"Would you rather attend without me?"

"Of course not."

"I think we should go. Since you've been tiring of my musician
friends, perhaps it's time we made some acquaintances with an
entirely new social set."

"That's not true. The Nettos, the de Mellos, and the others were my friends long before we were married."

"If that's so, why have you been criticizing the maestro so openly?"

"I apologize, querida. It's just that he talks incessantly about ideas I don't fully comprehend."

"His talent is so immense, he dwarfs the rest of us musicians as well. I expect he'll be off to Europe quite soon. He's applied to the Conservatoire again."

"You'll miss him."

"Certainly. He stimulates everyone."

"Stimulates, eh?" Erik arched his eyebrows meaningfully.

"Erik!" She punched her husband's shoulders playfully. "You're twisting my words. Besides, nobody can conduct the ensemble as well."

"With his long black baton."

"You're impossible! I think it's time we did make fresh associations!"

Erik groaned inwardly. Why was she persisting? "Well . . ."

Vicente Cardoso came into the room, wearing his usual slate-grey suit and high wing collar. "Dona Margarida, how delightful to see you!"

"Boa tarde. It's good to see you as well."

"How might I assist you?"

"I have a list of instructions . . ." She handed them to Cardoso and turned back toward Erik. "I'll take the invitation and write our acceptance, all right?"

Erik nodded mutely. He had far more important matters to deal with that day. When Margaret left, he turned back to the papers on his desk but couldn't concentrate. Although Tavares had given some indiscreet parties in the past, they'd mostly taken place around Carnaval time. This was probably going to be a harmless social evening, one they both might even enjoy, he told himself to put his mind at rest. Besides, he could count on his "jeito" not to fail him.

Jeito. This was a characteristic Brazilians claimed as uniquely their own and one they admired especially. It meant a peculiar knack for knowing when trouble might be stirring, the ability to fix, manage, and arrange complex affairs with apparent ease. Fortunately, Erik had been richly endowed with this intuitive sense, this innate cleverness. His timing in monetary matters was legendary; his guesses had brought him luck in the commodities market; and there never had been a woman he'd wanted that he couldn't have. All these successes he, as well as many others, attributed to his jeito. So, he thought as he turned to the accounts, it better not fail me now!

❧   ❧   ❧

The evening of the party Erik racked his brain for any plausible excuse not to attend. If Margaret looked the slightest bit fatigued, if Astrid were cranky, if the weather was foul . . . But no, Astrid had already been sent to her grandparents for the weekend, the weather was cool and dry, and Margaret, dressed in a masterful gown of violet pleats, looked ebullient. She wore a choker of the finest Brazilian amethysts, the size of quail eggs, in a baroque gold setting, with matching teardrop earrings. The only effect of her condition was a glowing skin that made her appear by far the most beautiful woman he'd ever seen.

"I replied to the address on the envelope," she said as they were getting into the Protos. "It's at a private club, not his home."

"Most Cariocas don't have homes as grand as ours or staffs that can handle large parties."

"Will we know anyone else there?"

"Augusto should make an appearance."

"Really? Francisca didn't say anything about it."

"You know she doesn't care to go out in the evenings."

"She would if Augusto wouldn't embarrass her by drinking so much."

"I can't do anything about that," Erik replied glumly. "Take Avenida Beira Mar," he ordered his driver.

"I'm sorry," Margaret apologized. She knew Erik had very little interest in discussing his surly brother-in-law. Augusto was an aggravating thorn in Erik's side, first because his marriage to his sister was not entirely happy and also because he was an extremely poor businessman. "Sometimes I think we should pay him to stay away from the office," Erik once complained privately.

Margaret leaned back on the comfortable leather seat, enjoying the glistening lights along the waterfront. They rimmed the scalloped bay like captured stars.

"I can't believe this section of the new roadway's finally open," Erik said in a grumpy voice. "At least the new Paulista knows how to finish a job as well as start one." Under the administration of Brazil's new president, Rodrigues Alves, the massive civic projects begun many years ago were finally being completed.

"Without that engineer, Pereira Passos, not much would have changed, would it?"

Erik nodded his agreement.

"Will your father be there tonight?" she asked to change the subject.

"No, I don't think so. This is a party for the younger set."

"What a pleasant change! I'm quite looking forward to . . ."

"Querida," Erik began seriously.

Margaret reached for his hand. "Is something the matter?"

"No, it's just that . . ." Deus! If only Margaret had noticed that the invitation had not really been meant for her. Only his name had appeared on the envelope and he was certain it had been delivered to his office, not his home, quite deliberately. How was he going to explain who might be attending tonight's gathering? Yet, maybe he was wrong. Events such as this brought together prominent men from all over Rio, and the connections they made were often invaluable. Women were only included for decoration, but everyone would certainly welcome his wife. Because she played in public several times a year, her name was well known. Erik proudly sat in the front row for every performance and clapped the loudest. The first bouquet she received was always from him: dozens of cascading white cymbidium orchids. An invitation to a private recital in his home was becoming a coveted social coup. Probably Celso Tavares was just hoping for his own turn. Erik looked over to where his wife waited to hear what was troubling him. Her eyes were bright, expectant, innocent. But she wasn't a child anymore. Since she'd blossomed into a sensual, knowing woman he'd found her even more desirable than when they were first married. He squeezed her warm hand. "It's nothing. I just want you to have a good time."

"I will, don't worry. Since I've cut back on my performances, I haven't been getting out for rehearsals as often. I guess I just needed a change."

He exhaled slowly. At least his wife was quite a different sort from the usual Brazilian wife, Erik consoled himself. How many other women had a musical career to satisfy their creative urges? Who else's wife had won acclaim for her own accomplishments, not just those of her husband? With her North American upbringing, Margaret also viewed his society in a different, more sophisticated way than someone who'd known nothing else. Usually she tolerated differences in attitude and culture as "foreign" concepts that need not apply to her and her life. At least that's what Erik tried to remind himself as they turned into the torch-lit driveway of the Náutico Clube.

The Nautical Club was decorated with ships' flags from around the world. A champagne bar had been set up on one side of the large reception hall. Men clustered in the center of the ballroom's polished teakwood floor, while the women hovered around the margins like trimmings on a cake. Erik and Margaret were greeted by Celso Tavares, a tall, slender man who appeared younger than Erik. He had an outsized mustache that turned up jauntily at the tips and wore an extremely tight, but finely tailored, white worsted suit.

"Celso, I'd like you to meet my wife, Margarida," Erik said with great precision.

"What an unexpected pleasure! You are the pianist, am I right?"

"Sim, obrigada. Muito prazer."

The fact that Celso squeezed his wife's hand a few seconds too long did not go unnoticed by Erik. He hooked his arm with hers and tried to lead her to another group of acquaintances. When Margaret looked away, Tavares raised his eyebrows with surprise, lifted his shoulders in an elaborate shrug, and smiled at Erik wickedly, as if to say, "All right, old boy, now what are you going to do?"

Erik searched the room for someone Margaret might know. There were a few familiar faces among the men, but the moment he scanned the women present he knew his instincts had been correct all along. If only he could get her alone for a minute to explain . . .

Someone clapped Erik on the back. "Erico, como vai? How's it going?"

"Aarão!" Erik spun around. "It's as usual . . . mais ou menos." He sculled his hand from side to side. "You know . . . so-so."

"I bet!" the man laughed. "So-so to you would mean a fortune to anyone else!" Erik was surrounded by men with whom he'd gone through school. He pushed his wife forward. "Margarida, I'd like you to meet an old chum, Aarão Rezende. He's Senator Leão Rezende's son. He'll probably be following in his father's footsteps, right, Aarão?"

Rezende bowed and kissed Margaret's hand. "Beleza . . ." he murmured. Erik wasn't certain if it was her bosom or her jewels he stared at so covetously. Whichever, he was annoyed.

Another man took Rezende's place. Erik introduced him. "I believe you've met Dr. Gil de Toledo Soares at Boa Vista, Margaret. His grandmother's house is just down the hill from ours."

"Oh yes, Doctor, I'm so pleased to see you again," Margaret said graciously. She'd always liked the shy bald-headed medical doctor and his petite wife, Maria Clara.

Just as she was about to ask where his wife was, Erik presented yet another acquaintance. "Querida, I don't believe you know Dr. Julio Velloso de Mattos. He used to live quite near us in Flamengo when I was a boy, but now his business takes him to Minas Gerais, where he's with the office of the public prosecutor."

"Muito prazer, Dr. de Mattos." Margaret smiled charmingly.

The dour-faced man did not melt under her spell. "It's my honor, Senhora Larson," he replied stiffly. "My mother knows Dona Guilhermina quite well and has heard you play many times." He stared at Margaret for a long moment as though he were debating whether to say what was on his mind. Finally, it seemed that he dared, so he added, "I also have known your sister-in-law for many years."

Erik shot an ugly warning glance at de Mattos. His lips curled inward as he walked away without another word.

Margaret and Erik were alone. "Odd man, isn't he?" she asked curiously. "Was there ever something between him and Francisca before Augusto?"

"Perhaps . . ." Erik replied darkly.

"Speaking of Augusto, is he here or not?" Margaret knew that Francisca rarely accepted social engagements outside the family and that her husband rarely refused one.

"I haven't seen him yet. He might be upstairs."

"Upstairs? What's there?"

"A deck overlooking the water. That's probably where the buffet and music will be."

"Now I remember. We came here for dinner with some friends of your father's a few years back. We were seated upstairs. The view of Sugar Loaf under a full moon was magnificent that night, wasn't it?"

"Yes, I think so . . ." Erik said distractedly. "Would you like a glass of champagne?"

"Maybe one. The bubbles seem to upset me lately."

"I told you we shouldn't have come! If you'd like to leave now . . ."

"A single glass, even two, won't hurt me. I'm feeling marvelously well tonight."

Erik swallowed quickly. "Well, we won't stay too long."

If Margaret wondered why she hadn't yet been introduced to any of the women, she hadn't said anything. At social gatherings it was not uncommon for the men to congregate in one place and the women in the other, mixing only for meals and dancing. He couldn't procrastinate much longer. Soon he'd have to go to his host and request introductions to some of the other ladies. Then it would be necessary to excuse himself and join the men for a few shots of stronger spirits at the outside bar or a cigar in the downstairs smoking room.

As if on cue, Celso Tavares was at his side. "Dona Margarida, I hope you are enjoying yourself."

"Very much. It's always a pleasure to meet new people and renew acquaintances."

"Por favor . . ." Her host graciously waved his hand forward in a gesture that meant he'd follow her toward where most of the women were gathered. "I understand you'll be performing at the

Lyric Theater in the near future," he chatted as they continued across the room lit with softly glowing brass ships' lanterns.

"Why yes, do you like concerts?"

"Very much, but alas, I attend all too infrequently. Now I will have more than one excuse to go." He smiled broadly at Erik.

"Why is that?"

"My company has the carpentry contract for the new Municipal Theater, so I need to study the Teatro Lírico's fine acoustics as part of my job and . . ." The grim look on Erik's face cut him off. "What will you be performing next? And when?"

Margaret gave a high melodious laugh. "It's at the end of August, but I'm afraid you may be disappointed. The concert will be a benefit for the crippled children's society. I'll be performing amusing pieces written for young people, selections from Schumann's 'Album for Youth,' for instance. Also, it will be the debut of a delightful contribution by our own Joaquim Freire called 'The Kite.' We're hoping many parents will bring their entire families."

"Well, even if I can't attend, I'll surely subscribe to tickets for such a noble cause," Tavares said in a flat voice. They were now standing near several women dressed in iridescent silks. "Dona Margarida Larson, it is my honor to introduce Dona Germana, Dona Clementina, and Dona Adriana." He stepped back to permit a waiter in a sailor's uniform to present platters of appetizers. When Margaret looked away from the women, he had disappeared, dragging Erik in his wake. "She'll have to . . ." was all she heard of her host's fading remarks to her husband.

"Oooh! These look delicious!" Clementina was saying. "Won't you try one?" she asked Margaret.

Disquieted by the odd introduction and the sudden departure of her husband, Margaret stammered, "Why . . . ah . . . certainly." She helped herself to a small stuffed cabbage and a few of the acarajés, small bean croquettes. She popped a croquette into her mouth. Suddenly her mouth began to burn. The acarajé had been dipped into a deceivingly hot pepper sauce. "Ai!" she choked.

"Dê-lhe uma xícara de agua!" Germana clapped her hands.

A glass of water miraculously appeared. Margaret drank it down. The heat in her mouth subsided somewhat. Now, unfortunately, she'd have to think of something to say to the woman. What had their last names been? she wondered, forgetting that Tavares had not mentioned surnames for any of the three. "Which one is your husband?" she began stupidly.

Germana, who had very ordinary, almost peasantlike features, but an enormous bosom, smiled shyly. "I'm with Renato Froes da Faria."

"Oh, I don't think I met him," Margaret answered warily.

"And I'm with Dr. de Toledo Soares," Adriana added.

Margaret turned toward the woman in the glittery pink gown. She had skin the color of palest milk chocolate and extraordinarily beautiful dark eyes surrounded by a fringe of black lashes. Margaret's gaze fluttered down to the woman's hands. She wore a large smoky topaz ring surrounded by pinprick diamonds, but no wedding band. She was certainly not her escort's wife!

Margaret felt as if she was awakening from a long dream. Erik had tried to warn her . . . He hadn't wanted to accept the invitation; he hadn't expected her to find any of her friends there. Francisca hadn't been invited. In fact, if the truth be known, she probably hadn't been invited either. Finally, she understood Erik's reluctance to accept. All along she'd thought he'd been embarrassed or worried about her pregnancy. That wasn't it at all! This party was for men and their mistresses, not their wives. How could she have been so stupid, and why ever had he let her talk him into bringing her?

Somehow a glass of champagne had found its way into her hand. She clutched the cool stem as though it might support her and pretended to be listening to some talk of a hairdresser who was now the rage.

All these men: the son of a senator, a public prosecutor, a doctor — many of Rio's leaders of industry and society — were unashamed to gather publicly with women who were not their wives! Why was she so shocked? She knew this sort of thing existed in Brazil. She'd heard stories of the men with second families; she knew wives who turned their backs on the matter, content with their privileged status. For the most part they lived quietly behind high walls, caring for their babies and households. Even Guilhermina once told her that she was proudest to be "the mother of a man." If her man, husband or son, had a few dalliances, it was not merely forgiven, it was obviously expected. Not that Margaret wanted so graphic a reminder of blatant indiscretion. She never should have come, she realized far too late.

"Would you like to go see the buffet upstairs?" Clementina asked in a low, sensual voice. "The club's chef does remarkable ice sculptures. I once saw a whole sailing ship carved on rolling waves!"

Margaret followed her rustling lemon-yellow skirt up a circular stairway. Clementina was a tall mulatta with flashing feline eyes. Margaret realized how attractive she would be to any man. Even Erik could be seen admiring women of her type, though Erik would certainly never . . . No! Maybe he attended this sort of gathering before their marriage, maybe when he was a younger man, but never since! Why, he hardly ever went out in the evenings without her and then only for family meetings or business suppers with visiting buyers. Erik with Clementina, Germana, or Adriana? Margaret closed her mind to the thought.

A huge buffet was set out against the far wall of the upstairs dining room.

"Ooooo!" Germana cried when she saw the array of artistically arranged foods. Two matched leaping dolphins sculpted from ice held a platter of caviar in their mouths. The center of the table featured a roast suckling pig surrounded by pineapples. Lavish side dishes included tripe with haricots, roast beef in brown sauce, stuffed crabs, and beef stew in fluted pumpkin baskets.

Margaret's attention was quickly diverted from the mouth-watering morsels. In the far corner of the candlelit room, Augusto was seated beside a pale mulatta with long black hair to her waist. He was stroking her arms so intently that, for the longest moment, he didn't realize his sister-in-law was in the room. When she caught his eye, his lips twisted cruelly. He deliberately reached over and kissed his companion passionately, his tongue lingering in her mouth.

Margaret felt dizzy. She reached over to the nearest table to steady herself. Germana was at her side. She looked over at Clementina and signaled her to fetch Erik. "A baby?" Germana asked wisely.

"Yes, in six months."

"Then you mustn't have any of the leitão assado. Pork is always bad for you during that time. Even the sight of anything so fatty used to make me sick. Is this your first?"

"Sim."

"Ótimo!"

"You have children?" Margaret asked queasily.

"Two. A boy and a girl."

"Sim." Margaret wondered idly who was the father of these children.

"Margarida . . ." Erik was beside her, his face ashen. He spoke shakily. "I told you we . . ." He caught sight of Augusto. "Deus!" he muttered. Augusto's hands had boldly wandered to his companion's cleavage. "Merda!"

Erik strode over to Augusto and whispered a few words. Augusto shouted back. "I don't care what you say!" It was obvious he'd had too much to drink. "Mind your own business or . . ."

"Or what? You . . . pau-d'agua! Drunkard!"

"For starters your father would probably be interested to know you've been seen with Julio de Mattos tonight. If not . . . your sweet baby sister would . . ."

Erik grabbed Augusto's lapels. "Preste atenção!" Erik spoke in a slow, deep voice. "Pay attention, you puny bastard, or you'll be out on the street."

"That's just what you and that bicha, that fairy, Raleigh are plotting, isn't it? Why does he get all the choice assignments, eh?" Augusto whined. "If you don't watch your own ass, he'll screw it soon enough!"

"Basta!" Erik warned. Out of the corner of his eye, Erik could see Germana and Clementina leading Margaret outside for fresh air. "Puta!" he spit. "You're a whore, Augusto. Everyone knows it."

"Don't start any trouble, my dear brother-in-law," Augusto was saying. He looked over his shoulder to see if Margaret was listening and seemed disappointed that she'd left. "Everyone, eh? Well, everyone also knows all about Isabel. I believe one of those 'ladies' with your innocent little wife is one of her oldest friends."

"You wouldn't . . ."

"Don't bet on it . . . Brother!" he spit.

"Vá pro inferno!" Erik cursed.

In the shortest time span possible, Erik had Margaret in the Protos. They rode all the way home in silence.

10 It was one of those bleak, aching August afternoons, so typical of the winter in Rio. The browned leaves of the tamarind trees shimmered like liquid coffee under the patina of misting rain. Almost the whole of Corcovado peak was wreathed in shifting clouds. Erik decided to take the Protos to his parents' house that evening for supper.

"Severino, take the car out for me. I'll be driving it myself."

"Sim, Seu Erico."

He carried Astrid to the car in his arms to avoid staining her white stockings with mud.

"I thought that the worst of the construction would have been completed while we were away," Margaret said grumpily. "All they seem to have accomplished is to move the piles of rubble from one side of the boulevard to the other."

"I agree that from above ground it seems as if there's been no progress, but you must realize how many kilometers of pipe are already in place. When the entire system is hooked together, it will be an engineering miracle."

Sighing mightily, Margaret leaned back in the seat and tried to get comfortable as the car swerved to avoid the largest of the ruts. "The miracle will be if we ever see a real roadway again."

"Papai, it's scary!" Astrid said as they drove through the billowing fog up to the Larsons' gate. The mansion at Flamengo looked like a glowing beacon wrapped in gauzy light.

"Will all those babies be there, Papai?"

"Yes, I suppose so."

"Even with Tio Raleigh away?" Astrid whined.

"I'm certain your grandfather sent the carriage for them."

"Why? They aren't *his* grandchildren!"

"No, but they belong to our family," Erik said firmly.

Margaret took Astrid's cool little hand in hers. "Astrid, querida, you were the first. That makes you very special to everyone."

As they pulled under the portico lights, Erik could see his daughter's obvious pout. "Come now, we're going to have a wonderful time."

When the door was opened for her, Astrid bounded out and rushed inside. Erik reached for Margaret's arm. "It's very slippery."

"In a way Astrid's right, Erik."

"How's that?"

"You speak as though my brother's children are to be counted with your family's heirs."

"I don't understand you." Erik paused at the top step. "I took a great risk by offering him the position in the first place, and I did it for your sake, not mine!"

"No one asked you to do him a favor. If you'd have consulted me . . ."

"Since when must I consult you on every decision? Besides, when are you going to get over your childish feud with your brother?"

"There's no feud. It's just that we're completely different personalities. Now we even have different religious beliefs."

"So that's what fuels your petty disagreements."

"They're not petty to Raleigh. Behind our backs he's said nasty things about my conversion."

"I'm only concerned with what is said to me directly. Frankly, your brother's been most cordial to me."

"That's because he wants to do well in the business," Margaret replied curtly.

"What's wrong with that?"

"You don't see . . ." she began, then stopped.

"Now, don't get overwrought. After the baby comes, you'll be able to think more sensibly about these matters."

"It's wrong to give my brother unrealistic expectations."

"Despite your worst fears, Raleigh's caught on quite rapidly. He took on the assignment to travel toward Recife with enthusiasm. Now, let's have a pleasant evening." He squeezed her close enough to feel the hard mound of her belly pressing into him. "You're looking even more lovely than usual tonight. Have I guessed that you're feeling better too?"

Margaret beamed her agreement as they stepped through the massive bronze doors that opened at their approach. Astrid had run ahead into the smaller drawing room where the children's toys would have been set out in anticipation. Instead of the joyful, noisy scene he expected, Erik found Zefinha comforting Emilia, Francisca's second child.

"Mila, Mila, o que é que há? What's the matter?" Margaret asked. The child was wearing only a simple cotton sleeping dress. Her hair was a mass of knotted tangles and her face was streaked with tears and dirt. Gathering the distressed toddler onto her lap, Margaret kissed her forehead and stared worriedly at Erik.

"Where's Dona Francisca?" he asked the maid sternly.

"Com sua mãe." Zefinha pointed upstairs.

Erik's eyes narrowed. "Stay with the children. I'll be right back."

Though Margaret wanted to follow him, she realized that the baby, still shuddering in her arms, needed her first. As she heard his shoes echoing their double-stepped ascent up the marble stairs, she felt a sinking feeling. Her own baby, perhaps aware of a crisis, flipped about inside her. Without warning, she began to weep. Little Emilia stared up at her aunt, touched the tears on her cheek, and then looked curiously at her tiny wet finger. Margaret forced herself not to make a sound.

She spoke to Zefinha. "Where are the other children?"

"Marcelino didn't come. His father wouldn't let him. The little one came in her mother's arms."

"Marianne and hers?"

"Upstairs as well. I kept Mila because she was screaming. Dona Guilhermina didn't want her to upset the others. When children cry it can be like a fire . . . It spreads."

Erik burst into the room. Never before had Margaret seen such fury on his face. "Pelo amor de Deus! I'd kill him myself if he were here!" His shouting rattled the china commemorative plates that decorated one of the walls. Emilia screamed again. In one corner of the room, Astrid stopped playing with the doll collection and listened intently.

Margaret pushed her husband into the hall. "Calm yourself." She took his hand. "The children are already so upset."

Erik pulled his hand away and paced so quickly toward the staircase that Margaret had to run to keep up with him. "Is Francisca all right?"

"They've sent for the doctor." He reached the first step, swung around, and paced back across the black-and-white squares of marble. "The worst of it is she's expecting again. Did you know that?"

Margaret followed him up the stairs. "No. It hasn't even been . . ." Hearing the convulsive sobs coming out of Dona Guilhermina's bedroom, she clasped a hand over her mouth. "Is she losing the baby?"

"Shhh . . ." Erik motioned toward Marianne's three-year-old daughter, Mary Lee, who sat sucking two fingers outside the door to the room. Erik lifted her up into his arms and kissed both her cheeks. "I'll wait here." He opened the door to let Margaret step tentatively inside.

Francisca was propped up in the center of her mother's large bed, wearing a dressing gown that was torn at the shoulder and exposed a bright red welt. Marianne sat on one side, with her infant child asleep at her breast, while Guilhermina patted a wet cloth across Francisca's face. Marianne stood to make room for Margaret and handed Guilhermina a freshened cloth. The moment the first was lifted, Francisca's battered face was revealed. Both her eyes were swollen, her nose was twice its normal size, and dried blood crusted on her upper lip. In the open *V* of her dressing gown, Margaret could see redness and swelling above Francisca's pale breasts.

"How did such a thing happen?" Margaret choked.

Marianne spoke in English. "Augusto hit her."

"Augusto did such a thing? Is the man crazy?" Margaret untied Francisca's robe. Her whole torso was dappled with the remnants of older bruises that had yellowed as they'd healed. "This isn't the first time, is it?"

Francisca moaned.

"Is it?"

She shook her head.

"Why didn't you say anything before?"

Francisca was too dazed to answer.

Margaret looked back at Marianne and Guilhermina and saw Zefinha tiptoeing into the room. She pointed her finger at Francisca's maid. "You must have known. How long has this been going on?"

Zefinha started to weep. "The senhor made me promise not to say anything."

"You've done nothing wrong, Zefinha," Guilhermina interrupted. "A husband has his rights . . ."

"Rights!" Margaret roared between gritted teeth. "No one has the right to do this to anyone!"

"D . . . d . . . d . . . don't . . ." Francisca's whimpering made Margaret stop.

"I'm sorry . . . I don't mean to make it worse for you, but why?"

"My fault . . ."

"Yours? You're the perfect wife. Already you've given him three children, another on the way . . ."

"If God wills it . . ."

Margaret shot a worried glance across the bed. Guilhermina crossed herself. "Some bleeding, very little . . . We called the doctor."

Erik moved into the room and stood beside the bedroom altar. Gilded plaster statues of Guilhermina's favorite saints were displayed in the velvet-lined niche. All his mother's prayers for her daughter had come to naught. Exhaling slowly, Margaret stood and went to join him. She crossed herself in front of the saints. Erik placed his hands around his wife and let them rest on her swollen abdomen.

"I can't imagine anything that she could ever have said or done to incite her husband to hit her even once, let alone . . . this!" she whispered hoarsely.

"Augusto drinks too much. If we can convince him to be more moderate . . ."

"That's no excuse!"

"Tomorrow he'll plead for her to come home and she'll go."

"Because of the children?" He felt Margaret suck in her breath.

"And because she cares for Augusto, she's grateful to him."

"Grateful!" Margaret's nostrils flared. She tossed her head so hard that pins went flying.

Erik grasped Margaret's hands and tried to think of some way to calm her. "There are some things that you'll never fully understand . . ." he said helplessly.

"Erik, please . . ."

"I can't . . . I promised."

He kissed her on the lips, as if that would bring the peaceful silence he desired. He couldn't answer any more questions. Not that night, not ever.

11 The curtains at the windows moved gently in the night wind. Erik woke thinking he could taste the salt from the sea. Once awake he was too agitated by the thought of his sister's injuries to fall back to sleep. He had so many matters to settle.

Before Margaret's baby was born he'd have to do something about Eulalia and Xavier. He'd insisted they learn to read and write, paying for a local cleric to tutor them, but if they were ever to receive a decent education, they'd have to leave the Parque Panorama to attend a proper school. Erik had considered sending them to boarding schools, but Isabel had rejected the idea.

"You cannot take *my* children from me!" she'd replied righteously. Erik knew that Isabel still resented losing Astrid.

The time had come for Isabel to move to Rio for the sake of the children. He'd found them a charming house on the Santa Teresa hill. When Isabel first saw it, she'd adored the bright yellow façade with the Portuguese tile trim around the doors and steps, the intricate iron gate, and the pretty patio garden overlooking the city. An excellent school was a short trolley ride to the base of the hill.

Only da Silva had objected. "Impossível! How can I run the hotel myself?"

Erik had thought he'd anticipated the problem. "Surely, Perna-de-Pau," he'd said without malice (for everyone called the man Peg Leg), "you realize that the hotel has never been as profitable as we'd hoped. In the city it will be easier for you to get around. The bonde stops right in front of the house. You could get a good job."

"Eu? Who would hire me when there are fifty two-legged men for every job?"

"I myself would help you . . ." Erik was beginning to feel uncomfortable. Ever since his marriage, da Silva had pressed him to the limit. Would he never be satisfied?

"O senhor, you are very kind. What work would I do for you?"

A position with him was not exactly what Erik had in mind, yet the more he thought about it, the more he realized that it might be better to know da Silva's whereabouts than always to be wondering what mischief he was stirring up. I need to get him away from Rio, away from Isabel and the children, he thought shrewdly before speaking. "Da Silva, I'm starting a new venture and will need a reliable foreman. As soon as you are settled at Santa Teresa, I'll discuss the matter with you. Until then, here's double Isabel's allowance to help settle your affairs locally."

Da Silva counted the bills. "Not enough."

Raising an eyebrow, Erik studied the man's leathery face. Must be gambling, whoring, or both. Damn him! He spoke between clenched teeth. "Your expenses are unusually large this month."

Without blinking, da Silva stared back. "I'm just a simple grandfather of two bastards," he said with mock humility. "You've no idea the quantities those children of yours can eat nor how quickly they need new shoes."

The old man sometimes pushed too far. Erik himself provided all their shoes, four pairs each per year, probably more than Perna-de-Pau had worn in his entire life, even when he had two feet. Deus! Would the man ever stop bleeding him? Erik had been able to mollify him up until recently, but for some reason, perhaps because the streetwise old leech sensed that Margaret didn't yet know about Isabel, his greedy demands had escalated. Erik counted out a few more bills into Peg Leg's grasping hand.

❧ ❧ ❧

Once Isabel was situated in Rio, the temptation to see his children more frequently was all-pervading. Isabel was a wonderful mother. Erik was enormously pleased with Eulalia's brightness. She obviously adored her father and clamored over him whenever he'd arrive for their brief meetings. Xavier was shyer, harder to know. When he progressed more slowly than they'd expected, his teacher suggested a vision problem. Erik personally took him to be fitted for spectacles.

"Now I know why there are poles," the boy had said on his way home from the optician. "And why the bonde has that funny arm on top." When Erik realized that Xavier was seeing wires and lines for the first time, he wept that his ignorance had hindered the child. Never again! From then on, his children would have anything they needed.

Arranging visits to Santa Teresa was not simple. Erik's habits had been too well set to change without arousing suspicion. The only part of his day that wasn't always accounted for was during the long midday meal. Three days a week he kept his usual date with his father and other wharfside merchants at the Café Leite; the other two he reserved for "banking."

On those days Severino would drive him to the financial district, then wait patiently at a café near the bank for a few hours. Erik would rush through a brief transaction, use a side door so that even Severino didn't know where he went, and hurry down a few alleys to where the bonde (called that because the trolley system had been financed by the sale of bonds) for Santa Teresa stopped. In five minutes he'd be at the gate of Isabel's house. She'd have a light luncheon prepared as well as a surprising array of interesting topics to discuss. Though entirely self-educated, Isabel read several newspapers and had a natural sense of what was popular and current in Rio at any given time. Once in a while he'd even bring fabric swatches for her opinion. A brown-and-white plaid his designer had rejected, but she'd adored, became the season's best seller.

By the time he'd finished his cafezinho, the children would arrive home from school, show him their papers, perhaps recite a few lessons. With astute planning, Erik found he could be back at the fábrica just before the older men returned from their three-course meal at the Café Leite.

One day, with nothing to keep him at his desk, he found himself leaving for the bank district an hour sooner than usual.

"You're early!" Isabel said, barely containing her joy. "The children won't be home until two. I'm making salada de quiabo."

"Okra, with the hot sauce?"

"Sim. Would you like a glass of vinho verde before?" She spoke unusually rapidly. "I could have the girl finish in the kitchen for me. She's cutting the fruit. I'll go tell her what to do."

Erik strolled onto the terrace. Isabel had covered the ledge with flowering plants that trailed down the rock wall. He grasped the rail and looked across the city. Smoke fires burned from numerous shack houses that dotted the lower hillside. Women and children walked the narrow trails with cans of water, sacks of beans on their heads. The growling of mongrel dogs scavenging in a heap of garbage competed with the squeal of a hungry infant.

Isabel reappeared in a clean dress and wearing the leather shoes that he had given her. Her curly black hair was wrapped in a bright pink bandana that matched the lace trim on the hem of the otherwise plain white dress. She handed him a glass of cool wine.

"Do you like living on Santa Teresa?" he asked.

"I must pretend."

"Pretend to like it here?"

"No, pretend I'm a widow. That's what I tell everyone. It's best I say very little, isn't it?"

"Yes, that's wise. Do they know who I am?"

"Your name, no. They know you come to see the children. They think you a very kind man."

"Will everyone notice I came earlier today?"

"Yes, they will. There's nothing to do for some of these people but watch who gets off and on the bonde."

"What will you say?"

"I will say nothing. They think what they like."

"What do you think?"

Shyly, Isabel turned to unwind the stem of a vibrant orange shrimp plant tangled with a Chinese jasmine vine. "I'm always happy to see you, senhor."

Erik stepped toward her. "Don't call me that!" His voice was momentarily harsh, then deliberately soft. "Do you remember how it was when I first spoke to you?" He recalled the young girl helping behind the bar that Perna-de-Pau had managed near the docks. She'd looked so fresh and tender in that rough district. When she was fourteen, a storekeeper who'd needed an unpaid clerk and bedmate had married her in a false ceremony — then, when he'd tired of her, had thrown her out. Erik had met her the first week she'd gone back to live with her father.

"You covered your eyes when I came up to you. At least you no longer do that."

"The way you looked at me, I thought I was under a spell."

"Me too. I wondered what you'd put in my beer."

"If I'd had a potion, I would've used it more often." She turned away from him and looked across the bay. "Those were very sad days for me. I'd rather not think of them now. I prefer . . . the better times."

"When were those?"

"Oh . . ." She closed her eyes. "When the children were very little babies you used to kiss their bellies to make them laugh." Isabel smiled calmly. "Are you ready for almôço?"

He stepped closer and turned her around to face him. "It's not lunch I'm thinking about."

She pulled her shoulders back and stared lovingly into the familiar blueness of his eyes. "You would like to rest first?"

His loins quivered their response. From their first hours together, Isabel had beguiled him with her simplicity, her warmth, her unselfish love. Everything he had given her was received with gratitude. Margaret. He tried to summon her face, but it dissolved in the bright sunlight that flooded the patio and reflected in Isabel's soft brown eyes. She tilted her smooth bronzed lips to him, and when he kissed her ever so gently she became limp and pliant in his arms. Her familiar musty smell was an overpowering temptation.

"Very much, I'm very tired . . . Por favor . . ." He allowed her to lead the way to the cool back bedroom, still shuttered and dark.

Isabel lifted her dress over her head. Erik hadn't remembered her body so smooth and voluptuous, her thighs so yielding, her ready wetness. He'd almost forgotten the glory and comfort of her dark nipples. Her breasts, now no longer swollen with milk, had a narrower, more conical shape. Isabel offered everything easily. Her hips undulated their welcome, her hands stroked his back rhythmically. Feeling as though he were being swept along by a great rushing tide, Erik drowned in her generosity, rested briefly, then, rejecting the waiting fruit and okra, decided to take the forbidden plunge once again.

❧ 12   By the beginning of the new year, Erik felt supremely content. In a few weeks Margaret's first baby would arrive. He'd never seen Margaret as healthy or cheerful. Only the happiest of music emanated from her piano. He'd been extremely gracious when the doctor had banished him from his wife's bed, though she'd wept at the news, denying that it was necessary. But he'd agreed with the doctor. "We can't take any risks with this child; we waited too long."

"How will you tolerate it?" she'd asked sincerely.

"I'll be brave. It won't be forever, you'll see." It was only when Margaret had hugged him with gratitude that he'd felt, for the first time, a surging wave of guilt.

Just for a short time longer, he promised himself. He'd stop with Isabel as soon as the baby was born. Compared to many other Brazilian men, he might be considered a monk; compared to Augusto, he ranked as a saint.

Augusto, suitably contrite over his violent outbursts, had agreed to a bookkeeping assignment in São Paulo for a few months. It would take Augusto less than an hour to find himself a woman in that town, Erik guessed. He must have had a hundred since his wedding day, which was fine as long as he treated Francisca with kindness. Francisca had recovered admirably, but she and the children had moved in with the Larsons for the duration of the pregnancy, which was proceeding normally despite the scare. With his mother in charge, Erik knew she'd be fine.

The new machinery for the factory had arrived from Europe, and Erik was supervising its installation. All his meticulous planning proved invaluable as each piece fell into place like a jigsaw puzzle. Now all he needed was the continuous supply of wood for the new mill and the imbaúba for the black powder operation. Raleigh's return from his long buying trip was anxiously awaited. Letters of postponement had arrived with brief explanations that matters were progressing, but omitting specific details.

The whole family was waiting at the factory docks when Raleigh's coastal steamer arrived during the second week in January. The man who stepped forward, though, was hardly recognizable as the one who'd departed almost five months earlier. During his travels, Raleigh had gained at least twenty pounds, his closely cropped hair had grown, and his trim mustache had blossomed into a wide, fashionable bristle.

Erik allowed Marianne and the children to have the first moments with him before stepping forward to clap him on the back, forgetting that Raleigh had rarely used Brazilian gestures of friendship. This time he responded in kind.

"How goes it?" he asked Erik genially. "Are you ready for what's coming?"

"So ..." Erik's eyebrows peaked upward. "You've had success!"

"Better than success. If I must say so, the trip was a triumph!"

Even Marianne was perplexed by her husband's uncharacteristic pride, but only said, "Raleigh, you look wonderful." She eyed the crisp white suit he was wearing. "Where did you get that?"

"I had it made in Bahia. All my clothes were too tight. It was important to go to negotiations looking presentable, don't you agree?"

"Certainly." Erik nodded.

Sven Larson stepped forward and shook Raleigh's hand firmly. "A few words, with your wife's permission. After that you must join your family."

"That's very kind, sir. But we've much to discuss." He patted Marianne's hand. "Would you mind if I joined you later? I'll get back as soon as I can, but it will be best if I spend most of the day here. There's much to explain."

"Not at all, Raleigh. Mother Larson is expecting us tonight, so why don't we all meet there?"

Raleigh agreed at once. "Show the men where to take the trunks, but have them bring my footlocker to Senhor Larson's office."

The men chatted amicably as they walked across the wharf to Larson's private quarters. Erik pointed out the progress on the new construction. "We're almost on schedule," he said brightly.

"For Brazil that's a minor miracle." Sven coughed. "When I first arrived from Sweden I used to take each delay as a personal insult. Now if things go too smoothly, I'm concerned that something terrible is about to happen." He stopped smiling and stared at Raleigh meaningfully.

He let his son run on about the theoretical profits in gunpowder as they waited for Raleigh's footlocker to be delivered. Sooner or later, Erik and the younger men would inherit the business, and when they did, they'd have to live with the fruits of their decisions. At least now he was still here to guide them if they made mistakes, to prevent minor errors in judgment from escalating into ruinous crises. Sometimes Sven wondered if they understood

how fragile a financial empire could be — the balance of payments, expenditures, sales, and collections had to work just so.
New ideas were fine as long as they were buffered by the secure
running of the strong central core of the business.

Two laborers carried in the heavy, battered trunk. "Set it beside the table," Raleigh directed. Taking a key from his pocket, he
started to open the lock. "I kept this with me day and night,
didn't care if anything else made it back. I even slept on it when I
couldn't get a bed or a berth. Everyone must've thought I was
carrying gold."

Raleigh lifted out a top tray that held a few personal articles of
clothing, two worn Bibles, and a small package wrapped in twine,
which he opened first. It contained specimens of precisely cut,
planed, and polished wood. "These are the best cabinet woods I
could find. You probably recognize this sample of jacarandá and
this mahogany. The trunks run fifty to seventy centimeters in diameter and from four to six meters in length. With hauling, saw-
ing, and transportation to the port, the cost amounts to thirty
mil-reis per metric ton. Add your freight to Le Havre or Antwerp
for a total cost of ninety mil-reis, delivered, but billed at more
than six hundred mil-reis."

Erik whistled. "That's a hefty profit!"

"We aren't in the business of exporting timber," Sven protested mildly.

"I realize that, sir," Raleigh said steadily. "I'm just asking you
to keep these numbers in mind while I describe what I've accomplished."

The second level of the footlocker contained roll after roll of
official-looking documents sealed with colorful government
stamps. "What are those?" Erik asked.

"I'll explain in a moment."

Sven reached down, picked one at random, and eyed it suspiciously.

"Let me show you the charts first." Raleigh lifted out a ragged-
edged map and spread it open. "This is the vicinity of São Mateus
in southern Bahia. The portions I've outlined in red are the timber areas where the most desirable trees are available. After some
of these districts are forested, young cacao trees are planted, giving the land a second lucrative use."

"That's very interesting," Sven began. "But what does that have to do with your wood purchases?"

Erik could see Raleigh wilting under scrutiny. With an unsteady hand he went back to the map. "In this particular area I negotiated with the landowners on the price of the trees we were interested in. They ranged from two to three mil-reis apiece. For the less valuable cedar and pine, somewhat less in larger amounts with long-term contracts. To me, those figures were exorbitant considering the quantities we'd be needing. With one particularly stubborn landowner, I pointed out that he was valuing his trees at ten times the worth of his land. 'Then make me an offer on the land,' he said in jest." Raleigh twisted his hands.

At once Erik understood the full meaning of all the rolls of paper. He took the one from his father's hand and broke the seal. "These are deeds!" He spun around to face his brother-in-law. "Are you saying you bought *land* instead of *trees?*"

The knobby Adam's apple at Raleigh's throat jerked wildly. "Yes. I bought the land for half the value of the timber in most cases, less in some."

"May I ask how you counted the trunks?" Sven's voice was slow and deep.

"I worked out a system of calculations . . ."

"But the cost!" Erik gasped. "How did you manage it?"

"Various notes. Sometimes I pledged one plot in a different district against the price of a second. The terms on all the largest pieces stretch over many years; a few smaller tracts could be had for the sum I had on hand. We now own those outright. One area in particular was very rich in imbaúba and very near to the sea. You could have a thousand tons shipped a week, if you required it. That alone would pay the debt on that piece in less than three years. After that, all the rest of the wood would be free and clear."

Raleigh misinterpreted the men's silence for interest and prattled on. "The best part of the plan came to me after I'd purchased the first two contiguous pieces, making one large plot of land. I decided that wherever possible, we should own adjoining sections, so eventually we would have the potential to link everything to the sea with private railroads. I didn't succeed entirely, but if you'll look at this larger section of map that takes in Bahia down to Vitória, you'll see how well . . ."

Sven Larson, ashen at the enormity of Raleigh's folly, could barely focus his eyes on the faded, fingerprinted map.

"This is figured in hectares?" Erik asked.

"No, kilometers."

Making a rough measurement between his thumb and forefinger, Erik choked. "Deus todo poderoso! Thousands of people must live on those lands!"

"The population is very sparse, Erik," Raleigh said in a comforting voice. "It's mostly trees — tall, stately, glorious trees. You've never seen such richness. There's massaranduba that the railways are clamoring to get and peroba, the shipbuilders' favorite, that grows over thirty meters high. Why, a single trunk weighs as much as forty metric tons! Also, there's beautiful pau-amarelo and the dark acapu for flooring — like the parquets in your home; louro for cabinet work; sebastião de arruda, which is considered the best wood for European inlay work; not to mention vast quantities of pau-brasil, which besides being used for their dyes is cherished for violin bows. It's no wonder they named this country after those fabulously profitable trees!"

"What I don't understand, Senhor Claiborne" — Sven Larson straightened his shoulders and virtually spat out the key words — "is what made you believe that *you* could undertake such an immense responsibility without consulting me? You've spent *my* money, used *my* name, saddled *me* with the responsibility for thousands of hectares of land and God knows how many people to look after. You were sent to buy *trees*, to provide wood to be burned for fuel or pounded into gunpowder, but not . . ." he sputtered, ". . . not . . ."

Unable to comprehend the extent of Larson's dismay, Raleigh listened without flinching. "With all due respect, sir . . ."

Larson, his pupils narrowing, placed his hands firmly on Raleigh's lapels. Erik took two steps back.

"I did it for the family. I thought that this was the most economical, sensible plan." Raleigh's voice wavered. "We'd own the land, forest it with modern methods, replant cotton or cacao. There's lots of willing labor that only needs proper management.

They've been treated so poorly for so many years. With only the slightest kindnesses . . ."

Sven tightened his grip on Raleigh's jacket until the fabric ripped under his fingers. "Helvete!" he swore in Swedish. "I don't understand how you had the audacity!" He pushed him backward so hard that Raleigh stumbled against the table. The map fluttered to the floor. Raleigh reached for one of the Bibles on the tray beside him and held it up.

"I still believe, once you are over the surprise of it, that you will agree with my decision. I prayed long and hard until I received my answer, here, in the Book of Joshua, the first chapter." He fumbled till he found the right passage. " 'Be strong and of good courage; be not afraid, neither be thou dismayed: for the Lord thy God is with thee whithersoever thou goest.' " He flipped the pages and pointed nervously to the Scriptures. "See, here's the part I took as a sign. 'Every place that the sole of your foot shall tread upon, that have I given you . . .' "

"Raleigh, I think that . . ." Erik interrupted. "Why don't we talk about it again tomorrow. It's more than we expected." Placing his arm around Raleigh's shoulders, he led him out of his father's office.

"You don't think I did the right thing?" Raleigh sounded amazed. "There's all the imbaúba you could ever want. Just the profits from the black powder would pay for everything in a few years."

"Yes, yes possibly. I hope you're right, but Father is very old-fashioned. He's mostly hurt that he wasn't consulted. Perhaps later we'll be able to convince him of the wisdom of . . ."

"Then you agree that it will work?"

"I'll have to study the papers before I can say. These matters are very complex; improper deeds are quite common. You may not have received legal documents. Large landowners must police their properties to prevent bogus claims and keep the peace. It will take some time to learn what we actually have here. Also, your financial transactions are . . . original, to say the least. We'll need to unravel the credit structure you've devised. Why, we don't even know how much you've actually paid or promised to pay, do we?"

"I assure you it will work. Once we start harvesting the wood, the payments will be easy to make. If worst comes to worst, we'll sell a parcel or two to settle our debts. But with this amount of land, we can afford to let some go."

Erik raised his eyes in mock prayer. "You really don't see what you've done, do you?" He shook his head in disbelief.

"What shall I tell Marianne? I can't let her know how upset your father is; she'd never forgive me."

"Don't say anything yet. I'm certain she's just pleased to have you home. Now, go. I'll speak to you tomorrow. Severino! Take Senhor Claiborne home, then take a message to my wife. Tell her not to expect me until very late this evening. I'll be going home with my father."

Erik turned and bounded up the private staircase to the office. His father was hunched over the maps, making his own calculations.

"Inacreditável!" Sven's jowls quivered. His wide bald pate was covered with perspiration. "The land he's purchased would be a kingdom in Europe."

"And you own it, Papai, so you know what that makes you?"

"To think it has come to this!" Sven began to laugh. He unbuttoned his vest and fell back into his favorite chair. "You know, I left Sweden over a political fight with my family. They objected to my going to antimonarchist demonstrations! What would they think to see me, fifty years later, the ruler of such territories? I never realized anyone could *own* that much land . . . let alone pay for it."

"Perhaps it's not exactly as he has explained. Raleigh is very inexperienced in such matters . . ."

"Ah, if it were so . . ." He wiped his shining forehead. "He's no idiot, but he must be watched much more carefully . . ."

"Yes, sir . . . Yes, sire!" Erik bowed, then doubled over laughing.

Sven roared for a minute and then, in a strange, inexplicable moment, his ebullience soured. He wiped his eyes and began gasping for breath. His head flopped over and began to turn a dusky blue. Erik rushed to loosen his collar. "Are you all right?"

Though his face was still flushed, with a purplish tinge around his ears, he seemed a bit better. "Yes. It's easing now. I'm not sure what happened."

"The shock of it . . . It will take time to understand it all, won't it?"

"My son, there are some things I'll never live to understand, nor do I think I wish to. At your age I'd have seen this as a challenge or perhaps as a game, anything but the massive problem it really is. You're younger, more flexible . . . so you'll have to take it on."

Lifting an armful of deeds from the footlocker, Erik agreed silently. I suppose I will. Erik felt his excitement mounting. I suppose I will.

Macumba

1   That February Rio was a city burning under an unrelenting midsummer sun. Carnaval preparations seemed slightly subdued in the enervating heat. Since the first of the year Erik had been eagerly anticipating the days when the mulattas paraded down the streets, wantonly flaunting their undulating thighs, jiggling breasts, and — the most delectable part — their arched bundas. Ah, the buttocks of the Brasileira! The perfect, rounded hearts of flesh on display for all to admire. Carnaval brought out all of Rio's beauty, all its exuberance, all its women! It always came as a great personal release for Erik when Rio cut loose from its moorings in commerce, order, and self-restraint, unleashing its wild, hedonistic soul for a few frenzied days of frolic and abandon. Even though Carnaval could never come soon enough to satisfy Erik, this year, the first he could remember, they had made no plans to celebrate. Their baby was weeks overdue. He worried how the excessive noise and stifling weather were affecting Margaret's lagging spirits. To make her more comfortable, he'd moved her from their house in the lowlands to his parents' Flamengo mansion, which at least was situated to capture any itinerant breeze. It also eased his mind to have Margaret, as her time approached, around his mother.

At noon on the last Thursday before Ash Wednesday, less than forty-eight hours before the "official" start of Carnaval, the Larsons' factories shut down for a week of festivities and recuperation. In the final hours, workers had begun to disappear. One moment a mill hand was adjusting a loom, the next he'd vanished. To secure the machines properly, Erik found himself working in the plant alongside a few of the most faithful and still sober employees.

Sven rushed into the huge spinning room where the bobbins and reels were unnaturally silent. "The stevedores have abandoned the new steam engine on the wharf!"

"Com os diabos!" Erik swore. He rounded up the few stragglers and organized them to move the huge crates inside. Heaving and cursing, they managed to drag the one containing Erik's long-awaited eight-foot flywheel, custom-built in Britain, but they didn't have anywhere near enough men to budge the copper-clad iron boiler or the two-cylinder steam engine.

Erik stood out in the noonday sun, contemplating the problem. "There's nothing to be done about it," he admitted to his father. "They'll have to remain outside all week."

"It's not as though anyone's about to come by and move them," his father said resignedly. "I'm only worrying about vandals."

"We could hire an extra vigia."

"We'll have to, but the chance of his remaining at his post is slim." Sven's overheated face had turned a pulpy red. His shirt was matted to his skin and his breath was labored. "Helvete! Förbannade shit!" From experience Erik knew that whenever his father swore in Swedish it was best not to interfere. "My blood has never adjusted to this kind of heat." He stumbled to a barrel filled with fresh water at the edge of the pier and instead of drinking a dipperful, dunked his head and poured the liquid over his upper torso. Erik couldn't remember ever seeing his father acting so unrestrained. "Papai!"

"That's better!" Sven beamed. "It felt like my brains were going to boil." He stared at his shocked son. "Gigo! You look as though you're about to faint yourself. Here!" He splashed water onto Erik's white linen slacks. Sven's deep bass guffaws were noticed by the few faithful workers still around.

"Ora veja! Os chefes!" They pointed to their bosses frolicking like street urchins."Carnaval! Carnaval!" they chanted, taking this as their cue to disappear.

❧   ❧   ❧

Boom-dah! Boom-dah! Ei-yi-yi! Ei-yi-yi! There's no rhythm in the world like the beat of Carnaval. It begins not on the eve of the festival but on New Year's Eve, called the "grito de Carnival," or "the first whoop of Carnaval." When he was little, the servants would tell Erik that he would be able to know when Carnaval was coming by the sight of the first black man chasing a stray cat. Cat skin was the best material for making the cuíca, an unusual percussion instrument. Even before January, the newest Carnaval songs began to be heard. Local neighborhoods prepared for the great event by meeting at terreiros, or rehearsal grounds, to practice an area's presentation. This year's most popular song was already so well known that Erik could sing along with the lyrics as his car made its plodding way through the streets that had been taken over by celebrants.

> Vem cá mulata
> Não vou lá não
> Sou democrata, Sou democrata
> Sou democrata de coração.

He liked the words. "Come here, mulatta, I'm not going your way. I'm a democrat, democrat deep down in my heart." The song reminded him of Isabel, his mulatta of the heart.

All women were attractive to him, never mind the color. Was he any different from the Portuguese explorers who couldn't resist Indian women or the plantation settlers who'd fallen for slaves? Weren't all Brazilians really democrats of the heart?

"Mulata ... mulata ... democrata de coração." The tin-can beat, played by the bateria of percussionists irrepressibly thumping down the thoroughfares, was contagious and impossible to forget. Erik's feet tapped out the rhythms on the automobile's carpeted floor. He yearned to join the ragtag groups practicing in the streets. The car swerved around a loosely organized group of dancers who concentrated on shuffling along at half time, learning the steps, picking up the beat, and swinging into a heel-and-toe, one-foot-behind-the-other variation. From the rear, the beautiful round female buttocks were swinging crazily, hypnotically. Deus, he loved Carnaval's excesses of sweat and sex and drink!

Erik could easily imagine the women carried away further, bumping and grinding with their legs well apart, tremors rippling down their thighs. Eventually, driving their men wild, the session would end as they'd break off in twos, returning home, falling into bed. Where did they get their energy for hours of practice after a full day's work in some marketplace or scrubbing a floor in a mansion not unlike his own? By the time the car passed through the double pineapples of the iron gates, Erik hoped no one would notice how Carnaval had already infected him.

❦ ❦ ❦

At the door Erik was greeted by a fluttering Guilhermina. "Thank goodness you're home early! With all the crowds on the streets, I worried you'd be quite late. It may have started."

Erik trembled. "You're not certain?"

"She's had pains like this for weeks. They come, they stop. If they continue a few more hours, we'll call for the doctor." His mother touched Erik's cheek with her fingertips. "Come inside."

Erik tried to curb his impatience while his father poured him a glass of cognac. "Drink this," Sven offered cheerfully.

The burning sensation revived him slightly.

"Shouldn't I go to her?"

"Give her a few minutes to prepare to see you." Sven pointed to the tooled leather sofa. "And sit down; it's too hot to pace about."

Erik obeyed his father, but his eyes darted toward the door.

"Tonight you will probably become a father . . . again."

Erik shook his head silently, wondering why this time it felt so different — so much more significant.

"You'd like a son?"

"Who wouldn't?"

Sven sighed. "I remember the night you were born. It changed my life. I . . ."

The sound of footsteps in the hall startled Erik. The cognac sloshed over the rim of his glass.

His mother called to him. "She'd like to see you."

Erik started to rush past his mother, but she caught his arm firmly. "Gigo, listen to me. Margarida is not Gunilla. What happened then was very unusual. If you want to help her, you'll have to be calmer. She has enough to worry about without you making it worse for her."

Erik tried to pull away, but his mother tightened her grip. "Do you understand me?"

"I'm not a fool."

"Then stop behaving like one." Guilhermina reached up and kissed her son on both cheeks, pulled back, and stared deeply into his cobalt eyes. "Go up to her now, but don't stay long. Whatever you do or say, be confident."

At the top of the stairs and at both ends of the hallway, Guilhermina had stationed kitchen servants with palm fans to create a slight breeze on the second floor. As he passed them, Erik barely noticed that they were already dressed for Carnaval.

Margaret had been settled into a corner bedroom because it had the best air circulation. Instead of the prostrate and agonized woman Erik expected, Margaret was sitting in the middle of the bed with her legs crossed in front of her, her hands resting easily on her huge mound of a belly as though it were a bundle quite separate from herself.

"You're home early!" Margaret grinned excitedly.

"Father and I had to close the fábrica ourselves. Carnaval rules the city already."

"Our baby must be a true Carioca! He's determined to join in with Carnaval. Already he's begun to do the craziest samba!" Margaret's delicate skin began to flush from her chest to her brow. "If only it wasn't so hot!" Her breath came in little pants.

"Even Papai couldn't take the wharf today. Deus, this city reeks this time of year. What we need are a few good nights of rain to clean out the culverts and cool the place down. Or move Carnaval to wintertime."

When Margaret didn't respond, he realized she was concentrating on something else. In less than a minute she gave a deep sigh and stared out the window at the cloudless sky.

"What is it?"

"The baby's coming, at least that's what they tell me, but it seems so unlikely." She placed Erik's hands over her belly. "Feel that?"

"It's very . . . hard and tight. Is that good?"

"I think so."

"You don't seem to mind it. I thought . . ."

"It's just a pulling feeling, like a very hard squeeze, and not terribly unpleasant at all."

Erik watched his wife's face freeze again into a questioning expression, then a grimace. Without a word, she slipped out of bed and into the side room, which had recently been modernized with European plumbing. Florinda followed behind and closed the door.

"What's happening?" Erik asked his mother, who had just come bustling into the room.

"Sometimes when a baby's coming there are all kinds of pressures. I always vomited, but Margarida seems to have the opposite problem. Don't worry, it's perfectly normal."

"Will she be in there long?" Erik stared at the closed bathroom door. "Isn't there something I can do?"

The door opened and Margaret stumbled back to bed. She was considerably whiter.

"They're getting stronger?" Guilhermina asked.

Margaret nodded. "I thought it was going to be so easy."

"Where does it hurt?" Erik knelt beside her.

"My back and sides. Not in the stomach where I thought."

"Shouldn't you call the doctor now?"

"Yes, it's time. Go downstairs and tell Severino."

"Then I'll come back here."

"No," his mother said firmly. "Not for at least one hour. By the clock."

"But what if . . ."

"Nothing will happen in an hour, I promise. Your wife needs to rest."

"You'll stay with her?"

"Every minute."

"You'll call me . . ."

"I promise."

"In an hour I can return?"

"Yes, but not a second sooner." Guilhermina impatiently gestured toward the hallway.

"Margaret?" Erik asked in a hopeless plea that the women would change their minds. His wife's back was resolutely turned from him and her concentration was centered somewhere on the faraway hills that loomed like bright emeralds in the flaming afternoon sun.

❦ ❦ ❦

To distract Erik as much as to add a few useful hours to the shortened workday, Sven opened up the ledgers in which he had tried to document Raleigh's land purchases.

"In theory it could work. Your brother-in-law's calculations were not inaccurate. For each parcel of land there is a payment scheme that, by itself, makes sense. In reality, however, it's a nightmare!"

Erik was only half-listening. He strained to hear if there were footsteps on the stairs, call bells for servants, anything that might mean that Margaret's ordeal would soon end. Not that she complained. Every time he had seen her she had been remarkably spirited, describing her pain as tolerable. Even when one gripped her while he was present, it seemed only to silence her instead of causing her the agony he'd remembered Gunilla enduring.

"If having babies were so terrible," his mother had said in the corridor, "no one would have more than one."

Unaware that his son's mind was elsewhere, Sven continued the financial discussions. "Now if we can change the promissory notes on the coastal sector and harvest the export woods first, we'll buy some time on refinancing the rest. Don't you agree?"

"I'm sorry?"

"Where have you been?" Sven asked tensely. Then he spoke more gently. "Can't you concentrate on anything else?"

Erik checked his watch. "I've been home two hours already. How long could it possibly take?"

"I remember that your birth took twelve hours, your sister's nine."

"Gunilla's was very long, more than a day. Two if you count the early pains, but Isabel . . ." He stopped himself.

Sven's eyes darkened. "Were you there for either?"

"No, she never sent for me."

"You see the children often?"

"When I can. I check on their schoolwork, their health. Both are very good students."

"Better than their father?"

Erik winced. "Perhaps."

"Your wife has never been told, has she?"

"No, I'm certain of that."

Raising one of his thick grey eyebrows, Sven continued. "Everyone has conspired to protect Margaret, but two children, two bright, attractive children who know their father to be their own, can't be kept a secret forever. You should be the one to tell her."

"How could I?"

"Better she should hear it from her husband than from someone else. In fact, I'm surprised you haven't had more problems with Isabel's father."

Erik nodded morosely. Perna-de-Pau, the old peg-legged scoundrel, had been after him to marry Isabel since the birth of their first child. When Erik was younger, he'd even begged his father for permission to do so. "You don't object to my bedding her, so why can't I marry her?"

"Are you crazy?" his father had shouted. In the end, Sven's will had prevailed. Isabel's social class had been more of a problem than her color. It was unsuitable, unthinkable, impossible to have such a woman in the family! However, understanding their son's need for a woman, his parents had never asked him to give up Isabel entirely. They'd encouraged him to meet his responsibilities by supporting his illegitimate children generously. But marriage? Never! Then, after Gunilla's death, when Erik, ostensibly to see Astrid, had renewed his visits to Isabel, Perna-de-Pau had escalated his campaign to get a wealthy son-in-law. By that time, however, Erik had matured. With a legitimate daughter of his own and the elevated social position that came with his job as second-in-command in the Larsons' enterprises, Isabel had been obviously unacceptable, even to him. Not that he'd desired her any less. Within weeks of being widowed, he'd found himself seeking comfort in her welcoming arms and solace at her milk-filled breasts. Some nights she'd suckled his motherless daughter on one side while he lavishly gulped at the other. His loins stirred at the memory.

Erik looked his father in the eye. "I promised Lucretia her daughter would never know about Isabel. How can I go back on my word now?"

"That was when your wife was very ill. It was a kindness then. Now that you two will have your own child, it won't mean as much to her. After all, Isabel's children were born long before your marriage to Gunilla or to Margaret."

Erik shuddered.

"Yes?"

"It's more complicated than that . . . now."

"You've been seeing her at Santa Teresa?"

"Just the last few months . . . when Margarida was unable . . ." Sven stared meaningfully.

"I didn't expect anything would come of it . . ." Erik rambled nervously.

"So, suddenly you forget where babies come from?"

Erik's chin drooped. For a moment he played the little boy caught in a naughty act.

Sven, no angel himself before his marriage and discreet thereafter, understood such matters, yet a father's duty was to discourage all behavior that could cause a rift in the family. "Are you admitting there's another on the way?"

"Yes, Papai."

Sven shook his head sympathetically. "The children can be more of a problem than the women, eh?"

"At least I've always accepted my responsibilities. Augusto . . ."

Instantly Sven became enraged. "Never compare yourself to him! Never!" He poured them both another cognac. After one long swallow he spun around and continued in a low, controlled voice. "Let's not speak of this tonight. But after the child is born, we'll take the proper legal precautions to protect all your children. You'll have to settle with Isabel once and for all. And, when your wife is stronger, you'll explain this to her."

"She'll never accept it!" Erik slumped miserably back into his chair.

Sven proffered his son the barely touched snifter, urging him to take a drink. Erik took several gulps before speaking hoarsely. "You've always said that some secrets should never be revealed."

Sven's tone became impatient. "Gigo! You obviously are too unsettled this evening to discuss this or any other important matter." He looked at his watch. "They should let you see Margarida again now."

"It's time?" Erik placed his glass on the marble table so forcefully that the stem shattered in his hand. As he wiped away the shards of glass that stuck to his moist palm, he saw a thin line of blood bubble to the surface. It would need bandaging; perhaps he'd have to remove tiny pieces with tweezers. Even the moderate throbbing was pleasantly involving. Finally he had something practical to do.

2 The child was christened Paulo de Lourenço e de Claiborne Larson. The first name had been chosen because there were versions of it in English, Portuguese, even Swedish; the surname, because it boasted of a triple heritage. In this parentela system, Brazilian children took their mother's surname as well as their father's, adding on the names of whichever relations might assist the child socially. But no matter the baby's lineage, Erik was not particularly impressed with his newborn son. The infant's scrawny limbs looked pitifully weak, his head was covered with only the sorriest strands of pale blond hair, and his buttocks were disappointingly angular. Even so, he had a son, a legitimate son of his own, and Margaret had weathered the birth masterfully. For all that he gave thanks.

While Margaret tended their infant, Erik's attentions were centered on unraveling Raleigh's land purchases. With the help of financial advisers, they were beginning to establish a plan for controlling the investment and making the payments to the landowners. Vital to the scheme was the harvesting of the lucrative furniture lumber for sale overseas. The second most profitable part was the use of the imbaúba for black powder. The original purpose of buying the lumber for fuel at the mill was, for the moment, of the least importance.

While Raleigh was kept busy making hardwood sales to European exporters, Erik designed the gunpowder mills. One of his initial ideas was to prove the key to making that business especially profitable. "Instead of transporting the imbaúba to Rio and then burning it into charcoal here, why don't we build the ovens on the forest sites?" he'd proposed to his father and Raleigh. The wisdom of moving the lighter charcoal instead of the huge logs was obvious.

It was Erik's responsibility to explain to the crews Krauss's method of producing charcoal. He took his father, Raleigh, and a team of men out to a field behind the house at Boa Vista to demonstrate what he'd learned. First, he directed a carvoaria, a large pit, to be dug in the ground. He showed the men how to pile the lumber vertically, the largest trunks on the bottom, the smaller on the top, with as little space as possible between the branches. The end result was an artful arrangement of wood with about one to two meters showing above the ground and the same amount hidden below. Next, the wood was covered with grass and leaves, then blanketed with a layer of sand or topsoil.

"It's important to set the fire in the proper manner," he explained. "You must light it from one side only, being certain you do so against the wind." The damp soil made it difficult for the twigs to catch, but after a few false tries, he seemed satisfied with the burn.

For three days he remained at Boa Vista to supervise the process, inviting his father and Raleigh to return to see the end result. "Carvão!" He showed off the long thin sticks proudly, directing the workers to break them into pieces to fit into burlap bags. When the first two were filled, he slung them over his shoulders easily. "How many trees do I have on my back?" he boasted. "Ten, twelve?"

Until that point Sven could not have been considered a supporter of the black powder plan. He picked up a charcoal stick and snapped it in two. "How are you going to guarantee that all the wood that's cut ends up as charcoal on our docks in Rio?"

Erik looked meaningfully at Raleigh.

"Since I'm the one who knows the area best now, I'd be willing to volunteer, sir," Raleigh offered.

"You've thought of everything, then?" Sven's tone was considerably warmer than it had been in the past.

Erik decided this was a good time to discuss the more complicated aspects of the scheme. "There are some difficulties. The saltpeter is one. Krauss makes his from organic material on his property. It would be too expensive to try to make it on the premises; besides, the climate factors are wrong. I'm still undecided about where to build the leeching barns and recrystallization vats. We need a large rural property and plenty of manure."

"Our closest farm is at Vassouras."

Erik allowed himself a thin smile. "The perfect place! It's near the railroad line and the final product is quite compact and transportable."

"Who would manage the operation?"

"We could always send Augusto," Erik quipped.

"Wish we could. He'd never be content in that place, nor could he handle the management without our direct supervision."

"You're not suggesting that I should go?" Erik asked.

"Of course not! How could I do without you here?"

As they spoke, the three men walked back toward the house for coffee. Teca, the ancient mother of Erik and Francisca's nurse, Zefinha, who lived permanently at Boa Vista, carried a wooden tray with fresh cups of cafezinho and a small plate of cakes.

"I've been thinking about Alvares Diniz. He's trustworthy, a good man."

Sven selected an elaborately iced slice of cake. "Do you think he'd go?"

"I understand his wife is fond of horses. If he'll agree to oversee the operation, I was thinking of sending another man to supervise the routine scraping of the barrels, the transporting of the shipments."

Sven admired a second cake decorated with swirls of chocolate. "You really should try one of these. Teca's still the best pastry chef in the Federal District."

"Não, obrigado, Papai. Lately all sweets leave a bitter taste in my mouth. I'll have some more coffee instead."

Sven licked the chocolate filling from his spoon slowly. "Who'd you have in mind for the second job?"

"Perna-de-Pau."

"How many times do I need to remind you to loosen your ties with that family? This would only complicate matters further!"

Raleigh was looking perplexed. Erik struggled to cover his

father's gaffe. "I suppose I've always felt sorry for the poor, one-
legged man."

" 'Charity shall cover the multitude of sins,' " Raleigh quoted
easily.

Sven exhaled loudly. "But that's for another discussion, isn't
it?" Calmly Sven lit a cigar. "How soon do you expect the powder plant to be in operation?"

"Two to three months, if I can arrange things at Vassouras."

"When do you go?"

"There's a train in the morning. I'll take Diniz and look
around. I seem to remember an old horse barn that would be perfect."

"I haven't been there myself in over five years. A pity, too. The
climate there is so delightful. Once I had a mind to start a racing
stable there." Sven's eyes began to twinkle. "Your grandfather de
Lourenço had a beautiful stud that I thought would have begun a
superb line."

"I remember him!" Erik was delighted by the sudden memory.
"A dappled grey named after a town somewhere in the south.
Nova . . ."

"Nova Aurora."

"Whatever happened to him?"

"He won some provincial competitions, then sired some interesting foals. Old man de Lourenço never saw much point in pursuing the matter, since Brazil doesn't have a racing association
organized to promote the sport."

"Why didn't you do anything about that?"

Sven laughed. He gestured to the wharf and mill. "I was too
busy building all this."

For a second Erik was filled with new insight into what some of
his father's yearnings and frustrations must have been. "It isn't
too late."

"No? I'll leave those pleasures for you younger men."

"You keep us too busy maintaining all this!" Erik mimicked his
father's sweep of the arm. "Why don't you take it up now?"

"Horse racing?"

"Why not? We need the manure in Vassouras!"

Again Sven laughed, happily at first, and then he began to

cough. "Give me a complete report on the barn," he choked. "Then we'll see."

Erik watched a flock of bright butterflies that had tired of the nearby lilies flutter curiously around the leavings of their cakes. Like visiting souls, they signaled with their bright orange wings and wafted upward. "Do you know what happened to those foals?" he wondered aloud.

"No, but if you ask around the fazenda, the old stable hands will know. All their names began with Nova, I recall."

One last butterfly alighted on his hand momentarily, then flew off with the others. "I'll do it tomorrow," Erik said, his eyes following the insect's curving flight. "Vassouras is looking better and better!"

3 "Astrid's been asking to see Isabel," Margaret said to Erik in their breakfast room. Heavy rains overflowed the gutters, forming wide sheets of water that pummeled the shrubbery.

"A fine day she's picked!" Erik was irritated that he'd have to discuss such a delicate matter over his coffee.

"Not necessarily today. She sees how much attention Paulo receives and yearns for Isabel more."

"Ridiculous! Children don't remember being babies."

"Erik . . ." Margaret's tone was soothing, not combative. "Astrid spoke to me from her heart when she told me how much she wanted to see Isabel and her 'sister' and 'brother.' "

The spoon in Erik's hand trembled. He stuck it forcefully into the jam pot and frowned. "The poor child becomes so confused every time she visits there. She has a real little brother now; what more does she want?"

"All those years together . . . The bonds exist whether you wish them to or not. Besides, she's put me in a difficult position over this."

Scrutinizing Margaret's every gesture, Erik tried to discover if his wife knew more than she was letting on. But the guileless expression in her eyes and the tilt of her tender upturned mouth appeared as innocent as ever. He drummed his fingers on the table. "You can't let her have her way all the time; you yourself taught me that."

"Let me explain before you decide," Margaret said steadily. "When Astrid first told me how much she wanted to see Isabel, I tried to dissuade her. Then she started to cry. 'If you were my *real* mother, you'd take my side at least part of the time,' she said. And she was right. I tend to defer to you when it comes to her, but with Paulo I use my own judgment about what is right. If the girl's ever to feel that she can trust me, she has to believe that I care enough for her to oppose you when I think you are wrong."

Deus! Erik realized he was trapped. If Margaret only knew the dangerous road she was traveling . . . "I suppose I could agree."

"Isabel's father is working for you now, isn't he?"

"How did you know?" Erik held his breath.

"Raleigh said something about a man with a wooden leg. How many could there be?"

"You think I shouldn't employ him?"

"On the contrary, you could never repay them for everything they did for Astrid."

Sometimes Margaret's kindness shamed him. She never went looking for the ugly or the devious, and when forced to confront someone's perfidy she did so with true shock. "Yes . . . well . . ." Erik stood and shook toast crumbs from his vest. He looked out the window. "The rains are getting worse. Might continue like this all day. You won't be going out, will you?"

"Certainly not. You don't have to send the car back for me."

"Aren't you discontent with staying home?"

"Everything I need is here. Paulo, my music. Now, if I could feed him and play piano at the same time, my life would be perfect."

"Don't you know any one-handed pieces?"

Margaret laughed. Erik reached down and kissed her firmly on the lips. She responded and stroked his hair, casually brushing a long lock over a thinning spot. "What shall I tell Astrid, then?"

"As soon as the rains clear, she may have an afternoon with Isabel. But be certain you tell her that I was against it. That'll keep her on your side and also have the effect of making her wait a bit longer before making the next request."

"Senhora . . ." Florinda stood in the doorway of the breakfast room.

Margaret looked up.

"The baby is calling for you."

"I'll go to him now. Join me when you've finished," Margaret said. She bent and kissed Erik's high forehead before going upstairs.

Knowing that Paulo was a restless baby who required feedings more often than most, Erik didn't object. Margaret suckled the child at her own breast during the day, but at night a wet nurse was brought in. Erik thought this an ideal arrangement.

"How much longer will he need?" Erik asked when he came into the nursery.

"A few minutes on the other side."

"Why don't you let Lilita finish him?"

"She's already asleep. Besides, I'd be miserably congested by the next feeding."

"It takes so much of your time."

"I don't mind, don't mind at all." Margaret stared reproachfully. "Why are you so impatient these days?"

"It's just that when I watch you with him I want you even more."

"Jealous of your own son?" Margaret teased. "Anyway, you have to leave for the mill soon."

Erik leaned back in the leather chair and closed his eyes. "I'll try to think of something else."

"Come, look at him for a moment."

Erik bent over the child cradled in her arms. Margaret lifted a tiny limp wrist. "He's so thin. I ask everyone if they think he's healthy and they all reassure me that babies grow at different rates." Her voice was high and wistful. "But Francisca's babies all plumped out a lot sooner."

"With Augusto for a father, what would you expect?"

Margaret didn't laugh. Though Paulo's cheeks sucked in and out in a placid rhythm, his feeding didn't seem particularly vigorous. With his fingertips, Erik stroked the silky skin of his arms, then lifted the withered soles of his miniature feet. "To me he seems bigger."

"He's not any heavier." Her chin jutted and she began to cry.

Erik sat beside her and tried to comfort her. "We'll ask the doctor to come, just to be sure, all right?"

Margaret sniffed and nodded.

"Look, he's already asleep." He touched the straggling hairs
that stuck out from his scalp in unlikely directions. "Shall I help
you put him to bed?"

"I say a prayer for him every time I lay him down."

So sentimental, Erik thought. While Erik held up the mosquito
netting, Margaret lowered the child into the intricately decorated
brass cradle in a rhythmic series of movements designed to keep
the baby asleep. She kissed him on the back of his neck and
tucked a satin cover around him.

"He's so tiny . . ." she whispered.

Erik silently agreed. The fragile baby looked as though a gust
of wind could blow him away.

I've almost lost her, Erik worried as he gathered his papers for
the office. Now it's Paulo's hunger or Astrid's demands that fill
her mind. Stop thinking like that, he warned himself, or you'll
turn into a man like Augusto who resents Francisca's consuming
interest in her children. Still, with Isabel it was different. Whenever she was with him it was as if nothing else in her life existed.
She never listened for the cry of a child when he made love to her
or talked about anything except what would please him. Not that
she was a stupid woman without a mind of her own. Lately she
knew a surprising amount about politics and had developed
strong opinions, even some fresh insights on local affairs. He'd
taken to bringing her books as gifts, and she reported on each one
that she read. If only she'd received a proper education when she
was younger, she could have raised her position in life considerably.

Isabel. He'd have been able to put an end to it sooner if there
wasn't this eternal complication with Astrid. If only he could disengage her from his second family, he might be able to keep
everything under control. Two women; four, almost five, children. It was too much for any one man to keep neatly organized.

Outside the front doorway the headlights of the Protos shimmered in the rain. Severino was running toward the house with
an umbrella unfurled. What a horrible summer! First the monstrous unrelenting heat, now the daily downpours that had
turned the neighborhood into a river of stinking sludge. In the
distance Paulo was crying. The boy should've been sleeping
soundly by now, Erik thought anxiously.

"Seu Erico." Severino slipped a rubberized black cape over his employer's shoulders.

Erik brushed it off.

"Muita chuva, senhor!"

"Estou bem. I don't need it!"

❧   ❧   ❧

On the way to the wharf the Protos stalled twice. Both times Severino had to pull over, remove the distributor cap, and dry the points and surrounding wires before it would start again. "Can't rely on anything!" Erik groaned. The chauffeur knew better than to open his mouth. Rarely had he seen the senhor in such a temper.

Erik was the last to arrive at the conference his father had called. Augusto and Raleigh sat at opposite ends of the table. Diniz, Cardoso, and Pinheiro, all senior executives with the firm, also participated. Cardoso and Pinheiro had been with the company since its early days and were due to retire at about the same time. Alvares Diniz was the first nonfamily member of his generation to be elevated to executive status. His long friendship with Erik and his unfailing loyalty had taken him far very rapidly.

Sven Larson's secretary read the month's report of transactions. The new stores in the São Paulo region were prospering better than expected, but the factory's production still was unable to keep them fully stocked.

"When phase three is completed in the new production line, we'll be doubling those figures the first week," Erik said.

"The installation of the looms is already three weeks behind schedule," his father pointed out. "I believe you've been neglecting the mill in favor of the powder sheds."

"I've left the workmen precise plans of what to do. If they'd only follow my . . ." He stopped. No sense in arguing; just agree, then do what he thought best in the end. "I'll try to see if I can speed things up. They probably don't understand the modifications on the new shuttles and bobbins."

Augusto took out a small knife and began to clean under his fingernails. After each scraping, he wiped the dirt from his knife by rubbing the blade across the blotter on the conference table.

Generally Erik tried to ignore his brother-in-law's boorish behavior, but this open display of discourtesy was too much. He swiveled his chair so he would not have to look in that direction. His father never asked Augusto's advice or opinion, something that Augusto obviously resented, but he was never excluded from these meetings, and his vote, when asked for, counted as equal to Erik's or Raleigh's.

After the routine reports had all been given, Sven began his planning for the next weeks and months. His management system divided everything into three plans — weekly, monthly, and yearly — but these were subject to change and revision at each meeting. He scratched a few notes on the chart in front of him and began his assignments.

"Diniz leaves for Vassouras at the end of the week. After re-evaluating the property there, we've decided not only to promote saltpeter production but to build three additional barns to handle future expansion. Alvares, you will supervise the saltpeter operations, sending samples to Rio for quality analysis weekly. By next month I expect you to have implemented recrystallization. My long-range goal is to have three barns in full production this time next year."

"Three empty barns . . . Isn't that wasteful?" Augusto spoke out of turn.

"I'm glad you asked that," Sven answered smoothly. "If you finish the warehouse inventory satisfactorily, Augusto, I'm considering putting you in charge of the management of my racing stable. My son thinks we might all benefit from raising horses. What do you say?"

Sven took particular delight as Augusto's jowly face registered his meaning. The man even had the sense to fold his knife away and sit up straighter. It was his fervent hope that Augusto might take a keen interest in the horses and become more responsible in general.

Next, he divided Erik's duties between the mill and the new powder plant. "You should accompany Diniz to Vassouras, introduce him to da Silva, and see that you are satisfied with the scraping operation."

"Yes, Father."

"Also, I want you to look into the feasibility of importing saltpeter from Chile. They say the mines there contain the world's richest and most reasonably priced source."

"That's years off," Erik answered respectfully. Inwardly, he was delighted that his father was looking at a long-range plan for the powder business.

"Next we must discuss the wood situation. I'm very pleased with the early orders for hardwoods. To make our payments on the land, we're going to have to harvest the most profitable trees first, along with the imbaúba for powder. Also, the whole operation will have to be extremely efficient. I don't want to see empty boats on the docks in Rio or idle lumberjacks in Bahia."

The men around the table nodded in agreement.

He looked directly at Raleigh. "I'm sending Claiborne, his family, and a small staff to oversee the operations in Bahia. Your drivers, guards, cook, and household people should all be nordestinos, Raleigh."

Augusto seemed peeved that Raleigh should be getting so much support. Until now, Sven had indicated only displeasure with the brash North American's purchases. Sven had fostered this image to keep Raleigh humble and cautious. Actually, after studying the documents and transactions, their financial and legal advisers had agreed that the deal was masterful and potentially the biggest asset the company had. Erik and his father had agreed, however, never to let Raleigh know quite how well he had done.

❧ 4 Astrid returned from her day with Isabel complaining of a stomachache. Florinda put her to bed with a compress of rosemary and garlic. In the morning, when she was worse, Dr. Bandeira was summoned. Erik stood by the child's bedside while the doctor palpated her abdomen. The doctor nodded gravely. "Do you know what she ate while she was visiting?"

"Astrid's a very particular child," Margaret interjected. "She rarely eats more than a few bites. She told me she was served some rice and beans and a small slice of chicken, which she didn't touch."

"Any sweets?"

"Now, *that* she'll eat!" her father answered. "Did Isabel give you any candy or cakes?" he asked his daughter gently.

Astrid was chalky white. Her blue eyes had paled to the color of running water. "Papai . . ." she said with a pleading tone.

"Now, now, no one is going to be angry with you, little Astrid," the doctor soothed. "We just want to help you."

"Some chocolates . . ." she whispered.

"What else?" Margaret asked. "Cakes? Jellies? Flan?"

Astrid's trembling chin bobbed in agreement.

"All of those?"

"Isabel always has my favorites."

Margaret pulled Erik aside. "That woman's made her sick!"

"It was your idea, remember?" Erik hissed back.

As soon as they realized that Astrid's eyes were darting back and forth between them, they stepped out of the room. Florinda covered Astrid and wiped her forehead.

"A simple case of sugar tummy," Dr. Bandeira pronounced. "Surely you have some caiapiá in the house?"

"Don't you have anything better?" Erik asked. "My mother gave that to me when I was a child."

"Sometimes the old compounds are still the most effective. Give her a dose every four hours. If that doesn't do the trick, send for me tomorrow."

"Thank you, Doctor . . . And one more request," Margaret said slowly. "Paulo, he has not been gaining as I expected. Would you have time to look in on him?"

"Certainly, Dona Margarida, though you probably have nothing to worry about. Every baby grows at his own pace."

Paulo was stirring in his cradle when they entered the room. Margaret lifted the baby.

"How old is he now?"

"Almost six months. Not anywhere near the size of my sister-in-law's babies at that age."

"You still give him your milk?"

"Yes, but he also takes from his ama de leite at night."

As the doctor handed the baby back to his mother, Erik immediately sensed his concern. "Two different milks might not be mixing in his stomach. Neither one may be absorbed properly."

Margaret was visibly upset.

"My advice is for only one woman to feed the child around the clock."

"You're suggesting I should be the one to stop?"

"Six months of feeding him is a praiseworthy effort for any mother. Most ladies of your position give it up in a matter of weeks."

Erik was nodding in agreement. "Whatever's best for Paulo . . ."

Tears stung Margaret's eyes. She pressed her face toward the baby so the men wouldn't see her cry.

❧ ❧ ❧

Astrid remained in bed several more days while the purgative did its work. Florinda brought hot packs to ease the cramps. By the fourth afternoon, Astrid was well enough to be cranky and demanding.

"Can't I have anything but green coconut water and bananas?"

"Not until tomorrow . . . Doctor said . . ."

"I'll ask my father when he comes home," she whined.

"Your father heard what the doctor said as well as I did, Astrid." Only to herself did Margaret admit she preferred the prostrate child who seemed grateful for every touch or kind word to the contentious recuperating one.

"Why don't you ever see my side?"

"Astrid, darling, I'm the one who convinced your father to let you go to Isabel's, if you remember."

"I had a horrid time!" Astrid pouted. "Santa Teresa was noisy with that bonde going right by the house all the time. It was too hot to play outside for very long and Isabel complained that her back hurt her."

"I had no idea she wasn't feeling well. We shouldn't have burdened her with a visit."

"She says it won't get any better until after the next baby arrives."

"Isabel's with child?"

Astrid nodded innocently.

"I thought she lived alone."

"Her father's there. He could be the baby's father, too."

"No, Astrid dear, a woman's father cannot be her baby's father."

Astrid stared quizzically. "Why not?"

"This is no time to discuss those matters," Margaret mumbled. "Now if you drink all your coconut water, I'll let you join us for some music and games this evening. All right?"

❦ ❦ ❦

Erik was waiting in the drawing room. He'd already had his sherry and was browsing through *Punch*, his favorite English magazine. "Is Astrid better today?"

"Her stomach seems settled, but her temperament's worse than ever."

"Have you two been quarreling again?"

Margaret's face flushed angrily. "Erik! I've spent the whole week nursing and coddling that child!"

He patted her shoulder in a gesture of conciliation. "Now, what has you so upset?"

"Did you know that Isabel is going to have another child?"

Erik's chest felt as though a heavy weight had begun to crush it. He willed his expression to remain serene, but a twitch at the corner of an eye threatened to betray him. "Who says?"

"Astrid is old enough to notice these things. How can we teach her properly if she's going to be influenced by the morals of a woman like that?"

"Isabel isn't a bad woman."

"How else did she manage to conceive two, almost three, children without the grace of marriage?"

"Her husband abandoned her; it wasn't her fault."

"Has he suddenly reappeared?"

"Astrid already knows that the servants have babies without being married. Look at the way Florinda and Severino have been carrying on! I wouldn't be surprised if he'd put something in her oven by now."

"Erik! Must you be so crude? You know Isabel is much more than a servant to Astrid."

"You're the one who encouraged the visit," he retorted.

"So, I was wrong!" Margaret was shouting. "From now on we must keep them apart at all costs."

"If you think it best."

"You should've heard the questions the child asked ..." She

choked. "Whether Isabel's father could be the baby's father. I couldn't begin to reply."

As Margaret rambled on, Erik felt a pervasive fear. If she ever discovered the truth, if she ever learned the paternity of Isabel's next child, he'd never find peace again. But how could he tell her now? "I'll go to Astrid . . . Talk with her. She's still so young to understand much of these matters, but maybe I can smooth things over for the moment."

"I'm hoping it will be easier to raise a son." Margaret sighed deeply.

"How's Paulo today?"

"The same."

"Will he be awake after supper?"

"I think it can be arranged," Margaret said brightly, for she always enjoyed watching Erik hold and bounce his baby. "But we'll have Astrid in first. I promised her. Then, when she goes to bed, I'll get Paulo. No sense in having him compete with her on her first time out of bed."

"You're so sensible," Erik said, wondering how sensible his wife would be if she knew the truth.

❀ 5 A few days after Astrid's recovery, it was clear that Paulo had contracted a similar complaint.

"He could hardly be accused of overindulging in sweets," Margaret said to the doctor, her light tone unable to mask her deep concern.

Dr. Bandeira admitted that his "bad milk" theory may not have been the whole cause of the baby's failure to thrive. "Usually it's the mother who's too nervous, causing the milk to become tainted. A wet nurse is often calmer, more reliable."

"My supply is now diminished," Margaret said anxiously. "Isn't it too late to change back?"

"I'm afraid so. I'll have Sister Piedade find a new nurse in case that's necessary. But I have some medications to treat the baby first." He uncorked a small vial and held it up to the light. "This is Warburg's tincture, a wonderful compound, though I've never tried it on a child as young as yours. If you give a modified dose four times a day, it should halt the dysentery by tomorrow."

"He's never been a strong one . . ." Erik's voice was raspy with emotion.

"Summer tummies are common and it's only in the poorest of neighborhoods that these complaints become epidemics. And Erico . . ."

"Sim, Médico?"

"I want you to supervise the medication. Your wife is too . . . worried. She might make an error, and this is not something that can be trusted to illiterate servants." The doctor removed his spectacles and rubbed his eyes. "This tincture is powerful. An overdose could do more damage than the disease."

"I understand. Write out the instructions and I'll follow them precisely."

❦　❦　❦

"I'm to do it!" Erik insisted.

"I don't understand why you don't trust me with my own child!" Margaret argued.

He slowly lowered the spoon containing the bitter liquid to his son's lips, but the moment the black fluid touched his tongue the baby spit forcefully enough to spatter Erik completely.

"He'll never swallow the whole amount, in any case," Margaret said. "Hold the spoon until I have his mouth open; then give it to me." She struggled with Paulo, who, even though he was weakened by his illness, had rallied enough to fight the invasion of his mouth. Deftly, Margaret tucked his feet under her armpit, pinned his arms to her side, and held his head in her left hand. With her right thumb she pried open his tight little lips. "Now!" She reached for the spoon and rapidly poured it down his throat, then sealed his lips closed. Stroking his neck, she forced him to swallow. When she released him, he howled and sputtered, but the job was done.

Erik was shaking. "It seems too cruel."

"That's why men aren't mothers," Margaret said weakly.

"Try to rest."

"How can I? He was up all night in great pain. I hate to see his little limbs drawn up."

"Astrid was also ill for two or three days. The doctor thinks he'll recover just as well as she did."

"Dr. Bandeira's been wrong before." Margaret reached out for him and began to cry uncontrollably.

"You're exhausted."

"If anything happens to him . . ."

In the intensity of her grasp, Erik felt her fear and need. "Do you want me to stay home with you today? I could be with him while you sleep. Perhaps having us both here . . ."

Margaret's eyes glistened through her tears. "Would you?"

"Certainly." For the first time, Erik allowed himself to dwell on the worst possibility. In Rio children died daily. How often had he seen their sky-blue caskets being carried through the streets by the older children of the family? Sometimes the parents and adults didn't even attend the burial. Children burying children. He'd always thought it a tender, pathetic sight. But those were other children. It was unthinkable that a son of his wouldn't survive!

He looked over at Paulo. The baby struggled irritably in his mother's lap. The first dose was inside his body, the blackness trying to bind his bowels and keep the fluids within. Surely the doctor knew just what had to be done. Surely Paulo was about to be cured! As soon as Margaret moved to settle him in his cradle, he began to cry inconsolably.

"I'll just hold you, then," she said softly, "if that's what you want." She picked him up and rocked him in her arms. "Erik, look!"

He studied the child's sunken eyes and sickly pallor. His skin had an odd doughy feel, as though all the moisture and life-giving fluids had been drained from his body. "What is it?"

"He cries without tears," she said slowly. "I wonder what that means?"

Erik took one of Paulo's delicate hands in his and held it with great tenderness. There was nothing else to do or say.

☙ ☙ ☙

The death of a child had to be God's most monstrous punishment. Erik wondered why his guilt should extend to Margaret. What had she ever done to deserve such a cruel chastisement? Paulo had lingered for only a week longer. No medicine had cured the relentless dehydration that the fever and diarrhea had caused. Finally, the infant had slipped from life as Margaret held him in her arms, growing icy before she'd allowed anyone to take him from her.

The funeral was held at sunset at the house in Flamengo. Augusto walked in front, carrying the cross; his eldest child and Astrid carried lighted tapers on each side. Next came the priest in a white-and-gold cope. Following the pale blue coffin covered with silver lace were six little cousins dressed in white, like angels.

Side by side Erik and Margaret watched the procession pass; side by side they listened to the consoling words of friends, heard Maestro Freire play a dirge he had composed especially. It was more calming than sad, with final chords that brightened into something promising and eternal. Erik wanted to tell Margaret what he heard in the music, to talk to her about the other babies they would have, even though he knew that Paulo would never be replaced, but Margaret wouldn't listen or speak to him. She seemed so terribly alone and distant. There was nothing he could do to reach her. Though he carried his own grief as heavily as she hers, his wife refused to acknowledge his, which pained him even more.

Side by side they said farewell to everyone who had come to mourn with them, and side by side they lay in their bed, his arms holding her close. Yet they were as far apart as they'd ever been before.

❦ ❦ ❦

In the days that followed, Margaret had difficulty sleeping. Sorrow had the opposite effect on him. His sadness only diminished when he fell into a dark, dreamless sleep that left him feeling heavy and sluggish in the mornings. What am I to do with myself? he thought silently. Only a week before, he'd learned that Isabel had given birth to a second son. She'd sent word that she wouldn't name the child until he'd had a chance to have his say about what he would be called, but because the only name that came to mind was Paulo, he'd never responded. As the days of mourning continued, he'd made a private decision. He wouldn't see the child, not now, not ever. Let no one believe that Isabel's child could ever replace Paulo. If God willed that he and Margaret would survive their grief and eventually unite to produce

another child, he'd have to remain faithful to her from then on —
in heart as well as body.

Even if Margaret had been beside him when he'd fallen asleep,
inevitably he'd find her in some other part of the house by morning. Half-awake, she stared blankly out a window, fresh tears filling her sunken eyes.

Three months after they'd buried their baby, he confronted
her. In the hazy violet light of dawn, her skin had a sickly greyish
tone. "You can't go on like this."

Too exhausted to argue, Margaret curved her body against his
and allowed Erik to put his arms around her. Her shoulders felt
angular. "You haven't been sleeping, or eating ... What am I
to do with you?" The words sounded hollow even as he said
them.

"I feel as if I'm recovering from another case of the dengue
fever," she said weakly. "Only then everyone permitted me to lie
in my hammock and stare at the flowers without thinking I was
acting strangely. Now they talk as though Paulo never existed.
They say things like, 'You must have another right away,' or 'It's
easier to lose a baby than an older child.' " Margaret's eyes blazed
with more color than Erik had seen in months. "Easier!"

"They don't mean to be cruel, although you aren't the first
mother to have lost a child. In Brazil more than half the children
don't survive the first year."

"One or fifty! It was my child that died!" Margaret pulled
away from him. Her silk dressing gown caught in the curved arm
of the divan and ripped at the sleeve.

"Our child ..." Erik reminded softly.

"It's just that" — her voice caught — "I'm tired of everyone
telling me not to be so upset. Why can't you all see that's what I
want to be?"

As Erik watched his wife storming about the room, her fury
palpable, he felt strangely relieved. This was much better than
her silences. The air was alive with her movements, her anxious
breaths communicating the awesome emotions she'd bottled
within. He followed her from room to room, until they reached
the drawing room. Pale yellow and white lilies bedecked the
piano. Joaquim Freire had sent fresh flowers each week in memory of the child, specifying to the servants that they be placed on

top of the piano. Somehow he knew Margaret hadn't allowed herself to play since the baby died. The fact that the composer understood irked Erik, though he tried to tell himself he was being ridiculous. Still, he felt a twinge of resentment every time a fresh bouquet was delivered.

"Don't know ..." Margaret sat down on the piano bench and began to weep softly. "Don't know what to do."

"You can't go on like this. There's no need to punish yourself by denying your music. You need to begin playing again."

"I can't."

Erik slid beside her and put his arms around her waist. "Why ever not?"

"It ... It hurts too terribly."

"You shouldn't be alone so much. Only yesterday Nicia Netto left her card. Isn't it time you saw some of your friends?"

"Too soon ..." She choked.

"At least you should have the courtesy to greet the maestro when he calls." Erik swallowed hard. Why was he encouraging her when her music inevitably took her away from him?

"Do you really think I should?"

"Yes, because you can't go on like this."

"I know ..." Margaret looked at Erik steadily, her eyes like beacons of light signaling sailors lost at sea. "Nothing I do could ever change ..." Her voice cracked. Tears, hot voluminous tears, cascaded down her cheeks. "I need to be with you more than anything!"

"And I need you!" He took her in his arms. "And we'll have more children. We'll have another, won't we?"

"Yes," she agreed. "Yes."

6 Still in mourning, Margaret rarely left her house, yet music now filled its rooms from morning to night. Up even before Erik, she practiced intensely for several hours, then bathed and had a light luncheon. Joaquim Freire arrived every weekday promptly at two and worked with her for the rest of the afternoon, except for Wednesdays, when the other musicians joined them for ensemble work. Not only was Margaret less despondent, she'd begun to make great strides in her musical development.

Though Erik was grateful for Margaret's recovery, he began to feel as if Joaquim Freire had become a permanent fixture in their lives. When Erik returned from the wharf every evening, Freire and Margaret were still at work in the drawing room. At first Erik took this for politeness on Freire's part. The maestro certainly did not want it to seem as though he came and went behind Erik's back. He'd stay long enough for one glass of sherry, but always depart at least an hour before the Larsons' dinner was served. Still, Erik could not help but wish Margaret would not have immersed herself in her music to the exclusion of all else.

When he'd complained privately to Francisca, she'd chided him. "Gigo, you must be grateful. Remember Dona Ermelinda?"

"But she was . . ."

"Crazy," Francisca finished. Both of them remembered the odd woman who, though she came from a fine family, sometimes wandered around Flamengo in a torn shift, stuffing garbage into a sack she carried on her hip. It was rumored she'd lost her mind after her eldest son had accidently drowned in the bay. They all pitied and watched out for her. If she was out after nightfall, someone, often Sven Larson himself, would see that she was taken home.

"I suppose you're right." Erik forced himself to agree with his sister.

One day a few weeks later, after a long but rewarding financial meeting with his father and Diniz, Erik had taken off early and rushed home to Margaret. The quarterly figures had almost leapt off the ledgers with the happy news that the land in the northeast was already beginning to be profitable. Prices for fine hardwoods had never been higher in Europe, and the initial harvesting had begun to pay off a sizable percentage of the land debt. To celebrate, he'd ordered dinner at a restaurant, invited his parents, Augusto, and Francisca to join them. He felt it was time for Margaret to go out, to participate in the real world once again.

In an expansive mood as he drove himself home in the Protos, Erik thought about inviting the composer to join them but realized this would be inappropriate, since no one besides the immediate family would be at the dinner. In any case, Erik was certain Freire would understand.

As he entered his house, the vibrant sounds of a piece Erik didn't quite recognize poured into the foyer. Is that Chopin? Erik wondered. Yes . . . I think so. Deus, it was frustrating not to have a memory for music! What did she call that style of piece? A mazurka? A polonaise? He listened for a moment to a few crashing, imperious chords. No . . . a scherzo! Erik was immensely proud that he'd figured it out. The sounds that tumbled from the room quickened; the music seemed to come boiling out of the piano in a frenzy. He stopped in the doorway and watched the intensity of his wife's arms wildly running up and down the keys as though they were hungry teeth ready to bite if she stopped for a second. Freire stood just behind her, bending to turn the pages.

Something about the tableau unnerved Erik. The tall, thin man was far too close to his wife. Their concentration on the work at hand excluded him. Even the music was too harsh, too complex. Erik didn't like its strong, almost demoniac quality.

Freire stopped Margaret from continuing with the next passage by placing his hand on her shoulder. "I think you're emphasizing the melody too much. It should be faintly breathed. Do you see my meaning?"

"Yes, I think so," Margaret replied. Her shoulders sagged. She seemed exhausted.

Just as she lifted her hands to the keyboard, Freire reached out and placed his wide tan hands at the nape of her neck. Instantly, he located the precise spot where Margaret frequently complained of pressure and pain, the one that Erik always soothed with gentle caresses. As Freire rubbed her pale skin with his fingertips, Margaret rolled her head around to ease the tension. "That's better."

Joaquim skillfully kneaded her spine. "Is it numb again today?"

"Just a little." Margaret straightened her back. "Ah, that's better."

"Shall we stop for now?" Freire asked gently.

"No, I'm determined to finish the . . ." was all Erik heard before a wave of fury engulfed him. He stormed upstairs and poured himself a glass of sherry but after one sip discarded it and poured another of the stronger cachaça. Maldito! I've brought this on myself! How could I have been so stupid?

From downstairs he could hear Margaret playing a bright, hopeful, romantic theme. Suddenly Erik felt as though he might cry. He sat down on the sofa and tried to understand what was happening to him. Margaret ... Joaquim ... the music. Music! He might not understand it technically, but he knew that its whole purpose was to stir feelings. Blindly he'd believed his wife's devotion had been so great that no other man could have tempted her. But seeing them together, so close — touching, stroking, whispering — was a revelation!

Erik went to the basin in his dressing room and washed his perspiring forehead. He changed his shirt, then slowly walked downstairs and into the drawing room without announcing himself. Margaret was making some notes on her sheet music. Joaquim was standing on the other side of the piano. Nothing in their manner revealed what had just transpired.

"Erik! You're home so early. Is anything the matter?" she asked.

"Not at all." He smiled charmingly. "I'm sorry to interrupt you, but we've had some awfully good news today and I've planned a small dinner to celebrate. I hope you won't mind stopping your work early, but we've got to prepare to go out this evening."

Though Margaret seemed surprised, there was something in Erik's manner that suggested she'd better not question him too closely.

"We've worked hard enough today to deserve a rest!" Joaquim replied heartily. He went to gather his papers from a nearby table.

"Do you have time for one drink?" Erik asked.

"I don't wish to keep you ..."

"I've changed already."

Margaret realized that Erik was waiting for her to excuse herself, so she did so hurriedly. As soon as she had left the room, Erik dropped his veil of manners. "I think it's time for us to talk about what's been happening here." He stared malevolently at the tall, elegantly dressed man with skin several shades darker than his.

Joaquim froze. A few sheets of music drifted to the floor, but he did not stoop over to pick them up. "I don't understand how I've offended you."

"Oh, don't you now? When another man spends more hours each week with another man's wife than her husband . . ."

"Erico! What could I have done to . . ."

"You've abused your friendship with me. I saw you touching her and . . ."

"But I've never . . ."

"Maldito! Don't lie to me. I saw your hands on her back, her neck."

"She works so hard, her muscles tense. I saw no harm . . ."

"No harm!" His voice broke.

Joaquim's mouth opened, then closed without a sound. He was very still. Erik watched the composer's knuckles blanch as he inadvertently crushed the remaining papers in his hand. Finally Joaquim spoke, slowly, as if measuring his words. "Without meaning to, I can see I've offended you. I may have spent far too much time with Margaret, but I beg you to understand that I did so because I believed she needed me. As you know, I've been planning to return to Paris and the Conservatoire for some time now. In fact, I've put off the trip on your wife's account. I thought that in a month or two she'd be feeling even better. Now I'll book passage for the first available ship."

As Erik listened, he realized that he might have been too harsh, though he was still too hurt to rescind his accusations. "If Margaret ever felt that I had something to do with your leaving . . ."

Joaquim didn't respond. Both men were silent for a moment. Freire finally bent and picked up the music sheets, gathered his tattered leather music case, and started for the door. "I hope you'll agree that your wife still needs a teacher to work with her."

"Who would you recommend?" Erik asked tensely.

"Flavio Queiroz is still the best in Brazil, but he lives in São Paulo and is quite" — Joaquim paused meaningfully — "elderly, although he might be convinced to come up to Rio, at least for part of the year."

The two men had made their way to the foyer. Erik waved the servant away and opened the door himself. Joaquim stared

at Erik. The golden glints in the center of his dark eyes flickered disturbingly. Erik thought the composer was going to explain something, but all he said was a crisp "Boa tarde" before
he strode out through the gate to a hired car waiting at the
curb.

He loves her, Erik mused unexpectedly. Impossible. He banished the preposterous thought. No, he admires her and she him.
In her grief, Margaret had needed affection and sympathy. But
enough is enough! At least I settled the matter now, before . . .
Once he's in France, all will be as it was . . . or better. I'll see to
that! Erik promised himself silently and hurried upstairs to his
wife.

17 On the first anniversary of Paulo's death, Erik and Margaret lit a candle at Nossa Senhora da Gloria and said a
silent prayer, as much for the baby due any day as for the one
whose thin face was but a hazy memory of a pink puckered
mouth and delicate pointed chin. Margaret kissed her gold pen-
dant that contained a lock of Paulo's hair and shed a few tears.
Afterward, Erik had sent Margaret home to rest, but when he returned that evening he wasn't surprised to find her at the piano
bench.

Sitting beside her was the potbellied teacher, Flavio Queiroz.
What a pair the two made side by side, the chubby, balding man
and his heavily pregnant student!

"Boa tarde, Professor."

"Boa tarde." Queiroz responded jovially and bade Erik to remain and listen. Margaret didn't skip a note. She was playing
"Marche de Nuit" by her fellow Louisianan, Gottschalk.

The professor went back to reading the unfamiliar music in his
lap, moving his lips as he counted the beats. Immediately Erik
had liked the man Freire had recommended. Fatherly toward
Margaret, yet stern and incisive enough for her to respect — they
made an admirable team. Erik agreed grudgingly that the maestro
had known exactly what was best for Margaret.

The song was finished. Queiroz cleared his throat. "Well executed, but not something for your concert repertoire, if I may say
so without giving offense."

"I value your honesty." Margaret allowed her back to sag

under the weight of the final days of pregnancy. "This piece was quite a favorite of Mlle Doradou's. I was drilled on it so extensively that I came to loathe it, but I thought you'd be interested in the ornamental effects and the Latin theme."

"Yes, it's a refreshing concept, especially for a North American to have written."

"Gottschalk spent more years in Europe and South America than in the United States."

"He died in Rio, didn't he?" Erik asked.

"A terrible tragedy! How well I remember it!" Queiroz said. "Two days after his opening gala at the Lyric Theater, Gottschalk suffered a collapse just moments before he was to make his entrance on stage. Three weeks later he died at the Hotel Bennett in Tijuca from galloping pleuropneumonia, the aftermath of a yellow fever attack, they say."

Erik walked briskly across to the piano and helped his wife stand. Her belly seemed even more immense than it had that morning.

The professor took the hint. "Your husband and I have agreed that this would be an opportune time for me to resume my duties in São Paulo. Of course, I shall return as soon as your confinement is over." Noticing Margaret's shock at his news, he continued quickly, "in say four to six months . . ."

"Six months. . . ?" she stammered.

"Yes, well . . ." Erik interjected. "My agreement with Senhor Queiroz has always been temporary . . ."

"But I thought . . ." She stopped and stared at the two men who had been humoring her for half a year. Incensed at the deception, she stormed from the room.

"I'm sorry if I spoke out of turn. I didn't realize your wife didn't understand the arrangement."

"No, I should apologize to you. Dr. Bandeira says women are always more sensitive in the last weeks. Would you care to join me for some sherry?"

The professor began to gather his music. "Thank you for your hospitality, but not today."

As soon as Erik saw the rotund gentleman out, he went to find Margaret, but the bedroom door was closed firmly to him. Florinda stood guard in the hall. As he stared at the maid, wondering whether to push past her or to wait until Margaret's mood lifted, he noticed a distinctive change in Florinda's shape. It was either a parasitic illness or a pregnancy. So, he'd been right about her! he thought wryly. He turned on his heel and went to confirm this with Severino; at least he was one man who could be trusted to tell him the truth.

                                  ✿   ✿   ✿

Just after dawn Margaret's labor began with a rush of water in the bed. Erik felt an odd mixture of revulsion and intimacy at the event.

"It's good luck," Florinda said as she bustled about, changing the linen while her mistress sat propped uncomfortably in her chair. "The baby will come very quickly now."

"Is it too early to call the doctor?" Erik asked Margaret.

"I don't think . . ." Margaret winced, bit her lip, and then began to moan uncharacteristically.

Alarmed by the intensity in Margaret's expression, Erik ordered Florinda to send for his mother, Francisca, and the doctor, and to wake the rest of the household. Before he'd finished, Margaret had doubled over once again. "My back feels as though it's splitting in half!"

"Lean on me. I'll help you back to bed."

"All right . . . No, I can't move . . . It's awful . . ." Margaret slumped to her knees and pressed her forehead into the pale Oriental carpet. "That's . . . better . . ."

"Minha querida, you can't stay on the floor." Erik tried to lift her.

"No . . . no . . . let me be here."

Erik became agitated. Something must be terribly wrong for her to be acting so strangely.

"Florinda! Isn't there something you can do to help her?"

The servant bustled out and soon returned with one of Margaret's slippers and a red lingerie ribbon. Before Erik realized what was happening, she placed the shoe, sole outward, inside Margaret's left thigh and tied it firmly with the ribbon.

"What the . . ."

"It helps to bring the baby to light sooner."

"Where did you learn that?"

"The curandeiro . . ."

He reached over to remove it. "Nonsense!"

Panting, Margaret pushed his hand back. "Leave it. I think I can move now. Please help me up." In less than a minute another pain had her clutching Erik's hand so tightly he felt as if he were saving her from drowning.

Severino knocked on the door and called into the room. "Dona Margarida, Sister Piedade is coming. The doctor is out at another house."

"Doesn't he realize who needs him?" Erik shouted. "I'll go see to this!"

Meeting the nurse in the front hallway, he began to ask about locating the doctor, but Sister Piedade stopped him. "I attend most of the births, not the doctor. Only in special cases is he ever needed. Even with your son," she crossed herself, "there was no need for the services of a physician."

"Dr. Bandeira has always had a special interest in my wife's health, and I'm sure if he knew her time had come, he'd want to be here."

Without disagreeing, Sister Piedade went directly to Margaret's room. Erik followed close behind. Everyone was so distracted by the forcefulness of the labor that no one bothered to shoo Erik away.

"Just in time . . . I was called just in time," the sister whispered conspiratorially to Margaret. Erik saw only the nurse's elbow peeking out from under Margaret's nightgown. "Do you feel the pressure here?"

Margaret groaned once, then screamed aloud.

"No, no . . . my dear . . . That will not do," the nun whispered, but Margaret seemed not to hear Sister Piedade. She took Margaret's lolling head in both hands and forced her to look at her. "Now, calm yourself. The baby's almost here. Push gently toward the bottom of the bed, then take deep breaths, but no noise. Nothing!"

Though Erik was annoyed to have his wife spoken to in such a firm voice, he realized these matters were for women to direct.

In the hallway there was more confusion. Thinking the doctor must have arrived, Erik opened the door. His mother bustled past him, then stopped abruptly when she saw how far the birth had progressed. A tiny dark head covered with a thin sheen of cream and blood was emerging.

Erik closed his eyes and only listened as Margaret made strange guttural noises. Next there was a wet sucking sound, and finally a sharp, fresh cry from the mouth of the newborn. Erik looked up.

"It's a girl, an ugly little girl!" Sister Piedade said joyfully.

"Feia?" Erik gasped. "My child ugly?"

"Shhh . . ." his mother ordered. "It's always said so the devil won't find the baby a temptation."

Margaret, her brow shining with sweat, beamed. Erik stepped forward. Florinda moved back to allow him to come to Margaret's side. "She's . . . bigger than Paulo, isn't she?" he asked.

The slippery child in Margaret's arms sneezed. Reflexively, Erik reached over to pat it, touching its warm wetness with his fingertips. "Isn't she cold?"

A soft knitted blanket was passed over and the baby's father wrapped her awkwardly.

"There . . . there . . ."

"You were here the whole time?" Margaret asked in amazement.

Erik smiled guiltily. "You aren't angry?"

"I guess not, though men aren't supposed to see this, are they?"

Sister Piedade spoke sternly. "Now there's more work for us to do. I must ask you to leave the room."

Erik looked dolefully at Margaret. "Must I?"

"For a while . . ."

Erik retreated without further comment. Outside the door, seated on a plush bench, Francisca was waiting.

"How long have you been here?"

She turned slowly, revealing a face covered with fresh welts. Fluid leaked from a wound at the corner of her bruised left eye.

"Chiquinha!"

"I didn't want to upset Margaret. Is the baby here already?"

"Yes, a daughter, graças a Deus. "I . . . I saw her born."

"You saw the baby born?"

"I did."

"Gigo . . . not really?"

"Yes, everything, her head coming through more and more,

then slipping out like a pea shooting from a pod. She's beautiful!"

"Good, that's all I needed to hear. I'd better go home. If Mamãe sees me she'll be upset and it would ruin Margaret's day. Let this be blissful for her."

"No, she'd want you here. Come downstairs. We'll see if we can make you presentable."

As Erik took his sister's hand, he forced himself not to let his anger at Augusto envelop him. Every few months it was the same. After a spell of drinking, something would ignite his brother-in-law and he'd attack Francisca. Later, when he'd realized what he'd done, he'd beg her forgiveness and ask her, in the name of the children, to return to him, promising he'd reform.

"I know he can't control himself. The worst is wondering when it will happen again, not if . . ." she'd said after the last attack.

In the kitchen he watched the cook treat Francisca's wounds. Not so bad this time. Her skin was only a pale yellow. It would be hours before it turned greenish-blue. With a bit of powder, they might hide it from Margaret for a while yet.

Erik felt a terrible thirst. Lately, a gravelly dryness sometimes came upon him without warning, followed by an acrid taste in his mouth that begged to be washed away. He poured himself a glass of water from the large stone filter jar built into a niche in the corner of the pantry. After three large gulps, the glass was emptied. He filled it a second and third time.

Seeing her brother frantic to quench his thirst, Francisca asked, "Do you always drink so much?"

"When I work long hours or am too excited." After the sixth refill, Erik finally put the glass down.

"I don't understand how anyone could drink so much so quickly."

"It's only water, not cachaça!"

Francisca was still concerned. "Have you seen a doctor?"

"Chiquinha! What is this? Just because I drink a great deal of water, I'm not ill." He began clowning, pretending he was swimming toward her. "You look so much better now! Come and see my new daughter. She's quite the most incredible baby you've ever seen!"

8 Everyone agreed that the baby Susana was unusually beautiful. Her alert eyes, Margaret's azure blue with a faint grey rim, followed every person who walked into the room. Privately, Erik believed Susana to be more of a real person than the pathetic Paulo had been.

One evening two weeks after the birth, Erik observed his daughter sleeping. She twitched and turned her head from one side to the other. As Erik fussed with the bedding, a piece of paper fell out from under the sheet. Though the superstitions of the servants usually repelled him, Erik wasn't about to forbid them to use their precautions to protect Susana. In an odd way, it was comforting. After all, no such amulets had been used in Paulo's crib.

He unrolled the paper to see what "magic" words were written on it. The charms were printed to form a block in which the rows of nonsense letters read the same forward, backward, downward, and upward.

```
S A T O R
A R E P O
T E N E T
O P E R A
R O T A S
```

"How do the curandeiros get people to believe in such utter. nonsense?" he muttered quietly.

Margaret, who had just bathed, came into the room. Her loose dressing gown opened invitingly at the neck. "Is she awake yet?"

"Only stirring."

"Then I'll wake her. She hasn't eaten for more than three hours." As Margaret came near him, she noticed the paper in his hand. "What's that?"

"Nothing." He crumbled it and placed it in his pocket. Susana opened her eyes. "Already she knows your voice."

"Every baby knows her mama's voice." He watched as his wife guided the baby's eager mouth to her nipple. Margaret had insisted on not having a wet nurse this time. In her heart she had always felt that there was nothing so right for a child as its own mother's milk. Now she was proven right; this baby was thriving.

While Susana sucked noisily, Erik discussed the latest ship-

ment of wood that Raleigh had sent, extolling the quality of the
hardwoods being harvested.

"So, has he justified the land purchase?" Margaret asked.

"In value for wood, I'd have to say yes. But other problems are
developing in the northeast. Those people are used to having a
local patrão to go to with their problems. Our local representa-
tives are being asked to undertake decisions that are beyond
them."

"What do you mean?"

"Questions about boundaries, negotiating conflicts ... The
violence is increasing."

"What about the policia?"

"The few that there are can be bought and sold. It's our responsibility to provide justice, protection, even medical care. But
in an area that vast, it's almost impossible."

"There must be some solution."

"Father is working on a plan, but it would be very costly. We'll
need our own ..." He paused. Better not discuss this with Margaret now.

"Yes?" She waited. Susana pulled her head back and looked at
her father expectantly.

"Even Susana wants to know! What am I to do with two curious women?"

"She just wants the other breast!" Margaret rearranged the
baby.

"The difficulty is having an authority that the locals will respect. Their own petty chiefs will take sides and bribes; outsiders
from the city are resented because they cannot possibly know the
long history of some of these feuds and the complicated inter-
family struggles in the villages."

"And so?"

"Father feels that someone completely different ... someone
who will immediately be respected might be ... a foreign officer."

"My brother is hardly ..."

"Not Raleigh! We're talking about professional military ...
European educated. Men with discipline and training."

"Why would they come to Brazil?"

"There are many retired officers living on modest pensions

who would jump at the opportunity for just such an adventure, particularly if they are well compensated. They'd be given parcels of land, tiny to us but immense to someone who's lived his life in the confines of a Prussian village."

"They wouldn't speak the language, know the customs . . ."

"They'd learn, but until then their mere presence would lend authority to our business dealings."

"They'd be armed?"

"Minimally. Just enough to impress the workers. Mostly they'd settle disputes, enforce peacekeeping. More important, they'd be a deterrent to squatters and bandits."

"Is there much bandit activity in that area now?"

"Worse than ever. The latest droughts have made life particularly hard."

Margaret touched Susana's silken cheek. She'd stopped sucking and was sleeping with the nipple just touching her lips. With her free hand Margaret covered herself, then lay the baby in her cradle. "She'll sleep all night, I think. She seems so much more content . . ." Her voice trailed. Paulo's name was too painful to mention aloud. Silently they each compared the two infants.

Margaret fussed with the blankets. Then she turned and began to speak nervously. "I've had another letter from Lizzieland. Father's extremely ill. He hasn't been out of bed in weeks."

"I'm sorry . . ."

"It's what I expected."

"What more can I do?"

"You've been very generous with them. At least they haven't had to worry about financial matters these last years."

"How's your sister Kate?"

"She's becoming my parents' nursemaid, I'm sorry to say. I don't understand why she was so reluctant to come to Rio. After all, Raleigh and I were here for her. I'm sure we could have introduced her to some fine young people."

"She still hasn't any prospects there?" Erik placed his hands around Margaret's waist and led her to their sitting room. A silver tray was laid out with glasses, tiny cakes, and their favorite fortified wines. He held the fine crystal decanter up to the light to study the ruby port's sedimentation.

"My baby sister's very particular, it seems."

He took a sip of the vintage port. By the discerning glimmer in his eye, Margaret knew he was pleased with the flavor. "Vilanova de Gaia ... It never disappoints. Shall I pour you one of your own?"

"Just a half."

"Unfortunately, women do not age as successfully as port. Little Kate should be encouraged to settle on someone, especially since your father is so ill. Wouldn't it be a comfort to him to have all his daughters well cared for?"

Margaret flushed. Wrong choice of words, Erik realized too late. His wife had mysterious ideas about what women could do or become. At least Kate was uncomplicated by music or education. "What I meant to say," he began again in a conciliatory voice, "was that we should extend a fresh invitation to Kate to stay with us."

"With Father so ill?"

"Whenever the time is right." He sighed aloud, drained his glass, and placed it on the tray. So many people to care about: his sister and her children, his wife's far-flung family, Astrid, Isabel's older children, and the latest faceless, nameless baby. Now Susana, his precious dimpled daughter. All of them were his familial responsibilities. And there were others who also required his money or time: Perna-de-Pau, who'd become increasingly difficult in Vassouras, the servants, the office workers, thousands of people on the lands in the north. His head pounded with the endless complications.

Margaret had left the room to wash. He heard the water running, smelled the rose scent she used in the basin. Unexpectedly, his mouth was peculiarly dry, his tongue felt thick, and he longed to drown the familiar galling taste. With a shaky hand he poured another glass of port and drank it quickly. Not enough. A full glass of water, a coconut cake, another glass of water. His thirst was unquenchable.

"Erik?" she called in her softest, sweetest voice.

He turned toward the doorway of her dressing room. His wife was absolutely naked, her creamy skin glowing in the pink lamplight. For a moment he forgot his concerns. The effects of

the latest baby were minimal, with only the roundness of her
stomach and fullness of the breasts proclaiming motherhood.

"Isn't it too soon?"

She smiled conspiratorially. "What does a few days matter?"

Erik walked toward her, feeling more weak than excited.

"Is something wrong?"

"Just tired." It was strange to not really want her. He felt
angry, then dizzy. He lay down on their bed and reached up to
pull her down on him, but she hesitated.

"Are you sure?"

He kissed her hand, then indicated that she should lie across
him. He touched her rounded buttocks lazily, stroked the perfect
hollow in her back. If only his breath didn't taste so foul or his
stomach feel so bloated, he could concentrate more on what he
was about to do.

Margaret had been as forward as she'd ever dared. Seeing his
resistance, she rolled over and covered herself with the embroidered sheet. Wordlessly, Erik undressed and slipped beside her.
As soon as his skin met with hers, a fiery uncomplicated feeling
reasserted itself, and for a few moments at least, all his desires
were satisfied, all his concerns melted away.

❦9 The death of Charles Claiborne, shortly after Susana's
second birthday, came as no surprise. He had suffered so
greatly for so many years that his wife and family had welcomed
his release. His burial, attended only by the few diehard colonists
left in the region, foreshadowed the demise of the tropical neo-
confederacies. If Margaret mourned her father, she did so quietly.
Any sadness was mitigated by her joyful days watching Susana's
precocious progress.

Erik's polite invitation to shelter his mother-in-law and her two
unmarried children was accepted at once by Lucretia. However,
his wife didn't react quite the way he'd expected. "We'll have so
little privacy," Margaret complained.

"It's our duty."

"Wouldn't it be better to get Mother a small place of her own?
Once she's under our roof, she'll never want to move."

"I don't understand you," Erik had answered testily. "Any

other woman would have kissed her husband's feet for making
such a generous offer!"

Margaret's lips had tightened into a thin line. "Is it so wrong to
want only one's husband and child and not a whole other set of
difficulties?"

"Obligations take precedence over selfish desires."

"What about Raleigh's house?" she'd suggested quickly. "If we
could open it for Mother, she could look after it for him!"

Why hadn't he thought of that first! Erik berated himself.
Sometimes Margaret was far more clever than he was. Had some
of his jeito begun to rub off on her? Of course, he'd agreed at
once. In a few weeks, he'd had the Claibornes established there. It
was Margaret, however, who was given the task of effecting her
family's adjustment to life in Rio. A teacher's college was found
for Kate, while Marshall was sent to MacKenzie College in São
Paulo, which had been started by North American missionaries.
Raleigh encouraged his mother to become active in the work of
the American Bible Society. At least twice a week she was driven
in the Protos to number 29, Rua Sete de Setembro, where she
worked in the book depository, finding satisfaction in helping dis-
tribute more than fifty thousand Bibles and religious tracts a year.

Erik's daily life was predictably complicated. If he wasn't arranging a car for his lonely mother-in-law or settling a dispute at
the mill, he was soothing matters between Francisca and Augusto
after one of his brother-in-law's rampages. Every time one problem seemed solved, another reared, and it was always Erik who
was asked to make the crucial decision.

Once she was settled, Lucretia Claiborne seemed, on the outside at least, content. But Erik sensed his mother-in-law could
become a troublemaker. None of her little "requests" seemed to
benefit her directly — all were designed to push Raleigh into
having more authority. Erik appeased her with generous gifts. "If
his family's content, a man will be content" was one of Sven Larson's favorite mottoes, one that Erik had taken to heart.

There were still others who required Erik's advice and benevolence. Even the servants hadn't the sense to handle their own affairs without needing his assistance. When Florinda's sixth child
was born, his chauffeur, Severino, accepted paternity. Unfortu-

nately, Severino's common-law wife was not inclined to take the situation so graciously. She demanded that Florinda be sent away or she would see to the matter herself. Erik assuaged her with a monthly "pension." And so it went.

More and more, Erik took refuge in his latest interest: the racing stables. With the barns at Vassouras begging for livestock, his father and Augusto had scoured the region for good breeding stock. One of the horses, Rio Alegre, had already begun making a name for himself. Erik vowed to make the Vassouras stables legendary, although his father had begun to worry that this hobby would begin to take him away from more serious business concerns.

"Ah, but Papai," Erik had said to appease him. "Whether we win or lose, the barns fill with manure just the same!"

However, saltpeter production was barely keeping pace with the needs of the black powder factory. "We'd better look into those mines in Chile," Sven reminded.

Though Erik had calculated that they should have been able to scrape and process enough to keep the powder mill well stocked, it seemed they were unable to efficiently extract what they needed. "First, I'll have to spend a few weeks at Vassouras myself to ferret out the answers to our problems there," he promised his father.

When Erik announced his plans, Margaret welcomed a trip to the mountains. "Vassouras . . . The name is soft and musical; does it have a meaning?" Margaret had asked.

"Yes, but not a very romantic one. A 'vassoura' is a broom."

"Why is it called that?"

"Don't know for certain. Someone told me a plant grows there that is used in the making of brooms, which makes sense, but I've my own theory."

"What's that?"

"The skies there are so clear, the air is so fresh, that I imagine that a great mythical sweeper has cleared the clouds and humidity away. Some say it has the most perfect climate in all of Brazil."

The journey over the fifty-year-old Central do Brasil railway was far more pleasurable than Margaret had expected. Since this had been one of the earliest and most profitable of Brazil's coffee-growing regions, the transport system had always been efficient and remained so even though the region had long since seen its day of economic glory.

Margaret held a squirmy Susana on her lap so that she could see out the window, but the endless rectangle of swiftly passing greenery kept the toddler's attention only momentarily. Florinda, busy nursing her Roberto, had little time to chase Susana up and down the aisle, so Margaret followed after her endlessly. "I didn't expect to *walk* all the way to Vassouras," she groaned.

Erik looked up from his *Jornal do Comercio*. "We should've brought Astrid along. At least she'd have enjoyed the journey."

"Better that she keeps up with her lessons. You know your mother will keep her very content and she won't miss us in the least."

"Yes, well . . ." Erik turned a page as Susana lurched in a different direction.

❧ ❧ ❧

"I had no idea . . ." Margaret said as the fazenda carriage wobbled its way up the long rutted driveway to the almost abandoned great house, its once-dazzling coat of whitewash streaked with dust and soot. "I expected something far less grand, a farmhouse more like the one at Boa Vista. How did your family ever come to own this place?"

"It was part of mother's dowry. Believe it or not, her father won the mortgage in a game of cards. However, he never cared much for the place. My father's made a few improvements, if just to keep it from falling into ruin, but no one has taken the time to care for it properly for ten years or more."

A row of imperial palms in the semicircular driveway dipped in the stiff mountain breeze that greeted them. Close up, the broken tiles on the roof and the disarray of the flower gardens were evident, but the basic construction reflected a permanence, stolidity, and strength that the recent decade of neglect had not quite erased.

Erik took Margaret's arm. "Let me show you the view from behind the house."

Margaret carried the sleepy Susana in her arms.

"Notice how they've set the house down into this little hollow in the hills to protect it from the sun and wind. The temperature inside is almost the same year round, with little need for fires or fans."

From the rise above the house, they could look across the valley to the Parahyba River. Margaret indicated a mountain range to the south. "What's that?"

"The Serra do Mar."

She had pointed to the loose chain of domelike hills formed from the ferruginous clay earth characteristic of the area. "It's like a sea of half-oranges."

"This alluvial soil has wonderful drainage. Perfect for the ripening berries, they say."

"Do you grow the same varieties of coffee as they did at the Krauss fazenda?"

"Only some of the oldest, most productive plants are still maintained here."

"Why is that?"

"Margaret, this is not a working estate. Right now its only cash crop is saltpeter for the factory."

"But this situation . . . the land . . . It must have great value."

"Potential value, minha querida. Since the days of abolition, it hasn't been profitable to work the fields in this region. Much better coffee lands exist in the south."

"Why?"

Erik shook his head thoughtfully. "Diniz knows all about that; you might ask him at supper." For a moment he wondered why his artistic wife had developed a sudden interest in agricultural matters, but then he remembered how fascinated she'd been with the Krausses' coffee plantation years earlier. Her curiosity, her diverse interests, never ceased to charm him. He felt himself a very fortunate man.

❧   ❧   ❧

Alvares Diniz had taken over the smaller manager's house instead of living in the casa grande as Erik had offered. "A better roof," his wife had readily admitted. A lively redhead who preferred country life to the stringent mores of Rio society, Maria Silvia had welcomed the move.

"Do you ride?" she'd asked Margaret the day she'd arrived.

"No, I never have."

Senhora Diniz seemed surprised.

"My wife is a city girl. The only thing she's ever ridden is the piano bench." Erik basked in the rippling laughter that ensued.

"Won't you teach me?" Margaret interjected in the lull.

Maria Silvia deferred to Erik. "Com a sua permissão."

"I don't think so," Erik replied seriously.

"But why ever not?"

"Because I said so!" Erik's eyes blazed forcefully. A mother of a young child could not take risks.

At least Margaret was intelligent enough not to insist. She'd turned to Diniz and was asking about coffee cultivation.

"Why did the early planters consider the area suitable in the first place?"

"Actually, they knew very little except common lore that spread by word of mouth. There were certain signs: the color of the soil, elevation of the terrain, and its exposure in relation to the sun. Mostly the redness of the earth attracted them."

"That's very interesting." Margaret leaned toward him eagerly. "But why is this soil considered desirable?"

Diniz leaned back nervously. "It has something to do with the decomposition caused by the tropical heat. When the lands are of the lighter color they say it will 'only raise snakes.' "

"But nothing is as it first seems," Erik interjected. "Many of what were once considered prime lands are now quite worthless; their fertility was but temporary. The virgin forest often had only a thin layer of vegetable mold, and after only a few years, the loose, gritty soil underneath permitted the rich organic matter to drain off. The fields never produced what was originally predicted."

"Like some women I know!" Diniz said jokingly, then stopped and flushed.

Realizing the man's tongue had been loosened by the wines they'd been drinking all evening, Erik pretended not to hear the remark. Still, he couldn't help noticing Margaret's hurt expression. How well he knew how much she yearned for a larger family of her own.

Maria Silvia tried to salvage the moment by mentioning the potential of several of the year's foals, but in a few minutes Margaret and Erik excused themselves and went to bed. Margaret stopped by the little room where Susana was sleeping with Florinda and baby Roberto.

"She hasn't stirred, Dona Margarida. Soon she'll stop feeding at night and you'll be able to dry up."

Margaret felt the hardness at the top of her breasts. "Maybe she no longer needs me, but what if I still need her?"

"In two or three days you won't be swollen anymore. If you wish me to awaken her . . ."

"No . . ." Margaret backed out the doorway. "Our daughter's growing so quickly," she said to Erik as she entered their room.

"Time to make another." He kissed her harder than she'd expected. Margaret pulled away. "I really would like to learn to ride."

"You heard what I said . . ."

"You'll permit Susana when she's older, won't you?"

"It's easier to learn when you're younger."

"Erik!"

"If you insist. But I don't think I or Maria Silvia should be the one who teaches you. Better the stable master, Felix da Costa. I'll have him select a suitable mount for you."

"That would be fine." On their bedside table a kerosene lamp glowed a dusky orange. Their shadows loomed across the freshly whitewashed plaster wall. "I like this room," she said suddenly. "The design reminds me of the Krausses' casa grande. The same wooden ceilings, tile floors, even the identical plan with four wings, like a cross. It could be quite a fine house again if someone would only care enough to bring it back."

"Diniz has sensibly understood the necessity of putting money into the barns and fences before beautifying the house."

"What a waste to allow this to disintegrate just because a mineral isn't crusting on its walls! This afternoon I found some old books stacked in a crate in the library. Do you know what happened when I lifted off the first one?"

"What?" Erik asked absently.

"The termites had eaten through the floorboards, into the bottom of the crate, through all the books, leaving only the top one intact. I'd be surprised if insects haven't destroyed the whole shell of this house. If they haven't, you'd better retile the roof to at least keep the wood dry, and to shore up the columns."

When Margaret spoke up on such unfeminine matters, Erik admitted feeling a vast confusion. It made him want her physically in a powerfully strange way. He watched her slip her long white nightdress over her head. "No, don't," he said, his voice catching in his throat.

She didn't seem to hear him, for she kept her body well covered and began primly braiding her hair. Once in bed, she continued to talk — something about a portico, roof tiles, a terrace. Erik fell alseep in the middle of her elaborate plans for renovation.

❧   ❧   ❧

By the second week of their stay in the mountains, Margaret was riding every afternoon.

"She's almost a fazendeira!" Maria Silvia announced proudly. She poured a glass of local beer for Erik during dinner, adding, "I'd never have thought she'd have learned so quickly."

"Persistência! My wife is the most determined woman in Brazil," Erik puffed proudly.

"Comes from my musical training." Margaret smiled demurely. "My teacher used to say that you could have anything if you paid for it with enough money; you could do anything if you paid for it with enough hours."

"Very wise," Diniz said thoughtfully. "Now, about that other matter . . ."

Erik picked up the cue and followed Alvares uphill toward the stables. In the soft twilight, a horse and rider could be seen cantering in their direction, the slight figure a perfect fluid extension of the animal. "It's Amara da Costa, isn't it?" Erik asked Alvares.

"Who else could handle a horse so well?" Diniz answered admiringly. "She's been on horseback since before she could walk."

Because their dark clothing blurred into the foliage, the rider didn't see the two men until the last moment. She reined her horse and stopped. "Boa tarde, Seu Erico e Seu Alvares." Amara's moist black skin glistened in the burnished glow of the setting sun.

"Boa tarde, Amara," Erik responded. He waved the girl on.

"She's turned into quite a little beauty, eh?" Diniz began.

"Is that what you wished to speak to me about?" Erik asked sharply, hoping to convince both Diniz and himself that he had not been aroused by the horse trainer's adolescent daughter.

"No," Diniz spoke easily. "I didn't know whether to tell you this or not, but since Dona Margarida has survived her first week in the saddle, I see no harm."

"Sim?" Erik asked curiously as they headed down a moonlit path toward the saltpeter storage area. "There's something you haven't told me?"

"Felix recommended Bambú, the gentle mare out of Albatroz, for her lessons. 'Is that an easy horse?' your wife asked the stable master. 'Of course, senhora,' he replied. So can you guess what your wife then did?"

Knowing Margaret, Erik sensed what was coming.

"She asked which horse would be the most difficult and demanded he teach her to ride him." They stopped in front of the first barrel shed. Diniz took a key from his pocket and unlocked the door to the storeroom.

"I've only seen her on Bambú."

"She didn't want you to know. If you had . . ."

"Which one has she been riding?"

"Raio."

"Thunderbolt!" Erik sputtered. "I'm amazed she wasn't thrown. At least he could have informed me!"

"Felix reports Dona Margarida has a very natural touch. That's not to say she didn't have a few . . . difficulties, but she's done well, hasn't she? You are proud, are you not?"

Erik muttered a few obscenities, but seemed to recover enough for Diniz to bring up what was really on his mind. "These past days you have personally inspected all the operations here."

"I'm pleased, Alvares, I've told you that before."

"Sim, senhor. You have seen the entire operation for yourself and have observed how I've handled my responsibilities, haven't you?"

"Alvares, what's troubling you?"

"My accounts always balance the number of barrels of saltpeter in inventory and the number shipped each month, yet we haven't generated the expected profits. I've been running the fazenda with less cash than we estimated; hence the repairs you wish are not always possible."

"A few broken roof tiles don't concern me. As long as there is enough saltpeter to meet my needs on the wharf . . ."

"You are very kind. But, I must do the honorable thing and tell you that there is a mysterious shortage which I have been unable to locate. If you feel another manager might better serve your . . ."

"Não faz sentido! You're too old a friend to speak such nonsense. If you have been wise enough to see the discrepancy, I need you to track the difficulty. Perhaps I could have Pinheiro assist you with an audit."

"The bookkeeping's quite accurate, I assure you. At first the figures appeared small, though now it seems that almost a quarter of the shipments are never received at the wharf."

"Perna-de-Pau escorts them personally . . ." Erik stopped. So that was the answer, the one Diniz had known but had wanted him to surmise independently! Erik berated himself silently. Nothing, short of marrying da Silva's daughter, ever would have been enough to satisfy the greedy bastard. What had become of the saltpeter? Its uses, except in making explosives, were limited. With the other two elements, charcoal and sulfur, readily available, it would be simple for Perna-de-Pau, once he had the rare saltpeter, to produce his own slightly more primitive version of the potent product. Though the sale of Larsons' Elefante brand pólvora, was well regulated, bandits and other criminals were always ready to pay dearly for an illegal supply of the explosive.

How had he been stupid enough to give such an untrustworthy man access to the crucial ingredient? He'd been blinded by the expediency of getting him out of Rio, of appeasing him so as not to create further difficulties with Isabel. Erik held his head between his hands as if to prevent his pounding temples from bursting. "The Parque Panorama? Do you think he goes there still?"

Diniz shrugged.

"We'll have to settle this once and for all, but without my wife knowing about it."

"You have my word, senhor."

Erik smiled crookedly, then placed his arms around Diniz's shoulders. "Alvares, do not be so formal with me. We're still friends and all friends call each other by their first names, do they not?"

"Sim, Erico . . ."

"That's better, much better. Let's go back and see if we can find some more of that excellent cerveja. I find I'm very, very thirsty."

❧ 10 "An unforeseen problem makes it necessary for me to return to Rio," Erik announced at breakfast the next morning.

Susana wobbled on chubby legs to greet her father. He picked her up and bounced her on his knee for a moment. Then she scrambled down and began running unsteadily down the steep path.

"Susana!" Margaret shouted, but the child persisted in the same direction. Lifting her skirt, Margaret started after her, but Erik noticed she didn't run as swiftly as she might have. In fact, she was limping! Perhaps Raio had given her a harder time than even Diniz had admitted. Deus! His wife confounded him, but that was part of the eternal attraction that hadn't diminished from the moment they'd met.

Finally, Susana turned around to see what kind of commotion she'd created, giving Margaret the advantage. She brought her child back to the house in disgrace. As soon as she saw her father, Susana began to cry pitifully. "You musn't run off!" he said in as stern a voice as he could muster.

Margaret's breath was short. "No use, Erik, she's just an active child, much like I was said to be. All we can do is watch her vigilantly." With her linen napkin, she wiped the grimy tears from her daughter's puckered face.

"Why isn't Florinda caring for her?"

"She's feeding Roberto."

"She should've left her baby at home."

"How can I ask another mother to leave her own child to take care of mine?"

"Yes, well, I won't argue with you about domestic matters. My only suggestion, then, is that you find one of the fazenda girls to help you more."

"None understand Susana as well as Florinda does."

"What's to understand? She's just a child that needs minding!" Erik checked himself. "You do as you think best, minha querida, but in any case there are some immediate matters for me to tend to in Rio."

"It's better for the baby if I wait here for you to return, don't you agree?"

"Muito bem. Alvares and I will take the train this morning. Maria Silvia will stay up at the casa grande with you, all right?"

"Certainly."

"Do you plan to go riding?" he asked meaningfully.

"Felix said he'd teach me cantering this week."

"As long as it's not jumping." He lowered his voice. "Because you never know when we might have started another blessed child. I expect you to take every precaution." After making his point, he stood up and smoothed his crisp linen jacket. "Only one thing more . . ."

"Sim?" Margaret tilted her chin innocently.

"I've sent word to Felix that you are not to ride Raio again."

"But I . . ."

"Always the most difficult piano piece, the most spirited horse. You love a challenge even more than I do." He smiled winsomely.

"That's why we married each other, isn't it?" Margaret laughed. The happy sound, so high, so musical, momentarily dissolved Erik's cares about the saltpeter thefts. "And you wonder why we have such a spirited child?" she added.

"Not really. It's only a surprise in a child with such an angelic face."

"Not all girls are as dainty as Astrid. By the way, I've asked Felix to get a little saddle for the pony. Perhaps Susana would like to learn to ride, too."

"She can hardly walk."

"We'll just get her accustomed to the animal, let her sit on its back. Felix has a sweet daughter, Amara, who has been riding since she was the same age. She'll be her teacher. Have you any objections?"

"And if I had?" Erik's eyes twinkled. "Just be careful, both of you."

Against the striking blacks and greens of the mountains, with cheeks pink from her rides in the afternoons, Margaret looked the healthiest that Erik had ever seen her. Until that moment, he'd believed she needed him to protect her.

"What are you thinking?" she asked sweetly.

He brushed the streaming hair from her face, thrilling to its softness against his coarse hand. "That you look so lovely, that ... that you are so strong. I don't have to worry about leaving you, do I?"

"It's my turn to worry over you. You haven't been sleeping well, have you? All these difficulties with the lands up north, the mill, now the powder business, are affecting your health. Even the horses seem to give you more problems than pleasure."

A wagon pulled by two roan horses drew up in front of the house. Diniz jumped down and called, "The train leaves in less than an hour."

"Do you need anything from town?"

"Yes."

"Then give the driver a list while I get my baggage." Erik kissed her perfunctorily.

As the wagon wound down the hillside, past the ragged, overgrown fields that had once produced the finest coffee beans in the region, Erik stared back at the disappearing roof of the great house. A feeling of emptiness enveloped him unexpectedly. Margaret and Susana, his wife and his child. Everything else that he once thought mattered were nothing compared to them. Did other men ever feel like this? There was no understanding of it, no help for it, no one to ask why he felt so alone without them.

❧ ❧ ❧

Erik wanted to confront Perna-de-Pau immediately, but Diniz found numerous faults with the plan.

"Even if you have evidence, that's not the way to learn how many others are involved. There might be someone at the factory helping him acquire the sulfur and the charcoal; he might have men producing and even selling the finished powder, and that's a matter for the police."

"Forget the police! This is a company problem." Erik had the door to his wharfside office firmly closed. Even Rico, his office boy, was warned not to disturb him. "First, I think we should go to Boa Vista and see what's going on around that old hotel. That would be the perfect haven for any illegal operation."

"If he's really producing powder there, it would be well guarded."

"What do you suggest?"

"Let's spend a few days gathering information; let's see if we can at least discover how many others we've trusted might be implicated."

Erik shuffled absently through the papers that had been stacked on his desk while he was away. "I can't very well question everyone on the payroll!"

"Will you permit me to take care of it?"

"Sim, obrigado, Alvares."

Just as Diniz headed for the doorway, Erik called him back. "One more thing! That daughter of Felix, the horse trainer . . ."

"Amara?"

"Sim, Amara. How much do you know about her?"

"Only that the girl is crazy about horses."

"Anything else?"

"She's a caboverde if I've ever seen one."

"What does that mean?"

"Someone not black enough to be called a preta, someone with straighter hair, thinner lips, a narrower nose. In Vassouras she's considered quite dark. In Rio, not particularly."

"Where is Felix from?"

"The da Costas have lived on the fazenda since anyone can remember. His mother was one of the slaves your mother's family freed when they took title to the land. There's an interesting story about that family."

"I haven't heard it. What's it about?"

"Rumor has it that the father of Felix was really the illegitimate son of the patrão."

"You don't think it's true?"

Diniz shrugged. "Who knows in these matters?"

"What happened to Felix's wife?"

"She was called Rozilda. She was the daughter of some morenos in the valley. It's said she had to run away with Felix because her parents were so upset that she was breaking the trend to lighten the family without marrying up financially either. You know the old saying, 'Money whitens best.'

"Anyway, Rozilda died when Amara was very young. A bad case of that parasite, the liver fluke. Why are you so interested?"

"Felix has asked me to take Amara back to the city. I don't know what to do with her, though."

"Isn't there room in your household for another servant?"

"Amara's only experience is with horses. She has quite a touch with them, doesn't she?"

Diniz nodded agreeably. "How are the plans coming to organize the Jockey Club?" he asked by way of making a suggestion.

"Excellent. Our first race is in twelve weeks." Erik stood and stretched. "The Jockey Club! Perhaps I could find Amara a position in the new stables."

"Sometimes these country girls don't thrive in the city . . ."

"Possibly not. But I owe her father too many favors not to agree to help him this once."

"I'll have Maria Silvia talk to her like a mother. Amara is a very gentle girl. And you'll have to agree that she's going to be an unusually lovely . . ."

Erik cut him off. "Yes, well . . ." He didn't need Diniz to extol the girl's attributes. Never before had he seen black skin so smooth, like ebony, her wide lips perfectly formed, her long body hardened by hours on horseback. The girl was agile, quiet, softspoken, but immensely appealing. She'd do well in Rio . . . He'd see to that.

❧ 11   The trail of the missing saltpeter led directly to Perna-de-Pau and the Parque Panorama hotel. Diniz had the damning evidence in less than a week.

"O malandro estúpido!" Erik was more annoyed than angry. "How can those characters have been so ignorant as to think we'd never discover them?" The two men were drinking beer at a wharfside café.

Diniz waited until two laborers passed their table before speaking. "It's precisely that they don't *think*, Erico. Da Silva probably figures, wrongly I'll admit, that your association with his daughter makes him immune to any consequences."

"We'll see about that!"

"Now shall I contact the police?"

Erik took a long, slow sip of the beer that had warmed quickly in the sun. "We don't know yet the extent of his dealings, do we?"

"Our sources say he is producing the finished powder and selling it illegally at an inflated price."

Erik signaled a waiter to refill both glasses. He spoke somberly. "He probably has no sense of the dangers involved. I know I didn't, at least not at first. Now I can't forgive myself for those three men we lost in the beginning due to our own stupidity."

"Now that we've gone back to earthen floors and trained the pulverizing crew in safety procedures, we expect no more accidents. Besides," Diniz added thoughtfully, "we've lost more limbs to the mill than to powder."

The second round of beer sparkled in the midday sun. Erik took several long, impatient swallows. "Cerveja just doesn't satisfy me the way it once used to."

"It's an unusually hot day; even for me, two are barely enough," Diniz agreed politely.

Erik smiled at his thoughtfulness. Though the man was his own age, his deference was faultless. "So, Alvares, how do we proceed on this?"

"Tomorrow night, Friday, we're to check out the Parque Panorama."

"Why must we wait till then?"

"Because there will be so many people around, we won't be conspicuous. Apparently, da Silva's turned it into a terreiro."

"A terreiro? Where they perform macumba rituals?" Erik was incredulous that da Silva would have anything to do with a spirit cult.

"Exactly."

"He's a believer in that superstitious nonsense?"

"More likely he uses it as a shield to sell his contraband. Otherwise all the comings and goings from the place would appear suspicious."

"Que diabo! That devil's smarter than I'd expected. So, we go tomorrow. Then what?"

"If we discover what we think is either hidden or sold there, I recommend, once again, that we call in the authorities."

Erik sipped his beer and idly noticed that the dockworkers were taking care not to exert themselves unduly in the noonday sun. In front of almost every warehouse, men slept in doorways. Even the seagulls seemed to hover instead of fly. What would Father do in this case? he wondered. The incessant heat made it difficult to think clearly on the matter, as did the rough conversation at the next table.

"Those nigger cunts are too rough. Give me a fat mulatta anytime!" an inebriated sailor was saying. "Lots of sweet flesh to hold onto, brown tits the size of jugs."

"Pico rola! What do you know about women?" his companion jeered. "With your puny prick you've never touched the sides of a skinny or plump one, so how can you compare?"

A third member of the same crew came over to defend the first one. "Que é que você quer, pedaço de bosta, com meu homem?" he swore. "What do you want with my man, you piece of shit?"

"Onde está a dificuldade?" the owner asked in a conciliatory voice.

"Always over a woman!" Diniz muttered.

Erik agreed silently. Even in his own case, if it hadn't been for Isabel, this matter would have been something he could've discussed with his father and the police. Diniz probably believed Sven would've turned such a matter over to the authorities immediately, but Erik knew that there had been times when his father also believed that "private solutions" were best.

"Vá pro inferno!" the sailor who preferred fat women yelled. When the owner's back was turned, he spun around, lifted a cane chair, and threw it across the room, where it crashed atop an empty table.

Diniz shook his head at the stupidity of the enraged man. Erik prayed for wisdom.

❧   ❧   ❧

Severino parked the Protos on a dirt road that ran parallel to the main entrance to the hotel. Then the three men walked back to the highway, following the faithful worshipers who made their way on foot toward the terreiro. Erik, who had rubbed shoe polish in his hair and dressed in the shabby suit of a minor civil servant as an attempt at a disguise, stopped and picked up two decapitated statuettes that had been tossed under a fig tree.

"It's dangerous! Put them back!" Diniz said nervously.

"You believe in this nonsense?" Erik snapped.

"I don't practice . . . but then I don't deny it, either. My own mother is still a great believer and some of her experiences with the cult defy logical explanations. One of their healers cured her of an eye complaint when the doctors had given up."

Erik replaced the statues where he found them. "You know the meaning of all this?"

"Some of it."

Along the road, despachos, or offerings, were laid in ceremonial patterns. The three men avoided the burning candles and headless chickens. From the sounds that echoed inside the dilapidated hotel structure, they could tell the macumba ceremony had already begun.

"Severino will check out the back of the hotel," Diniz said, taking charge. "You stay with me, Erico."

"Severino? I thought he'd go back to the car."

Diniz patted Erik on the shoulders. "Calma, Erico!"

Unsettled by the odor of incense, fresh-cut leaves, and the sound of the primitive music that seemed to give the building an eerie pulse, Erik was not about to argue.

Inside, the old hotel had been renovated to fulfill its spiritual purpose. The walls had been papered with an odd blue-and-white design, then painted with coarse representations of Christ, Saint George, and Lazarus, as well as signs: circles filled with crosses; stars, crescents, and arrows representing the macumba gods. The crumbling roof beams were hidden by a false ceiling made of thousands of tiny colored paper flags strung on threads. In all the corners of the room candles burned on saucers.

The former dining room was divided by two low barriers, each with an opening at the center. Diniz led Erik to the side where spectators and faithful followers were permitted.

"Who are they?" Erik nodded at the participants seated oppo-
site.The women were dressed in long pleated white skirts, fluffed
out by layers of elaborate petticoats, and white puff-sleeved
blouses appliquéd with tiers of lace. Their heads were wrapped in
white turbans.

"They are the Daughters of the Gods. They translate messages
from the Other Side."

At the far end of the room there was an altar covered with
plaster figures of saints, vases of flowers, candles, blue satin ribbons, chipped flasks of perfume, and, next to an ornate cross, a
large box of cigars.

"Where does the crucifix fit?" Erik asked hoarsely.

"Macumba has African rituals combined with Christian elements and a bit of quimbanda, black magic."

Three men in white shirts and pants walked across the center
of the floor, which had been strewn with freshly cut leaves. They
carried elaborately painted cylindrical drums and began to pound
out a beat. A wizened black man with a white mustache came
forward and began to chant:

> I greet the ways of Umbanda,
> Saravá Ogum, Iemanjá,
> Saravá Oxossi,
> Xangô and Oxalá!
> I salute the ways of Quimbanda,
> the ways of the East,
> the Caboclos and the Preto Velhos.
> I greet Exú and his family,
> and the family of souls,
> Saravá! Welcome!

A second man, thin and energetic, came into the room bowing
to all the celebrants. As soon as he'd passed the area where they
were sitting, Diniz hissed, "Pai Jerônimo, the Father of the
Gods."

The drummers took their position in the corner of the room
and began a different beat while some of the older women in
white drew diagrams on the floor with chalk.

Diniz kept his voice barely audible. "When the pictures are
complete they will place candles in each circle. Then the Gods
can be summoned."

"Isn't it time to check with Severino?"

"Be patient, it's just beginning."

Eric squirmed in the ill-fitting suit he had borrowed from the brother of Vicente Cardoso. "Do you think anyone will recognize us?"

Diniz touched his fake beard and chuckled quietly. "Hardly!"

At the end of the song, the rhythm changed again. The mediums began to sing, shifting their weight from one foot to the other in time to the slow, plaintive music. As the words began building in speed and intensity, the dancers' feet moved faster and faster until they'd formed a tight, liquid circle around the Father of the Gods. His eyes remained half-closed, concentrating on the tip of a large, odiferous cigar. The drum beat continued to build in tempo and volume. Some of the women seemed to vibrate with the music. Then one of them, her face glazed with perspiration, broke away from the group. "Ai! Ai! Ai!" She clutched her head, stumbled, and fell to her knees. When she stood again, she turned her eyes to the ceiling and began to spin, her many layers of white skirts flying around her. Pai Jerônimo came toward her calmly, reached out his hand to steady her, then blew a mouthful of cigar smoke in her face.

Erik sat forward expectantly and watched her ecstatic dance. The woman's dark bronze color reminded him of Amara. Sweet little Amara must taste like the sapoti fruit, its juice like honey. He thought of her riding across a hot plantation field, as tall and proud as a swaying palm.

Just as the dancer settled back on the floor in a trancelike state, another woman stepped out of the group, screeching in a strange language. One of the assistants handed her a lighted cigar and she began puffing smoke around herself.

"Where's Severino?" Erik asked nervously. "Shouldn't we join him now?"

"We can't leave until the others move onto the floor for their consultations."

The room had begun to darken with the sultry smoke of more than a dozen cigars. Candles had burned down and dimmed. The mediums took their places next to the individual circles of chalk. Cult members from the gallery began to move forward to select someone to whom they could unburden themselves.

Erik was surprised at the varied classes of people who were in attendance. There was a mother with two grown children; all seemed to be equally distraught. Erik guessed they were concerned about the father, who was notably absent from the group. The daughter, who was dressed as though she were going to a fashionable party, walked forward with a lavish set of gifts, mostly candles and rum, to lay before the altar.

A fat man, in a custom-tailored white suit, walked forward in bare feet and timidly stood by the plumpest of the mediums. She blew smoke in his face. He leaned over and whispered something to her.

"What is he asking her?"

"He tells her his problems, probably something marital."

The medium puffed on her cigar, spat on the floor, and questioned the man again. When she seemed to understand his difficulty, she blew smoke on his neck, his shoulders, finally his thighs.

"See" — Diniz nudged Erik — "I told you where the problem was!"

"What happens next?"

"She'll say a prayer, give him a few suggestions about what to buy in the way of herbs, ribbons, and candles."

"Alvares, can you honestly tell me that this nonsense works?"

"I do not exactly disbelieve," he said obtusely. "Come, this is a good time to leave."

Outside, the men had to stand close together to be heard over the pounding drums. "Did you notice anything peculiar about one of the mediums?"

"They all were peculiar to me!"

"The one nearest the altar spent very little time with her cases. When someone would come to her, she'd only blow smoke in his face, then send him out the back without giving him advice. Isn't that the route to the old kitchen?"

"No. It leads to a small building where sacks of rice, beans, and dried meats were stored."

"Show me."

The men cautiously walked around the perimeter of the hotel. All along the broken pavement, scores of candles flickered in the darkness. A small group congregated on the front porch around a black man stripped to the waist and swathed in glass beads.

"What's he doing?" Erik asked.

"He's there to pacify Exú, the devil, and his woman, the prostitute known as Pomba Gira. They're two of the most fearsome members of the spirit world and accept only special sacrifices."

Erik drew closer. All around the black man were crockery bowls containing the corpses of black chickens with their throats cut. In the center basin lay the severed head of a goat marinating in its own blood, its sightless eyes gleaming like jewels in the eerie light. Sickened, Erik turned away and wordlessly followed Diniz around to the back of the hotel. As soon as they heard voices, Diniz pushed Erik behind a sable palm. He managed to hide himself in the shadows but still be able to glimpse what was happening.

"Sim, chefe, se Deus quiser," a tall, thin man was saying to Perna-de-Pau.

"It's him! Some man just called him 'boss'!" Diniz murmured into Erik's ear. "Da Silva's giving him a box and he's swearing some kind of oath."

"Let me see!"

Diniz pushed Erik back against the wall and signaled him to be quiet. The man who'd received the box walked back around to the front of the building. As soon as he was out of sight, another took his place.

"I see money exchanging hands," Diniz mumbled. "Listen! Do you hear that call, like the mother-of-the-moon bird?"

"I think so."

"That's Severino's signal. It's coming from behind the shed."

"Now what?"

"We were going to surround Perna-de-Pau, but let's wait until the sales are finished."

"Could go on for hours."

"Don't think so. Only a few others were waiting to see that same medium."

"What if someone recognized me and tells da Silva?"

Diniz pointed to Erik's slick black hair. "You don't look much like a galego to me."

Erik sighed uneasily. He drew his arm across his chest so he could comfort himself with the feel of the revolver he carried. He tried to remember their plan to confront Perna-de-Pau with what they knew and scare him into obedience. In the bright light of his wharfside office the scheme had seemed simple; now, in the dark, with the scent of snuffed candles and dried blood from the macumba rites reeking in the damp night air, he felt foolish and inadequate.

A door banged at the back of the hotel. Diniz dropped to a defensive position. Erik saw a glimmer of moonlight flash on the metal barrel of his gun.

"Não!" Erik cried out.

Perna-de-Pau turned and whipped out a revolver of his own.

Without thinking further, Erik leapt out into the clearing between the hotel and the shed. "Da Silva!"

In the lemon light that streaked out from the old hotel, Erik, with his blackened hair and baggy pants, was almost unrecognizable, but his distinctive voice was entirely his own.

Perna-de-Pau blanched. "What are you doing here?"

"Paying my respects to Iemanjá, Iansá, and Omulú."

"You? A believer? Who would have thought it?" Perna-da-Pau spat on the ground.

"Who would have thought I'd have noticed the shortages in the saltpeter, eh?"

Da Silva looked up contemptuously and squinted at Erik. "You think your three bastards can be supported by the pittance you pay my daughter?"

"Why didn't you come to me? You never were shy in the past."

"Isabel won't beg and neither will I! Va para o diabo!"

"Terei muito prazer em ajuda-lo. I've always been willing to help you out. But not this way. You've picked too dangerous an occupation, you don't understand . . ."

"Espere um pouco! Wait, you understand! This is my business, see? You will not interfere. If you do . . ."

"Yes?"

"Your fine wife, the vaca, will be paid a visit by three bastardinhos calling you Papai and covering you with kisses. Eh? You think your Norte Americana cow would like that?"

Erik was so furious he could barely keep from jumping forward

and striking the evil man. "Da Silva, that's not the way . . . If it's
money you want, we can talk." Erik forced his voice to remain
smooth and conciliatory. "I've always been fair . . ." he seethed.
"Merda!"

Erik noticed that da Silva was no longer pointing his gun at
him. If he could grab his arm, it would be easy to knock the one-
legged man over. In a second Diniz and Severino would jump out
and help him. "Escute . . . Listen to me . . ." he began just before
he lunged.

Though the revolver dropped from his hand, da Silva was
quick. With his elbow he jabbed Erik in the chest; then he made a
run for the partially open door of the shed. Diniz appeared from
behind the bushes, his gun pointed directly at da Silva, just as
Severino jumped out from the far side of the low tile building.

"Don't!" Erik cried to keep Diniz from shooting. "Pólvora!
Powder!" From where he stood, Erik could see box after box of
explosive material lining the shed's shelves. There was even a
thin trail of the sparkling black dust running along the tile floor
and out the door.

Perna-de-Pau backed inside.

What happened next was a horrendous blur. The worshipers
inside had just been singing their last song of the night in praise
of Omulú, macumba's counterpart to Saint Lazarus, god of sickness and cemeteries. Later the locals were to explain the tragic
events of that night as the time Omulú returned from the dead,
mightily rumbling the earth and taking two sons back with him.

Erik pieced it all together differently. Since Diniz never fired
his gun, he came to believe that the source of ignition must have
been da Silva's wooden leg itself. He remembered seeing Perna-
de-Pau back up so that he could close the heavy shed door behind
him. The nails that held the leather pad at the base of his wooden
leg must have scraped the tile floor, exploding the loose trail of
powder, for the door never closed. It sailed through the air, with
Perna-de-Pau following its path but landing, in several bloody
pieces, a hundred yards beyond in a thorny glade. All Erik actually remembered, though, was being thrown clear of the buildings. When he turned back, the shed had burst into a thousand
splinters.

He'd found Diniz, with a dangling broken arm, clutching a

mango tree trunk at the far side of the house. The terreiro had
been filled with so many hysterical, screaming devotees, Erik had
thought there'd been a massacre. But though the shattering glass
had caused a few injuries, fortunately the explosion had frightened more than maimed. The only fatalities had been da Silva
himself and the innocent and trusting Severino. His body had
burst so completely there were no remains large enough to warrant burial.

❀12 Erik's "private solution" had such disastrous consequences that he came to wish he'd let the saltpeter
shortages go unnoticed. Once the matter of da Silva's illegal business had been explained to the police, they dropped their investi-
gation entirely. Erik ordered the old hotel torn down once and for
all. Sven Larson, after hearing Erik's brief report of the incident,
never mentioned it again, a consideration for which Erik was
especially grateful.

He'd had to go and see Isabel. There was no point in adding to
her grief by explaining the extent of her father's crimes. She'd
accepted his story of the accident passively and with few tears.
When he had finished, she introduced him to his infant son.

"I call him Armandinho, but his real name is Armando."

Erik had lifted his son. He was a cute, chunky sort of child with
dark soulful eyes.

Isabel claimed she understood why Erik had avoided her. She
showed no signs of anger.

"I have something for you . . ." Erik took out an envelope that
contained enough money for her to live well for a year and
handed it to her quickly.

"Obrigada. You are always too generous," she said, tucking it
into her pocket without even opening it.

Isabel kept a far more forceful hold on him with her perpetual
acquiescence than overt demands would ever have accomplished.
When he'd left her, he'd felt his tie to her and the children an
even stronger one than before and was racked with the immensity
of his endless duties. Was there no way he could satisfy all the
people in his life?

On returning to Vassouras, Diniz arranged for a cart at the station. As they left the dust-blown market road, taking the narrow

path that wound along the edge of the deep ravine, Erik began to feel the magical presence of the forest renewing his shattered nerves. From the depths of the gulleys, trees shot up more than a hundred meters before sending out lateral branches to form a vivid canopy that shaded the entire valley. Erik marveled at the enormous trunks of the wild fig trees whose composite veinlike structures reminded him of flying buttresses. He wished he could clip some of the huge trumpet flowers growing on lianas that encircled trunks thirty meters in diameter and take them as a gift for his wife. Far below, the sinuous streams echoed in the lowlands; above him loomed the hills that had, in the waning light, taken on feminine forms. He was tempted to ask Diniz if he also saw spread thighs and voluptuous breasts sculpted in red stone, but realized the more conservative man would probably think less of him if he mentioned it.

At the battered gates of the estate, Margaret greeted him on horseback. Right behind her came Amara, holding Susana in the saddle in front of her. His little daughter's corolla of sunshine curls was set off starkly against the sheen of Amara's ebony skin. As the horse pulled alongside, Amara lifted Susana down to kiss her father.

"See me ride fast, Papai," she said.

With one firm hand, Amara drew her back into the saddle and prodded the horse up the trail in the direction of the house.

"Papai! Papai!" Susana's gleeful calls could be heard in the distance.

Margaret caught Erik's proud glance at his daughter and smiled. She kept her horse in step beside her husband's cart as it ambled up the furrowed road.

"What has occupied you while I've been gone?" he asked. Expecting only the briefest report, he was greeted with an enthusiastic avalanche of details.

"Did you know that over eighty slaves used to run this plantation?"

"I knew there had been slaves, but . . ."

"That doesn't include the free men who served the original family of Barão Antônio Gomes Ribeiro de Avelar, who had it when it was at its peak."

"A baron?"

"Apparently, the imperial government conferred those non-hereditary titles during Pedro II's reign. They say that de Avelar won his for his financial contributions to the Paraguayan War."

"How did you learn about this?"

"All the owners kept records. There are huge account books filled with the most fascinating minutiae: the number of copper pans and three-legged stools in the kitchens, the available bill-hooks and digging sticks in the sheds, the contents of the chapel. Even each tile fired in the olaria was counted. Do you know that the roof of our house has seven thousand three hundred and eighty tiles?"

"Have you counted to be certain?"

"Erik! Seriously, I've just been impressed with how well-managed this place once was."

"Those were very different times, minha querida. No one could run a fazenda in the old way anymore."

"It could be managed more profitably, in any case." She stopped to see the effect of her words on her husband and Diniz, who rode beside Erik in the cart. "Take the making of mandioca flour or the harvesting of the coffee plants, for instance."

Diniz brushed the ruddy soot from his jacket before he spoke. "You aren't wrong, Dona Margarida. There are many ways to improve this fazenda, but no one has had the interest, the time, and, may I add, the money to put into it for many years."

"A pity, don't you agree?"

"I myself have several suggestions for improvements. Dona Maria Silvia and I have been working on a list . . ."

A child's cry silenced Diniz. "Susana?" Margaret kicked her horse and galloped forward. In a few moments she was beside her daughter. From the distance, Erik watched her jump down from her horse and gather her child into her arms.

"What's the matter?" Erik asked as his carriage pulled along-side.

"Nothing serious, senhor." Amara spoke in a whispering voice. "The horse smelled something, perhaps a snake, and threw his head back. Just scared the baby, nothing more."

Erik took Susana into his arms. The snuffling child buried her head in his shoulder. He looked sternly at Margaret. "I told

you she was too young to be on a horse," he said crisply. "I'll
carry her back to the house."

Angered that her husband blamed her, once again Margaret
kicked her horse and galloped down the narrow trail that was a
shortcut to the barn.

❧ ❧ ❧

"I'm surprised you've taken such an interest in this old fazenda,"
Erik said later.

"Why ever not? It's a shame to let it rot back into the hills."

"It's just that you seemed to have no love for Lizzieland."

"That was a place without promise. But this . . ." She gestured
across miles of rolling view. "We could raise a fine species of coffee, perhaps not vast quantities, but specialize in the rare beans
that get so much more at market. The mandioca mill could be
resurrected and worked more efficiently. And . . ."

"Who would undertake the task of overseeing all this?"

"I could."

Erik smiled crookedly. "Now you're intending to live here?"

"Not year round. Alvares and Maria Silvia could take over for
me when we're not here, but we could spend at least six months,
the summer months, here, don't you think?"

"What about your music? You can hardly expect the members
of the Academy, let alone Queiroz, to come to you. There isn't
even a piano within one hundred kilometers of the place!"

"Yes, I've thought of that," Margaret said slowly. "We'll have
to order one when the house is restored."

"A piano!" Erik sputtered. "How do you expect to get one up
the mountain trail?"

"I'm sure with proper planning it can be accomplished."

He began to laugh, a teasing, testing laugh. "For a moment I
was beginning to take you seriously."

"I am serious!"

Erik's mirth turned sour. "I don't mind you occupying yourself; after all, caring for a child only two years of age cannot be
all-consuming, but for you to make decisions about how this fazenda is to be managed . . ."

"Many women have done exactly that!" Margaret's voice was

filled with tension. "When the old baron died, his widow ran the place successfully for twenty years."

"I have no immediate plans to make you a widow . . ." Erik stopped. "What are they doing?" He pointed to some men making repairs he hadn't authorized.

"There are leaks in the roof. During the rains, water runs down the wall and soaks the rafters. If they rot, a whole section of the roof could fall in."

"Wasn't there some molding along that roof line?"

"Yes, a series of wooden corbels that anchored the eaves to the outer wall. It was so elaborately carved, I'm having some difficulty finding someone who can match it."

"We'll have to worry about that some other time," he said more steadily. "We will be returning to Rio next week."

"When will we come back?"

"Not this year."

"Won't you even consider my plans?"

"Oh, querida, there's so much you haven't thought out completely. What about Astrid? Your mother and sister and brothers? Francisca and her children? My parents? You're being completely impractical."

"I guess so, but there's one more difficulty. Florinda's taken Severino's death very, very hard. I find her hiding in her room and crying when she should be working. Going back to the city will be hard on her. Perhaps if she stayed on here for a while . . ."

"We can't reorganize our life to suit the needs of a grieving servant, minha querida."

"I know, I just thought . . ."

"I'm pleased you like Vassouras so well, really I am. Florinda can stay on for a few weeks if you think it best, but I need you to come home with me." He placed his arm around her and walked her slowly back to the big house.

☙ ☙ ☙

After the noon meal, Margaret took her rest. Florinda usually minded Susana at that time, but since Erik was feeling ashamed that he hadn't been more sensitive to the servant's plight, he didn't call her from her room. He'd promised to show Susana the pony she'd learn to ride when she was older, but she was still too tired from her nap to walk, so he carried her in his arms. Every few minutes he'd stop, hike her up, then sniff the sweetness of her freshly washed tangle of daisy-yellow curls. Passing the barn under construction, he noticed that the workers had almost finished the foundation, using granite from a local quarry to make it sturdy and promote the coolness needed for the saltpeter production. Coming down the road on a two-wheeled cart drawn by a pair of yoked oxen were the hand-squared beams for the esteios, or corner posts. It had been Erik's own idea to have the part of the trunk that would be sunk into the ground left covered with bark for protection against decay.

"Seu Erico." A workman waved him over to where the beams were being laid atop the stone foundation to form the base of the outside walls. He leaned the droopy Susana against the half-finished wall. Still dazed from her nap, she remained obediently where he put her. "Be right back, sugar." He kissed her on the forehead. The English endearment had become Erik's special name for the child. He'd taken it from something he'd heard Margaret say in the nursery: "Sugar is sweet and so are you."

The foreman on the job pointed to the center of the building where the largest beam, the via madre, was supported by piled stones. "One meter square, patrão." The carpenters hewing beams with finely sharpened adzes stopped to see if their boss approved.

"Muito bom. Perfeito!" He nodded to them. They grinned back.

"And the other? Are you pleased, senhor?"

Erik walked with the foreman across the rutted road to where a smaller building, a new extraction shed, was almost complete. The walls were constructed of the traditional mud and wattle, but Erik had asked him to add a layer of revestimento, made of mud and sand, for a more finished appearance. Today, one group of men was applying the final white coat of caiação while another was working on the telha-vã roof of red tiles, laying them in such a way as to allow air to circulate inside and encourage the evaporation that would take place in the vats below.

"Everything's in order." Erik smiled. "Even the spacing between the tiles is as I required."

The foreman, smiling at the compliment, went back to his beams.

"Susana! Time to see the horses!" Erik walked back to where he'd left her, idly wondering if Amara would be at the stables. Amara was a nice name, but typical of dark pretas. If Felix had thought more about her future, he'd have named her something more ordinary, more Brazilian. Where was the child? He blinked in the violent sunlight. "Sugar!" he called. "Sugar, call to Papai!" He listened intently. Nothing could be heard but the twitter of birds in a banana tree.

Where would she have gone? Back to the house? No, she wanted to see the horses. Erik spun around and hurried to the stables, calling all the way, "Sugar? Where are you? Susana! Sugar!"

Running in the hot sun, he began to perspire so freely that sweat poured down his forehead, blinding him. He stopped to wipe his face on his shirt sleeve, then rushed into the barn. Amara, alerted by his cries, was mounting her own horse, a stocky chocolate mare with a patch on her forehead.

"Have you seen Susana?"

"No! Maybe she went back to the house."

"Take the lower path to the casa grande. I'll go back to the barns. Perhaps she was just hiding from me, but if I find her . . ."

"Sim, Seu Erico. Don't worry, she couldn't have gone very far."

Frantically, Erik ran back in the direction he came. His shouts brought out all the construction workers. "Susana? Have you seen her?"

"Não, senhor." They shook their heads and joined the search.

Back at the wall where he'd left her, one of the roofers noticed a puddle. He touched it with his finger and brought it up to his nose. The smell was unmistakably that of urine. "Coitada! Poor little thing . . . Frightened."

"Maldito!" Erik cursed when he saw the wet spot. If she's hiding from me, it will make things even more difficult.

"Susana . . . Sugar! Papai isn't angry with you! Come back, sugar! Come back!"

In the distance he heard Amara's horse coming toward him. She's found her! His heart pounded uncontrollably. Running to greet his child, to gather her in his arms and tell her that there was nothing to worry about, he stumbled into a palmeira wood upright loosely placed in the newly drilled holes in the foundation. Both he and the tottering post fell over. Amara reached him just as he stood up unsteadily.

"She wasn't at the house, senhor. Her mother is frantic, but I promised we would find her. Seu Erico . . ." She pointed to his forehead.

He felt an egg-sized lump beginning to form. Though it throbbed, he was much too concerned about his child to worry about it. "There are so many places she might have hidden." He pointed to the thickly forested area behind the new barn. "She wouldn't have dared to go in there, would she?"

Amara spurred her horse forward to the edge of the greenery. "Susana! Your pony's ready for you! Susana, aren't you ready to see him?" she called in a high, friendly voice. Nothing. She came back to where Erik stood, his hand shielding his eyes from the sun as he scanned the area, looking for a likely hiding place.

He pointed at the damp spot in front of the wall and explained to Amara why the child might not be responding. "We've never punished her for making a mistake."

"She's very smart, she wants to do what's right. Why, she copies everything you do. That's why I can't understand why she'd run off. I'd have thought she'd have followed you."

Followed me? Erik thought. I was in the new barn, then in the extraction shed. He ran back into the barn, looked behind a pile of beams, then rushed across the road to the shed. He cupped his hands and shouted again. "Sugar! Sugar! Diga 'Alô, Papai!' Call to me, sugar!"

A sound . . . a bird . . . a voice? "Listen! Do you hear it?" he called to the others. "Susana! Say it again. Tell us where you are!"

"P . . . P . . . Papai . . ."

"Did you hear that?"

Amara dismounted from her horse. "Where's it coming from?" she asked the workmen.

They each pointed in a different direction.

"Susana! Sus . . . Sus . . ." Erik's voice began to crack.

"P . . . Papai . . ." The little voice echoed in the treetops.

Erik stared up at the orange-capped hillside that loomed behind the buildings. "Could she have climbed up there already?"

"Not without crossing the stream on the other side of those trees. She couldn't have done it in so short a time."

"But her voice came from up there!" Erik choked.

"In these hills sounds can trick you."

"Susana! Sugar! Tell me where you are!"

Nothing. He was running to the other side of the shed to search for the trail up the hill when an overturned bucket of whitewash caught his eyes. He followed the wide splash to the foot of one of the roofer's ladders. Then, knowing what he would find even before he dared look, he gripped the base of the ladder and wordlessly began to climb.

Lying in the valley that formed at the side of the L-shaped roof was Susana. She'd crawled up, either to hide or to have an adventure. Even if she had wanted to come down, there was no way she could have recrossed the peak and descended the ladder safely. It was important not to frighten her. A sudden move and she'd slip off. Standing on the top rung of the ladder, Erik could just touch the roof's peak. If she could crawl to him, the rescue would be much easier; if she tried to get away from him she could tumble to the ground.

"Are you my little monkey?" Erik forced his voice to sound playful. "You climb like a monkey, don't you?"

Susana tilted her head curiously. Was her father angry? Maybe not. She grinned. "Mon . . . key . . ."

"Monkey! Monkey!" Erik kept up. "My sugar monkey. Climb to your father, all right? Can you do that?"

Susana began to crawl up toward the peak of the roof.

"That's a good little monkey . . ." Erik encouraged. His heart was pounding rapidly. From the periphery he could see Amara and his workers encircling the building. With his eyes he willed them not to scare the child. Understanding instinctively, they crept forward silently. There might be enough of them to catch her if she fell, Erik guessed. He prayed they wouldn't need to try.

"That's my sugar girl, that's my monkey!" He smiled encouragingly as she reached the top. "Now put your feet over here. Papai will get you."

Her chunky legs swung around, the way she maneuvered

down steep stairs. "Boa menina, now come toward Papai."

Using his knees and abdominal muscles to brace himself against the building, Erik reached up with both hands to grab her ankles. Another few feet . . . "Let go, I'll catch you."

Afraid of falling, Susana scrambled back up toward the peak. "N . . . Não . . ." Her foot dislodged a tile, which went hurtling back in the direction of Erik's face. Quickly, he grabbed the gutter with one hand and guarded himself with the other, deflecting the tile with his elbow.

Susana looked back and began to cry.

"Deus!" Erik shouted. "She won't come to me!"

Then, unexpectedy, from the other side of the roof's peak, he could see Amara's face. She'd gotten another ladder and had scrambled up onto the roof. In an instant she'd pried the child's hands from the tiles, stretched her own long arms as far as they would go, and lowered the baby to Erik. He grabbed her around the waist and hurried her down the ladder. As soon as she was safely on the ground, he began to chastise her.

"Never, never climb a ladder again!" Then he spanked her tiny bottom very firmly.

Susana poked out her lower lip but didn't cry.

Margaret, who'd seen the rescue, rushed forward. "How could you have let her . . . ?" She gathered the grimy child in her arms and kissed her from head to toe, crying hysterically.

In a moment Florinda caught up with them and, hearing the story from the workmen, got a wild look in her eyes and fell down on the ground. "Must have been a spirit! Probably Iansa with the wind and rain. She travels the forest, flying over the hills. Here comes Iansa, queen of the wind and rain!" Her voice rose eerily.

"Enough!" Erik shouted. "The child is fine. Can't you see how you are upsetting her?"

Amara took Florinda away from the family and the workmen shuffled back to their tasks.

Susana's arms were tight around her mother's neck. Erik wanted to hurry them back to the house, to get out of the sun and away from the commotion, but his own arms and legs were so heavy he could not move. He could barely breathe, it was so hot. His heart still hadn't stopped pounding its ferocious beat. The faces in the crowd blurred. "Enough," he repeated weakly, as though the word might still something inside him that was breaking apart.

A few moments later, Diniz was at his side, saying words he couldn't quite hear. A glass was placed in his hand, but his rigid fingers dropped it. Margaret was beside him. He looked up. He was lying on his back inside the new barn; the light dappled through the half-finished roof beams.

"Sugar?" he asked. Was she safe? No . . . He had to find her. "Sugar, must . . ."

"She's already back at the house . . ." Margaret's voice reverberated queerly. "Can you stand?"

"Stand?" he repeated senselessly, closing his eyes against the rushing light.

Sugar. He had to tell her. It was all right about the puddle. Now someone was forcing him to drink, but he couldn't swallow. His skin was dry and he flushed crimson. Deus! His mouth tasted like the bottom of a spoiled bottle of wine. He tried the coffee again, but this time a pain began to balloon in his stomach. A crazy pain, like a cat clawing from the inside. He staggered to his feet, stumbled outside the barn, and heaved violently. The afternoon sunshine dimmed, the redness of the hills became a long chalky blur, and everything faded into a blankness that was more comforting than anything, even sleep.

🌿 Part III 🌿
FRANCISCA
1905-1907

🌿

Ah! as the heart grows older
It will come to such sights colder
By and by, nor spare a sigh
Though worlds of wanwood leafmeal lie;
And yet you will weep and know why.
— Gerard Manley Hopkins,
"Spring and Fall: To a Young Child"

The Lizard

1 Francisca was propped up in bed, her white island awash on polished marble floors. She stroked the fine embroidered edge of the coverlet, enjoying the silky feel of the threads between her fingers. Though the shutters were still closed tight, she could hear the calling voices of her children wafting from the courtyard.

Her house was the plan she'd always wanted: a perfectly square two-story box with an atrium cut out of the middle that contained a garden planted with diminutive roses, heliotrope, and honeysuckle arbors to perpetually sweeten the air.

"Dona Francisca?" Zefinha called from the doorway.

"Sim?"

"A senhora quer chocolate?"

"Quero, sim."

Francisca's usual breakfast, the menu identical to the one she'd preferred as a child, was laid in front of her on a wicker tray: hot cocoa sprinkled with cinnamon, soft white rolls, butter swirls, a cut-glass jar filled with guava jelly, and slices of freshly picked pineapple.

Her old nurse opened the shutters. The sounds of the children floated higher and closer. Sun streamed across the coverlet in bright slashes. Francisca wouldn't be disturbed again unless she dressed and went downstairs. Zefinha understood she'd stay in bed all morning. Augusto called her lazy and stupid; her mother thought she was wasting her life away; and Margaret guessed she was sickly. Francisca didn't care what they thought about her. She knew only that it was so much easier to think in bed, where, without the world intruding, everything was so very simple. And, even if she wasn't physically active, she participated in the life of her household mentally and spiritually. Just listening to her children's faraway voices she believed she knew more about them than a mother who spent every waking moment watching and playing with them. Her children were little lights she carried within herself. The flames burnt high and hot when they were active, dimmed when they were sad, flickered when they were hurt. She had only to concentrate to know exactly what each was doing or feeling.

A lizard skittered across the shutters. Stupid women had their servants kill the house geckos, called lagartixas, afraid they might crawl over them while they slept or get into their clothing or food. Francisca believed that lizards not only protected people from the bites of insects, they kept a house safe from more, from much, much more.

Francisca scratched the sheet with her fingernails. Attracted by the sound, a curious one hurried across the mound of her legs, then paused. Its bulging eyes stared hopefully. As she watched, its skin color began to bleach to match the bedclothes. Francisca thought again how wonderful it would be to blend into any background, to adapt and go unnoticed anywhere she went. She dipped a piece of bread in her cocoa and placed it on her hand. The long darting red tongue, faster than a spurt of blood, snapped it before she could blink. She offered a second bite, but it skittered toward the floor.

"Stay!" Francisca pinched its tail imperiously. The creature released it into her grip and scurried away. Francisca studied the neat separation point of the short green tail in her hand. To be able to drop the offending or trapped part, then grow back a newer, fresher one, was a remarkable skill. That's why she believed their tails were talismans.

Francisca folded the severed tail in her napkin. Later, when she

left her bed, she'd place it with the other ones in her collection.
By now she had more than a dozen shriveled black sticks lined up
on the velvet bottom of her jewelry box. Nobody else knew that
under the sapphire bracelet her mother had given her when she
was married, under the topaz earrings that Augusto liked her to
wear, under all that glitter and gold, lay her real treasures: her
lucky little lizard sticks.

Outside, a cheerful baby laugh quickly dissolved into tears.
The sound was too sporadic to be seven-year-old Marcelino's, and
too mature to be the toddler, Tulio's. Must be one of the girls,
probably Mila. Francisca closed her eyes. The sound died to a
sputter. If anyone had really been hurt she'd have known it even
before hearing the cry. A mother knew.

Zefinha was back at the door to dress her even before Francisca'd finished her tray. Why? Oh, yes, now she remembered!
She'd promised Margaret that she'd go with her to the Botanical
Gardens. Margaret felt it was her duty to plan little excursions for
her. She'd go because her sister-in-law needed her more than
she'd ever admit.

Downstairs she looked over her brood of children and decided
that Emilia would be the one she'd take along that day. Emilia the
screamer. Give the others a rest from her.

"Mila, we're going to the Gardens." She took out her lace
handkerchief and wiped it across her four-year-old daughter's
smudged face. The child grimaced while her mother rubbed. She
was the darkest of the brood, with long black braids and the high
flat cheekbones of a Cavalcanti. "Hardly worth the effort. She'll
be into the flowers and bushes as soon as we arrive," she said to
Zefinha.

Margaret was at the door. Emilia bounded to her aunt and received a generous hug. Francisca's other children sulked in the
background.

"Only Mila's coming today?" Margaret asked sweetly.

"One at a time. That's my rule."

"I know you like to take each separately," Margaret said, her
lips turning down in disapproval. "But . . ."

Francisca pushed past her, refusing to argue.

Knowing that Francisca didn't like the Protos, Margaret had
come in her carriage. Even though Augusto now had a car of his

own, she rarely agreed to ride in it. "Only trust an animal," she'd
stated flatly, and nothing would change her mind.

Astrid sat up front with the driver while Susana and Emilia
were tucked in between Margaret and Francisca. Immediately the
two little girls began nudging, poking, and giggling so noisily that
Francisca had to raise her voice to be heard.

"How's Gigo this week?"

"The doctors are being very strict with him. As long as he fol-
lows his diet, he's perfect."

"There's no question that he has the disease?"

"Over the past year or so his attacks have followed those expected of a diabetic quite exactly. It's so hard on him, though.
He's forbidden sweets, most fruits, port, sherry, cider, cachaça —
all his favorite foods and drinks. Since he had an aggravated attack after shellfish, they've banned oysters, crabs, most fish, even
rice and beans. It makes him very cross at mealtimes."

"I imagine so. What other treatments does he receive?"

"A whole shelf is filled with his medicines. He must wear flan-
nel next to his skin, be dry-cupped twice a week, and measure his
water output. At first it was almost three gallons a day; now he's
down to less than one."

Francisca looked at Margaret gravely. "It sounds so very complex and time-consuming, but I suppose it must be done. Will he
ever be cured?"

"We've been warned not to expect that, although cures are
possible for some. When Erik's feeling well, he thinks it will be
forever and does whatever he wants, completely unmindful of the
consequences. Last week he had only a small glass of wine with
supper, then suffered all night. The next day he went right back
onto his milk diet and tannic acid cure, but that has a strange effect on him."

"In what way?"

Margaret bent over and whispered. "It makes him very amo-
rous, but that's not good for him either, so it's all very complicated."

Francisca winced. Good thing Augusto abhorred milk. That
something might make Augusto even more demanding was not
appealing.

They passed in front of the new headquarters for the Jockey

Club. Through the iron gate they could see the horses being exercised.

"Sometimes Erik brings Susana and Astrid here on Saturday mornings. Amara shows them the stables and lets them pet the horses."

"Amara has a remarkable touch, doesn't she?"

Francisca was silent. Margaret was so innocent sometimes. Funny, everyone believed the opposite, thinking *she* was the one who knew so little about men and worldly matters, and Margaret, because of her talents, because she'd come from another country and had married a more powerful man than Francisca's husband would ever be, was the one who knew all about life. Nothing is quite as it seems, she mused. Nothing.

A bonde was heading to the downtown district. Little boys in torn shirts hung on the outside straps, their bodies leaning against the sway of the curves. "Is that the streetcar that goes to Santa Teresa?" Astrid was asking the new driver, Valentim.

He shook his head, "Não, Senhorita Astrid."

Astrid turned around to Francisca, "Have you ever been to Santa Teresa? There are wonderful views of the city from there! You can even see the old aqueduct. But Ridi and Papai won't let me go there anymore." She pouted.

Francisca watched Margaret's expression curdle. Astrid knew just how to jab her. Her niece was a difficult child to care for, but Francisca, realizing the girl's gaping needs were even more vast than her own, had always tolerated her. Hungry. Astrid was as starved as a beggar's child. Because she'd been denied a real mother, everything she said and did was but a plea to be nourished. Though Margaret had made a valiant effort, no one yet had been able to satiate her. Probably no one ever would.

The carriage pulled up at the Botanical Gardens. Francisca took Astrid's hand and squeezed it tight. "You're looking just beautiful today. Did you pick that blue dress? It's a perfect match to your eyes."

"Ridi did."

Ignoring her niece's petulant tone, Francisca said, "I've some matching ribbons for your hair." She tugged at Astrid's white-blond braids. "Remind me to give them to you when we return home."

Kicking the pebbles in her path, Astrid trailed behind the others as they set out to walk the Street of Triumph at the entrance to the Gardens. Francisca adored the two gigantic rows of royal palms, looking like columns of a thousand-year-old Greek temple. Emilia skipped ahead. Framed by the vista of majestic trees, the little girls looked picture perfect in their pastel dresses and matching petticoats. Watching them, Francisca felt buoyed. How wonderful to be so young and carefree! Astrid still dragged behind.

"Shall we wait for you?" Margaret called over her shoulder.

Astrid shook her head from side to side.

Francisca wanted to tell her sister-in-law not to try so hard, though she never criticized, for to do so might etch a line in their friendship.

"Well, then," Margaret said in a resigned voice, "meet us at the water lilies." She turned back to Francisca. "We'd better catch up with the little ones."

"They can't get into trouble here. That's why I like it so much. This is my idea of a jungle, all the beauty and none of the horrors."

Margaret laughed. "I think I prefer my trees without printed labels. There seems so much more enjoyment in the unexpected."

"Pain is unexpected, sorrow is unexpected," Francisca said solemnly. "When I can, I'll choose order over randomness."

"Aren't you inconsistent?"

"Why do you say that?"

"You once told me you preferred the wild gardens of Boa Vista to the tailored ones at Flamengo."

"That's different." She sniffed. "Both are examples of choices. One gardener selects a symmetrical pattern, the other imitates the best of nature's whims. Each eliminates chance, disorder, chaos, ugliness . . . Don't you see?"

To change the subject, Margaret said, "Florinda's coming home from Vassouras next week. I didn't realize how much I depended on her until she was away. Nobody else can manage my clothes as well."

"She's recovered completely?"

"I hope so. In any case, Diniz thinks it's time she returned to Rio."

"Her five other children must have missed her."

"They have. Her eldest, Carlota, is coming along quite nicely. She's wonderful with Susana, amuses her for hours. But Diniz told Erik that Florinda had met some odd characters from the village near the fazenda. They may have had a bad influence on her."

"Didn't know there were types like that around Vassouras. It always seemed a town left back in another century."

"Neither did I. In any case, I'll be glad to have her home."

Around the next bend Susana and Emilia were darting between specimen clusters of bamboo. As soon as their mothers came into view, they bounded up the stone staircase beside a diverted stream and hurried to the Oriental pagoda built at the top of a rise. By the time Margaret reached the steps, Susana was already waving down from the railing. "As ... tree ... d!" she shouted to her half-sister below.

"Don't chase them," Margaret suggested. "Let them run up and down the steps and exhaust themselves. They'll sleep better this afternoon."

"You're right," Francisca agreed.

A slight breeze stirred the blossoming shrubs splashed with blood-red, purple, and golden blossoms. In front of where they stood a huge jaca fruit plummeted to the ground with a hard thud. Francisca lifted it to feel its rough exterior, then placed it back beneath its tree just as the younger children emerged from under a dark arch of wisteria vines.

Francisca pointed to the bench beside the pond where Astrid sat dangling her legs back and forth. The Victoria regia water lilies were everybody's favorite. Their ruffle-edged pads appeared strong enough to cradle a baby. A water bird with stiltlike legs and very long toes walked from one to the other with impunity. However, the little girls seemed more interested in running back and forth over a humped bridge than enjoying the sight of the immense floating flowers. Francisca and Margaret took a seat on either side of Astrid.

"I'm thirsty," she whined.

"There's water in the carriage."

"Can't wait."

Margaret looked helplessly at Francisca, who said, "I've some barley candy. Would you like some?"

Reluctantly, Astrid smiled. "Obrigada, Tia Chiquinha."
After sucking on the sweet for a few seconds, she asked, "When can I go to Santa Teresa and see Isabel again?"
Margaret winced. "You know how your father feels about that."
"It's not fair! Just because I got sick there once a very long time ago!"
"It's more complicated than that," Margaret added softly.
"You never let me do anything!" she whined. "If it was Susana who wanted to go, I suppose you'd let her!"
Her stepdaughter's jealousy was so blatant sometimes that Margaret didn't know what to say. "Astrid . . ." she began.
"Besides," Astrid interrupted, "I've never even seen her baby, and you know I love babies."
"He's older than Susana, so you'd hardly call him a baby."
Once again Francisca marveled at Margaret's naiveté. Just as she was wondering anew how Erik had managed to keep his secret for so long, Astrid's words took a turn that, though unexpected at the moment, had been inevitable.
"It's so unfair of Papai! He promised Isabel he'd take care of her!"
"You're not to talk that way," Margaret chided. "Your father's been more than generous to that family. Why, he's even been kind enough to educate her children."
"Why shouldn't he? They're Papai's family, too!"
"Astrid . . ." Margaret said kindly. "I know you *feel* that way, but you're old enough to separate those childish ideas from the truth. Your father is really Susana's father because he's my husband. The father of Isabel's children is some other man."
Trembling now, Astrid stood and shook her fists as she spoke. "That's not true! I know Isabel isn't my mother. I know my mother is dead and I'll never, ever see her. But my father is also the father of Eulalia, Xavier, even the new one they called Armando. Isabel told me and she would never lie. Never!"
"Who told you about Armando?" Francisca asked excitedly.
"Perna-de-Pau did, a long time ago when he still came to visit me. Now I can't get to see him anymore either."

"Francisca?" Margaret waited for her sister-in-law to contradict Astrid's story.

"Da Silva won't come again," Francisca started hesitantly. "He was very sick and . . . even so, he never should've come to see you without your father's permission," she finished lamely. Although she was referring to Isabel's father's seeing Astrid without permission, Margaret, in her confused state, heard the words differently.

"Erik shouldn't have . . . Are you saying . . . ?"

Francisca felt trapped.

"My father's done nothing he shouldn't have except marry you!" Astrid shouted at her stepmother. "If you hadn't come, he would've married Isabel and we'd all have been one family!" Now Astrid was screeching. Her face contorted and turned deep crimson. "You're the one who ruined everything." She jumped up and ran back toward the pagoda on the hill. Margaret started to follow her, but Francisca held her back.

"Let her go and cry it out."

"But . . ." Margaret's face was stricken. Francisca was not refuting the child's accusation. Everything must be true. The color drained from her cheeks. "All these years . . . How could I have . . . ?" she gasped.

Francisca held very still. Inside she felt everything her friend, her brother's wife, was feeling. It was as though a brightly burning candle had been blown out. The pungent scent from the vats of red begonias that lined the walkway was suddenly nauseating. One day someone had to tell her. The only surprise was that her brother had managed to keep his secret for so long. Francisca blamed Erik. He should have told his wife the truth from the beginning.

Finally Margaret began to speak. "The older two, they were here before Erik married Gunilla?"

Francisca's silence answered for her.

"And the littlest? He must've been born after Paulo, wasn't he?"

Oh, why had she been chosen to witness this horrible moment? Francisca wondered. Without saying a word, she was hurting her friend irreparably. Someone was crying. Either Susana or Emilia

had fallen down. The sound was plaintive, but not serious, so
Francisca remained at Margaret's side. Without turning her head,
she looked toward the pavilion. A flash of silvery hair behind a
post betrayed Astrid's hiding place. From the expression on the
child's watchful face, Francisca could tell Astrid was feeling pleasure rather than pain.

Emilia and Susana came into view, the older child supporting
the younger one. Susana had bruised her elbow and knee. "She
fell," Emilia announced unnecessarily.

"Mamãe, not hurt . . ." Susana faced her mother's worried expression.

Margaret stood serenely and straightened her skirts. "It's all
been a lie, hasn't it?" She lifted Susana and hugged her too
tightly.

32 Erik stood in Francisca's parlor, ashen and contrite. "I
never wanted to deceive Margaret. I'm sure I could make
her understand if . . ."

There was nothing Francisca could do or say. Margaret had
gone home, spent the night with Erik without mentioning what
she knew. The next morning she'd packed secretly and taken Susana to Vassouras. Erik had come to Francisca as soon as he'd
heard that Margaret had gone, so she'd had the unpleasant duty of
explaining what had happened at the Botanical Gardens.

"Don't rush to her, not yet. You must realize that Margaret
purposely kept herself ignorant of these matters. If she'd wanted
to know the truth, she would have figured everything out years
ago. When she comes to realize this about herself, there might be
a possibility of reconciliation."

"Why would she choose Vassouras of all places?"

"She feels safe there."

"How do you know that?"

Francisca gave Erik a crooked little smile. "How could you not
know it?"

Erik stared out at Francisca's atrium. The rains that year had
come late, but now they were making up for the drought by slicing the sky daily. Swollen droplets linked together to form sheets
of water that cascaded down the gutters, creating muddy rivers in

the garden. "The weather's probably even worse at Vassouras. The mountain roads might be impassable. How will Margaret manage by herself?"

"Alvares and Maria Silvia Diniz are still there, aren't they?"

"But what will she *do* with herself? There isn't even a piano! If she knew how I . . ."

"There's no way you can help, at least not yet," Francisca stated flatly.

"I must talk to her, I must explain . . ." Erik was silenced by his sister's stony disapproval. He walked over to the small table in Augusto's parlor that contained a pitcher of water and several bottles of imported whiskey. He started to pour himself a drink.

"Gigo! You're not permitted!"

Ignoring her completely, he took a sip. "There's no reason to abstain now, is there?"

"Stop talking foolishly!" She took the drink from him.

Erik sank into the deep-cushioned armchair, lay his head back on the lace antimacassar, and closed his eyes. "Doesn't she realize that she's my whole life?"

"You also have children, Gigo. Five children, if I've counted correctly."

"Children might be enough for women, but a man needs . . ."

"Nonsense! Men and women are not so different. There are two types of people, those who care more for their spouses and those who care more for their children. One can't help the way one feels. If you think about it, you'll agree I'm right."

"Our parents? Which were they?"

"I have come to believe that they cared more for each other than for us. Mother tended us with great devotion, but if she ever had to choose, it would be Father over us."

"What a horrid thought! Why would anyone have to choose?"

"In a fire perhaps, or if a boat was sinking and you could only save one."

"Thank God people rarely have to make such choices, but if they did, I believe they would reach out to save the closest one."

"I myself have already had to make the choice."

"That's different. You've never loved Augusto the way I've loved Margaret."

Francisca sighed. "It's not as simple as that. No matter whom we married, we both would have preferred our children. It's our nature."

"Our nature? I don't think or feel as you do about anything!"

"That's what you haven't yet understood about yourself. Long ago you decided to shield Isabel's children at the risk of losing Margaret."

Erik's eyes burned with anger. "I was protecting Margaret!"

"No, you're wrong. If you had cared for her feelings, you would've told her the truth many years ago. How could you have believed that such a secret could be kept forever?"

Francisca watched Erik's face as he struggled with the ideas she'd presented. Perspiration had formed across his upper lip, tiny beads that betrayed him.

"Perhaps if she'd agree to travel with me, somewhere away from Brazil, for a while. After Paulo died, I was willing to let her go to Europe to study music, anything to help her overcome her grief. I could take her myself. Do you think she'd still like to go to Paris?"

A crash of thunder echoed through the house. The storm excited Francisca, making her heart beat faster. "Gigo, you're not being sensible."

Erik raised his voice to be heard. "You could talk to her for me, you could try to explain . . ."

The rains fell more furiously, clattering on the tile roofs and making dents in the packed earth walkways. Somewhere upstairs a shutter, blown open, rattled against the house in an uneven rhythm. Francisca started from the room.

Erik leapt up and followed. "If you won't help me, who will?"

At the bottom of the staircase, she turned to face her brother. "Why would your wife listen to me? She blames me as well. She thinks I should've been honest with her before her marriage, and maybe she's right! She trusted me, she trusted you. We're both implicated in the lie. The whole family is!"

An eerie wind pulsated through the house, lifting curtains and rattling hinges. Francisca rushed upstairs. The lace curtains in her bedroom were blowing horizontally, and dead leaves from the roof were swirling around on the floor. Her first attempt to close the shutters against the wind was unsuccessful. A splash of rain drenched her. Erik stepped forward and slammed them forcefully. "It's unusual for it to blow in from the south, isn't it?"

"Yes. There's rarely even a breeze through here when we need it." She touched her dripping hair. "Now I've got to change. You'd better go home. It's not right to leave Astrid alone. She's suffering as well."

"She seems happier than ever."

"You're wrong. She got her wish, and that can be devastating for a child."

"What do you mean?"

"In a secret sort of way she's always wanted to get rid of Margaret. Margaret was the reason she was taken from Isabel, and Margaret took some of your attention away from her. But she knows that Margaret was always good and fair with her, so now she feels, as she rightly should, responsible for losing her. She's also terribly afraid that you'll blame her for what's happened."

"I do blame her."

"You mustn't. It's you, dearest brother, who has made all the errors in this matter. Astrid did nothing more than speak honestly. You must forgive your daughter, just as you hope your wife will forgive you."

"I see that it's easier to ask someone for pardon than to actually give it yourself." Erik paced the room anxiously. "What must I do to win her back?"

Francisca was pleased that he was seeing the situation more realistically. She walked to a tall carved chiffonier, opened the left side, and removed a large towel. She rubbed her soaking hair and continued. "You're still very confused, partially because of what happened and partially because of the effects of your illness."

"My illness is under control!" he retorted.

"Not if you continue to drink, not if you don't get proper rest," she said caustically. Francisca sat down on the edge of her bed and tied the towel into a turban on her head. Under its bulk, her face looked peculiarly small and frail. "I'm sorry. I shouldn't have spoken so harshly."

Erik took her hand. "No, I'm glad you did. I haven't been fair to you. You've lost a dear friend through no fault of your own."

"As I said before, I am partly to blame. Now that I admit it, I should help set matters right, shouldn't I?"

"If only you could!" He squeezed her hand tightly.

"She might listen to me before she'd see you."

"Do you remember that I ordered a new piano for her from France as a surprise about six months ago?" Erik's voice rose excitedly. "The Pleyel that she always wanted! It's at the docks now. I could take it to her in Vassouras. She's always wanted a piano there. You could come with me when it's delivered and . . ."

Francisca considered this. For once her brother had arrived at a sensible plan. She could just imagine Margaret's delight with the instrument. Surely she'd see it as proof that her wayward husband had her best interests at heart. "Perhaps . . ."

"You'll accompany me, then?"

"If Augusto permits."

"Augusto? What say does he have in this?"

"I prefer not to anger him unnecessarily."

"He'll do as I say!"

"Gigo, when will you realize that every time you suggest that his position's inferior, it irks him immensely? He's like a spirited child who, when punished, puts more energy into the revenge than into mending his ways."

Erik eyed Francisca warily. "I think we've all underestimated you. In your own quiet way you've been studying everything and everyone most thoroughly, haven't you?"

The corners of Francisca's bow-shaped mouth turned downward. "Silence is the best way to hear what's left unsaid."

Erik started toward the bedroom door. "I'll see to the arrangements for the piano immediately. Shall I ask Augusto's 'permission' for next week?"

"No, not next week. Margaret will need more time."

"Two weeks, then?"

"We'll see. First write her, let her know how you feel. If you arrive with the piano too soon, it might be too great a shock."

"I suppose you're right, but I'll never rest until she sees my side of it. You'd better get into some dry clothing."

"It's you who needs to take better care of yourself."

"I'm seeing Dr. Bandeira tomorrow."

"Good ..." She waved good-bye in the doorway. "Good," she repeated under her breath as Erik walked away, haggard and weary.

❧ 3 Erik had long been planning an eighth anniversary gift for his wife. The matter of the perfect piano had consumed him for some time. Francisca had believed that Margaret would have been happy with any reasonable-sounding instrument, but Erik had heard his wife speak so lovingly of the Pleyel that he'd insisted that be the one for the surprise.

Francisca dimly remembered the piano in Mlle Doradou's New Orleans parlor. It hadn't appeared very special; the Queen Anne legs had been battered and the scratched English walnut finish never retouched. As a schoolgirl Margaret had always treated it with reverence and claimed it was the greatest piano she would ever play.

"It was the piano Gottschalk brought back with him from France. On his early concert tours of America he never traveled without his own Pleyel. Later, though, he came to promote the Chickering. When he left for South America he left his first Pleyel in Mademoiselle's care. When he never returned ..."

"Did Gottschalk prefer the Chickering?" Francisca had asked Margaret in her teacher's presence.

"I doubt it. It was more convenient for him to promote an American piano. Wherever he went in the United States, the Chickering company would provide one. A French manufacturer couldn't arrange such a service so easily."

"So he chose a piano for expediency, not merit?" Francisca had suggested boldly.

Mlle Doradou had been piqued by these comments. In a slow, unusually pompous tone, she educated the foreign student. "This is the finest piano in the South, if not in all the land. Its tone and action are beyond reproach. Modern pianos may have more elegant lines, fancier stenciling, many exterior improvements, but from a musician's point of view none can compare to a Pleyel. Unfortunately, Margaret will be unlikely ever to have another piano so responsive, so right for her particular touch."

Whether the piano had been superior or not, Francisca would never know. Only one thing was certain: Margaret truly believed the Pleyel to be the finest. Erik couldn't have planned a more perfect gift, nor timed its arrival better. Perhaps the piano might just be the key to mending their rift.

❦   ❦   ❦

A month later, Francisca's children and Astrid were sent to Boa Vista for a brief holiday while Francisca and Erik set out to deliver the valuable cargo to the mountainside fazenda. Because Margaret had returned all Erik's letters unopened, Francisca had impressed upon her brother the wisdom of not expecting too much of the reunion. In her heart she feared, piano or no piano, Margaret would never take Erik back.

On the date of departure, Francisca met Erik at the wharf because she was curious to follow the logistics of moving the three-quarter-ton piano and crate. From the comfort of Sven's office, she watched the complex loading operation. Erik had explained how it was to be moved, but she hadn't expected to be so impressed with the foresight and ingenuity of his plan.

A specially outfitted wagon pulled by two sturdy horses was waiting. Six stevedores, stripped to the waist and ready for work, sat deferentially on the ground beside the huge crate, awaiting Erik's orders. Francisca didn't understand why Erik was having the wagon brought so close to the dock's edge until she saw it being chained to the pilings so it wouldn't move. Next, long metal rails were leaned against the loading end of the sturdy wagon and solid timbers were nailed across its length to create a secure bed for the precious freight. Erik marched round and round, suggesting that the rails be moved first to the right, then to the left, centering them exactly. He fussed at the alignment for more than thirty minutes until finally he seemed satisfied. From Francisca's position, the centimeter or two he was concerned about seemed insignificant. Coconut grease was slicked on the rails. Wondering why this was being done, Francisca hurried out onto the quay. The September day wasn't especially warm, but Erik was already drenched with sweat.

"More grease on the underside," he ordered. "Idiotas! Watch the rail positions!"

A dockworker tried to reset the rail quickly, but it slipped from his fingers and clattered to the ground.

Erik lashed out and kicked the clumsy man. Realizing what he had done, he tried to apologize immediately. "Desculpe . . ."

Though Francisca was shocked by Erik's temper, the worker, unmindful of either the reprimand or the apology, went right back to resetting the rails.

A few minutes later, Erik ordered three hands up on the wagon where a winch had been improvised across its width. A rope was tied to the crate and the burliest stevedore set to work turning the winch crank. Three others stationed on either side of the crate slid it up the greased rails. At first it seemed not to move at all, but suddenly a tightening from the winch rope dragged it forward and it started inching up the incline. The dockworkers, their chests glistening from exertion, let out a rousing cheer. Anxious to take advantage of the momentum, Erik yelled, "Turn, turn! Push, push!"

In the excitement, Francisca squeezed her hands together so tightly that her nails dug into her palms. As soon as the piano was safely on the wagon bed, she let out a grateful sigh. In a short time, the crate was centered and blocked to prevent it from shifting on the journey to the train depot. The wagon was unfastened from the pier, and they were on their way.

At the station, Erik examined the possibilities for transferring the cargo to the flatcar he'd ordered coupled to the train. "I didn't anticipate the wagon bed would be two feet lower than the floor of the railcar."

"You could use the greased rails again, couldn't you?" Francisca suggested.

"Perhaps there's an easier way. If we could raise the wagon to the exact same level as the flatcar, the box could be pushed across."

"Ótimo!" Francisca clapped her hands, thinking she'd underestimated her brother's cleverness in the past.

After the workmen had laid down the boards so they equaled the height of the railway car's flooring, Erik directed the horses until the wagon's wheels were aligned with the tracks. Then the horses were walked forward slowly. The wheels crept up the makeshift incline until they reached the top. Next, the wheels were blocked to prevent slippage during the transfer, the greased rails were laid out horizontally, and finally the huge crate was pushed across the gap. After it was positioned in the center of the railway car, it was tied down with abundant amounts of sturdy rope.

A whistle blew. Erik helped his sister into the first-class car. From his yearning look back at the flatcar, she had the feeling he'd rather have been riding with the piano. They settled themselves in the plush seats and accepted the coffee served immediately by a whitejacketed steward. Brother and sister were too tense to speak as the train sputtered and jerked out of the station.

The train quickened pace rapidly. It passed the meager houses at the outskirts of the city, then the cattle abattoir. Francisca turned away from the sight of hundreds of vultures hovering above a pile of bloody bones. They traveled through the notorious swampy area where many people lost their lives during the construction of the Central do Brasil railway, arriving at the foot of a great mountain rise. As the air became cooler and the train ride more vertical, Erik seemed to relax.

An old memory caused Francisca to smile. "I wonder if there will be any surprises when we open *this* crate," she said.

Erik's cobalt eyes twinkled. "Are you thinking about 'Canelinha,' our 'Little Cinnamon'?"

"Exactly. One of Papai's men found her in a crate of mill equipment, didn't he? I always wondered how she got inside."

"Father guessed she must've come aboard when the ship stopped in Pernambuco or Bahia because there're usually animals for sale at those docks: parrots, coati, monkeys, and marmosets like our Canelinha."

"Mamãe wouldn't let us keep her at first, remember?"

"But you convinced her . . . with lots of tears!"

Francisca giggled. "Wasn't she the prettiest creature! We made that nice little home in the gardener's shed and when we'd come to see her in the morning, she'd chatter as though she were angry for being left alone. But as soon as she had her grapes or guavas she'd be all over us."

"I remember how much she loved insects. I caught spiders and bottle flies that whole summer. She'd only eat them if they were alive, biting off the heads first, then picking at the legs before crunching the body."

Francisca made a face. "I wonder what really killed her.

Mother thought it was the bees. We'd feed her sugar water and they'd buzz around the little dish. Do you think a bee sting could actually have done it?"

"Don't know." Erik shook his head sadly. "But if a bee can kill a man, surely a little animal that was small enough to sit in your hand could be stunned by even the smallest amount of the toxin."

Sobered by the memory, Francisca turned her head and looked out the window as the train lumbered up to the hilly region outside Vassouras. Her mind swirled with recollections of the adorable pet with its tufted ears and long, ring-striped tail. The marmoset had an amazing acrobatic ability to climb ropes and scamper through the trees. Francisca had loved it immensely. She'd bury her nose in its musky fur and kiss its soft underside much the way she nuzzled her children in later years. To feel so much for an animal had probably been ridiculous, yet she'd never felt as deeply for a pet again.

Erik noticed his sister crying openly. "Don't . . . We're almost there."

"I can't help it . . ."

"Please, Chiquinha . . . Don't . . . Don't . . ."

She dried her eyes slowly and stared at her brother, who was weeping also.

❧   ❧   ❧

The first wagon waiting at the Vassouras station was far too small for the task. Erik impatiently sent men scurrying to find something stronger. The driver of a cart piled high with bananas was offered a week's wages to unload his wares and make the trip to the fazenda.

"His horses, they don't appear as . . . robust . . . as the ones in Rio, do they?" Francisca asked uneasily.

Erik shooed several skinny dogs that had been sniffing his boots. "Don't be misled by a coating of red dust."

After the crate was transferred to the banana wagon, Francisca began to worry once more how Margaret would receive them. She knew her friend would be overjoyed with the piano, but would it be enough to break down the barrier between her and Erik? The driver of the banana cart urged his horses forward. Thinking they were pulling their usual load of fruit, the animals

started off brightly, but they stopped suddenly after only a few
steps.

"The load's too great for just these two!" Erik shouted.

A third horse was commandeered and hitched to the rig.
"Ready?" Erik asked in a husky voice.

Francisca nodded. The wagon lumbered under the weight of
the piano. Erik and Francisca followed in the small cart that had
been hired originally. Finally the precious piano was on the last
phase of its tedious journey, one that had begun in a factory
oceans away in France.

"Damned piano better play after all this," Erik swore under his
breath.

"Oh, Gigo!" Francisca admonished lightly as they passed a
cluster of pastel-colored colonial buildings with red roofs, blue
doors, and blue shutters. "I haven't been here in so many years
that I'd forgotten how enchanting the area can be. No wonder
Margaret fell in love with it."

A sudden sound changed Erik's focus from the twilight-dap-
pled cane slopes to the piano crate. "Meu Deus! Não!"

The wagon's right rear wheel had fallen into an unexpected
soft spot and it swerved calamitously. Wooden carriage wheels,
though wonderfully strong under a downward load, were over-
stressed by a lateral force. Francisca and Erik watched helplessly
as the wheel wobbled, twisted, then split at the top of the hub.
The crackle of the breaking spokes echoed ominously just before
the wagon bed heaved to the ground. The piano crate slid inexorably downward, slowing only when it reached the muddy slope
of the bank.

Erik's face had turned a dusky purple. He caught his breath
and began screaming orders. The men ran to the crate and tried to
pry it from the mud, thinking that was what Erik wanted, but the
weight was impossible for even five men to lift.

After much confusion, Erik managed to get some planks underneath it to keep it from sinking further. He sent one man on
horseback after additional help. "Get me oxen!" he shouted after
the dust cloud that disappeared back down the mountainside.

Erik shuffled round and round the crate, looking for obvious
damage. "Damn that banana driver! What were those wheels
made from, matchsticks?" He kicked the dust in frustration.

"Calma, Gigo, calma. Be glad it wasn't a wheel on the other side." She pointed to the cliff.

"I hate it when people try to make light of one misfortune by thinking of something more disastrous," Erik seethed. " 'Good thing he lost his left hand, he works with his right,' " he mimicked cruelly.

Francisca forgave her brother's temper. She started to calculate whether anyone could return from town with oxen and another wagon, then reload the piano and get it to the fazenda before dark. She looked at the sky: not exactly clear, but the scudding clouds were high, light, probably not precursors of rain. Suddenly, she felt a sharp pinch.

"Ow!" She began batting at her ankles. "Gigo! Help me!" Ants were crawling up her skirts faster than she could shake them away.

Erik came running. "Saúvas!" Without concern for her modesty, he shook out her skirts and pulled the clinging creatures off her thighs. "Go sit up on the seat!" He pointed to the tilting wagon. "Take off your underthings and check them well."

All the men turned their backs so she could undress. A few renegade ants had already burrowed in her panties and slips. "What else can go wrong?" she muttered.

The banana cart driver pointed to where the leaf-cutter ants had dug tunnels under the road. "Here's the reason the wheel sank in." The other men came over to see the big formicarium the driver was excavating with a stick. "Look at this." He showed them.

One of Erik's men from Rio peered down into the maze of passages and chambers almost four meters deep. "What are they doing?"

"The saúvas carry the leaves and pack them together to create a funguslike growth that they later eat, like farmers making cheese," Erik explained.

Cautiously, Francisca walked over to the edge. "We had the same ants in Boa Vista, didn't we?"

"Yes, but I've never seen anything the size of these!"

A line of ants carrying pieces of green leaves twice the size of their little black bodies marched by. "If only men could work so efficiently," Erik muttered.

As the ant column drew closer, Francisca scurried back to her high seat. At least his interest in the ants had diminished Erik's rage somewhat. Soon he was regaling the men with stories of the even fiercer army ant. "I've heard it said that when one of their columns, which sometimes are as much as several feet wide, approaches a house, the occupants must abandon the place for several days."

The burliest of the workers smiled broadly. "Sim, Seu Erico. But you know that after the ants pass the house is much cleaner. Not a single roach, mouse, snake, centipede ... Nothing is left!"

Francisca cringed and rubbed the welts on her leg where the less vicious, vegetarian ants had squeezed her flesh.

"Here they come!" one of the men shouted. In the distance the new cart oxen were making their way up the road.

Erik hurried the men to place ropes about the crate. Improvised levers worked the sunken end out of the boggy mire; while the oxen pulled from the front, Erik directed the placement of the rails in different positions. After a few mighty heaves, the ropes strained. The men, their muscles bulging, raised the low end of the crate onto the firmer portion of the roadbed. Erik ordered the ox driver to move his beasts just so much to the left, then so much to the right, until the crate was lined up with the new wagon.

Erik inspected all the sides of the wooden box until he was confident that it had withstood the trauma of the fall without damaging the contents. Finally, he directed the oxen's owner to move them back to their position at the head of the replacement wagon. So involved was he in the mechanics of the loading that Erik paid little attention to the restlessness of the two milky-white oxen as their ropes were being untied.

From her perch on the disabled vehicle, however, Francisca realized what was bothering them. The oxen were standing just where Francisca had been attacked by the ants. She could see the black dots swarming around the oxen's hoofs and moving up their legs to their tender underbellies. Later she knew she should have said something, but what could anyone have done at that point? No one, least of all she, expected those docile, sturdy creatures to have bolted in quite the manner they did.

One moment they were straining forward under their driver's command; the next they stumbled backward into the crate. Their immense weight cracked the battered case. One of the clumsy beasts fell on its side with one hoof piercing the polished wood of the grand piano's lid.

Erik had been hit in the face by a flying splinter of wood. Blood streamed from his upper lip and a welt formed above his left eye. Several other men were pulling splinters from their clothing, and the ox driver was nursing rope burns on the palms of his hands. The pathetic corpse of the piano was strewn all over the road. Its elegantly carved legs had snapped in two, its strings and hammers were disemboweled, the black and white keys were scattered everywhere. The only sound was the pathetic bleating of the writhing injured ox.

Erik turned a frightening shade of crimson. Francisca held his clammy hand. "You've not eaten enough or had proper fluids today, have you?"

Dazed, he watched as the one healthy ox was led away and didn't respond.

Suddenly she was in charge. "Hitch up the good cart. We must get the senhor to the fazenda, pronto!"

As soon as they rounded the bend, a single gunshot rang out. The ox with the broken leg had been destroyed. Erik leaned against his sister. When they approached the fazenda's great iron gates, he made an effort to present a dignified appearance to the vigia.

"Seu Erico! Boa tarde." The guard touched his cap respectfully.

When they stopped in front of the casa grande, Erik took a deep breath. "Let me help you," Francisca whispered.

"No, I'm fine . . ." he protested. But, as he descended from the cart, his limbs seemed to melt. Before he could reach the first step to the verandah, he fell prostrate on the ground. Francisca touched his face. It felt moist and was alarmingly pale.

Susana fell on top of her father. "Papai! Papai!" Margaret ran forward to find her estranged husband drooling uncontrollably. His breathing was so shallow he could barely speak. His arms and legs were trembling. Poor brother, Francisca thought, this is surely not the way you intended your reunion to begin!

Margaret had the sense to take Erik's pulse. "Full and bounding . . ."

"What?" Erik groaned.

"The doctor said that if his pulse was weak we were to give
medication, but if full and bounding we were to" — she furrowed
her brow, trying to remember — "feed him!"

A bowl of rice and overripe bananas, food more suitable for a
baby than a grown man, was ordered from the kitchen. Propped
up against a porch column, Erik was slowly fed by Margaret.
"When was his last meal?" she asked Francisca.

"We only had some coffee this morning on the train."

"Has he had anything else to drink since then?"

"Only some water at the station."

"Are you trying to kill yourself?" Margaret demanded harshly.
He turned from her without replying.

"I'll find him some aniseed tea." Margaret stalked into the
house.

4 Francisca followed Margaret into the dining room and
wearily fell into a chair. Margaret asked that the tea be
made for Erik and a meal served to Francisca. The cook brought
her a lukewarm plate of rice, beans, and cheese and left them
alone. As she took a few bites, she tried to explain to Margaret
what had happened.

"The piano is ruined." Francisca choked. "He wanted so much
for you to have it!"

"It seems he needed not only something to bring but someone
to act as intermediary. Didn't he trust himself to speak with
me?"

"I don't believe he thought you would listen to him, perhaps
not even see him, unless someone first explained how sorry he
was."

"Sorry!" Instead of the diatribe on the injustice of her brother's
actions that Francisca expected, Margaret broke into sobs.

"Mamãe!" Susana cried from the kitchen doorway.

The cook, who had been trying to keep the child away from all
the commotion by feeding her sweets, attempted to restrain her,
but Margaret motioned her into the dining room. The confused

child climbed into her mother's lap and put her thumb in her mouth.

"Did you see the way she ran to her father? She's missed him terribly, asked about him every day. I've felt like a monster keeping her apart from him." Margaret spoke in English to maintain their privacy in front of the child.

"He missed her very much."

"He has Astrid and . . . the others."

"Astrid's been through a terrible time, and he never sees Isabel's children anymore. Why are the children made to suffer for the stupidities of their parents?" Francisca paused for a minute to wonder if she should go on. The time had finally come to speak directly about painful subjects. "When Gigo first met Isabel he was a very young man. It was what all boys at his age did. In fact, it was *expected* of them."

Francisca struggled to think of what to say next. Margaret clutched Susana on her lap as though the child could somehow protect her. Francisca took a deep breath and continued speaking in English. "I know you believe that if Gigo had only been truthful before your marriage you might have accepted the situation. Even he wanted to explain everything, but everyone advised against it. They said you were too weak, that there would be time later. I, for one, thought they were wrong."

"You were right." Margaret rocked her tired daughter in her arms. "I'll never understand why I wasn't told . . . or" — she choked —"how the third one happened, especially when I was so . . . attentive . . . to him . . . So willing."

Francisca's nervousness increased. "You were having the baby, you were advised not to."

"I waited!"

"For a man, they say, it's different."

"It's not!"

Flustered by an argument she couldn't begin to tackle, Francisca bowed her head. Why was she the one who had to do this? The words finally tumbled out. "Because you have so many talents you pretend that you can live without a man. Even here on the fazenda you play out a little game of running a farm and telling everyone what to do. But do you think anyone would listen to

you if you were not Senhora Larson? Even your Mlle Doradou
won her income and protection from . . . men."

Margaret was aghast. "That's not . . ." She blinked her eyes
furiously to stop the tears from forming.

"There's more . . ." Francisca caught herself in time. If she ever
revealed herself completely to Margaret it would not be in this
way or for this purpose. But there was one piece of information
that should be told — now.

She looked over at Susana, who had become a sleeping weight
in her mother's arms. Florinda came in to take the child. With
Susana out of the room, Margaret slumped in her chair and
placed her head in her hands, as if to quell a throbbing head-
ache.

"I already said that Erik wanted to tell you the truth, but you
didn't believe me, did you?"

Margaret shook her head numbly.

"Mothers," Francisca began simply. "We're both mothers now.
Much of what we do for our children comes from our own perception of what *we* believe is right for them. I've made hundreds
of mistakes with mine, you must have also, so we each should understand how a mother, thinking she knew what was best, could,
without meaning any harm, have made the wrong decision for a
child, couldn't we?"

"My mother!" Margaret stood unsteadily.

Francisca half rose to follow her, then sank back in her seat.
"And mine." She stared at the polished floor. "The two of them
decided that you shouldn't be told. They convinced Erik they
were right, and he was so . . . so desperate to have you that he
agreed to do as they wished. He has always found it difficult to
refuse any woman's request. It's been his great strength, and his
defeat."

Margaret was obviously shocked. "How did you learn all this?"

"I've listened, I've asked a few questions."

"I should've known it was my mother!" Margaret pounded her
right fist into her left palm. Thinking she needed something, a
servant, trained to respond to clapping, came into the room. Margaret waved her away. "If my mother hadn't tried to make me
into a musician, I never would have been crippled by so many

useless dreams; if she hadn't separated me from my family for so many years, I might have . . ."

Might have what? Francisca wondered. No one ever knew where another road might have led. But she let Margaret rail on without comment.

Margaret looked crazily around the room. "Don't know anything . . . Don't know what to do. Without him it's been so . . ." She leaned against the wall for support.

Francisca came toward her with arms outstretched and Margaret willingly leaned against her friend's shoulder. "I know . . . I know . . ." she comforted.

"What else do you know?" Margaret asked close to her ear. "Do you know what I should do with him now? I can't go back to the same house, the same bed. Everything's different, everything's ruined."

"Different perhaps, ruined no. Everyone makes compromises."

"I . . . can't."

"You can and you will, just as I do all the time."

Margaret stood back so she could look at her friend's pale, concerned face.

Stroking Margaret's damp hair, Francisca said tenderly, "Do you know what else I know?"

Margaret shook her head slightly.

"You cannot leave my brother out on the porch all night. His wounds, though minor, need tending. With his disease he tends to get infections easily, remember? And we can't allow him to get a chill."

"What shall I do?"

"Just take care of him for now," Francisca stated firmly. "The rest will come — slowly, but it will come."

❧5 Erik's condition after his diabetic attack was serious indeed. No matter what medications or dietary changes they tried, he could not be stabilized. Francisca stayed on to help nurse her brother. She was able to observe not only his physical healing but the beginnings of a new friendship budding between husband and wife. Initially Margaret had thought she couldn't leave a man as sick as her husband; later it was obvious that she didn't wish to.

The changes Margaret had effected on the farm were impressive for anyone to have accomplished so quickly. She'd put all her energies into analyzing the profitability of the fazenda, believing that she might make a life there without Erik. Worried by the drastic fall in coffee prices on the international market, she decided to pay less attention to its production. Some of the biggest growers were afraid this bust might be as disastrous as the ones for cotton and rubber in recent years.

"Last year at this time the average export value per bag of coffee was 4.09 British sterling; last month it was 2.91," Margaret had quoted accurately, much to her husband's surprise.

On her own she had begun to apply innovative ideas to making other crops more successful. Erik had been especially amazed by Margaret's rearrangement of the casa de mandioca, where manioc roots were converted to the farinha that Brazilians used widely in their cooking.

"I've reorganized the whole system," his wife announced blithely as she escorted brother and sister into the enlarged mud-walled hut. "I've made it more economical for us and more efficient for the workers."

Inside, women and children as young as six were peeling the large tuberous roots with razor-sharp peixeiras. Francisca was alarmed to see the rapidity with which the youngsters flicked the blades, though they seemed almost as skilled as their mothers.

"Every day farmers bring maniocs, but we don't open the building unless the pile reaches here." Margaret pointed to a mark on the wall. "It isn't worth lighting the fires or running the presses unless we have a full day's production since there is so much start-up and then cleaning time, no matter how much is finally bagged."

Walking around to the pile of peeled vegetables, she pointed to a small kerosene-powered grinder. "I don't know why they kept this in a barn almost a kilometer away. They used to bring the manioc here, peel it, carry it to the grinder, then return the pulp. What a waste!"

Erik was amused by the simplicity of her plan. "Why didn't Diniz or someone else think of it before?"

"Sometimes it just takes a new pair of eyes to see what's obvious."

"But who expected them to be as lovely as yours?" Erik remarked playfully.

Hiding her pleasure at this open flirting, Francisca had looked out at where the manioc juice, a poisonous by-product of the pressing process, was running into a stream. "What a convenient place for it."

Peering over the short wall that permitted air to circulate in the building, Erik commented, "I don't remember water being here before."

"We diverted the sluiceway from one of the ponds after I noticed how much water formed in these gullies after a storm. Better to have the streams flowing than stagnant."

Margaret pointed out the newer, more powerful press, which removed the last of the moisture in the process, and the large firebox under the roasting area, which permitted one man with a long-handled paddle to keep the entire day's production turned and stirred on the flat oven plates. At the far end of the building, the finished flour was being scooped into bags by the children who had finished peeling the raw root.

"You certainly have made all these people into willing workers," Erik complimented.

"That's because they share in the proceeds differently. Before this, we would pay them a small daily wage and allow them to use the casa de mandioca for their own produce once a month. Now I permit them to use it the same days we do our own crops. For efficiency's sake it's better to have more manioc to process. They pay us back twenty percent of what they receive at market; we pay them twenty percent of what we receive for their labor. Most families have doubled their income, but our profits have done even better."

Erik's left eyebrow raised expectantly. "How much better?"

"Eight, maybe ten, times better."

"Amazing!" He whistled. "You're amazing."

❦   ❦   ❦

Margaret had become so involved with the fazenda, Francisca feared that she would not wish to leave it, but after four weeks it became clear that Erik had recovered sufficiently to travel. The day before all were to return to Rio the two women lay side by side in hammocks on the verandah, watching blackening clouds in the valley move ever closer to their district.

"Wonder if it will rain here," said Francisca idly.

"It will miss us," Margaret replied with certainty. She clapped her hands to call for tea and seemed visibly annoyed that Florinda didn't come at once.

"How can you be so sure?"

"I know the pattern. It will come over that hill to the south, then turn and pummel the area toward the east. The soils are far too wet on those slopes because of it."

"You've really studied everything: the soil, the climate, the crop records."

"I've needed to do something productive," said Margaret, clapping for Florinda once again. "Where could she've gone?" she asked impatiently.

"You know as well as I . . ."

"I knew I shouldn't have brought her back here with me. She's like a child who can't be trusted. Every opportunity she gets she sneaks off to be with that man she met soon after Severino died. Alvares was right to be worried about her."

"How can some affection hurt the poor girl?"

"Diniz says he's a very bad character."

"Diniz is probably jealous!"

"Francisca!" Margaret pretended to be irate, then giggled. "I just hope she'll be back to her old self when we get home to Rio."

"She adjusted last time. She will again."

"Probably better than I will."

"Aren't you ready to return to the city?"

"Not really."

"What about your music?"

"My music often frustrates me far more than it satisfies."

"Did you know that Maestro Freire is returning from Paris? I think he'll be back in time for Carnaval."

Margaret's head popped out of the side of her hammock. "How do you know?"

"I met one of your musician friends, Nicia Netto, a few weeks ago. She lives in our district and she frequents the park where I

sometimes take the children. Apparently Freire's been an enormous success in Europe."

"I'm not surprised."

"He's sure to ask you to perform with him again."

"Not if he hears me now."

"With a few weeks of practice you'll be back in good form."

"Don't know," Margaret said morosely. "Don't know if I still
have the . . . energy for it now. Rio is so . . . draining. Here I feel
very different, very strong, energetic, lively . . . needed. In the
city I'm just another piece of furniture that requires dusting and
maintenance."

"Erik needs you more . . ." A thunderclap buried her last few
words. The air had turned several degrees cooler. A curtain of
hard pounding rain moved closer each second. Moments before a
wet wind sprayed the verandah, Margaret and Francisca rushed
to the doorway. "I was wrong . . . about the rain," Margaret admitted.

Francisca laughed at Margaret's wrinkled expression. "I don't
know if I've ever heard you use those words before. Then again, I
don't think I've ever heard my brother admit he was at fault,
either. The trouble with you two is that you're far too much alike.
Whoever would've thought that a woman and a man could be so
similar, eh?"

26 "Alô, lagartixa," Francisca greeted the plump lizard that
stared at her from her nightstand. "Lagartixa," she repeated with a little laugh. Around Vassouras the colloquial expression "lagartixa linda" had meant a pretty, supple, slender
young woman, but the green reptile didn't look particularly feminine to Francisca. Wasn't this the one who'd lost its tail most
recently? While she was away it had grown back almost completely, but there was still a dark line at the site of the fracture.

"I guess I'm a bit like you," she said aloud as she pulled back
the covers. "No matter how many times they try to break me, my
tail grows back." Perhaps that was the reason she had such affection for the creatures.

Upon returning home, Francisca was no longer content spend-
ing so much time in bed. She was buoyed by a sense of accom-
plishment because she had contributed to the new understanding

that flowered between Margaret and Erik; the journey had bene-
fited her immensely.

On her way downstairs, Francisca tiptoed by her husband's
suite. From the hall she could hear Augusto snoring mightily. It
was clear he'd not missed her. Obviously he had enjoyed the additional freedom of having both her and Erik out of town. Not
that he hadn't taken every opportunity to assert his marital rights
once she returned. Even her first night back he'd come to her and,
without even caring that it was an immodest time of the month,
insisted she satisfy him. She cringed as she remembered how he'd
humiliated her.

"Been to the farm, have you? Did you learn a few tricks from
the stallions?" He'd forced her down on the floor on her hands
and knees and taken her from behind. When she cried that he was
hurting her, he'd thrust even harder. At the last moment he'd
made her take his penis, swollen, wet, and bloody, into her mouth
to finish him off the way he preferred. It was a wonder she'd ever
conceived her children! After all this time she should have been
accustomed to his demands, but it continually surprised her
to rediscover how brutal and unfeeling the man she'd married
could be.

Even her children had not been overly responsive when she'd
returned. No wonder, she realized. They were quite accustomed
to a mother who spent much of her time away from them. Because she'd missed her children dreadfully, Francisca had begun
to bathe them, read to them, and spend long hours in their company. Soon she was berating herself for having left so much of
their care to servants in the past.

Other matters that had been left to the help began to interest
her as well. She became familiar with the peddlers who came to
the kitchen door hawking their fresh wares. When she realized
that there were so many choices, she wondered why her cook had
settled for the same two or three items each week. Enchanted the
first time the meat man had displayed his board for her, laying
out slabs of thick liver, honeycomb tripe, and yards and yards of
oxtails, she'd bought far more than the cook could use before the
meat spoiled.

Soon the fish man became her favorite. Long before he'd arrive
at the house she could identify him by his long guttural cry,

"Peixe e camarão, fish and shrimp." As soon as the gatekeeper let him in, a retinue of cats appeared to rub his legs and beg a sample of his wares. He'd put up with the purring troupe until Francisca appeared; then, in order to be able to show her the fresh seafood properly, he'd quickly lift a cover off a basket and toss, as far away as possible, his smallest sardine, which immediately became the center of a brief but hard-fought feline battle.

Augusto certainly noticed no change in either his menus or his wife. Occupied with managing the stables, at least he seemed happier. His status in the family was less of an issue now, and his salary was increasing every year. Maybe this explained why he was drinking less. In any case, the more sober he was, the less likely his temper might flare.

There was another, unmentioned reason for his contentment. Because Augusto was required to fill many of Erik's more visible duties during his convalescence, Erik's illness had placed his brother-in-law in a stronger position among the Larsons. But as soon as Erik felt well enough to take his usual, more active role, Augusto was openly annoyed.

"Your brother wants to establish some races with large enough purses to attract horses of international merit," Augusto said scornfully after dinner one evening.

"What's wrong with that?" Francisca asked. Dressed demurely in a cream-colored silk gown, she was making a special effort to have a pleasant time alone with her husband. The children, fed earlier, had been sent to be bathed. Soon they would be permitted a few minutes with their parents before bedtime. Augusto preferred to see his children when they were at their clean, mannerly best. The balance of the time, Francisca permitted them to become as rambunctious and scruffy as they chose. "Children must have a chance to be children first before they can be expected to mature" was the dictum she followed privately. Fortunately, Augusto had few child-rearing ideas of his own.

"How can your brother expect breeders to risk their finest horses on ocean crossings?"

"I expect you're correct about that." Francisca was making an effort to be agreeable. "Yet if the incentive is a sufficient amount, it might encourage more than you think."

"It's all vanity," Augusto scoffed, then lifted his glass of cognac and held it to the light. "Inferior color," he sniffed and placed the glass down with a clatter. "Your brother just wants the club to be a monument to him. I've seen that kind of pride in older men, but in him it's . . . revolting."

Swallowing her vexation, Francisca lifted a small silver tray of peeled fruit and offered it. "The pineapples are especially good tonight."

Augusto looked at the perfectly arranged pieces. "Save them for the children."

Francisca tried to bring the subject back to something that interested Augusto. "Do we have any horses that could really compete?"

"We have a very long string of perfectly mediocre horses. A matched dozen," he muttered. "Of course, your family wouldn't think of letting *me* have a say in the horses' selection. Why, they even take that stable girl's word over mine."

"Amara?" Francisca had seen the dark little beauty exercising the horses when she'd gone to meet Augusto.

"Sim. You should see the way she can twist Erico with a tiny word."

"She must know the horses better than anyone."

"A child! A spoiled child, that's all she is!"

Somehow, without meaning to, they'd strayed to another area of contention. Francisca hoped the children would be ready soon. Any diversion would be better than the strain of actually having to talk with her husband.

"There's only one . . ." Augusto began talking as though she weren't in the room. He rubbed his thumb over his rough lips, which were almost always chafed from his mannerism of chewing on them nervously. "Nova Esperança." This young horse had been named New Hope for a city in the northernmost section of Paraná.

"Then that's who I'll put my money on!"

"*Your* money?"

Though Francisca was only trying to support her husband's favorite horse, another sensitive point had been touched upon unwittingly. While the assets of most Brazilian women were automatically under a husband's complete control, Sven Larson had cleverly managed to keep a good portion of his daughter's assets under his own supervision. Just in time, the parlor doors burst open and scattered their four children: Marcelino, Emilia, Heloisa, and Getulio. The four-year-old bounded to his mother, lifting his arms for her to hold him.

She pushed Tulio toward his father first, and the cherubic child, following the example of Marcelino, bowed respectfully and held out his hands with his palms upward. "A bênçâo, senhor," he said, asking for his father's blessing in the traditional way of Brazilian children, but then giggling at the silliness of it all. Despite himself, Augusto laughed and patted his younger son's dark blond head. Of all his children, this was the only one who truly resembled Francisca. He took special pride in the fact that the rest had retained the tanned skin and wide-set dark eyes of the Cavalcantis. "More Brazilian; they fit in better," he'd been heard to remark often, even though many, including his own mother, would have preferred to have seen the strain lighten considerably.

After Francisca had passed the fruit tray once, she called to Zefhina, who waited outside the door. "Bring some more abacaxi and uvas. And a knife to remove the seeds."

The children sat on the floor and licked their sticky fingers. They knew they were not permitted to sit on the satin chairs when they were eating and obeyed without complaint.

"Tulio!" Augusto barked the instant his son let his hands stray to the leg of a chair. The child withdrew his fingers quickly, but not fast enough to avoid a slap on his arm from his father.

"We've been practicing a song for you, Papai," Emilia said.

"Have you now?" Augusto reached for his discarded glass of cognac, this time finding it at least passable enough to take a few loud sips. "Won't you entertain me, then?" he asked expansively.

"Marcelino is supposed to play the piano," Emilia added.

The painfully thin eight-year-old was hunched over, trying to stay out of trouble. While Francisca was at Vassouras he and Augusto had clashed several times. It seemed the boy could do nothing right.

"Well . . ." Augusto turned in Marcelino's direction.

He looked at his sticky hands.

"Here comes some more fruit," Francisca said, taking the tray and knife from the maid. "Marcelino, why don't you have a few grapes before washing your hands? Then, when the other children have finished their treat, we can have the songs."

Marcelino stood by his mother and looked at her soulfully. His dark eyes shimmered with a patina of tears. "I'd rather not play tonight, Mamãe."

Augusto took a step forward and pointed a finger, fat as a sausage, at his elder son. "What is the purpose of all these lessons if you won't even play for your parents?"

The boy stepped closer to his mother. Francisca reflexively put her arm around him. "If Marcelino doesn't feel ready, he doesn't . . ."

"The child is just being defiant. If *I* want him to play, then he *will* play!" Augusto's face contorted menacingly.

Abstractedly, Francisca counted the number of drinks her husband had taken that evening. She'd only seen him take a moderate amount of wine with the meal and then the cognac. He must have had quite a bit earlier to be acting so contentiously.

Augusto grabbed the bunch of red grapes from the boy's hand. "Now get over to the piano and play!"

Francisca's skin prickled with fear, for she was long accustomed to having these tirades directed at her. She had a finely tuned sense of when violence would erupt, but few skills to prevent it. Although she'd seen Augusto annoyed with the children before, she'd never caught such an abusive tone directed at anyone but her. As he marched the terrified child to the piano, Francisca saw the reddening of her husband's thick neck and the tension in his clawlike grip on Marcelino's bony shoulders. "Don't . . ." she gasped. "Don't hurt him."

Hearing her frantic voice, Marcelino shrugged himself clear of his father and looked helplessly at his mother's twisted face. Heloisa started to cry. Exasperated by Marcelino's resistance, Augusto lost control of himself. He lunged for the child, wrapped his hands around his frail neck, and began shaking him. Marcelino's eyes began to bulge in terror; then his face turned a dusky purple.

In a panic, Francisca lifted the knife from the fruit tray and, without a second's thought, plunged it into Augusto's beefy back. The short-bladed knife lodged a few inches into his armpit, just far enough to get him to release his grip on his son.

The maid, hearing the screams of the children, ran into the

room, but Augusto ordered her out. With one loud crack of his
fist into her abdomen, he had his wife on the floor. "No bruises,"
he said. "This time, no bruises for anyone to see."

Francisca looked up and saw blood oozing down the side of his
shirt, saw his leg raise up and then come down on her in one
crushing blow to her belly. The agony was not unlike the last
phase of childbirth. She lay limp and silent. Waiting. What would
he do next?

He reached over and felt the warm stickiness of his own blood
on his shirt, then stared at the quantity that pooled in his hand.
"You're . . . you're mad! Trying to kill me? You're . . . insane."
He paused and licked his lips. "In . . . sane . . ." He said the word
so slowly it seemed as if he were tasting it. He turned and walked
purposefully out of the room.

Francisca lay on the carpet quite a while longer. Finally Zefinha and the children's maid slipped in and escorted the frightened children out. Then Zefinha returned to comfort Francisca.

"He tried to hurt Marcelino! I couldn't let him . . ." Francisca
sobbed on Zefinha's shoulder. "Could I?"

The devoted old servant crooned words of comfort, agreeing
that she couldn't have let anyone touch the child; at the same
time, she tried to determine how seriously Francisca herself had
been injured. When it was clear that she could walk, Zefinha
helped her to stand.

As they reached the staircase, Augusto, still wearing the same
bloody clothes, came rushing down. When he reached the bottom, he spun around and shouted, "How can I trust a madwoman
with my children? I may not be in charge of the purse strings
here, but I am still the legal guardian of my children and my wife.
None of your father's maneuverings can change that, can they?"

Francisca gripped the banister and looked down at the man
who was screaming at her.

"I'm going to the police, my dear wife," he was saying more
calmly. He pointed to his wound. "This will demonstrate what
you have attempted. While I'm out, you might as well prepare
yourself, for you'll not spend another night under this roof.
You're too great a risk . . . to me . . . to the children . . . to yourself." The front door slammed behind him.

What was he saying? Francisca wondered as she stared at the

blood that had dripped on the foyer floor. Women of her class were hardly ever sent to jail, even for murder. And this, this attack had been justified! She had only been trying to protect . . . She stopped that line of reasoning as she suddenly realized what Augusto had been thinking. "In . . . sane" is what he had said. A sudden heat roared inside her head. Everything around her flashed bone white.

"Deus do Céu! God in Heaven!" she cried piteously and collapsed into Zefinha's generous arms.

Carnaval

1 The rules of the Santa Casa da Misericordia, the Holy House of Mercy hospital, permitted but one visitor each day. Francisca's week was marked by the people she was allowed to see. Mondays were reserved for her mother, whose distress at her daughter's confinement was so blatant Francisca had to be the cheerful one. Tuesdays belonged to Erik, although business appointments frequently caused her brother to miss his day. Wednesdays were best of all, because Margaret came. At least with her friend she did not have to pretend anything. Thursdays were saved for sessions with her doctor. Fridays brought a visit from her father, who usually raged against the laws that gave a husband rights that took precedence over a parent's. Margaret's sister Kate had volunteered to come Saturdays so Francisca would have company. Francisca liked the forthright Kate, who'd rejected all suitors, preferring a life of charity work teaching poor children to read. If she'd been a Roman Catholic, she'd surely have become a nun, Francisca guessed. Sundays ... Sundays were for the immediate family, but because she refused to see her husband, Augusto wouldn't permit the children to visit her. Not that she wanted the children to see their mother in such a place.

The section she was in, set apart from the rest of the Hospício

Pedro II asylum for the insane, housed those patients who could pay for private care and accommodations. From the small barred window in her stark room, Francisca could see down into the courtyard where the less fortunate charity patients were left outdoors in pens to be exercised — one for the female inmates, one for the males. They were kept naked for sanitary reasons. Every afternoon they were hosed down like animals before being let in for the night.

Animals! That's what their noises — screams, groans, and the incessant rhythmic knocking on the walls and bars — sounded like. The orderlies herded them about, more like zoo keepers than hospital workers. At least the nuns on her floor, members of the French Sisters of Charity, spoke mostly in soft voices. But not always.

All too often, someone in her section would become unmanageable. From a distance she'd hear the running feet, a nun shouting for help, the scuffling, the dull thumps of someone being restrained from . . . from what? From themselves, from the demons rising up and demanding to be released, from the horrors of their loneliness.

Though Francisca believed most of the inmates were actually crazy, sometimes she wondered what caused a normal person to slip into madness. She sensed that brutal forces or ill-fated circumstances twisted a person's fragile self beyond recognition, because as a mother she knew how delicate a child could be; as a mother she knew that it took vast quantities of unconditional love to nurture a healthy person.

The woman across the hall, Dona Carmosina, had tried to hang herself two times and when that was unsuccessful had swallowed some horrible caustic that had burned her throat so severely she could only grunt syllables. Francisca wished Dona Carmosina could speak so she could tell Francisca about her life, her childhood, her marriage. Desperately Francisca wanted to know what unspeakable terror had caused the inmate to stare at her with that odd glazed expression. Even if she didn't know what caused Dona Carmosina's torment, she did understand that the woman regretted she'd been saved from her suicide attempts. Sometimes it seemed that the Santa Casa's purpose was to prolong rather than to heal misery.

Nobody seemed to recover or even get appreciably better. The very nature of their confinement made them sicker. Sometimes Francisca wondered if anyone else had arrived in the same unfair manner as she had, only to deteriorate into madness at the horridness, the hopelessness of it all. She wouldn't, she vowed. For the sake of her children her mind had to remain clear.

Even with all her visitors, even with three meals in the dining room and an escorted walk around the palm-lined gardens twice daily, most of her day was spent in utter boredom. Sometimes she read the books her parents brought her in French and English as well as Portuguese. The other languages kept her mind sharp — maybe too sharp, so mostly she slept. At first she could only sleep seven or eight hours a night, perhaps lie down for an hour after lunch. With practice, however, she'd managed to extend it to twelve hours a night and three hours for a nap, leaving only nine hours to stay awake in her tiny whitewashed room.

From home she'd brought only a few pieces of clothing, her silver-backed hairbrush and comb that she'd had since she was a child, and a looking glass, but they'd taken it away immediately. Tucked in with her lingerie she'd managed to hide one of her lizards, and without having to compete for the multitide of itinerant insects, the little green reptile had thrived in the solitude of her cell, adapting, as always, better than she had.

"Come here . . ." She called it, then tapped on the edge of her metal bed. The little green head jerked out from a corner of the washstand. Francisca placed a few crumbs she'd squirreled away from breakfast on the cold tile floor and he scurried forward immediately. Before he was through, Francisca checked a little ant trap she'd made by filling a matchbox with sugar. She'd opened it long enough to permit the ants to find their way inside and tied it shut with a silk stocking. This kept them alive until she was ready to serve the lizard.

"How many do you feel like today?" she asked the lizard. "How about ten nice plump sweet ants, hmmm?" She removed the stocking and opened the box. Anxious ants began to scramble out. Francisca watched the frantic movements of their forelegs trying to skitter over the edge just before she dumped them in front of her pet. Her father had always called this species the formiga louca, or crazy ant, owing to the fact that they didn't keep on a track but wandered to and fro in a most irregular and seemingly foolish fashion. "Appropriate." She chuckled aloud. "Crazy ants in a crazy house." As soon as the lizard's red tongue darted forward and captured each ant, Francisca felt satisfied. Never liked the little black creatures, never liked them at all. They seemed tiny and inoffensive, but just think of the damage they could wreak! There were disgusting saúvas like the ones at Vassouras that had ruined the piano as well as hideous army ants that could decimate everything in their path. Brazil must have more species of obnoxious ants than anywhere in the world!

Francisca reclosed the ant trap, then lay back on her bed, remembering that they used to actually eat the tanajura, the female leaf-cutter ant. Disgusting if you really thought about it, but all the servants' families did it, so Erik and she had just joined in.

Every year, in late September, a great swarm of tanajuras would take to the air, flying around Boa Vista looking for mates. From faraway they seemed a noisy cloud, but close up they were formidable-looking creatures, not unlike hornets, entirely brown, eight centimeters across the wing and over three centimeters in length. The neighboring village children would run out with buckets and nets and begin gathering them while chanting a traditional song:

> Cai, cai, tanajura,
> Amanhã tu amanhece dura.
> Fall, fall, flying ant,
> Tomorrow you'll be stiff.

After the mothers scalded the insects in hot water, the children ripped off the wings and gave back the succulent abdomens to be fried in fat, then sprinkled with salt and pepper. The resulting treat smelled like roasted nuts and tasted like crunchy prawns.

Where had that girl, that adventurous, spirited child who would try anything, gone? Francisca pondered just as someone knocked at the door.

Sister Lourdes always arrived punctually for her exercise period. "Nice to see you aren't sleeping away the whole afternoon for a change," she said brightly. "It's not so hot this afternoon, so I thought we could stay out a bit longer."

Why bother? Francisca wondered. To walk the same trampled

path around the same dismal foliage eight times instead of six? They could sit on the north bench for fifteen minutes, then the south bench for fifteen minutes. She could nod to five or six other shuffling inmates or hope that one of them might break out of his or her pattern and do something diverting. Francisca did not dare say what she was thinking, since everything she uttered became part of her record. If anyone even guessed that she looked forward to an act of violence or perversity, it might harm her chances for being released in a reasonable amount of time. Time. No one knew how long she would be required to live at the asylum. Augusto, wielding all his legal rights as a husband, had managed to have her locked up for an unspecified duration. Though her parents were working to have her placed in their custody, even they admitted that it might take a year for her case to be settled.

"Why don't you punish Augusto by firing him?" Francisca had asked her father when he last visited.

After the first few weeks, Sven had managed to remain calm when he visited his daughter, though he vented his frustration on everyone else around him. His lawyers had counseled that patience and time were his best weapons, but seeing his child confined unfairly was an outrage he couldn't overcome. Still, for her sake, he pretended that matters were under control.

"I think we can manage Augusto better if we permit him to go on as usual. That way we'll know what he's up to," Sven had explained. "Then, when his anger has subsided, we'll be able to reason with him."

"Reason with Augusto?"

"Let me put it this way," her father had said with resignation. "You're still Augusto's wife and he has every right to keep you here if he so chooses. We must persuade him to give your custody to us by using certain subtle enticements."

"And my children? Will I have my children?"

Sven avoided her eyes. "They are Augusto's cards to deal as he wishes." Her father's jaw sagged.

Francisca began to pity him.

"Without the children, what have I to live for?" she moaned. She shouldn't have said that, even to her father, because the next few weeks had been horrible. She'd been moved to a windowless room and watched constantly, even in the toilet, until they'd decided she wasn't going to harm herself.

Sister Lourdes was tapping her foot on the hard floor. "Today I thought we'd go to the smaller atrium outside the doctors' offices. It should be very quiet and pleasant, all right?" Francisca nodded. She straightened the pink cotton dress she'd been wearing. It hung from her limply without the bright patent leather belt that was a part of the costume, but belts weren't permitted. Because she spent so much of the time indoors, Francisca's skin had taken on the waxy, chilly whiteness of a magnolia flower. Thin and pale as she was, though, her hair was still a vibrant light chestnut, her hands were delicate and almost transparent, and her eyes, now her most notable feature, were large, deep-set, and absorbed all that she saw.

"You look just lovely, my dear," Sister Lourdes said, wrinkling her prunelike face into what she thought was a smile.

Francisca had nothing against the nun. Sister Lourdes was an odd, displaced character who had a thankless job maintaining mostly pathetic cases. Francisca believed the nun knew that she wasn't crazy like the others, but after years of working with the insane was wary enough not to be certain, at least not yet.

"Obrigada," Francisca replied.

She steeled herself for the walk through the corridors past the barred cells that held the more aggressive male patients. Sometimes the men lay on their metal shelflike beds, leering at her when she passed. Sometimes they came up to the bars, pressing their distorted faces at her. She had to be very careful to walk right down the hall's center so a waving arm couldn't grab at her. She had to force herself to stare directly ahead so she wouldn't see their obscene gestures or exposed genitals poked at her. Whatever she did, though, she couldn't block the hideous inhuman sounds they could make. Please don't let them scream at me today, she prayed silently, just don't let them scream.

❧ ❧ ❧

Madness. Francisca thought a great deal about it, inventing theories of who was susceptible, who was not. If she were going to go mad, she'd have done it years ago. She wasn't the type, she

decided. Though she locked away her own share of pain and secrets, she saw life for what it really was and lived it, day to day, in
her own plodding, imperfect way. Others seemed born to madness, needing but an excuse, a denial, an incident to trigger the
response.

"Do you remember Sister Cecilia?" she'd asked Margaret during one of her first visits. That afternoon Margaret had been
dressed to perfection in a white linen suit with a lacy collar and
cuffs. Francisca was embarrassed to greet her in the loose grey
hospital shift.

Margaret had pulled her lips into a strong, disapproving line at
the mention of the nun who'd taught them embroidery at the
convent school.

"I remember I couldn't help watching her. She always made
me feel afraid."

"Why?"

"She didn't fit my image of a nun. She was so powerful, like a
peasant woman in a Brueghel painting; she should've been sitting
in a farmyard with chubby children around her knees instead of
decorating priests' vestments with embroidered scrolls and
leaves."

"I remember her melancholy eyes. I thought that if I ever
asked her something about herself she'd burst into tears," Margaret added.

"Did you notice that the other nuns never trusted her with us
completely? There'd always be a second one hovering by. Maybe
something happened before we came."

"I don't think it does any good to . . ."

Francisca rambled on, even though Margaret was decidedly
uncomfortable with the memory. "Well, I think Sister Cecilia
was bound to go mad. She'd become a nun to try to stave it off,
but it hadn't worked that way. You remember that terrible night
before Good Friday, don't you?"

Margaret nodded.

"I still hadn't fallen asleep, though you'd been dreaming for
hours."

"Dreaming, how do you know that?"

"By the way you twitched in your sleep." Francisca demonstrated by tossing on her bed. Margaret couldn't help laughing.

"Then it came, that unforgettable shriek. It sounded as though she'd been stabbed ..." Francisca choked, but she disregarded Margaret's motions to forget the rest of the story.

"The next morning Sister Paulette tried to explain what had happened as 'a special fever of the brain.' At the time I believed she was making up something to mollify us; now I agree with her. These people" — she pointed toward the high window in her room that looked out over the rooftops of the asylum — "are suffering from something like a fever. It's not just ... weakness."

"They did finally send her back to France, didn't they?"

Francisca nodded. "But for weeks they kept her in the nunnery, in some faraway room that Sister Paulette told us was padded so she wouldn't hurt herself. I remember Sister became very angry with me when I asked whether the room had always been padded or if it had been so fitted especially for Sister Cecilia."

"Did you ever learn the answer?"

"Yes. It had always been padded. I'd think about that often. Maybe somewhere deep inside I knew I'd end up in a place where many of the rooms were padded. Think about it, Margaret! The world is filled with padded rooms waiting for the small number of us who are going to need them."

"You can't possibly believe that you belong here!"

"Of course I don't. I would never go mad, neither would you. We know others who are more likely ..."

"Who do you mean?"

Francisca spoke slowly, enunciating every word. "My husband, for one. The idea to put me here came from his own fear of insanity. You've never actually seen him when ... when he's had too much to drink. Before he attacks me, his whole face changes, becomes crazed, wild."

"Yet you've permitted it." The minute she'd said the words, Margaret regretted them. "Not that you could've ... Augusto's so much ..."

"Shhh," Francisca soothed. "I'm not offended. It's just so difficult ever to know what really happens when two people are alone. As close as we are, I can't imagine you with my brother or ..."

Margaret blushed. "With us there's nothing to imagine. After Erik's last attack ... the doctor said ... He forbade all excitement."

"That's ridiculous!"

"No, not really. It's something to do with his glands producing more toxins. It's best if he remains calm, and so . . ."

"I can't imagine my brother restraining himself."

"He makes it very difficult. Almost every night he comes to me saying 'Just this once' and I have to refuse him for his own good. You can't know how awful I've felt."

"He's too young a man not to . . ."

"The doctor says he could die from this illness, so . . ."

"What if he's wrong?"

Margaret looked stunned. Apparently the idea of an inaccurate diagnosis or alternative treatment hadn't occurred to her. "I don't think . . ."

"What if Gigo doesn't believe. . . ?" Francisca stopped herself. Though she didn't trust Erik herself, to revive Margaret's distrust in him could be an even worse misfortune. Her brother's sexual appetite had always been hearty. Now she feared how he might react if he was denied at home.

The friends were interrupted by a knock at the door. Sister Lourdes signaled that visiting hours were over. Docilely, Margaret prepared to leave, then, as a parting gesture, flung her arms around Francisca and held her close.

"Until next Wednesday . . ." Her voiced trailed into the hall.

Francisca turned to face the wall so she wouldn't have to see the door closing. "Until next Wednesday."

42 Sven Larson's petitions to gain custody of his daughter had apparently landed on some nonexistent official's desk. After four months of waiting, none of the Larsons could find out what was happening in the case. A third of a year had passed without Francisca seeing her children. Though she tried hard to remember their little faces, their images were blurring. In her mind Tulio looked like a young Marcelino and she'd place Heloisa's curly hair on Emilia's head.

If she didn't get to see her children soon, Francisca believed she might truly go crazy. The last time they'd seen her, Augusto had been beating her brutally. How had they felt about that? Did they mourn her absence? Certainly the servants could see to their everyday needs, but who else knew what to give Tulio when he'd

eaten too much fruit? The usual remedy, green coconut water,
never worked for him. He needed mashed papayas and rice. And
Marcelino. How had he survived the catastrophic evening when
she'd wounded Augusto to protect him? Did the poor child feel
partially responsible for creating the disturbance? Francisca
wanted to take him in her arms and tell him that no one, least of
all his mother, blamed him.

On her bed, looking at the light that reflected on Misericordia's
gilded dome, she felt as though the aching for her children was
making her physically ill. Twice that week she hadn't the
strength for her afternoon walks, and she'd developed headaches
so severe she'd vomited from the pain. If she only knew exactly
how they were doing, she'd be able to rest easier, but nobody
could tell her for certain because, instead of permitting the Larsons to care for his children while he worked and traveled, Augusto had sent them to his own parents. Behind the high walls of
the Cavalcanti estate, the children were probably being gorged on
sweets and permitted to do as they pleased. Inquiries as to their
health were ignored.

On Monday, Guilhermina told Francisca about seeing her
grandchildren outside the church. "Your father has arranged for
us to visit them in this way at least once a week, although Augusto protested at first. 'What's the matter?' he'd said unkindly to
your father. 'You think I'd harm them? They're my children and
it's for their protection that I am doing this.' "

Francisca shook her head wildly. "He said that?"

"That's not the worst of it. He said his only concern was
that the children's mother would do them harm. The children's
mother, that's how he refers to you. He never uses your
name."

"How did they look? Did Mila get her tooth? Has she lost any
more? And Marcelino, does he still practice the piano? I wouldn't
want him to forget what he's learned from Margaret."

"Augusto won't permit the lessons. Says they're wrong for a
boy." Guilhermina took out her handkerchief and wiped her eyes.
"Soon this will be over. We'll have you and the children at our
house. It'll be a new life for all of you."

"I don't believe I'll ever leave this place."

"Don't talk like that! You're not crazy!"

"I know that and so do you, but that's not the law. Augusto wants me here. That gives him everything: his position at the factory, my money, my house, my children. Best of all, no one will condemn him for anything he might do. They'll say, 'Poor man . . . no wife . . . no possibility of remarrying!' All his debaucheries will be excused."

Her mother refused to let the conversation continue. The truth of it had been too painful for her to bear. Once she had spoken them, though, Francisca began to believe her own words. She forgot about her dream of freedom and concentrated on getting what she most wanted: to see her children.

❧ ❧ ❧

"You haven't eaten a decent meal in days." Sister Lourdes pushed some beans on a fork toward Francisca's mouth. "No wonder you're too tired for our walks."

To forestall an argument, Francisca opened her mouth and allowed the food to be spooned in. She held it there until the nun turned away, then spat it back onto her plate. She'd promised herself she wouldn't eat until she was permitted to see her children.

By the seventh day of her fast, she had become obviously dehydrated. The authorities were alarmed enough to call a conference with her parents and Dr. Luiz de Souza, the director of the private asylum.

"We no longer consider your daughter dangerous," Dr. de Souza pronounced from his end of the long mahogany table.

"Never was!" Sven Larson snorted.

The doctor stared at the mound of documents in front of him. "Yes, well . . ." He cleared his throat and pushed his glasses back up on his nose. "She did attack her husband with a knife, did she not?"

"How many times had he . . . ?" Guilhermina began before her husband cut her off.

"Let's not open the whole case now. We're here to solve one particular problem."

"As I understand it," the doctor continued, "Senhor Cavalcanti has agreed to permit the children to visit their mother once a month on the grounds of the hospital."

"The children are very young and sensitive. Their mother is more concerned for their welfare than her own in this matter. She feels that seeing her here, seeing some of the other patients, would be too distressing for them."

The doctor looked grave. "I see."

"Also, Augusto . . . ah . . . Senhor Cavalcanti . . ." Sven corrected himself nervously. "He has insisted that he accompany the children, but you'd have to concur with us that, knowing my daughter's history, that . . . that would be unwise."

"Over four months without seeing her children . . ." Guilhermina continued plaintively. "You must understand how this would benefit our daughter, give her a reason to go on."

"We are planning to force-feed her as soon as her husband signs the permission papers."

Guilhermina gasped. "Please . . . With everything you know, you could not possibly consider holding her down, shoving food . . ."

"We can't allow her to starve to death. I'm sure you understand that we have a responsibility to the patient's husband, her official guardian. Until a higher authority rules otherwise, my hands are tied in this matter."

Sven Larson jumped up. "Dr. de Souza, are you saying there's nothing you can do?"

"Not exactly. Within certain restricted limits and if I am willing to accept full responsibility, a patient who has shown excellent progress can be permitted brief, supervised trips away from the hospital for therapeutic purposes or special occasions."

"The Grande Prêmio!" Sven said at once. "The Jockey Club is running the biggest race of the year next week, the newly formed 'Grande Prêmio Brasil.' Her brother is responsible for having a purse this large offered in Brazil for the first time, and our family has a horse entered. Perhaps you and Senhora de Souza would like to be our guests in the steward's box?"

The doctor repressed his excitement by thumbing through some of the documents in front of him. "That's a possibility, if my patient would be well guarded in that section."

"Certainly she would."

"The children could be at the racetrack?"

"Before the race, perhaps in the women's lounge."

"I think something could be arranged," the doctor answered slowly. "Give me a few days."

"You'll have our eternal gratitude, Doctor," Guilhermina said, stepping forward to shake his hand.

❧ 3 The morning of the first Grande Prêmio race, Francisca's excitement even surpassed that of the holders of invitations to the coveted steward's box. As she dressed, she was not unmindful that she would probably be the only person there with not a whit of interest in the outcome of the running. The blue dress that Margaret had ordered for her from Ottiker, the most fashionable dressmaker, was ingeniously designed. An undetachable grosgrain ribbon belt had been securely woven into the basic design. The same ribbon had been worked into double bands for the neckline, wrist, and hemline, then trimmed with the most delicate embroidery, a perfect example of the Brazilian art. The dress not only fit beautifully but minimized Francisca's unhealthy thinness.

Once she was dressed and waiting, Francisca wondered what time it was. Dr. de Souza was due just about noon. Idly she touched the embroidered flowers and birds on her sleeve. The dress was very beautiful, but also fragile. How could she ask her babies to be mindful of her clothes when all she wanted to do was pick them up, hug them close. Surely they'd all pile on her, cover her with kisses! Why, Tulio still drooled when he was excited, didn't he? For a moment she thought about changing into something more practical, but she stopped herself when she realized how much her appearance might mean to the children. She touched her hair. Without a mirror in her room it was impossible to tell if anything was out of place. In order to see herself, she'd have to ask one of the sisters to hold a hand mirror for her. This one time she decided it was worth the humiliation. Francisca found her brush and extra pins, then walked resolutely through the dining area to where Sister Lourdes was filling out a stack of forms.

❧   ❧   ❧

Though they'd arrived two hours early for the first race, Francisca and the de Souzas were already part of a large crowd at the gate.

"We have passes to the steward's box!" The doctor waved impatiently from the window of his car.

"Luiz, can't you see that the guard is taking each in turn?" his wife said to him patiently.

From her seat in the middle, Francisca pretended to look straight ahead calmly. She was really worrying about whether Augusto would have the children there at the promised time. As the car crept through the massive gate with the words JOCKEY CLUB BRASILEIRO forged in wrought iron, her heart beat so loudly she feared the doctor would find her unfit to stay. If only she could trust her husband; if only she could believe that her four precious babies would be there, waiting to rush to her and hug her tight! Tears welled, but she fought to control herself. Mustn't appear sad, mustn't appear too anxious.

Finally it was their turn to enter the compound. Their driver was being directed where to discharge his passengers and the doctor was being shown which doorway to enter. De Souza glowed openly when he realized the guard was pointing down the crimson carpet to the members' entrance.

"Senhora Cavalcanti," he said, taking Francisca's arm. "Anita." He smiled genially to his wife. "What good fortune for me to be personally escorting the two most beautiful ladies in Rio this afternoon."

His wife, an unusually tall woman with a wide, toothy mouth, smiled with her lips tightly closed. Francisca liked her more than she expected she would. Inside the members' lobby, a clock on the wall indicated that it still wasn't twelve. The doctor had been overly anxious, too!

She turned to him and smiled as brightly as possible. "We've arrived early, but it's just as well. The crowds later would have been even worse. Since it isn't time to meet the children or my brother yet, we could visit the stables if you like."

"Is it permitted?"

"Not generally" — Francisca beamed at being able to turn the tables by granting a privilege to the man who kept her locked away — "Unless you're an owner. Would you care to see the horse destined to win the big race?"

"I would." As he followed his patient through a side door that led to a private passage, the doctor laughed. "You're very confident that your horse will win."

"So's everyone else. Nova Esperança is the favorite. But you can still double your money."

"Luiz is not a man who gambles."

"Even on a certainty?" Francisca chided merrily.

"As a doctor I know that there are no 'certainties,' " he replied more seriously than necessary.

Francisca ignored the remark. "Here's the section belonging to our greatest rivals, the horses of the Bezerra family from Rio Grande do Sul. Their horse, Castelo, is in his prime, but . . ."

"Not as good as your horse, is he?" Anita de Souza kidded as they stopped in front of a heavily guarded stall.

The Bezerra trainer was gazing nastily at Francisca. Dr. de Souza steered her away. "I didn't realize you were so knowledgeable about horses."

"I've learned a bit in the last few years, though I'm far from having 'an eye for a horse.' " Francisca pointed down the row of stalls where young boys, dressed in blue-and-white checkered jackets, were filling water buckets. "Most of these are my family's horses, although a few may be boarders."

The doctor's wife peered into one of the commodious paneled stalls. "Why, these horses have better accommodations than some of the patients . . ." She stopped herself.

Francisca had already moved down to the corner stall where Nova Esperança was expected to be. She recognized Erik's favorite groom outside the door. Hercules was the man's real but ironic name, since he was a dwarf. His way with the animals, though, was undisputed, and the Larsons had no qualms about putting him in charge of their most precious horse flesh. Hercules, armed with a pistol, slept in his charge's stall each night. Only Hercules drew his water, only Hercules handled his grain. Once, when Augusto had offered Nova Esperança a cube of sugar, Hercules ordered him never to touch the horse again. Furious, Augusto had lifted Hercules by his trousers to bring him to eye level and

berate him just as Sven Larson arrived. Augusto had almost been
sent back to the factory for that incident, but Hercules had defended Augusto's actions as an innocent game. So Augusto had
escaped a reprimand.

As Hercules called to her in his husky little voice, "Bom dia,
Dona Francisca!" she remembered what he'd later said about the
incident with her husband. "A man my size can't afford ene-
mies." Suddenly she felt a deep empathy for the physically pow-
erless little man.

When she moved toward the stall, Hercules seemed to be
blocking her way. Francisca tried to go around him, but this time
the interference was obvious. "We're trying to keep the horse
from becoming too excited, Dona Francisca."

"Hercules!" Francisca laughed. "Not even me?"

"Your brother's orders. After the race, please come back and
spend as much time as you wish with the winner."

Francisca looked down at him and met his gaze. The face on
the distorted body was surprisingly handsome. "This is my doctor . . . from the hospital . . . It means so much to him . . ." she said
with pauses between the phrases for emphasis. Even as she spoke,
she wondered why she was pressing the point. It wasn't important to see the horse, but suddenly it seemed vital that she should
have her own way in this.

Hercules kept his dark eyes fixed on hers for a long moment,
long enough for her to skitter around him and run toward the
stall. Just before the end of the row, a second door, which led to
the room where the horse's tack was kept, was partially open.
Francisca knew there was a bench inside for the trainer to rest on,
as well as a desk where stable accounts were handled. Sometimes
Augusto worked there. Perhaps, she thought quickly, Augusto
was there now and that was the reason she was being kept from
that part of the building. Out of the corner of her eye she saw a
leg dangling from the bench, and she heard a muffled, though familiar, voice.

"Gigo!" She flung the door open. "Hiding from *me?*"

Erik quickly closed the door behind them, shutting out the
doctor and his wife. In the vast silence, Francisca could hear
Hercules trying to rescue the situation by taking them to Nova
Esperança's stall for a private showing.

Francisca gaped as her brother hurriedly pulled his trousers over his naked buttocks. His dress shirt, vest, and jacket were neatly hung over the training bridles. She had caught him undressed with Amara, who now clutched a horse blanket in front of her bare body. Even with her eyes closed, Francisca would have known what had just transpired. The sweetness of the hay and grain, the leathery aroma from the reins, the pungency of the pomades and polishes, could not disguise the sexual reek in the room.

"You're much earlier than I expected," Erik excused himself lamely.

"I'm sorry, Gigo. I . . ." Francisca stammered. She couldn't help thinking that her instincts had been right. Denied Margaret's attentions, Erik had ignored medical advice and gone elsewhere for satisfaction. Embarrassed, she turned away from her brother's guilty expression.

The horse trainer's daughter looked different somehow. Francisca couldn't help thinking of the first day she'd seen Amara exercising Torres. She'd thought of the girl as an extension of the animal, both of them rippled with muscles and tension, both black and shining with sweat. She'd admired their bodies to the point where she jokingly had suggested that Amara be selected as the horse's jockey. "A matched pair," she'd said to Erik, without meaning to be unkind. He'd taken great offense at the remark and she'd never found the exact words for an apology. Today Amara seemed rounder, softer, and even more beautiful than Francisca had remembered. Tears shone on her ebony-black face. Francisca could feel her acute humiliation and pitied her deeply. All of Augusto's ugly insinuations about Amara had been true, and yet, seeing how young she was, seeing how she looked to Erik for consolation, Francisca felt no anger toward her. Her brother had brought her to Rio without thought for her future and had been unable to resist her fresh adolescent beauty. Erik could never disappoint any woman. That was his charm; that was his downfall.

Francisca dropped her eyes from the girl's face to the way the blanket wrinkled around her hipline. For a girl as young and as athletic as Amara, her belly was surprisingly rounded. At once she knew. Sometimes such knowledge, such awareness, was a curse. She turned away. "But with your disease . . . It's been hard on your wife . . . I know . . . I could sense it . . . but you . . ."

"For a man, it's different." Erik placed his hands lightly on her shoulders and turned his sister's face so she had to look into his eyes.

Erik's faraway, sea-blue, riveting eyes. How they'd captivated Margaret and every other woman he'd set out to win! They wouldn't win her over, not now, not when he only thought of himself and his pleasures. To him life was a game to be played. From childhood the world had been offered to him like a platter of sweets from which to pick and choose as he wished. Her brother meant no harm, that she knew, but neither did he think through the consequences of his actions. Poor Amara would soon be living like Isabel, with bastard children and no real life of her own. Who'd marry her now? And the child! Isabel's darker, mulatto children were enough of a problem, but Amara's skin was as purely African as any left in Brazil. Even her name was that of a slave! Francisca's eyes darted anxiously between the couple. What chance would Amara's child have to better itself? And Margaret. Deus! There'd be no way she'd ever accept this folly.

"Amara's going back to Vassouras next week." Was this Erik's way of asking her not to reveal anything to Margaret?

"Senhora Cavalcanti!" Dr. de Souza was knocking impatiently.

As Erik opened the door, he swung his sister around and held her by the shoulders. "Doesn't Francisca look wonderful!" He smiled down at her, then back at the doctor. "Such an improvement! You don't know how happy the family is to have her with us today!"

If the doctor noticed Erik's state of undress, he didn't register surprise. Probably thought he had been working with the horses. Francisca craned her neck to see what had happened to Amara, but the girl had disappeared into the supply room. When she turned back, the doctor was staring at his pocket watch.

"It's time to go to meet your children," he said.

Francisca's face was completely blank.

"Your children . . ."

"Can't you see how nervous she is?" Anita asked kindly. She reached for Francisca's hand, but Francisca withdrew it and placed it behind her back. She trembled from head to foot.

"Now ... now ... let's not get too upset," the doctor soothed.

Francisca tried to calm herself, but the world seemed to be exploding around her.

Finally Erik saw what he had done. He couldn't allow them to take Francisca to see her children in that state. Somehow he'd help cheer her. He'd always been able to do so in the past, hadn't he? "I promised I'd come along, but I wasn't ready. If you'll give me a moment ..." He pointed to his clothing on the hooks.

The doctor led Francisca out and shut the door. "As you wish, Senhor Larson, as you wish."

❧ 4   Almost every seat in the grandstand was filled an hour before the first race. In order to get to the women's lounge, the foursome had to cross in front of the bleachers, an aisle where everyone's attention was focused on who was with whom and what the women were wearing. If Francisca had been in a less agitated state, she might have enjoyed the manicured crowd, even smiled at old friends. Instead she kept her eyes on Erik's back as he pushed his way through the throng.

At the stairway they were forced to pause as the stream of people moved up and toward them.

"What a beautiful view! I had no idea there was so much to be seen from here!" The doctor's wife pointed across the racetrack to the mountains that surrounded the lagoon. "Look, you can see Corcovado on one side and the Morro dos Cabritos on the other."

Erik turned to the older woman and smiled charmingly. "From the highest seats you can even see the surf at Ipanema. We're thinking of building a restaurant at that level in the new clubhouse next year."

"Alô! Erico!" A man wearing a full-dress morning suit and carrying a jewel-encrusted cane slapped Francisca's brother on the back. Francisca recognized him as one of the owners of a shipping line the company used to send textiles to Europe. "My money's on 'Toes Out.' " He said the words affectionately. Only a few insiders knew the story of how Felix da Costa had come to purchase Nova Esperança at a bargain rate because his original owner,

Thales Quintana, had been mistakenly told that the horse lacked
the good straight forelegs needed for the track. Felix had seen the
slight imperfection as something that the extremely long-legged
colt would correct as he developed.

"So's Quintana's money! Don't think he has put even a mil-reis
on Diamante." The man was referring to Quintana's own entry
in the race.

"Neither of you will be disappointed," Erik said heartily as he
herded his party through a break in the wall of people rushing to
their seats.

They passed the long row of betting booths underneath the
stands. Lines extended outside the gates. Erik glowed with the
success of the Jockey Club and the excitement building toward
the Grande Prêmio. A bell rang. The booths closed for the start of
the first race. A roar lifted from the great crowd as the horses took
off. Anita de Souza looked toward the stands longingly. Her husband touched her shoulder.

"I'd take you back myself, but I've promised to accompany the
senhora."

"I know, Luiz," she mumbled, then followed Francisca
through the carved wooden door to the women's lounge.

Francisca was blinking in the dark room. Where were her children? Erik spoke to the servant who tended the silver samovar
that was kept filled with tea for the ladies. "Have you seen some
children here?"

"Não, senhor."

Panic filled Francisca's eyes. The doctor checked his watch.
"So many crowds, perhaps they are late."

Anita held Francisca's hand consolingly.

Erik rubbed his thumb across his lips pensively. He looked
around the lounge one more time. "There are several other places.
It would be more private . . . more prestigious to have them in the
steward's room. Perhaps Augusto felt . . . demeaned coming here.
I should never have suggested it."

"Of course, you're right! Augusto would never come into the
women's lounge!" Francisca agreed too enthusiastically.

The four climbed back across the bleachers just as the first
race's winners were being posted. "Velocidade!" Erik looked
pleased. "Well, Bezerra can have that one."

"Didn't you have a horse in the race?" de Souza asked.

"Natal. He didn't even place. Didn't expect him too, either. I put my money on Velocidade!" Erik laughed aloud. "The day looks very, very promising," he said, thoughtlessly forgetting his sister's troubles for a moment.

He turned in Francisca's direction. She was bone white with anxiety. "The children are around here somewhere," he said soothingly.

The steward's room was empty. Even the bartender was at the window, watching the start of the second race. Erik called him back. "Have you seen Senhor Cavalcanti?"

"Sim, Seu Erico. He was here a few minutes ago with his children."

"He left?"

"Sim, he said it was getting too late."

"Where'd he take them?" Francisca asked frantically.

The white-haired man shrugged. "He's not likely to have left the racetrack this early."

"Are children permitted in the stands?" the doctor's wife asked.

"Not really, but older children are sometimes brought for special races like the Grande Prêmio," Erik responded.

"That's where they'll be," the older woman said matter-of-factly. Everyone hurried toward the Larsons' box in the center section.

Marcelino was standing on his seat, screaming the name of the Larsons' entry in the second race. "Curi . . . ti . . . ba! Curi . . . ti . . . ba!" The little girls, dressed in matching pink dresses, jumped up and down, while Tulio, clinging to his father, had covered his ears to block out the thunderous noise of the crowd.

Francisca stopped in the aisle so she could just watch them, oblivious to the pounding hoofs that passed beneath her on the grassy turf.

"O vencedor: Governante!" The loudspeaker shouted as the pink-tinged dust on the track cleared. "O segundo: Curitiba! Terceiro: Primitivo!"

Hearing his horse's name, Marcelino was clapping for joy. First or second, it didn't matter to him.

"Marcelino!" Francisca called to get her son's attention. The boy, obviously not expecting to see his mother, looked stunned.

The girls called "Mamãe" in unison. Tulio only clutched his father more tightly.

Augusto remained silent. Beside him his mother, his father, even his brother and sister, formed a united Cavalcanti front. They all looked at Francisca disdainfully. For support she turned to where the Larsons sat with Astrid. "Tia Chiquinha!" Astrid called gaily. "Come sit with me!"

"Later . . ." Erik answered abruptly.

Seeing what was happening, Margaret slipped out of her seat and came around to stand beside Francisca, who was trying to decide what to do. She felt trapped in an impossible situation. Behind the short barrier of the box, her children were almost as remote here, less than a meter from her, as they had been while she'd been locked away. Why was this so . . . public? What had happened to her dream of holding them in a quiet room, crooning to them, telling them that she loved them and would be back with them soon. Among the Cavalcantis they looked like Cavalcantis, had the same sallow skin color, the same black hair, and, except for Tulio, the same dark Portuguese looks. Only if they lived with her, if they learned from her, could she ever influence the people they'd become. With her gone, with them receiving the same kind of upbringing that had produced an Augusto . . . it was hopeless!

When Francisca didn't move forward, Erik detached Tulio from his father's arms and handed him to his mother. The child began to struggle, but Erik was firm. "Go to your mother!" This only confused the boy further. Erik helped Francisca hold him. She didn't flinch from his kicks. She placed her face against his and drew in a deep breath. "Tulio . . . Meu Tulio . . ." she whispered. He smelled of an oily hair cream she didn't use, not like the sweet little boy she'd been remembering. His breath wasn't milky . . . but bitter. She didn't want to hold him any more than he wanted her to.

"Give him back," she whispered to Erik and went to talk to the girls. "You are all looking very pretty today. Mila, where did you get that new dress?"

"Avó Cavalcanti." Emilia pointed to her grandmother, who sat, unsmiling, behind her.

"It's lovely." Francisca faced Antonieta Cavalcanti's severe expression as bravely as she could.

"Heloisa, I like the way you've done your hair. Did you know that's how I wore it when I was little?"

"Did you, Mamãe?" the child chirped sweetly.

Francisca closed her eyes for a second. When they opened, her daughter's face was glowing, like a small lamp. I wonder what she thinks of me. Whatever I do, I mustn't allow anyone to ruin her pure little thoughts.

Instead of looking at his mother, Marcelino was pretending to pay attention to the ceremonies in the winner's circle. Francisca touched his shoulder lightly, then bent to whisper in his ear. "I'm not angry with you, my darling. I hope you're not with me."

Augusto moved forward to pull her away, but Erik grabbed his arm. Marcelino flung his arms around his mother's waist and pulled her to the wooden fence, sobbing.

"She's upsetting the children," Antonieta Cavalcanti muttered. "Doctor, can't you do something?"

Dr. de Souza had been trying to stay in the background, but now, thinking that he somehow had been publicly caught neglecting his duties, he moved forward. "Senhora Cavalcanti . . ." He touched Francisca's arm lightly.

Francisca wheeled around. "No! No! Let me be with my children!" She caught Margaret's expression of horror at her outburst. Do something to help me, Francisca pleaded with her eyes.

Can't, Margaret seemed to answer.

"The Grande Prêmio is next," Erik spoke brusquely. "Perhaps we could all take our seats. Then, afterward . . ." He pulled his sister toward the best section in the grandstand, beside her mother and father. The horses were parading in front of the spectators. On the track, a line of twelve men in orange suits, carrying wooden blocks on poles, tamped the turf back into place in preparation for the race.

The standing crowd had swelled to the point where it seemed a sea of bobbing heads. Francisca raised her eyes to Corcovado. The hunchbacked mountain had begun to cast long violet shadows across the oval track, and at the same time, the sky had darkened perceptibly with a threatening rainstorm. None of this

mattered to the excited crowd who cheered as each horse was announced.

"Numero um: Marimacho. Numero dois: Projetil. Numero
três: Nova Esperança . . ." Now the noise was deafening. Their
horse was definitely the favorite.

"It's the best horse in Brazil!" Erik bragged. "Best in the world,
for that matter."

"If we win, Gigo," his father broke in, "everyone will think
the race isn't a fair one. After all, you've organized it, found
the money for the purse. Perhaps it would be best if one of the
others . . ."

"What are you saying? Nova Esperança will win and I'll send
him to Europe, to the Grand Prix de Longchamps, to the Derby,
or anywhere else it takes to prove he's the best in the world."

Sven Larson looked amused. "I hope you do." He then looked
over to where his daughter was staring, eyes fixed on a distant
spot on the horizon.

❧ ❧ ❧

The race was closer than anyone would have expected. In the last
quarter, Nova Esperança boldly claimed his lead, though it was
quickly shortened by a long shot, Rei Arturo, who was ahead
momentarily at the turn. But the Larsons' stable won. Bezerra's
horse, Rapazola, meaning "overgrown boy," came in a close second, with Rei Arturo third. A good race, an exciting race. Everyone was pleased.

Margaret tried to talk to Francisca, but her sister-in-law had
little to say to anyone, least of all her closest friend, betrayed by
her own brother not hours before. For a while Francisca allowed
her mother to hold her hand while her children were sent home
with their father's mother. All of the Larsons acutely felt they
had lost to the other family, the other side.

Although the rest of the races that day were anticlimactic, the
doctor and his wife showed no interest in leaving. Francisca was
grateful Erik was too busy with the festivities surrounding his
Grande Prêmio winner to return to the stands, for she found
his presence an embarrassment. Finally, when the rains made
their inevitable appearance, Francisca was almost relieved to be
escorted back to the hospital and returned to her room.

In bed she curled into her sleeping position, hands tucked between her knees. It hadn't been at all like she'd expected or
dreamed. She needed to be with the children, play with them,
have a meal with them, tuck them into their beds. She needed to
be their mother, not a visitor at a public event. Somehow she'd
arrange to see them again; somehow she'd recapture them, win
them back. A mother's love, a mother's word . . . No one else
could give them what she could.

She squeezed her eyes tightly to block out the images of Tulio
crying, Marcelino needing her to console him, and the bright,
hopeful, yet confused eyes of her daughters. Think of something
else . . . anything else, she ordered herself. The only image that
came was Amara. Amara and her brother on the bench, naked,
rolling together, their hair mattted with straw, the girl riding Erik
like she'd ridden the stallion, with a frightening intensity and
concentration in her muscles. It was easy to imagine Erik gripping her buttocks, kneading them; Amara leaning over him — her
conical brown breasts dripping into his mouth. Francisca trembled. This was the clearest, boldest sexual image she'd ever permitted herself to envision.

The black of Amara's skin, the white of her brother's. Legs intertwined, hands stroking each other. The hot smell of their lust
commingling. Amara and Erik, shuddering together, grasping
each other. In her mind she saw it all: the soles of Amara's feet
were so pink, with tiny black lines in the creases; the strength of
her body was so beautiful, so different from Margaret's long, delicate limbs. She imagined her brother's pleasure from the tightness of a woman who's never borne a child, from the immature
breasts of one who's never suckled a babe.

Probably her brother thought no more about it than a stallion
did. Francisca faced the wall. The images in her mind didn't fade,
they began all over again. Amara and her brother, in the stable, in
the bed he'd slept in as a child, at Boa Vista, in the kitchens of the
house in Flamengo. The two of them thrusting, twisting, pumping incessantly. Erik and Amara . . . together . . . joined infinitely.
She couldn't stop the thoughts tumbling out, though the visions
seared her. Their imagined voices whispering passionately caused
her to quiver in a curious kind of way. She covered her eyes with
her blanket as if that could blot out what she didn't wish to know.

The feelings of pain and helplessness churned violently. She began to shake so intensely that had she been in any other place, she might have permitted herself to scream. Here, though, where everyone else screamed, she could not. She suffered in exquisite silence.

❧ 5 September brought the beginnings of further miseries for Francisca. The increasing heat made life in her little room more unbearable because sleeping half the time away was impossible. Her visitors still came by the same schedule, but in the weeks since the Grande Prêmio she'd found it increasingly hard to be with Margaret now that she knew about Erik and Amara. She thought Margaret deserved the truth, yet she couldn't hurt her, nor could she break Erik's trust, especially now that he was quite ill once again.

Francisca herself was so distraught after the races, Margaret had not told her the details of Erik's difficulties for many weeks, until she'd had to explain why Erik had missed so many of his visits.

Francisca had been shocked by the news. "He told me that he hadn't had a single attack since Vassouras."

"That's correct if you realize he doesn't consider himself ill until he's lost consciousness! There are many other symptoms of imbalance: his skin itches, there are boils, he gets up hourly at night, why, even his vision is too blurred to read the newspapers. Dr. Bandeira says this is all part of the same disease. If he doesn't stop drinking completely, if Erik doesn't stop asking me to . . ." Her voice quavered.

Oh, Margaret, if you only knew, Francisca thought. But instead she said, "We've spoken of this before. My brother's a vital man . . . just in his early forties. You can't expect him to stop living."

"I did listen to you! I permitted him to come to me . . . in moderation. Now look, he is sicker, just as the doctor predicted. He must take care of himself, if only for the sake of his children. Since we've been reunited, I've noticed quite a difference in the girls. Even Astrid has been thriving."

Francisca was relieved the subject had changed. "Astrid looked lovely at the Jockey Club. I can't believe she's almost twelve."

"Old enough to go away to school."

"You'd send her away?"

"Her father's been talking about it. He wants Astrid to know the Swedish side of her family."

"What does Astrid say?"

"Surprisingly, she's very receptive — enthusiastic, in fact. Her mother's family's gifts have been unnecessarily elaborate and generous over the years. She probably imagines living like a spoiled princess over there."

"Will you speak against it?"

"No. Maybe she'll appreciate more of what she has here when she returns. If nothing else, it's *warmer* here." Margaret laughed heartily.

"She's been a great burden for you." Francisca eyed Margaret steadily.

Margaret didn't flinch. "She's a child, innocent, unthinking. I've always forgiven her . . . for everything. People who understand the consequences and then still choose an unconscionable action . . . those are the ones I find difficult to pardon."

"Not impossible, though."

Margaret looked painfully sad. She swallowed hard. "Not impossible."

"I'm glad you took him back. Now, if you could accept him for what he is . . ." Amara! Why couldn't she put that girl out of her mind!

"I've done my best . . ."

"Yes, certainly you have . . ." was all Francisca dared say.

When Sister Lourdes checked, as she was supposed to each half-hour, she'd ended the interview because she saw that Francisca was disturbed. "Mustn't upset her now, it only makes the treatments more difficult," she'd clucked as she led Margaret out.

Anxiously, Francisca waited for Margaret's return visit. Next time she wouldn't show any emotion. She'd try to be the cheerful, smiling patient they wanted. Sometimes she wondered whether they marked the number and quality of her laughs on one of their report forms. If so, perhaps there was a magical tally — one hundred chuckles and forty straight days without tears — that would ensure her release. If only she knew the formula, she was certain she could demonstrate it ... if only she knew it.

❧ ❧ ❧

The following Wednesday Margaret brought a basket of freshly baked rolls, Danish butter because Francisca had complained about the rancidness of the hospital's offerings, and hibiscus honey from Vassouras.

"It's in a tin, I'm sorry. They wouldn't permit a glass jar."

"I know."

"I hope it won't spoil the flavor."

"I'll eat it too quickly for that to happen ... and I'll share it. Most of the others don't get as many gifts."

"You're looking so much better!" Margaret commented cheerfully. "The last few weeks ... Frankly, I've been worried about you."

"It was only the disappointment over the way it went with the children. Now I realize that the important thing was that I saw them and they're healthy. I'm looking forward to a better time with them at Christmas. Papai promised to make the arrangements."

"And he is," Margaret said so flatly that Francisca didn't dare question her further.

Instead, she was filled with inquiries about their friends and family. All the minutiae of the world outside her barred window fascinated her. "Do you think Kate will ever marry?" Francisca asked curiously.

"No, I don't think she will."

"A pity, she's such a kind girl, and attractive in an unusual sort of a way."

"It's easier to marry when you're younger, when you've formed fewer ideas."

"Wouldn't you choose Gigo again?" Francisca asked playfully.

"I'm sure I would. He's as dazzling now as he was then. But would you have been so agreeable to Augusto's offer if you'd been older?"

"That's different," she said curtly. "We're talking about Kate."

"Every year her chances are slimmer, not that she cares. She's not even looking for a man."

"I see," Francisca said thoughtfully. "What would your mother do without her if she did marry?"

"I don't know. My mother thinks she's her old age insurance. The trouble is that Kate won't rebel against waiting on her hand and foot."

"If they're both content . . ."

"I don't know," Margaret said restlessly. "I just wish Kate would find something that's important to her; it wouldn't have to be a man."

"And Marshall, the brother I hardly know. Does he still do well in his studies?"

"Much to everyone's surprise, he's become quite a scholar. We expect him to finish his degree, thanks to Erik's generous support."

"Do you think your sister Nell will ever come to Rio? I liked her so much when she was here at the time of your wedding."

"Maybe in a few years, when her children are older. She complains all the time about missing us."

"Not like Marianne. She's never been one to fuss, even with all the troubles they've had up there in the forests lately."

"How did you know about that?"

"I ask everyone to tell me what's happening and they each tell me a part of the story. Then I put it together like puzzle pieces. Each of you has a different idea about what I should and shouldn't hear."

"What do you mean?"

"From Erik I heard how your brother's used religion to advise and control the peasants and landowners. Papai, on the other hand, is still worried about the soundness of the entire venture in the north. He sometimes thinks that your brother has become a little too — how shall I say? — despotic? He's afraid some of his policies might cause a revolt."

"And your mother, what does she say about all this?"

"She worries about Marianne and the children. She'd like them all back in Rio."

"She's so infinitely kind and caring. You're fortunate to have her as a mother and so am I!" Margaret offered Francisca a piece of candy from her purse. "It's from France. Maestro Freire sent it in a box containing one of his latest piano pieces. He wanted me to learn it for when he returns."

"Nicia Netto wrote me a letter and said they expected him early next year. Is his music as fine as Nicia hinted it is?"

"It's brilliant. He's working on a complicated 'Forest Concerto.' It's terribly modern, using bird calls and jungle themes as a counterpoint to more classical forms. But the piano part is very complex. I doubt whether I'll be able to do it justice."

"I don't believe you! Why, I've been told that Freire's been writing with just your touch in mind."

"Who'd say a thing like that?"

"I think Nicia knows him a wee bit better than you do. They've worked together for years."

"I hope he won't be disappointed with me after all the great musicians he's worked with in Paris."

Francisca began to tidy her gifts. Everyone who visited brought her something. The room was always cluttered. There was only one item she really wanted: the signed release paper. Nothing else would do. Suddenly the room seemed unbearably close. "Shall we ask the sister to take us down to the garden?"

"Actually, I've already arranged something special." Margaret winked mischievously.

For a second Francisca's heart soared with hope. The children, she's brought one of the children! Almost reading her mind, Margaret quickly continued, "My cook's prepared some of your favorites: sopa de siri, empadão de galinha, and for dessert, merengue de banana. Dr. de Souza's going to let us eat in the superintendent's private atrium. Won't that be grand?"

The garden table was beautifully set with the peacock china from Margaret's home. She'd brought Florinda along to serve. The first taste of the soup, swimming with minced crab meat in a garlic and cream sauce, brought a strange sensation of well-being. Despite her disappointment, Francisca beamed at the meal's prospects. "If the doctors see this, they're sure to be jealous. I hope you brought enough for de Souza at least."

"Not of the soup, but the banana meringue perhaps. You like him, don't you?"

Francisca grimaced. "Does a prisoner ever like her jailer?" She sipped the soup without further comment. "It was thoughtful of you to bring Florinda, makes it seem more homelike."

"To be truthful" — Margaret spoke in English to ensure their privacy — "I didn't bring Florinda only for that reason. I'm watching over her these days."

"You don't trust her, after all these years?"

"Not right now. Ever since we returned from Vassouras she's acted strangely. Why, we've been relying more on her children than on her."

Francisca had always thought Margaret's maid was an unusually sensual and attractive woman. Her body was still trim, with the high, undulating buttocks that Brazilian men seemed to favor. Though Florinda was modest around her employers, Francisca remembered seeing her flirt surreptitiously with Severino.

"Poor girl, she's had a tragic life. The two men she's loved have died horribly, and now she probably misses that man she met in the mountains. Why don't you see if he'll marry her?"

"That wouldn't be wise. You know he has a bad reputation."

"As far as I've been able to tell, that's all rumor and hearsay. You should be glad for her."

Margaret shrugged.

"Margaret! For someone as kindhearted as you, you hardly understand your servants at all."

"And you do?"

Francisca stood up and paced around the atrium's large pots of freshly watered ferns, their fronds glistening in the late afternoon sunshine. "I think so. Why should Florinda be denied a full life of her own? All it might mean is bringing the man to Rio, finding him a job."

"Apparently he's already in Rio."

"Then you must take him on. Better to have them both under one roof than to worry about her running off."

"I'm certain he's not a good influence on her. Since we've suspected he's been around, Florinda has been acting strangely, neglecting her children."

"Erik can set them straight."

"It's complicated. It's been rumored he was once involved with some of those men in the backlands . . . bandidos . . ."

"Bandidos! This family's been obsessed with criminals ever since that time your necklace was stolen on my wedding day by a brazen street urchin."

Margaret knew Francisca had never been told about the shooting on the steamer. In fact, she'd been protected from the tale of the killings on Raleigh's river barge as well. The Larsons had always united to guard their sensitive daughter, and this was hardly the time or place to break their confidences.

"Let me tell you something," Francisca began darkly. "If Augusto's a gentleman, then just who is a bandido, eh?" She laughed shrilly at her allusion.

Florinda approached to serve the chicken and palm heart stuffed pastry. "Come sit down and finish your meal," Margaret insisted. "We'll worry about that other matter some later time."

Francisca tasted the pastry. "Oh, it's perfect!" Florinda poured a glass of Portuguese rosé. "Wine's not permitted."

"Today it is."

"Why, what's so special?" she asked warily.

"We're just trying to . . . to . . . make your life more pleasant. If you have to be here, then we're determined you shouldn't suffer unnecessarily."

Now Francisca understood what was on Margaret's mind. Her release had been delayed. More trouble with papers and courts. This was not a celebration but an expression of helplessness. "What's gone wrong?"

Margaret looked down at her plate. "Your father . . ."

"Is that why he didn't come yesterday?"

"Yes. He couldn't face you, not after he got the news . . ."

Francisca felt her hands becoming icy. "What news?"

"All his petitions have been denied. It's not the end, but this session is over. Next year he'll have to start again."

"Next year!" Francisca leapt up. Her wine glass crashed to the cobblestone floor.

"Nobody's more upset than your father. He became hysterical . . . He . . ."

Francisca froze. "What's wrong! What aren't you telling me?"

Francisca was surprised that instead of shouting, her own voice had become slow and deep.

"He had an attack. There's not much to tell now. He's so much better that you needn't worry. At first we thought it might be his heart, and I stayed at Flamengo with Erik until the danger had passed. But now the doctor has decided it was just a very severe case of indigestion."

"He'll recover?"

"Yes, he will, as long as he stops eating spicy foods such as his favorite, stuffed crab and duck with manioc and pepper sauce." Margaret sighed heavily. "Now come and sit down and have your meringue and some tea."

"You'd tell me the truth about my father?"

"Francisca, your father will recover fully, I promise you! Drink some of this lovely China tea. It's the kind you always asked me to serve."

Francisca decided that Margaret had no reason to lie to her. She'd already given her the bad news about the petitions. She touched the rose decoration on the white teapot. "This looks like your music teacher's old teapot."

"It is. It's *the* 'Gottschalk teapot.' Mademoiselle gave it to me as a farewell gift."

"Did he give it to her?"

"Don't think so. He probably drank one cup of tea that was poured from it and it became, like the rest of her mementos, a precious reminder of his existence. I once calculated that she'd never spent more than a total of a month with the musician, yet she dedicated her whole life to him. Can you imagine, a few days changing a whole life?"

Francisca was feeling very peculiar. At first she thought it was the shock of the news about her father and her case; then she attributed it to being unaccustomed to rich foods. But it was something else. The little courtyard, though appealing and quiet, had never felt quite right, and now the discussion about the piano teacher had touched some vital nerve.

Margaret poured herself some tea. She seemed extremely tense and concerned. New lines had begun to etch little grooves along the sides of her mouth; the cleft in her chin seemed deeper, her facial bones more pronounced than ever before. Francisca be-

lieved Margaret had grown more beautiful as she aged. Maybe
that was because Francisca loved her so, even though she was
sometimes stubborn, willfull, self-absorbed by her music, or
blinded by her odd veneer of innocence.

If Margaret could be made to see the world as she saw it —
incredibly imperfect with only a few pleasant moments set between months of agony — she'd be more willing to be practical
and flexible. The Lord in Heaven knew that she would have to be
sensible again soon, when the inevitable news about Amara surfaced.

One reason Margaret had so much more difficulty with unpleasant realities than Francisca did was the simple difference between their cultures. Brazilian women were brought up to accept
their lesser status. Brazilian women knew men required and demanded certain freedoms that the more puritanical North Americans didn't grant as easily. That time when Erik had been foolish
enough to take his wife to Celso Tavares's party at the Nautical
Club, she'd had to listen to Margaret's shocked description of the
guests for weeks afterward. What had her brother been thinking
of? He had to know that there were things about life in Rio that
Margaret could never fully accept. If only Margaret knew the
truth about some of the men she'd probably met that night . . .
Maybe if she did know . . . Francisca wrestled with her grimmest
thoughts while Margaret sipped her tea.

Innocence was for children! Children were purposely buffered
from hard truths until they were strong enough to understand
them. The greatest mistake adults made was that they never knew
precisely when a child, or anyone else for that matter, was ready
to know about the realities of life. They never explained anything
because of the pain the teller knowingly inflicts on the listener.
Nobody understood that better than she did; nobody was more
guilty in her silence than she'd been with Margaret.

Margaret was sitting quietly, arms folded in her lap. She
seemed to be listening to some faraway music. Her golden hair,
sunlit from behind, appeared to glow.

Francisca spoke once again in English. "You've got to let
Florinda have that man if she chooses him. So few of our desires
can ever be fulfilled that we must not prevent anyone else from
taking any happiness that's within their grasp . . . as long as no

one else is harmed." Francisca's plaintive tone made Margaret put down her teacup and listen. Francisca knew she was speaking queerly; her voice sounded tinny to her own ear. Now that she had Margaret's full attention, she could go on with the rest — the whole of it. An immense pressure, an incredible constriction, was lifting. A breeze parted the leaves of the highest tree in the garden, permitting a wide crack of sunlight to spill over the high wall and blind her momentarily. Francisca shut her eyes tightly. A few long seconds later, she opened them and began to reveal her secret tale from the beginning. Others had told it many times, that she knew. One of the nuns had repeated Francisca's story in confidence to Mlle Doradou, possibly to explain her extreme shyness. Not that Mademoiselle had ever said anything to Margaret or anyone else, but Francisca had seen the knowledge of it in the music teacher's eyes: the sympathy, the sadness of an experienced woman for a terrified girl. That's what she hated most, the eyes of those who knew. And there were far too many of them.

Now, for the very first time, she'd tell the story herself.

16 "When I was almost fifteen I began to be invited to the parties given to introduce the girls to society; that's the age Brazilian young women are traditionally presented as marriageable."

Margaret nodded. "Astrid's received invitations already, but Erik won't allow her to go yet." Margaret seemed to be trying to make the confession into a conversation. Francisca humored her for a bit.

"As well he shouldn't! Though I'm certain she is just as anxious as I was at her age. You wouldn't have recognized me then; I was so different, more like Astrid than you'd think. My mother never disciplined me too harshly, and I followed Erik around like his shadow. I wanted to be exactly like him — brave, independent. I did crazy stunts: walked the high walls around Flamengo without falling, went swimming in the sea during a thunderstorm, even drove the charrette at Boa Vista down the mountain without permission.

"You?" The shock on Margaret's face was gratifying. "You dared?"

"I did . . . and more . . ."

"I can't believe this is the Francisca I know! What else?"

"All sorts of little tricks to get attention. My father spent all his time with Erik, since he'd be the one to inherit the business. They just expected me to wait out the right number of years and docilely marry a suitable man."

"That's why you were sent to the convent school? To discipline you?"

"No, that's not it."

"Then why? It always seemed so peculiar that they sent you so far away when there were fine schools in Brazil."

"I'm telling you, I'm telling you now." Francisca closed her eyes and willed herself to go on.

"It was one of those coming-out parties. You are friends with the girl who was being fêted; you know her family; in fact, you've met most everyone who was there that night. Rio's a very small community, really. That's why no one could believe anything like that could've happened. Those troubles did not occur among good families. Proper children did not behave that way."

Margaret crossed her arms. "What are you talking about?" The sunlight had completely disappeared from the garden. The air had a faint chill. Francisca, however, perspired openly.

"There were really two parties: one for the children and one for their parents. Papai didn't attend; he'd had meetings that evening. Mamãe had come with Zefinha, and of course Erik had been invited also. That night Mamãe didn't even look in on me; she thought I would enjoy the independence. If I didn't have a dancing partner, Gigo promised to ask me and so had several of his friends. Mother always reminded me how fortunate I was to have an older brother.

"Once we arrived, Zefinha recombed my hair and fluffed my dress, then went into the kitchen, where the maids bragged about whose little girl was prettiest and who would marry first. Mother went to the parlor, where they were serving champagne for the parents. This very well established old Portuguese family was the equal to ours at that time." Francisca stopped herself from giving away any further identifying details.

"From the start the party was . . . I suppose you'd say it was wild. The boys were very rough with each other — teasing, joking, like very young children, although most were over sixteen and some, like my brother, were in their twenties. The point, you understand, was to introduce the new girls to the boys, to help make arrangements for marriages or to solidfy unions the parents had been planning for years. I knew the families from which my mother wanted me to choose a husband. I even liked several of her favored boys, but I had a strong feeling for one who was a schoolmate of Gigo's."

Margaret's brow formed a quizzical arch. "Who?"

"He no longer lives in Rio," Francisca responded flatly. For a moment she wondered if she could continue. The tea in her cup was cold and stale, but she took a sip to delay her tale.

"Don't you think we should go inside?" Margaret asked anxiously.

"This won't take much longer."

After one glance at Francisca's intense face, Margaret shifted in her seat but remained silent.

"The dress I wore that night was probably the most beautiful I've ever owned, prettier and more expensive than my wedding dress by far. It was the first time my mother had permitted me to wear a bodice without a high neck. It had handmade silk lace at the neckline and little cut-out areas filled in with crocheted flowers. It was cool and floating. I was also given my first silk stockings and satin slippers with Louis Quinze heels, even a hand-painted ivory fan, full-length kid gloves, and a gardenia for my hair. I felt beautiful, and everyone, not only Mother and Zefinha, told me I was. I saw it in the faces of other mothers who hated me, just a bit, because I was the only one with fair hair and eyes, the only one with so splendid a dress. The sons from the most respected families lined up before me to request the honor of a waltz. I can't say that I didn't glow from the heat of all that admiration.

"Gigo didn't have to dance with me. But by midnight I was exhausted. I hadn't sat down even once. Then this boy, the one I liked especially, came up to me when he saw me sitting with the other girls. I told him I was too tired to dance. He agreed it was too hot inside and invited me out on the terrace. I asked a few of the girls who were sitting beside me if they'd like to come outside with us, but no, they wanted to dance, or they didn't want to go with me because they were jealous, or maybe they wanted me to get into trouble by being seen unescorted with a boy. I think about that moment the most — the tiny second when a life changes. If one of the girls had been willing to join me, or if I had resisted the temptation of being alone with him . . ."

Francisca took a deep breath. "So I decided to go without them. After all, it wasn't far, just outside the door, and he *was* the one I liked the best."

Margaret's eyes were bright, expectant pools, like those of a child waiting for the happy ending. Why was she doing this to her sister-in-law, her closest friend? Margaret had no idea that the words she was about to hear would, even if only in some small way, change her forever. She'd never go out in Rio society again without wondering who had been there that night or who knew; she'd never look at another Brazilian of a certain age without thinking that he might have been one of them. Now, as Francisca was rethinking the wisdom of telling the story, she realized it was far too late to turn back. Secrets have been what have hurt Margaret far more than the truth. I'm finally doing what's right, she reminded herself and plunged ahead.

"When we were just outside the ballroom door, he reached over and touched my hair. 'You're so beautiful,' he said. Never before had I felt anything like what I felt then: a crazy rushing sensation inside my chest. The boy I'd picked over maybe twenty others had selected me as well! At that moment I thought I was the luckiest girl in the world. It made me bold. I told him that I liked him, too. As soon as I'd said the words, he acted surprised, but pleased nevertheless. He put his arm around my shoulders and pulled me behind one of the pillars on the portico and kissed me, or rather brushed his lips across my cheek. I'd never felt anything so thrilling boiling inside me.

"Then we heard laughing people coming close. We didn't want to be discovered alone together, so I made a move to hide until they'd passed. Hidden behind the column, our bodies were close together for a few seconds, face to face. I felt him . . . something poking my leg. I thought it was his hands until I realized he was holding both my shoulders. I remember trying to figure out if it was his knee, but it was too high . . . I really didn't know . . . so, I touched it."

Margaret looked as though she was about to laugh. Everyone

had similar embarrassing youthful moments, but the complete lack of humor in Francisca's narrative made her stop.

"Even then, when I realized what was in my hand, I didn't know exactly what I'd done; I just knew I had to get away from him. I ran quickly back into the bright room where the music was playing and went right up to someone I knew, a brother of a schoolmate, and reminded him that I'd promised him that dance. He was flustered, but began the waltz, clumsily. I wasn't exactly able to keep in step either, because I knew the boy from the terrace was watching me.

"When the music stopped, I went to find my mother because I wanted to go home. She wasn't with the other ladies. The senhora of the house said that I should hurry back to the party, since they were just about to serve the cake and begin with the gifts. She promised to tell my mother I needed to see her. Gigo had also disappeared.

"In the ballroom, all the girls were clustered around the daughter of the house. Most of the boys were in the background; a few were out on the terrace, sitting on the railings. When I passed close by the door, my 'friend' grabbed my arm and yanked me outside. He said I owed him at least another kiss. Before I could pull away, he pressed his lips to my mouth, right in front of several other boys. They were laughing. Then the first boy held my arms behind my back so tight they ached, while he told them what part of him I'd touched. He said I wanted him so desperately that I couldn't keep my hands to myself. Another boy pretended to unbutton his pants, saying I could have his, too. All the boys went on like that, teasing me while the first boy held me fast. Because I knew my mother was coming to get me, that she'd be there in a minute, I didn't scream or fuss. Finally, down the steps that led to a very steep hillside garden, I saw two men, one who, in the light from the party, looked just like Erik. I called to him. The boy let me go. I ran as fast as I could, but the two men disappeared before I reached them. There was a second stairway that led to an even lower terrace with a magnificent view of the city below. I thought Erik had probably gone down there. But when I got to the landing, I realized I was alone. I decided to go back to the house as quickly as possible, to find my mother, but I never got up that first step.

"The boys surprised me; they held me down. Someone pulled up my dress. The skirt was so long it went over my head, trapping me inside. Another boy held my head and stuffed my skirt into my mouth. The fabric in my throat choked me so badly that I thought I was going to suffocate.

" 'Let's give her what she wants,' one of the oldest ones said.

" 'Hey, you go first,' someone said to the boy whose genitals I'd touched. 'It's your right, isn't it?'

" 'Go, go, go . . .' they chanted as he went inside me. The other boys all helped him, made it easier by holding my legs . . ." Francisca's voice faltered.

Margaret rushed to her side and clutched her hands. "No . . . no . . . Why . . . ?"

Margaret's agitation forced Francisca to regain her eerie, calm storytelling expression. "Listen to me . . ." Margaret was shaking her head. "I need to tell you now. I should've told you years ago. Listen to me . . ." she pleaded.

Margaret was crying. Francisca pressed a napkin from the table into her hand and continued in a rapid, detached voice. "The worst was my back; it was being pounded onto a rough gravel surface and my legs were being stretched in an impossible position. I didn't even know what they were doing, not completely. I couldn't see anything. I could just feel all this pressure, all these hands on me. Some were on my breasts, some between my legs. I know the first one got off me quickly. My legs were slippery and wet. Then there was another. He was bigger, he took longer, and he hurt much more. The others were quieter when he did it, like students at a lesson. I cried, but they stuffed my dress down my throat further.

"I heard the voice of my 'friend' telling the others that I was getting only what I'd asked for and they were agreeing. Then the third boy fell on me. He was so heavy, so fat . . . I thought he'd crush me. At the last moment, though, he jumped off me and yelled at the boy at my head to make me look. They pulled off my dress, but my eyes were shut.

" 'Open your eyes,' he ordered. Then I saw it; even in the dark he was obviously huge. He poked his organ in my face and the stuff spurted all over me . . . my eyes, my hair. The others loved it. They cheered. From then on they let me see what was happening."

"How many?" Margaret croaked.

"I never knew. Some may have come back twice. It went on for a very long time, till I was so sore and weak I was passing out. I was so wet with blood and everything that the last few complained. One wanted to stick it in my mouth, but the others were afraid I would scream. They began to talk about what to do with me, threatened to kill me — or cut out my tongue, blind me — if I ever told who did it."

"You knew them all?"

"Most of them."

"Margaret held Francisca's hands between hers. Her tears flowed openly. "They just left you there . . . like that?"

"Not exactly. One of them, the biggest, fattest one, kicked me. Another picked up a handful of dirt and threw it between my legs. It stuck in the wetness and gave them ideas. They covered my dress with the muddy dirt, streaked me with it . . . my face . . . my hair. One of them urinated on me and another . . ."

"No! I don't want to hear any more!"

Francisca pushed Margaret aside and stood up. "They opened my legs and filled me, jammed me full of pebbles, dirt, and sticks. I couldn't walk or stand. Then they left me there, left me to be found by Erik. It *had* been Erik I'd seen. He'd gone walking with one of his friends. They'd gone up the hill into a nearby favela to meet a whore his friend frequented. The other boys had known he'd left the party; that's why they knew they could do what they wanted with me. When Erik came back he heard me crying, and when he found me he acted like a lunatic, went wild. At first he thought I was dying. He carried me exactly the way I was up the stairs, across the terrace, into the brightly lit ballroom. Everyone saw me — the mud, the blood, even the sticks falling out from under my dress!"

Without realizing it, Francisca had been standing in a narrow flower garden, her back pressed against the wall. In her hand she clutched the vine of a hanging plant and was twisting it to shreds.

"Did you ever say who did it?" Margaret asked in a voice that dreaded any answer she might hear.

"Yes, eventually. My parents forced me to tell. They promised I'd never be harmed. I gave every name I knew. I told everything. As soon as I was better — it was only a matter of weeks — I was on the boat for New Orleans. I was happy to leave, happy never to see any of those people again."

Margaret covered her face with her hands. "Now I finally understand."

"What do you understand?" Francisca challenged. "It's impossible for anyone to know what it was like, to have your life begin and end on the same night. To have all the trust and hope murdered, destroyed, torn from you." She looked at Margaret's crushed face. "I'm only telling you so you won't eternally wonder about me and why they are making me stay here. I don't want you to feel sad about my past; I only want you to realize how hopeless the future is for some of us and to show you why you must make more of your own good chances."

"What are you saying?" Margaret was truly confused. She looked at the sky, now streaked with the pinks and greys of a spectacular sunset. "They'll ask me to leave soon, but I can't go without . . ."

"It's not a long story from here on. The facts are very simple. I lived in New Orleans as long as possible, until my parents felt that people would have forgotten the worst of it, until most of the young men and women were already married, settled, until the boy . . ."

As Francisca paused, Margaret's mind raced to the school friends of Erik's she'd met over the years. For some reason a few of the men at Tavares's party came to mind. "The one you liked? What happened to him?"

"He's dead."

"But how?"

"I've never really been told. They say it was some unfortunate accident about a year after the attack. But I'm certain it wasn't. My father . . . he'd promised he would see that they were punished, all of them. Yet he couldn't kill every one of them, could he? One . . . one life . . . Perhaps he decided that was fair enough. So he picked the first one, the one who'd begun it."

"Your father killed him?"

"I'm certain he wanted to do it himself, but it's more likely he just made arrangements. It was probably very expensive. In fact, the whole matter was very costly to him. All those people to pay so they would never speak of it again. I'll never know what he actually did, but none of the families of the other boys prosper any longer. *None* of them," she said with vicious emphasis. "Then there were the Cavalcantis . . ."

Margaret gasped. "They were involved?"

"No, no, of course not! That's why Augusto was chosen for me. No member of their family was there that night. That's why . . ."

" . . . he married you?"

"Actually, he married me for a great deal of money, more than you'd ever believe. He'll get three-fourths of my father's estate. Erik agreed to settle for a smaller portion to see me married well."

"There's more than enough for everyone," Margaret said generously. "But how could Augusto ruin such good fortune by treating you so horribly?"

"If you think about it, Margaret, you'll now realize exactly why he behaves as he does. Can you imagine how he felt when he was pressured into marrying a woman who was as used as I was? I had been with how many men? Six? Ten? And everyone knew it!"

"But . . . you were violated . . . You didn't . . ."

Francisca cocked her head haughtily. "Didn't I? All the girls saw me rush out into the darkness with him happily. Everyone knew how and where I touched him when we were hiding from the others. Everyone thought that I ran down the stairs onto the lower terrace because I wanted to be alone with all the boys, to see them, to touch them, too."

"That's what they said?"

"They did."

"But after what you looked like, how injured you were, how could anyone have trusted their word?"

"There were so many of them, and everyone knew I had a reputation for being a bit 'wild.' "

"You were a child!"

"Augusto has never believed my version of the story, that's for certain. When he's angry or has had too much to drink, he makes accusations. He thinks I'm incurable, that I'm always looking for

other men. He's hit me for talking to a servant, accused me of
taking the gardeners into my bed. Why, he's even hinted that
Gigo and I had . . ."

"Erik!" Margaret was incensed. "He's crazy! Erik! How could
he!"

"No, Margaret, you forget, *I'm* the one who's crazy. That's
why I'm here. He told the authorities when he committed me
that I've gone after the children, my little boys!" Now she was
choking and raving. "My sons! My brother! He claims the rape
made me insane, permanently insane. Even the doctors, the mag-
istrates, all of them think that, some more than others. They wonder, 'How could a woman, so young, from such a fine family, go
through all that and not finally go mad?' You see? It's a delicate
problem. If I can live a good life, I must be warped; if I can't, it's
understandable, but it still makes me a lunatic. That's why I'll
never get out of here, never! They all believe I *belong* in an asylum."

"But you don't . . ." Margaret moaned. The knowledge, the
truth of it, was so intense that she felt her head was going to ex-
plode with it.

Sister Lourdes was at the gate. How long had she been there?
Not that it mattered. Certainly Sister Lourdes had known most of
the story from the day Francisca was admitted. From the first the
sister had stared at her with a compassionate yet knowing gaze.

"Senhora Larson, your driver has been waiting."

"One moment longer, Sister, por favor."

Margaret wrapped her arms around Francisca. "You're
wrong," she whispered in English. "They can't blame you for
any of it any more than you can blame yourself. It was something
done *to* you, not something you did." She stopped to wipe her
flooding eyes. "I never knew . . . You know that . . . I never knew
any of it!"

Francisca murmured. "Someone else should have told you a
long time ago."

"No, nobody else could have, I realize that now."

Taking Francisca by the arm, Sister Lourdes said, "Thank you
for coming, Senhora Larson; your luncheon was a lovely idea. I'm
sure Senhora Cavalcanti had a wonderful day. Didn't you, dear?"

Francisca's mouth tightened sardonically. She looked to see if

Margaret had also found the sister's remark ironic. But Margaret had a totally different yet unmistakable expression. Francisca recognized the heavy lids, wide pupils, luminous whites, lashes fluttering lightly. There it was, pasted on her best friend's face, the awful permanence of it: pity.

❧ 7 The carpenters' pounding began at six in the morning, waking every inmate in the asylum. Four smaller cubicles across the ward from Francisca's room were being converted into one larger suite with a sleeping area, private dining room, and day parlor. Without being told, Francisca realized the rooms were being readied for her. Intead of cheering her, though, the project was so disheartening she could rarely be persuaded to leave her bed.

"You always liked the little atrium," Sister Lourdes coaxed. "If you'll let me help you get dressed, we'll have our morning coffee, read for a while, or do stitchery there today."

Stitchery? Francisca's interest was roused. Although they knew she was talented at embroidery, they hadn't permitted her to have needles or scissors before. She supposed the sister was expected to guard her closely.

The day was particularly clear and cool for summer. Over the garden walls Francisca could see the sun shining on the sides of the emerald hills that jutted majestically into a cloudless sky. She almost admitted that it was a pleasant change to have left the ward, now choked with plaster dust and noisy saws because of the construction.

"When will they move me?" she asked in a natural voice.

Not missing a beat, the sister answered, "Before Christmas. Dr. de Souza promised your family it would be ready in time. You'll be so much more comfortable."

Comfortable! As though a bit more space could make the difference! The contrary was true, for the very effort of the renovations convinced her that her chances of ever being freed without Augusto's approval had narrowed considerably.

Once they were settled on the stone bench in the courtyard, Francisca set to work on the small circle of fabric she'd been given. From the limited colors, she noticed the range of red threads matched the hues of some of the flowers in the garden.

Without needing a pattern, she quickly stitched the outline for her design.

"What are you working on?" Sister Lourdes asked.

"A Christmas gift for my mother." Francisca pointed to the waxy anthuriums growing by the garden wall. "In English they call antúrios 'painter's palettes.' I've never seen as many shades of reds and pinks before. My father grows some white ones as a border in his orchid garden, but as a child I never liked them."

"Why is that, my dear?"

"I thought them ugly. The long protruding spike in the center seemed as though it would hurt if you touched it. I've always preferred his orchids. Nothing is more beautiful than his own crossbreeds. He's bred a pure white cattleya, and he has a world-famous collection of *Phalaenopsis*. I'd even prefer a cactus; at least their spines are more honest."

Francisca turned over her cloth and tied off her thread. After briefly admiring how quickly she'd done the thickly scalloped petal outline in a Portuguese stem stitch, she began to thread a different needle.

"Why would you choose a distasteful flower as your subject?" Sister Lourdes probed.

"My mother likes them. She sees them differently. 'Like hearts,' she used to say to get me to appreciate them." Francisca's voice rose defensively. "Besides, the colors are good for Christmas." She knew she'd just sounded childish, but often it was too much of a strain to impress the sisters and doctors with perfectly moderated actions.

Not that anything she did mattered anymore, but at least they thought they could trust her with a needle for a few hours or leave her in a less secure, larger suite of rooms. Think of it that way, she'd remind herself whenever she was becoming especially despondent. In the end, though, her own sensible arguments couldn't diminish the hollow feeling that gnawed at her perpetually.

❧   ❧   ❧

Francisca's new suite of rooms was cooler and remarkably quieter. Instead of overlooking the inner courtyard where the wild, naked patients were kept, she now had a view across the park that surrounded the institution. In the morning, the grounds were filled with the orphans housed in the building across the street. Nuns, dressed in grey-and-white habits, wheeled carriages, each filled with up to six small babies. From Francisca's third-story view, their veils appeared to be sails, blowing the children across a sea of green.

One morning Sister Lourdes found Francisca gazing down at the orphans when she'd come to deliver a small parcel of books in English and French that her father had ordered for her. "You are watching the parade of the children?"

Francisca nodded. She didn't turn away from the view.

"After I took my final vows, I used to work at the orphanage."

"Didn't you like being there?"

"On the contrary! I adored the children!"

"Why aren't you still with them?"

"It's not for me to decide where my Lord needs me to serve."

"Surely they consider the wishes of a sister!"

"Wishes can create a disobedient attitude. From the infant ward I went directly to the west wing on the first floor."

"With the men? The violent ones?"

"They needed my love and care as much as any child."

Francisca thought she understood Sister Lourdes better. Until that moment she'd seen the sister as her keeper, her jailer, not as a person with any feelings of her own. Now, as she looked at the nun's ethereal yet somewhat vacant gaze, she was touched by the ordinariness of her suffering. Their lives were not so different after all. She was beaten down by an autocratic husband, while the nun was controlled by an inflexible religious order.

"Tell me about the babies. Where do they come from?" Francisca spoke more gently to Sister Lourdes than she ever had before.

"These days we accept them all and ask no questions. A few years ago we tried to find some way to help a mother keep her child. Then we discovered our mistake. Babies we'd turned away would be found floating in the sewers. At last Sister Domingas had the revolving wheel installed."

"What's that?"

"A wheel with a cradle attached, which is built as a part of one of the windows that faces the thoroughfare. It revolves on a perpendicular axis and is divided into four triangular compartments. One side is always open, thus inviting the approach of any so heartless or so desperate as to wish to part with an infant. The mothers leave unobserved after turning the wheel, and the foundling passes anonymously to the safety of the convent. The receiving sister has no means of identifying a mother unless she chooses to reveal herself. Since the wheel was installed, that part of the hospital has become known as the Casa da Roda, 'House of the Wheel.' We'll never know how many babies' lives the wheel has saved. Only last week we were given the care of tiny twins, their cords still attached."

From that moment on, Francisca thought continually about the orphaned babies. A few days before Christmas, Sister Lourdes arrived with a small package containing the green embroidery threads Francisca needed to finish her mother's gift.

"Shall we work in the garden this morning?" the nun asked.

"That's not necessary; I'm only filling in the leaves." Francisca waited for the encouragement she knew would follow.

"But you need to get out."

"I know," Francisca replied sadly. "Isn't there someplace else we could go?"

"Only Dr. de Souza could authorize leaving the grounds, and he's not available this morning."

"Not off the gounds, someplace else, like the orphanage. I've been so anxious to see the newborn twins you told me about. Are they well?"

The nun looked at Francisca curiously. "I don't really know . . ." Suddenly she smiled mischievously. "Let's go and see."

Nothing had prepared Francisca for the sight of several hundred babies under two years of age lined up in metal cribs in one huge room.

"Easier to watch them all this way," the ward sister explained apologetically. "There's only six of us on duty at any one time, fewer at night. By having them all together we can see immediately who needs tending."

The youngest babies lay six to eight on a bed. On the far side of the ward, only two or three of the older children shared each mattress. Although all the sisters were busy changing diapers, the fecal smell in the room revealed how impossible it was to keep everyone clean. Worse were the apathetic looks on the children.

"Are they all normal?" Francisca asked.

"Most of them. It's hard to tell at this age."

"But look . . . From the size of that one he must be almost two, yet he isn't standing or walking, is he?"

"They learn to walk quite late, since they must be kept in bed so much of the time. Can you imagine if we had a hundred little ones stumbling around? They'd surely injure themselves or each other."

Francisca knelt down and peered through the bars. A wide-eyed baby stared vacantly past her. Francisca clapped her hand and the child started. Once she had her attention, Francisca began to sing. A smile crept across the little face.

"What's that one's name?" Her voice caught in her throat.

Sister Lourdes went to the bottom of the crib and looked at the tag. This is four hundred eleven, female."

"A number, not a name!"

"Some of the favorites have little nicknames, but we reserve the naming as the right of the adoptive parents. They also have secret baptism names that are kept in the records."

Francisca looked horrified.

"You must understand that we are saving these children from infanticide, from cruelty, hunger. When you realize the numbers we take in each year, you will agree that we are doing if not a perfect, still an exemplary, job."

Lifting number four hundred eleven, Francisca was amazed to feel how light and relaxed the child was, more like an infant than the one-year-old that she was. As she stroked the child's smooth neck and back, an idea began to form. "Could I come here to be with the babies? I could talk to them, sing to them, help them learn to walk."

Sister Lourdes pursed her mouth tensely. "I don't think so. We'd never get permission for one of our patients to visit with the babies on a regular basis. I'm sorry."

"But why?" Francisca questioned shrilly.

"Your documents have you listed as potentially violent; you know that, my dear."

"But you can't believe . . ."

"No, I don't."

"Then, couldn't you . . . ?"

Sister Lourdes watched the baby beginning to cling to Francisca. The child's arms were tightening at her neck. "No, I couldn't bring you here. Too many would see you walking across the courtyard, and we must account for your whereabouts every hour of the day."

Francisca spun around so the sister could see the transformation taking place on this one baby's face. Now she was cooing and drooling, pointing to the windows and making happy sounds. "Look at this child and tell me I couldn't do something for her!"

"For her? Do you like this one especially? Or would you like another? Perhaps you could select two or three. They'd never be missed."

Was the sister teasing her in some particularly unkind way? Francisca noted nothing unserious in her words. "You're saying that I would be missed, but a few of these children wouldn't? You're saying that I can have them with me?"

Sister Lourdes's greying eyebrows began to arch merrily. For the first time Francisca saw her as a co-conspirator. "Shall I help select a few?" The nun's arm swept across the room, indicating that Francisca could have her pick.

There they were: hundreds of children! How could she choose just a few of them to love? Still holding her first choice in her arms, Francisca began to walk the rows. Every shade and color of child was on display, from ebony black to the fairest blond. She stopped by a row of children who were just beginning to sit up. One had extremely dark skin but unusually light green eyes with yellow flecks. He bounced merrily as she approached. "That one . . . What's his number?"

The sister looked at the tag. "Nine zero nine. Do you want him?"

Francisca nodded. The sister lifted the baby and followed after. "Where are the twins?"

"In the far corner. The youngest are kept right by the nursing station so they can be observed more closely."

Francisca peered into the basket at the frail babies sleeping side by side. "Boys or girls?"

"Two girls."

"I want them, too."

The sister's head turned away as she spoke. "No. I can't permit it. They aren't expected to live."

"Why not?"

"They aren't doing well on the goat's milk we feed them. If we get them a few months older, they live with more certainty."

"If you give them to me, I can promise they'll survive."

"But how?"

"I'll have their milk bought from an ama de leite. Surely the orphanage can't undertake such an expense."

"Four babies . . . That's certainly enough," Sister Lourdes said seriously. Then, looking at Francisca's determined face, she added, "For a start, considering the exceptional needs of the twins."

"All right, four," Francisca agreed, "as a start."

8 Baby four hundred eleven was named Carolina, nine zero nine was called Rodolfo, and the twins became Adelpha and Gilda. Francisca made an effort not to give them names that would be considered too unusual, yet picked those that were special to her. As she did so, she realized that her own children's names had been selected by Augusto without any consultation.

Francisca's nursery was set up in her new sitting room. All the clothing, special milk, and food was provided by the Larsons, who were convinced that the babies were excellent therapy for Francisca. The truth was that the work the children entailed was completely exhausting. Francisca never complained. Now there was never a minute to be bored, to worry about herself or her problems, for even if she had one of them down for a rest, at least two others would be demanding her full attention. Each twin required feeding every three hours, taking almost an hour for the complete cycle of eating and changing. Carolina was rambunctious as she crawled about the room, pulling herself up on her chunky little legs, then walking hand over hand as far as the furniture would take her. Rodolfo was quieter. He'd sit, sucking his fingers for long periods of time while he watched the commotion in the little room. But once in a while he'd let out a shriek and wouldn't be stilled until he was lifted up and cuddled against Francisca's body. At night, unknown to the sisters, Francisca would take him into her bed, where he'd sleep plastered under her nightgown. Away from her he'd toss and turn, getting her up hourly. Next to her he was completely content.

With maternal feelings blossoming, Francisca thought of little else but her own children, reliving the moments when they were the same ages as her tiny new charges. The orphans were time-consuming, they were lovable and tender, but their presence made Francisca acutely aware that they were not and never would be her own children.

Quietly, with Dr. de Souza himself volunteering to escort her, Francisca had been allowed to be with the Larsons for Christmas, to attend mass at a neighborhood church in Flamengo where her presence would not be unduly noticed; she was then whisked back to the hospital. Augusto had not been informed.

"We'll keep this our little secret," Dr. de Souza had made her promise. But in so doing, she was denied the possibility of seeing her children.

By late January, her parents had begun to make some progress with her court case. "We've been promised a hearing in March," her mother explained. "There's every reason to believe that Augusto will cooperate." Francisca didn't contradict her mother, who had deluded herself from the beginning.

"At least you're still truthful with me," Francisca said to Margaret on the next Wednesday afternoon. While she entertained her guest, she spoon-fed Carolina. Rodolfo was playing at her feet. "Sometimes I wish they'd end all this talk of legal hearings and writs and just tell me, once and for all, that there is nothing more to be done."

"I don't agree with what you're saying, but I understand why you feel as you do. Even criminals have a determinate sentence. But Augusto . . ."

"Don't talk to me about him!" Francisca said so forcefully that Carolina spit up her rice gruel and began to wail. Wiping the mess with one hand, Francisca gesticulated with the other. "Augusto is the happiest man in the world. His wife is alive and well, but completely out of the way. Nobody would look twice at any indiscretion of his because they see him as a man without a woman. Also, he has complete security. Do you think my father or brother would dare to upset him, anger him, even question his judgment? No! They mollify him, treat him like a pampered child. The man has never had more power in his life! 'Make my life difficult,' he says without needing to mouth the words, 'and I'll *never* let Francisca out. Keep me happy and then . . . well . . . perhaps . . .' " She lifted Carolina down and went to change Gilda's pants.

Looking at the soiled diaper, Francisca commented to Margaret, "The milk you've arranged agrees with her so much better. Before . . . the color was greenish black, now it's back to normal."

Margaret turned away from the child's stool. "Don't you have any assistance with the babies at all? I don't think I ever remember seeing you change one of your own babies."

"Sister Lourdes helps me when she can. She adores them almost as much as I do, but her superiors have chastised her for neglecting her other patients. Besides, what else do I have to occupy my time?"

That something so mundane as the state of an orphan's bowels was her friend's sole interest these days was pathetic to Margaret, yet the motley group of castaways in her care had done for Francisca what no one else had. They had given her a reason to go on living, fighting the horror of all that had happened to her. For that Margaret was pleased.

"You're right," Margaret said suddenly. "Augusto is playing this like an expert. Frankly, I hadn't given him credit for being so clever. Nobody can take away from him your children or the income he receives from your dowry!" Margaret helped uncap the bottle of purchased breast milk that had been kept on ice and poured it into a waiting nurser with a long black rubber nipple. "Let me," she said, then proceeded to feed Gilda while Francisca paced nervously.

"Papai must understand that he's taken the wrong tack with Augusto."

"Your father's doing his best to get Augusto to voluntarily have you released."

"Father's ideas would make sense *if* he were trying to convince someone with intelligence. The fact is that Augusto's a very stupid man."

To relieve some of its air, Margaret had lifted the baby to her shoulder, but Francisca said, "She doesn't like that position. Sit her on your lap and just pat her back for a few minutes."

Margaret followed directions and soon was rewarded with an extraordinarily loud belch that made her laugh. "Sounds more like a man's than a baby's!" She began to feed the hungry baby a second time. "What *do* you suggest your father do?"

"I think he — or better still, Gigo — should order Augusto to do a task he won't like. Send him to Bahia to work with Raleigh, take him away from the horses, just make his life unpleasant."

"He'll refuse."

"Of course, we'd expect that. Next, find out where one of his important investments is and manipulate the money so that he loses a significant amount."

"Lose money, purposely? Who would agree to that?"

"It's the only way to apply pressure and begin to prove that he can't make it without our family's approval and guidance. It could be done, couldn't it?"

Margaret thought quietly for a few seconds. "Yes, I'm certain it could, but . . ."

"Bom! Then, Father should order him to permit my children to go to Flamengo for Carnaval. When Augusto resists — as we know he will — Papai can explain about the money Augusto's just lost, thereby proving the power he still has over Augusto. My dear husband will relent on this crucial point, the very first since I've been here."

"I don't see how that solves your situation."

Francisca's eyes twinkled brightly. This was the first time she'd been able to articulate her ideas, and it was gratifying to see they were making sense to someone else. "Dr. de Souza would not object to my making another visit to Flamengo . . . especially at Carnaval."

"But Chiquinha, you're talking about a few hours. Isn't the idea to bring you home once and for all?"

"It can't be done so quickly. Let Augusto see forces working against him from the other direction. Let him know that he doesn't hold all the strings in one hand. Once he truly sees the limits of his options, he will be more receptive to having me released. It will, in the end, become a business transaction, as my marriage was in the first place. Some shares, probably a large number, enough to guarantee him an income without his having to work, will have to be offered. Then I'll bring the children to Flamengo to live, and Augusto will be a very happy, very free, and very wealthy young man. What more could he want?"

Although Margaret's face twisted with disgust, she realized Francisca had outlined a workable, if expensive, plan. She looked down at the baby who'd fallen asleep in her lap. Withdrawing the bottle so as not to disturb her, she looked back up at Francisca's placid face. Her paleness was as appealing as a fragile camellia, and just as pathetic because, like the flower, she bruised at the slightest touch.

"Shall I tell Erik, or do you want to . . . ?"

"No, you do it. They always listen to you."

29 Carnaval! Francisca remembered once asking her mother what it meant. "It comes from a contraction of *carne*, meaning 'meat,' and *vale*, 'to take away,' as from the table. It's a farewell to meat in anticipation of the forty days of abstinence that follow it. But they've turned it into the 'loucura,' the insanity that has become the Carnaval of today."

"Does everyone in the world have a Carnaval?" she'd asked.

"Many places do, but not quite as we have in Brazil. It gets crazier every year." Guilhermina never hid her disgust for the overblown, frantic festivities that took weeks to prepare for and recover from. "It's just an excuse for immorality and excess, if you ask me. Do you have any idea how many are injured, even murdered, during the madness? The cost in time and suffering is too great to justify it," she'd said, defiantly taking an unpopular stand against one of Rio's most treasured traditions.

Not that this ended Carnaval participation in their home. Sven Larson, perhaps because he was a foreigner from a much more restrained culture, was enchanted by the celebration, refusing to miss the lavish society baile at the Teatro Lírico, even though his wife refused to accompany him. His Carnaval costume was legendary. He always dressed as Thor, the Norse god of thunder. Years ago he'd had a silversmith fashion an elegant version of the god's magical hammer that returned when it was thrown and a matching wide belt and gloves of silver mesh that he wore over a golden tunic. How Francisca loved the sight of her handsome father dressed for the baile, and how she had wished she'd someday be old enough to attend it with him.

"When you're sixteen," he'd promised. But her sixteenth Carnaval found her in a convent school in New Orleans.

It was not necessary to count the days until Carnaval. One had only to listen to the beat echoing down from the hillside favelas. As it grew louder, more insistent, the day neared. Though theoretically Carnaval officially began on the evening of Sábado Gordo, or Fat Saturday, and ended at midnight on Shrove Tuesday, unofficially it had begun weeks before.

Once, when she was about twelve, Francisca had observed a much younger and slimmer Zefinha practicing for Carnaval with one of the cook's assistants. They were doing a special samba called a gafieira, a kind of honky-tonk or low-class dance. Eduardo, the cocky, skinny boy in the kitchen, was transformed at Carnaval time by his special position as the mestre-sala, or master of ceremonies, of his samba club. He'd won this position because of the incredible acrobatics he'd taught himself.

Eduardo could do any step that he'd been shown, in double time, making it seem effortless. Zefinha would dance around him, letting him be the center of the show; then, when he'd lean way back, with his head inches from the floor, he'd extend his arm, wriggle his fingers toward her, beckoning suggestively. She'd advance with her hips pumping, her generous buttocks keeping time in the rear. Finally, Zefinha and Eduardo would hold each other tightly, but off center, so that as they spun about they used their bodies as counterweights. Eduardo would lift Zefinha and bounce her rhythmically from one side to the other, so erotically that Francisca remembered a tightening sensation between her own legs that was excruciatingly pleasant. From then on, the coming of Carnaval was always fraught not only with the impending excitement of the celebration but with a nameless anxiety that the fulminating energy stirred within Francisca.

But this year was different. This year Carnaval meant her day of freedom, her day alone with her children in a safe haven, a day to tell them all of her love for them and explain the unexplainable. This year every beat from the tamborim drum, every vibration from the cuica, every pulsation from the hollow-sounding surdo, brought the crazy days closer and closer. And for once Francisca welcomed them fully.

❧ ❧ ❧

Dr. de Souza stood in the doorway to Francisca's little visiting room that was now primarily a nursery. "I'm afraid I have some very difficult news," he said slowly.

Francisca was holding the littler twin, Adelpha, in her arms. Patting the child's wiry head as she listened, she tried to remain calm.

"The plans . . . for Carnaval . . ." His voice was hoarse with emotion. "They must be canceled."

Francisca started so violently the sleeping baby woke and began to cry.

The doctor looked at the distraught woman sympathetically. "We tried to make arrangements, but your husband became suspicious about the children being at your parents' house. He's gotten a document to prevent your release until the next hearing."

"How did he know of our plans?"

The doctor shrugged. "I suspect he paid someone for information, either one of your servants or someone here. It's hard to resist a few extra coins, especially at Carnaval time."

Francisca was pathetically silent as she mulled over her limited choices. The baby's whimpering had stopped, so she laid her down on her mat and covered her with a gauzy blanket.

"It was my one chance . . ."

"I've done all I can, Dona Francisca," he said respectfully.

Looking up at the swarthy man, Francisca saw compassion and kindness in his drooping eyes. If only he were a cruel administrator, it would be easier, she thought unexpectedly. If she could only hate him or Sister Lourdes, but no, they both were unfailingly kind.

"My father is pursuing the legal matters more forcefully,

so . . ." To prevent the doctor from noticing the tears welling up in her eyes, she quickly turned toward the window. Outside the far gate a street peddler was hawking coconut candy to the beat of a samba tune. She turned back to where the doctor still waited uneasily. He seemed not to know where to position his feet.

"I'm afraid it's going to be very hot for Carnaval this year," he began finally.

Adelpha let out a little cry, then turned herself over and quieted. " 'February's the worst month of the year,' my mother'd always say. She never participated in Carnaval, never permitted me to either."

"You've never been to a baile?" he asked.

"No, never. My brother has always gone, and Augusto, even Margaret, but I . . . I just couldn't."

Knowing as much as he did about her past, the doctor nodded glumly. "There's enough of a show in the streets to satisfy any Carioca, eh?" he said lightly. "Here at the hospital we have a little Carnaval of our own. We all wear costumes, staff and residents alike."

"It must be difficult to tell who is to be locked in at night, isn't it?" Francisca's tone was only slightly ironic.

The doctor started to reply, then stopped. He walked across the threshold and closed the door firmly. "That's really why I've come. You'll be needing a good costume, something that disguises you well, like an old colonial gown, plumes, something very festive."

"But I've told you I don't . . ." Francisca stopped abruptly and stared at the doctor in disbelief.

His eyebrows curved upward jauntily. "That's the trouble with Carnaval . . . All the confusion . . . Only half the staff covering the floors. Impossible to keep track of any but the most dangerous and difficult cases. One person, costumed for Carnaval, could so easily be missed for a night . . . even two."

"But how. . . ?"

"A door left carelessly open, a momentary lapse, that's all it takes."

"Oh! Dr. de Souza, how can I ever . . . ?" Francisca rushed forward and kissed both his hands.

❧ 10 The week before Sábado Gordo, Margaret arrived at the asylum with a costume made over from one she'd worn early in her pregnancy with their first child. Francisca remembered that Gigo had been a gorgeous Bacchus that year, draped in a toga of bronze lamé that perfectly complemented his lightly tanned skin and golden hair, while Margaret, as Diana, had worn a matching fabric that tied at her shoulders, then draped discreetly over her expectant belly. It had been a private joke for her to go as the goddess of women and protector of childbirth even before the announcement of her pregnancy.

"It was the easiest to alter," Margaret said as she unwrapped the dress, "because it wasn't fitted at the waist. Besides, it was the most modest one I still have."

Francisca was grateful that Margaret realized she wouldn't want to bare as much of her body as was the custom these days. For one or two nights a year even well-bred ladies were not averse to exposing large areas of torso or bosom.

As they spoke, Rodolfo crawled toward them and began pulling on something in the box. Margaret gently uncurled his fingers from around the snakeskin sash that was designed to bind the folds of the dress in a Grecian fashion.

"You'd better hide that. I'm not supposed to have belts, you know."

"Ridiculous!"

"Of course. Look around you." Her arms encompassed the nursery. "With all the babies' clothing and bedding I could fashion any style of rope I should want."

Now Rodolfo had discovered a second box and was biting the lid.

"Não, não . . ." Margaret diverted the chubby baby in the opposite direction. She opened the box and showed Francisca the headdress of black and white ostrich plumes with a matching mask. She put it up to her own face and giggled as the feathers fluttered around her face. "This will do marvelously, won't it?" She handed it to Francisca, who played peekaboo with the mask. Instead of being amused, Rodolfo screamed in fright.

Francisca put the mask down and went to comfort him. "Now, now . . . it's all right. Mamãe's here."

"Mamãe?" Margaret spoke without thinking.

"Every child needs to have someone to call Mother," Francisca replied defensively. "It makes me feel better, too. Truly, though, I live only to see my own. Now that it's so close, I'm terrified."

"Don't worry, all the arrangements are settled, thanks to Dr. de Souza."

"It's not that; it's the children themselves. Surely Augusto and the Cavalcantis have not been truthful with them. Perhaps they've been told I'm some kind of monster."

"When you're alone with them, you won't need words. Remember how close you were to each of them? I've seen them recently and they haven't changed. Each one is as healthy and beautiful as ever."

"You saw them? Where?"

"They were brought to Flamengo on Sunday. Your father insisted. He's getting tougher with Augusto, as you suggested. If your husband doesn't come around soon, your father will be sending him to Bahia to work with Raleigh. But of course Augusto's resisting that."

"He'd hate the backlands — no racehorses, no Carioca women. Anyone would. I really don't understand how Raleigh and Marianne have withstood it for so long."

"Raleigh likes the freedom of it, the responsibility. He's the ruler of a little kingdom, makes decisions independent of everyone, even the law sometimes. When I lived at Vassouras the peasants would come to me to settle disputes. I know what it's like to have them look to you. You're a Solomon. The power — it can be intoxicating. However, I don't think living in the north has been as good for Marianne as it has been for my brother."

"Why?"

"She's a very sensitive woman. In her letters she writes about the terrible drought on the sertão. The peasants suffer terribly; there are many deaths. It's a hard life for most of them."

"But Raleigh has a large house, doesn't he? They should want for little."

"They have what they need ... and more. That's part of Marianne's problem. She's so kindhearted that she can't bear the suffering of those around her. But no matter how much she does or gives, there's a hundred more who have nothing. I think she's eternally frustrated."

"Frustrated!" Francisca pointed to the bars on her window and began to laugh in an odd high-pitched way. "How many Brazilian women do you know who aren't frustrated? My mother's been cloistered behind the high walls of privilege all her life. And what about you? Hasn't your life been one of exquisite frustration? You were left in New Orleans against your will, sent to Brazil in opposition to your wishes, married off before you were well enough to decide for yourself."

"But I . . ."

"Come, now," Francisca said forcefully, "you and I. We're finally beyond not saying what we mean, aren't we?"

"I would've married Erik even if I never had that fever."

"If you had known about Isabel?"

Margaret pondered for just a moment. "Yes, I believe I would have, if he'd told me about her himself. At that time I didn't worry about Astrid, so why should I have worried about the other children?"

"Their mother wasn't dead, Margaret."

"If he'd promised me . . ."

"Maybe he wouldn't have."

Margaret began to redden, but she kept her temper. "I don't understand why you are saying all this when you worked so hard to reunite us. Now it sounds as though you are trying to destroy what's been rebuilt."

"Has it really?" Francisca's tone was unusually sour. "I thought there were parts of your marriage that were closed."

"That's only because of his illness."

"You're making a mistake to follow the doctor's orders."

"Francisca! Erik's been better now than he has been in months. He's planning to go to England for the Derby after Easter. I wouldn't want to ruin that for him."

"What's being ruined for you?"

"That part of a marriage isn't important to me — not anymore."

By the tightness around her lips, Francisca knew she wasn't telling the truth. "Isn't it?"

"You know me too well." Margaret forced a smile.

"Well enough to give you advice. You must go to England with Erik, you must stay with him as much as possible. You must bring him back to your bed. Have more babies. Susana isn't enough for you."

"I think he's fathered enough children, don't you?"

An image of Amara floated in front of Francisca. She blinked to dissolve it. "So that's it," she said slowly. "You are using his illness as an excuse to punish him. No more children. Once I talked to Erik and explained that there are two kinds of people: those who love their children best and those who love their spouses best. The greatest difference between you and my brother is that you are the kind of person who will always love her husband more than her children, yet he's the opposite!"

"I don't agree with you, but I don't wish to argue. If everything were as simple as you make it seem . . ."

"If you weren't so stubborn, it could be simple. Few of us have the choices you do. Marianne's trapped in Bahia, I'm here . . ." One of the twins was stirring. Francisca began to speak more rapidly. "You're the only wife in our family who has choices, the only one who can speak for herself, who can make more of her life."

"What can I do?" Margaret spoke in a tiny voice.

"You can choose your music, your child, your husband. You can have all of them, or some, or none."

"I've always wanted them all! Erik too! You're right. I desire him still, but I keep away from him because I'm afraid to hurt him. He gets sick so easily; it's more of a problem than he lets on. Any excess affects his illness: food, drink, passion, anger. Lately he's so impatient. He's actually jealous of my music. Soon, when Maestro Freire returns, I'll be asked to perform his new works, take a more active part in the Music Academy. When I do, Erik could get upset, could get sick."

"Perhaps you can't have it all." Francisca went over to see which of the babies was awakening.

"Then . . ."

"Then you have the luxury of decision." Francisca touched Gilda's soaked gown. "Make your choices for yourself and also . . . make them for me."

❦11

Viva o Zé Pereira
Viva o Zé Pereira
Viva o Zé Pereira
Nos dias de Carnaval!

Boom! Boom! The drums pounded, the horns blasted. Carnaval officially opened with the classic marcha, paying homage to the famous Portuguese musican of the 1850s with the flowing mustache who marched through the steets of Rio pounding a big bass drum. Now every samba club had its own version of Zé Pereira, coxswain of the beat. Even the asylum had its own Zé, an orderly known as much for his good humor as for his viselike grip, which could restrain even the most ungovernable patient.

The big bass drum woke Francisca at dawn the morning of Carnaval Sunday. Zé was leading a group of revelers who had decided to serenade the inmates after a long night on the town. Francisca looked down at the exhausted crowd all dressed in colorful Zouave uniforms and carrying signs saying they were from the Tenentes do Diabo club.

When they had the attention of a hundred or more patients, they put on their entire presentation, the one they hoped would win them a prize in the competition that night on the Avenida Central. Their imaginative theme was based on the jôgo do bicho, the popular lottery that used animals and numbers to select the winners. Members of the samba club were dressed in fantastic costumes portraying a baron and his zoo of beasts, finery that had taken women weeks to sew and had cost the club almost as much as their members could earn in a year.

"Incredible waste!" Guilhermina Larson had always scoffed.

"Think of the people who are employed ... from the seamstresses to the mill workers who must produce the fabric," Sven Larson had retorted heartily. His own line of inexpensive but glittery satins sold particularly well for Carnaval costumes.

After the samba club had danced its routine, the patients began screaming down in appreciation, "Já ganhou! Já ganhou! You've got it made!" When they danced off finally to get some rest before the big parade, the patients sang their theme song after them.

Only a few more hours, Francisca told herself. The excitement,

the music, all were mounting to the point where Francisca wondered how she would be able to get through the day. Fortunately,
there were diversions by the hour. A bateria began in the men's
inner courtyard. All day long she could hear the yelp of the cuica
and the percussive bursts from the tamborim, while on the other
side of the barrier, where the dangerous women were penned,
came the whoop, whoop, whoop sound of their dancing and
shouting. Francisca tried to imagine what would happen if, on
this festive night, the two groups, kept naked, sometimes even
shackled, were permitted to commingle. Ah, what a Carnaval that
would be!

A small, pathetic party was organized for the women in her
wing during the afternoon. Everyone dressed up, if only in a
draped sheet or paper plume. Francisca felt ridiculous gowned as
a goddess at midday, but she saw the charade as a necessary ad-
junct to her evening plan.

Tables dotted the lawns between the royal palms in the patients' garden. The February sun beat relentlessly on the west
side of the building, then reflected off the white linen cloths.
Platters of sweet coconut cakes, candies, and fruit jellies shimmered and melted while the residents padded around in mock
merriment.

"At least it shouldn't rain tonight." Sister Lourdes chattered
kindly as they each sipped an orange juice. "Nothing sadder than
a rain-soaked Carnaval parade, don't you agree?"

"Yes, you're right about that." Francisca was trying to concentrate on being pleasant. Only a few more hours, she reminded
herself. It was so hot that even the looseness of Diana's gown, still
unbound by the snakeskin belt, was impossible to bear. The humidity was so thick that all the pores of her skin seemed to open
in order to find relief. "If it doesn't cool off soon, how will they be
able to dance without collapsing?" she wondered aloud.

"Last year we cared for a group of dancers who, when they
wound their way downtown through the narrow shaded streets
out to one of the sun-drenched boulevards, scorched the skin off
the soles of their feet. *Jornal do Brasil* had it on the front page as
the 'tragedy of the year' because the whole escola de samba
troupe had been too injured to perform for the judges; a year's
work had been lost."

"Let's hope that more are spared this year," Francisca replied sympathetically.

"Every year there's always something!" The nun sighed. "You know that mischief makers are only locked up for the duration."

"They say that's the worst punishment of all."

"At least they're off the streets for a few hours. They're always let out the morning of Ash Wednesday without further persecution, no matter the crime."

"Once after Carnaval we were driving by the jail and my father pointed out the people waiting in front to see if their relatives were inside. He called it the 'Que é que vou dizer em casa?' or 'What am I going to say at home?' bloco, or Carnaval group. If you were looking for someone you lost during Carnaval, the jail was the most likely place to find them. If they weren't there, you'd next try the hospitals or the morgues."

Sister Lourdes nodded. "I treated a stabbing victim a few years ago. Later I heard that his attacker had been charged with 'inserting foreign matter into the human anatomy,' then released with the rest."

A commotion near the food had Sister Lourdes up and running, her grey habit floating behind like a wayward cloud. An obese patient had flung herself across one of the tables and was smearing herself with pastries. It took three nurses to restrain her.

A few minutes later an overheated patient poured fruit juice over her head. Seeing this, a few others tried it on themselves and each other until the flinging got out of hand. When some red juice was splashed on Sister Lourdes's white veil, the offenders were finally hustled inside. Nauseated, Francisca looked the other way, past the padlocked gates to the broiling street.

To live behind bars, walls, gates! No one outside could imagine what it was really like. Francisca stared at the top of the wall where shards of glass were embedded in the mortar to discourage escapes and watched a large green lizard skitter across the vertical surface, oblivious to the obstacle, then crawl to the trunk of a palm on the other side and scurry up toward the nuts.

She tilted her head way back to look high up, where the malachite-green fronds touched each other like stars in a crowded sky. Because the trees had been planted in two neat rows, the canopy they formed was a perfect rectangle with a slice of burning sunlight pouring through. This vision, so perfectly symmetrical and pleasing, relaxed her. She breathed slowly in and out in rhythm with the light breeze that swayed the tops of the trees. The blue hole in the sky was like a promise of freedom, sucking her up and into it. A few more hours, she said on an inward breath, then let it out slowly and closed her eyes. A few more hours. Then she'd be . . . what? Away for a night, possibly two? No! She opened her eyes and followed a brilliant shaft of light down to where it illuminated the gate, the wrought iron dazzling silver in the glare. I won't go back! Papai and Gigo will find a safe place to keep me until this is settled. Possibly Vassouras, even Bahia, someplace where the governor of Rio and all of Augusto's writs will be worthless. Why hadn't she thought of this before?

She felt a gentle hand on her shoulder. "It's time to go in," Sister Lourdes was saying.

Francisca was beaming. "Sim, it's time."

❦ ❦ ❦

Beyond the three sets of gates that their keepers had temporarily deserted to join the festivities blazed a spectacle so glorious that to Francisca the incandescence was like sunshine without the heat. It would have been thrilling enough just to have been alone on the street, liberated, but also to have exultant crowds streaming past, singing, dancing, shimmering with abandon, was such a fresh sensation that Francisca found herself transported with the sheer novelty of it.

Here she was, the mother of four children, almost thirty-two years of age, and she couldn't remember ever being alone on the streets of Rio before, not during the day, not during the night, certainly never at Carnaval. Always she had been chaperoned by her mother, a friend, her husband, or a servant. Her mother had taught her a saying in the nursery: "A woman and a hen shouldn't go out walking; a hen gets eaten, a woman sets folks talking." Though impetuous at times, she never dared to disobey this dictim, for being seen alone in the city would have ruined her reputation forever.

As quickly as possible, Francisca moved away from the Santa Casa walls toward where the Protos was supposed to be waiting for her on the corner of the Rua Santa Luzia. The plan had been to meet Erik and Margaret at the earliest possible hour after darkness fell, which in this tropical zone was always quite close to nineteen hours. As best as she could estimate, it was just about that time, but the clock tower chimes had been drowned out by the omnipresent songs and shouts of Carnaval.

Though it was still early in the evening, dense throngs had already begun moving to the marshaling point for the parades. Whole blocos, temporary neighborhood groups organized to compete for prizes, filled the street as they rehearsed for the greatest moment of the year, now only a few hours away. The Rua Santa Luzia was one of the main arteries leading toward the plaza where the secondary clubs were grouped. As soon as Francisca arrived at the appointed corner, she realized the hopelessness of their choice for a rendezvous. Seas of satin-covered bodies bursting with sequins and baubles replaced the usual carriages and automobiles. Francisca searched for any sign of the Protos but was pushed aside by a tide of black men costumed in swallow-tailed coats and wide breeches called bombachas. The moment she stepped out on the street, she was pushed and shoved down several narrow alleys before she realized she'd never get back in the other direction. Her one chance would be to follow the masses who were converging on the judging stands. At least there she could find a car for hire that would take her home to Flamengo.

With renewed confidence she followed the edge of the swaying rancho, a strolling group of dancers dressed in glittering silver-and-black costumes, as it undulated down the avenida. She felt like a tiny boat being carried along by a buoyant wave. Ahead of her she could see the plaza illuminated by Bengal torches filled with incandescent powders that burned in lurid pinks, oranges, and purples and gave off great puffs of acrid smoke. At first glance, the writhing crowd bathed in the ghoulish light seemed like an illustrated sermon on the horrors of Hades, but a closer look at the innocent merriment transformed the scene into something wondrously inviting.

"Cuidado com a cabeça!" a dancer shouted, pushing Francisca out of the way of a flag bearer whose spiraling pole had almost hit her in the head.

Francisca dutifully ducked away from the demonstration of twirling colors. "Obrigada!"

"De nada," the dancer, shining from a sheen of sweat, said. Then, to keep Francisca, who was obviously not a member of the rancho, out of the mainstream, she placed her hands around her waist and sambaed with her to the curb. At first Francisca was flustered, but when she realized that it was easier to dance her way out than to walk, her right foot picked up the beat.

"Ôpa! Ôpa!" The dancer clapped in appreciation while Francisca finished the samba. "Next year you must join us, eh? Our rancho's called the Flower of the Avocado!" The dancer laughed so forcefully that one of her barely concealed breasts shimmied loose from her corset. Without missing a step, she tucked it back into her colonial costume and patted her elaborate powdered wig festooned with flowers and brightly colored jungle birds. Just before she floated off with her troupe, she blew kisses to Francisca.

While Francisca let them pass around the corner, she tried to ascertain where she was. Once-familiar streets looked different in the fantastic illuminations. Garlands of flowers hung from baroque buildings, pointing up the fancy wrought-iron work, flamboyant domes, and roof statuary beloved of Iberian architects. Signposts were bedecked with paper serpentines, making them impossible to read. Francisca felt a spasm of terror tighten in her chest when she realized she was lost. The only familiar landmarks were the curlicued lightposts that bisected the Avenida Central, glowing in a steady orange line in the distance. At the opening of the street, however, the way was barred by helmeted police who were permitting only the slow corso of touring cars to parade down the avenue. Now, at least, she thought she had her bearings. As far as she could see, Rio's most elegant automobiles were lined up with elaborately costumed revelers standing on the seats to toss confetti and paper flowers at the spectators. The drivers were wearing immaculate white suits and Panama hats, and most sported pencil-thin mustaches of such uniformity of thickness and length that they must have been false.

One of the waiting cars, a huge black Packard with a rolled-down canvas top and shiny brass trim pulled alongside Francisca. "Going to the grandstand?" the driver asked politely.

Francisca stared at the well-groomed gentleman whose dark hair was so well greased it shone like patent leather. His car was already filled with at least eight young men and women in eighteenth-century court costumes, carrying baskets of freshly picked roses.

"Sim, but there's not room." Francisca gestured to all his other passengers.

Wordlessly, one of the men lifted her onto the running board. In a few seconds she glided past the guards.

"Oh, look at that!" one of the women called excitedly. "Formidável!"

Down the Avenida Central the alegorias, or floats, were passing by. The first construction was a Viking ship with a bank of fifty oars on each side moving in time to the music. Alongside it came hundreds of dancers carrying yards of diaphanous cloth that represented the ocean. When the music changed, their gentle waving motion became a turbulent, writhing sea that won cheers and whistles from onlookers and participants alike.

"Magnífico, eh?" The driver called over to Francisca, then winked. "Who are you, anyway? The sun goddess?"

"Não, Diana."

"But of course." He smiled brilliantly.

One of the women touched her dress. "Beleza," she said, rubbing the fine lamé between her fingers. She touched the snakeskin sash. "Elegante!" she complimented. "Have you lost your companions?"

"Sim. They should be in a car."

"Do you think you would recognize it in this crowd?"

"It's a Protos."

"A very large one, yes, but in all this . . ." The standing woman swept her lace-bedecked wrist back to a line of hundreds of vehicles that followed them and across to as many or more ahead. Serpentines of streamers being thrown between the slow-moving cars had them intertwined like links in a great moving chain. Under all the paper and confetti it was difficult even to recognize where one car began and another ended.

Francisca sighed audibly. "I will just have to find my own way home."

"Alone? In the midst of Carnaval?" The woman, whose face was painted in metallic hues, patted her hand. "Why don't you join our party?"

Before she had a chance to reply to the offer, a torpedo burst a few feet from the car. Everyone screamed at the noise and flare. Just after it came a new float, a giant hearse drawn by a dozen mules with grey plumes like puffs of steam jutting from their heads. In the hearse was the figure of death, with a scythe in one hand and an hourglass in the other. His mask was a skeleton's face, but he had flame-colored hair. Surrounding him were dozens of half-naked cannibals calling out to pretty girls that they wanted to eat them. More firecrackers blasted in their wake.

Someone screamed. Francisca saw a young boy holding up a scorched hand from a misfired torpedo. He was carried away to the edge of the crowd quickly enough for the cars to continue their slow crawl without braking.

Inside her head Francisca could hear her mother's voice complaining about the number of senseless Carnaval injuries. Thinking of her, and everyone waiting and worrying about her at home, renewed her desire to find a way out of the crowds as quickly as possible. "Obrigada!" she called to her new-found friends as she stepped from the running board when it stopped to let a group depicting Neptune riding a giant fish pass by.

"Até logo, Dee . . . ah . . . nnna! A noite e uma criança!" the driver shouted affectionately as he put his car in gear. "The night is still young!"

Francisca pushed her way through a tangle of children dressed as little fish who were part of Neptune's retinue. If she could only get to the far side of the judging area, she was certain to find a car for hire that could maneuver down a side street and get her on the beach road to Flamengo. The closer she came to the spectator stands, though, the more frenzied the celebrants became. She squeezed her way through the few interstices in the shoulder-to-shoulder crowd, her heart beating wildly. Got to get home, got to get home, she thought in a panic.

Here the peculiar smells of Carnaval were an overwhelming

mixture of sweat, beer, and the sickly sweet ether odor of the lança-perfumes, the most traditional objects of the festival. Derived from the ancient Portuguese tradition of the entrudo, the original lemon-shaped wax balls had been filled with perfumed water if one was lucky, or urine if one was not. Officially banned sixty years earlier, the entrudos were now only glass tubes of ether that were squirted at passers-by as a harmless way to get attention. Servant could squirt master with impunity; a politician could be sprayed without retribution. As children, Francisca and Erik had been permitted small vials of the stuff to use on each other and their nannies. Erik had shown her the peculiar, not unpleasant effect just sniffing the vapor could have. However, at that moment, the odors of the crowd and the lança-perfumes were equally upsetting. Got to get home, she told herself once more, inching her way forward.

A shout, which had begun half a mile away, seemed infectious. From group to group the call was coming. "Fen-i-anos! Fen-i-anos!" The chant grew louder and louder as the most popular club, winners of the top prize for the past several years, came into view. Some young boys standing next to Francisca started to climb on each other's backs to get a better view.

"Here they come!" one shouted and pointed down the Avenida Central. At his cry, the crowd surged forward. Francisca stumbled, then tried to turn back out of the way. Just as she spun around, a squirt from someone's nearby lança-perfume bottle hit her in the face, stinging her eyes severely. Wiping her face on her sleeve, she stumbled blindly toward the underside of the grandstand. Opening her lids to see where she was, she groped for a rough-hewn wooden support and leaned against it, blinking her eyes to tear out the irritating poison.

In a few seconds she could see clearly again, but she decided to wait until the confusion of the Fenian extravaganza had passed. From the howls and cheers in the rows of seats above her, she could tell they were being well received. Looking upward, all she could see, however, were hundreds of feet pounding the planks in time to the fast-moving samba march named after someone called Filomena and featuring long, plaintive choruses of "Ai, ai, ai!" The hollow beats of a hundred drums seemed to come in layers.

Under the grandstand the "whoop, whoop, whoop" from the bateria in the performing arena sounded like a cacophony of jungle birds.

The music ended. A great silence, then exuberant booming cheers screaming, "Mais! Mais! More! More!" The crowd above her thumped their feet with enthusiasm.

The Fenian bateria began their song once again, doubling the time of the first version. "Filomena! Filomena! Ai, ai, ai!" Everyone in the grandstand joined in with the chorus, pulsating faster and faster. "Filomena! Filomena!" The beat had the compelling steadiness that promised it would go down as one of the most popular sambas. Even Francisca found herself stamping her foot on the pavement. She guessed that the beautiful young Brazilian girl, most probably from a humble family, who'd inspired the song was in her glory that night.

> Filomena, Filomena,
> Ó vem comigo,
> Vem, minha santinha . . .
> Come with me,
> Come, my little saint . . .

A sound like nearby thunder rolled above her. For a second Francisca thought that a sudden shower would soon dampen the festivities, but then a closer crack of splitting wood proved it was something else. Dust, grit, falling objects rained around her. She brushed the dirt from her hair and, confused by what was happening, peered up through the cracks in the grandstand.

Though the pounding footsteps above her had sounded one last throbbing whomp, the next beat never followed. In that silent second Francisca looked out toward the street, which glowed with torches and colors, then again up at the swaying above her. An enormous funnel filled with boards and sand was cascading on top of her.

"Filomena . . . come my little saint." The words hung in the air as her vision of a bronzed and shimmering young mulatta dancer was replaced by that of the carved wooden saint in her mother's bedroom altar. Its plaster face, its gilded crown, dissolved into a dusty cloud.

"Fil . . . o . . . men . . . a!"

Francisca couldn't move. A great weight pressed the breath from her. She couldn't suck air in or out. Her nostrils flared once as though feeling for a clean breath, then tightened against the choking sand.

"Filo . . ."

"Mamãe!" she sputtered. Something warm, wet, and iron-tasting flowed freely from her mouth.

"Ai, ai, ai!" The words were now a communal scream. Yet for Francisca, instead of getting louder, the last sound was but a diminishing echo at the end of a long, obscure chamber, before it ceased forever.

❧ Part IV ❧
JOAQUIM
1907

❧

Brazil will be a great nation only when
you can look at any Brazilian without
being able to distinguish the race from
which he sprang.
— José Bonifacio de Andrada e Silva,
father of Brazilian independence

The Kite

1 The square in front of Nossa Senhora da Candelária appeared to undulate in the glare of the midmorning sun. Already several of the mourners waiting to gain entrance to the cathedral had fainted from the intensity of the heat. Joaquim Freire looked up at the gleaming white marble dome that seemed like an immense eyeball focused on heaven. The brightness bothered him. He wondered if his tropical vision had been ruined forever by the pallid European skies to which he'd become accustomed during his three years abroad. Shading his face with his hands, he searched for his friends in the immense crowd that had gathered to pay their last respects to Maria Francisca de Lourenço Larson Cavalcanti.

"Quincas!"

He turned to see Delgado de Mello walking in his direction with a decided limp. "Delgado, what's wrong?"

"A touch of the gout." De Mello patted the guitar that Freire had slung across one shoulder. "So, you did agree to play?"

"Sim, but I'll play some simple pieces by Fernando Sor, not my own. Everyone will agree that vanity has no place today."

"Everyone?" De Mello raised his eyebrows meaningfully. "Wasn't it Dona Margarida who made the request?"

"Yes, when I went to pay my respects to the family."

"How did Erico receive you?"

"Politely. I don't think he holds any grudges. A tragedy like this tends to put all else in its proper place, doesn't it?"

"Indeed."

The two men walked side by side up the cathedral steps, de Mello even more round and paunchy than before Freire had left for Europe; Freire slimmer, more intense in appearance, more nervous in gesture. They paused before the church's three baroque solid bronze doors. Freire read the inscription on the base of the life-sized statue. "It's Saint Genevieve. I never noticed that before. Odd, isn't it?"

"Why's that?" De Mello stood aside to allow a large group of mourners to stream into the sanctuary.

"She's the patron saint of Paris. Wonder what she's doing here? Do you think she came all this way to haunt me?" He frowned.

"Aren't you being a bit melodramatic, my old friend?"

"Perhaps. Still, this is not the homecoming I'd imagined. I waited until Carnaval because I wanted to arrive in a burst of laughter and music."

The crowd pushing from behind forced them into the nave. De Mello leaned against a column of green marble and stared at the cathedral's elaborately gilded ceiling. "When this tragedy passes over, we'll have a proper welcome for you: concerts, balls, perhaps even a gala at the new Teatro Municipal."

Joaquim stroked his guitar's back as if he were comforting it. "Que pena! A whole family, crushed by the weight of this disaster. How must old Sven Larson feel to have had so much good fortune in business and so little with his children. It's like a curse."

The door behind them opened and they were ushered into the narthex. "So you've been told about Erico's problems?" de Mello whispered.

"The Nettos said that his disease has worsened considerably."

"What else did they tell you about the Larsons?"

"All about the troubles between Erico and Margarida. They're not rumors, are they?"

"I wish they were," Delgado said morosely.

They moved toward the wall to allow a cluster of nuns, all wearing the habit of the same order, to pass. Each was dabbing her eyes with a white handkerchief.

"Who are they?" Joaquim asked.

"The sisters from Santa Casa, the hospital where Francisca was a patient."

"Weep they should. It's their negligence that caused this!"

"Quincas, its more complicated than that."

"What's to understand? The poor, sick woman disappeared during Carnaval, was missing from the hospital for three days before they finally found her crushed under the grandstand on the Avenida Central. I only hope she didn't suffer for too long."

"A terrible accident, truly, but there's more to it. She was on her way to see her children. It had all been arranged. Didn't anyone explain?"

Joaquim recognized Lucretia Claiborne in the crowd, being supported by Margaret's younger sister. He walked forward to greet them. "Senhora and Senhorita Claiborne, my deepest condolences."

Lucretia stared at the composer's proffered hand, then turned away without a word.

"Obrigada, Maestro," Kate whispered as she passed by.

An assistant priest stepped forward and touched Freire's shoulder. "You may begin at any time."

De Mello followed Freire and the priest to where a raised platform had been set across from the north transept. Self-consciously, Freire tuned his guitar, a Bouchet that he'd bought in France after being inspired by the playing of Francesco Tarrega, and slowly began the first chords of Sor's Etude in B Minor. A hush fell over the mourners as the bell-like notes echoed through the vast cathedral. The shafts of light that streamed down the center aisles were snuffed out as the doors to the street were closed to bar the curious. Francisca's mother, supported on one side by her gaunt and weary husband and on the other by her son, proceeded forward. Margaret followed behind, holding the hands of Francisca's two eldest children. She was pathetically thin, with dark sunken eyes. Just after her came Zefinha, carrying Francisca's littler boy and holding the hand of her younger girl.

At the sight of the children, Joaquim's fingers faltered. He struggled through the next few bars but then brought Sor's work to a swifter conclusion than the composer had intended. Only Delgado de Mello noticed the musical interruption, for at the entrance of the motherless children, the sobs in the cathedral rose to cover the music.

2 Joaquim stood in front of the mirror, adjusting his high stiff collar and practicing what words he might use when Margaret arrived for the first meeting of the Music Society since his return. After speaking only the nasal, clipped French language for several years, he was finding it a palatable pleasure to roll his tongue around the hushed, suggestive consonants of his native Portuguese. He well understood the reason he worked so hard to make the right impression with his euphonious speech: it was far easier to change the tone of one's voice than of one's skin. Even in Brazil, where "classismo" meant more than "racismo," Freire continued to be apprehensive that his color put people off before he'd proved himself.

Smoothing his curly, close-cut hair back of his ears, he studied his face. From his father he'd inherited his handsome Portuguese facial structure, with high cheekbones, a thin nose, and a strong square jaw, but he couldn't deny that he still was first categorized by his mother's pale sable skin. In a peculiar way, his race had been an asset in Paris. "The Brazilian composer," they'd whisper when he passed. Once, after he'd met Henri Rousseau, he'd been told that the painter had remarked later that he had admired "the graceful honey-skinned savage." Freire had laughed along with the taleteller, but the fact that the great man had referred to his skin and not his talent had not left him unscathed.

With more than an hour to wait until the Fluminense Music Society members were due, he doubled-checked to see that his old housekeeper, Jacobina, had followed every order he'd given over the last few days. More than once that day he'd overheard her complaining that he was worse than a woman with all his fussing. Still, since this was also the first time Margaret Larson would be seeing his home, he wanted to make the precisely correct impression.

"Do you think it proper to even invite her?" he'd asked the Nettos at dinner recently.

"I can't see why not. It's not as though she's as reclusive as she was after her baby died. I know she's already organized a school at Boa Vista for all the family's children."

"Remarkable," Freire had said. "To undertake the care of so many when only one is her own. How many are there altogether?"

"There are Erico's two, Francisca's four, plus the four orphan babies."

"Orphan babies?" Freire'd asked.

"Francisca adopted them at the asylum. She was a woman of rare goodness. And then" — Nicia had paused meaningfully — "there are the three others. I believe that makes thirteen in all."

"Do you mean she's also taken in Erico's bastards?" Freire had long known about Isabel da Silva. Her house was only half a mile down the Santa Teresa hill from his own.

"After Francisca's death, Margaret promised to start a school for *all* the family's children, so I suppose she's only keeping her vow."

That anything should deter such a talented pianist from a rigorous course of study was a tragic waste to Joaquim, especially when he needed her. So much of his new music had been written, not unconsciously, with her particular touch in mind. Freire looked out onto the street expectantly. At least Nicia Netto had promised she'd bring Margaret to this meeting. Though there was only a slim chance Margaret might agree to his plan, his heart beat too quickly just thinking she might react positively. But it was far too early to expect anyone yet. "Maldito!" he cursed. He closed the shutter that looked out onto the Rua Monte Alegre, the tree-lined street that was an oasis above the noisy, dirty city below. Groaning with anxiety, Joaquim fell back into his cane rocking chair, the only place he could sit comfortably. He'd had a bad back since a childhood fall, and it had worsened in the damp Parisian climate.

As he closed his eyes, the memory of the day he'd injured himself burned freshly in his mind. He'd grown up in Olinda, a captivating seaside town where the residents had just enough of a liberal bent to accept his parents' irregular marriage. Joaquim's patrician father, Delfim de Holanda Freire, had been educated in the best schools of his day: first the Pedro II College in Rio, later law school in São Paulo. There he became close friends with Joaquim Nabuco, who was to become the eloquent abolitionist not only for whom Delfim named his son but whose antislavery cause he joined and advocated the rest of his life. Eventually, in 1868, Delfim influenced his own father to free his slaves and, that same year, married Maria-Elisa, the musically inclined mulatta daughter of a slave his grandfather had owned.

When he was ten, Joaquim had been running on the beach at Olinda, flying one of his kites. He'd always had kites: simple tissue paper triangles made for him by the servants, elaborately painted birds and dragons bought by his doting father. This one, a purple parrot from Rio, was a particularly stunning flyer, the envy of all the other boys, who chased after him trying to tangle his string with theirs to bring it down. Freire had run along the narrow slice of beach remaining at high tide to rescue his kite from the pursuing throng, his eyes on the sky, not on the ground. He'd never seen the jetty of rocks that tripped him. When he fell, his thoughts were only for protecting his kite, not his body. The kite string had stayed tight in his hands, but he'd broken his back.

Six months of bed rest had been ordered. Knowing how much he'd always enjoyed his mother's piano lessons, his father had arranged for a musician to come to his bedside to teach him theory. Young Joaquim surprised everyone with his grasp of abstract musical concepts. He read every book he was given, then began writing down the music he heard in his head. All the bright child's energy soon was concentrated on writing little songs. When he'd finished one, he'd beg his mother to play it while he thought of how he could change and perfect it. His back had healed and Joaquim had never stopped composing.

"Seu Joaquim?" Jacobina asked softly as she came into the room carrying a basket of hard-boiled quail eggs.

He opened his eyes. "Ah . . . everything's in order?" He stood on stiff legs and went to inspect the table. The cut-glass sherry glasses and decanter were placed to one side of the bouquet of

jasmine blossoms; the matching pitchers for water and juice were
ready but unfilled. After straightening the Bahian lace tablecloth,
there was nothing further to do. Freire went to the piano and
played the "parrot theme" from his new series of Brazilian studies. It was novel, amusing, and melodic, perhaps the best he'd
ever composed from the standpoint of originality and appropri-
ateness. Would Margaret see in it what he'd hoped? If only he
didn't care so much for her approval . . . If only . . .

The front door opened. Voices spilled across the drawing
room. Late . . . but no, they were precisely on time, Rio time, that
is. If the hour of an invitation was eight, no well-mannered
Carioca dared show before nine. Joaquim adjusted the jacket of
his tweed suit. Though the suit's fabric was not the least bit sensible for the tropics, it was considered especially fashionable to
wear woolens and tweeds in Rio.

He stood to receive his first guests. Gustavo Meira, director of
the recently dedicated Teatro Municipal, entered the room and
gave him a firm abraço. Next came Julio Goulart, the aging conductor who'd led the orchestra even when Gottschalk performed
in Rio thirty-eight years before; he was accompanied by his son
Tristão, whom he was grooming as his successor.

"I suppose I win the bet," Meira laughed.

"What's this all about?" Joaquim asked.

Tristão Goulart coughed and explained, "Some of us didn't
think you'd ever come back, at least not permanently."

"Thought that Paris would have ruined you for us," his father
added.

"I was right on another matter," Meira pointed out. "He's
come back without a woman."

Just then the de Mellos arrived and jumped right into the conversation. "If Gabriela Braga wouldn't suit, no one would!" Constança de Mello said. For years she had spearheaded the campaign
to find Joaquim a wife, endlessly matching him with unsuitable
relatives or music students. Before he'd gone to France, she was
sure she'd found the answer in Henrique Braga's darling niece,
Gabriela. But he'd been far too absorbed in other matters, including helping Margaret over the loss of her child, to have even considered the alliance.

"Even if you missed an 'affaire d'amour,' Quincas, you managed to witness 'l'affaire Ravel,' didn't you?" Constança de Mello's white hands fluttered like little birds as she tugged at her dress to cool herself. "I'm so anxious to hear your version of what happened with last year's Prix de Rome."

"It was an amazing incident," Joaquim began, "one that proves that nothing, not even the art of music, is free from the strings of politics. In fact, that was what finally convinced me to come home."

Freire was interrupted by the arrival of the Nettos. Because they were supposedly escorting Margaret, he turned around to see where she was.

Nicia Netto knew exactly what he was thinking. "Margarida is coming later. Her husband has agreed to accompany her tonight."

"But I thought . . ." Joaquim hoped the waver in his voice went unnoticed.

"Erico seems to think less of the rules of mourning than she does. In fact, I believe he's encouraging her to go back to her music."

"I'm delighted." Joaquim was able to recover himself and speak more smoothly.

Nicia Netto stepped forward and introduced an unfamiliar young woman. "This my niece, Aida Alves. She's studied cello with Fabricio Rosas for many years, and now she's come to live and work with me."

"Delighted to have you here with us, Senhorita Alves." Freire hoped his voice was charming the young woman with the soulful dark brown eyes and bright pink cheeks. "Tell me, did your mother have a particular interest in Verdi?"

"Why, yes, how did you know?" the girl replied. "Oh, my name . . ." She giggled delightfully.

"Did your aunt tell you that I always write especially nice passages for the cello?"

"Sim, Tia Nicia told me," Aida said guilelessly. "I've already learned part of your . . ." She stopped short. Most everyone in the room was focused on the entrance of the Larsons. "Is that the pianist?" Aida gasped as Margaret walked into the room. She was wearing a long-sleeved black silk dress with a black scarf trailing almost to the hem of her skirt. Her golden hair was parted simply in the middle, braided, and severely pinned into an intricate chignon. Aida sighed. "She's beautiful."

Joaquim nodded. "Yes, yes, she is."

❧ ❧ ❧

After Gustavo Meira gave a short welcoming speech, he asked Joaquim to tell them what they'd all assembled to hear: the direction his new musical compositions were taking.

"One very frigid day in France," Joaquim began nervously, "I suppose I was purposely thinking warm thoughts. What came to mind were the bumba-meu-boi dances I'd seen as a child on Saint John's Day. The central character's the bull, with two or three others dressing up as cattle herders. I'm certain you all know that familiar beat: 'Eh boi bo-ni-to; eh bum-ba ... boi!'" Freire clapped and sang a few bars. "The rhythms came to me while I was working on a more classical composition and I wove them into the main theme. One phrase led to another. My fingers couldn't play it as fast as I heard it ... It was coming from a place so close to me that I knew every note." Joaquim paused and took a deep breath. Would his friends understand that he had taken a totally different approach to his music, breaking many of the rules of classical composition?

He walked over to his piano. "I'm combining these smaller works into a larger whole called Estudos Brasileiros, studies on regional folk songs. The first section is 'Bumba-meu-boi,' the second is based on the desafio, a type of musical duel, and ... well, you will hear for yourselves momentarily."

Freire rubbed his hands anxiously. Though his audience had always respected him as a young prodigy, he hoped he now could prove he'd begun to mature as an artist. He took a seat on the piano bench. "This first study is for piano, brass, flute chorus, soprano solo, and six cellos ..." Joaquim smiled at Aida. "Desculpe, seven cellos."

When the young girl realized he'd singled her out, she flushed and turned away.

"I'll only play the major theme, because frankly the piece is too difficult for my clumsy hands to do it justice." He grinned amiably and passed out the scores. "The strength in the opening sec-

tion is in the horns, then the piano begins the folk theme. Next
comes a dissonant bass ostinato, same voice, same pitch. Do you
see how it works?" His powerful fingers hit the keys and played
the parts of the various instruments. "After the fiery coda, we
pause and go into the flute solo." He played the graceful dénoue-
ment on the treble keys and sustained the last sad note with the
pedal.

Gustavo Meira led the applause. "Your best ever. A triumph,"
he announced. "Our gala to welcome you home will be a landmark in Brazilian music. You must tell us more. I've heard
rumors of a symphony."

"It's just in the earliest stages. I'm calling it Os Três Rios."

"The Three Rivers?" Tobias Netto asked.

"Yes, the first movement is the mighty Amazon, the mysterious, sinuous, primitive jungle river; the second, the Iguaçu, culminating in its magnificent cascading waterfalls; and finally, the
false river, Rio de Janeiro — vibrant city of diversity, city of the
future. It will take me years to complete."

Freire stopped talking as Margaret moved forward to join those
congratulating him; the silk of her dress rustled like water. "The
folk themes of your studies will speak for Brazil to the rest of the
world. It's a masterpiece."

Joaquim's gaze met hers during the long compliment. It
seemed that the once-vibrant blueness of her eyes had dimmed
somehow, but her stare was as steady and honest as ever. She
would not praise him excessively; she meant what she was saying.
"Muito obrigado. Your opinion matters greatly, for I'll need your
enthusiastic cooperation if this can ever be performed in Rio."

"Maestro, you know that I cannot be the one, no matter how
much I'd be honored. It would be unseemly for me to appear in
public for at least a year."

"Of course I've thought about the proprieties, but I think I
have a plan that would not offend anyone."

Erik had moved to his wife's side. His hair had thinned, he'd
grown a Kaiser mustache, and his Nordic skin had tanned to such
a dark shade that it was lined and leathery. "Now what have you
conspired?" he asked Freire genially.

"Not only me, but the Music Society has . . ."

Gustavo Meira stepped forward to aid Freire with his proposition. "The maestro wishes to dedicate his Estudos to the memory of your sister, Dona Francisca. The proceeds from the gala would benefit the orphanage at Santa Casa."

Freire tasted an acid flavor in his mouth as he waited for Margaret to respond. She looked at Erik, then back at Meira. If Erik was still worried about his working closely with his wife, Joaquim knew he'd never permit this; if, after all this time, he'd been forgiven . . .

Larson inched closer to where his wife was standing. Freire sensed a need for them to touch before either answered. "I think it would be a great honor to my sister's memory," Erik began haltingly. "When our child died" — he stopped and cleared his throat — "and you wrote the lovely piece for him, Francisca said it was the most touching act of sympathy she'd ever known, that your music expressed what we all felt but could not say." Erik swallowed hard. Those close to him could see him blinking away tears.

So as not to embarrass him further, Joaquim averted his eyes and in doing so caught a glance from young Aida, who was watching with the stillness of a startled mouse.

Meira stepped forward to discuss the rehearsal schedule with Margaret. Without having to be told, Jacobina was serving the sherry. He'd done it! They had listened to his new work and genuinely seemed to like it! Even Erik approved Margaret's participation. All his dreams were coming true. Why, then, wasn't he excited? Why wasn't he accepting the congratulations and joining in on the grand plans in the making? Why, when everything he'd always wanted was happening, did he feel, instead of the intense pleasure he'd imagined, a hollowness that ruined it all?

❧ 3 "I love you, Quincas," Margaret was saying as she bent over and kissed him with welcoming lips.

His hands reached up and traced the outline of her loins, then felt her nipples ripen under the faintest brush from his fingertips. "I love you, Margaret," he replied, and the sudden truth of it consumed him. He pressed his body against her full length, praying she'd draw him within her without hesitation.

The knock on the door woke him instantly. "Seu Joaquim, bom dia."

He rolled over onto his stomach and groaned at the interruption. The dream had been so real . . .

"Maldito!" he cursed. He rose from the bed in a state of acute frustration. It will pass. It must, he warned himself. Already his concentration was slipping. Yesterday he'd forgotten to check the orchestrations for the string section, hadn't remembered his fitting with his tailor or to leave the menus for Jacobina. Minor lapses, yes, but indications of how his feelings were beginning to take control of his life.

As he shaved, Joaquim tried to organize the events of the day in his mind: go over the music with the arranger at the Teatro Municipal at ten. At noon he'd return to Rua Monte Alegre for the soloists' rehearsals and Margaret.

Humming, old Jacobina walked into the room, carrying her master's cafezinho without a thought to the fact that he was standing naked in the center of the room, trying to decide what to wear. Nor did she avert her eyes when his genitals revealed what had been on his mind. By the time he'd reached for his towel, she'd lumbered back into the hall.

Without dressing, he drank his coffee in a few quick gulps. Even though the sweet roll on the plate looked dry and unappealing, he took a bite. His stomach twisted nervously and he began to sweat. He clapped for Jacobina. "I'll bathe before I go out. Have the tub filled and brush my blue suit."

"Sim, senhor," she replied flatly.

By the time he'd finished his bath, he was running late. Jacobina had sent the kitchen boy to the foot of Santa Teresa for a hired car. His music was neatly stacked on the hall table next to the pearl-grey fedora that he preferred with his blue suit. The neck of his monarch collar chafed. For a moment he debated changing into a shorter, less formal style, but there was no time.

I'll do it before I see Margaret this afternoon, he decided as he rushed out the door with Jacobina shaking his music after him.

Later that day, the Larsons' wide Protos pulled through the narrow stone gateposts with only a few centimeters to spare. The elegant car was kept as brightly polished as the week it had arrived from Germany. From the entryway, Joaquim observed

Margaret being helped out by her chauffeur. Unexpectedly, she was followed by Astrid, who carried Margaret's leather music case.

Joaquim stepped out to greet them, too effusively perhaps. "Ah, Astrid, how nice of you to join us this afternoon."

"I hope you don't mind," Margaret said easily. "Astrid's quite bored with all the younger children in her class, so I'm taking her out with me now and then."

"School was tedious to me, too, until I went to the Conservatoire, that is. When you discover what it is that you want to learn, it will be a pleasure."

Jacobina held the door open and, when Astrid walked past, reached down to stroke the child's fine flaxen hair. "Linda! So pretty," she murmured in admiration.

The composer was thinking exactly the same as he studied Margaret's graceful costume. Still in mourning clothes, she had made the best of the situation by wearing a grey tunic trimmed with black ostrich feathers over a hobble skirt. It warmed him to see that she hadn't neglected stylish clothes. This, coupled with her relentless attention to the concert preparations, gave him hope that she was emerging from her cocoon of melancholy.

Astrid, who appeared delightfully fresh in her immaculate white dress tied with a black sash, bounded energetically into the dining room and then back into the hallway and asked, "Is it true what they say about this house?"

"What is that, little one?"

"About there being a lake on the inside?"

"Yes, it's true. Would you like to see it?"

"Oh, sim!" Astrid clapped her hands.

"Come, I'll show you both. Your stepmother's never really seen that part of the house before."

"Is there really any other room but the one with the piano?" Margaret gave a high, liquid laugh. "Astrid, look!" She pointed out Freire's unusual piano through the open doors of the drawing room. "Have you ever seen a square one?"

Astrid stared at the instrument, which occupied a carpeted podium at the far end of the room. "Não, Ridi."

Freire tried to hide his surprise that the girl would call her stepmother by a nickname. "My father bought it for me from the estate of the Viscountess de Caula," he said genially.

"Does it sound as good as a curved one?" Astrid asked.

"You'll see for yourself when Margaret plays for us, eh?" Joaquim smiled at the child who was at an awkward age, with long legs out of proportion to her immature body. At least she seemed a calmer, less intense child than she'd been before he went to France.

"If you'll come this way . . ." He gestured the ladies to walk in front of him down the narrow hallway. "When the house was built over seventy-five years ago, they installed the bath on the ground floor adjoining the kitchen because they feared a leak upstairs might injure the woodwork below."

Freire opened the double doors to reveal a room entirely tiled in bright blue azulejos from Portugal. The walls used the design in blue and white, while the pool itself was done in a reverse of the same pattern.

"Look!" Astrid pointed to a winding staircase that led from the bath to a narrow inside balcony. "Can you get to the bedroom without going out into the hall?"

"Sim, wasn't that clever?" Joaquim murmured. He was certain that Margaret knew that his house originally had been built for a mistress of the emperor. A leading architect of the day, Pierre Alexandre Cavroe, had drawn the plans to please a man with decidedly eccentric whims.

In the 1830s the place was a showpiece. Though rectangular and undistinguished in design on the outside, it followed the lines of French neoclassicism that Joaquim thought eternally pleasing. Graceful iron-grilled balconies bulged from the upper floor, while strictly utilitarian bars protected all the windows at street level. Inside, however, the architects left no doubt that this had been an imperial lovers' bower. The beveled panes of glass inserted in all the transoms above doors and windows were, symbolically, heart-shaped.

While Astrid wandered about, exclaiming at the faucets gracefully wrought into a swan's head and neck, the tall built-in majolica stove that provided warmth during the chilly months of late July and August, and the stained-glass panels that led out to the bougainvillea-bordered garden, Margaret took the opportunity to

speak softly. "I wanted you to know one of the reasons I brought
the child today. Her father and I have decided to send her to
school in Europe. In a few months she'll sail with Erik's father to
Sweden. Sven would like to see his relatives once more, and he
thinks that Astrid should become acquainted with her mother's
family. Afterward, he'll settle her in a school where she can learn
both Swedish and English."

"Does she wish to go?"

"She seems enthusiastic, but then Rio has had some unpleasant
moments for her lately. She worshiped her aunt and . . ."

"Ten people could have taken a bath here at once." Astrid giggled as she came bounding back.

Freire laughed out loud, the sound echoing off the hard tiled
walls. "There's a wonderful story about this room. It was known
that the lady of the house so enjoyed the pool that she bathed
here every single day. Because of this she was considered very
naughty indeed. You see, fifty years ago, it was considered im-
moral to wash so often!"

Astrid appeared perplexed. "I can't see why."

"Neither can I." Joaquim laughed even louder this time and
was delighted to hear Margaret join him.

When they passed through the pantry area, Astrid asked, "Is it
true that you made a gramophone recording, senhor?"

"Sim, with the French National Orchestra. Would you like to
hear it?"

"Por favor!" the thirteen-year-old exclaimed.

"I don't think we'll have time today," Margaret interjected.
"Soon the others will be here, and I don't feel it's fair to have
them wait for me."

"Might I suggest that we work now on the Aria and the Fanta-
sia and then play the Odeon gramophone for Aida and Nicia
when they arrive. I'm certain they'd like to hear it, too. Frankly,
the contraption is just a novelty. The reproduction of sounds is so
inferior to those in performance that it will never find an audience."

"But everybody wishes they could have a gramophone!" Astrid
insisted.

"Only the violin sounds anything like its real tone. That's because the instrument can be placed close up to the mouth of the

recording horn. All the others suffer a terrible loss in the higher frequencies. The piano reproduces the least successfully of all. But you'll see what I mean after we rehearse, all right?"

Astrid's lower lip jutted petulantly. Margaret led her firmly back to the drawing room. To cheer her up, Joaquim said, "Astrid, you may go out to the back garden and introduce yourself to Wolfgang, my pet parrot. Ask Jacobina for some grapes to feed him. He might even sing or do a little dance for you."

"Really?" Astrid smiled warily. "What does he sing?"

"Only classical pieces, I'm afraid. He's named for Mozart, after all."

"Quincas, don't tease her."

"Go see for yourself," Joaquim encouraged.

When Astrid left, Joaquim thought he could feel the tension between him and Margaret increase. Had she also come to cherish the few brief hours they were alone each week? If only he could speak his feelings . . . and she hers. And yet he had to accept the possibility that they probably did not share anything besides their mutual love for music.

Margaret's hands were poised above the piano's keys and wavered perceptibly. Joaquim loved the way she approached his music with such intensity and vigor. All at once she burst into the opening trill with magnificent precision, breathing life into dead notes, the sounds exploding with feeling. He watched as her face was transfigured with concentration. Her hands swept effortlessly across the keyboard, first a gentle caress, later a fierce rebuke. Her eyes were closed halfway, her mouth seemed to be tasting the music. This is how she must be with a lover, he thought. Joaquim willed himself to concentrate on the nuances of the score.

Most people must suppose that a pianist is subjugated to the will of the music, he thought. But nothing is further from the truth. How dependent a composer is on the performer! From Margaret's interpretation he was learning a whole new aspect of his work. She was drawing out beauty and knowledge rather than merely playing a lifeless instrument. He admired her steel fingers, merciless in their virtuosity as they infused his sweeping crescendos with a complete spectrum of emotions. Perhaps this piece is too intense for the beginning of the concert, he worried. I should discuss its placement on the program again with Meira. Plans crowded his mind, gently blunting the passion that churned just beneath the surface. If Margaret ever guessed how I suffer in her presence, Joaquim thought silently, she'd never permit herself to work with me. Yet without these brief moments, life would be infinitely more excruciating.

❧ ❧ ❧

The program for the concert was a continued cause of anxiety for Joaquim. Only when Gustavo Meira was asked to change its order for the seventh time did he protest.

"What difference does it make if the second guitar solo comes before the first?" he asked. The two men were having coffee together at a small café just across the plaza from the Teatro Municipal.

"The second solo is slower, more appropriate for the opening of a memorial concert." Joaquim's finger idly ran around the chipped rim of his demitasse cup as he spoke.

"To me the program is perfect."

"Don't you see that there's nothing on it which is really evocative of Senhora Cavalcanti?"

"What do you have in mind?"

"Something like Ravel's *Pavane pour une infante Défunte*, or Fauré's new requiem."

"The whole idea is to introduce your new work to a wider audience. If you insist on a requiem, you'll have to write one yourself."

"There's not time, even if I wanted to," Joaquim had protested, but later that night the idea had come. He could write a simple musical eulogy by using just a few words of the Introit that were said in the *Missa pro defunctis*. The passage "Requiem aeternam dona eis, Domine" stuck in his mind. "Give them eternal rest, O Lord." He rolled the words over slowly. They had a presence, a movement of their own. "Requiem. Re ... qui ... em ..." The syllables formed notes in the key of B-flat minor almost effortlessly. A simple piece for the piano. A slow, methodical poem, an ode to a lovely, tragic woman. The melody came more quickly than he could transcribe it. He wrote for two days straight, hardly resting until it was finished. When the last notes were down, he yearned to show it to Margaret and to win not only her approval but her promise to perform it. Quickly he dressed in his Parisian tweeds and prepared to call on her at her home in the Gloria section.

At the bottom of the Santa Teresa hill Freire easily found a motorcab and gave the driver the address. Carlota, Florinda's eldest daughter, explained that Margaret was at Boa Vista with the children.

Miscalculating how long it would take to get to Boa Vista, Freire arrived at the gate just before dusk. He rang the bell next to the fern-draped stone wall. "It's the maestro!" Astrid called out as the guard unlocked the rusty gate. "Boa tarde, senhor." He tipped his hat.

Astrid skipped over. "Ridi's up at the house. Isn't that who you've come to see?"

"Why, yes, and what is that?" He was startled by something moving on the child's shoulder.

"Oh!" She giggled merrily. "That's Lento, our sloth. I was just out finding him fig leaves. He loves them so! Do you want to hold him?" Astrid began to disengage the sloth's two long curved claws from around her arm.

"Não, obrigado." He quickened his step up the path.

Chaos of a most attractive kind filled the downstairs of the rustic house. Two tiny children, wet from their bath, raced through the parlor and hid in a corner, only to be chased back to the kitchen by Zefinha. "Momento, Seu Joaquim. I'll call Dona Margarida."

From the center hallway, Joaquim could see a girl with long dark braids sitting on top of the piano, swinging her legs wildly to the thumping of her older brother's noisy march beat. A crawling babe with cocoa skin and surprising green eyes blocked his path momentarily. Joaquim walked around him and headed for the only chair in the cluttered parlor not covered with clothing or toys.

"Maestro!" Margaret called with surprise as she entered the room. She was wearing a simple black gown covered by a sensible striped smock. "I must apologize . . . If I'd known . . ."

"I shouldn't have come unannounced, but . . ."

"Is there something the matter?"

"Não, don't worry. I just wanted you to be the first to see what I've just written."

Margaret looked concerned. "I don't believe you've come all this way to show me a composition. There must be some other . . ."

Was she so accustomed to hearing bad news? "I've made a mistake arriving so impetuously, but I needed to hear your reaction as soon as possible."

"Like Brahms asking Clara Schumann to play his work first?" Margaret's eyes sparkled merrily.

"Well . . . I . . ."

"Is that it?" Margaret pointed to the music folded under his arm.

"Sim. I thought it might be on the program for the concert — that is, if you approve."

Margaret held out her hands. "May I see it?"

The boy and the girl near the piano were kicking each other mischievously. "Marcelino! Mila!" Margaret warned them with a scowl.

"Requiem for Piano in B-flat Minor," she read aloud. Without looking up from the notations, she walked over to the piano and sat beside Marcelino. "Mila, will you please get off the lid. Now!"

The child slid down. As Freire came around behind Margaret to point out a few directions in the music, he couldn't help noticing the factory mark on the piano. "A Pleyel! In Rio!"

"My husband gave it to me for our anniversary this year. It's the second one he ordered, but the first to reach me."

"Sim," Freire said sympatheticaly, "it's so difficult to get shipments from Europe these days."

Margaret turned away with an obtuse smile on her face but didn't answer. Instead she gave her concentration to the music. The requiem was easy to play, its beauty reflected in the simplicity of the theme. Even the children quieted after the first phrase and listened all the way through. When she'd finished, her head remained bowed. At first Joaquim thought he might have displeased her.

Finally Margaret spoke. "It's very short." As she looked up at him, her eyes glistened with tears.

"You'll perform it, then?" he asked hesitantly.

"Certamente, Maestro!" She hugged Marcelino close. "You're staying for dinner," she added with such finality Joaquim didn't even dare begin a polite attempt at a refusal.

❧ 4 On the afternoon of his last private rehearsal with Margaret, Joaquim waited eagerly. He fussed with the vase of fragrant orange blossoms on the piano, rearranged the needlepoint cushions on the sofa, then opened the shutters so a precise amount of light would illuminate the keyboard without creating a glare. He looked at the mantel clock for the tenth time in an hour. This time she was definitely late.

He worried about her. Could she be ill? It was crazy to have so much feeling invested in a woman he could never have as his own. Maybe the Nettos and the de Mellos were right; maybe he, for some unexplainable reason, required someone unattainable. Otherwise, why had all the other women he'd been attracted to been impossible choices?

When well-meaning friends and family had questioned his bachelorhood, he'd compared his dedication to music with a priest's to God. Yet he knew it was his total unwillingness ever to compromise — to be satisfied with an imperfect chord, a second-rate musician, an untrustworthy friend — that had made it impossible for him to settle on a wife. If he couldn't find one to whom he could dedicate his life with at least as much passion as he gave to his music, he would have none at all. Not that there hadn't been a few significant women in his life. Because he'd had public presence as a composer and performer from a very young age, he'd been very discreet in all his alliances. There'd been the usual ones who'd offered themselves after performances, but the first woman he'd really loved had been Brigida de Farias, the young widow of old Dr. Leão de Farias, who treated his father. Joaquim had taken her as one of his piano students as a favor to his mother.

"She needs an outlet for her grief. You'd be doing a great kindness," his mother had said to convince him. "It's always a tragedy when a woman marries a man so much older. The man gets a bargain, the woman a misery for the rest of her life."

Though the woman had no talent for music, he'd been so desirous of her body, so smitten with her charms, he might have married Brigida if she would have had him, but her own experience in marrying someone older than herself had convinced her that it would eventually harm him to have a wife almost ten years his senior. For five years Joaquim had been loyal to the widow until he'd met Stella Dias, the aristocratic daughter of Laudelino Dias, who then held the title of Rio's Promoter of Public Justice. In order to woo her with all the intensity he felt her due, he'd given up his "lessons" with Brigida. The Dias family, knowing Joaquim was quickly rising to prominence in the musical community, did not dissuade his interest, thinking the association a flattering one that might lead their daughter to other influential and intellectual prospects. So it had come as an immense surprise when Stella, who'd always been warm and engaging with Joaquim, suddenly cooled the moment his intentions became serious.

"I cannot go against my mother's wishes," she'd said, her cheeks moist with tears. "If you were only a bit lighter . . ." she'd added honestly. It wasn't his parentage that they questioned, but the fact that his particular racial mix had been from too dark a palette, compromising generations of breeding more European and less native blood into their line. Only a few months after they parted, Stella had married a professor who now occupied the chair of geometry at the Military College. Then, shortly after Stella's marriage, Margaret had arrived in Brazil. Beside the talented North American with the golden hair, every other woman had seemed bland.

The mantel clock chimed half past the hour. Now Margaret was an hour late! It was unlike her to be tardy by more than a few minutes. Today they'd planned to review the short requiem that was to be the finale to the program. When she played it, the music became something quite apart from what he had composed. She'd taken his simple phrases and turned them into a poem. She understood the first movement to be an angry struggle against death, the second fateful and gloomy, and the third filled with an assuaging tenderness, an enigmatic memory. Today he wanted to work especially on measures thirty-five to thirty-nine. He didn't think she'd changed all the C-flats to C-naturals, which he'd done at the last minute on his copy. Not that these details mattered to

anyone but him. What was important was that she was able to
bring to the little requiem a spark of originality that set the stan-
dard for the piece.

Finally, Joaquim heard the unmistakable whine of the Protos
coming through the gates.

"My deepest apologies," Margaret said as she was ushered into
the parlor.

Joaquim tried not to seem unduly distressed. "I was concerned
that you had difficulty with the automobile."

"In a sense, I did. Florinda, my maid, has been missing since
last night. I sent the car to Boa Vista to see if anyone there knew
her whereabouts."

"Has this happened before?"

"Yes, but she's always come back by morning. There's a
man . . ."

"Ah, always the same . . ."

"Yes . . . and no. The other servants have warned her and us
about him. I believe he's a bandido from Vassouras. That's probably where they've gone."

"How would you know about men like that?" Freire began to
laugh, but the piercing look in her eyes stopped him short.

Margaret moved around to the far side of the piano and deliberately waited three beats. "Once I shot a bandit who'd attacked
me."

Now it was Freire's turn to pause. Disbelief was clearly written on his face, so she quickly went on to tell him about Tubarão.
"I saw him one last time. The day of Francisca's wedding he
stalked me and spat on me. Sven Larson always said it was because I'd wounded his pride."

"I should say!"

"Since then I've always worried that he might return."

Joaquim began to shuffle through music stacked on the piano.
"I'm sorry to bother you with these trivial matters. It seems
that the pull of my responsibilities at home is always with me."

"You could be mistaken. She might return in a few hours."

"I doubt that. She's taken much of her clothing and left messages for her children."

Margaret signaled she was ready to begin work by seating herself at the piano. "For now, I'll just worry about the concert next week. When it's over, I'll try to get Florinda back. Perhaps by then she'll be missing her children enough to return."

Joaquim opened the music to measure thirty-five. "Shall we begin?"

❧ 5 Special trams marked TEATRO were put in service the evenings of performances. As a courtesy to the ladies who dressed elegantly for the occasions, the Rio de Janeiro Tramway and Light Company placed white satin covers over the leather seats and hung a bright garland of ribbons on the rear of each vehicle.

Early in the evening of the memorial concert the crowds began to converge in front of the Teatro Municipal. Those without tickets enjoyed the spectacle of Rio's most prestigious families in their finest regalia. Joaquim had spent the entire day strolling around the theater to see if any item — from an unpolished armrest to a misprinted program — needed his attention. To him the building's whole design was but a derivative copy of the Paris Opéra. He would have preferred one that reflected more of Brazil's colonial and tropical heritage, a place to motivate Brazilian musicians and artists to look to their own country for inspiration. Don't be so condescending, he chided himself. Just think how fortunate you are to have such a magnificent hall in which to give your works their debut and a music-loving audience eager to listen!

Only last week the theater's season had opened with the São Paulo Opera Company's sold-out performance of Carlos Gomes's *O Guaraní*, perhaps the one uniquely Brazilian work known worldwide. Secretly Joaquim hoped that eventually he might inherit Gomes's position as Brazil's musical interpreter, but he was clutched with the fear that he'd far overestimated the impact his music might have.

At last he could hear the hum as the first members of the audience were taking their seats. For most it would be their first opportunity to see the inside of the new theater. He knew they'd be awed by the frescoes and friezes that decorated the great hall, impressed by the Verlet chandeliers and the Bernadelli sculptures, and appreciative of the excessively romantic painting on the great backdrop while they waited for the performance to commence. But for him the minutes dragged.

A half-hour later he checked his watch against de Mello's. "Margaret was to be here at nineteen hours. Have you seen any sign of her yet?" The maestro mopped his brow and began to pace behind the sky-blue cyclorama.

Henrique Braga came running. "Larson's car has been seen at the entranceway. You'd better come!"

"Just escort her backstage, Henrique," de Mello answered.

"But Senhora Larson isn't in the vehicle."

"What?" Joaquim hurried out a side door. He diverted Erik and his daughters as they were halfway up the staircase that led to the first tier of boxes. "Where's Margaret?"

Erik appeared completely dumbfounded. "She was to come by carriage. I went to Boa Vista for the children."

"When did you last see her?"

"This afternoon."

"Was she feeling all right?"

"A bit nervous, as you would expect. When I left after lunch, my mother was helping her make a final decision about which jewels to wear. Without Florinda to help, she was a bit disorganized, but still she should have been here an hour ago."

"What shall we do now?" Freire's voice rose in panic.

"Let's double-check to see she hasn't come in through a different entrance; then, if she really hasn't arrived, I'll take the Protos home to see what this is about. Won't take but thirty minutes." He looked at the watch in his vest pocket. "The performance doesn't start for almost an hour. If I'm late returning with her, could you change the program so all her pieces come at the end?"

"Not very easily. The order of the music is strategically arranged for maximum effect. And it would be too much strain on Margaret to have her play all her pieces consecutively."

"I see." Erik rubbed his mustache anxiously. "Astrid, take Susana to our box. Grandmother and your cousins will be there shortly. I'm going to find Margaret and will join you as soon as I return."

"But, Papai," Astrid whined. "Don't leave me alone!"

"Astrid!" Erik said sternly.

She lowered her eyes. "Sim, Papai."

A search of the theater and discussion with the guards at all the entrances failed to locate Margaret. Erik had already sent someone to find his driver, so the Protos was waiting by the stage door entrance. "I'll be back with her as soon as I can," Erik called to Joaquim, Henrique Braga, and Delgado de Mello as they stood on the loading dock.

Just as the driver closed the door behind Erik and walked around to the front seat, Joaquim jumped down, reopened the back door, and slid in beside Erik. "I'm coming too."

❧ ❧ ❧

Carlota greeted them in tears. "Oh, Seu Erico! There was nothing I could do!"

Erik began to shake the terrified girl. "What do you mean? Where is she?"

"They took her. The two men and . . ."

"Took her? What are you talking about?"

Carlota began to scream uncontrollably. Joaquim loosened Erik's grip. "Calma, calma . . . por favor. Who took her and where?"

"The two men and — " she began to wail even louder — "my mother!"

"Florinda?" Joaquim shouted. To Erik he said, "Your wife told me how worried she was when Florinda ran off. I tried to make light of the romance, but she insisted she was mixed up with a bandido. Could she possibly have been right?"

"He looked like just an ordinary favela jagunço to me," Erik said.

In a few moments, all the servants gathered around with their own versions of the story. Two hours earlier, Margaret had been almost ready for the concert when Florinda arrived.

"She claimed she'd returned for us children," Carlota said between heaving sobs. "Then Dona Margarida heard what was happening and began to argue with her."

"Sim, Seu Erico," the cook continued. "While this was going on, the two men came into the kitchen and began shouting as though they were fighting. I was very frightened and called in the vigia and the gardener from above the stable."

"It wasn't a real fight," the guard continued, "because as soon as we were all inside, they turned a gun on us and marched us upstairs. They locked all of us in the bathroom, even Carlota and Florinda's younger children. When we finally broke down the door, everyone was gone."

"Everyone?" Joaquim asked.

"The two men, Florinda, and Dona Margarida."

"What did they look like?"

Carlota answered slowly. "One had a large ugly nose with a hook in it; the other wore dark gold-rimmed glasses."

"You've seen that one before, haven't you?" Erik asked.

"Sim, Seu Erico. He visited my mother many times. He always brought me sweets."

Joaquim spun around and faced Erik. "What would they have wanted with her?"

Erik's hands were up to his temples as if he were trying to keep his head from exploding. "The jewels, they must have heard about the jewels. Last week my mother took all her best pieces from the vault, but because Margaret still hadn't selected which dress she was going to wear, my mother promised to bring back the emeralds and the pearls studded with diamonds so she could make her final choice."

"How many people knew of this?"

"Only my parents, Margaret, me, and Florinda, of course. She was still here then. She's never stolen anything from us; not a piece of bread was ever missing from our home. But she knew the jewels would be here today."

"But what could they possibly want with Margaret?" Joaquim asked anxiously.

"Has anyone called the police?"

"Não, Seu Erico," the cook answered. "We only just broke down the door."

"If . . . anything . . . happens . . . to . . . her . . ." Erik said in a slow, threatening voice.

"No one would harm her," Joaquim shouted, as though his words would make it true. Suddenly he realized that there was no possibility of holding the concert that evening. Seventeen hundred disappointed patrons would have to be sent home. "I must

go to the theater . . . make an announcement . . ." he said to Erik,
who only stared blankly.

"Yes, the theater. We'll go back in the car."

"First the police . . ."

"Yes, the police . . . First the police."

"Does anyone know who the men were or where they were
from?" Joaquim asked.

"Carlota might."

"Wasn't the man from Vassouras?"

"Vassouras? How did you know that?"

"Margaret said she thought Florinda went to Vassouras when
she ran away."

"If they're headed for the mountains, they wouldn't dare travel
by rail. We could beat them there, have the roads closed off. We
could wire to the local deputies . . ." His mind raced.

"But, Erico" — Joaquim reached out and touched his arm —
"it's not so simple. We can't do anything that would alarm them
or cause them to hurt Margaret. My guess is that they've taken
her as protection or to hold her for ransom."

"So, she's been kidnaped . . . She's . . ." Erik's voice faltered.
He stumbled forward. Joaquim watched helplessly as the man
he'd known as one of the most vigorous, hardy, and expansive
men in Rio fell to his knees.

6 The square in the center of Vassouras appeared tranquil
on days when there was no market. By eight in the
morning, long blue shadows from the church at the far end of the
plaza still streaked across the grassy park as the sun just barely
made its appearance over the curtain of ragged mountains to the
east. Two barefoot children were filling pottery jugs with water
from the well a few yards to the right of the police station. Erik
watched as the older girl helped the younger steady her vessel
atop her head, before lifting her own with a practiced grace. As
they walked down the dusty lane, the little one's jug overflowed,
leaving a trail of splotches on the thirsty red soil.

"It's a very bad business," the regional police commissioner,
Major Miguel Paraiso Borges, was saying in his dark office in the
Vassouras municipal building. "From your descriptions the

hawk-nosed one is probably Tubarão; the one with the glasses, Limoeiro."

"Florinda's daughter described her mother's enamorado as a man who never took off his dark glasses!" Erik said excitedly.

Horacio, the youngest police recruit, brought over a tray with cafezinho. He served his boss first, next the police colonel who'd just arrived from Rio, and finally the two men who'd come after the woman — one brown as cocoa, one pale as milk. They'd not be forgetting this case for many a year, he was thinking to himself.

Erik yawned. "This Tubarão. Could he be the one my wife wounded many years ago?"

"The colonel was just filling me in about that incident." The major smiled. "We can't be entirely certain because when one of these cangaceiros dies, their nicknames are sometimes taken by a new member of the group in an attempt to conceal their losses. But to answer your question, I would think he's probably the same one."

Joaquim dared to ask the question that most concerned him. "Do you think, Major, that they've taken her for ransom or just for vengeance? Surely they can't have held a grudge against Senhora Larson for all these years."

Major Borges sipped his coffee noisily. He placed his cup down with a clatter. "Hard to say, Senhor Freire. The unusual part of this story is the role of the woman, Florinda. I believe that if she thought any harm would come to the senhora, she would never have participated."

"She's a stupid girl from the backlands herself. They could have duped her to get anything they wanted," Erik interjected harshly. "I'm convinced those bastardos went after her purposely. They befriended the servant to get to her mistress!" A sheen of sweat covered his forehead. "If they harm her, I'll . . ."

"These men are not necessarily as violent as you might think. They have a code and a pride of their own. I remember an amazing tale a few years back when several members of one of the gangs went to a house where they'd heard an old enemy was hiding out. The mother of the man they wanted was a woman whom the bandits respected from the days when the two families were friends. She told them her son was not present and begged them to spare her and her other two sons. The bandits went into the house to talk to the brothers and, on their vow never to pursue them again, spared their lives. Later, though, when they caught up with the one they'd been hunting, he met a ruthless death."

The story made Erik even more agitated. Joaquim attempted to calm him. "I don't think we need to consider the worst. Let's take this one step at a time."

"Excellent," replied Colonel Orlando Feitosa, leader of the Rio contingent of thirty men that had been posted on this crucial case. "Now what's your plan?" he asked the Vassouras major, who, though his rank was lower than his, had the authority to act in his region over him.

Crude maps of the area were laid out on the table. "This is Desengano. They've made camp there in the past." The major indicated a red spot. "That's because many of their coiteiros live around there."

"Coiteiros?" Joaquim asked.

"Protectors. You see, the rural population is almost defenseless against these culprits, so they make — how shall I say it — accommodations. The ranchers pay the 'taxes' demanded and, perhaps reluctantly, assist the bandidos with the purchase of provisions and ammunition. For this the cangaceiros pay well in both money and protective services."

"And if they refuse?" Erik asked.

"To refuse a favor is to invite almost certain reprisal."

"What do the police do to prevent this illegal aid?" the colonel from Rio asked pompously.

Major Borges shrugged. "Out here we operate a bit differently than in the city, my friend. We must understand the predicament of some of these landowners and poor farmers who are given no choice from either side."

Impatient with the background talk, Colonel Feitosa pointed to the dot on the map. "If this is really where they're hiding out," the colonel began, "with my forces alone we have enough men to surround the place easily."

"Desculpe, Colonel," the major replied with as little deference as he dared, "but it's our intention to return Senhora Larson unharmed."

"What are you suggesting?" he argued belligerently. "We wait to hear their demands, then meet them?"

"You are at least partially correct. Time is our friend. We must weigh the advantages of giving in to them now so the senhora is returned unharmed, then pursuing them aggressively later."

"I'd prefer that myself," Erik said rapidly.

"It's completely against our policies to negotitate with criminals." Colonel Feitosa's palm hit the table. The empty coffee cups rattled. Officer Horacio, thinking he was being summoned, ran in with a steaming pot of fresh coffee.

As the two officers argued for control of the mission, Freire realized why they were jockeying for power. Neither man could afford to fail in the rescue, and both wanted the credit in a case that would make national headlines. "Gentlemen," Joaquim began, his eloquent voice sounding weaker than he hoped it might. He felt as uncomfortable in that tiny municipal building as he'd ever felt in a grand Parisian salon. "May I make a suggestion?"

"Since you seem to know so much about these matters, Senhor Freire, what do you propose?" the major asked abruptly.

Freire swallowed hard and tried to explain what he had been thinking. "Colonel, you have your own troops here and can formulate plans that involve them, and Major, you know this area and the ways of the bandidos best. I suggest that you each separately make a strategy. There should be pieces of each plan that will be workable, or perhaps when they are compared, it will be obvious which one will be best."

"That's ridiculous!" Major Borges said, rising out of his seat in anger. "Nobody tells me how to run my district!"

The colonel was pacing the back of the room. "You've given me an idea, Senhor Freire. This could be a joint effort. One group will set up a diversion, the other the rescue."

"A diversion . . ." Major Borges tested the word aloud. "It just might work . . ."

※   ※   ※

"Vengeance is mother's milk to the babes of the cangaceiros." The major was explaining the history of banditry in the area later that night in the dining room of the small hotel where the Rio

contingent had taken all the rooms. "Feuds continue for generations. One of the longest involves the family of Casimiro Carvalho and Virgulino Mesquita, a violent mulatto who ran off with
Casimiro's daughter more than twenty years ago. After a bitter
and prolonged conflict, Virgulino was killed by Casimiro. It is the
Carvalho band with whom I believe your Tubarão and Limoeiro
are now aligned. Over the years there have been so many fights
involving cousins and uncles that it would be impossible to find a
family in the region unaffected by the violence. Casimiro's own
brother was slaughtered by a Mesquita. Their reprisal was the
rape and killing of Mesquita's two young daughters a few years
back. Since that time, the conflicts have escalated, though only
they know the score."

"What does this have to do with my wife?" Erik asked. "I can't
believe they would've taken her all this way for vengeance."

"I agree with you," the major said. "I'm explaining this so as to
plan our diversion. If we can get the Mesquita family to cooperate
with us, they could be invaluable. No one knows the patterns and
whereabouts of the Carvalho clan better than they do."

"You'd trust a criminal?" Joaquim asked naively.

"With respect, Senhor Freire," the major said slowly, "there
are many roads to the same end, some straighter than others. Permit someone who knows the territory to pick the swiftest, eh?"

Erik stared at Joaquim sympathetically. "If the bandits are so
interested in their own petty feuds, why would they want my
wife?"

"My guess is that this case is similar to one a few years back
involving the Baroness de Campo Belo. They held her for ransom
until her husband parted with a fortune in gold and jewels. That
exploit made news all the way to Rio. After that there seemed to
be a shift from crimes perpetrated on the ranchers to enable the
bandits to survive to blatant attacks on wealthy members of the
community for money or jewels."

"If it's jewels they want, they've taken a small fortune from us
already!" Erik groaned.

The major stood, loosened his belt, then shamelessly rearranged his genitals in his trousers. "Information is already being
gathered from many sources. By morning we'll have some news
in the case."

Major Borges left the room and his men followed. A few minutes later Colonel Feitosa bade Joaquim and Erik good evening.

"Now what are we to do?" Joaquim asked Erik.

"We could go out to my fazenda tomorrow, but I don't wish to be so far away in case something happens."

"I'm sure you're right," Joaquim added morosely.

Erik snapped his fingers and ordered another round of beers. Two hours later the proprietor dimmed the lamps in the dining room and noisily cleared the bottles. The two guests still didn't move from their seats.

"I know in the past we've had our difficulties . . ." Joaquim began.

"We adored the same woman," Erik said aloud, surprising them both.

Joaquim sucked his breath in so quickly that he almost choked. "I've always admired your wife's talent, but perhaps I've pushed her too hard. She might have been more content not to have pursued her music so vigorously. But you know that I've never stepped beyond . . ."

"I know. I hope you will forgive that time I was unfair to you. It was . . ."

"I've never held it against you. In fact, I should have thanked you. It was the push I needed to leave for France."

"No, I should be thanking you. You've given Margaret so much of what has made her happy. Without music . . ." Erik stopped as if trying to remember what he was going to say. Then he blurted unexpectedly, "We've both been unfaithful to each other, haven't we?"

Joaquim felt himself trembling. "I don't believe Margaret ever could've been unfaithful to anyone."

"Not purposely, of course. If she was unfaithful, it was to her first love, her music. Her marriage vows were false. She could never forsake everything else. And I didn't demand it of her because I couldn't. Some have wondered how another woman could please me when I was fortunate enough to have Margaret, but there have been . . . temptations. You'll never know how many I've resisted, but there have been a few" — Erik raised his empty glass — "who've made it impossible."

"You must remember I also live on Santa Teresa hill," Joaquim said softly.

Erik's tired eyes began to twitch. "Only the night before last . . ." He muttered something unintelligible. "She's been so good to me lately, ever since Chiquinha . . . ever since . . ." His words slurred.

"We'd better get some rest, Erico. Tomorrow will be difficult enough . . ."

"You know, Maestro, I'm glad you're here. I trust you." Erik stood unsteadily and peered down at Joaquim, blinking his eyes to focus them. All his youthful exuberance had faded. He pushed his chair back, clapped Joaquim across the shoulders, and walked him to the stairs. "Our rooms are across the hall from each other, aren't they?"

"Yes, numbers four and five."

On the landing they parted. "In the morning . . . wake me." Erik's voice dropped with fatigue.

"Sim. Boa noite, Erico," Joaquim whispered, then opened his own door.

Joaquim was so overcome with the events of the past two days his heart pounded mercilessly. He glanced around the simple room. There was one rickety chair and a lumpy bed. Even if Margaret comes back safely — when she comes back safely, he silently corrected himself — she'll go home to Erik, to his bed. She'll go back to their immense brood of clamoring children, but never to him. He'd rarely see her except for Music Society meetings, brief concerts, social engagements. Not enough! he roared to himself. Not enough! He tore off his clothes and lay down on the musty bed. He tried to summon Margaret's flowery smell, but it would not come. Closing his eyes, he forced himself to think of something else. The theme of his requiem flooded his mind, the slow, minor melody rising above his anguish. He played it through three times in his mind before falling into a fitful sleep.

7 Grim-faced, Erik joined Joaquim in the dining room before either the major or the colonel arrived. Cocks crowed on the hillside behind the hotel, but no employees yet stirred.

Erik spoke first. "I can't help believing that if Florinda's still with them, they won't harm Margaret."

"What could she do to stop them?"

"Don't know," Erik admitted. "It's just a feeling, that's all." Joaquim's own fears were so intense that he decided not to contradict Erik. Maybe he's right, he tried to convince himself.

Major Borges, wearing a crisply pressed uniform and freshly polished boots, strutted into the room. His mustache had been waxed to a point and his hair slicked back with a too-fragrant pomade. "Bom dia, gentlemen." He smiled humorlessly.

Joaquim and Erik nodded an informal greeting.

The major pulled out a chair from the next table, turned it backward, and straddled it with his enormous thighs. His stomach sagged against the rail of the chair. Taking a large inward breath, he began. "My men have not been idle. Yesterday several teams were instructed to discover the bandits' whereabouts. Since we suspected them to be in the vicinity of Desengano, they" — he coughed for a few seconds before continuing — "questioned the coiteiros in that region. I'm pleased to report that we achieved a high level of cooperation." He smiled thinly.

"What happens now?" Joaquim asked gravely.

"Already I've sent the good colonel from Rio and half of his troops to the river. I wanted them in position before sunrise. They'll stay hidden until we command them to go in. I've several of my best men moving closer. The riverside location makes it more difficult, but the plan is a very strong one."

"What part do you play?" Erik wondered aloud.

"I'm waiting for reinforcements from several districts to the north, men who are accustomed to this terrain. When they arrive, I'll lead them down to the Mesquita ranch."

Erik's fingers drummed on the table. "I don't understand what Mesquita's got to do with this."

"Mesquita's cooperating because this is a convenient way to eliminate his most despised rival. One of the coiteiros has gone to the camp at Desengano with news for Casimiro that the Mesquitas, who supposedly know nothing of the kidnaping, are planning a raid tonight. When Casimiro hears this, we hope he'll feel honor bound to stage an attack first. This will break up the forces at the camp, which, my sources tell me, are not substantial in the first place."

"If I understand you," Joaquim said with an involuntary shudder, "once they leave to attack the Mesquitas, you'll move in for the rescue."

"You're not talking about some hypothetical maneuver, Major, you're playing with the fate of my wife!" Erik's voice rose angrily. "What makes you think that Casimiro would believe this wasn't a trick? I think we should wait, see what they're asking . . ."

"You're wrong, my friend," the major insisted in a firm but controlled tone. "Right now they're in hiding, they're confused. In our experience these groups are more disorganized than you'd guess. They live like hunted animals, fearful and stupid. It's to our advantage to reduce any time they might take for scheming."

"How are you planning to protect my wife?" Erik spat out the words.

The major stood to make his point, his chair falling back with a clatter. "We've paid several coiteiros to go to the camp and look after her welfare. The rest of the details I cannot divulge, not even to you. My apologies, senhor."

"When do we leave?" Joaquim asked.

"Leave?" the major asked.

"When do we go to the camp?"

"You?" The major sounded as though he were chastizing a new recruit. "I'll have enough problems without having to worry about you two!"

"Um momento!" Erik pounded the table forcefully. "I may be needed if negotiations begin. I have money with me and our family is willing to pay if . . ."

The major studied the two tense men — the darker one with the elegant voice and gestures, the lighter one clearly accustomed to dictating, not following, commands. It would be an amusing business if there were not so much at stake. Still, he hadn't the authority to forbid them to join in the rescue, and if they were incorporated in the plan, he'd feel more secure knowing where they were at all times. "Ai-Jesus!" he moaned under his breath.

"You will follow my instructions!" He spoke an order, not a question.

❦ ❦ ❦

A low, dark mist hung over Vassouras all that day. The major ordered one of his men to escort Joaquim and Erik on horseback through the woods to a rendezvous point. The clouds from the encroaching afternoon storm dimmed the light so that at midday the path under the trees could barely be followed. As they passed small settlements, emaciated dogs ran out to bark at the hoofs of the horses and bare-bottomed children waved from the doorways of palm-thatched shacks.

"Where are we going?" Erik asked.

"I'm not certain," Lieutenant Vasco, their escort, replied politely.

Erik seethed. "So this is the major's idea of how to keep us out of the way!"

"Não, senhor. I am just following my instructions. We take this road until we come to a house where two children will be flying kites as a signal. At that place we will be among friends."

Erik seemed mollified for the moment and prodded his horse on. Lagging behind, Joaquim tried to appear at home in the saddle, but the jarring, bumpy ride, combined with the damp, changing atmosphere, had irritated the old injury in his back. It throbbed so severely he contemplated quitting this foolishness and returning to a bed and hot-water pack in Vassouras. Joaquim admired Erik's bearing on his mount ahead of him. Larson had undoubtedly been one of the most handsome men of his day. He and Margaret had been a golden couple who had seemed, on the surface at least, blessed with riches, talent, and beauty — but nothing was as it seemed on the surface, was it? Unexpectedly, a line from Homer flashed through his mind. "The lot of man; to suffer and to die." Erik and Margaret had already lost a child, had marital difficulties, and now this calamity.

The horses slowed as they began the ascent up a slope planted with banana trees. Oversized leaves draped across the trail, brushing their shoulders as they rode past. Erik reached up and picked several ripe bananas and tossed one back to Joaquim. He peeled and ate it, reveling in its natural sweetness.

"There it is!" Lieutenant Vasco pointed to a clearing where two white kites could be seen above the trees.

"That's where we're to wait?" Joaquim asked.

"Sim, senhor."

Joaquim sighed with relief, for his sciatic pain was so severe he doubted he could have withstood more than a few more minutes on horseback.

After their animals were tied up in a wooded glade behind the banana grower's modest house, the lieutenant warned, "You're to stay inside until I return for you."

"Do you think he's abandoning us here?" Erik asked under his breath.

Lieutenant Vasco had heard Erik's remark. "I have my orders to follow," he said in a clipped voice. More softly, he added, "Although, I do know that we've been given a position within sight of the camp. I just need to see if the boat's ready for us."

Erik gritted his teeth and turned back into the house.

"You can put the kites away now," the planter said to his two oldest children, who were enjoying the brisk wind that whipped their kites around in a most satisfactory fashion.

"Oh, Papai!" they complained in unison.

"Come inside now!" he demanded in a voice that had a strange whistling sound because he had so few teeth in his mouth. His wife sat on a crude stool just inside the doorway, nursing a scrawny baby and shooing flies from around its face. The hut smelled of burnt beans and damp bodies.

From the window, Erik and Joaquim watched one of the children's kites become tangled with his brother's as they pulled them down. "Children are children everywhere," Erik said absently. "Did you have kites?"

"Always. Before I went to school I made my own from paper and twigs and flew them daily in the fields behind our house. When I was older, I'd take them down to the beach at Olinda, where there was always a wonderful sea breeze."

"I was never permitted out alone," Erik said wistfully. "Until I was twelve I could only fly mine in the garden at Flamengo. Sometimes I'd get so lonely I used to pretend I was tiny and could ride on my kite and look down at everyone and everything."

"When my father would travel south, he'd always bring me back a new kite. I loved the papagaios from Rio, those brightly painted parrot kites."

"That's what I had, papagaios. When I was older" — Erik's voice became more animated — "I'd tie razor blades to the beaks of the birds and my sister and I would try to slash each other's kite strings in the air." He paused. "Didn't you once write a piece of music about a kite?"

"Yes, it seems so long ago. Margaret played it at a children's concert." Joaquim sighed nostalgically.

The lieutenant returned to the clearing. "Tudo em ordem. We go now."

Erik headed to where the horses had been tied. "Não." The policeman waved him off. "We walk."

Joaquim could barely hide his relief.

When they were deeper into the forest, Erik asked, "What happened at the Mesquitas'?"

"Don't know. I haven't spoken to anyone yet."

A rushing sound drowned out even the wind. A few more steps led them to the edge of the river just as the downpour finally spilled from the fomenting clouds. Fat drops pounded broad palm leaves with a steady rat-a-tat. Though it was not very wide, the river moved at a tremendous speed, scudding into foam as it passed over sharp boulders.

"This must be the Rio Parahyba," Erik told Joaquim. "It forms in the valley just below our fazenda. It's usually not this swift."

The sky thundered, then let loose with double the volume of water. It became impossible to see across to the other bank.

"We'll cross downstream," the lieutenant explained.

The rain pounded their backs like bullets. The lieutenant's cap flew off and was washed down the river before he could grab for it. As the wind whipped Joaquim's clothes and the rain lashed his back, the pain in his leg throbbed so insistently he couldn't keep up with the other men's pace. Soon they were so far ahead they appeared but faint outlines in the curtain of greyness. The mud along the river bank sucked at his feet and the heavy, wet branches scratched at his face.

Lieutenant Vasco whistled a signal. An echoed whistle was

heard from the opposite bank. Out of the swirling water and mist came a small dugout canoe.

"It's Horacio, the recruit who served coffee yesterday," Erik said, brightening.

"They must have commandeered everyone who can still breathe today," Joaquim muttered as he caught up. "I hope he knows what he's doing."

The three men, their legs slick with stinking mud, clambered into the boat. Lieutenant Vasco pushed off and asked Horacio, "Has the major crossed already?"

"Almost an hour ago. He said to tell you that Casimiro didn't go to Mesquita's, but he sent a small band led by his nephew."

"And?" Erik asked.

"We got them all, não ha problema."

"But not the chief?" Erik asked.

"Não. Nobody really thought Casimiro would've left so important a hostage. They say he's the brains of the clan." He pointed to his head. "Limoeiro's the heart; Tubarão, the guts."

In the whirling river the boat was making more progress downstream than across the current to the other bank. Lightning right above them made a bright slash in the grim sky. Horacio had to concentrate on paddling with great force. As soon as they were near the other side, the lieutenant reached for an overhanging branch and pulled the boat to shore. Erik helped Joaquim out, then, head down to keep the lashing rain from his eyes, leapt onto the slippery bank. He tripped in the mud and fell on one knee. Cursing, Erik stood and followed the two policemen and Joaquim as they headed back upriver. At least under the canopy of the forest, the rain couldn't pummel them quite so hard.

When they reached the edge of the wooded margin along the river, the storm was abating. They listened to hear if anyone was nearby, but the loudest sound was the droning of mosquitos.

Erik stared out onto a flat plain between mounded hills. "Where are we?"

"Desengano," Horacio replied.

"Disillusionment?" Erik translated.

"Sim, senhor, Desengano. I'm from very near here, the place they call Ubá."

"At least I understand why that name was given, eh?" Erik smiled. *Ubá* meant a dugout canoe, similar to the boat they had just used. "Where's the camp?"

"Just over the next hill. It's the site of an old mission," Horacio explained. "There's a church and several smaller buildings. I went to school there as a young boy."

"So you know it well?" Erik asked hopefully.

"Sim, senhor."

Erik shifted his feet impatiently. "What are we waiting for?"

"We aren't to move until sundown," the lieutenant replied.

Joaquim leaned against a tree trunk and tried to rest. His clothes stuck to his skin and he was remarkably hungry. Erik appeared even more miserable. His pale lips were lined with blue and the skin around his eyes had a curious ashen tone. In contrast, young Horacio seemed especially bright-eyed and animated.

In about an hour, the lieutenant stood and smoothed his wrinkled uniform. "Now we go up the hill, very quietly, no talking," he directed. "Major Borges will be bringing most of his men from the south, although some will be coming from Mesquita's to the north. The colonel from Rio will direct activities to the east. We're coming from the southwest because it's unlikely the bandits would head our way and risk being trapped by the river, compreende?"

Joaquim didn't understand exactly, but he was impressed with the coverage the plan appeared to afford. As they approached the crest of the small hill, they were ordered to crouch down. A smudge of smoke rose from the other side.

Slowly Joaquim maneuvered himself to where he could peer over the ridge. Down through rows of freshly planted sugar cane he could see the encampment in the distance. People around it were discernible in their movements, but at that distance no individual could be singled out. In front of the old stucco church with a crumbling roof, a campfire had been lit and a carcass of meat was being roasted on a makeshift spit. Candlelight inside the church spilled a pale orange flickering through myriad cracks in the roof and walls. To the right was a smaller building with a roof but no walls. From one side Joaquim could see rows of benches.

"The school?" Joaquim asked.

"Yes," Horacio answered. "On the other side's the old stable; behind are some storage sheds."

"Which building is my wife in?" Erik asked.

"The major knows," the lieutenant replied confidently.

Joaquim began to count the number of people he could see in the compound. At least four women, none of whom resembled Florinda or Margaret, were tending the fire. Six guards, wearing the familiar crossed-bullet belts of the bandit, were stationed at the perimeters. Two more guards stood in front of the church.

"That's where they must be keeping Margaret," Joaquim said. "None of the other buildings are guarded."

"I believe you're right!" Erik spoke excitedly.

He looked up at the sky. The rain clouds had blown off just enough to permit the faintest golden glow of sunset to dapple the hillside. In a few minutes nightfall covered them like a benevolent blanket. Now they could begin.

A man crossed the courtyard, carrying buckets of water to the horses. A horse whinnied. The man looked about, then shouted an alarm. At once a dozen others came running from the different shelters, waving their guns. Before they had a chance to assemble and confer, Colonel Feitosa's group fired from the east. Two bandits were hit — one in the back, one in the head. Joaquim thought he could feel the earth shudder as they fell.

From the crest of the hill, Joaquim and Erik watched as the outlaws swiftly took cover in and around the buildings. Since they were expecting more gunfire from the forests to their left, they were totally surprised when a flank of men moved in from the south, firing forward continuously. Several more bandits fell and lay writhing in the thick mud. Hidden behind the sheds, gunmen shot random volleys back in the direction of the police, but the troops were well camouflaged in the dark forest and no bullets found their mark.

"I can't see what's happening!" Erik groaned. Completely disobeying orders, he crouched down into the cane field and scrambled closer to the compound.

"Deus todo poderosa!" Lieutenant Vasco exclaimed when he saw Erik leave. "Horacio, you stay with this one!" he ordered fiercely before following Erik to the base of the hill.

From his high position, Joaquim could follow their movements between the columns of cane. Thankfully, Erik and the lieutenant had taken cover behind several high bushes without attracting any attention. He exhaled with relief and tried to move his stiff body into a more comfortable position. A sharp pain pierced his back and traveled down to his toes. He bit his lip so he wouldn't cry out.

After the brief calm, Feitosa's policemen rushed into the square, shooting a curtain of bullets ahead of them. Some fell. Joaquim could tell which casualties were the cangaceiros only if they wore the distinctive wide-brimmed cowboy hat. Now a new flank of guns moved in from a third direction. Joaquim guessed that these must be the balance of Borges's men coming from the Mesquita camp. This was a surprise to the bandits, who'd figured the attack was coming from only two sides. A half dozen more of their men fell under the withering fire. Their wounded staggered for shelter.

Now there was a period of respite as each side tried to figure what move to make next. At first Joaquim didn't notice the movement in the shadows out of the range of the campfire until something in his area of peripheral vision swayed. A crouched bandit was moving toward the bush where Erik and the lieutenant were hiding. Surely they saw him! No! "Cuidado! Be careful!" Joaquim shouted to warn them.

Lieutanant Vasco lifted his gun a second too late. A bullet hit the side of his head and he keeled over. From his position high above the bandit, Horacio had a clear shot and hit the outlaw squarely in the chest, then ran down to help his fellow officer. Joaquim clambered behind him.

The lieutenant had been killed instantly. Erik was unharmed, more furious than frightened. "Jagunços! Hoodlums!" he railed as a burst of gunfire drowned out his words. "This is crazy! How do they expect to get Margaret back alive?"

Horacio clapped his hand over Erik's mouth. "Hush!"

For less than a minute everything was quiet. Then there were three rapid shots from the east, followed by three from the south. A signal, Joaquim surmised. Suddenly, from all sides, more than forty men burst into the courtyard. Several policemen carrying buckets doused the fire, which hissed in protest and sent smoke billowing out along the ground. This misting screen enabled the police to take closer positions around the buildings. After the vapor cleared, a faint light remained from the embers. Everything was still.

"Erico." Joaquim gasped and pointed to a shadowy outline in the church window. "Margaret's in there!"

"I'm going after her . . ." Larson pulled away.

"Não!" It took all the composer's strength to hold him back.

A loud blast roared from inside the church. Two men hurled a body through the front door and called out, "Here's your coiteiro, scum of the earth!"

"That's Casimiro's voice," Horacio croaked. "He's murdered the rancher we sent to warn him about Mesquita."

"The one you paid for help?" Erik asked.

"Yes. He was to ask for a few moments with your wife as his reward."

Erik was enraged. "You offered my wife?"

"Não, senhor! If he got her alone, he was to tell her the plan for her escape. We weren't even sure if they would let him near her because they usually save the women for themselves."

"If anyone has touched my wife . . ." Erik's voice was far too loud. Horacio clapped his hand over his mouth once more.

"They have rules to govern these matters. Rape is reserved as a punishment for the women of rival bands. If they only want money, they'll treat her kindly . . . Besides, there hasn't been time."

Joaquim wanted to ask how much time the young recruit thought it took to commit a rape, but he kept blessedly silent.

"I'm coming out!" Casimiro shouted. "With the women! If anyone shoots, they're dead."

Three men, the ones they called Tubarão, Limoeiro, and Casimiro, came forward, Florinda and Margaret pinned in front of them as shields. Margaret looked unharmed but confused. Florinda was stumbling so badly they had to kick her to make her move her feet.

"You can have them if you want them, but in exchange you'll

have to leave three men as our hostages and one hundred contos de mil-reis."

"Fifty contos is all we have with us" came the voice of the major from the tree line.

Before the bandits could answer the counteroffer, shots from Major Borges's forces at the rear hit the men on the ends almost simultaneously in the back and they both dropped.

"Não!" Florinda screamed and reached out toward Limoeiro as he fell.

Casimiro hugged the two women together to keep them from running off. He pointed his weapon to Margaret's head. As he shifted his pistol, he slightly loosened his grip on Florinda, who seemed to have had a swift transfer of loyalty back to Margaret and lunged for the gun. In the confusion, Casimiro stumbled for just a second.

"Run, Margaret!" Erik shouted. "This way!"

Dazed by the sound of her husband's voice, Margaret looked around for him. Realizing that she couldn't see him in the darkness, Erik ran toward her the moment Casimiro recovered his stance. The bandit's gun pointed at him, but Florinda pushed his arm off center just as the blast was fired. Instead of hitting Erik in the midsection, where it had been aimed, the bullet penetrated his shin. Erik fell, face first, into the mud.

Horacio had leveled his revolver at Casimiro, but Florinda, after knocking his arm, was now squarely in front of him. The sleek bullet from the young recruit's gun entered the hollow of her neck. Blood spurted like a fountain. Without thinking, Joaquim ran forward, lifted Margaret in his arms, and carried her back to the safety of the bushes while Horacio dragged Erik to the same spot.

Now a hail of bullets poured into the compound, mowing down every bandit who could be spotted. There was a brief pause. The remaining outlaws surrendered. Moments later, Colonel Feitosa was at the Larsons' side, examining Erik's wound. "Not so grave, eh?"

Erik was pale and shaking from the loss of blood, yet his sense of humor bubbled to the surface unexpectedly. "Do you throw such wild parties often, Colonel?"

Joaquim watched as Margaret held Erik's head in her lap.

Tears poured down her cheeks and she moaned, "Florinda . . . Florinda . . ." Erik reached over and stroked her limp hand.

"My deepest apologies, senhora." Horacio wept openly. "I didn't mean to hit the girl. I beg your forgiveness."

Joaquim could see the boy was shattered.

"She was a lost cause in any case, Margaret," Joaquim tried to console her.

"She died a noble death," the colonel added. "Without question, she saved Senhor Larson's life and possibly your own."

"My husband saved me," Margaret said. Nobody dared contradict her. In the confusion it would be impossible to really ascertain who had done what. All they knew was the cost of the rescue had been great. Dead were Florinda, Lieutenant Vasco, and how many others? There were too many bodies and wounded to even count that night.

Major Borges's troops milled about the mission courtyard, shooting into the brush to mow down the few desperadoes who were trying to escape into the forest. In front of the church, three of the major's men were holding Casimiro prisoner while his jubilant soldiers looted the bandits' treasures and mutilated the dead, cutting off ears and genitals for trophies. Major Borges walked among his men, not saying a word about their barbaric behavior.

Joaquim turned from the ghastly scene and concentrated on the man who was preparing a litter for Erik. Finally, Margaret looked up from her wounded husband and seemed, for the first time, to be aware of his presence. "You've been here through it all?"

Joaquim's eyes met hers, but she wasn't really seeing him. She looked back at her husband. "He'll need a doctor right away. An injury like this can aggravate his diabetic condition."

"We'll take him back to town immediately," Joaquim agreed aloud, but he was thinking how precariously close Erik had come to never needing a doctor again.

8 "Have you seen this?" Delgado de Mello showed Joaquim the item in the newspaper featuring the release of Casimiro. He'd bought it at Rio's train depot while waiting for their luggage to be unloaded. "The story's still front-page news."

"Why would they make heroes out of criminals?" Joaquim

asked as he studied the sensational photographs of the decapitated heads of Tubarão and Limoeiro next to those of their slain
comrades. They were surrounded by the trophies taken by the
police: cartridge belts, hats, and guns. The headline read, "The
Tears of Desengano." Under it was a close-up photograph of
the Larson jewels with the words "The Teardrops of the Rich."
The final picture on the page was Margaret's most recent portrait,
the one that had been used to publicize the memorial concert. She
was identified only as "Margarida of the Bandidos."

"Disgusting!" Joaquim threw the paper down on the steam-
misted platform. A sickening feeling twisted his stomach. "To
think that swine's free again! It would've been better if he'd died
with the rest of the outlaws."

"Then they would have deified him," de Mello replied. The
noise of a train pulling out of the station covered most of his
words.

"This just proves you can buy justice in the backlands!" Joaquim raged.

"Enough, it's over!" Nicia Netto chided as she stepped off the
train. "Aida, did you get your satchel?"

"Sim, Tia Nicia."

The composer shook his head sadly. "It will never be over for
me."

The door of the train compartment opened once more to permit Olympio Baptista, the young, flashy student of Flavio
Queiroz who had taken Margaret's place on the tour, to hand
down the two cellos. Aida beamed at the pianist. The two youngsters were so charming, Joaquim thought. They'd attempted, unsuccessfully, to hide their blossoming affection for each other all
during the month-long trip to six southern cities.

"Well, Olympio," Joaquim asked cheerfully, "are you ready to
win raves from the Carioca critics as well as those in the prov-
inces?"

"Well . . . I . . ." Olympio stammered. He removed his glasses
and wiped the lenses purposefully.

Joaquim observed every gesture of the boy's hands, the only
graceful part of his gangling, untried body. At twenty his thinness and pallor were the results of years spent on a piano bench

instead of in the sun, but his persistence had been rewarded by the praise he'd won during this important debut. His success had been especially remarkable considering he'd had to play before audiences disappointed they weren't hearing "Margarida of the Bandidos," for Margaret had remained in Rio to tend her wounded husband.

"Margarida of the Bandidos!" How Joaquim loathed that epithet! It made her sound as though she had become a willing accessory to the bandits, when nothing had been further from the truth. They'd bound her and threatened to kill her. She'd been harassed by the guards, who teased and fondled her but — graças a Deus! — nothing more. Terrorized, she witnessed the slaughter of rebels and police alike, the horror culminating in the slaying of the tragically misguided Florinda.

Yet, to the many who knew only what they read in the press, the last stand at Desengano was becoming a folk legend that glorified the ambushed criminals and denigrated the fine strategy of the police. "Desengano." Was there ever a place so aptly named? Desengano, where all his illusions had been shattered. Perhaps that's why he'd accepted the offer of a major tour so soon. He'd needed distance from the calamitous events; he'd needed to be as far away from Rio — and Margaret — as possible.

Francisca's memorial concert, rescheduled for June, had been a grand, if anticlimactic, success. Instead of a one-night gala, tickets had been sold for two full weeks of performances to meet the demands of everyone who wanted to see the woman who'd been kidnaped by Casimiro's gang and lived to tell the tale.

Freire's participation in the events around Vassouras had given him the notoriety he'd dreamed of having as a composer. At moments he regretted that his newly won fame had derived not from the brilliance of his art but from his role as one of her rescuers. The themes from his "Estudos Brasileiros" and "Requiem for Piano" were already being played by street musicians in Rio and São Paulo, and copies of his sheet music were being sought nationwide.

Though initially Joaquim had complained about the popularizing of his serious works, Delgado lectured him to be grateful. "A composer writes for as many ears as he can find to listen, even if it means tying the bodies to which they're attached down in their seats to force them to hear his work. Fortunately, you've been spared the expense of the rope!"

At least he rejoiced that his music had met with critical as well as mass approval. Some of the most influential of the reviewers called it "stunning in originality," "the essence of the Brazilian spirit transformed into ethereal art," and "the voice of Brazil to the world"; they applauded Freire's break with European traditions and reminded others in Brazil's artistic community to stop emulating French culture and begin expressing their own unique heritage. Even his few detractors had done much to publicize him, by labeling his pieces "outlaw tunes" and "bandit bravado." Though his reputation soared, it galled Joaquim to think that an incident that caused so much pain and cost so many lives had caught the public's morbid fascination. These Robin Hoods of their day were, in reality, despicable characters, not heroes. Their only saving grace was that they hadn't physically harmed Margaret once the attack began.

"Quincas!" De Mello was calling him out of his reverie. "Henrique's going ahead with the instruments and will meet us later at Erico's."

"What?"

"Quincas? Haven't you heard a word I've said?"

"I'm sorry. I'm just exhausted. Perhaps I'd better just go on home."

"But don't you want to see for yourself how Erico's feeling?"

"Yes, of course I do."

All along the way to the Gloria district, Joaquim steeled himself to make his duty call with the other musicians. Before he'd left for São Paulo, Erik's shinbone had stubbornly refused to heal.

"The doctor warned us wounds are more serious in someone with my husband's disease," Margaret had explained. "Blood doesn't flow to the ankle very profusely, even in normal people, but for a diabetic the lack of a strong blood supply makes healing more difficult."

On his last visit to the Larsons' before the journey, Erik had shown Joaquim his festering sore. The blackened tissue around the bullet's entry site had to be scraped daily, and the swelling from a persistent infection had moved almost to his knee. But that was many weeks ago, Joaquim reminded himself. When they arrived at the mansion on the Gloria square, they saw a small crowd surrounding the Larsons' gate.

"What's going on here?" Joaquim asked.

"Don't you know?" the driver answered. "This is where Margarida of the Bandidos lives. They say it's good luck to see her."

"Who are you?" a woman asked Joaquim as he stepped down from the carriage. Suddenly she touched her forehead with recognition. "Ai! It's the maestro who was there too." She tugged on Freire's sleeve.

Joaquim pulled away and hurried to the front door, which was immediately opened. "How long do they wait there?" he asked the servant who took his hat.

"All day. The children stay at Boa Vista now because the crowd frightens them."

"It frightens me," Joaquim said under his breath. "Terrible business!" he muttered as he was shown to the drawing room.

Margaret offered her hand. Its coolness was like an icy stab. "I've read all about your great success."

"You know how those southerners love to exaggerate." He laughed uneasily. Then, after a deep breath, "So, how's Erico? All recovered?"

"Not exactly. We expected a slow healing process, but no matter how much of the skin they cut away, the contamination extends to a larger and larger area."

At the unexpected bad news, Joaquim's heart pounded fiercely.

"Is he in much pain?" de Mello asked.

"Yes, but he bears it well. He's so weak that he has no appetite. The doctors would prefer" — she stopped, took a breath, then jutted out the point of her chin bravely — "to amputate past the knee."

Aida reached for Olympio's hand.

"Is that what's planned?" de Mello dared ask.

"Not yet. They feel that the risks of surgery are very poor right now because his blood is poisoned."

"What are they doing for him?" Joaquim wondered aloud.

"He takes his powders and medications hourly, and they work on the skin infections with the maggots."

"Maggots?" Joaquim's hand went to his mouth.

"First they let the worms in to eat away the bad parts, then they pick them out with tweezers. I can't bear to watch it. They say it's the best way to clean the wound."

Joaquim blinked quickly. "I'd like to see him."

"Now's a good time. His fever's down in the afternoons, and he slept well this morning."

De Mello and Joaquim followed Margaret up the elegant wrought-iron staircase, with its fanciful motif of cherubs and grapevines, to the upstairs drawing room where her harpsichord was kept. Ten-foot-high French doors opened onto a narrow iron balcony where Erik lay on a settee, his leg propped on cushions for an airing. He was wearing a blue silk dressing gown and reading the financial pages of the *Jornal do Comercio*.

"Look who's here, querido!" Margaret announced brightly.

Erik turned slowly, but when he saw who it was, his face was wreathed in smiles. "The maestro of the cangaceiros! Conqueror of the southlands!" He laughed. "Is it true that a baton is mightier than a gun?"

De Mello threw back his head and roared a bit too loudly. Joaquim joined in with less enthusiasm. Both were trying to hide their shock at Erik's disastrous appearance. All his exposed skin surfaces were covered with huge, pustular eruptions. His leg, which was open to the fresh air except for the loosest of cotton bandages, was more than twice its normal size, with blackened patches visible on the toes and shin. To think that a tiny bullet had wreaked so much damage! Joaquim was nauseated, not only by the sight, but by the sickeningly sweet odor of some medicant that was used in a vain attempt to mask the all-pervasive smell of rot.

De Mello nudged him. "The box . . ."

"Box?" Joaquim asked stupidly, then remembered and reached into his vest pocket. "Seu Erico," he began respectfully, "with your permission we've brought your wife a small token of our disappointment at not having the pleasure of her company on the tour."

"From what I've read in the journals, young Baptista replaced me quite adequately," Margaret interrupted. In the tone of her voice Joaquim heard more than a hint of regret.

"Nobody could ever replace my Margarida, eh, Maestro?" Erik added smoothly.

"Exactly," Delgado de Mello said protectively.

Erik studied the green velvet box Joaquim was inadvertently stroking between his strong brown fingers. "What is it, then?"

Joaquim awkwardly handed the gift to Margaret. "Something I ... we noticed you didn't have. Perhaps this will change your luck."

With a shy smile, Margaret opened it. Inside was a figa, a uniquely Brazilian charm, carved from a piece of native amethyst and banded in gold. A matching gold chain was attached to the loop. Margaret lifted it out and touched the talisman in the shape of a clenched fist with thumb between the first two fingers. "I've always wanted one."

"I never knew you were so ... superstitious ..." Erik's voice trailed absently. He closed his eyes.

Joaquim thought Erik was upset with the present until he noticed the tenseness of the invalid's facial muscles and his clenched fists. The man was suffering physical pain too intense to hide.

In a high, quick voice, Margaret asked, "Why is the figa supposed to be so lucky?"

Delgado de Mello responded first. "Originally the African slaves used them as a symbol of masculine fertility; today most all Brazilians carry one as a good luck charm." He took out his own watch chain to prove he had a small gold figa dangling near the winder. "They say no harm can come to someone who wears it faithfully. I don't know if it's true or not, but I'm not taking any chances." He chuckled uneasily.

"Then I must put mine on immediately," Margaret said. "It's time my luck began to improve." Sitting on the edge of her husband's couch, she bent her long, swanlike neck forward so Erik could close the clasp on the chain. "There!" She fingered the coolness of the stone. "Now I'm safe."

"Dona Margarida." Carlota's voice captured her attention.

She stood to permit the girl to set Erik's tray of medicines and bandages down. Margaret poured a powder into a glass of water, turning it a chalky white, then added three drops of a strong-smelling liquid. When she handed Erik the glass, he grimaced but

swallowed it down. "Now you'll have another sleep," Margaret
said as she stroked his brow.

Delgado and Joaquim quickly said their good-byes.

"I'll be downstairs in a few minutes," Margaret said and turned
back to tend her husband's leg.

9 "It seems as though your parlor has become the official
Fluminense Music Society meeting hall," Delgado de
Mello said as he tried to greet Margaret cheerfully a week after his
return from Rio.

She ushered him and Joaquim in. "I don't mind at all. It's been
a blessing to be surrounded by all our dearest friends. In fact,
you're the last of the 'members' to arrive today."

"I see everyone's in his regular place, too!" Joaquim smiled at
the assembled troupe, each in a familiar seat.

Against the principal wall, facing the door, sat Nicia Netto
with music scattered about her on the sofa. On her left, in one of
the two matching wine-colored plush sofas, sat Olympia and
Aida. The vigil at Erik's bedside had become their decorous excuse to be together so frequently. Joaquim delighted in the
youngsters' romance. It was healing for him to watch them blossom while he willed himself to care less for Margaret.

"I'll be back shortly," Margaret said. "Help yourself to the coffee, won't you?"

"She looks so pale and exhausted. Doesn't she ever leave the
house?" Joaquim asked Nicia Netto.

"I don't think she's been away from his side in weeks."

"Where's Tobias?" Joaquim asked Nicia as she poured him a
cup of Margaret's special chicory-flavored coffee. Her husband,
the liberal attorney, had developed an especially close relation-
ship with Erik. They'd become friends initially when they'd
sought each other out as a refuge from their spouses' incessant
musical discussions. Now their long association had led to
Netto's handling some of Erik's legal interests.

"Upstairs. Erik's arranging to send that horse of his to
England."

"So, Tobias has become indispensable," Joaquim noted in
what he thought was a kindly voice.

Nicia frowned. He hadn't meant to imply that her husband had been improperly ingratiating himself with an invalid, but that was how he'd sounded. Before he could apologize, Margaret's mother and brother were ushered in. All the men in the room, as well as young Aida, stood respectfully to greet the older woman.

"Dona Lucretia." Joaquim stepped forward and gave a little bow.

"Maestro Freire," she said coolly. He noticed that she didn't extend her hand. "You remember my son, don't you?"

"It's a pity my sister couldn't travel with you on your latest tour," Raleigh said, remaining at his mother's side.

"We're all in agreement on that," Freire answered stiffly. As he introduced Raleigh to the others in the room, Joaquim studied his appearance. Nobody would guess that the swarthy man with the huge ears and slightly disreputable expression was Margaret's brother, he thought.

After a few minutes of polite banter with the musicians, Raleigh asked, "Who's with Erico now?"

"Your sister and my husband," Nicia Netto replied.

Raleigh raised a dark, bushy eyebrow. "The attorney?"

"I told you we should have come right over last night," Lucretia replied tensely just as Margaret returned, even more wan than she'd seemed earlier.

"Mother!" She kissed Lucretia on both cheeks. Someone hugged her from behind. She started and turned. "Raleigh! When did you get here?"

"Late yesterday."

"Where are Marianne and the children?"

"I left too quickly to bring them with me. They'll be following in a few days."

Margaret continued to stare at her brother worriedly. "What's wrong?"

"Nothing, they're all well."

"No, what's wrong with you?" She studied his face curiously. "There's something the matter with your eyes, isn't there?"

"You're the first to notice."

Lucretia came around and stared up at her son. "Notice what?"

"In the north there's this shrub that grows along hedgerows called avelós but nicknamed dedo de cão, meaning 'devil's fingers.' It has a white sap that blinds. Unfortunately, when I tried to cut a few branches for kindling, I got some in my eye. The burning was horribly painful. Since then I've been blind in that one."

Lucretia grabbed his arm. "No! Completely?"

"My right eye is still perfect."

"Thank God!"

"Look." He pointed to the back of his suntanned arm. "See those light splotches? That's where the sap tattooed those marks on my skin permanently."

"My poor darling! Why didn't the locals warn you? What kind of people . . . ?"

"Mother, there was no one else around at that moment. Besides" — his eyes looked upward, as though indicating Erik upstairs in his bed — "there are far worse crosses to bear . . ."

"Would you like to see him now?" Margaret broke in.

"Of course, that's why we're here," her mother said testily.

With an apologetic nod to her other guests, Margaret led her family out of the room. When she returned a few minutes later, she perched on the long padded satin cushions placed between the bay windows. From the expression in her darting eyes and the faint twitch around her mouth, Joaquim could tell that she was much more agitated than she'd been before.

"Is there anything I can do?" Nicia asked softly.

"It's just . . ."

"Your mother and brother?"

Margaret nodded.

"Families can be so difficult," the cellist began sympathetically.

"I hope they won't upset Erik. Today hasn't been one of his best."

"Tobias is still there?"

"Yes."

"Bom! I'm certain he'll be a mediating influence. He's the calm one in our family."

"What a surprise!" de Mello said to break the somber mood.

Margaret acted as though she hadn't heard him. "You're right about Tobias. For some reason my brother was rude to him right off, but he pretended not to be insulted. These financial matters are always such a problem, especially in a family business, aren't they?" She sighed deeply.

Out of respect for Margaret, everyone in the room was quiet.
Her feelings of melancholy were so great they were obvious to
her friends. With her face in the soft shadows and her hair outlined from the sun behind her, Margaret seemed ethereal, almost
saintly, to Joaquim. If there were only something he could do or
say to bring her comfort! But no, he had to remain in the background, helpless, yet culpable for his own part in the events that
had led to Erik's injury and her unbearable distress.

❧   ❧   ❧

Joaquim found excuses to stay away from the Larsons for the
next few days. Finally, when his absence would certainly have
been noticed, he reluctantly ordered a car and arrived at Gloria
quite a bit later than his usual hour.

"Am I too late to visit with Erico?"

Margaret looked ashen, but thankfully, she didn't ask why he
hadn't been visiting. "Not at all. You may go up anytime. He's
much improved and was very jolly with everyone this afternoon."

"Well, that's great news!"

De Mello bit into a slice of guava topped with a creamy white
cheese. "His jokes are still in terrible taste."

Joaquim smiled thinly while eyeing de Mello to ascertain any
hidden meaning in his words, but there was nothing in his manner to indicate that Erik hadn't indeed undergone a reversal in his
illness. "I'm so pleased! I can't wait to see for myself."

"His lawyer's with him," Raleigh interjected curtly.

Margaret bit her lip. "By now he'd probably welcome a break
from all those tedious matters."

As Joaquim turned down the hall, a nurse, carrying a covered
bowl, was leaving Erik's sickroom. She motioned him to go right
in, but he stood in the half-open doorway, trying to prepare himself for whatever he might see.

"How can you ask me to do that for you?" Tobias Netto's
voice bellowed through the doorway. Clearly he was appalled by
some request. Since it seemed like a bad time to barge in, Joaquim
remained outside, his hand on the edge of the door, waiting for a
break in the conversation.

"She'll have to know about Malvina in any case," Erik's voice
insisted.

"Then you tell her."

"If she hears it from me, she won't be able to react. I expect her to be angry, but how can she lash out at someone in my condition?"

"Suddenly you've become extremely considerate. If you'd thought more and done less . . ."

Erik broke in, laughing. "Dr. Netto, my esteemed attorney, I should have sought your advice before unbuttoning my pants, but since you were unavailable, I made my own decisions in that matter."

Joaquim was shocked, not only by the coarse talk but also by the difference in Erik's manner. Only a few days ago he'd had little energy even to greet his visitors, let alone argue with them.

Joaquim shuffled his feet to draw attention to his presence.

"Maestro!" Tobias Netto motioned him to enter the room.

When Erik did not turn in his direction, Joaquim moved around to the far side of the bed. He was shocked to see Erik's skin was silvery, almost iridescent, as though he'd been touched by a light frost. At first he thought the man was covered in sweat, but the sheen was quite dry and unusual. Whatever it was, it did not harm his appearance, and the glow could even be considered becoming if it hadn't been for the strong putrid smell that still pervaded the room.

"Tomorrow is the day that Erico's horse leaves for England," Netto said in an overly loud voice.

"Without me . . ." Erik groaned theatrically. The nurse returned and efficiently placed some medicine bottles on a tray. "He'll win! He'll show the world what a Brazilian horse can do!" Erik bragged to Joaquim, then pointed to the file on the attorney's lap. "Do you have my letter to Lord Wavertree?"

"Yes, it's right here," Netto replied. As an aside to Joaquim, he added, "Lord Wavertree owns the stables where Nova Esperança will be housed."

"Who's accompanying the horse?" Joaquim asked.

"Felix da Costa and his daughter," Erik said matter-of-factly. "We were just talking about them when you arrived. There's only one complication that must be settled . . ."

"Erico!" Netto glared as if to warn him not to speak.

Joaquim glanced meaningfully at Netto. He thought this had

something to do with the horse trainer. Nobody knew better than he how the dark-skinned Brazilian would be received among the British racing crowd.

"Why shouldn't he know about Malvina? I've never meant to keep her a secret from my friends. And who would understand about her better than he, eh?"

"Malvina?"

"Amara da Costa's infant daughter . . . and mine."

Joaquim could not control his shocked expression. "You had a child with her?" It must be the illness, Joaquim thought at first. The fevers had gone to his brain. How else could he explain Erik's smug and cocky smile and the fact that he wasn't sensing the displeasure of both the other men in the room? Each had his own reasons for not wanting to know about this untidy business — Tobias because of the legal complications, Joaquim because he instinctively felt what Margaret's horrified reaction would be and took it for his own.

"For goodness' sake, Quincas, don't tell me you can't count a handful of bastards of your own," Erik continued too lucidly for a man who had to be speaking out of delirium.

"Can't say that I have ever had . . ."

"Bicha . . ." Erik muttered under his breath. His eyes began to water profusely. He mumbled some other unintelligible remarks that didn't seem to be directed at anyone in particular.

Joaquim clenched his fists and fought for self-control. To have Erik call him a homosexual was utterly insulting, but considering the man's condition, there was nothing he could do or say.

"She's a beauty . . ." Erik said wistfully. "A body tight as steel, warm as a dove . . ."

"How could you . . . ?" Joaquim finally choked.

"Just as your father could, Quincas," Erik interrupted. "Lucky for you he had a taste for dark meat, too, eh?" Erik cocked his head and lifted his eyebrow provocatively.

Joaquim moved around to where the attorney sat. "Does he know what he's saying?" he muttered under his breath.

"In a way he does," Netto responded quietly. "Sometimes he speaks crazily, sometimes he's perfectly reasonable. In either case, he doesn't seem to or doesn't wish to understand the consequences of his remarks." Tobias Netto stopped and stared at

Erik. His eyes had an odd glazed expression, and he began to breathe too rapidly. The nurse quickly mixed a medication and forced Erik to take a few sips. Erik closed his eyes and fell back on his pillows.

Netto murmured, "One minute he's absolutely charming, full of tales, bright ideas. Then, without warning, he's unintelligible." He looked down at Erik. It seemed he'd dropped off into a deep sleep.

"It's not true, then . . . this daughter of his . . ."

"True? Oh, it's true enough, I'm sorry to say. It's what he wants me to do about it that's the difficulty."

"You could wait, couldn't you?"

"Wait for what?" Erik shot upright in bed. "Wait for what?" He repeated himself like a silly child.

He's mad . . . Joaquim thought for a second, but changed his mind. Erik always liked to tease, to keep you off balance. Whatever it was, he was doing a superb job of it now.

"Waiting! I'm tired of waiting! Nurse! Nurse!"

The nurse patted his head. "Senhor Larson?"

"Call my wife!"

"Are you in pain?"

"A party . . . Today we'll have a party in my room. I'm tired of everyone tiptoeing about."

"I can't allow it, senhor. Doctor will be here soon . . ." the nurse said weakly.

Erik pouted. "A toast! Who could deny me a toast to my horse? What do you say, Tobias, my friend?"

The attorney looked nervously at Joaquim. "I can see no harm . . ."

"No harm! How could anything harm me now?" Erik pulled the covers off his legs. "They're getting better, I feel it! There's no pain anymore!"

The nurse caught the sheet before it hit the floor and rapidly moved to put it back in place, but not before Joaquim got a good look at the swollen, blackened mass that obviously could never again support the man's weight. All his anger dissipated into compassion. Deus! he thought, he's half-dead already.

❧ ❧ ❧

As Joaquim returned downstairs he overheard Olympio saying,
"Que pena! What a pity Senhor Larson won't see his horse run
the Derby."

"Would you have gone with him, Dona Margarida?" Aida
asked easily.

Margaret, who had taken a particular liking to the young cellist
with the soulful dark eyes, sighed. "No, I have far too much to do
here with all the children . . ." Her voice trailed wistfully.

"Wouldn't you like to travel, though?" Aida persisted. "Play in
European concert halls, see Paris, meet Ravel, Debussy, and
Fauré, or even visit North America again?"

Margaret sucked in her lower lip and hesitated a few beats.
"Certainly, but not now. My teacher in New Orleans once told
me that musicians are some of the few people who become better
with age. When our children are grown, there will be time for me
to see these places. Perhaps by then I'll have improved sufficiently to play for those sophisticated audiences. If not, I'll still be
able to listen, won't I? Would you like to travel?"

"I'd like to see the whole world!" Aida answered brightly. She
turned to Olympio, who smiled his agreement.

"My teacher would have approved of you two together."

Aida spun around.

"She used to say that musicians should marry each other, since
they were already married to music first."

"Did she marry one?"

"No, but she devoted her life to the memory of Gottschalk and
his music."

Aida's radiant eyes filled with tears. "How sad!"

Tobias Netto, looking quite drawn and upset, entered the
room. He went directly to his wife's side. "I must stay with Erico
a bit longer. He has many questions, papers. Do you mind?"

"You're looking so tired."

"There's aways tomorrow," Margaret agreed gently.

"He won't rest until everything's settled regarding Nova
Esperança's insurance and documents."

Nicia glanced at Olympio and Aida fondly gazing at each
other. "We can't expect them to remain here all day."

Delgado de Mello cleared his throat loudly. "It's a wonderful
afternoon for a walk along Praia Vermelha, eh?" He beamed at

the young lovers. "Or even a trip up the cable car to Pão de Açúcar?"

"Senhor," Olympio began respectfully, "will there be time for a trip all the way up Sugar Loaf?"

"Sim, sim. I'll take you myself. But I don't care for the cable car, so you'll have to permit me to wait for you at the base of the hill."

Aida seemed anxious. This would be the first time she would be alone with Olympio without any chaperone. Nicia Netto forced a laugh. "How much can happen on a cable car? Go! I won't write your mother any letters!"

When Aida was out the door, Tobias Netto patted his vest pocket as some sort of a sign to Olympio.

"What was that all about?" Margaret asked.

"What?"

She pointed to his pocket.

"Oh, that . . ." He formed a circle with his right thumb and forefinger and slipped it over his ring finger meaningfully. "When they get to the summit, he has a gift that he hopes the young lady will accept."

Margaret clapped her hands gleefully. "É a verdade? How romantic! Maravilhoso!" Her mood changed quickly. She was studying Netto for a clue to what might be happening with her husband. "Is he . . . better?"

"We were able to go over many vital matters today," he said smoothly. "You know Erico, he's very exacting."

Margaret didn't press the attorney for more details. She knew better than anyone her husband's pessimistic state of mind. "I'm so glad he has you now. I, for one, trust you more than any of the other advogados he's hired in the past."

Netto appeared uncomfortable with her praise. His wife, however, radiated with pride. Of all the marriages Joaquim knew, the Nettos' was the one he admired the most. They seemed to be two distinct halves of a very interesting whole.

"So," Margaret said after Tobias Netto returned to Erik's bedside, "as you see for yourself, there's been some improvement — lower temperatures, less sweating." She smiled optimistically and waited for her friends to agree.

What could he say to her? He was still recoiling from Erik's uncalled-for insult. All the veneer of the charming gentleman had fallen away for a brief few minutes, his tongue loosened by pain or medicine. Deus, this was awful! Not only that, but Erik had managed to transfer his own guilty secret to him and now Joaquim carried it like a weight within him. "I'm certain you're right," he mumbled.

"The doctors have always felt that his body could reverse the infection; now it seems they were right." Margaret spoke as if mouthing the words could make them true.

Tobias Netto had returned to the drawing room. He took his place beside his wife. Margaret immediately noticed his somber expression. "What's wrong?"

"He's just . . . resting. I'm afraid I've tired him out."

Raleigh, who'd been sulking in the background, stepped forward. "Can I go up now?"

Margaret responded with great gentleness. "In an hour, perhaps."

"Don't you realize I've important matters to discuss as well? There are thousands of hectares of land under my control and an equal number of problems, I assure you."

"Why don't we sit down together and discuss your greatest concerns," Tobias suggested. "Then, when Sven Larson returns this evening, we'll be prepared, not only with the problems but with several solutions."

"I don't mean to be unkind, Dr. Netto, but some of these are family matters."

Lucretia came up behind her daughter and smiled wanly. "Let's not quarrel. We all are praying for your husband's quick recovery from this terrible affliction."

Tobias looked at Margaret with great sympathy. "Well, Senhor and Senhora Claiborne, if you don't require my assistance now, I promised Erico I'd get to the docks." He forced a slight chuckle. "He's asked me to say bon voyage to his horse!"

Nobody smiled. Joaquim felt the fear that had gripped Margaret. "I wish you'd stay . . ." she said weakly.

"I'll return after supper," Tobias promised.

Margaret held the attorney's hand a second too long. "Isn't there anything else you can tell me?" she asked in a pleading voice.

Netto cleared his throat nervously. "Are all the children coming to visit tomorrow?"

"No, they come on the weekend usually. Why?"

"Could they possibly come tomorrow?" he asked softly.

Joaquim watched helplessly as Margaret's mouth formed a silent cry. Her face crumbled. Netto helped her into a chair and called for the nurse. When her mother kneeled by her side, the musicians backed away into the dining room like guilty thieves. Still, they could hear every ugly word that followed.

"You can't permit those bastard children to come at a time like this!" Lucretia said sharply. Though they were speaking in English, Joaquim could follow most of what they were saying.

"They're his children, Mother," Margaret said in a thin voice. Then, lower, as though she were speaking through her teeth, "Anything you could have done about them, you forfeited years ago by not telling me what you knew. However, I don't see why innocent children should be hurt by Erik's folly or yours!"

Lucretia became more placating. "It's one thing to keep them out at Boa Vista, but to bring them into your own home is . . . improper at best!" Her voice rose shrilly. "I'd have gotten rid of them years ago!"

"How, Mother? They're not stray cats you can drown!"

"He could've paid them all off! Why not? His family's done it before, haven't they? How else did they get rid of that leech Augusto?"

"That was different."

"But not your husband, he wouldn't give up a precious penny, would he? If you only knew what the Brazilians say about him!"

"About my husband? What do *they* say?"

"That he's as tightfisted as a parrot sitting on thin wire."

"What!" Margaret sputtered. "Where'd you ever hear an expression like that?"

"I'd rather not say."

"Raleigh! Is that your contribution?"

"It's well known that he's stingy with his workers, but of course that's part of being a good businessman." Raleigh covered himself masterfully.

"How can *you* talk about my husband that way when he's been so generous to every member of our family?"

Lucretia began to weep copiously. "You're right. I don't know what I'm saying. I know what it's like to lose a husband, don't I? This is hard on me too, but nobody thinks of me!"

"Mother . . ." Raleigh comforted.

Joaquim and de Mello strolled back into the room. Lucretia quickly departed, dabbing her eyes.

Raleigh took a seat opposite Joaquim, made a tent with his fingers, and pressed the point to his mouth. Joaquim crossed his long legs, leaned back, and stared at the center of Raleigh's beady pupils, attempting to determine which was his bad eye. Neither spoke a word.

❧ 10 "Estou chegando . . . Coming!" Jacobina went running to answer the rude knocks on the front door. Through the glass side panels, the unexpected visitors were bathed in the eerie purple light of dawn.

"Senhor Joaquim . . . por favor," Tobias Netto asked somberly.

Jacobina raised her hand to her mouth to silence her scream.

Joaquim stumbled downstairs, wrapping a towel around his naked waist as he ran. Seeing Nicia in the pastel shadows, being supported by her husband, he knew immediately.

"Dead? Already?"

Tobias nodded.

"But how could that be? Yesterday he was so . . ."

"So crazy," Tobias answered for him. "I knew then it had to be close, but didn't know how to tell you. The doctor had warned that there might be a drastic personality change near the end."

Joaquim's first thoughts were for Margaret. "Did she know it was so close?"

"She wanted to believe he was beginning to recover."

"Please . . . Come in! You haven't slept, have you?"

"No, we were called back again late last night."

"Why?"

"Erico had asked for some . . . musicians . . . Carnaval players to be brought to his room. His father was so worried by these requests, he sent for us."

"I can't believe . . ."

"You heard him yesterday, he wanted a party . . . Music!" Tobias could barely speak. "When we got there he was sitting up in bed, the band was playing old favorites like 'Vem Cá Mulata' and 'Ó Abre Alas.' Erico said, 'See, Tobias, I told you I'd do it; I'd fix it somehow. Dá-se um jeito!'"

"Jeito," Nicia repeated under her breath. "If that doesn't perfectly describe the man!"

Joaquim barely heard any of this. "How's Margarida?"

"We barely saw her. She never left his side. They sent for the children in the middle of the night, but they arrived too late." Nicia began to weep loudly.

Jacobina served cold coffee from the night before, but no one noticed.

"What can I do?" Freire asked in a pathetic voice.

"When you're dressed we'll take you to Gloria with us."

"Wouldn't it be wrong to go to her now?"

"Why?" Tobias asked.

"Her family wouldn't want me around."

"That's ridiculous!" Nicia answered firmly. "You'll always be welcome in that house."

"I'm a bit too dark for the Claibornes' tastes, don't you think?"

"Margaret's never cared about anything but your friendship," Tobias added.

Joaquim stared at him, trying to comprehend all that was happening. Erik was dead; Margaret was now a widow. Their professional association had been acceptable only so long as her husband was alive. Suddenly he wanted to be alone to think this out. His brain wouldn't accept his conflicting thoughts.

"You need to help me," Tobias Netto was saying slowly.

Help him? "How?"

"As you know, I have some very difficult news for Margaret."

"You can't tell her about that child! Not now!"

"It's more complicated than that."

"I don't care what it is, there's nothing to be gained by hurting her with that information."

"It can't be kept a secret . . ." Nicia interjected.

"Why not? At least for a few more months."

"You don't understand, Quincas . . ."

"No, I don't!" He jumped up from his chair and flung open the shutters that had been bolted for the night. The first pale rays of sunlight slashed across the room.

"Tobias helped rewrite the will. He must explain it to Margaret." Nicia spoke slowly, as if to a child. "We think you should hear what it is about."

"It's not my concern."

"You've always been able to talk with Margaret. You could help her understand why Erik did this."

"I'm sure she's a very rich woman and won't suffer any hardships . . ."

"You're wrong!" Nicia said forcefully. "Listen to me, Quincas, it's not what any of us expected. At first Tobias didn't want to do what Erico had ordered, but in the end he wrote it because he thought that he could at least moderate his unusual requests."

Joaquim felt his stomach churning wildly.

"He's left everything to his children," Netto said simply. "Nothing to his wife."

"All his children," Nicia added. "All!" she emphasized. "He has legally claimed six: Astrid and Susana, of course, Isabel's three, and the new one, Malvina."

"Malvina," Joaquim echoed. He hadn't forgotten the name from the day before. "Does Margaret suspect anything about this one?"

Nicia's face had turned chalky. "No, we don't believe she does. If he hadn't listed the child in the will, she might have been kept blissfully ignorant. Now, when these documents are made public . . ."

"I don't understand why Erico . . ." Joaquim railed.

"Come now, Quincas, how many men do we know personally who have at least two families? My father had a friend who had more than twenty children by several women and his brother had over thirty."

"But for Erico to have left his fortune to the children . . . to wish to neglect his wife when she has been so devoted . . ."

"It wouldn't have surprised Erico's sister," Nicia added. "Francisca once told me that there were two types of parents: those who cared more for their children and those who cared more for their spouses. Francisca believed that Margaret had married a man for whom his children would always come first. I argued with her then. Now I'm certain she was absolutely correct."

"What will Margaret do?"

Tobias spoke slowly. "It's not as disastrous as it seems at first. She may live in the house as long as she wishes, and she is to manage the Vassouras fazenda and keep any net income. Further, her well-being is ensured, since all the children's estates will pay her, as sole trustee, generous management fees."

Joaquim was incredulous. "I can't believe . . ."

"Erico trusted her to do what was right. She's even been given the care of Francisca's own and orphan children. All told, there are fourteen youngsters, not to mention" — he choked out the names — "Isabel and Amara. He's empowered Margaret to protect them financially. Why, he's covered everyone; even Florinda's underage children are to be given a stipend."

Nicia was aghast. "Tobias, you never told me that part!"

"Inacreditável!" Joaquim whistled.

"He was very clever."

"Clever, in what way?" Nicia asked angrily.

"Erico was certain there'd be sufficient income from the trust fees and Vassouras to keep Margaret more than comfortable. And" — he paused for a long breath — "he believed it would burden her unfairly to have too much Larson money of her own."

"A burden?" Joaquim almost shouted. "The wealth would increase her attractiveness to almost anyone."

Tobias gave Joaquim a knowing glance. Almost anyone . . . So that was it! What Erik had done was to ensure that the next man who came into Margaret's life would not seek her wealth. It had been a risky concept, but at the core it was an idea conceived not with enmity but with love. "Now I think I understand . . ." Joaquim groaned. "But will she?"

"Not at first," Tobias answered. "Even I tried to dissuade Erico from making the terms so harsh. Just last week we discussed it again. He insisted. 'The little ones cannot be made to suffer for anything their parents did or did not provide, so I must ensure their protection,' he explained and went on to say, 'Yet, it's much more complicated to protect a woman's future. The most important gift I can leave Margaret is the freedom to have a life of her own.' "

Joaquim could almost imagine Erik saying the words, his merry eyes crinkling at the edges, his smile a tease and a promise.

The last time he'd seen him the old spark had been rekindled, his mood had been euphoric . . . for a while. All at once he'd seemed to change, he'd insulted him cruelly without any reason or provocation. Or . . . was it really an insult? Had Erik been attempting to give Joaquim a message that could be said in no other way? "Bicha!" The ugly word echoed in his mind. Erik knew it wasn't true, so why the accusations, why the need to upset and hurt him? What, in the end, had Erik wanted from him?

Nicia touched his arm. "Why don't you get dressed now?"

Joaquim seemed to have forgotten that he was wearing only a towel. "One more question. How did he die?"

"We were downstairs. His father says he finally fell asleep after the musicians left. Margaret sat by his side; so did his parents. He never awoke."

They were quiet for a few moments. Finally Tobias Netto broke the silence with the kind of comment that Erik himself might have fashioned. "He thought he was doing what was right . . . Perhaps he'll live to regret it."

But nobody laughed.

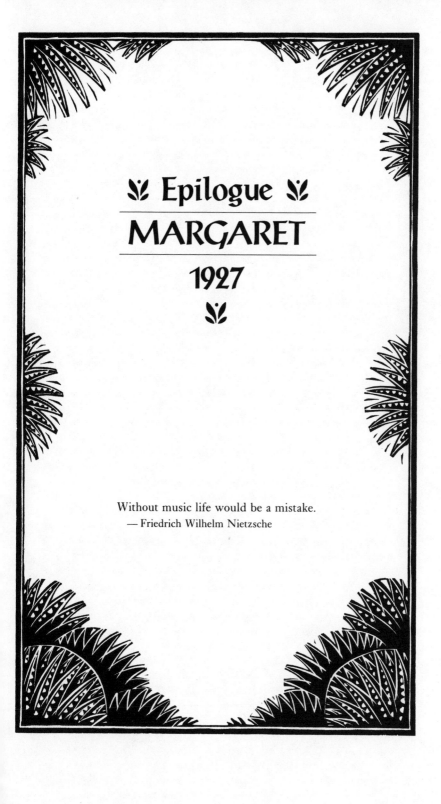

❧ Epilogue ❧

MARGARET

1927

❧

Without music life would be a mistake.
— Friedrich Wilhelm Nietzsche

River of January

1 Margaret drove down Rua Cosme Velho Silvestre and into the funicular station for the ride up to Corcovado. Spying the enormous vehicle, two street urchins ran forward. The older elbowed the younger out of the way so he could open the driver's door first. "You will need a guard, lady?" he asked.

"My car will require two vigias." Margaret smiled as the ragamuffins walked reverently around her gleaming black Isotta-Fraschini. They stroked the brass headlamps, the oak door trim, the leather wheel covers of the elegant Italian touring car that Margaret had brought back from her European tour two years before. She drove it herself, a skill in which she took great pride. She was the only Brazilian woman she knew who had a license.

The taller boy took a cloth from his back pocket and set to work polishing the brass plate that read, "Cesare Sala, 8-A." The other opened the rear door to let the young passengers out. Margaret studied the skinny boy with his huge black eyes and a protruding belly that signified undernourishment. "I will need you to guard the inside," Margaret said firmly. "What's your name?"

"Manoel, senhora. My brother's called Mario."

"All right, Manoel, will you promise to stay with the car the whole time we're gone? It'll be several hours."

"Sim, senhora."

"Muito bom." She hurried off to the platform where the children were waiting for her. Manoel looks so tired, she thought sadly, I hope he'll sleep in the car while we're gone. Street children, she shuddered. How many of Rio's youth were tossed out of their homes at age five or six, to live by their wits or starve? How she wished she could care for them all!

"Lucia!" Margaret caught up to her granddaughter. She reached for her just as the train was pulling into the base station.

The child's soft little hand squeezed hers back. "Is it our turn now, Avó?"

"Sim, Lucia. Cecilia, come with me." She looked around for the others. "Otavio, Evangelina . . ." she called.

The two eldest rushed for the front seats on the train. Lucia clutched Margaret's hand even tighter as she stepped gingerly across the gap between the platform and the door. That's the difference between the cautious four-year-old and the bold adolescents. Margaret smiled to herself. Each is so predictable, so lovable, though fours are far less of an intellectual challenge.

The small red rail car jerked forward as the cogwheel moved along its rack. Lucia scrambled onto her knees and peered out the window. "We're not very high."

"Not yet, but wait till we get to the very top."

"Then you'll see the whole world," Cecilia said in the knowing voice of someone who's almost eight.

"Whole world," Lucia echoed. "Grandmother, do you come here every day?"

"No, not every day." Margaret laughed at the simplicity of the question.

"Auntie's brought me here a hundred times," Cecilia bragged.

"Well, maybe not a hundred. Look!" Margaret pointed to the moss-covered aqueducts paralleling the route of the train. Wild orchids and ferns sprouted from the cracks in the ancient stonework. "Isn't that lovely?"

"Did you ever take my mummy here?" Lucia piped in her high little voice.

Margaret had forgotten how many questions young children asked at that age. "Yes, sometimes."

"Will I be able to see my mummy on the ocean?"

"No, not that far. But we might see other boats." Margaret

tried to imagine where Susana and Hugo might be at that moment. They would have landed in Southampton by now, might even be in London. Margaret liked Susana's husband immensely. When, at age nineteen, her daughter had asked to marry a man ten years her senior, Margaret had objected. She'd wanted her daughter to finish her linguistics course at the University of Leeds, for Susana was already fluent in not only English and Portuguese but also French and German, and she might have had a career as a teacher of languages. But at a party at the Brazilian Consulate in London she'd met Hugo Hargreaves, a diplomat who had charmed her away from her studies and married her at the first opportunity. Margaret had come to agree that Susana had made a wise choice after all. The young couple had just visited Rio for three months and now were moving to Lisbon, where Hugo would be a new attaché at the British Embassy, his first important post. In order to give Susana the time necessary to set up a new household, she'd agreed to care for Lucia, their only child.

It seemed that people were always leaving children in Margaret's care. Odd, since she hardly ever thought of herself as a maternal person. Not that she hadn't been an admirable parent. All the children were thriving in the world — all over the world, too.

The train, creeping forward at a forty-degree angle, reached the Corcovado Hotel stop.

Margaret had to restrain Lucia from running out the open door. "No, we're not there yet." As the train lurched forward again, she stroked the child's auburn curls. Lucia favored her British relations, though the child had certainly inherited Erik's broad brow and his particular color of sea-blue eyes and was destined to be a very pretty little girl. Unfortunately, Cecilia, Francisca's youngest granddaughter, retained the swarthy complexion and stocky build of the Cavalcantis.

Almost ten years earlier, her mother, Emilia, had married a general's son who was also pursuing a military career. They now had six children, including a set of identical twin boys. Today Francisca would have been the grandmother of sixteen children and the foster grandmother of five more. If only Francisca could have seen them all! She would have been especially proud of the orphans. Rodolfo was an officer in the Brazilian navy, Carolina was the wife of a banker in Recife with five young children, Adelpha had married the owner of a small hotel in the outlying beach district of Ipanema that she helped him manage. Her twin, Gilda, had joined the order of the Sisters of Charity and was assigned to a geriatric ward at Santa Casa de Misericordia.

"Oh! Oh! Oh, my goodness!" Lucia exclaimed as she looked down more than seven hundred meters toward Guanabara Bay.

Margaret hugged her. "Here we are."

A stiff wind blew Margaret's skirt between her legs. She protectively buttoned her silk jacket and tightly tied the scarf with the delicate floral border. "Now don't climb up onto the wall," she warned the children as they followed the sightseers to the summit.

All of Rio lay before them like a tapestry woven in every tropical hue. Bright red roofs dotted the verdant greens of the valleys and forests, the bay sparkled in shades of emerald and azure, and beyond, the ocean was a deep violet, tipped with creamy caps.

"Dona Margarida! It's Margarida of the Bandidos!" A group of well-dressed ladies had recognized her. She had found it useless to try to hide from the curiosity seekers who easily spotted her distinctive silver-streaked hair pulled back into a braided chignon. The older children flanked her protectively, but she waved them off.

"Dona Margarida." The plumper of the ladies almost curtsied. "My husband and I were fortunate enough to hear you play at the Debussy recital last year. You were magnificent."

Her companion spoke nervously. "Every time I hear you play Freire's 'Requiem for Piano' I cry. It's my favorite piece."

"You're both very kind. I think you'll enjoy the première of Freire's symphonic work, 'Os Três Rios,' in March."

"Will you be playing?"

Margaret smiled enigmatically. "Perhaps."

The admiring ladies moved away. "Does everyone know you, Avó?" Lucia asked.

"Of course they do!" Cecilia answered proudly. "My auntie's the most famous woman in Rio!"

"Why, Lila, who ever said that?" Margaret asked gently.

"My mother."

"Oh, I see. When your mother was your age, I taught her to play a few songs on the piano. Don't you think it's your turn now?"

"She doesn't play anymore."

"No," Margaret admitted. "But you could try." Of all the children in the family, only Francisca's Marcelino had shown any talent. After his mother's death, though, he'd refused to study. Not that it mattered. He had become an artist of another sort, a painter of landscapes. He was very good, but still, without the money from his trust fund, he'd have starved. Evangelina and Otavio had demonstrated musical aptitude, as well they should. Both played a passable piano and violin, but Margaret refused to push them. If they wanted musical careers, there was still time for them to choose.

Cecilia pointed to an oval track next to a large lagoon. "What's that big circle down there?"

"That's the Jockey Club. Your grandfather helped build it. You've been there to see the horses many times, haven't you?"

"Oh, yes! I love the story about the horse that went to England and won the Derby. What was he called?"

"Nova Esperança." Margaret felt a sharp pain as she said the name. If only Erik had been able to see the horse's triumph! His win had placed Brazilian racehorses in world-class competition and had vindicated the Larsons' stables completely. The horses . . . The grandchildren . . . There was so much she wished she could have shared with Erik. How he would have adored Lucia's curly red hair and bright little voice! He'd have loved and been proud of all the rest as well.

Isabel's three children had all bettered themselves. Eulalia had married the son of the Federal Deputy of the state of Santa Catarina, a childhood friend she'd made at school. Xavier had been taken into the textile business and now was export director. The youngest, Armando, was still being educated at a university in Portugal.

Amara da Costa remained in Vassouras and managed the racing stock along with Felix, her invalid father. Her daughter, Malvina, was currently at school in Switzerland, the same one Susana had attended seven years earlier. The privileged daughters of nobility and wealth from many nations were enrolled at the alpine school, so the color of Malvina's skin would not be the darkest, but Margaret often wished she could have seen the expression on the headmistress's face the day the second Larson daughter, whose appearance was so different from her half-sister's, arrived.

All Erik's children had received European educations. It had been his specific wish that they be sent abroad "by the time they are fifteen if at all possible and with their assent." His last will and testament had been a complex and far-sighted document that not only delineated a financial structure for his holdings but provided philosophical guidelines as well.

"I bequeath to my wife, Margaret Claiborne Larson, her own life and the freedom to choose for herself," he had written. "I humbly request her to permit each of my children a life of his or her own choosing as well, though painful or expensive this may be. I ask that she see that each child is given the best education that his individual talents and temperament warrant, and that upon his majority he be permitted to fulfill his own promise, to make his own choices, financial as well as personal, for that will be the ultimate expression of my love for each of them."

Only Astrid hadn't followed her father's guidelines. Instead of having but a year in Sweden and moving on to the British school he'd selected, Astrid had never left Stockholm. She still lived there with her husband, Hans Nillson, a physician, and their four children: Francisca, Gunilla, Erik, and baby Sven. Less than a year after Erik's death, Sven Larson had kept his promise and taken Astrid to his homeland. Shortly after their arrival, Sven had suffered a series of debilitating strokes, and after a brief illness, he'd died. Guilhermina said his system had been shocked by the cold winter weather and blamed herself for permitting him to travel in his state of bereavement. Astrid, mourning the loss of her father and grandfather in the same year, found solace in the home of her maternal grandparents. Though she never returned to Brazil again, Margaret had seen her stepdaughter several times during her European tours, and the two maintained a steady correspondence over the years.

"Maybe her problem was that she was never really meant to be a Brazilian," Lucretia often said. Margaret had disagreed, believing that Astrid thought Brazil contained too many painful memories. The clue to her true feelings could be found in the names of her children. She'd had one to replace all the important people she'd lost in her life. Poor darling! Margaret still thought of her as the thin, lovely, difficult child who'd sailed away instead of the mature woman of thirty-three years she was today.

"What's that growing out of the water?" Cecilia pointed across to the beach at Copacabana, now the fastest-developing section of the city.

"They're constructing another hotel. The white building just before it is the Copacabana Palace." Margaret grinned. She'd purchased the land under that hotel as part of the children's trusts almost twenty years earlier, when nobody thought real estate on the south beaches would ever have much value since the area was virtually inaccessible. A few years later, after tunnels had been blasted through the huge rock mountains that separated the old city from the seashore, the value of the land on Copacabana had risen dramatically. She'd continued investing in seaside properties farther down the coast, buying prime pieces along Ipanema and Leblon. She still held on to many parcels that bordered Avenida Atlantica, planning to sell them very slowly so that there would still be raw, inflation-proof land in the trusts of her grandchildren when they married.

Every one of Erik's and Francisca's children, whose fortunes she also managed, was very rich. But Margaret, as sole trustee, took great pains to hide the full extent of their wealth from them. She doled out their portions in yearly payments they considered generous but that amounted to only a fraction of the interest earned in their accounts.

The family's holdings now included investments in land and buildings all around the city, shares in diversified industries from coconut oil to shipping, more than seven hundred Casas Margaridas, six fabric mills, two black powder factories, not to mention the vast land holdings in the northeast that Raleigh had acquired.

The little girls ran away from the southern viewing platform to the one that looked directly across Guanabara Bay. "I see Sugar Loaf! I see the forts!" Cecilia shouted. "Where's my school?"

Margaret came up behind her. "Look to the left of Sugar Loaf.

The first curve of water is Botafogo, the second Flamengo. Now
do you see the house on the pier?"

"Yes."

"Just to the left of that . . . on the little hill. Do you see it now?"

"Yes! I see my school!"

All the children of the family, Cecilia included, attended the
Escola Francisca Larson in the family's Flamengo mansion. After
Sven had died, Guilhermina moved into one wing and had insisted the children be brought from Boa Vista to attend school at
her home. "So I can see them every day," she'd explained. Under
the guidance of Margaret's sister Kate, who had been the school's
headmistress for almost twenty years, it had become one of the
most prestigious preparatory schools in Rio. Graduates attended
universities throughout the world. In fact, a fair number of the
alumni were sent to Tulane in New Orleans where today Margaret's baby brother, Marshall, was a distinguished professor of
American history.

At the age of eighty-five, Guilhermina was still attended by
Zefinha, Francisca's servant, who slept in her room and puréed all
her food. Every morning the grande dame of the family greeted
the pupils as they arrived at her front door as though they were
honored guests in her home, and every afternoon she presided at
tea for the oldest girls in her drawing room. "They are the reason
I go on," she'd say and proudly display scrapbooks of photographs and letters from favorite students of years gone by.

Kate Claiborne never married. "The school is my husband, the
students my children," she insisted. Margaret guessed her sister
probably had a happier life than most of the married women
she knew and was pleased that she'd found such a rewarding
vocation. She was a superb administrator as well as an inspiring teacher. Evangelina worshiped her, as Susana had before
her.

Nell had remained on her plantation. She and her husband,
Royce, managed one of the largest operations in the region, with
diversified holdings in rice and other crops. With astute management, they'd weathered the coffee bust of 1906, which had ruined
many of their neighbors and, in fact, made marginal operations
like the Larsons' at Vassouras impossible to run competitively.
Vassouras was now a breeding stable for racehorses and nothing

more. All the saltpeter needed for the black powder factories was imported from the mines in Chile.

Royce Burrows had worked to develop the national coffee valorization plan, a price-raising scheme whereby the state governments undertook the purchase of a large percentage of each harvest and withheld it from the market until a compensatory price level was reached. Every year the region around São Paulo alone produced more than twenty-one million bags, enough to supply the entire world demand. So that Brazil could control the price of coffee on the world market, it was imperative not to allow the sale of inexpensive coffee. Export quotas were stringently regulated by the government, and surplus beans were burned or dumped into the sea. These strict export laws spawned a network of professional smugglers willing to take the risk of fines and stiff sentences, for if a load of coffee could be sold across the border or out at sea, the price of the bean tripled.

One entrepreneur who'd succumbed to the lure of quick profits was Augusto, whose name had long been associated with other questionable enterprises. It was rumored that he bankrolled gambling operations and owned the most exclusive house of prostitution in Rio. He probably could have continued with these iniquitous endeavors by bribing the authorities indefinitely, but his avarice had led him to mastermind one of the more elaborate coffee smuggling operations. He had been caught and prosecuted and was currently serving a ten-year sentence. The investigator who'd gathered the evidence against Augusto had been none other than Orlando Feitosa, leader of the raid on Desengano and now chief of police. From where Margaret was standing on Corcovado's summit, she could see the outline of the prison tower where Augusto was incarcerated. When he was arrested, she'd refused to come to his aid, and she felt no pity or remorse now. Augusto would probably learn that the state's vengeance was but a mild taste of what was awaiting him in the next world.

After Sven had not returned from Sweden, Lucretia had become despondent. "I don't want to die in a strange land either! I want to be buried with the Davises in Iberville Parish, not in some jungle cemetery."

Margaret resisted sending her mother back to the United States because both her mother's brothers had already died and she had no close relations to care for her. But Lucretia became increasingly belligerent and difficult. She had never approved of Margaret's second marriage, which had taken place a discreet two years after Erik's death; she refused even to come to the lavish ceremony attended by leaders of society as well as the artistic community. Even afterward, Lucretia rarely visited Margaret's home, and she wouldn't live with Raleigh or one of her other daughters, requiring a house and servants of her own. And still she was never content.

Then, Mlle Doradou passed away at the age of seventy-two, bequeathing to Margaret her home and possessions. Marshall, who had been teaching in São Paulo, decided to do graduate studies in North American history. He took his mother to live in Mademoiselle's French Quarter home while he attended and later taught at Tulane.

Margaret had seen her mother only once again, when she'd returned to New Orleans during her 1922 concert tour. Marshall, still a bachelor at that time, had taken exemplary care of their mother on the generous funds that Margaret sent, but the old woman was bedridden and senile. A nurse had carried Lucretia into Mademoiselle's parlor and propped her patient in her wheelchair while Margaret had entertained her mother by playing Gottschalk's Pleyel.

How far she'd come from that docile, willing student Mlle Doradou had molded into a professional musician! As she played the familiar keys, she'd strongly felt her old teacher's presence, almost hearing the hoarse voice criticizing the position of her fingers, the interpretation of the piece, the tempo. At least she'd please her ailing mother, who always took such pride in her achievements. When Margaret had finished her vibrant rendition of Brahms's "Variations on a Theme by Paganini," the number in her repertoire that had won her the loudest ovations in Europe, she'd turned around to see the expression on her mother's face. Lucretia's head had lolled to the side; her mouth drooled slightly — she'd been asleep.

Lucretia died two years later. Marshall, who by then had written several important works on Louisiana history and was editing a Civil War journal, opened his home to academically talented

Brazilian students. He finally married one them. Maria Victoria de Macedo Soares was one of Kate's protégés and the daughter of one of Rio's most prominent journalists. Shortly before Marshall's and her first child was born, her father helped publish her first book, *Diary of a Foreign Student*. Margaret had a special feeling for the journal because her younger sister-in-law, in writing about her own adjustment to a new culture, had captured the essential confusion and loneliness she'd felt upon her arrival in Rio thirty years before.

Margaret stared out at a ship passing near the Raza Island lighthouse and entering Guanabara Bay. "It's like another sea!" she'd said to Francisca as they had stood side by side at the rail of the *Oceania*, each filled with her own expectations and dread. She'd imagined Brazil a horrid country and had resisted coming. Now, though she'd traveled through Europe and North America extensively, she would choose to live nowhere else. She reached out and patted Lucia's thin shoulders.

"The very first day I came to Rio your grandfather promised to bring me here."

"Did he?"

"No, not that day."

"Why, Avó?"

Why . . . She couldn't quite remember. "I don't know, but we did finally come here together later. Just the two of us. It was early in the morning and . . ." Lucia had lost interest and run after Cecilia, who had spied some kites being flown from the western observation area.

Though Erik had been gone for twenty years, she thought of him every day and felt "saudades" for him — the Portuguese word that so wonderfully described an overwhelming yearning, a longing. She still reached out to him, though she had no desire to change the fulfilling life she had today.

Now the ship Margaret had been watching had crossed the white lines of foam and was anchoring in the bay far below. On board must be others who were seeing this marvelous city for the very first time. Margaret envied them.

"Rio de Janeiro actually means 'River of January,'" Francisca had explained, her timid voice almost lost in the wind on that long-ago day.

"It isn't really a river?" she'd asked. "But why did they keep the city named after something that doesn't exist?"

"Perhaps to remind us that nothing in Brazil is as it first seems." Margaret could almost hear Francisca laughing at the paradox. "Perhaps to remind us . . ."

"Uvas!" Evangelina called. The little girls ran to take the wooden sticks speared with grapes and dipped into a sugar syrup that she had bought from a candy seller.

"Evangelina! You should have asked me first!"

"Avó?" Lucia looked up to see if Margaret really wouldn't permit her to have it.

"All right!" she relented. "But we must go down soon."

"We haven't seen everything yet!" Cecilia whined.

"No matter how many times I come to Corcovado I still see something new. And so will you. Rio's changing every day. Look over there!" She pointed out a wharf near Gloria. "When I first arrived in Rio that was nothing but swampland. Your grandfather and I moved near there when we were first married."

"Where?"

"Do you see Nossa Senhora da Gloria on the hill?"

"Yes."

"Just below, on the plaza. See the house with two turrets?"

"Oh, yes."

"That's where we lived." And Erik died, she thought to herself.

"Who lives there now?"

"It's now the Academy of Music, but Olympio and Aida Baptista live upstairs. You remember, Dona Nicia is Aida's aunt."

"The one who always plays music in a wheelchair?"

"That's right." Suffering from brittle bones, Nicia Netto had been confined to a wheelchair for more than five years, but she was still an active cello teacher and never missed a performance. "How fortunate I picked an instrument that had to be played sitting down!" she'd say to make light of her affliction.

Cecilia and Lucia had lost interest in the scenery and were soon pursuing large white butterflies. Their delighted squeals wafted upward with the fluttering wings of the almost-caught insect as the lights along the harbor began to illuminate. Soon it seemed the bays were rimmed with a twinkling necklace. Lamps and cooking fires dappled the hillside compounds called favelas. Although Carnaval was more than a month away, the sounds of the samba beat could already be heard. Favorite songs of years past competed with the ones being tested for 1927. Music goes on, Margaret realized; it lives far beyond its players. She spent her life bringing the work of dead composers to the ears of new audiences, and when she was gone, someone else would do the same. The fact that a piece of music had an eternal life was a great comfort. Some day a great-great-grandchild of Evangelina or Lucia might hear "Vem Cá Mulata" or Schumann's "Papillons," or even Freire's "Requiem for Piano." Yet no one would hear the same bateria playing that Carnaval song in years to come; and just as Clara Schumann's hands were stilled, so hers would also be.

Margaret took Lucia's sticky hand in hers and called to Cecilia. "It's time to go." Evangelina and Otavio seemed to have disappeared. She passed the candy seller and asked the woman wearing the typical turban of Bahia if she'd seen where they went.

"Sim." The woman pointed down a flight of stairs that led to a lower platform, then looked back at Margaret with recognition. "Dona Margarida? Ai!" The woman pulled on Margaret's sleeve.

Margaret took a deep breath but didn't pull away. Though she understood that people touched her for luck, she sometimes found it difficult to be gracious and permit strangers to take this liberty. After her captivity at Desengano, she'd been frightened by the attention paid her and resented becoming an unwitting public figure. Eventually, though, she'd learned her notoriety was the best protection she could have. How many other Brazilian women could drive their own cars or walk the streets of Rio with impunity? Because she was Margarida of the Bandidos, nobody would dare harm her.

Sometimes the weight of never being able to be a quiet, private person was all-consuming; sometimes she needed to get away. So, each year she toured Europe and North America. She'd met Debussy and Ravel; she counted the pianist Marguerite Long among her personal friends; but she always returned to Rio and her complex and diverse family, for only in Brazil could she find acceptance for both her private and her public life.

In a few minutes Margaret found Evangelina and Otavio sitting on a rock wall, watching the moon begin to rise from the sea.

The night cloaked them with its velvet-soft tropical warmth. The navy blue of the faraway Atlantic horizon melted imperceptibly into the darkening canopy of sky. Silhouettes of palms swayed in front of the rising lunar globe and a liquid haze moved in across the land in tiers. "We've got to go home."

"Oh, no!" Evangelina groaned. "Can't we stay and see the stars come out? Please! We've never been up here at night before."

An exhausted Lucia leaned against Margaret, her eyes closed. "I'm thirsty," Cecilia complained.

"I'll take Lucia," Otavio offered. He carried his niece down the long flight of concrete to the rackrail station.

Lucia slept during the entire ride to the base of the hunchbacked mountain. By the time they reached the bottom it was completely dark. The two little brothers guarding the car had also fallen asleep. Mario was stretched out on the running board, Manoel on the back seat. Margaret tapped them gently and gave them each a coin. Then she started the Isotta-Fraschini. It sputtered and purred. Evangelina and Cecilia scrambled to sit beside her in the front. Otavio looked as though he was going to argue for a moment, but seeing Margaret's stern expression, he slipped quietly into the back and snuggled Lucia in his lap.

Before putting the car into gear, Margaret touched the amethyst figa that always hung around her neck. The well-worn stone was her talisman. She never took it off, not even to bathe. "Are you ready?"

"Yes," the children chorused. Manoel waved sleepily as they drove off.

There was nothing Margaret enjoyed more than steering her long, sleek car through the city at night. She approached driving with the same concentration she gave to her music, turning the wheel, pressing the clutch, shifting the gears with grace and ease. She prided herself on never jerking the car or coming out of a turn too early. She drove in smooth defiance of those who thought a woman shouldn't. If Francisca could see me now! she thought as she drove through the Catete section of the city. Why, Francisca had almost always refused to ride in a car, trusting only horses to be reliable forms of transportation. Yet Margaret knew that Francisca would have approved of the Fraschini. She braked at a cross street quite close to Francisca's old corner.

"I see Tio Raleigh's house!" Cecilia called. "Are we going there?"

"Not this evening. Your mother is probably wondering where you are by now. She was sending her car to meet you at our house."

Raleigh and Marianne had moved into Francisca's house in Rio shortly after Sven's death, to help manage the company. Because he understood the complex management of the lands in the northeast better than anyone, Raleigh soon controlled that portion of the Larsons' holdings. Under his leadership, the mills and stores did not continue to expand, but they did function efficiently. Eventually, he'd become the company's chief executive. But, as executor for the children, the sole owners and proprietors of the Larson enterprises, Margaret had the power to appoint all the directors. Although she herself did not serve on the board, Margaret selected conservative, mature men, including Alvares Diniz and Tobias Netto, who were not easily swayed by Raleigh's more outlandish schemes. So while her brother had the overt power, all major decisions were either approved or vetoed by Margaret before they went into effect.

Raleigh remained quite religious and tithed his earnings to the missionaries who served in Brazil. Tragically, Marianne and their son Ethan had been two of the first victims of the Spanish grippe epidemic of 1918 that had killed thousands in the city. Their other son, Lawrence, moved to the northeast and now ran the timbering operations there. He'd married a local girl, converted to Roman Catholicism, and had six daughters of his own. Mary Lee had married the son of one of Raleigh's missionary friends and had been called to a mission post on the Orinoco River in Venezuela, much to her father's consternation, for he'd have preferred to have his only daughter closer by and living in greater comfort. As Margaret passed her brother's home, she reminded herself to visit him the following week. Lately his health had been very poor. Years ago in Bahia he'd contracted schistosomiasis, a parasitic disease caused by a liver fluke, which had infected him after he'd bathed in the streams that bordered the woodlands. His chronic bouts of cystitis and dysentery had taken their toll, and Raleigh left his home only a few hours a week to sign documents at the downtown office of Larson International Ltd. He needs

Marianne now more than ever, Margaret thought sadly as she drove to the base of Santa Teresa.

"I see the crocodile!" Cecilia called when they rounded the first bend of the hill. Margaret wished Otavio hadn't told the impressionable child that the view from Santa Teresa was of a hungry reptile. He'd showed her how the mouth of the harbor looked like open jaws, the rocks like jagged teeth.

Margaret preferred Santa Teresa to any other quarter of the city. While renovations had modernized most of Rio's beautiful old neighborhoods, the residents of Santa Teresa restored their houses and steadfastly refused to widen the narrow lanes or pave the cobbled streets. Artists, writers, and musicians all gravitated to the hill. Here she could live without a huge domestic staff, and her children were free to have friends from a varied group of families. And considering the eccentricity of her life and marriage, it was best that she lived unpretentiously. As if that were possible! Strangers still paused by her gate when they toured the quarter. Even guidebooks listed her home as that of Margarida of the Bandidos.

"When we're both dead this house will still be standing," she'd say to Joaquim. "The bronze plaque that the visitors will read will not have my name. It will say, 'Home of Joaquim Freire, Composer,' and I'll have been forgotten completely."

❧ 2 Margaret was late, much later than she expected. Joaquim would be fretting. Erik had hated waiting — perhaps most men were the same. From boyhood they were rewarded for quick decisions, speed, activity, while girls were praised for docility, passivity, patience. Perhaps if Joaquim had been busy with his work that afternoon, he'd not have missed her too much. One reason she'd taken the children for such a long excursion was to give him the peace he needed to concentrate. By organizing the debut of his long-awaited symphony "Os Três Rios" in just two months, he was forced to finish the last movement, the one that had been incomplete all these years. The first section, "The Amazon," was already of world renown; the second, "Iguaçu," was less popular, perhaps because it didn't stand alone as easily as the bolder, more volatile, first movement.

Margaret pulled into the driveway, which had been widened

slightly for the benefit of the Fraschini. Emilia's driver was waiting for Cecilia. "Boa tarde, Auntie!" She hopped into her waiting
Mercedes. "Oh, obrigada!" she called as an afterthought.

Januario, Florinda's son, opened the back door of the Fraschini.
Otavio handed Lucia out to him and he carried the exhausted
child inside.

"Celinha, are you asleep too?" Margaret asked when Evangelina didn't leave the car quickly.

"You know I hate that nickname!" Evangelina moaned.

"I'm sorry, I forgot. What shall I call you, then?"

"Evan . . . ga . . . lyne, without the stupid 'a'!" She pronounced
her name with as North American an accent as she could muster.

"Yes, well, I'll try to remember, querida. But you know, the
fine lady you were named for called herself Evan . . . ge . . . leen
Doradou." Margaret's exasperated tone sounded strangely like
Lucretia's. Why was she fighting with the girl? At least she could
let her have her own way when it came to her name. Mothers and
daughters . . . Was it always the same?

Joaquim poked his head outside the front door. "Margarida! Is
anything the matter?"

"No, we're coming."

Sulking, Evangelina moved toward the house. She kissed her
father on both cheeks perfunctorily.

"I've asked Otavio to go to the music room. Won't you join
your brother there?"

"Of course, Papai," Evangelina replied. There was nothing she
wouldn't do for her father.

Joaquim reached for Margaret's hand. She knew from the softness around his eyes, the suppleness of his mouth, that he was
pleased with how his work had gone that day. "So?" was all she
asked.

He bobbed his head and smiled. "I finished it."

Margaret's hands fluttered to her mouth. "Already!"

"It's been almost twenty years . . ."

"Papai, have you really been working on one piece for so
long?"

"Your father began it many years ago, but he hasn't worked on
it the whole time."

"There's a lesson in that. Speed is not necessarily an asset in art." Joaquim placed his arm around Margaret's waist. Together they walked into the music room, which had been added to the back of the house. It held three pianos and rehearsal space for a small orchestra, and it was acoustically as perfect as could be achieved in so small a space. Otavio and Evangelina were sitting on the sofa where guests listened to rehearsals.

"Otavio, Evangelina, have you heard any music in the streets today?"

"Sim, Papai," they answered in unison.

"Well, that's what started my new perception of how to complete the symphony's last movement. I heard the beat of the tamborim, the drone of the cuica, the boom of the big bass drum, and thought — January's here, Carnaval's coming. So I threw out my false starts and began with the quick, bright march theme from Zé Pereira."

"Zé Pereira in a *symphony*, Papai?" Evangelina asked incredulously.

"Just the first few beats, querida. Listen." Joaquim went to the piano and began to talk his way through the piece. "Now the percussion section keeps the Carnaval beat in the background while the orchestra takes over with my 'theme of the false river.' Here's where I had my breakthrough. Before, I was trying to evoke Rio as a city — vibrant, growing, a part of the modern world — but that was the wrong approach entirely."

"I don't understand, Quincas," Margaret said.

"Come sit beside me. I'll show you."

Evangelina smiled and nudged her brother. She loved to see her parents, her mother with the silver hair, her father with the white, side by side at the piano bench. It was so romantic, and it made her feel secure.

"The false river theme," Margaret read. She played a few tentative phrases of a haunting, lyric melody.

"Do you hear my meaning now? This 'Rio' is not a real city. It's a river of dreams, of imagination. Listen . . ." Joaquim played some chords. "This would be supplemented by a chorus of women's voices, like sirens luring the explorers to the shores of Brazil."

"Oh, it's lovely!" Evangelina said rapturously.

"Next the sailor's song: bright, bold, bawdy. Tambourines here,

cymbals, xylophone." He looked back at his son, who was helping pound the beat with his foot.

Margaret turned the page, eager to read on. "The mood
changes here. Why?"

"Dawn, the approach to the harbor. What will the adventurers
find? A new continent, a new world? Fearsome dragons? Beautiful women!" Joaquim spoke in his rolling, hypnotic way. Margaret remembered how captivated she'd been by his voice from
the moment they'd met.

"Here an oboe introduces a slow passage of discovery. The
harp joins in, then the strings. All is revealed." Joaquim was
speaking more quickly than he could play. His fingers brushed
the piano to highlight the musical passages. Pages flew down
around the piano. "Rio de Janeiro, the misnomer. There is no
river, but a finite bay. We go round and round looking for another outlet. There's frustration, anxiety, crushed desire, and finally . . ."

Margaret took over and began to play phrases, test the chords
that were suggested.

"Now all is still. A long pause. The theme of the false river is
reprised in woodwinds and a flute. The vision of the Europeans is
a mythical river, one of infinite possibilities, of faith for the future."

"It's so sad, Papai."

"No, it isn't," Otavio insisted. "Listen."

Margaret played on, her right hand smoothly touching individual treble notes as if to draw forth the gift of everlasting life. "It's
inspiring, it sings itself," she whispered.

Joaquim turned the page.

Margaret played a series of complex seventh and ninth chords
and blended the impressionistic harmonies with the damper
pedal. Joaquim turned to the final page of his symphony. "The
mystical river, flowing onward, endless as the stars in the sky . . .
One long aching violin . . . The piano sounds the last echoing
note, a promise of more to come."

Everyone was quiet for a moment. "Well?" Joaquim dared.

"Yes." Margaret smiled. "It's precisely right."

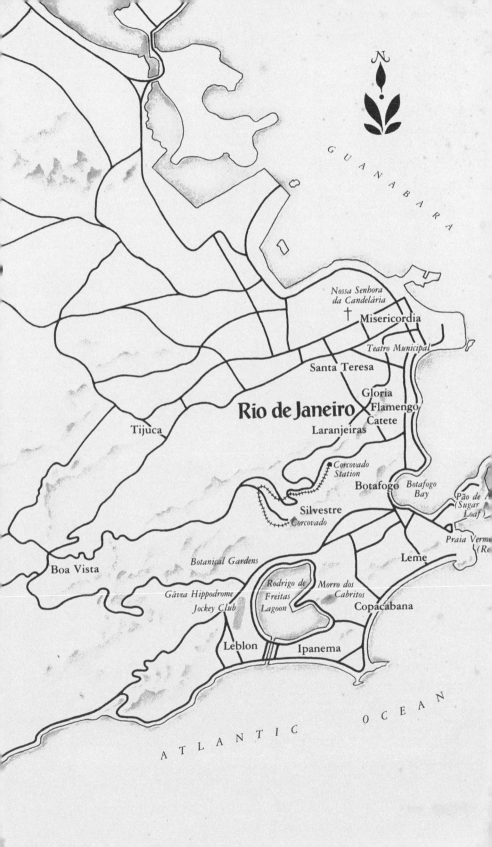